# Introduction to Management

# Introduction to Management

**Gerald A. Silver**
LOS ANGELES CITY COLLEGE

WEST PUBLISHING COMPANY
ST. PAUL  NEW YORK  LOS ANGELES  SAN FRANCISCO

## PHOTO CREDITS

**Cover Photos:** *Top, left to right:* **1.** Courtesy of Sperry Univac. **2.** Paul Crosby. **3.** Courtesy of Honeywell. *Middle, left to right:* **4.** Courtesy of the Minnesota Department of Economic Security. **5.** Paul Crosby. **6.** Courtesy of the Minnesota Department of Economic Security. *Bottom, left to right:* **7.** Paul Crosby. **8.** Paul Crosby. **Text Photos: 2.** Bob Gaylord. **8.** Courtesy of Stock Boston, Owen Franken. **16.** Bob Gaylord. **27.** Bob Gaylord. **32.** Courtesy of IBM. **33.** Historical Pictures Service, Inc.—Chicago. **35.** Historical Pictures Service, Inc.—Chicago. **37.** The Bettmann Archive, Inc. **52.** © 1979 Robin Hoyer from Black Star. **56.** Courtesy of Stock Boston, Jeff Albertson. **67.** Freelance Photographer's Guild, Sam Bass. **78.** Freelance Photographer's Guild, Tom Carroll. **86.** Freelance Photographer's Guild, David Attie. **100.** Freelance Photographer's Guild. **103.** Freelance Photographer's Guild. **121.** Courtesy of Magnum Photos, Inc., Rene Burri. **128.** Courtesy of Jeroboam Inc., Rose Skytta. **135.** Freelance Photographer's Guild. **138.** Jerry Bushey. **148.** Jerry Bushey. **151.** Courtesy of Jeroboam, Inc., Mitchell Payne. **158.** Jerry Bushey. **168.** Courtesy of Stock Boston, Cary Wolinsky. **180.** Courtesy of IBM. **181.** Courtesy of Control Data Corporation. **182.** Courtesy of Digital Equipment Corporation. **183.** Courtesy of Control Data Corporation. **184.** Courtesy of NCR Corporation. **185.** Courtesy of Burroughs Corporation. **192.** Courtesy of Jeroboam, Inc., Kent Reno. **203.** Courtesy of Stock Boston, Michael Hayman. **209.** Courtesy of Jeroboam, Inc., Peeter Vilms. **218.** Freelance Photographer's Guild. **225.** Courtesy of NASA. **242.** Courtesy of Stock Boston, Owen Franken. **250.** Courtesy of Focus on Sports, Inc. **256.** Courtesy of Magnum Photos, Inc., Abigail Heyman. **264.** Bob Gaylord. **271.** Bob Gaylord. **277.** Bob Gaylord. **292.** Bob Gaylord. **304.** Courtesy of Control Data Corporation. **314.** Bob Gaylord. **322.** Bob Gaylord. **325.** Courtesy of Jeroboam, Inc., Suzanne Wu. **338.** Courtesy of Focus on Sports, Inc. **344.** Bob Gaylord. **353.** Frank T. Schneider. **360.** Bob Gaylord. **366.** Bob Gaylord. **373.** Bob Gaylord. **382.** Courtesy of Jeroboam, Inc., Suzanne Wu. **385.** Courtesy of Stock Boston, Inc., Owen Franken. **399.** Bob Gaylord. **408.** Bob Gaylord. **411.** Courtesy of Black Star, A.V.L. Owen. **420.** Charles L. Farrow. **430.** Bob Gaylord. **442.** Bob Gaylord. **447.** Bob Gaylord. **454.** Jerry Bushey. **459.** Bob Gaylord. **468.** Bob Gaylord. **476.** Courtesy of Jeroboam, Inc., Kent Reno. **489.** Courtesy of Image Bank, Jules Zalon.

COPYRIGHT © 1981
By WEST PUBLISHING CO.
50 West Kellogg Boulevard    P. O. Box 3526    St. Paul, Minnesota  55165

All rights reserved
Printed in the United States of America

**Library of Congress Cataloging in Publication Data**

Silver, Gerald A

   Introduction to management.
   Includes index.
   1. Management.   I. Title.

HD31.S528    658    80-27283
ISBN 0-8299-0415-8

1st Reprint—1981

# Contents in Brief

Preface xix

## PART ONE   INTRODUCTION   1

1   The Role of Management   3

2   The Evolution of Management Theory   27

3   The Environment and Social Responsibilities of Business   53

## PART TWO   THE PLANNING FUNCTION   77

4   Fundamentals of Planning   79

5   Applied Planning   101

6   The Decision Making Process   129

7   Quantitative Tools of Management   149

8   Management Information Systems (MIS)   169

## PART THREE   THE ORGANIZING FUNCTION   191

9   Fundamental Organization Principles   193

10   Applied Organization Principles   219

11   Group Dynamics and Informal Organizations   243

## PART FOUR   STAFFING   263

12   Human Resources Management   265

13   Management Development and Training   293

**PART FIVE  THE DIRECTING FUNCTION   313**

   14   Organizational Development and Change   315

   15   Motivation   339

   16   Leadership Organizations   361

   17   Principles of Communication   383

**PART SIX  THE CONTROLLING FUNCTION   407**

   18   Control Process Fundamentals   409

   19   The Financial Control Process   431

   20   The Nonfinancial Control Process   455

   21   Controlling the Multinational Corporation   477

Index   499

# Contents

**Preface** xix

**PART ONE  INTRODUCTION**  1

**1  The Role of Management**  3

Need for Professional Managers  4
Some Common Goals of Organizations  6
Key Terms  8
Levels of Management  10
Real World: That New Santa Fe Travail  11
Management Functions  11
Activities of Managers  13
The Manager's Fund of Knowledge  15
Why Study Management?  17
Can Management Be Learned from Books?  17
Facts and Statistics on Management  18
Review of Some Popular Management Philosophies  19
Real World: Advertisement for Ford Motor Co.  21
Postscript: A Boss Takes His Job — Personally — and His Persons Expect It  22
Summary  23
Review Questions  24
Case Incident  25

**2  The Evolution of Management Theory**  27

Early Management Theories  28
*Greek, Roman and Chinese Civilizations*  29
*Medieval Influence of the Roman Catholic Church*  30
*Industrial Revolution and Reorganization of Work Force*  31
Real World: Liquid Gold  31

*Richard Arkwright, Charles Babbage, and Others 32*
*Max Weber's Bureaucracy 33*
Scientific Management Theory 33
*Taylor's Principles 34*
Other Early Theorists 35
*Henry L. Gantt 35*
*Frank and Lillian Gilbreth 35*
*Henri Fayol 37*
*Hugo Munsterberg 38*
*Mary Parker Follett, Alan C. Reiley, James D. Mooney, and Lyndall F. Urwick 38*
Human Relations Theory 38
*Elton Mayo 39*
*The Hawthorne Study Conclusions 39*
*The Hawthorne Effect 40*
*Chester I. Barnard 40*
Behavioral Science Theory 41
*Abraham Maslow 41*
*Douglas McGregor 42*
*Frederick Herzberg, Victor Vroom, and Rensis Likert 43*
Quantitative Theory 43
Systems Theory 44
*Feedback Loop 45*
Real World: A Guide to Taking Charge 45
Postscript: Japanese in No Hurry for Five-Day Week 46
Contingency Theory 47
Summary 49
Review Questions 49
Case Incident 50

**3** **The Environment and Social Responsibilities of Business 53**

Governmental Environment 54
Union-Labor Environment 55
Social Environment 56
Economic Environment 56
Major Trends Which Affect Management 57
*Basic Economic Trends 57*
*Basic Labor Force Trends 58*
Growth of the Credit Economy 61
Growth of Government Influence 62
Growth of the Multinational Firm 62
Management and Social Responsibility 63
*Business Ethics 64*
Real World: Stinging Nuns 64
*Consumerism 66*
*Employee Safety 66*
*Affirmative Action Programs 67*
Real World: How Bob Rowan Served His Time 68
*The Energy Crisis 70*
Postscript: Job Titles Reinforce Sexist Attitudes, Barriers to Women 72
*Environmental Pollution 73*
Summary 75
Review Questions 75
Case Incident 76

## PART TWO  THE PLANNING FUNCTION  77

**4  Fundamentals of Planning  79**

Need for Planning  80
Benefits and Advantages of Planning  80
Key Terms  81
Major Organization Goals and Objectives of Profit-Making Organizations  84
Real World: The Jumbo Flies High  85
*Sales or Marketing as a Goal*  85
*Nonprofit Organizations*  86
Measurement of Achievement  86
*Measurement Criteria*  88
Use of Plans  90
*Types of Plans*  90
*Steps in Developing and Implementing Plans*  91
Real World: P&G's New New-Product Onslaught  94
Planning at Various Levels of Management  95
Summary  95
Postscript: Soviet Factory Outmaneuvers Planners  96
Review Questions  98
Case Incident  98

**5  Applied Planning  101**

Time Element  102
Major Management Plans  104
*Plans Based upon Scope of Task*  106
*Interrelationship of Plans*  107
*Hierarchy of Plans*  107
Real World: Looking for Longer Horizons  107
*Good Plan Design*  108
The Planners  109
*Planning Departments*  109
*Selecting Planning Personnel*  109
Basic Planning Tools  111
*Budgets*  111
*Statistics and Descriptive Data*  111
*Ratios*  112
Real World: Billionaire Ludwig's Brazilian Gamble  115
*Forecasting*  116
Management By Objectives  119
*Advantages of MBO*  121
Postscript: 'Tinker Toy' Approach to Plant Design Saves Costly Errors  122
*Limitations of MBO*  123
*Example of MBO*  124
Summary  124
Review Questions  125
Case Incident  126

**6  The Decision Making Process  129**

Decision Making as a Process  130

Decision Making Defined   130
Approaches to Decision Making   130
*Qualitative Decision Making   131*
*Quantitative Decision Making   132*
Scientific Approach to Decision Making   132
Real World: Paperwork and Regulations   134
Advantages of the Scientific Approach to Decision Making   136
Programmed and Nonprogrammed Decisions   137
*Programmed Decisions   138*
*Nonprogrammed Decisions   139*
Decision Trees   139
Decision Tables   140
Real World: Blue Collar in the Board Room   142
Decision Making Factors   142
Group Versus Individual Decisions   143
Postscript: Notable & Quotable   144
Summary   144
Review Questions   145
Case Incident   146

## 7  Quantitative Tools of Management   149

Key Terms   150
Quantitative Techniques   151
*Modeling and Simulations   152*
*Critical-Path Method (CPM)   153*
*Program Evaluation and Review Technique (PERT)   154*
*Linear Programming (LP)   155*
*Probability Theory   157*
*Queuing Theory   157*
Real World: There's Big Business in All That Garbage   159
*Game Theory   159*
*Break-Even-Point Analysis   160*
Summary   163
Real World: A Guide to Golconda in a Wavy Sole Shoe   163
Postscript: Could Computers Have Kept Chrysler Healthy?   164
Review Questions   164
Case Incident   166

## 8  Management Information Systems (MIS)   169

Key Terms   170
Pressures on Business Organizations   171
Trends in the Number of Computers in Use   172
Real World: Managing the Unmanageable   173
How Computers Are Used in Management   173
Advantages of Computers   174
Management Information Systems (MIS)   175
Major Elements of the MIS   175
Real World: How Detroit Got Stuck with All Those Cars   176
Advantages of MIS   177
History of Computers and Data Processing   178
Early Computers   178
What Is a Computer?   179
*Input System   180*
*Central Processing Unit (CPU)   180*

    *Secondary Storage System*   181
    *Output System*   181
    Computer Systems   182
    Computer Programming   182
    Evaluating Computer Systems   183
    Problems of Security, Access, and Cost Control   184
    Postscript: Computer May Be Wonder or Thief   186
    Summary   188
    Review Questions   189
    Case Incident   190

## PART THREE   THE ORGANIZING FUNCTION   191

### 9   Fundamental Organizational Principles   193

    What Is Organizing?   194
    Organizing Existing or New Structures   194
    Real World: The Right Mood   195
    Key Terms   195
    Basic Principles of Organizing   197
    *Steps in Organizing*   197
    *Division of Labor*   201
    *Authority and Delegation*   203
    Real World: Producers in Revolt   204
    *Accountability and Responsibility*   204
    *Organizational Shape*   205
    *Levels of Management*   206
    *Unity of Command*   207
    *Staff Function*   208
    *Departmentalizing*   209
    Postscript: Family Businesses Challenge to Managers   214
    Summary   216
    Review Questions   216
    Case Incident   217

### 10   Applied Organizational Principles   219

    Central and Supporting Functions   220
    Basic Organizational Structures   221
    *Line Organization*   221
    *Line and Staff Organization*   222
    *Committee Organization*   223
    *Task Force (Project) Organization*   225
    Real World: Learning to Do It All   226
    *Matrix Organization*   226
    Contingency Organizational Structure   227
    Centralized Versus Decentralized Structure   228
    *Influence of the Computer*   228
    *Factors Affecting a Decision to Centralize*   228
    Real World: Sidetracked Sisters Tackle Success   230
    Documenting the Organization   230
    Major Problems and Failures in Organizational Design   232
    Postscript: Paper According to Form   236

Summary 238
Review Questions 238
Case Incident 239

## 11 Group Dynamics and Informal Organizations 243

Key Terms 244
Real World: Stockholders' Meetings — Assured Calm 247
Why Do Informal Organizations Exist and Grow? 248
*Job Dissatisfaction and Boredom* 248
*Need for Rewards, Security, and Social Outlets* 249
Types of Groups 249
Interrelationship of Groups 250
Methods of Studying Groups 251
The Grapevine 252
Bavelas' Communication Network 253
Group Norms and Goals 255
Group Sanctions, Discipline, and Rewards 256
Informal Leadership 257
Real World: Firms Allow Employees to Set Their Own Hours 257
Postscript: How to Boost Power in 'Brainstorming' 258
Using Informal Groups to Advantage 258
Summary 260
Review Questions 261
Case Incident 261

## PART FOUR  STAFFING  263

## 12 Human Resources Management 265

Human Resources Management 266
The Staffing Function 267
Overview of Human Resources Planning 267
Real World: Court Upholds Ruling on Bias of Dress Code at Chicago S & L 268
Human Resources Planning 269
*Differing Approaches* 269
*Job Design* 269
*Compensation* 271
Human Resources Inventory 274
*Computer-Based Personnel Inventories* 274
Human Resources Acquisition 274
*Recruitment* 274
Real World: Sexual Harassment Lands Company in Court 275
*Sources of Applicants* 275
*Testing and Screening* 276
*Selection Process* 279
*Orientation to Job* 280
Other Personnel Functions 281
*Evaluating Employee Performance* 281
*Termination of Employees* 282
Union-Management Relations 284
*Collective Bargaining* 284
*Labor Contract* 285

*Resolving Disputes* 285
Postscript: 'Loaning Workers Assures Japanese of Lifetime Jobs' 286
*Other Issues* 288
*Summary* 288
Review Questions 289
Case Incident 289

## 13 Management Development and Training 293

Real World: How the Japanese Do It 295
Key Terms 295
Management Development and Training 296
*Need for Management Development* 296
*Benefits of Management Development* 297
*Desirable Abilities Developed by Management Training Programs* 298
Staff Development 299
How People Learn 301
Applied Training Techniques 303
Real World: Sears Searches for Success 306
Executive Development 307
Postscript: Firm's Goal Is to Make Training Cost-Effective 308
Summary 310
Review Questions 311
Case Incident 311

## PART FIVE   THE DIRECTING FUNCTION 313

## 14 Organizational Development and Change 315

Change 316
*Impact on Organizations* 316
*Internal and External Change Forces* 317
Real World: Now for the Greening of Pillsbury 318
*Rate of Change* 319
*Attitudes Toward Change* 320
*Resisting Change* 321
Conflict in Organizations 322
*Introduction of Conflict* 323
Real World: Women Rise as Entrepreneurs 323
*Kinds of Conflicts* 324
Organizational Development 325
Characteristics of Organizational Development 326
*Unfreezing, Change, Refreezing* 326
*Force Field Analysis* 327
*Greiner's View of Change* 328
*The Management Grid* 328
*Leavitt's Change Model* 331
Postscript: Rules & Regulations to be Observed by All Persons Employed in the Factory of Amasa Whitney 332
Tools of Organizational Development (OD) 332
Summary 334
Review Questions 335
Case Incidents 335

## 15 Motivation 339

Key Terms 340
Historical Views of Motivation 341
*Classical Theory: Carrot and Stick* 341
*Human Relations* 341
Real World: One Dollar a Year? 342
*Money as a Reward* 342
*Job Rewards* 343
*Design of the Job* 343
*Morale* 344
Contemporary Views of Motivation 345
*Behavioral/Reinforcement Theory* 345
*Need Theories* 347
Real World: Compensation Woe; How to Pay? 350
*McGregor's X and Y Theories* 350
*Herzberg's Two Factor Theory* 351
*McClelland/Atkinson Need Theory* 352
*Equity Theory* 353
Postscript: Well Pay; Bonuses for Just Showing Up 354
*Expectancy Theory* 354
Summary 356
Review Questions 356
Case Incident 357

## 16 Leadership in Organizations 361

Key Terms 362
The Environment of Leadership 362
Sources of Power 363
Real World: A Movie Mogul Eats Her Words 364
Major Leadership Theories 365
Trait Theory 365
Behavioral Theory 366
*Lewin's View of Leadership Styles* 367
*Likert's Systems* 368
*Ohio State Studies* 369
*Tannenbaum and Schmidt's Contribution* 370
Real World: Bunker Hunt's Comstock Lode 372
Contingency Leadership 373
*Vroom and Yetton* 375
Postscript: Wistful View from the Corporate Heights 376
*Reddin's Three-Dimensional Model* 378
Summary 378
Review Questions 380
Case Incidents 380

## 17 Principles of Communication 383

Importance of Communications 384
Key Terms 384
The Communication Process 385
One-Way and Two-Way Communications 387
Real World: Crocker National Bank's Thomas R. Wilcox 387
Communications Networks 388
*Internal Communications Flow* 389

# CONTENTS

*External Communications Flow*   389
Formal and Informal Communication Networks   390
*The Grapevine*   390
Principles of Semantics   392
*Symbol Selection*   392
*Words as Holders of Meaning*   392
*Language*   393
*Personal Perceptions*   395
Communications Media   395
*Written Communication*   395
Real World: Black Beauty   396
*Oral Communication*   396
*Nonverbal Communication*   396
Barriers to Good Communication   397
How to Improve Communications   399
Transactional Analysis   400
Postscript: Firm Raps with Workers   402
Summary   404
Review Questions   404
Case Incident   405

## PART SIX   THE CONTROLLING FUNCTION   407

### 18   Control Process Fundamentals   409

Key Terms   410
Need for Control   411
The Basic Control Process   413
Feedback Loop   415
Basic Control Tools   416
Real World: Rent-a-Suit   418
Key Areas of Control   419
Applied Aspects of Control   421
Major Issues in Control   422
The Hawthorne Effect   423
Real World: Federal's Nighthawks   423
Postscript: The Ten Worst Guesses of Experts   424
Real-Time Control Systems   424
Summary   426
Review Questions   426
Case Incident   427

### 19   The Financial Control Process   431

Key Terms   432
Real World: The Solid-State Linguist Makes Its Debut   433
The Basic Accounting System   434
The Basic Accounting Statements   435
Ratio Analysis   438
*Developing Ratios*   438
*Comparing Ratios*   438
Real World: Autumn Binge   440
Budgetary Control   441

*Purpose of the Budget* 441
*Staffing the Budgetary Effort* 442
*Types of Budgets* 443
Postscript: An Embarrassment of Riches; A Look at Big Oil's Big Profits in Third Period 448
Applied Budget Considerations 448
Summary 451
Review Questions 451
Case Incidents 452

## 20 The Nonfinancial Control Process 455

Key Terms 456
Overview of Nonfinancial Control 456
New Product Development 457
Market Control 458
Production Control 460
Real World: The Fast-Feeding of America 462
Quality Control 463
Inventory Control 464
Real World: Camping It Up 466
*Optimum Size of Order* 466
*Optimum Time to Order* 468
Postscript: Productivity Is Key, Eastern Says 470
*Turnover of Inventory* 470
Distribution Control 470
Personnel Control 472
Summary 472
Review Questions 473
Case Incident 473

## 21 Controlling the Multinational Corporation 477

Key Terms 478
Growth and Interdependency of World Trade 479
Factors Favoring World Trade 479
Economic Associations 480
*European Economic Community (EEC)* 481
*European Free Trade Association (EFTA)* 481
Real World: A Made-in America Japanese Car 481
*Other Economic Associations* 482
Growth of Multinational Corporations and Joint Ventures 482
*Advantages of Multinational Corporations* 483
*Limitations of Multinational Corporations* 486
*Problems and Risks Faced by Multinational Corporations* 487
Organizing and Structuring the Multinational Corporation 489
Real World: Wickes Corporation's Retailing Triumph in Europe 492
Managing and Controlling the Multinational Corporation 492
Staffing Multinational Corporations 493
Postscript: Government in Industry — No Small Deal 494
Summary 496
Review Questions 497
Case Incidents 497

## Index 499

# Preface

This text is designed to provide the student with a solid foundation in the principles of management. It is a fundamental text aimed at students taking management courses in universities, business schools, community colleges and in on-the-job training programs.

The book is useful to any student interested in gaining an understanding of the basic principles of management. A grasp of management theory is valuable to those who must work with others, supervise employees or manage organizations. Students entering business for the first time, or even managers and subordinates with many years of business experience will find the fundamentals presented here of practical use.

This book is organized to follow the tried and tested pattern widely used by instructors and professors. Major sections of the book include planning, organizing, directing and controlling functions. This sound organization lends itself to a logical and complete presentation of the subject. This book fits well into most introductory management courses which approach the subject from the functional viewpoint. Those using the systems and contingency approaches will have little difficulty in using the book as the foundation of the instructional program.

The contents of this book include the fundamentals of management, with emphasis upon basic concepts, principles and widely accepted theory. There is stress upon basic terminology and vocabulary. Key terms and concepts are presented in an understandable, easy-to-read style.

This book surveys many of the new and rapidly developing areas of management including management information systems, computers, situational management, zero-based budgeting and management by objectives (MBO). It blends contemporary theory with a review of classical and fundamental principles.

One of the most interesting aspects of this book is the colorful and vital method of presenting material. The student is invited to enjoy a visual treatment of the subject including photographs, cartoons and drawings, in addition to clearly written prose.

Each chapter includes many human interest features, stories and pictures which touch upon the people and events of today. This added material helps the student grasp the theory of management as a contemporary, changing discipline.

The following features are included in this book to make study easier, more interesting and efficient:

— Learning objectives are given at the beginning of each chapter. These define the information the student should have learned upon completing each unit.

— Generous use of illustrations, artwork and pictures to convey key concepts and reinforce material presented in the textual explanation.

— Two color format including many headings, lists, numbered series and visual aids to help the students remember key concepts:

— Stress on vocabulary. Basic terms are printed in a second color the first time they are introduced in the text. A key-word list at the end of each chapter refers the student back to the point in the discussion where the term is first introduced or defined.

— Easy-to-read style. Concepts are presented in an easy-to-read narrative style, without complex terms or excessive footnoting.

— Use of cartoons, humorous stories and anecdotes to add a touch of interest and humor.

— A group of boxed inserts "Postscripts" are presented, one per chapter, to focus on the contemporary and human aspect of management theory. These inserts are drawn from real life situations which depict the problems, successes and failures of people in actual management situations.

In addition to these key features, the basic text is supported by a complete learning package. The package includes a thorough study guide, a test bank and transparency master set. A complete teacher's manual outlines each chapter and includes a group of role play or situational episodes which may be used in the classroom.

This book is the result of the efforts of many people who have assisted in editing, reviewing and producing the finished book. I would like to thank personally the following people for their valuable and constructive comments and suggestions: Robert M. Fischco, Middlesex County College, New Jersey; Herb Genfan, Ithaca College, New York; Janie Lawhorn, Miami-Dade Community

College; John Martin, Mount San Antonio College, California; Douglas Mollenkopf, Southwest Texas State; James R. Myers, Pensacola Junior College; Mike D. Rice, Santa Barbara City College; George H. Sutcliffe, Central Piedmont College, North Carolina; Robert L. Wallace, Western Michigan University.

Gerald A. Silver

## ACKNOWLEDGEMENT

The Real World examples used throughout this book are derived and rewritten from many news sources: Fortune, Time, Business Week, The Executive, Forbes, and others. The cases describe real people, organizations, dollar amounts and management situations. They give the student an insight into real life management problems and decision making.

# Introduction to Management

# PART ONE

# Introduction

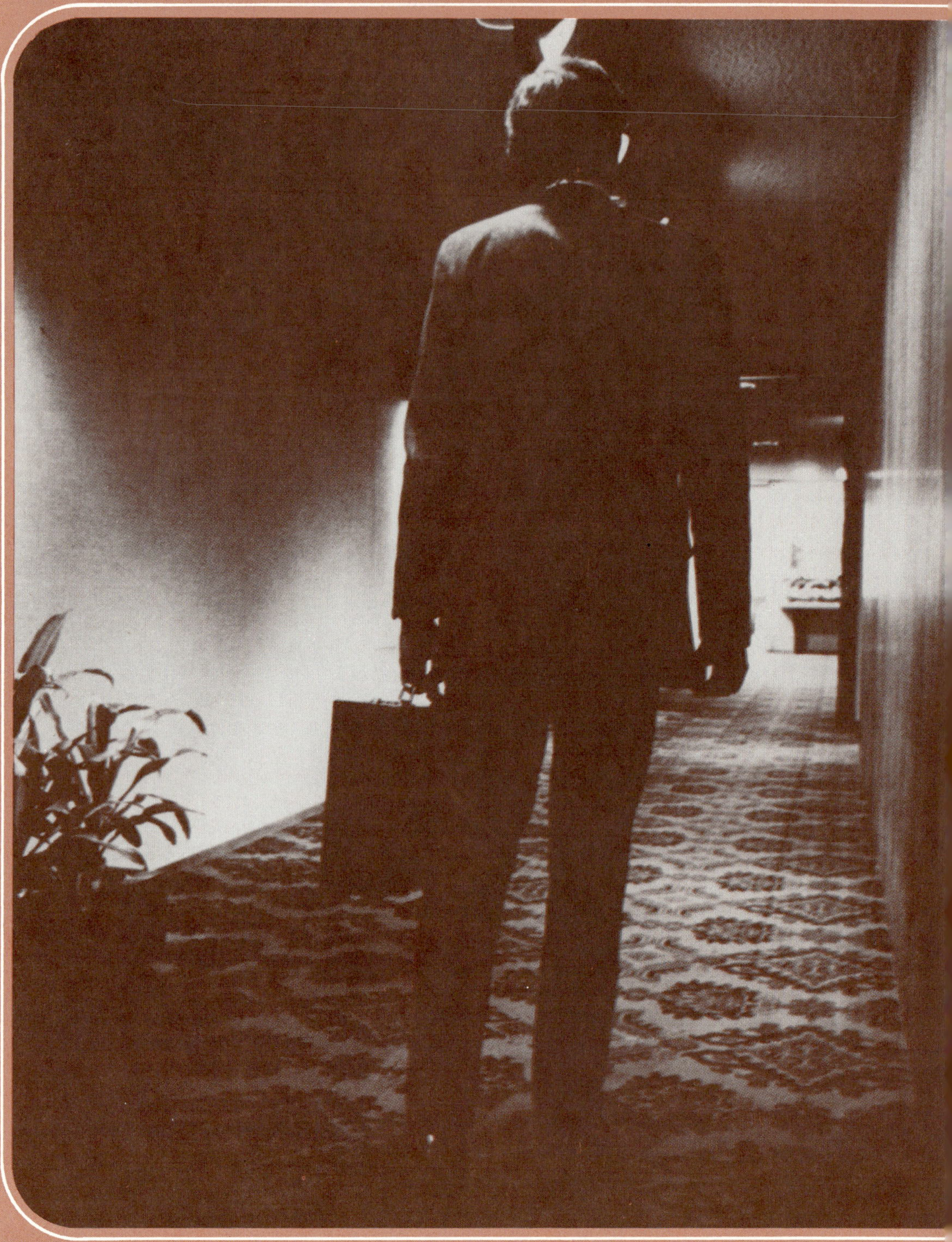

# 1
# The Role of Management

**LEARNING OBJECTIVES**

After studying this chapter, you should be able to:
1. List some common goals of organizations.
2. Define basic terms used in the study of management.
3. Identify five major management functions.
4. List some specific activities of management.
5. Summarize the types of knowledge possessed by successful managers.
6. Cite current facts and statistics for the management profession.
7. Contrast some popular management philosophies.
8. List several reasons for studying management.

An interplanetary space probe races toward a pinpoint in the heavens .. a skyscraper towers above the bustle of the city .. a computer program with the calculating power of a thousand mathematicians is written on a silicone chip the size of a match head. All these achievements are products of human effort, knowledge, money, machines, and raw materials. They have one common denominator: they require management to guide them to a successful completion.

You are about to begin a study of modern management. From this book you will gain an understanding of one of the most powerful forces in human activity: the ability to lead and direct people and organizations.

The management function is found in almost all organizations. Management is the cement that binds together all parts of an organization, moving it toward a goal. In every business office, manufacturing plant, hospital, military installation, school, and social organization, the need for management exists.

Your study of management will involve a variety of interesting subjects, including psychology, human behavior, group dynamics, motivation, communication, organization theory, budgeting, finance, personnel training, systems thinking, and the decision-making process.

The purpose of management is to coordinate many divergent resources, including people, technology, money, and raw materials, to work toward a common goal. The manager monitors all aspects of the enterprise and, as shown in figure 1-1, guides their direction.

## NEED FOR PROFESSIONAL MANAGERS

If a business organization exists with only one person, as in a sole proprietorship, there is no need for outside management. In this case, the owners, man-

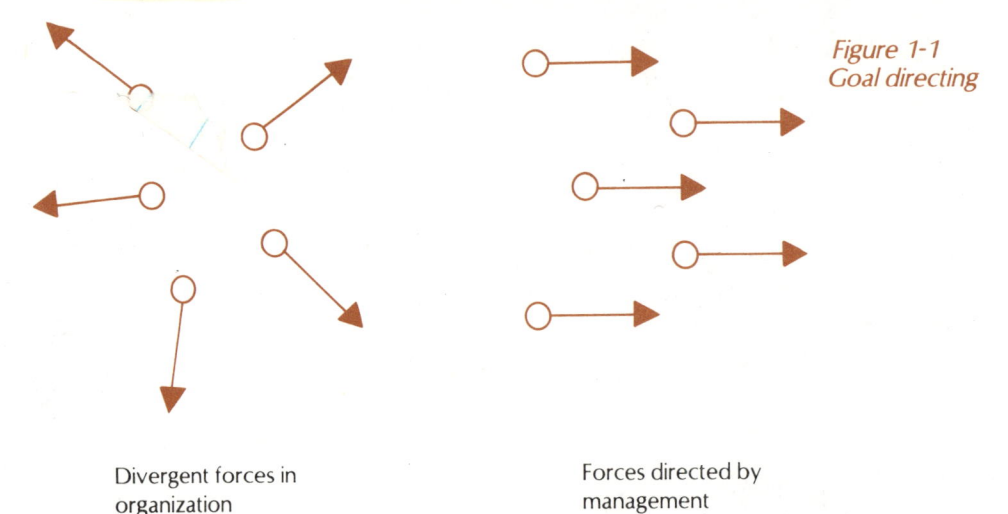

*Figure 1-1
Goal directing*

Divergent forces in organization

Forces directed by management

# CHAPTER ONE  THE ROLE OF MANAGEMENT

agement, and production personnel are all the same person (fig. 1-2). The sole owner directs his own activities and efforts to the goal he selects. He performs all tasks necessary to run the business and, hopefully, to make a profit.

However, most modern organizations are more complex. Many employ thousands of people who work in different offices and locations and carry on a variety of activities. A firm may employ accountants, scientists, researchers, machine operators, typists, clerks, truck drivers, salespeople, and many others. The efforts of all these people must be coordinated and directed towards the common goal, as in figure 1-1. This requires management.

A distinctive feature of the modern corporation is the separation of roles and the division of labor. There are three distinct categories of participants in the corporate structure (see figure 1-3): the owners (shareholders), the managers, and the workers. The owners may wish to reap a profit from their investment without participating in the actual production of services and goods or in the management of the firm. The task of management is turned over to professional managers, who make the decisions and carry out the day-to-day operation of the enterprise. The workers who produce the goods and services seldom take part in the management of the firm and usually do not own any part of it.

Figure 1-4 illustrates the structure of the modern corporation. The owners or shareholders appoint a board of directors. This group handles the principle management activity of the organization. The board of directors establishes ba-

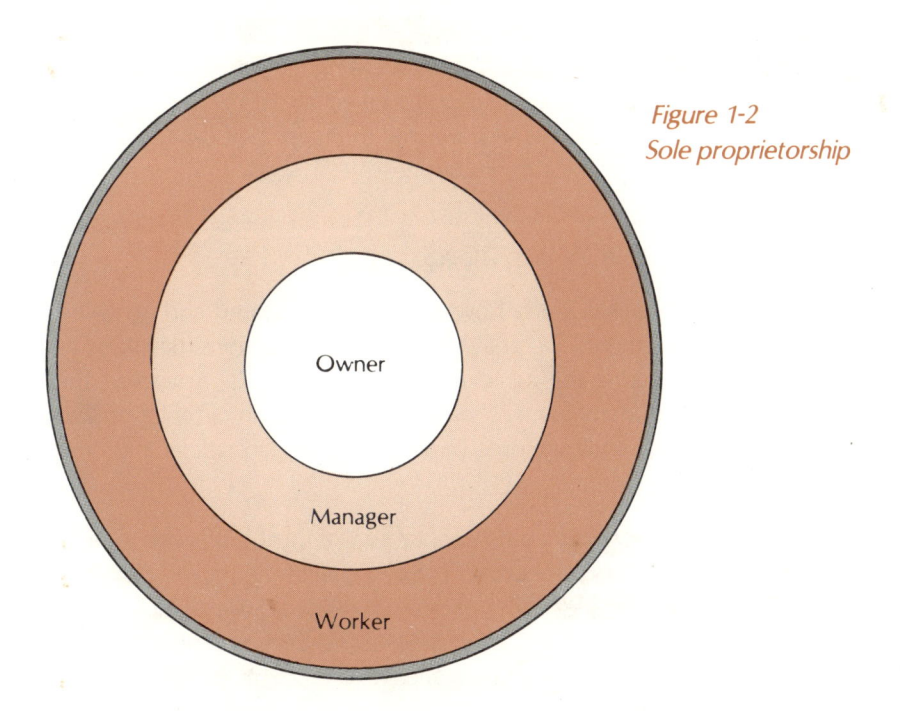

*Figure 1-2*
*Sole proprietorship*

*Figure 1-3 The corporation*

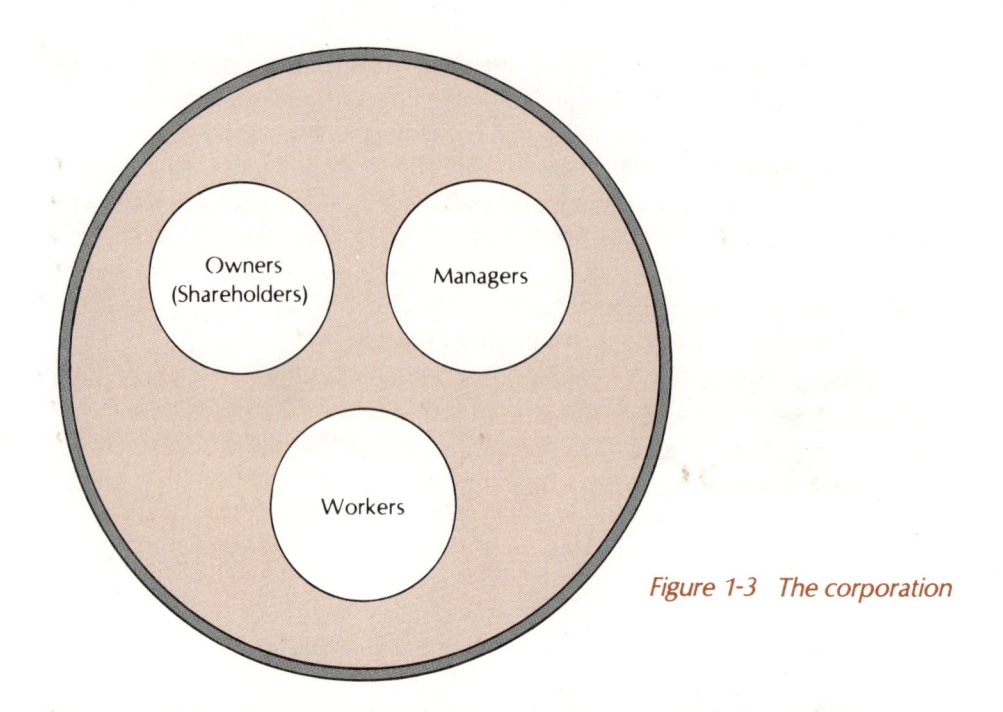

sic policy and, in turn, employs a group of officers who manage the daily activities of the firm. These officers usually include the president, vice president, secretary, and treasurer.

This division of labor between the owners, workers, and managers gives the modern corporation much of its power by allowing for specialization of effort. Skilled managers can be employed and moved about, workers can be placed where needed, while the owners are free to invest their capital without being involved in the actual running of the business.

## SOME COMMON GOALS OF ORGANIZATIONS

In the chapters ahead we shall study how goals are established and achieved through effective management. The goals of various organizations may vary, as may the means of measuring the achievement of these goals. However, the concepts and methods of management may be very similar in differing organizations. It is worthwhile to look at some basic goals of organizations and how they differ.

1. *Profit.* The making of money is a fundamental goal of most business organizations, and most attempt to maximize profit. The end goal of the organization is to return as much money as possible to the investors or owners. Success, counted in dollars returned to owners, provides a simple and convenient means of measuring organization performance. In practice, organizations seek to achieve

optimal profit *in the long run.* They try to maximize the current value of expected future returns.

2. *Growth and productivity.* A goal of some organizations is stimulated growth or increased productivity. This may result in a long-term increase in profit, but in the short run they seek to increase their physical size, share of market, or hourly output.

3. *Satisfaction of customers.* Success may also be measured in terms of customer satisfaction. The satisfaction of wants or nonmonetary needs of customers provides a useful yardstick, and it may later affect long-term profits. For instance, a school system may measure success in performance of students on a test, in the percentage graduating and going on to a higher level of schooling, or in the number placed in jobs.

Hospitals and medical systems may measure success in terms of patient care, number of beds, or reduced mortality rates. A government agency may measure success in terms of miles of paved streets, the number of books in libraries, or the number of traffic signals installed.

4. *Social returns.* Another measure of the success of an organization lies in its ability to achieve some greater social good. The performance of nonprofit and nonbusiness organizations such as schools, hospitals, social institutions, government agencies, and charitable groups, is not measured in terms of profit alone.

For example, a civic group formed to promote and build a new park or daycare center is working for the benefit of others. Its management and organization success may be measured in terms of the number of acres of new park

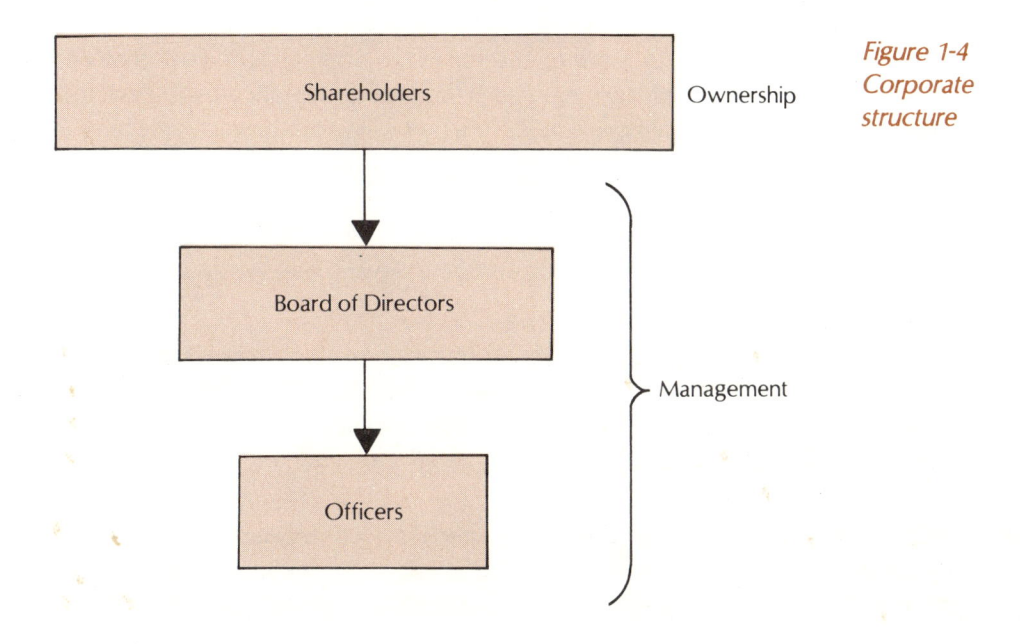

*Figure 1-4 Corporate structure*

Increased productivity is a common goal of many corporations.

grounds available or the number of children in the program. The goals may be noneconomic and can only be measured in terms of social standards. They all require a high level of management skill on the part of the organization directors.

## KEY TERMS

You should understand the definitions of the following basic terms used in the study of management.

— *Management.* Management is the coordinating process by which an organization achieves specified goals. Management involves molding into common action all resources of the organization, including human, financial, production, and distribution elements. It is the process of achieving predetermined objectives through others.

— *Manager.* A manager is anyone who performs a management function. A manager plans, organizes, staffs, controls, leads, or directs people or organizations. Managers are those who are given control and authority over others. Managers are charged with the responsibility for making decisions and carrying out plans.

— *Subordinate.* A subordinate is anyone who is directly responsible to someone at a higher level in the organizational structure. A subordinate receives direction, instruction, or guidance and is responsible to a manager for his actions. A subordinate may at the same time be a manager of others who are lower in the organizational structure.

— *Organizational hierarchy.* Modern organizations can be viewed as a pyramid (fig. 1-5). This pyramid is often called the organizational hierarchy. It defines the position of each person in the structure. At the top of the pyramid is the president, board of directors, or any individual or group with ultimate responsibility for the organization. At the bottom of the pyramid are the workers, who must carry out the orders. At varying levels on the hierarchy are managers who must direct subordinates.

— *Goals and objectives.* Goals and objectives are the end results toward which all effort is directed. They are the termination point of planning and production.

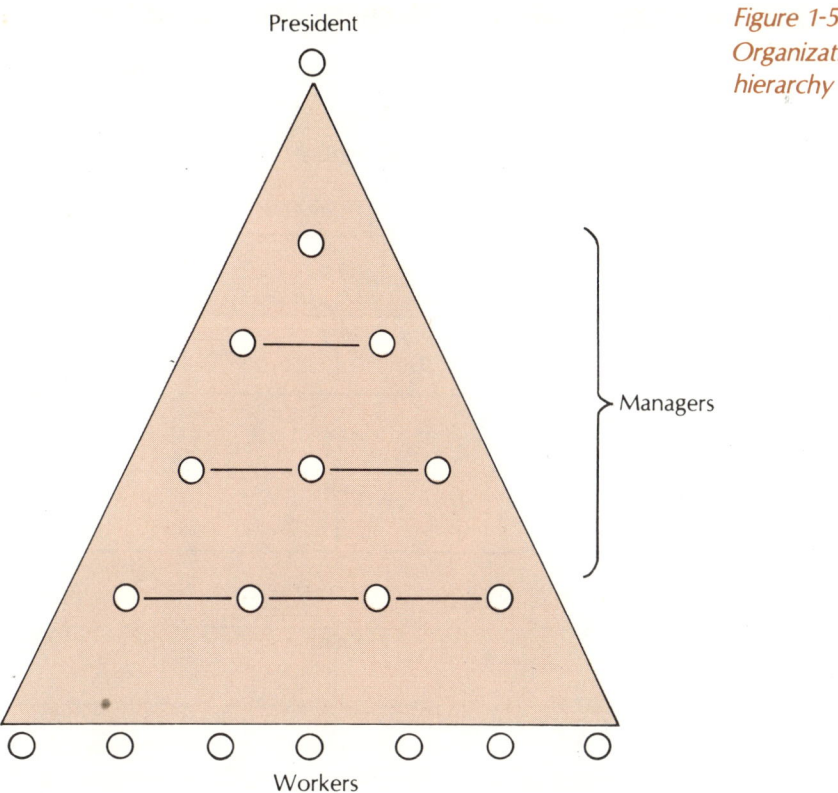

*Figure 1-5
Organizational hierarchy*

Some management authorities prefer not to draw a distinction between the terms *goals* and *objectives*. However, in this text a *goal* is defined as a generally stated end with no time limit. An *objective* is a more precisely stated end which will be achieved within a definite period of time. Goals and objectives are explained more fully in later chapters.

## LEVELS OF MANAGEMENT

In most organizations, it is possible to define loosely three levels of management. The definitions which follow are somewhat general. The dividing line between levels is not clearly delineated in many organizations. Figure 1-6 illustrates these management classifications.

1. *Top-level management (executives).* This group includes the top executives and decision makers in an organization. Top-level managers are generally those who wield the maximum authority and power. They establish the major long-range goals and plans and make the key decisions. They select key personnel to staff the mid and upper levels of the organizational hierarchy. These managers are highly paid individuals with major responsibilities. They may have only a limited number of subordinates with whom they work directly, such as mid-level managers, but they are responsible for the overall performance of all subordinates in the organization.

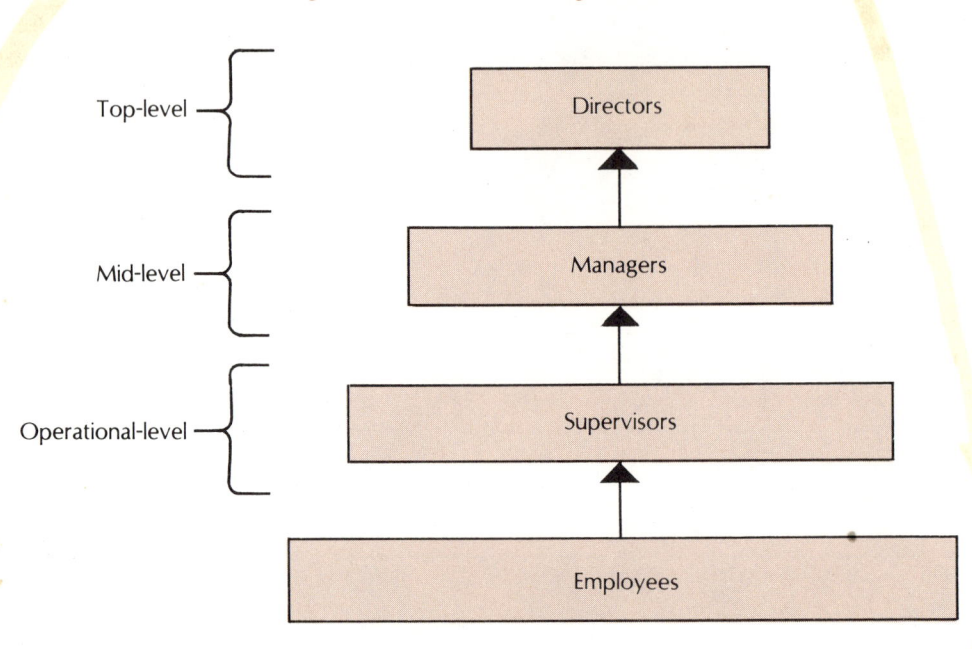

*Figure 1-6 Levels of management*

- Top-level: Directors
- Mid-level: Managers
- Operational-level: Supervisors
- Employees

> **REAL WORLD**
>
> ## That New Sante Fe Travail
>
> A combination of a unique and specialized product and management skills have thrust Robert Ozuna into a profitable and rapidly growing business. He founded New Bedford Panoramex Corporation of Santa Fe Springs, California. The firm assembles and produces a line of specialized instrument control panels for nuclear plants, pipelines, and oil drilling rigs.
>
> Using knowledge gained from night classes and on his job at an electronics firm, Ozuna decided to start his own business. He mortgaged his house and, with a handful of tools, began operations in 1967. In a little over a decade his firm has grown to sales of over $3.5 million and employs forty-one people. Ozuna's success is a product of the oil boom. But he doesn't look for any government contracts or federal business because there is too much paperwork and too many complications to make it worth his while.
>
> Adapted from *Time*, 5 May 1980, p. 85.

2. *Mid-level management (managers).* This group is subordinate to the top-level managers. Mid-level managers are charged with the task of carrying out the major decisions made at higher levels. Typical of this group are plant managers, division managers, and heads of major sections or departments. Mid-level managers often have several subordinate managers reporting to them. This level of manager is concerned with shorter-range plans and goals than is the top level.

3. *Operational-level management (supervisors).* At the lowest level of the management hierarchy are the supervisors, forepersons, and leadpersons. They are located closest to the people on the line who actually carry out the work load. These managers are sometimes called first-line management. They are responsible to the mid-level manager and are charged with implementing short-range plans and policies established by mid- and upper-level managers. They are usually responsible for several subordinates, from a small group of two or three to a larger group of twenty, thirty, or more.

## MANAGEMENT FUNCTIONS

Many authorities have attempted to define the specific functions which managers perform in their day-to-day activities. A *function* is a group of related activities contributing to a larger action. Most authorities agree that these functions include planning, organizing, staffing, directing, and controlling.

1. *Planning*. Planning involves setting goals and objectives. The planning function also includes devising a design, scheme, or program for the orderly achievement of an objective. Planning is always the beginning point of a sequence of activities and efforts designed to reach a specific goal. Planning may include either long-range or short-range plans. By definition, it is always oriented to the future.

2. *Organizing*. The organizing function involves developing a structure by bringing together many parts into a structured whole. Thus, organizing seeks to pull together many related activities into a united effort. For example, organizing consists of assembling the human resources, equipment, money, and raw materials necessary to reach an objective. Using charts to show the relationship of various individuals in the organization, (fig. 1-7), the manager gathers and maintains the needed staff and trains people to work as part of the united whole.

3. *Staffing*. Managers often have the responsibility of selecting staff to fill positions in the organization. They interview prospective employees, assess their qualifications, and place people where they can do the most good. The manager may be the one who introduces the new employee to the job or trains the employee for the position.

4. *Directing*. This function involves leading people, by showing or pointing the

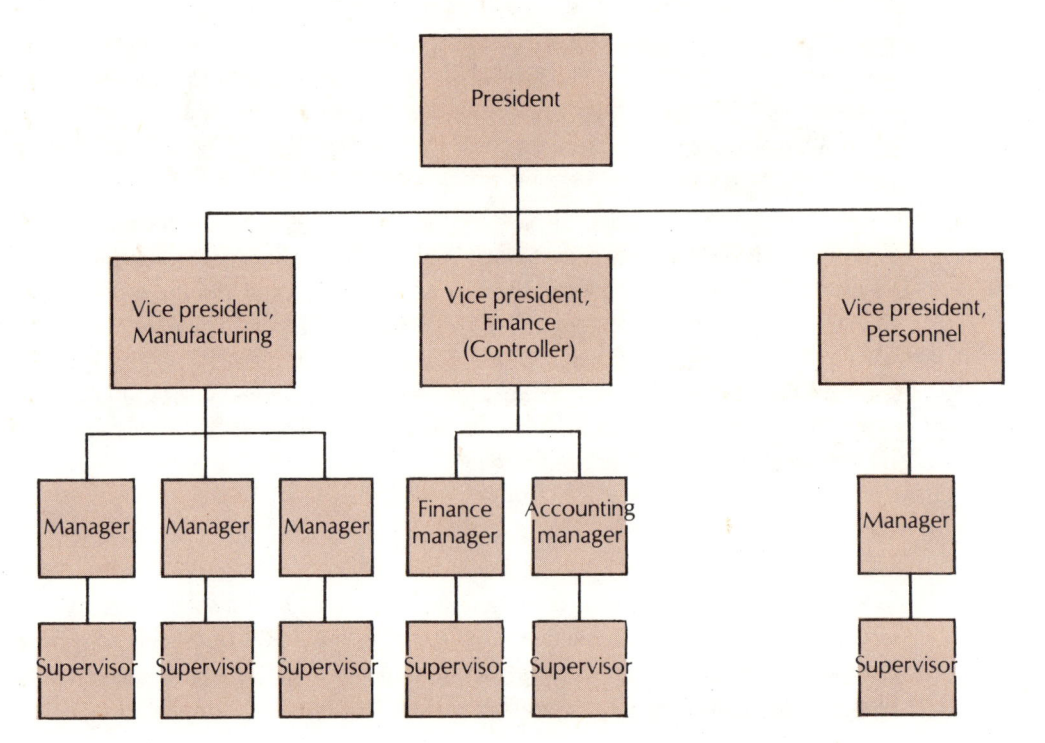

*Figure 1-7   Line organization chart*

# CHAPTER ONE   THE ROLE OF MANAGEMENT

way to the desired outcome and charting a course that others may follow. The key to this function is leadership. The manager points out the type and amount of effort needed to reach an objective. Part of the directing function involves motivating subordinates to reach the specified goals. A major part of directing consists in communicating with subordinates and conveying by example, illustration, and explanation, how an objective is to be reached.

5. *Controlling.* Controlling is the measurement of progress against standards and the redirection of activities to achieve objectives. It involves monitoring the progress of the organization against standards established during the planning stage. If progress is not in the anticipated direction and of the expected magnitude, the manager must redirect efforts. Control can be exercised in many ways. A major form of control is in the allocation of funds. By giving more funds to one activity and less to another, the manager can redirect the progress of the organization. The control function stresses measurement and comparison of progress against predetermined bench marks.

## ACTIVITIES OF MANAGERS

In order to better understand the five major functions just described, let us review specific activities performed under these categories. Figure 1-8 is a typical page from a manager's desk pad. It gives some clues regarding what specific activities are performed by managers in their day-to-day work.

1. *Policy making.* The manager often must define specific courses of action. The establishment of policies is a prime executive activity. Managers set the operating policies which subordinates are expected to follow. Policy making looks toward the future and is therefore a planning function.

2. *Decision-making.* A principle activity of the manager is decision-making. Managers are continually assessing alternative courses of action, then selecting from among them. This decision-making process is a fundamental management task and is also a planning function.

3. *Evaluating personnel.* Managers periodically review personnel performance to insure that employee performance is consistent with company objectives. If not, employees' efforts must be redirected. Managers often retrain employees or provide in-service training to update skills. This is both an organizing and a controlling task.

4. *Evaluating overall organization performance.* Managers assess the total effectiveness and performance of all facets of the organization. To do this, they study financial statements, personnel reports, sales data, warehouse records, and performance ratios. If performance is not what it should be, the manager must redirect efforts of individuals or whole departments. This is a control function.

14   PART ONE   INTRODUCTION

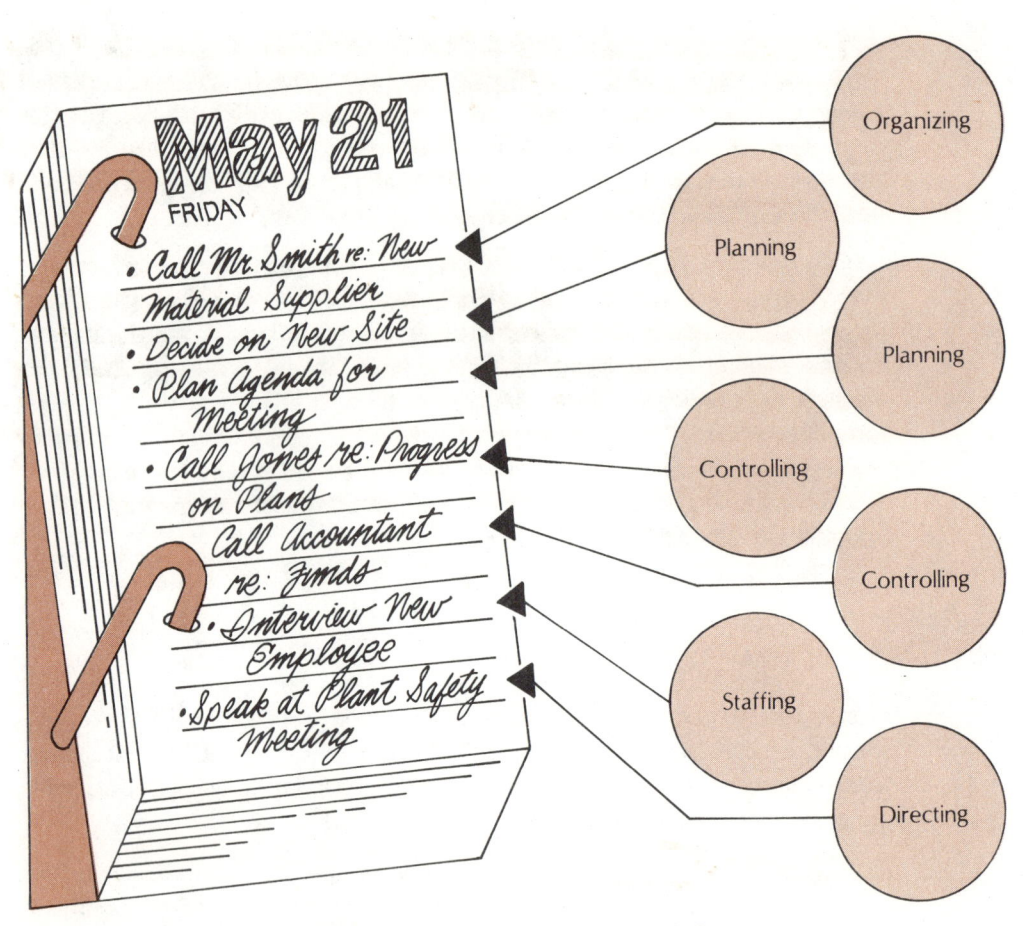

*Figure 1-8   What do managers do?*

5. *Establishing short- and long-range plans.*  Managers and executives make plans and chart courses of action for the organization. Short-range plans may specify what will be done for a period of a few weeks or months. Long-range plans may chart a direction which will be followed for many years. This is a planning function.

6. *Communicating.*  Both written and oral communication are part of the manager's job. The manager must devote time to communicating plans and policies. This involves talking to subordinates on a one-to-one basis and speaking to groups. Written communications include letters, memos, reports, and bulletins.

7. *Leading.*  A manager must often set examples for others to follow, and must instruct, train, and guide subordinates. The manager may use a variety of leadership techniques to motivate employees, and must lead the way in coping with the changes facing the firm. Leading employees in accepting and adapting to new technology and methods is a directing function.

# CHAPTER ONE   THE ROLE OF MANAGEMENT                           15

8. *Coordinating.* An especially important activity of managers is coordination, in which the manager attempts to make all parts of the organization work together.

## THE MANAGER'S FUND OF KNOWLEDGE

To perform successfully, the manager must possess human relations, technical, and conceptual skills. (See figure 1-9.) Because the job involves working with people, money, and organizations, the manager must have a basic understanding of human behavior, the group process, finance, and organizational behavior. Following is a list of major areas of knowledge which the manager should possess to perform effectively on the job.

1. *Psychology.* The manager must have a solid understanding of the psychology of human behavior in order to know what motivates people and how their fears, hopes, and aspirations affect their work. A grasp of motivation theory, driving forces, value systems, and basic human nature is essential.

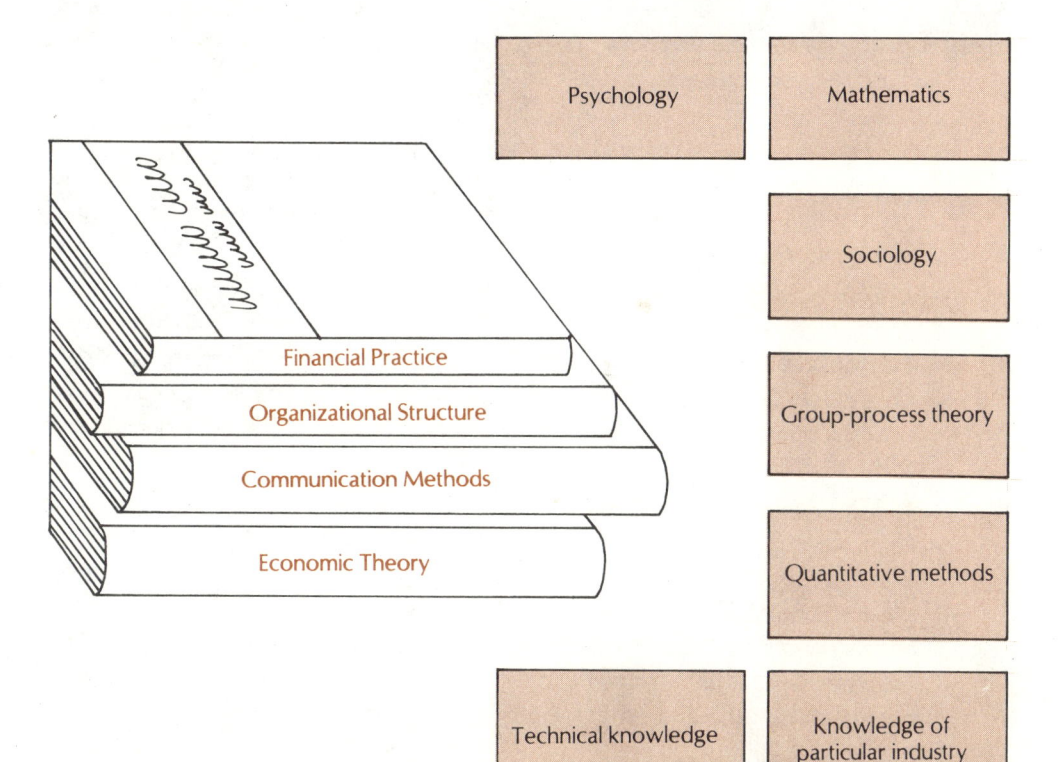

*Figure 1-9  Managerial knowledge*

Books labeled:
- Financial Practice
- Organizational Structure
- Communication Methods
- Economic Theory

Boxes:
- Psychology
- Mathematics
- Sociology
- Group-process theory
- Quantitative methods
- Technical knowledge
- Knowledge of particular industry

Oral communication is an important managerial skill.

2. *Group process.* The manager must understand how people interact in groups. Much time and effort is spent working with people who perform in a group setting. An understanding of the group process, roles, rewards, peer influences, and leadership is important.

3. *Quantitative methods.* Many decisions made by managers are based upon quantitative, or numerical, data. As the financial stakes in an organization grow, the manager must take all possible care to make the correct decision. Managers have come to rely more and more upon mathematical and quantitative tools, including operations research, probability theory, and statistics. An understanding of these subjects is essential for good decision making.

4. *Economic and financial theory.* The manager should have an understanding of finance, microeconomics, and macroeconomics. Microeconomics principles are used to run day-to-day internal affairs of the manager's business firm. Macroeconomics explain the relationship of the manager's firm to the larger national economic picture. An understanding of the laws of economics and finance help the manager understand the principles of marginal cost, supply and demand, budgetary control, and other aspects of the organization dealing with money matters.

5. *Organizational structure.* To successfully assemble groups of individuals into

working units, the manager must understand the principles of organizational structure. The manager must know how to delegate responsibility and authority, establish a division of labor, and organize people so that relationships are clearly defined.

6. *Communication theory.* The manager must communicate plans, goals, and directions clearly to subordinates. In addition to writing well, the manager must speak effectively with small and large groups of people and on a one-to-one basis with subordinates. The manager must be a good listener and reader as well.

## WHY STUDY MANAGEMENT?

You may ask why it is necessary to study management. Why is a management course often found in the curriculum leading toward undergraduate and graduate degrees in business and administration? Management is a part of virtually all endeavors which involve groups of people working toward a common goal. Here are some of the benefits from taking a course in management.

1. *To gain an understanding of the fundamentals of the management discipline.* A course in management will help you learn the basic principles of the discipline. An organized study will systematically cover the fundamentals necessary for successful performance on the job as manager.

2. *To learn basic vocabulary and terminology.* The study of management will enable you to understand management literature. It will facilitate communication with managers by teaching you the commonly accepted language of the trade.

3. *To prepare for further study.* A class in management is often an introduction to the study of business and a foundation for other courses. The study of management provides you with the theoretical knowledge and concepts you will need in further academic work.

4. *To gain practical off-the-job skills.* You will soon learn that you can apply much of the skill and knowledge obtained in a course in management in activities away from the job. This information may help you in your relationships in social, school, and other groups. Anyone involved in a common endeavor or in charge of motivating or directing people can use basic management knowledge.

5. *To become a better employee or subordinate.* Your first entry into the business world will likely be as a subordinate, and you will be responsible to others for your actions. An understanding of management principles will help you understand your role in the total organization, and how managers seek to achieve goals through others.

## CAN MANAGEMENT BE LEARNED FROM BOOKS?

Many useful skills and concepts about management can be learned from an academic study of the discipline. While books cannot replace practical knowledge or on-the-job experience, they can provide the necessary support and background to make the best use of your practical knowledge.

The effective manager must draw upon many resources. Academic knowledge is only one part of the manager's arsenal of skills. This book offers the results of research and other people's experiences, and should be useful in guiding your study and progress in management as a career.

## FACTS AND STATISTICS ON MANAGEMENT

Managers play an important role in the makeup of the American labor force. This section describes the number of persons employed as managers and administrators, including a survey of their median earnings. These statistics will give you an idea of the scope and importance of the job performed by managers.

There has been a gradual increase over the years in the number of persons employed as managers and administrators. While it is obvious from table 1-1 that the number of persons employed as managers has increased, it is also clear that the basic relationship between men and women has continued, with substantially more men than women employed in this category.

In 1970, the full-time weekly salary for managers and administrators was $190; in 1978 it was $323.[1] Females' salaries were substantially lower than males', though the gap is closing slowly. As a group, managers and administrators are

### Table 1-1. Employment of Managers and Administrators, 1960–1979

In thousands of civilians 16 years old and over

| Occupation Group and Sex | 1960 | 1965 | 1970 | 1974 | 1975 | 1976 | 1977 | 1978 | 1979 Jan.-May |
|---|---|---|---|---|---|---|---|---|---|
| Total managers and administrators[a] | 7,067 | 7,340 | 8,289 | 8,941 | 8,891 | 9,315 | 9,662 | 10,105 | 10,296 |
| Male managers and administrators[a] | 5,968 | 6,230 | 6,968 | 7,291 | 7,162 | 7,373 | 7,511 | 7,744 | 7,805 |
| Female managers and administrators[a] | 1,099 | 1,110 | 1,321 | 1,650 | 1,729 | 1,942 | 2,151 | 2,361 | 2,490 |

[a]Excludes farm.

Taken from table 685, "Employed Persons, by Major Occcupation Group and Sex: 1960 to 1979," *U.S. Statistical Abstract* (Washington, D.C.: Government Printing Office, 1979), p. 415.

---

[1]Taken from table 691, "Full-Time Wage and Salary Workers — Weekly Earnings and Index of Earnings: 1970 to 1978," *U.S. Statistical Abstract* (Washington, D.C.: Government Printing Office, 1979), p. 420.

among the highest paid employees. They surpass even professional and technical workers.[2]

## REVIEW OF SOME POPULAR MANAGEMENT PHILOSOPHIES

By 1962, dozens of differing management theories had been put forth. The world of management theory was described by Harold Koontz, a management authority, as a "management theory jungle"[3] of conflicting and inconsistent approaches. In this section, we shall briefly review some of the popular management philosophies. Later chapters will expand on these theories.

1. *Born managers.* One very old school of thought holds that managers are born, not made. This philosophy theorizes that the ability to manage is an inborn talent. Management is not learned from books, schools, or other people. Extensive research has failed to uncover any consistent basis for this theory.

The world has seen born leaders and managers, people with a gift of charismatic leadership. They have successfully led great companies, institutions, and nations through turbulent times. These managers appear to have an intuitive feel for the management discipline. They manage people and organizations effectively, though they do not hold graduate degrees in the subject. They have gained skills by personal experience and contact with other people rather than through extensive formal education. Some examples of great charismatic leaders are Winston Churchill, Franklin D. Roosevelt, and Martin Luther King. We shall not expand on this theory, since it has little academic foundation.

2. *Scientific management.* Another school of thought developed about the turn of the century. Frederick W. Taylor espoused a scientific or analytical approach to the study of work which formed the basis for much of modern industrial engineering. Taylor's approach[4] was based upon the assumption of primarily economic motivation of workers.

The scientific manager seeks to discover the *one best way* to do a task and applies it to all situations. Those who support this theory believe that most people inherently work because of economic rewards. Taken to an extreme, money is the principal motivator. It is a carrot offered for good work. A stick may also be used, such as threats and coercion.

Today, most managers believe that human beings are not governed by such

---

[2]Ibid.

[3]Harold Koontz, "The Management Theory Jungle," *Journal of the Academy of Management* 4, no. 3 (Dec. 1961): 174-188.

[4]Frederick W. Taylor, *Principles of Scientific Management* (New York: Harper and Brothers, 1911).

"Don't be ridiculous, Higgins — I always see two points of view on a subject . . mine and the one that's wrong."

Reprinted with permission of *Graphic Arts Monthly*, 1978.

simple principles and that more complex theories must be applied to the understanding of people and organizations.

3. *Human relations school.* This school, born in the 1930s, holds that the role of the manager is parental. The manager must look after subordinates' welfare, assist them, encourage them, and pick them up when they falter. This theory holds that fair treatment of subordinates evokes positive behavior. Employees, recognizing the benevolence and good intentions of the manager, will follow the manager's directives. This theory also does not take into account the complex makeup of the human organism.

4. *Human behavior school.* This school of thought emerged from the works of such important behavioral scientists as Abraham Maslow[5] and Douglas McGregor.[6] Their work led to the theory that the key to management is found in the study of people as individuals and in groups. This school is heavily influenced by individual and social psychology. Those who support this management theory view people as part of a complex socio-psychological system. The study of psychology, human behavior, responses, and the interaction of individuals with their environment is necessary to management. This theory stresses communication, leadership style, and an understanding of human motivation.

5. *Decision theory school.* This philosophy emerged out of the World War II ef-

---

[5]Abraham H. Maslow, *Motivation and Personality* (New York: Harper and Brothers, 1954).
[6]Douglas McGregor, *The Human Side of Enterprise* (New York: McGraw-Hill Book Co., 1960).

forts to apply advanced mathematics, statistics, and quantitative analysis to solving production problems. It was soon applied to the understanding and control of people and organizations. The task of the manager is to determine mathematical relationships and apply logical rules of statistics and probability to the understanding and control of enterprises.

6. *Systems school.* The late 1950s and 1960s saw the development of still another school of management thought, systems theory. This school holds that the basic rules of systems analysis can be applied to the human organism. A system is a group of related parts which function as a whole and move toward a common goal. Thus, systems theorists believe that people, procedures, policies, and methods are subsystems. These subsystems make up a total system. As such, it is predictable and controllable and follows prescribed laws.

7. *Contingency theory.* The contingency theory, sometimes called *situational management,* was developed because none of the preceding management theories worked in all situations. It became abundantly clear that no one theory could be applied to all situations.

---

**REAL WORLD**

# Advertisement for Ford Motor Co.

Ford Motor Company believes that communication is an important part of its relations with consumers. It is doing something about it in the Southern California area. Ford Motor Company has introduced a "consumer appeals board." It is made up of Mary J. Solow, President, Consumer Federation of Los Angeles; Howard H. Board, President, Board of Ford Co.; Ronald Melendez, Director, Office of Consumer Affairs, Santa Ana; Helen Sachs, President, Sachs Lincoln-Mercury, Inc.; and Billy L. Meyers, Chairman, Department of Mechanical Technology, Citrus College, Azusa.

This independent review board is designed to help consumers iron out problems with the Ford Motor Co. It has been delegated the authority to bind the Ford Motor Co. in service-related problems. The board is empowered to make decisions that are binding on Ford and its dealerships, but not on the customer.

Consumers are encouraged to use this board when they have reached an impasse with their local dealer. The Ford management hopes this will boost sales by eliminating the frustration some customers feel at the hands of giant corporations.

Reprinted with the permission of Ford Motor Co., from October 29, 1979.

**POSTSCRIPT**

# A Boss Takes His Job Personally—and His Persons Expect It

### BY ELLEN GOODMAN

I know a man who is a boss. Not a Big Boss, and not a very bossy boss. But he does have a title on his door and an Oriental rug on his floor, and he takes his job very personally — which is the problem.

You see, when this boss was in business school he assumed that management was a question of profits and losses. Now he finds himself spending a great deal of time worrying about the cost-accounting of personnel problems. Personal personnel problems.

Moreover, he says, it's going around. He keeps reading articles about "corporate irresponsibility" toward private lives. He hears how often business plays the heavy in family crises. But from where he's sitting, in a corner office looking down on the rest of the city, he sees something else.

He sees employees who want to be treated strictly professionally one moment, and then personally the next moment. He sees the conflicts faced by his employees, but also the conflicts of being a boss. He is often in a no-win situation.

The boss had three stories to tell me.

The first was about his secretary. Last January, when he interviewed her, he was warned by the personnel office to keep the questions strictly professional. On pain of a lawsuit, he could not quiz her on her marital status or child care. So he stuck to the facts, just the facts — stenography and typing and other work experience. Then last month, when one of her children was home sick, he was expected to understand why she had to be home. He saw the situation this way: One month he wasn't allowed to ask if she had children, the next month he was supposed to care that they were sick.

Then there was the junior executive whom he wanted to promote. The man

©1978, The Boston Globe Newspaper Company/Washington Post Writers Group.

Out of the dozens of divergent philosophies came the contingency theory. These management theorists hold that there is no single set of rules or universal laws which can be applied to all situations. They believe that the task of managers is to select those methods or rules which appear applicable to the given situation. Instead of a set of universal rules, the manager must begin with an analysis of the situation and work back toward a method of management. This contingency

CHAPTER ONE    THE ROLE OF MANAGEMENT

was clearly ambitious and good. The boss had judged him on the basis of his work, he had groomed him and watched him. Then he had handed him a big promotion to the Southwest. But the junior executive asked to be excused. He didn't want to make this trip, because he just couldn't move his family at this time. But, the boss said, the man had never described himself as immovable on account of teenage children. Now the boss was asked to make allowances.

The third story was actually somewhat ironic, because it happened in the personnel department itself. The assistant director of personnel was a man who administered the most careful, scientific, professional testing service that the boss had ever seen. It screened people in and out of the company, up and down the hierarchy, on the basis of multiple-choice answers. But now this man had just obtained custody of two small children. He had come in to ask for flexible hours. Under the circumstances, he wanted to know whether he could make some special arrangements that would help his personal life.

This particular boss isn't a Simon Legree. Nor is he the sort of man who treats people like interchangeable plastic parts. So he adjusted to his secretary. He adjusted to his junior executive. He adjusted to the assistant director of personnel. He did it because, well, a happy employee is probably a productive employee and all that.

He did it because a person's private life is a factor in his professional life, and all that. He did it because he believed that business should be more flexible. To a point.

But he feels a certain frustration. People want him to treat them professionally when it's to their advantage, and personally when it's to their advantage. While he understands the family-business conflict, he also understands the conflict that comes with the title on the door and the Oriental rug on the floor.

Every day this boss has to decide at what point the best personal interests of his employees conflict with the best business interests of his company. Where is it writ, he asks, that business increasingly has to deal with personal personnel issues? How do you balance the needs of the company and the needs of the workers?

Sometimes this man is afraid that he's running a family agency instead of a corporate division. Other times he's afraid he's being a heel.

The boss doesn't expect any sympathy. He doesn't want his name in the paper. People don't sympathize with bosses, anyway, he says, because it's hard to sympathize with someone who has the power to hire and fire you. He understands that.

But the fact is that he's responsible for 150 lives and one corporate balance sheet. And he takes both these jobs very personally.

theory has gained many supporters during the past several years. They are broad-based in philosophy and draw upon a rich variety of management thought.

## SUMMARY

There is a need for management wherever organizations exist. Organizations are composed of managers who direct and control subordinates. Some common goals of organizations include maximizing output while minimizing costs, satisfaction of clients, and social returns.

Management is divided into three levels: top-, mid-, and operational-level management. These categories include executives, managers, and supervisors. Five major functions of management are planning, organizing, staffing, directing, and controlling.

In carrying out the management responsibility, managers perform a variety of activities including planning, decision making, staffing, evaluation of personnel, and overall organization performance. Managers must possess skills and knowledge of psychology, group process, quantitative methods, economic and financial theory, organization structure, and communication ability. They must also understand the technology of their industry.

There are a variety of reasons for taking a course in management, including transfer and preparation for further study, practical on- and off-the-job skills, and the need to become a better employee or subordinate.

A variety of management philosophies have been advanced, including the concept of born managers, scientific management, and human relations, human behavior, decision theory, systems, and contingency theory schools.

## KEY TERMS

| | |
|---|---|
| Profit  6 | Staffing  12 |
| Manager  8 | Directing  12 |
| Subordinate  9 | Controlling  13 |
| Organizational hierarchy  9 | Policy making  13 |
| Levels of management  10 | Decision making  13 |
| Planning  12 | Communicating  14 |
| Organizing  12 | Coordinating  15 |

## REVIEW QUESTIONS

1. Describe some common goals of organizations.
2. How does the role of the manager differ from the role of the subordinate?
3. Describe the differences between various levels of management.
4. Explain the planning function.
5. Explain the organizing function.
6. How does the task of directing differ from controlling?
7. Can you describe several common management activities?
8. In your own words, summarize the knowledge and skills which the successful manager must possess.
9. Give four reasons for studying management.

10. Do you believe that management ability can be learned from books? Why or why not?
11. Contrast several major management philosophies.
12. What are the major premises of the contingency school of management theory?

# Case Incident

Andrew Tennison sat in class taking notes and thinking about the problem his professor posed on the first day of class. "Define manager and describe how a person gains skills and knowledge necessary to perform management responsibilities," said Professor Steele. The professor went on to discuss the various traits that most managers possess. She discussed group processes, learning to understand people, social psychology, and the nature of organizations. Professor Steele closed the lecture with an assignment to ask three people their definition of what makes a good manager.

Andrew left the class thinking about his first day's assignment and feeling unsure about what he would learn. The first person Andrew talked to was the manager of the supermarket, who said, "Everybody knows that managers are really born, not made. Either people have what it takes or they don't, and you really can't learn it from books or on-the-job experience."

Next Andrew decided to talk to his father, who was very clear about his feelings on how one becomes a good manager. "You obviously learn this in school. You are taught management skills through in-service programs, exercises, and training. It's something you learn by studying, since there are certain basic skills and abilities that all managers must possess."

Finally, Andrew decided to approach his Aunt Ruth. Ruth had her own opinion about what makes a good manager. "There's only one way to become a good manager, and that's through lots of practical, real-world experience. You've got to live it day in and day out. You must manage people and face the problems and frustrations involved in the job to understand what makes organizations tick."

## PROBLEMS

1. Explain how you think a manager gains the necessary skills.
2. How important is experience in a manager's repertoire of skills?
3. How important is academic training in learning management skills?

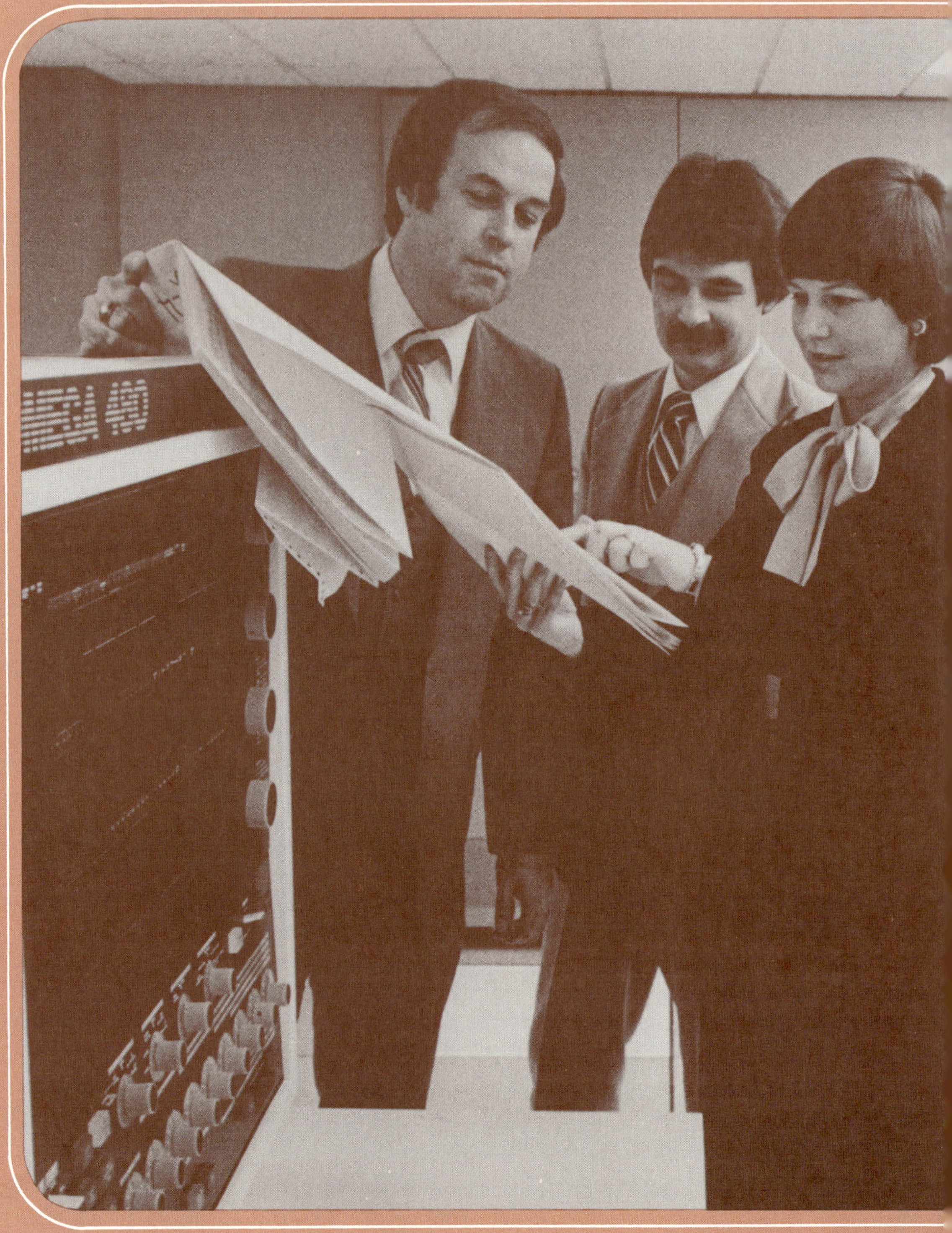

# 2
# The Evolution of Management Theory

**LEARNING OBJECTIVES**

After studying this chapter, you should be able to:
1. Contrast major management theories.
2. Summarize the contributions to management theory of Weber, Taylor, and Fayol.
3. Describe the scientific management theory.
4. Explain the importance of the Hawthorne studies to management theory.
5. Describe the behavioral science theory of management.
6. Describe the quantitative theory of management.
7. Describe the systems theory of management.
8. Describe the contingency theory of management.
9. Identify key individuals who have made major contributions to management theory.
10. Contrast the roles of managers and subordinates under various management theories.

This chapter traces the historical development of management theory from its earliest beginnings to contemporary management thought. The evolution of management theory is the result of countless contributions from individuals who have studied, analyzed, and managed people and organizations.

Table 2-1 contrasts management theories and lists some of the individuals who have influenced each school. The following outline will help you see a structure to the development of management theory.

*Premodern Theories*
    a. Early management theories
    b. Scientific management
    c. Human relations

*Modern Theories*
    a. Behavioral science
    b. Quantitative/decision theory
    c. Systems theory
    d. Contingency (situational) theory.

## EARLY MANAGEMENT THEORIES

Theories of management have been applied since the dawn of civilization. Someone probably advanced a management theory the day two or more human beings first joined together to achieve a common goal. The selection of a goal, the deployment of resources, and the direction of others is an attempt at management.

Early roots of management are found in efforts directed at organization of the work force, communication of plans and goals, and leadership of others. All of these activities are found in ancient tribes. Individuals were assigned a task by tribal leaders. They were expected to perform a job, and their work was coordinated and directed by others. Thus, we find delegation of authority, responsibility, and channels of communication. Many early management efforts were attempts by monarchs, kings, and other rulers to govern and control subordinates or subjects. The control of subjects by heads of state and government predates the role of management in business and private enterprise.

Since almost every business enterprise was rooted in the home or on the farm, there was little need for elaborate management systems. It was not until the 1750s, when manufacturing moved from the farms and cottages to the factories, that the real need for business management developed. The earliest attempts at management focused on building roads, protective city walls, palaces and citadels, and aqueducts. These were generally government-sponsored projects and did not involve private enterprise.

CHAPTER TWO    THE EVOLUTION OF MANAGEMENT THEORY    29

**Table 2-1. Management theories contrasted**

| Theory | Role of Subordinate | Role of Manager | Theory Based upon; | Individuals Who Made Contributions |
|---|---|---|---|---|
| Scientific management | Follow the manager's *one best way* and *one best time* | Discover the *one best way*, direct subordinates | Early scientific principles | Charles Babbage<br>Frederick W. Taylor<br>Lillian and Frank Gilbreth<br>Henri Fayol |
| Human relations | Part of the family of workers | Managers as parental figure | Simple human needs | Hugo Munsterberg<br>Elton Mayo — *Hawthorn effect*<br>Chester I. Barnard (transitionalist) |
| Behavioral science | Psychological animal | Understand psychological nature of worker | Human motivation, needs, wants | Abraham Maslow<br>Douglas McGregor |
| Quantitative decision making | Laws of statistics and probability | Understand and use laws of statistics and probability | Mathematics, statistics | P. M. Morse<br>G. E. Kimball<br>Joseph McCloskey<br>Herbert Simon |
| Systems theory | A subunit, part of a larger system | Understand total system behavior | Systems theory, feedback loop | Fremont E. Kast<br>Ludwig von Bertalanffy<br>Kenneth Boulding<br>James E. Rosenzweig |
| Contingency theory | Varies with situation | Varies with situation | Eclectic; no universal rules apply to all situations | Joan Woodward<br>Fred E. Fiedler |

*(Handwritten annotations: "pre modern" bracketing Scientific management and Human relations; "modern" bracketing Behavioral science, Quantitative decision making, Systems theory, and Contingency theory)*

## Greek, Roman and Chinese Civilizations

The early Greek, Roman, and Chinese civilizations involved governing large numbers of people and guiding them toward common goals. The construction of great Roman cities, the Coliseum, and the Great Wall of China required a large amount of resources and workers.

Through the years, a natural system of management evolved. Selected individuals with leadership ability gave orders to their subordinates. In turn, these mid-level managers delegated responsibility to others, who carried out the work load. Before long, a complex hierarchy of subordinates developed.

As far back as 5000 B.C., recorded attempts are found which establish rules and policies governing the work force as well as the social structure. Around

1800 B.C., the Babylonians produced the Code of Hammurabi, which laid down significant laws concerning the rights of citizens, business, and organizations. This code was an early effort at management. It involved the classical functions of planning, organizing, directing, and controlling an entire empire.

Early Roman and Chinese efforts at management were often directed at military strategy and maneuvers. One of the most significant of these was the "Art of War," a treatise written by Sun Tzu in 500 B.C. This document laid down basic military principles which formed a foundation and structure for managing people. It gave instruction in methods of delegating authority and stressed the need for planning.

## Medieval Influence of the Roman Catholic Church

The Roman Catholic church had a great influence on the development of management thought. The church, more than any other social structure of the time, defined rules of organization, responsibility, staffing, and authority. A hierarchy was established by the church which laid out the division of labor and implemented the functions of planning, organizing, directing, and controlling.

Figure 2-1 shows the hierarchy of the Catholic church. All over the world

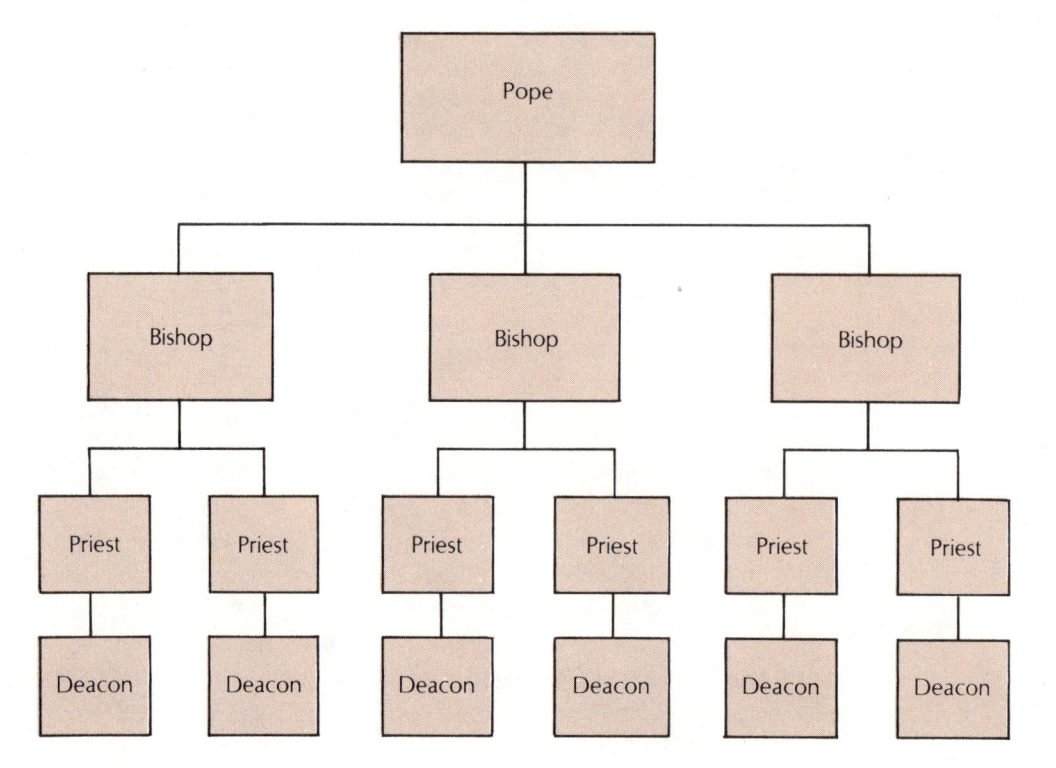

*Figure 2-1    Roman Catholic Church Hierarchy*

churches, abbeys, monasteries, and missions were built. The construction of these buildings required the coordination of labor to implement and control the successful completion of these projects. The clearly defined hierarchy of the Catholic church parallels the chain of command found in the military.

## Industrial Revolution and Reorganization of Work Force

The Industrial Revolution had a significant influence on management theory. The Industrial Revolution began in England in 1750 and spread to the United States by 1820. It was characterized by a shift from hand labor to machine production, and from horse power to steam driven machines. Several inventions, including the power loom, steam engine, spinning jenny, mechanical harvester, and sewing machine, fostered the revolution.

The Industrial Revolution brought the factory system and the demise of the cottage industries. Prior to the Industrial Revolution, most goods were produced in the home (cottage) or on the farm. With the introduction of machines, it became necessary to build factories. These factories soon spread throughout England and became the focal point of manufacturing. Soon the work force reflected this change, moving to the cities and away from the homes and farms. Large numbers of people started working in factories. The need for improved management practices became imperative.

---

**REAL WORLD**

# Liquid Gold

Managers often overlook the simple and obvious in favor of the complex. But Bette Nesmith Graham saw the obvious need for a simple and inexpensive product — a little bottle of correction fluid which she called Liquid Paper.

In 1951 she was employed as a secretary and was constantly plagued by typing errors. Using a formula she concocted, and $500, she conceived Liquid Paper, a product that is now commonplace on virtually every secretary's desk. Because of her innovation and creativity, a product was brought on the market that earned over $3.5 million on $38 million of sales in 1979.

Adapted from *Fortune*, 5 November, 1979, p.32.

Babbage's Difference Engine

## Richard Arkwright, Charles Babbage, and Others

There were many individuals who influenced management thinking during these years. Richard Arkwright developed a loom and built a factory which employed hundreds of people. He soon realized the need for management of his work force and pioneered personnel management methods.

In the 1830s Charles Babbage, a mathematician and scientist, experimented with a mechanized means of managing and processing data. He developed plans for his analytical and difference engines which would automatically perform mathematical calculations. These machines were never actually built, but they laid the foundation for a mechanized means of processing data. Babbage's concepts influenced management theory. He believed that the manager's tasks included analyzing the manufacturing process, measuring output by scientific means, using printed forms, and studying the manufacturing process, materials, and work force to maximize production. Babbage emphasized rational methods of study and observation to increase output.

### Max Weber's Bureaucracy

During the 1890s, Max Weber, a German sociologist, studied how organizations are controlled and function. Weber became interested in how an organization's bureaucracy worked, and how it could be used to manage the large numbers of people who were now leaving their homes and farms to enter civil service.

Weber saw a logical framework for organizations, and certain rules and principles which could be implemented to improve output. His understanding of bureaucratic structure influenced later management theorists.

Weber defined several essentials of a bureaucracy. He theorized that the basic form of an organization is analogous to a pyramid. This pyramid, or hierarchy, is governed by specific rules. For instance, he believed there is a need for accountability of resources by management, the need for putting things in writing, and the need for reliance upon professional managers to direct the organization.

## SCIENTIFIC MANAGEMENT THEORY

One of the most influential contributors to the field of management was Frederick W. Taylor. Taylor began his work in 1879 and spent several decades attempting to find better ways to manage workers and improve productivity. Taylor considered the worker as primarily motivated by money, an *economic man*. He saw scientific management as a way of maximizing the fulfillment of workers' needs as well as those of management. Taylor became known as the father of scientific management, and his work influenced management methods for many years.

Taylor developed the theory of the *one best way*. His idea was that there is one best way to perform every job. The responsibility for discovering and implementing this one best method lies with the manager, rather than with subordi-

Frederick W. Taylor

nates. Taylor believed that the planning of a job and the actual execution should be separate functions. He viewed the manager's job as planning what to do, while the worker would simply follow this plan. The worker, freed from the planning task, could concentrate on carrying out the orders. Taylor instituted a differential rate incentive system, where workers with high output were rewarded by receiving extra pay. This would benefit the company and the worker.

Taylor began his work at Midvale Steel Company as a machinist, and worked his way up to chief engineer. During his years at Midvale, Taylor experimented with work measurement and output. He first attempted to systematically study a job, such as the work performed by a lathe operator, and to analyze the time and motions needed to perform it properly.

In the early 1890's, Taylor moved to Bethlehem Steel Company, where he conducted further research into time and motion studies and job design. His work at Bethlehem centered on measuring worker performance and improving output. In one experiment he examined fatigue factors and controlled rest periods for the loading of pig iron. In another study he sought to maximize output by finding the optimum shovel size for various materials.

Taylor established what he considered to be the *one best way* and *one best time* to do the job and required employees to follow his specific recommendations. He also agreed to give the employees a piece work, or differential incentive pay bonus, as a reward for increased production. The results were immediate and positive. The men following his method increased output substantially, thus saving Bethlehem thousands of dollars. Taylor was summoned before Congress to testify on work measurement and output, and published several books which became milestones in management theory.

## Taylor's Principles

As a result of his studies, Taylor defined four major principles of scientific management:

1. Use scientific methods in studying each job. Avoid rules of thumb or guesswork.

2. Workers should be selected and trained carefully. The manager should analyze each task and select the proper employee for the job. The worker should be schooled in the *one best way*, rather than being allowed to choose any method.

3. Workers' output can be improved by increasing motivation through bonuses and incentives. Minimum output standards should be established, and workers who exceed these should be rewarded financially.

4. The task should be divided between the manager and the worker. The planning function should be performed by the manager, so the worker is free to do the job.

Taylor's methods worked so well that they were soon copied by other industries all over the country. Before long, Taylor's scientific management became the standard industry management method.

## OTHER EARLY THEORISTS

### Henry L. Gantt

A fellow employee with Taylor at Midvale Steel was Henry L. Gantt. Gantt was also interested in work measurement and output. He believed that workers should not be treated in an arbitrary manner, and that the manager should be more responsive to the individual needs of each employee. Gantt felt that there were some employees who would not increase output if money was the only incentive offered.

Gantt devised a system of scheduling production using a chart (Fig. 2-2), which listed tasks horizontally. This chart showed the relationship of events over a given period of time. Managers were able to see the sequence of events necessary to complete a task. Gantt charts are still widely used to control production and schedule manufacturing operations.

### Frank and Lillian Gilbreth

A husband and wife team made the next important contribution to the understanding of management theory. The Gilbreths expanded upon Taylor's theory by further refining each job into a carefully planned series of steps. The Gilbreths used time and motion studies extensively. They reviewed each task,

Henry L. Gantt

and after an analysis they detailed the exact order and movement of hand and eye which should be followed.

This approach later became characterized by the stereotype of an efficiency expert with a stopwatch standing over an employee. The Gilbreths instructed employees in the proper way to grasp, hold, or move a part. Soon many business managers adopted this motion study approach to job analysis.

The Gilbreths' methods were implemented by managers, who gained immediate improvements in productivity. The Gilbreths outlined a series of basic motions or work components which became known as *therbligs* (Gilbreth loosely spelled backwards). The following elements greatly influenced managers during this era.

1. Employees were to be carefully selected for a job and then given specific instructions on how to do it.

2. Employees were then to be left alone, so they could perform the work.

3. Regular reports were to be completed by the employees to record their output.

A humorous insight into the work of the Gilbreths was dramatized in the motion picture, *Cheaper by the Dozen.* The Gilbreths applied their rules of management to their own family of twelve children. Each child was assigned a specific job to do and instructed in the proper way to perform it. The Gilbreths brought precision measurement of work right into their home.

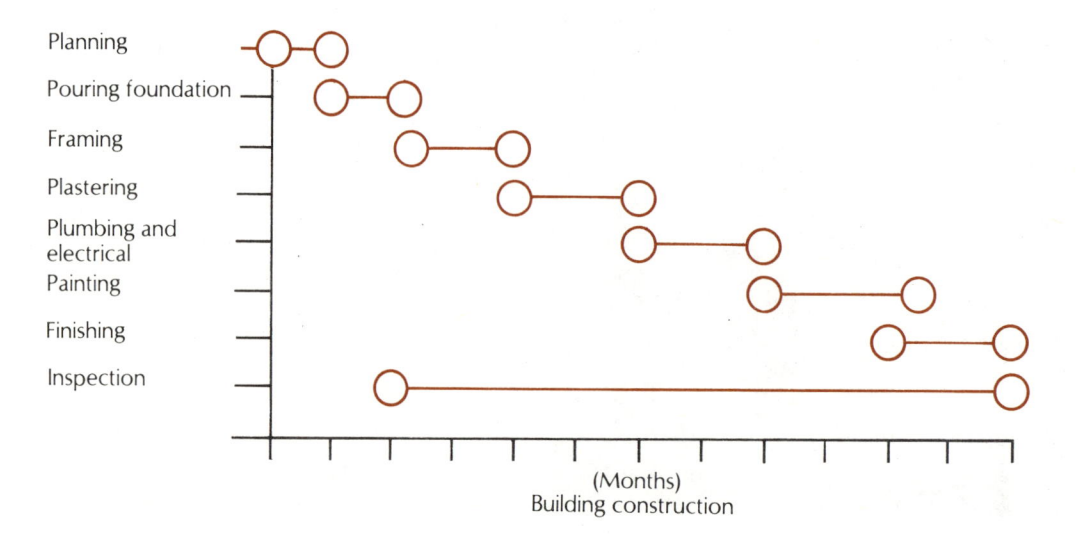

*Figure 2-2   Gantt chart*

(Months)
Building construction

Frank and Lillian Gilbreth

## Henri Fayol

In the early 1900s, a French mining engineer, Henri Fayol, became interested in identifying the basic building blocks of an effective organization. He believed the French government could improve productivity of workers by paying more attention to administrative management.

Fayol concerned himself with administration and organization principles, and isolated six important elements in any work task:

1. technical operations;
2. commercial operations;
3. financial operations;
4. security operations;
5. accounting operations;
6. administrative operations.

To Fayol, the essence of management was in planning, organizing, designing, coordinating, and controlling the activities of subordinates. Fayol's work profoundly influenced management thinking for generations to come. He structured a framework upon which may be built a sound theory of management. Fayol stressed the basic elements of planning, organizing, commanding, and controlling. These still form the underpinnings of most management concepts. For example, he believed there should be authority, discipline, and a division of labor. A unity of command should be followed, where each subordinate answers to only one manager. He also believed there should be a chain of command and equity in dealing with staff.

### Hugo Munsterberg

Hugo Munsterberg made a contribution which changed the emphasis of management theory. Munsterberg was employed as a vocational testing counselor. He sought to match an individual's abilities and aptitudes with a job. Munsterberg designed several interesting experiments, including the famous trolley experiments of 1911. Through these experiments, he developed a series of aptitude tests to find trolley car operators who were suited for the work. He found that certain individuals who passed his visual and written tests became safe, competent operators, while those who failed were unsuited. Munsterberg concluded that there is a link between an individual's aptitude and quality of job performance. His studies focused on the psychological aspects, differences between people, and how people relate to their jobs. Munsterberg became known as the father of industrial psychology.

### Mary Parker Follett, Alan C. Reiley, James D. Mooney, and Lyndall F. Urwick

During the mid 1920s, a number of management theorists made significant contributions. Mary Parker Follett impressed managers with her simple and logical idea that government could increase the productivity of employees by the application of sound management principles. She emphasized the need for a democratic, fair-handed, human relations approach to handling subordinates. She believed that the manager and subordinates should work together and avoid conflict.

Alan C. Reiley and James D. Mooney expanded upon Fayol's work by drawing a distinction between the task of assembling an organization and its actual management. In their view, the function of the organization was to coordinate overall activities, while the manager's job was to lead and direct subordinates in carrying out these activities.

Lyndall F. Urwick was influential in popularizing and disseminating many of Fayol's principles. He developed a logical structure from the theories of Fayol, Mooney, and Reiley. Urwick believed that the major theories were all interrelated and should be treated as a whole.

## HUMAN RELATIONS THEORY

The emphasis of management theory up to this point was on treating people in a relatively mechanistic and nonhumanistic way. Generally, scientific managers viewed individuals as work-producing units that could be guided and controlled by simple rules or principles. Such theories put little emphasis on human needs, wants, and inner psychological motivations. Most of the efforts by early management experts were on studying the job or task and identifying universal rules or principles. The psychological aspects of people and how they relate to their jobs were not taken into consideration.

## Elton Mayo

The next major contribution was made by Elton Mayo, an industrial psychologist from Scotland. He was on the faculty of Wharton School at the University of Pennsylvania, and later joined the faculty of Harvard University.

Mayo influenced the development of the human relations school of management. He was trained in the basic principles of scientific management. During the late 1920s, many industrial psychologists were seeking to improve worker efficiency by applying scientific management.

Elton Mayo had been experimenting with rest periods, and how they affected worker morale and labor turnover at the Hawthorne plant of Western Electric. Mayo and others also conducted a group of studies involving relay assembly procedures and bank wiring operations, and later did a series of interview studies. Each of these produced some profound insights into management theory and practice.

A group of experiments relating to illumination had revealed some interesting observations. Some assembly workers had been observed and their output studied. When illumination in the room was increased, the employee's output went up. A further increase in light illumination resulted in another increase in output. The researchers concluded there was a significant relationship between light level and the amount of work produced.

To confirm their findings they decided to reduce light levels and see whether less work was produced. When they reduced the lighting in the test room, they discovered that output went up, not down! (See figure 2-3). Reducing the lighting levels even more, they observed another increase in output. This raised many questions regarding the worker and the job.

## The Hawthorne Study Conclusions

There are many psychological and social interactions at play in the work place. These have great influence on the worker's output. The human side of the worker must be considered as much as the physical aspects of the job. The personal and social interactions between the worker and peer group are important. Mayo recognized that people respond to their work environment as human beings and as part of a social group, and that psychological elements and attitudes

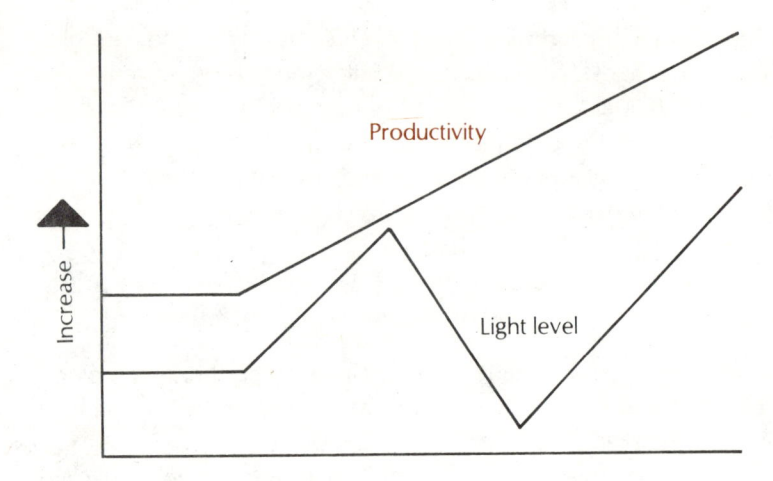

*Figure 2-3 Productivity study with varying light levels*

greatly affect the worker and the quality of work. Mayo concluded that the employee's attitudes, peer group, informal relationships, and relationship with the manager could not be ignored.

## The Hawthorne Effect

As a result of these studies, managers became aware of the *Hawthorne effect.* Conclusions drawn from studies made under test conditions are often distorted. Workers who are being timed or observed as they work may increase or decrease their output merely because they are the objects of a study. Employees may assume that their employer has a personal interest in the subordinates, and as a result they frequently produce more work than they would under normal conditions.

As a result of the Hawthorne studies, a new theory of management, the human relations school, was born. This school spread throughout industry in the 1930s and 1940s. Human relations became the management philosophy in many companies. Managers became aware that employees were human beings with a psychological makeup and a response to their peers and their environment.

## Chester I. Barnard

In the late 1940s and 1950s, Chester I. Barnard, president of New Jersey Bell Telephone, expanded the fund of management knowledge. While he was not strictly part of the human relations movement, Barnard is considered an early behavioralist. He analyzed various companies and determined that all organizations have certain elements in common. In his studies, Barnard pointed out that the willingness of the subordinate to accept authority is a crucial element in management. According to Barnard, subordinates have a *zone of indifference* in which they will accept a given amount of authority. Anything within this range will be agreed to. Directives which go beyond the zone of indifference will be questioned. The astute manager must understand this zone and use it in guiding and controlling subordinates.

Barnard viewed an organization as a cooperative system, in which management provides the authority and inducements, while the subordinate is free to accept this authority. He stated that the mere exercise of authority was inadequate. An employee must receive something in exchange for accepting authority. An employee who will not gain personal benefits will not accept directives.

## BEHAVIORAL SCIENCE THEORY

During the 1950s and early 1960s, much research was done on the human behavior aspects of people in organizations. Behavioral scientists studied human responses, group interaction, motivation, need, and reward systems. Two behavioral theorists, Abraham Maslow and Douglas McGregor, stand out in this effort to understand human behavior. Douglas McGregor defined his X and Y theory of motivation, and Abraham Maslow developed a basic theory of human needs.

Adherents of the behavioral science theory of management believe that the laws of science apply to the understanding of human behavior. Management focus should be on social psychology and human motivation. Their major goal is to understand the socialization and interaction process and apply it to management.

### Abraham Maslow

An important theory of human motivation was espoused by Abraham Maslow. Maslow stated that human motivation is based upon a hierarchy of needs. He believed that each human being has basic needs that must be met for that person to be productive and function well. A human being's primary motivator is the lowest unfulfilled need on a hierarchy. When that need is fulfilled, it no longer acts as a motivator.

Adherents of Maslow's theory believe that the role of management is to provide an environment which satisfies the basic needs of people. Maslow's hierarchy of major human needs, shown in figure 2-4, is as follows:

1. *Physiological needs*. The need for food, shelter, rest, and sex, the basic and primary needs of all human beings.

2. *Safety needs*. The need for physical security and personal protection.

3. *Social needs*. The need to be accepted by others as part of a family or work group.

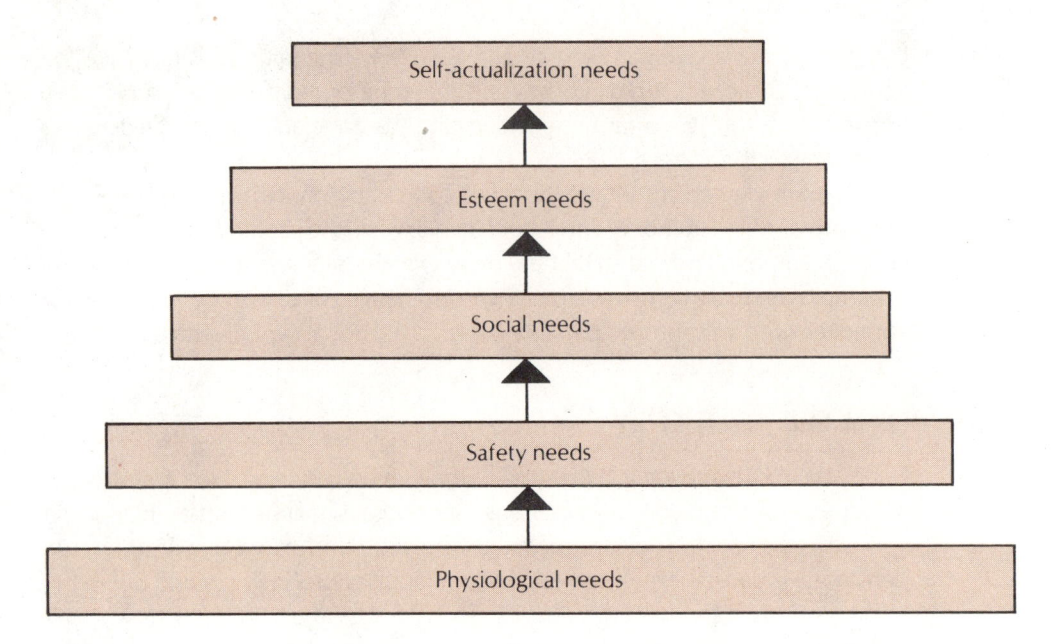

*Figure 2-4   Maslow's hierarchy of needs*

4. *Esteem needs.* The need to be recognized and responded to by others.

5. *Self-actualization needs.* The need to be a complete, creative person, and to fulfill one's maximum potential.

## Douglas McGregor

In the early 1960s, Douglas McGregor framed several ways of looking at people at work and attitudes of supervisors. He called these the X and Y theories. Each theory made widely different assumptions about human nature and work. (See table 2-2.)

— *Theory X.* McGregor's X theory assumes that most people dislike work and will avoid it if they can. Since people do not like to work, they must be coerced, controlled, or threatened to produce. Managers who follow theory X believe the average employee would rather be directed, would like to avoid responsibility, has little ambition, and above all, needs to feel secure.

— *Theory Y.* This theory assumes that people prefer to work, and that the expenditure of physical and mental effort is natural. Threats or coercion are not necessary to make employees strive toward organizational goals. Theory Y assumes people want to use self-control and be self-directed. The average employee seeks and accepts responsibility. There is a high degree of imagination and creativity in the average human being. Adherents of theory Y believe that modern

**Table 2-2. Theory X, Y assumptions**

|  | Theory X | Theory Y |
|---|---|---|
| Nature of human being | Other-directed | Self-directed |
| Attitude toward work | People avoid and shun work | Work is as natural to people as rest or play |
| Attitude toward responsibility | People avoid responsibility | People seek responsibilty |
| Role of manager | To coerce and threaten subordinates to enforce obedience | To allow subordinates freedom to create and to be self-directing |

industrial life forces employees to work under conditions which use only a small part of their intellectual abilities and potential.

Theories X and Y are diametrically opposed to each other. If a manager assumes that subordinates are governed by theory X, then the manager will exercise a high degree of control on subordinates. If a manager assumes that theory Y applies, then the manager's function is to stimulate subordinates' innate need to work. For those who accept theory Y, a good manager allows a subordinate to use the desire for achievement as a motivating force.

### Frederick Herzberg, Victor Vroom, and Rensis Likert

Other important figures who influenced the behavioral science school of management were Frederick Herzberg, Victor Vroom, and Rensis Likert. They believed that great power lies within the group or social unit. Managers must focus on the group process and peer influences in resolving human conflicts. These theories are explored more fully in chapters 16-18.

## QUANTITATIVE THEORY

The first electronic computer, invented in 1946, gave a new dimension to business, industry, and government. The computer brought with it an increased emphasis on mathematics, statistics, and quantitative tools for solving problems.

At first, the computer was used by managers for accounting and later for solving production problems. The computer became a valuable tool for scheduling work, finding the best combination of ingredients in a complex mix, and balancing work loads.

Next, managers began using the computer and statistics to solve management problems involving people, motivation, and decision making. Among these management theorists were Herbert Simon, P. M. Morse, G. E. Kimball, and Joseph McCloskey.

A group of sophisticated mathematical tools known collectively as operations research (OR) were developed and later aided by the computer. These techniques include mathematical modeling, program evaluation and review technique (PERT), critical-path method (CPM), and others. Decision-making and quantitative tools of management are explored more fully in chapters 6-8.

Adherents of this school of management believe that the laws of mathematics, statistics, and probability apply to the management of human enterprise. They place less emphasis on motivation and human relations, and more on quantitative patterns of human behavior. Once a cause and effect relationship is discovered, the solution to a management problem can be found by applying logic and quantitative methods.

## SYSTEMS THEORY

The next major theory of management to evolve was the systems theory. A system is a collection of elements which function as a whole and behave according to predictable laws. A system is composed of subsystems, which interact to affect the total performance. Business organizations, human organisms, and the natural environment are all systems which exhibit certain common traits. Figure 2-5 illustrates the systems concept.

Ludwig von Bertalanffy was a pioneer in systems theory. He proposed systems as a basis for ordering biological processes. Kenneth Boulding, Fremont E.

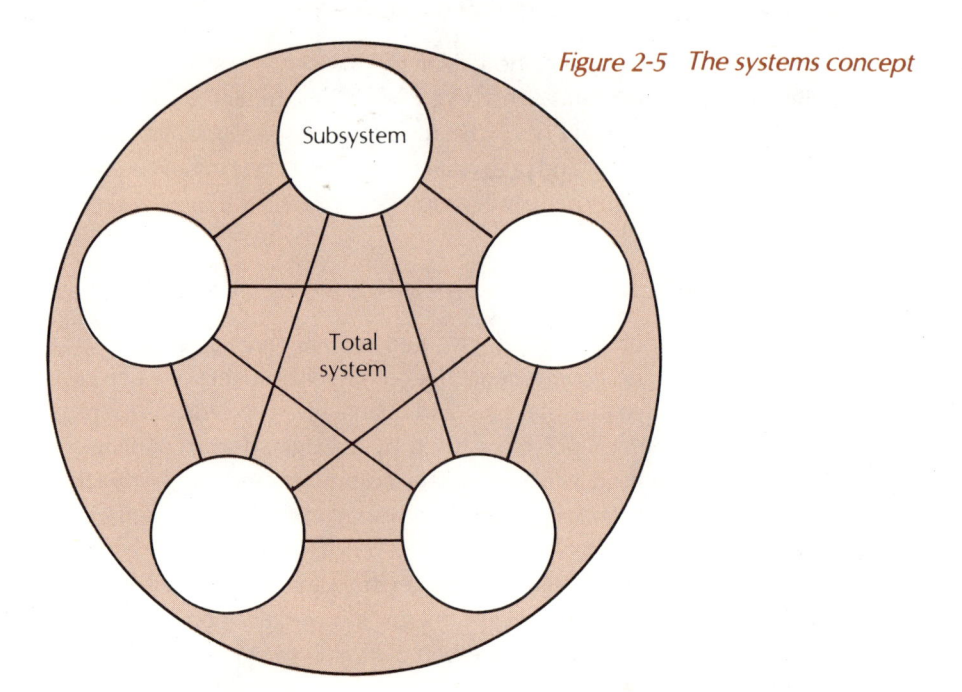

*Figure 2-5 The systems concept*

CHAPTER TWO    THE EVOLUTION OF MANAGEMENT THEORY    45

```
Input  →  Processing  →  Output
  ↑_____|
         Feedback loop
```

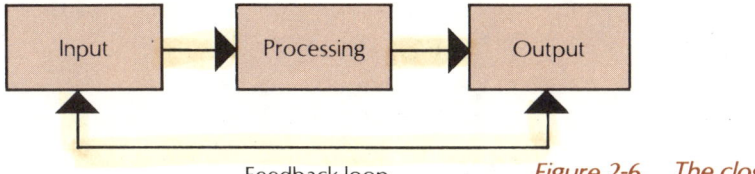

*Figure 2-6   The closed system*

Kast, and James E. Rosenzweig applied the systems theory to management. During the late 1960s, the systems view of management gained popularity in many areas of business, science, and industry.

The systems theory views an organization as a total interrelated entity, composed of many subsystems, and itself a subsystem of a larger system. Each subsystem functions as an interrelated part of the whole. The net result is that the sum is greater than the parts. Subsystems in an organization include personnel, finance, marketing, production, and distribution. The efficiency of each of these subsystems affects the total performance of the organization.

## Feedback Loop

A system is sometimes diagramed with several elements: input, processing, output, and feedback loop (Fig. 2-6). The output is used to control the input, so that

---

**REAL WORLD**

# A Guide to Taking Charge

Some interesting guidelines for success in management have been laid down by Charles Knight, who heads the family-run company of Emerson Electric. Knight learned much of his management theory from his father, who taught him the importance of sound management philosophy. Knight has laid down a series of important ground rules for managers. Among them are the need for a sense of urgency. Also essential for managers are attention to detail, commitment, and not wasting time worrying about things that cannot be changed. Knight also believes that managers cannot succeed unless they are willing to risk failure.

Other rules set down by Knight include the need to be tough but fair with people and to solve tough problems rather than delegate them. He also thinks that the manager must enjoy the work, and must set rules and demand standards of excellence from subordinates. Knight heads a firm with sales of over $2.6 billion a year, which makes it a serious challenge to Westinghouse and General Electric. Knight's advice deserves to be seriously considered.

Adapted from *Time,* 25 February, 1980, p.82.

## POSTSCRIPT
# Japanese in No Hurry for Five-Day Week

### By Sam Jameson

TOKYO — Six years ago, partly in response to criticism from abroad, Japan officially urged private business to give its workers more time off, to cut back to a five-day week by 1980.

The experiment has not been much of a success. The government itself has dragged its feet, but a more important reason lies with the workers themselves.

They seem to like to work. They are extraordinarily devoted to their jobs and to their employers and, when given Saturday off, many of them go down to the office anyway.

"You can't call it the Christian work ethic," RCA executive Charles B Jennings said in an interview, but he added that it is certainly a work ethic of some kind.

It even applies to Japanese who would not be expected to give much thought to the philosophical aspect of work. A young Tokyo waiter who gets three days off a month and no vacation at all said in reply to a reporter's question:

"What would I do with another day off?"

Foreigners who are critical of the Japanese attitude toward work think their criticism is justified. As recently as 1970, when Japan's trade balance was widely envied, some foreign officials were referring to the Japanese as "economic animals," a people motivated by economics alone in everything they did.

Talk of economic animals is no longer heard, but attitudes have not changed much.

For example, according to RCA's Jennings, KDD, Japan's international telephone company, gives its employees three

Reprinted from the Los Angeles Times, 18 February 1977

the system behaves in a balanced, controlled manner. Adherents of the systems theory believe that in nature, for example, a balanced system is the norm. A healthy, functioning organization should also strive for a balanced system.

The manager's job is to see that inputs (money, materials, human resources) are properly processed (manufactured) to provide output (finished goods). The task of management is to control the feedback loop and to bring the output in line with desired results.

Saturdays off a month, "but many of them come in to the office anyway — without overtime pay — when there is some big job that has to be done."

In Japan the work ethic is traditional, pervasive. It makes for resistance to the five-day week even in the few companies that have adopted it. Masaya Miyoshi, an official of the Federation of Economic Organizations, said that what the five-day week has done for him is give him more time to read books and other material related to his job.

He said that although the federation's working day ends officially at 4:45 P.M., almost everybody is here until 6 P.M. or later. I guess it's a sense of belonging."

Not everybody agrees. Jennings thinks it may "have something to do with the ancient concept of loyalty to one's feudal lord. The peasant served the lord unquestioningly and received protection in return. Today the company has become the lord."

And not everybody believes that the work ethic always means hard work. Frank E. Salerno of the Chase Manhattan Bank admits that Japanese put in long hours, "and they work very steadily, but I don't think they work all that hard."

Still, whatever the popular attitude toward work and the five-day week, the government is not doing much to carry out its own directives.

Government offices are required by law to be open on Saturday mornings, as are the banks. But neither the government nor the banks — not even the unions that represent the people who work for them — has sought to change the law. To do so, they fear, would offend public opinion.

Major opposition comes from individuals who do their banking on Saturday and from the great number of small firms that continue to resist such innovations as cash-dispensing machines and night deposit facilities, Saito said.

On the local level, Koganei city, a suburb of Tokyo, tried the five-day week — and officials there were even more timid than the national government. They divided workers into an intricate pattern of "groups" and "sections" to be given one Saturday off every six weeks.

The result kept ninety one percent of the workers on the job every Saturday and gave no more than one Saturday off every seventy two weeks. The ultimate goal is to work up to where everyone will get one Saturday off every month.

Kiyoshi Honma of the city's personnel office told a reporter:

"People around here still work a six-day week and until the five-day week becomes more widespread, the public won't tolerate civil servants taking Saturdays off. Besides, if the city hall is closed on Saturday, what would happen if someone needed to register a death?"

## CONTINGENCY THEORY

By the early 1970s, one fact became clear to management theorists. There was no single set of rules or approach to management which could be applied successfully in all situations. While any one theory was logical and consistent, it could not be applied universally. This reality led to the development of the modern contingency philosophy of management. Much of this school of thought was devel-

"You know very well WHAT chair!"

©*Industrial Research,* April 1977, p.58.

oped by Fred E. Fiedler. Joan Woodward, an English management researcher, explored the ways in which various companies dealt with management problems. She found that no one best way existed. Different management methods were used in each situation. Her work led to the evolution of the contingency theory, which stresses that managers must work out a management theory based on the particular situation which exists in their organization. The theory must fit the facts, rather than the facts being manipulated to fit the theory.

Thomas J. Burns and G.M. Stalker isolated two distinct forms of management styles. Some managers applied a rigid set of rules in all situations. Other managers were more flexible in their methods and used fewer rules. Burns and Stalker defined these two opposite management styles, which influenced the development of the contingency theory as *mechanistic* and *organic*.

—*Mechanistic.* A rigid set of management rules applied by the manager. This is best used when management conditions are static and predictable.

—*Organic.* No fixed, unbending rules or structure. Managers use the methods that work best in each situation. This approach is best applied when the manager is faced with lack of structure and rapidly changing conditions. Contingency theorists are drawn from many management schools. The contingency theory has gained popularity in the 1970s, as many managers recognize the need for flexibility and responsiveness to individual situations.

## SUMMARY

Modern management theory is the result of an evolutionary process. Theories can be categorized into premodern and modern philosophies. Premodern theories date back to Greek, Roman, and early Chinese civilizations. Egyptian, Syrian, Babylonian, and other early cultures had major influences on management theory.

During the late 1800s, the scientific management theory became popular, which stressed the *one best way* and *one best time*. Frederick W. Taylor was influential in bringing the scientific approach to management.

The human relations school of the 1930s emerged as a result of several studies dealing with the human aspects of the worker, peer group, and attitudes of supervisors.

Later the behavioral management philosophy developed, influenced by Maslow, McGregor, and others. These management theorists focused on human needs and motivation. Other management theories also developed. The quantitative theory stressed the role of computers and mathematics; the systems theory stressed the view of the organizations as an integrated whole. The contingency theory stresses the the need for analysis of the situation before implementing a theory of management.

## KEY TERMS

| | | | |
|---|---|---|---|
| Industrial revolution | 31 | Inputs, outputs | 46 |
| Bureaucracy | 33 | Mechanistic view | 48 |
| Hawthorne studies | 39 | Organic view | 48 |
| Zone of indifference | 40 | Contingency theory | 47 |
| Theory X and Y | 41 | Statistics | 43 |
| Feedback loop | 45 | Law of Probability | 44 |
| Hierarchy of needs | 41 | | |

## REVIEW QUESTIONS

1. Contrast several premodern theories of management.
2. What are the major beliefs of adherents of the human relations school of management?
3. What beliefs are held by adherents of the behavioral science school of management?
4. What tools and methods does the quantitative decision theory school use?

5. Summarize the fundamental concepts of the systems theory of management.
6. Explain why the situation is important to contingency theorists.
7. Summarize the role of Frank and Lillian Gilbreth in the development of management theory.
8. Discuss the major contributions of Henri Fayol.
9. What contributions did Hugo Munsterberg make to management theory?
10. Contrast the differences between mechanistic and organic views of management.
11. Discuss the role of the computer in management.
12. How did the work of Elton Mayo affect management thought?

# Case Incident

Business in the past year has been very good for Thompson Engineering. Jeff Thompson, the owner, is pleased to announce to his staff that he plans to open two more engineering departments due to the increasing number of contracts that they now have underway. Jeff has talked at length to two of his best supervisors, whom he is now promoting to managers.

Arlene Atkinson, while relatively new to the company, graduated with honors from a highly regarded local college of engineering. She was at the very top of her class and was heavily recruited by several employers. Howard O'Connell has been with Thompson Engineering for over twelve years, and he has been actively supervising engineers for the last six years. Howard has shown his abilities many times in supervising employees.

Jeff talked to Arlene about her plans for managing her department. She is eagerly looking forward to the challenge and said that she intends to lay down some basic rules, policies, and procedures which are important to insure that the new department gets off to a good start. Knowing that employee relations will be critical, she has carefully worked out a set of procedures for promotions and evaluations of the engineers who will be under her charge. She said, "Since I have never been a department manager, after these rules have been in effect for one year, I will evaluate their soundness and modify or change them as necessary."

Howard O'Connell said that, rather than form initial rules, he is going to take a wait and see policy in his new department. "I will not set down any hard and fast rules until after my people have a chance to work with me and the others in the department for a while. That way I can best develop my own rules and procedures to fit the kind of people I'm working with and their needs."

**PROBLEMS:**

1. What problems does Arlene Atkinson face in applying her approach?
2. What problems does Howard O'Connell face in applying his approach?
3. Discuss your own views on how to establish rules and policies for the new department.

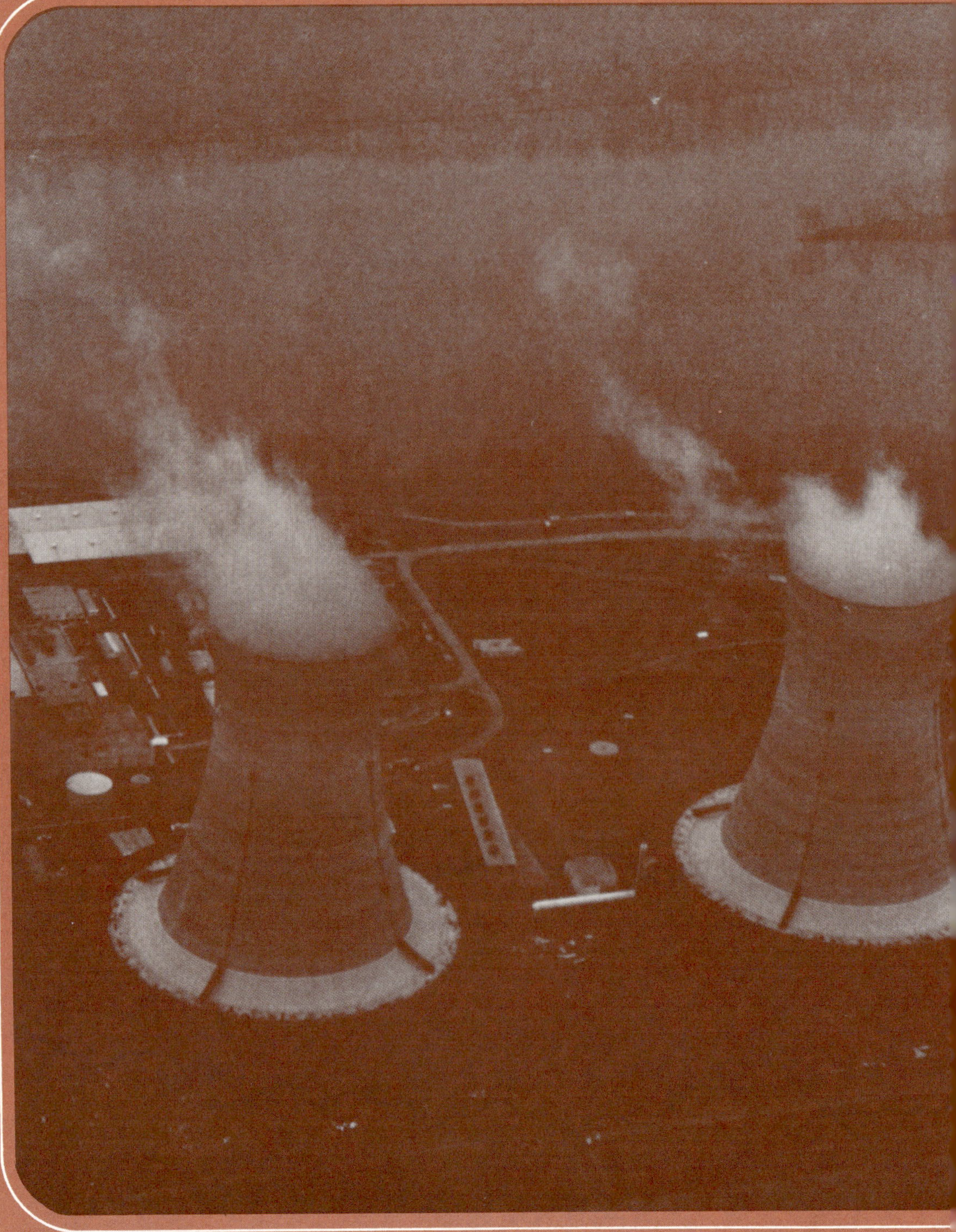

# 3

# The Environment and Social Responsibilities of Business

**LEARNING OBJECTIVES**

After studying this chapter, you should be able to:

1. Describe types of governmental regulation of management.
2. Describe the union-labor influences on management.
3. Describe the social influences on management.
4. List some of the major economic trends which influence management decisions.
5. List some of the labor force trends which influence management decisions.
6. Summarize the growth of government influence on management.
7. Describe the impact of multinational organizations on management.
8. Summarize the growing interest in social responsibility and business ethics by managers and what has brought this on?
9. Discuss the changing role of women and minorities in management.

At first glance, one might think that managers are free to make decisions based exclusively upon their own judgment, experience, and knowledge of management theory. In reality, the manager's freedom of choice is greatly limited. There are many external and environmental factors which determine the course of action, reduce freedom of choice, and limit the activities which the manager pursues. The manager is always walking a fine line between what he wants to do or feels is right, and what he must or should do.

Table 3-1 and figure 3-1 outline the relationship of a business organization to the environments in which it operates, listing these environments and the areas of involvement of each.

Let us consider these environments and how they influence organizational goals and affect management's decision-making authority.

## GOVERNMENTAL ENVIRONMENT

The government, courts, legislature, and regulatory agencies are charged with the duty of establishing a legal and political framework which controls, regulates, and assists business. Management is not totally free to make decisions, but must work within a carefully balanced legal and political structure.

The government passes laws and establishes regulations which affect those who go into business. Reporting of profit or loss, insurance requirements, taxation, labor controls and regulations, product safety, land use, building permits, and many other phases of business are affected by these rules. Decisions which managers make must consider this complex and controlling influence.

Some of the government agencies which influence management decisions are the Federal Trade Commission, Interstate Commerce Commission, Civil Aeronautics Board, Food and Drug Administration, and even the Justice Department. The Justice Department, for example, is charged with enforcing such laws as the Sherman Antitrust Act and the Clayton Act, which regulate monopolies.

**Table 3-1. Relationship of business to other factors in its environment**

| Environment | Concerns |
| --- | --- |
| Governmental | Laws, including the legal and political structure of management decision making |
| Union-labor | Concerns of the work force, including hiring, promotion, working conditions, safety |
| Social | Equal opportunity, social benefits, ecological considerations |
| Economic | Financial institutions, credit, cash flow, profit, national economy |

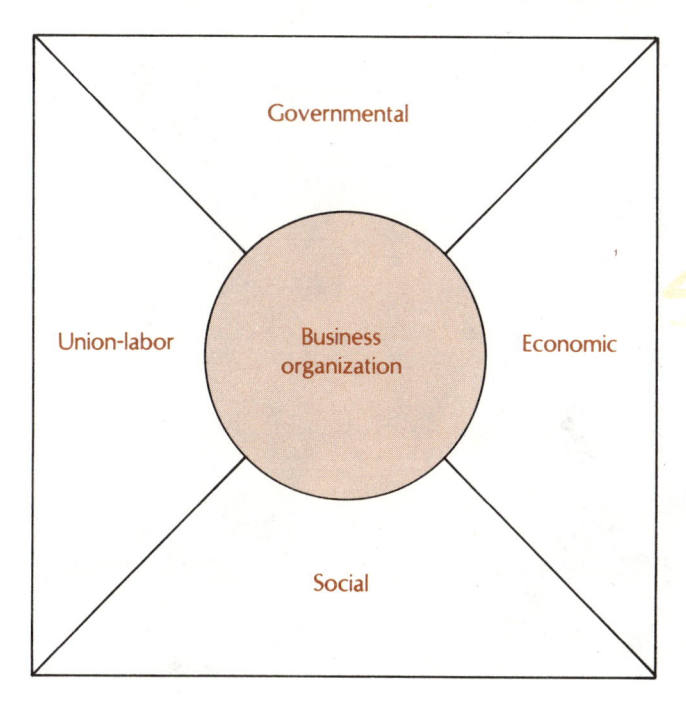

CHAPTER THREE   THE ENVIRONMENTAL AND SOCIAL RESPONSIBILITIES OF BUSINESS   55

*Figure 3-1
Environments of business*

Local, state, and federal agencies may wear several hats. A government agency may act as a supplier (atomic materials), as a customer (military aircraft), or as a competitor (parcel post). Thus, government may assist business, acting as a customer, or compete with it, while at the same time controlling its actions as a regulatory agency.

## UNION-LABOR ENVIRONMENT

Business management operates within the constraints and boundaries established by its relations with unions and its work force. Decisions concerning working conditions, promotions, hiring, and safety must be made within the context of the union-labor relationship.

Labor contracts spell out wage rates, bonuses, and incentives. These contracts cover discipline, firing, and suspension proceedings. Matters dealing with seniority, pension plans, overtime rules, and grievance procedures are also included in these contracts.

To a large extent, collective bargaining makes the union a partner with management in the decision-making process. The manager must take the impact of all these factors into consideration when making decisions.

Unions are a powerful force in the modern business environment.

## SOCIAL ENVIRONMENT

Business organizations operate within the context of the total society. In recent years much emphasis has been placed on the social consequences of business actions. Business is not free to do what it wants, but must consider the impact of its decisions on the nation's social institutions. Business decisions affect employment, housing, education, transportation, and welfare costs.

While business decisions affect society, social changes also affect business. Government plans regarding federal employment, minimum wages, retraining programs, urban renewal, housing, and transportation have a great impact on business. There is an interaction between business, government, and social institutions which must be considered. The day a business could operate without concern for the social environment is long gone. Many business decisions are made in conjunction with government officials, housing authorities, educators, social planners, and others.

## ECONOMIC ENVIRONMENT

A major determinant of management direction is the financial environment in which business operates. Decisions made by managers must be based upon consideration of the economic and financial world in which they exist.

The economic environment includes the money supply, wage rates, inflation, business cycles, balance of trade, balance of payments, and interest rates. It would be foolhardy for management to make decisions without giving serious consideration to the economic conditions. The nation's economic health has great impact on whether a business chooses to expand, enter new markets, and increase imports or exports.

Conversely, business decisions have an impact on the nation's economic health. When a large industry fails, reduces its labor force, or transfers its operations to an overseas plant, there is a direct impact on the country's economic health.

## MAJOR TRENDS WHICH AFFECT MANAGEMENT

The fundamental environments just described are not static, but are constantly changing. The student of management should be aware of the major economic, social, and demographic trends which affect business and society. These trends and statistics influence the direction which managers may follow in guiding an organization. A review of key statistics follows.

### Basic Economic Trends

The major trends and statistics which influence the manager in the economic environment are the Gross National Product (GNP: the total amount of goods and services produced in the country in one year), the rate of inflation (the rate by which the buying power of the dollar changes each year), interest rates (the cost of borrowing money), and capital investment (the amount of money invested by industry in new plants and facilities).

1. *Gross National Product (GNP).* The GNP is the total dollar value of goods and services produced in one year in the United States. In 1978 it exceeded $1.4 trillion. (See figure 3-2.) Adjusting for inflation, the GNP in 1975 was almost double what it was in 1960. The United States had experienced a continued increase in GNP until recently. Today the U.S. GNP rate of growth is declining, while foreign competitors' GNPs are growing more rapidly.

2. *Inflation rate.* An element in the manager's decision making is the inflation rate. The inflation rate in this country has ranged from below six percent to over twelve percent during the past decade. As the buying power of the dollar declines due to inflation, management must pay higher wages to labor and charge a higher price for the goods and services it produces.

It should be noted that the United States inflation rate, while higher than some industrialized nations such as Japan and Germany, is substantially lower than that of other industrialized countries.

Trillions of 1972 dollars

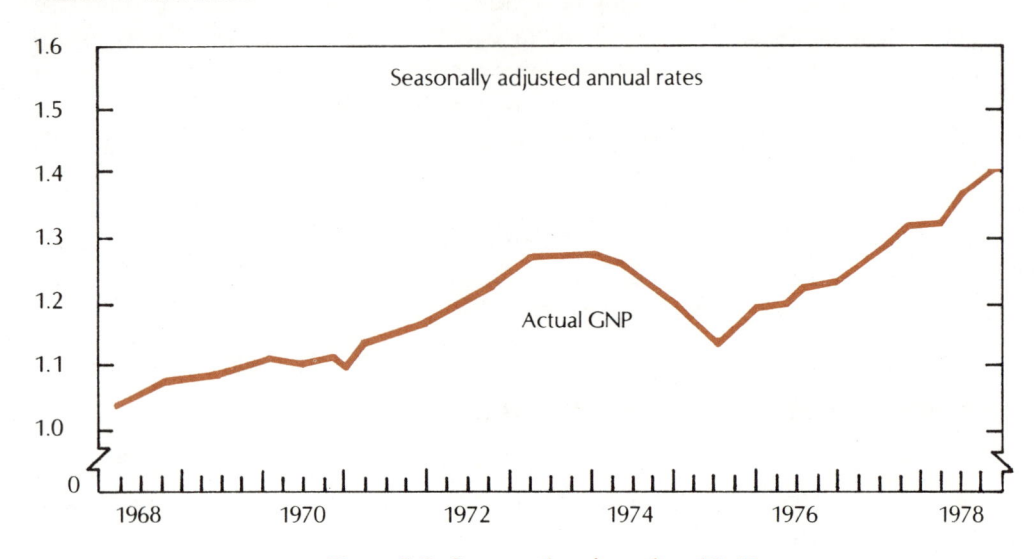

*Figure 3-2 Gross national product (GNP)*

Adapted from the *Economic Report of the President,* January 1979, p. 75

3. *Interest rates.* Business firms often borrow money to acquire new assets such as buildings, factories, and machinery. Figure 3-3 illustrates the prime interest rate banks charge their best customers for borrowing money. The prime interest rate has ranged from below five percent to over twenty percent during the past decade.

When interest rates are low, the cost of acquiring new capital is reduced, and firms are more willing to invest in new facilities. When interest rates are high, there is less incentive to invest in new equipment or buildings. Interest rates and rates of inflation are both influenced by government fiscal and monetary policies.

4. *Capital investment.* There has been a continual increase in the amount of money invested in real estate, new inventions, plants, and equipment.

Capital investment is a function of the tax laws, tax and interest rates, and the amount of money available for investment. Low tax rates, tax credits, and supportive legislation, coupled with a large money supply, means that firms are willing to invest more in capital improvements. Conversely, when taxes are high and money is expensive to borrow, many firms are reluctant to invest in capital goods. New Tax Laws

## Basic Labor Force Trends

The cost of labor is an important consideration in management planning. Managers must hire personnel, train people, evaluate their performance and pay their salaries. Labor costs are often the major expense item in the production of goods and services.

The student should understand the basic trends in the labor force, since these are major influences that affect the manager's decisions. The key factors include productivity and the composition of the labor force.

1. *Productivity.* Productivity is the amount of goods and services produced in one hour by one worker. Productivity is a measure of how effectively labor is being used. Productivity is measured annually on an index based upon a base year. Figure 3-4 shows the productivity index in the private domestic business economy between 1948 and 1976. The continual increase in productivity during this period is the result of improved factories, tools, management methods, and technology.

Productivity is a key factor in raising the general standard of living and controlling inflation. If payment to labor increases faster than productivity, the result is higher costs and less profit for the employer, who must then raise prices, starting an inflationary spiral.

2. *Composition of labor force.* The composition of the labor force is influenced by the number of white and blue collar workers and the sex and age of employees.

There has been a continual shift in the makeup of the labor force from blue collar workers to white collar workers. (See figure 3-5.) In 1950, blue collar work-

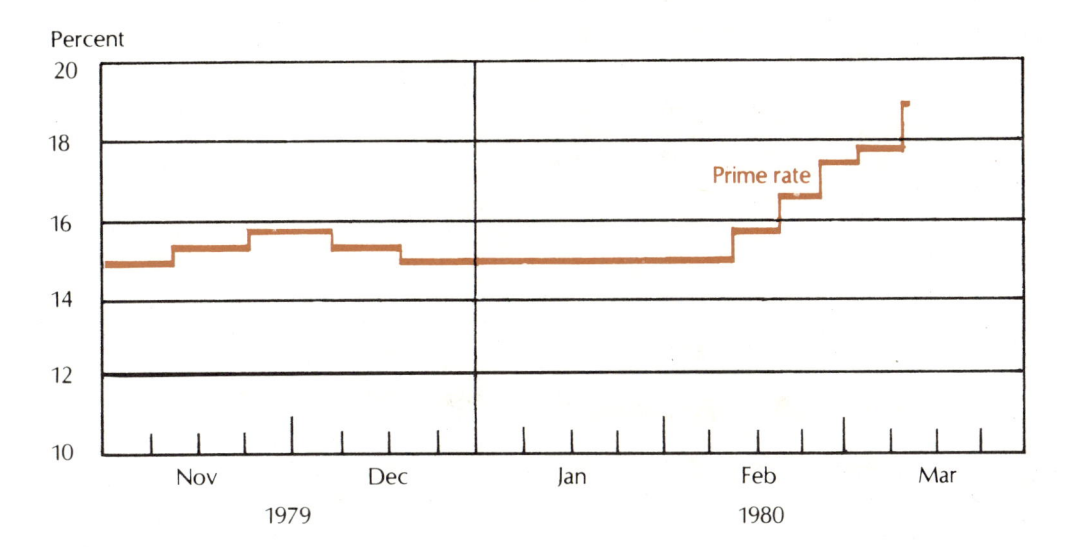

*Figure 3-3 Prime interest rate*

Reprinted from *Federal Reserve Bank of New York,* Spring 1980, Vol. 5, No. 1, p. 32

Units of output
(per labor hour)

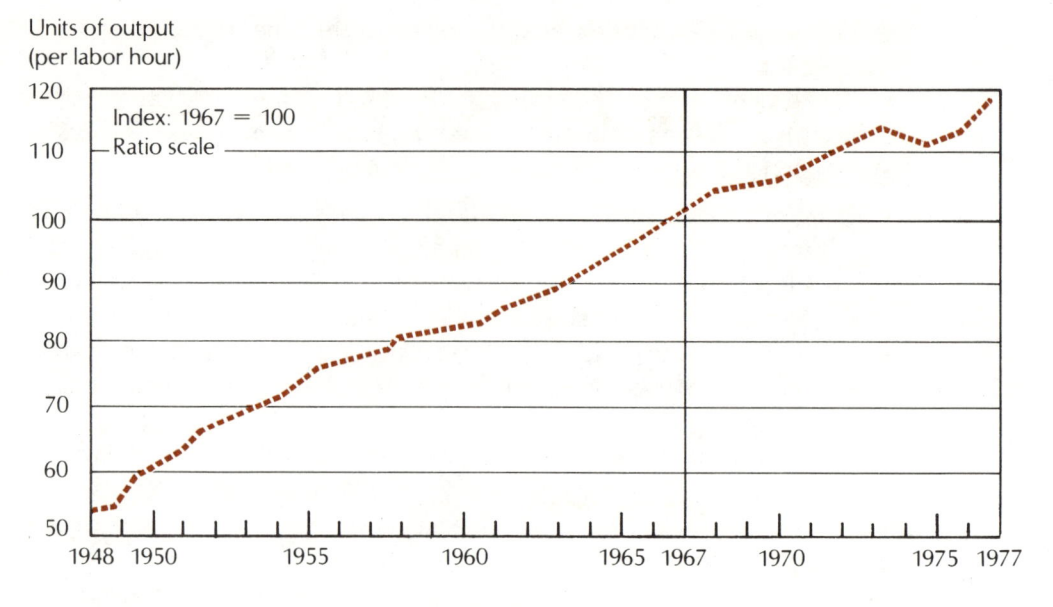

Index: 1967 = 100
Ratio scale

Figure 3-4 *Productivity*

Adapted from The Conference Board, *Road Maps of Industry,* nos. 1822-23, January 1978.

ers (mechanics, machine operators, and other manual laborers) made up the major portion of the work force. White collar workers (managers, salespeople, and clerical workers) were in the minority.

In 1956 those employed in white collar jobs in the United States outnumbered blue collar workers for the first time. This trend toward more white collar workers is expected to continue. The major causes of this shift in the work force include automation, computers, increased emphasis on services, and a deemphasis on manufacturing.

In addition to these changes, during the past several decades women have entered the labor force in great numbers. (See figure 3-6.) In 1950 the labor force consisted of 54 million people, of which 18 million were women. By 1975, the labor force had grown to 80 million, with 36 million women, about forty-six percent of the work force.[1] Although the number of working women continues to rise, the proportion of women in high-level management positions has not kept pace with this increase.

The age makeup of the labor force has also undergone change. Workers in the twenty to fifty-four age group are expected to show an increase in the num-

---

[1] The Conference Board, *Road Maps of Industry,* no. 1794, November 1976.

ber employed, while both older and younger workers are expected to show a decline.

The number of people who will become professional and technical workers is expected to expand. Managers, proprietors, clerical, sales, and service workers will also increase in number. On the other hand, the number of farm workers and laborers is expected to decline.

## GROWTH OF THE CREDIT ECONOMY

The United States is becoming a cashless society because of a continual shift toward credit buying. The electronic funds transfer system (EFTS) and increasing use of credit cards affects management decisions regarding retailing, merchandising, and credit reporting. In 1974, over $190 billion of consumer credit was outstanding because of installment buying and noncash purchases.[2]

---

[2]Ibid., no. 1760, April 1975.

*Figure 3-5 White and blue collar workers*

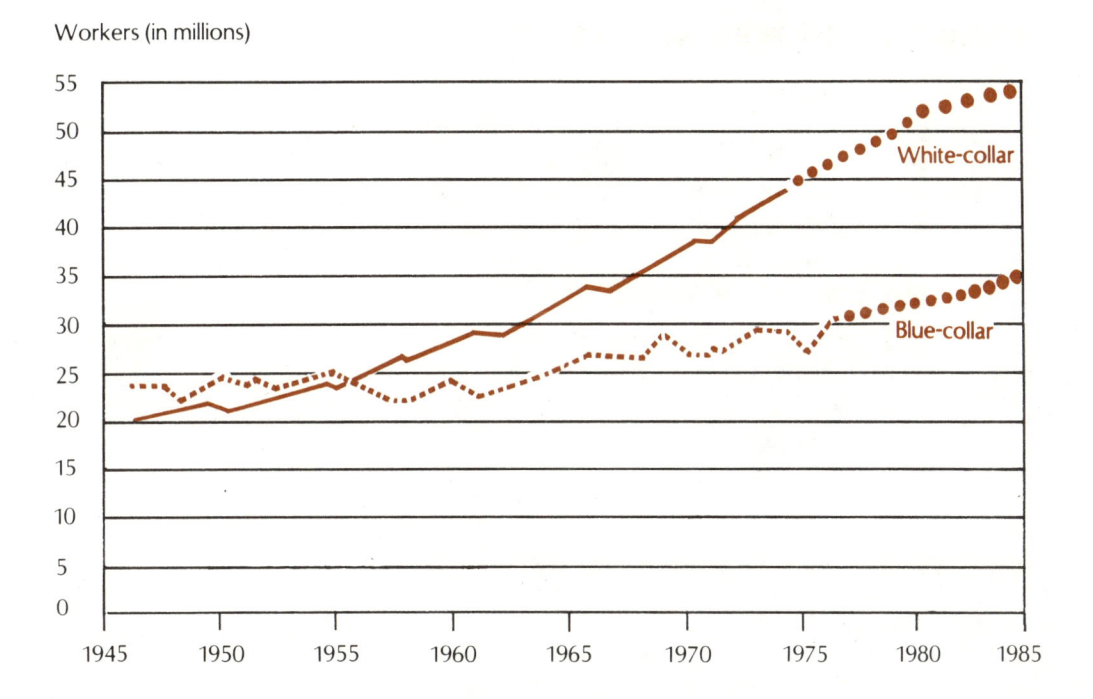

Reprinted from *Occupational Outlook Handbook, 1978-79*, U.S. Dept. of Labor, p. 23.

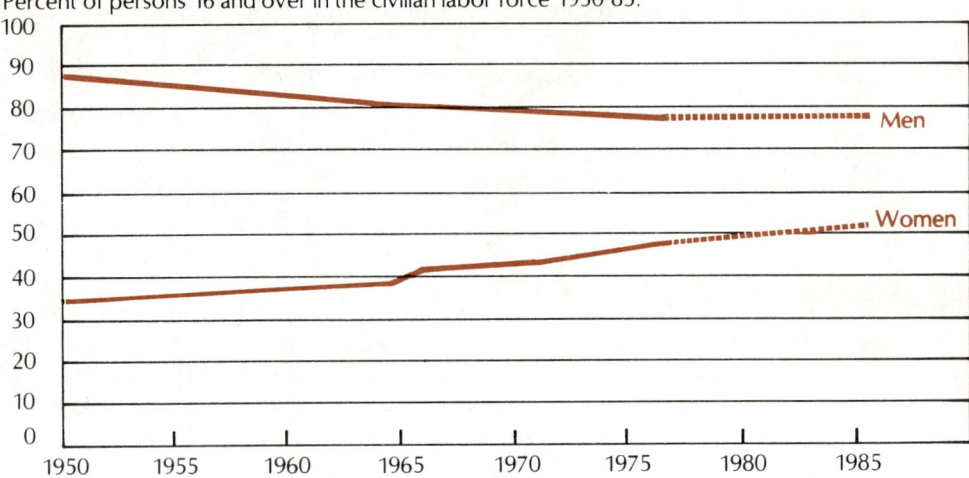

Percent of persons 16 and over in the civilian labor force 1950-85.

*Figure 3-6  Men and women in labor force*

Reprinted from *Occupational Outlook Handbook, 1978-79*, U.S. Dept. of Labor, p. 20.

## GROWTH OF GOVERNMENT INFLUENCE

Government is an increasingly important element in the management of business organizations. It influences business by establishing minimum wages, work rules, and regulations. Government also has an impact as an employer. Figure 3-7 illustrates the trend toward an increased number of government workers. In 1950, the government accounted for a little over 13.3 percent of the work force. By 1975, 19.2 percent of the working population were working for local, county, state, and federal government agencies.[3]

Government influences business from another aspect. The federal government continues to expand its controls and regulations over business and industry. Assemble almost any three letters of the alphabet and you have the name of a government agency: FTC (Federal Trade Commission), FAA (Federal Aviation Administration), ICC (Interstate Commerce Commission), and numerous others.

## GROWTH OF THE MULTINATIONAL FIRM

Management must now take into consideration the growth of the multinational business enterprise. A multinational business firm is one that operates in the home country and in at least one other country, and that has a management philosophy

---

[3]Ibid., no. 1808, June 1977.

CHAPTER THREE    THE ENVIRONMENTAL AND SOCIAL RESPONSIBILITIES OF BUSINESS    63

that is worldwide. Chapter 21 explores the subject of multinational corporations more fully.

There has been a continual increase in the number of multinational firms. (These include General Electric, IBM Corporation, and Mobil Oil.) Managers of multinational firms must now be responsible for a staff which is spread all over the world. They must deal with subordinates in many lands who speak different languages, use different currencies, and have different ethnic and social values.

## MANAGEMENT AND SOCIAL RESPONSIBILITY

During the past decade, management has had to recognize its social responsibilities and respond to new challenges. Business organizations all over the country are now beginning to recognize the ethical and moral responsibility they have to the total society.

No longer can a manager make a decision based solely upon the economic benefits to his own firm. New legislation, and an increasing awareness by the public and business people, has created a demand for management to shoulder the burden of social responsibility. Management is expected to institute constructive policies and to make decisions which consider the impact of these policies on society.

Social responsibility deals with ethics, consumerism, equality in hiring and

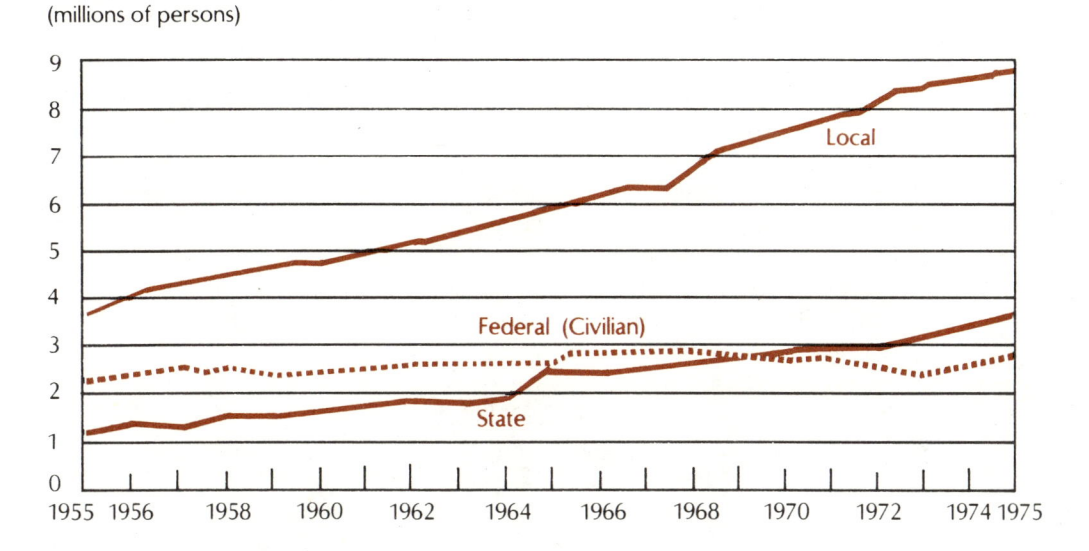

*Figure 3-7 Government employment*

Reprinted from The Conference Board, *Road Maps of Industry,* no. 1808, June 1977.

promotion, and product safety. Let us review some of the major social responsibilities which management must face.

## Business Ethics

Ethics deals with moral principles, standards, and obligations which govern the conduct of an individual or group. There was a time when the general philosophy of business management was, "What is good for General Motors is good for the country." However, the years of the Vietnam war, the despoiling of the environment, poverty, decaying inner cities, and rising crime rates have forced a new look at business and social goals.

Business management must face these issues and establish a moral and ethical code which exerts a positive effect on society. Business goals must extend beyond merely making money. Some firms are taking the initiative and instituting *social audits*. These are critical internal assessments of their products and practices, measuring their impact on society. They are scrutinizing themselves very carefully and measuring progress against stated goals. However, not all companies do this. There are firms that take little stock of themselves. They do the minimum required by law or the courts.

Ethics and moral standards of management differ from country to country. This is one of the problems which management must consider. Table 3-2 lists

---

### REAL WORLD

# Stinging Nuns

The world of corporate critics is all too real for the Blue Diamond Coal Co. Managers for this Tennessee-based coal producer have found themselves embroiled in squabbles and legal hassles with consumer groups. Leading the fight against Blue Diamond Coal Co. is the Sisters of Loretto, a teaching order based in Denver. These nuns are attempting to bring a stronger sense of corporate responsibility to business organizations.

The nuns have attacked the Blue Diamond organization for many alleged sins, including union busting, environmental abuses, and unsafe operations of its mines. Led by Sister Eileen Harrington, a law student, the sisters are now going to court to force Blue Diamond to acknowledge them as shareholders of record so that they can work from inside the organization to bring change.

The company is fighting back, declaring the nuns are not bona fide stockholders and should have no say in the management of the company. The nuns, on the other hand, want the company to show greater corporate responsibility.

Adapted from *Time*, 1 October 1979, p. 78.

some of the major American companies and the bribes they have allegedly given to foreign government officials. In many foreign countries bribery is expected, accepted, and often the only way to obtain licenses and permits to do business.

### Table 3-2. List of American firms accused of foreign bribery

Nearly forty large American corporations have been accused of paying bribes or questionable "commissions" to win contracts overseas. Ten of the biggest admitted spenders:

| | |
|---|---|
| *Ashland Oil, Inc.* | Admits paying more than $300,000 to foreign officials, including $150,000 to President Albert Bernard Bongo of Gabon to retain mineral and refining rights. |
| *Burroughs Corp.* | Admits that $1.5 million in corporate funds may have been used in improper payments to foreign officials. |
| *Exxon Corp.* | Admits paying $740,000 to government officials and others in three countries. Admits its Italian subsidiary made $27 million in secret but legal contributions to seven Italian political parties. |
| *Gulf Oil Corp.* | Admits paying $4 million to South Korea's ruling political party. Admits giving $460,000 to Bolivian officials — including a $110,000 helicopter to the late President Rene Barrientos Orutno — for oil rights. |
| *Lockheed Aircraft Corp.* | Admits giving $202 million in commissions, payoffs, and bribes to foreign agents and government officials in the Netherlands, Italy, Japan, Turkey, and other countries. Admits that $22 million of this sum went for outright bribes. |
| *McDonnell Douglas Corp.* | Admits paying $2.5 million in commissions and consultant fees between 1970 and 1975 to foreign government officials. |
| *Merck & Co., Inc.* | Admits giving $3 million, largely in "commission-type payments," to employees of thirty-six foreign governments between 1968 and 1975. |
| *Northrop Corp.* | Admits in part SEC charges that it paid $30 million in commissions and bribes to government officials and agents in Holland, Iran, France, West Germany, Saudi Arabia, Brazil, Malaysia, and Taiwan. |
| *G.D. Searle & Co.* | Admits paying $1.3 million to foreign governmental employees from 1973 to 1975 to "obtain sales of products or services." |
| *United Brands Co.* | Admits paying a $1,250,000 bribe to Honduran officials for a reduction in the banana export tax. Admits paying $750,000 to European officials. Investigators say the payment was made to head off proposed Italian restrictions on banana imports. |

Copyright 1976, February 23, by *Newsweek* Inc. All Rights Reserved. Reprinted by permission.

## Consumerism

Consumerism is the term applied to the reaction by consumers to inferior goods, unsafe products, and lack of adequate user information. During the 1960s and 1970s the nation experienced a growing awareness of consumer demands. Spearheaded by Ralph Nader, consumer groups were formed all over America. They fought back at shady business practices, poor quality merchandise, lack of adequate warranties, poor labeling, and unsafe merchandise. They forced new legislation and controls on business.

For years some firms have marketed unsafe or harmful products or did not provide adequate information on the proper use or maintenance of goods. It was an era of, "Let the buyer beware!" Automobiles with safety defects remained on the road, even though manufacturers were aware of these defects. People were killed or injured unnecessarily. The consumer movement is forcing management to respond with greater responsibility. It is now becoming an era of, "Let the seller beware!"

As a result, many companies have undertaken extensive product recall campaigns when goods have been suspected of being unsafe. Firms use product recall to provide greater safety for consumers.

## Employee Safety

A major concern of management and the public is the health and safety of employees. This concern dates back to the turn of the century, when worker's compensation insurance laws were mandated by Congress. Prior to the passage of these laws, the injured industrial worker or his family was forced to bear the financial brunt of industrial accidents, injury, or death.

With the passage of worker's compensation laws, management became aware of the need to compensate the worker or his family for lost wages and medical expenses, regardless of fault. Today, worker's compensation insurance is an accepted responsibility of management. Now, the cost of industrial accidents and lost time is borne by the entire industrial society, not merely the injured worker or his family.

**Occupational Safety and Health Act**  In 1970, the Occupational Safety and Health Act (OSHA) was passed by Congress. OSHA placed a heavy demand on employers to provide a safe and healthy working environment for employees. OSHA set standards on the job for noise levels, safety gear, rest requirements, equipment guards, and similar protective measures.

Initially, OSHA was looked upon favorably by labor. Now labor and management have become disenchanted because of the stringent safety rules. The regulations have slowed down the worker and reduced productivity. This has resulted in higher production costs and reduced output in some instances.

Companies must meet tough OSHA safety and health standards or face heavy fines.

## Affirmative Action Programs

One of the most difficult aspects of social responsibility is correcting the long-standing problems and injustices on the job. Forces in society are demanding that the employer be concerned with correcting these problems through equal opportunity hiring and promotion programs.

The Civil Rights Act of 1964 deals with many areas of unlawful discrimination, including hiring, firing, and promotion practices. This major piece of legislation requires that there be no discrimination in hiring practices in government and in all those organizations employing over twenty-five people.

The Justice Department has taken an active role in prosecuting violators under this act. A result of this vigorous prosecution effort is the affirmative action programs established by many organizations. An affirmative action program sets out in detail a set of goals and a plan of action to bring a balanced ethnic, minority, and sex ratio to the staff.

Managers must bring in new groups of workers, many of whom have not previously been in the mainstream of the labor supply. Managers must hire new employees from the ranks of women, minorities, and other traditionally

> **REAL WORLD**
>
> # How Bob Rowan Served His Time
>
> Bob Rowan was the articulate president and chief executive office of Fruehauf Corporation. Then he became involved in a scheme to gain a competitive edge in the truck-trailer business by defrauding the United States government of $12 million in excise taxes. He was caught and convicted. But he wasn't sent to jail. Instead he was ordered by the judge to work forty hours a week at the Sacred Heart Rehabilitation Center for alcoholics.
>
> Rowan left his $403,000 a year job as president and took on the task of managing the rehabilitation center. He approached the job with his usual vitality and thoroughness. He brought professional management to the center, which was being run by recovering alcoholics. Rowan believes that when corporate officers are convicted of white collar crime, their knowledge and experience should be used to help society. However, many federal prosecutors don't agree and think that jail is more appropriate than a public service sentence.
>
> Adapted from *Fortune*, 27 August 1979, p. 42.

underemployed people. They must actively seek out potential job candidates to fill positions. This requires a fresh look at the labor market. Years of stereotypes and negative attitudes toward groups that have been discriminated against in the past must change.

Businesses are establishing special training programs to give instruction to potentially qualified applicants. Many of these applicants lack the traditional language and job skills for entry into the labor market. As less qualified people are brought into the work force, others, more qualified, who cannot find jobs, are accusing management of reverse discrimination. Management is faced with the delicate and difficult task of bringing about equal job opportunities for all employees without alienating anyone.

**Women and minorities in the labor force.** Minorities accounted for seventeen percent of the population in the United States in 1969.[4] Yet minority-owned business firms accounted for less than one percent of the total business receipts. Most minority-owned business firms were small companies such as laundries, dry cleaning establishments, and beauty salons.

---

[4]Ibid., no. 1701, November 1, 1972.

CHAPTER THREE    THE ENVIRONMENTAL AND SOCIAL RESPONSIBILITIES OF BUSINESS            69

In 1975, women accounted for 39.9 percent of the labor force and men for 60.1 percent. Yet businesses owned by women accounted for only 4.6 percent of the business receipts in the country. Women and minority workers are the last to be hired and the first to be fired in case of layoffs. One of the major challenges to management in the years ahead will be to see to it that women and members of the minorities are allowed to share in business prosperity.

One of the principle problems management must face is the difference between what is paid to men and what is paid to women. Figure 3-8 shows the median weekly earnings for full-time employees between 1970 and 1978. Although women have gained substantially in numbers employed over the years, their median wages are still considerably below that of men. In actuality, the gap continues to widen.[5] The fact that many women work in lower echelon jobs, and many work only part time, partially explains the lower wages. In spite of legislation requiring equal pay for equal work, a large amount of discrimination still remains.

---

[5]Ibid., no. 1795, November 1976.

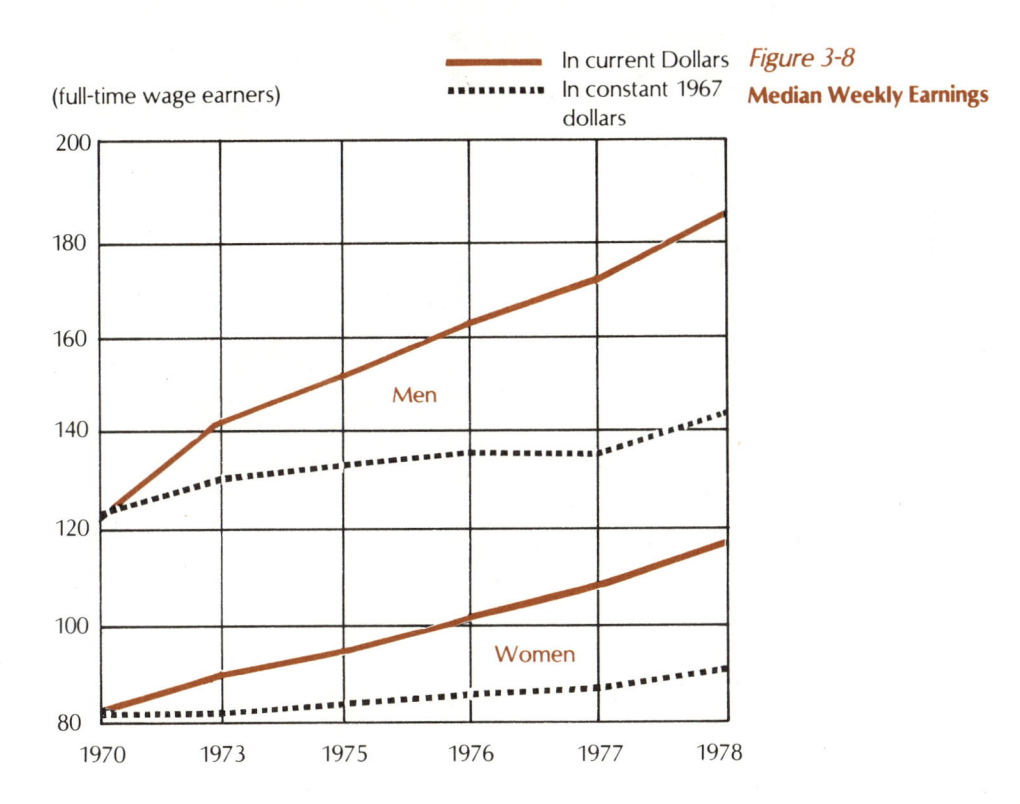

*Figure 3-8*
**Median Weekly Earnings**

Adapted from *U.S. Statistical Abstract, 1978*, p. 423.

**Correcting stereotypes.** Management has a variety of tools which can be used to overcome these disparities. These include programs to hire more minorities, women, and the hard-core unemployed. Management will need to implement more on-the-job training and special community recruitment programs and provide training and education for jobs which require special skills.

Management must take a closer look at revising testing programs which have been traditionally biased toward middle-class, white standards. These changes will not come easily or be quickly accepted by some sectors of the labor force, which have a vested interest in protecting their jobs.

## The Energy Crisis

The energy crisis is of major concern to American industry, as well as to the general public. A growing population, and increasing consumption of energy in the face of limited resources, has created a severe energy shortage. The United States must find creative ways of dealing with this energy deficiency.

Energy consumption in the post-World War II period is characterized by a continued rise in demand, accompanied by a substantial shift toward the use of oil and gas, and away from coal. Between 1947 and 1976, total demand for energy increased at an annual rate of 2.8 percent.[6]

Recent declines in the production of oil and gas in the United States, coupled with a steady rise in consumption, have resulted in a growing dependence upon foreign energy sources. Figure 3-9 shows the total United States energy production and consumption.[7]

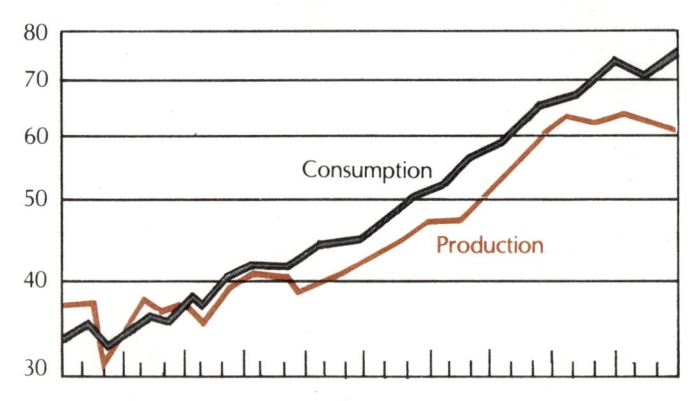

*Figure 3-9*
*Energy production (Quadrillion Btu)*

Reprinted from The Conference Board, *Road Maps of Industry,* no. 1820, December 1977.

---

[6]Ibid., no. 1821, December 1977.
[7]Ibid., no. 1820, December 1977.

CHAPTER THREE    THE ENVIRONMENTAL AND SOCIAL RESPONSIBILITIES OF BUSINESS                71

*Figure 3-10. Mobil Advertisement*

## The national guilt complex • Achievement or original sin • Production vs. atonement

Judging by some of what we read and hear, self-flagellation seems about to become the order of the day. Much of whatever Americans do or achieve or enjoy is termed immoral or otherwise indefensible, and what people in other countries do is hailed as the shape of the future, morally speaking.

Well, now.

A lot of this national guilt complex depends on how things are put.

Suppose, for example, we ask you, "Do you think it's right for the United States, with only 5% of the world's population, to consume 28% of its energy?" That might be your cue to beat your breast and cry, "Heavens to Betsy, no! How could we do such a thing? And how can we atone?"

Suppose, however, we rephrase that question and ask you, "Isn't it remarkable that the United States, with only a twentieth of the world's population, can produce a fourth of the entire world's goods and services? And that we have become the industrial and agricultural breadbasket of the world...a prime purveyor to the hungry and the needy abroad?"

"Gee," you might say. "Just shows you what the old Yankee ingenuity, along with hard work and clean living, can do."

We can stomach breast-beating or a hair-shirt demonstration, if that's what gives the other fellow his kicks. But the point we want to make is that nobody in this country has to beat himself over the head just because he's adequately fed and clothed. Mankind has always striven for a land flowing with milk and honey, not a land short of necessities and barren of luxuries, long on deprivation and longer on austerity.

This is not a plea for devil-may-care hedonism. On the contrary, we are trying to make two points:

(1) Gratuitous martyrdom is an exercise in futility.

(2) When someone tries to make you feel guilty because our country has achieved to a considerable degree what _all_ countries strive for, don't leap to the bait. Remember, it's possible to state even the most positive accomplishments in a way that makes them sound like original sin.

We get the distinct impression that most of the people who berate this country for its productivity are themselves quite well fed, well clothed, well housed, and, possibly as a result, feeling guilty. We cannot believe that Americans can solve, or even alleviate, the problems of this country and the rest of the world through starvation diets or by sleeping on a bed of nails. A refrigerator or a loaf of bread or a pair of shoes not bought and used in the United States is not automatically going to end up in some less-developed country.

The point is that our country is so productive, despite all the roadblocks thrown up by government and others, that it can turn out an almost unbelievable volume of goods—enough to supply the domestic market and still have a lot left over to export. If you want _more_ U.S. money and food and other goods sent to needy peoples abroad, fine; tell your Senators and your Congressman so. But don't feel guilty about living well if you already do, or about wanting to if you don't.

We are not trying to promote gluttony or even conspicuous consumption. We _are_ trying to deflate what strikes us as nonsense. Life is short, and people who work hard and productively shouldn't reproach themselves over their rewards, especially since producing for plenty makes society a lot more comfortable than sharing unnecessary shortage. To some people pleasure may be a little sinful, but if there were no sin in the world, what would be the benchmark for virtue?

Mark Twain once commented that on the basis of the information reaching him, his choice would be heaven for climate and hell for good conversation. Maybe he had something there.

**Mobil®**

©1978 Mobil Corporation

Reprinted from *Fortune,* 10 April 1978, p. 27. ©1978 Mobil Oil Corporation.

## POSTSCRIPT
# Job Titles Reinforce Sexist Attitudes, Barriers To Women

### By Joan Beck

What name you give to a job — foreman, salesman, cameraman, congressman, anchorman, repairman, scrubwoman, hat-check girl — makes an important difference in who gets it. Male-oriented job titles have historically created conscious and subconscious barriers that shut women out of economic equality.

How deep such ingrained sexism goes is evident from all the jokes and jabs about efforts to switch *chairman* to a sex-neutral term. (It's ironic that the same chauvinist males who swear they cannot mouth a nonsexist substitute will, as chairmen themselves, blithely say, "The chair recognizes . . .")

To show how easy it is to give jobs nonsexist names, the U.S. Department of Labor has deliberately taken the sexism out of almost every one of the twenty thousand jobs listed in the new, fourth edition of the massive *Dictionary of Occupational Titles.* Comparing new entries with those in the previous 1965 edition point up how sexist our job talk is.

For example, the 1965 *Dictionary of Occupational Titles* had several listings for *cameraman* (news, commercial, portrait, TV, film, scientific, special effects), but only one for *cameragirl,* who takes photos in night clubs. The new edition replaces these sexist designations with matching categories of *photographer.*

The newspaper job of *rewrite man* in the 1965 edition becomes the updated *rewriter* or *newswriter* or *associate editor* of today. *Legman* is absorbed into the *reporter* category.

What sounded like male-only jobs dominated the public relations field in the 1965 book: *public relations man, promotion man, publication man, public events man,*

Reprinted, courtesy of the *Chicago Tribune,* © 1978.

---

Many large American firms have taken a major interest in the energy problem and have launched massive public relations programs. One firm, Mobil Oil, states that the United States has only five percent of the world's population, but consumes twenty-eight percent of its energy. However, the situation is mitigated when one considers that the United States also produces twenty-five percent of the world's entire goods and services.

Industry must develop more efficient products, such as automobiles that give better gas mileage, and alternative sources of power. Part of management's

CHAPTER THREE    THE ENVIRONMENTAL AND SOCIAL RESPONSIBILITIES OF BUSINESS    73

*dealer contact man,* and *sales-service man.* The new volume refers to *public relations representative, sales-service promoter, public information officer,* and *lobbyist.*

Various *salesman* categories filled pages of the 1965 book of job titles, with only an occasional *salesperson* selling flowers, cosmetics, home furnishings, or clothes for infants and women. The new volume for *salespersons* of both male- and female-oriented products, *sales representatives, sales clerks, sales agents,* and *sales engineers*—but not a single salesman or salesgirl.

The word *woman* was almost never used in the 1965 edition with the exception of terms like *charwoman* and *scrub woman.* Except for *restroom matron,* the usual designation for a job most often held by a female was *girl* as in *26 girl, bakery girl, cigarette girl, cash girl,* and *cleaning girl.* Typically, a *fountain man* did the same work as a *fountain girl.*

Instead, the new book uses *char* and *scrubber* and *restroom attendant.* Employees of both sexes are included in *gambling dealer, food salesperson, cigarette vendor, cash clerk,* and *cleaner. Fountain man* and *fountain girl* are both absorbed into *fountain server.*

Thousands of industrial and technical jobs listed in the 1965 edition carried titles that implied male-only—including hundreds of *foreman* designations and an enormous variety of specialist work described by terms ending in *man,* such as *set-up man, metal man, parts control man, oilroom man,* and *line-up man.*

All have been replaced by nonsexist names. The new edition uses *supervisor* instead of *foreman* and combines all of the specialist industrial job titles with endings like *operator, setter-up, machine tender, assembler, controller* and *maker.* Often, it's as easy as changing a work ending in *man* to *er*—as *workman* becomes *worker.*

The reason it's important to make these changes in the way we talk about jobs is not just a matter of semantics, but of salary and opportunity. It's easier for employers to consider hiring women for jobs called *drafter* rather than *draftsman* or *repairer* than *repairman.* And it's more difficult to continue the usual discrimination in pay between men and women if both not only do the same work but carry the same job descriptions.

The new *Dictionary of Occupational Titles* shows how easy it really is to use nonsexist words for work, to change job titles that imply women aren't eligible for thousands of kinds of lucrative jobs simply because of what we call them. In fact, it's so easy to use nonsexist substitutes that it's now fair to assume those who don't, really want to display their prejudices against women.

responsibility will be to educate its employees and consumers to the need for energy conservation.

## Environmental Pollution

Environmental pollution is a problem which is directly related to the energy crisis. Each year, American industry substantially pollutes the natural resources of the country. Millions of tons of debris are dumped into the air and water. Noise assails

"O.K., then, it's settled. We present it to the public with all its pros and cons, we let the media chew on it for a while, we go through a lot of soul-searching, and then we go ahead and do it."

Reprinted from the *New Yorker*, October 10, 1977, p. 221.

our ears, creating subliminal irritation.

Environmental pollution comes from many sources, including vehicles, solid wastes, industrial processes, and stationary fuel consumption. Money is being spent to improve the quality of the environment. However, there is a price that must be paid to ensure a cleaner, healthier environment. Prices will be higher, some jobs will be eliminated, and some plants will be relocated or closed. Reduction of environmental pollution will, on the other hand, reduce medical care needs, improve recreational facilities, and make our natural resources once again fit for human consumption.

To illustrate the trade-offs between pollution and cost, the management of major automobile companies face a dilemma in producing automobiles marketed in California. California has strict air pollution control laws. Automobiles built to meet this standard have resulted in substantially reduced mileage due to the antipollution equipment required on the automobiles. An exchange between reducing pollution and increasing consumption of fuel had to be made by management. This is typical of the problems faced by all facets of the manufacturing industry.

Business has responded to the need for reducing pollution by encouraging the recycling of waste paper, chemicals, and by-products. It has developed water purification plants and scrubbers to cleanse factory air emissions. Indications are that industry will continue to find ways to make even more improvements in the years ahead.

CHAPTER THREE    THE ENVIRONMENTAL AND SOCIAL RESPONSIBILITIES OF BUSINESS

## SUMMARY

Management is limited in its ability to make decisions because it operates in a complex environment. Management decisions are influenced by business, government, social, and economic trends, and by labor-union relations.

Government influences the laws and regulations which control management, while labor limits its personnel options. Economic aspects play a role in matters dealing with finance, plant expansion, the money market, and other related areas.

The major trends which managers should be aware of include the Gross National Product (GNP), inflation rate, interest rates, and amount of capital investment. Labor force trends in productivity, and the makeup of the labor force, are watched by managers.

In recent years there has been an increasing awareness by managers of their social responsibilities and business ethics. The consumer movement and the Occupational Health and Safety Act (OSHA) have played a part in influencing management. The employment of women and minorities, and the energy crisis have also impacted the task of management.

## KEY TERMS

| | | | |
|---|---|---|---|
| Gross National Product (GNP) | 57 | Multinational corporation | 63 |
| Inflation rate | 57 | Consumerism | 66 |
| Interest rate | 58 | Occupational Safety and | |
| Capital investment | 58 | Health Act (OSHA) | 66 |
| Productivity | 59 | Affirmative action program | 67 |
| White and blue collar workers | 59 | Energy crisis | 70 |
| Credit economy | 61 | Environmental pollution | 73 |

## REVIEW QUESTIONS

1. Summarize the influence of labor unions on management decisions.
2. List the major economic trends which affect management.
3. Discuss the growth of government and its influence on management.
4. Describe how attitudes of managers toward business ethics and social responsibility have changed.
5. Summarize the changing role of women and minorities in management.
6. How do stereotypes affect management's view of women and minorities?
7. How has the energy crisis affected management?
8. Why is productivity important when assessing labor output?
9. Discuss the product recall and how it is used.
10. List efforts management is making to address itself to improved business ethics and social responsibilities.

11. Discuss the international implications of business. What problems have multinational firms brought to management?
12. List the four major environments which managers must consider. How do these differ?

## Case Incident

Dental Products Company maintains a staff of sales representatives who call on dental laboratories throughout the city. Dental Products sells a variety of supplies, equipment, and tools used in the dental profession. Ronald Wilson, national marketing manager, has outlined an aggressive new marketing plan for the company. According to Wilson, employee incentives and bonuses will be given to top-ranking sales representatives for outstanding performance.

K. Randolph Hartman, one of Dental Products' oldest and best clients, has told Wilson that he does not want a female sales representative calling on him or anyone else in his company. Hartman said, "They don't stay with our account long enough to learn our individual needs and desires. Also, I have found that many of them don't really know the important technical aspects of the business. With the volume of money that we spend on dental equipment, these technical details are very important."

Joan Klein and Bob Chavez, two of Dental Product Company's top sales representatives, would both like to call on Mr. Hartman. The obvious reasons are the dollar volume and the loyalty of his company's account. Both know that with such an account in their territory, incentives and bonuses for their performance will be much greater.

Joan Klein has said that she will leave Dental Products if she is denied the opportunity to call on Mr. Hartman, and that it would be a clear case of sexual discrimination. She knows that she can overcome whatever prejudices Mr. Hartman has toward female sales representatives. It would be both a professional and a personal challenge to her.

### PROBLEMS

1. How should Mr. Wilson handle the conflict between Klein and Chavez?
2. What social and ethical issues does this problem present? Explain.
3. How could similar problems be avoided in the future?

**PART TWO**

# The Planning Function

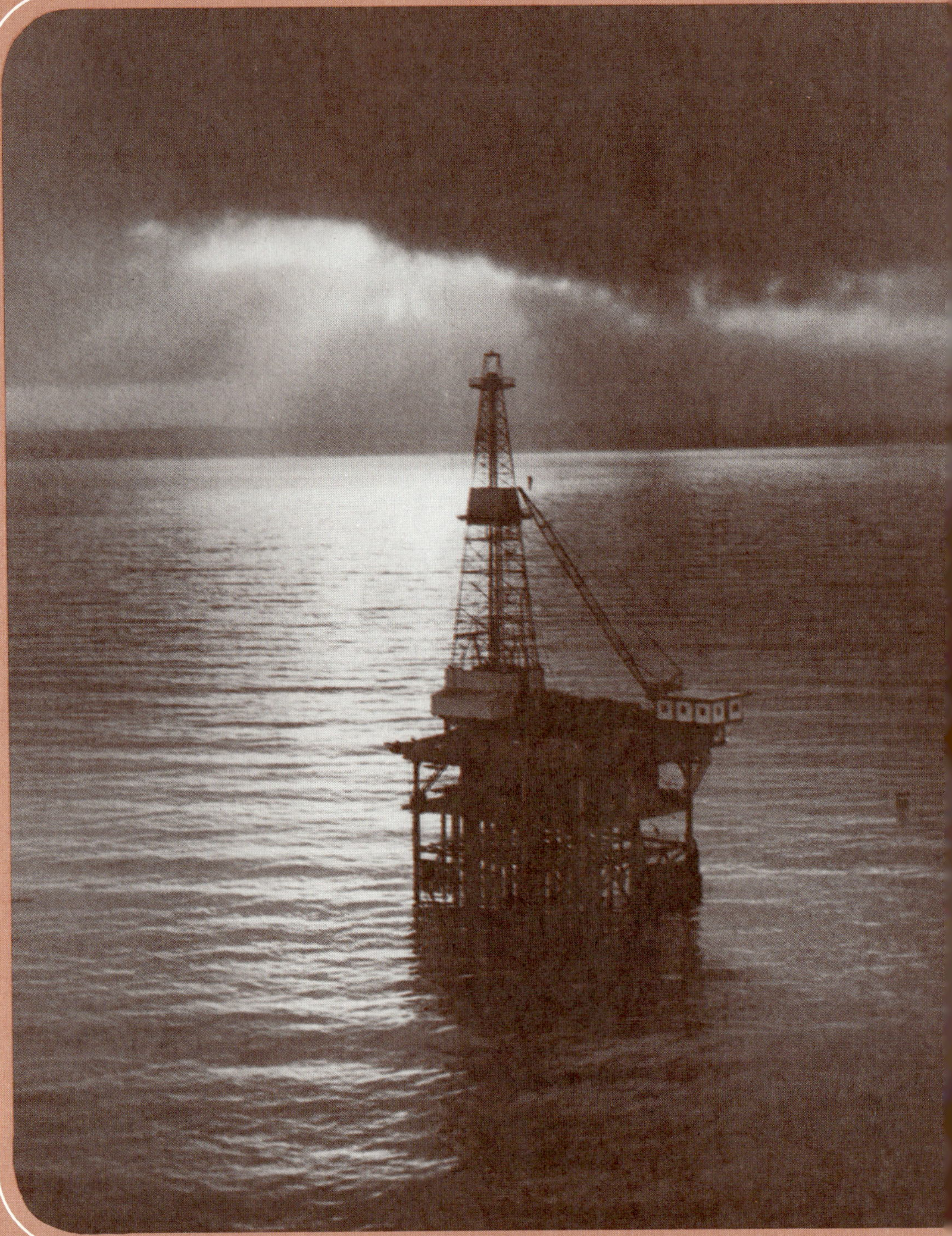

# 4
# Fundamentals of Planning

**LEARNING OBJECTIVES**

After studying this chapter, you should be able to:
1. Summarize the need for planning.
2. Define major terms used in planning.
3. Be able to give examples of goals, objectives, policies, and statements of rules and procedures.
4. Discuss the differences between goals of profit-making and nonprofit organizations.
5. Summarize the need for quantitative measurement of achievement.
6. Contrast the difference between qualitative and quantitative measures of performance.
7. Contrast the difference between basic and supporting plans.
8. List the steps in developing and implementing plans.
9. Discuss how the planning effort differs at different levels of management.
10. Describe the three basic elements necessary in evaluating a plan.

**P**lanning is any forward-looking activity which precedes a decision or course of action. Planning involves projecting future behavior and changes. It is a tool to help management control the growth and direction of an organization.

In this chapter we consider the need for planning, important definitions, planning fundamentals, goals, and objectives and how they are implemented. In chapter 5 we review the applied aspects of planning, including selection of specific goals, types of plans, and hierarchy of plans. Then, in chapter 6, we consider the quantitative aspects of planning, including various mathematical and computer planning techniques.

## NEED FOR PLANNING

Years ago, an organization could either ignore planning or make informal plans, as the need arose. The stakes were generally low. A major investment in office equipment might be a desk for under $50, or a typewriter for under $100. In today's business environment office machines, communication equipment, duplicating machines, and computers may cost hundreds of thousands of dollars.

## BENEFITS AND ADVANTAGES OF PLANNING

Modern organizations have heavy investments of money, equipment, real property, and personnel in their operations. This huge investment of resources requires careful planning to maximize benefits and reduce costs.

A rational approach to planning has many benefits for an organization. These include the following:

1. less effort and expense by avoiding duplication and wasted resources;
2. better control over the direction and growth of an organization;
3. selection of the right tool for the job, so that management can achieve its goals;
4. standards and guidelines by which management can measure organization progress;
5. standards and guidelines by which managers and subordinates can measure their own progress.

Planning is a key task of management. While planning activities may not seem to have the glamour and immediate rewards of such functions as directing or organizing, they are vital to the success of an organization. Without planning, an organization is a ship without a rudder. It lacks the ability to guide and control its course. Planning provides management with the rudder, or guiding force, which directs an organization.

# CHAPTER FOUR  FUNDAMENTALS OF PLANNING

## KEY TERMS

Before proceeding with our study, let us define some key terms. These terms are basic to the planning function and should be understood by the student.

*Goal.* A goal is the achievement toward which effort is directed. It is a long-range statement of the end result or condition which an organization wishes to achieve. Goals are broad statements which do not have specific deadlines. They indicate in general terms where the owners or managers of an organization wish to go.

> *Statement of goal:* This organization will be a leader in the field of solid-state electronic memory devices and will command a major share of the market.

This statement is very general and does not include specific information such as the date of attainment; neither does it define *major share* of the market. The statement does not address itself to profitability, specific products, or customers whom it wishes to serve. Obviously, such general goals must be further refined before they can be implemented on a day-to-day basis by subordinates.

Major organizational goals include the following:

- survive in a competitive market;
- maximize net profit;
- maximize sales;
- increase dividends to shareholders;
- provide increased public service;
- provide greater employee benefits;
- expand share of market;
- effect market innovation;
- influence government regulations and legislation.

*Objective.* An objective is a statement describing the specific behavior or condition which an organization wishes to achieve within a specified time and under specified conditions. Objectives are more specific than goals and define deadlines and desired results in a precise way. A major difference between goals and objectives is that objectives are measurable. Some management authorities prefer not to draw a distinction between goals and objectives, saying simply that both are statements of ends of organizational behavior.

> *Statement of objective:* By 1985, this organization will be a leader in the manufacture of computer disk memory devices sold to original equipment manufacturers (OEM). It will command a twenty percent share of this market

and will return fifteen percent to investors for their investment of capital in the firm.

This is more specific than the statement of goals. The objective gives a specified time period, a specific product to be sold, a targeted share of the market, and the end-user market. It also defines the anticipated return on investment for shareholders. One could further refine the statement of objectives by specifying such things as the number of units to be sold and profitability to the firm in terms of dollars. However, these details are often left for formulation in plans.

— *Plan.* A plan is a procedure, method, or means of doing something to reach a stated end or result. A plan consists of a list of activities or courses of action which will cause an organization to reach a goal or objective. Plans are like road maps; they spell out routes to take in order to reach certain points. The selection of destination is left for the statement of goals and objectives.

Plans may be simple or very complex. They may involve hundreds of pages of documents, drawings, timetables, sequences of events, or lists of activities. They may be focused on the activities of sections of the organization, such as marketing, production, or research and development. Plans may be grouped into either strategic (basic) or operational (supporting) plans. (See figure 4-1.)

— *Strategy.* The term *strategy* is derived from the military usage, which describes the deployment of military forces, personnel, and materiel to reach a military objective. In management usage, a major long-range strategy is a plan, tactic, or program of action used to pursue or reach a goal. Plans and strategies are similar. The plan is the tactic which supports the logic, or plan of attack, defined in the strategy. Both define steps and procedures for reaching a predetermined end. For example, an organization may develop a complex, and detailed strategy for the expansion into a new market. In this effort they may develop long and short range plans, define a specific set of tasks or steps such as designing a new product,

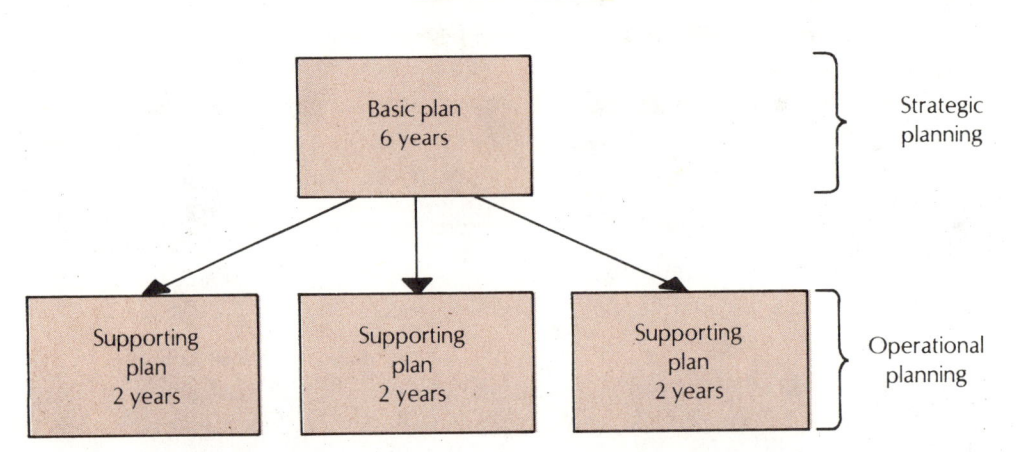

*Figure 4-1   Plans*

```
                    ┌─────────────┐
                    │ Basic plan  │  ⎫
                    │   6 years   │  ⎬ Strategic planning
                    └──────┬──────┘  ⎭
              ┌────────────┼────────────┐
              ▼            ▼            ▼
        ┌──────────┐ ┌──────────┐ ┌──────────┐  ⎫
        │Supporting│ │Supporting│ │Supporting│  ⎬ Operational planning
        │   plan   │ │   plan   │ │   plan   │  ⎭
        │ 2 years  │ │ 2 years  │ │ 2 years  │
        └──────────┘ └──────────┘ └──────────┘
```

opening new stores, etc. Once the new product has been introduced, or new stores opened, the strategy may call for introduction of related products, or additional retail outlets.

— *Policy.* A policy is a defined method or course of action to be taken in light of a given set of conditions. Policies guide future decisions and specify what is to be done under certain conditions. Policies give latitude, discretion, and choice to a decision maker. Thus, a policy is a statement which is to be relied upon by others in making a decision. It is the laying down of guidelines which others are expected to follow in selecting among alternative courses.

Policies save subordinates time and effort, since they can rely upon established policy to make a decision. Policies also assure management that decisions will be made in accordance with defined goals and will be consistent throughout the organization.

*Statement of policy:* Collect telephone calls are not to be accepted by company personnel unless they are directly related to the organization's sales and marketing operations.

This statement of policy guides employees in deciding whether to accept a collect call. Collect calls for the sales department will be accepted, while calls to any other department will not be accepted. Thus, an employee has a clear-cut, established policy to guide this decision.

— *Procedure.* A procedure is a series of steps which are to be followed in a specific order. Procedures lay down the acceptable, established way of doing things for a set of circumstances. Procedures are generally prepared by management and given to subordinates to follow. They outline the series of steps, or actions, the subordinate is expected to take. Procedures are similar to policies in that both direct future behavior. However, a policy addresses itself to anticipating a single decision, while procedures address themselves to a series of steps.

*Statement of procedure:*

1. Upon receipt of a service complaint, the employee will log in the date, time, and the name and phone number of the customer.

2. A complaint report outlining the nature of the complaint will be given to the service manager.

3. The service department will attempt to service the customer and resolve the complaint.

4. A follow-up report will be sent to the division manager, outlining the complaint and its ultimate resolution.

Note that the procedure specifies a sequence of activities. It leaves little room for doubt. The follow-up report is always sent to the division manager after the service department has acted upon the complaint. The procedure guides subordinate behavior and lists the acceptable way of handling the complaint.

— *Rule.* A rule is a regulation or law which is laid down by management and is expected to be followed. It is a statement of practice, custom, or habit which the manager expects the subordinate to observe without question. The difference between a policy and a rule is that a policy is general and establishes guidelines for a category of decisions. A rule is specific and leaves no room for discretion. Rules are often used to control the conduct of employees in an organization.

*Statement of rule:* Employees are not to use a company automobile for personal business except in emergencies.

This is a rule or statement which management uses to regulate the usage of company automobiles. Rules are stated in a manner which gives little room for interpretation, question, or judgment.

— *Standard.* A standard is a statement of an established model against which something is measured. Standards are provided by management as examples by which subordinates can measure their performance or behavior.

*Statement of standard:* The standard output for each operator in the finished assembly department is twenty-six tested and approved units per day.

This clear-cut statement provides a quantitative measure of the expected output of the subordinate, who can easily determine whether his productivity is above or below that which is expected by management. Standards provide baselines for a judgment of whether something is acceptable or unacceptable.

## MAJOR ORGANIZATION GOALS AND OBJECTIVES OF PROFIT-MAKING ORGANIZATIONS

The goal of some business organizations is to make the optimum amount of profit. However, this is a very general statement and must be further refined to be meaningful. What is meant by *optimum profit:* to make the most profit in one year, or over the long run? Is this profit to accrue to the benefit of the shareholders and owners of the organization, or is it to remain in the firm as a surplus? Is the money to be used for investment in new equipment and plant facilities which will make even more money later? Managers must define their goals in clear terms which can be communicated to others in the organization.

*A profit of $500,000 this fiscal year* is a clearer statement. A profit is what remains after all expenses for the period have been paid. In establishing an organization goal or objective, it is necessary to define the period of time which is to be considered when judging whether a profit was made.

It is possible to make a large profit in one year, then reinvest it in new equipment and plant facilities. Thus, the organization will show almost no return to its

# REAL WORLD
# The Jumbo Flies High

Bigger is often better. Especially when you are talking about jet airplanes. No one knows this better than Thornton Wilson, chairman of Boeing Aircraft. His long-range planning saved Boeing from near bankruptcy.

Back in 1966, Boeing designed the 747, a jumbo jet which was to offer the lowest seat-per-mile operating cost of any plane. For a while it looked like the long-range plans for producing the jumbo jet would fly Boeing right into bankruptcy. However, management overcame the problems. What the airline industry needed was a big plane for high-volume hauls with low operating costs.

During the 1970s dozens of airlines have recognized the sound economics behind Boeing's design. Over the next three years Boeing has orders totalling $60 million. Boeing management's plans were so well conceived in the 1960s that they should keep the company economically sound building and selling these jumbo jets until the turn of the century.

Adapted from *Fortune*, 31 December, 1979, p.30.

investors during that year. However, in future years the investors may reap substantial profits because of the new facilities.

Profit earned by a company can be invested or spent in different ways. A firm can spend its profit on improved facilities for personnel, pay higher wages, or give more benefits. In this instance, a major goal of the organization, in addition to making money, is to provide an increased level of benefits to its employees. This may result in higher morale and a more cooperative work force.

## Sales or Marketing as a Goal

Some managers define the goal of an organization in terms of maximizing sales. Their principal consideration is to sell the most products possible. The successful attainment of this goal may place them on top of the list of sales competitors, but they may also find themselves at the bottom of the list of profit makers because they have exceeded their physical ability to sell, distribute or ship the goods.

Other organization goals may be to increase product acceptance, introduce new products into the marketplace, or create a large number of satisfied customers. Organization goals can also include building a firm's prestige in the eyes of the public, customers, or the government.

The goals of an organization can, therefore, range beyond monetary profit.

A firm may provide many social benefits to the community, which are bought at the price of reducing its return to investors.

### Nonprofit Organizations

A nonprofit organization exists to provide a service to the community, the public, or a special group. It may show an excess of benefits over costs, but this surplus is returned in the form of benefits to the public or to its sponsors.

A nonprofit organization may have as its goal building a hospital, providing benefits for the handicapped, or providing family services for members of the community. These organizations require a high level of management expertise and planning skills to achieve their goals. Yet their productivity cannot be measured in terms of dollars alone. They measure their output in the number of available hospital beds, hours of free counseling given the public, or other social units.

## MEASUREMENT OF ACHIEVEMENT

Regardless of what goals are selected, organizations need quantitative means of

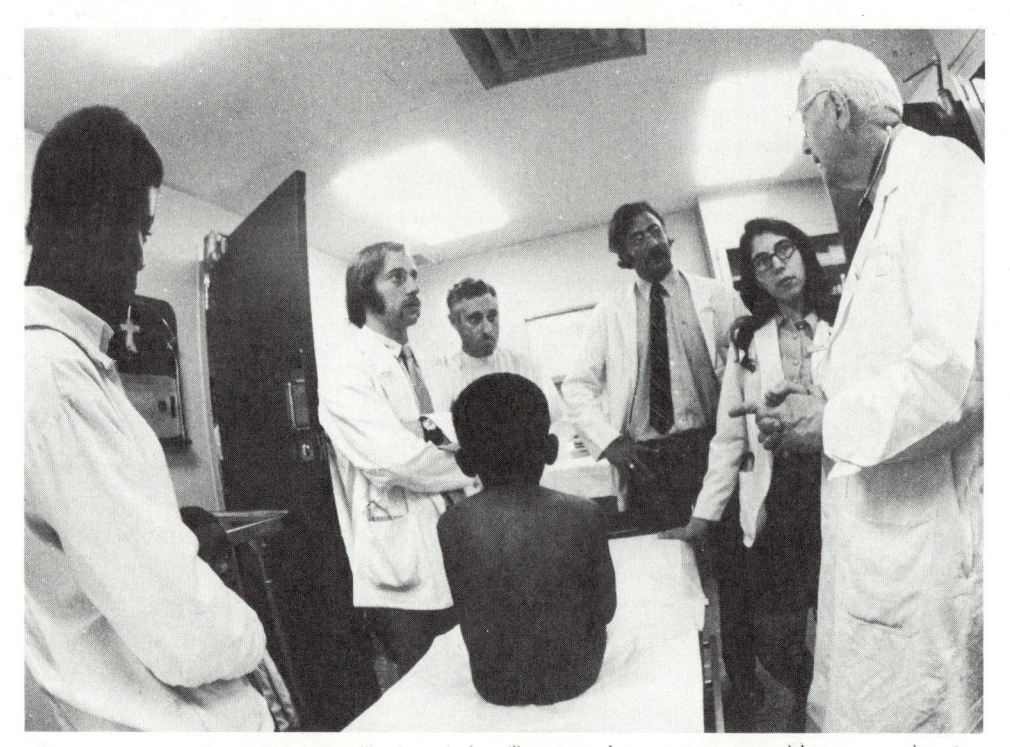

Non-profit organizations like hospitals will use surplus money to provide new services to the public.

### Table 4-1. Qualitative versus quantitative goals

| Qualitative Goal (subject to wide interpretation) | Quantitative Goal (subject to narrow interpretation) |
|---|---|
| Make money | Net a profit, after all expenses, of $500,000 in one year |
| Satisfy employees | Reduce employee turnover rate by twenty percent |
| Gain major share of market | Control forty-two percent of market in the greater Chicago area during the next calendar year |
| Satisfy customers | Seventy percent of customers return to buy again during next 90-day period |
| Maintain equipment | Assembly line will shut down less than five percent of time during next ten days due to equipment failures |
| Reduce dropouts | Seventy percent of freshman class will complete semester with GPA above 3.0 |

measuring their progress. To illustrate the difference between *qualitative* and *quantitative* measures of output, table 4-1 lists some qualitative and quantitative goals and objectives of organizations.

*— Qualitative measurement.* Qualitative measurement seeks to denote results in terms of qualities and is subject to wide interpretation. This approach uses a verbal, rather than numerical, description of productivity. For example, a qualitative description of a firm's profit for the year might be described as *excellent* or *better than average*. No attempt is made to quantify or describe the profit in dollars.

*— Quantitative measurement.* Quantitative measurement seeks to describe results in terms of numbers or discrete quantities and is more narrowly interpreted. It avoids general verbal statements in favor of more precise quantities, such as dollars, hours worked, complaints handled per week, or tonnage of shipments in transit.

It is said that before one can control an activity, one must be able to measure it. In recent years, much of the emphasis in management theory has been on the quantitative aspects of management. Most businesses seek to measure their attainment of goals in terms of dollars. Government may use dollars or other criteria, such as miles of paved roads, number of takeoffs and landings at an airport, or gallons of drinking water delivered by the city water system. However, managers must be aware that quantitative data is still subject to interpretation. It can be manipulated and made to mean what we want it to mean.

There is nothing wrong in using qualitative measurements in management. However, they lack the precision which is necessary to control most business organizations. For example, it is much easier for a personnel manager to grant raises or promotions to an employee based upon an objective quantitative measure of

*"So you finally have an idea that's worth quitting us for."*

Reprinted from *Machine Design*, 22 November, 1979.

performance. A report which states that an employee's attendance on the job has been *fair* is less meaningful than, *The employee was absent five times out of thirty working days and arrived late on the job four times.*

## Measurement Criteria

Suppose an organization wishes to introduce a new product to the market and sell ten thousand units during the first year of sales. It plans an extensive advertising and marketing effort to attain this sales objective. Can it be said that the objective has been reached if at the end of one year, sales of the new product are ten thousand units?

In a limited sense, the goal has been achieved as soon as ten thousand units are sold in the first year. However, this simple statement does not consider all the circumstances leading to the sale of the ten thousand units. Consider the effects of the following factors upon the sales of the new product during the first year:

1. sales price (high or low);
2. amount of money spent on advertising and promotional efforts;
3. the number of competing products on the market;
4. the amount of money spent by competitors in advertising and promoting their goods;
5. the sales price of competing goods;
6. the general economic conditions affecting consumer behavior (per capita discretionary income, tax rates, and so on);
7. laws and government regulations affecting the sales or distribution of the product.

Many of these factors might have accounted for the firm's reaching its sales goal of ten thousand units. It is quite possible that despite a strenuous marketing effort, poor sales may follow because of low-priced competing goods or government regulations restricting the flow of goods.

Conversely, a weak or poorly planned marketing effort could result in an excellent sales record. But this may be due to the lack of strong competition in the field, excess consumer purchasing power, or government regulations which encourage the sales of the goods.

A plan which merely states the end results of an organization's endeavors is inadequate. The plan must also state the conditions under which the goals and objectives are to be reached.

Finally, can it be said the sales effort was a failure if in the first year the firm only sold 9,900 units, instead of 10,000? What criteria are to be used to measure the successful attainment of the goal?

To effectively evaluate any plan, it is necessary to define three basic elements: end results, conditions, and criteria of acceptable performance.

1. *End results.* The products, services, or results which will be achieved upon reaching the goal.

2. *Conditions.* The conditions under which the results will be produced must be specified. These include such factors as the number and types of competing products, their sales price, general economic climate in the country, interest rates, etc.

3. *Criteria of acceptable performance.* The degree of attainment which will be considered as fulfilling the goal should be stated. The percentage of profit, number of items sold, and return on investment which will be considered successful, should be specified.

To measure the success of an organizational plan, you must specify the end results, the conditions under which it will be achieved, and the criteria of acceptable performance. (See table 4-2.)

**Table 4-2. Conditions of performance**

| End Results | Criteria of Successful Attainment | Conditions under which Results Are Produced |
|---|---|---|
| Sales of new line of vacuum cleaners (10,000 units in first year) | Ninety-five percent of sales goal reached (9,500 units) with five percent maximum cancellations | Cash sales Eight percent advertising budget Competition with brands A, B, and C |

## USE OF PLANS

### Types of Plans

We have discussed how goals are achieved and measured. Let us now turn to the means of reaching an end. A plan, or strategy, is generally used to guide an organization to its ends. Ends are reached as a result of a step-by-step effort outlined by management, which guides organizational behavior.

Organizations use two fundamental types of plans: basic (strategic) and supporting (operational).

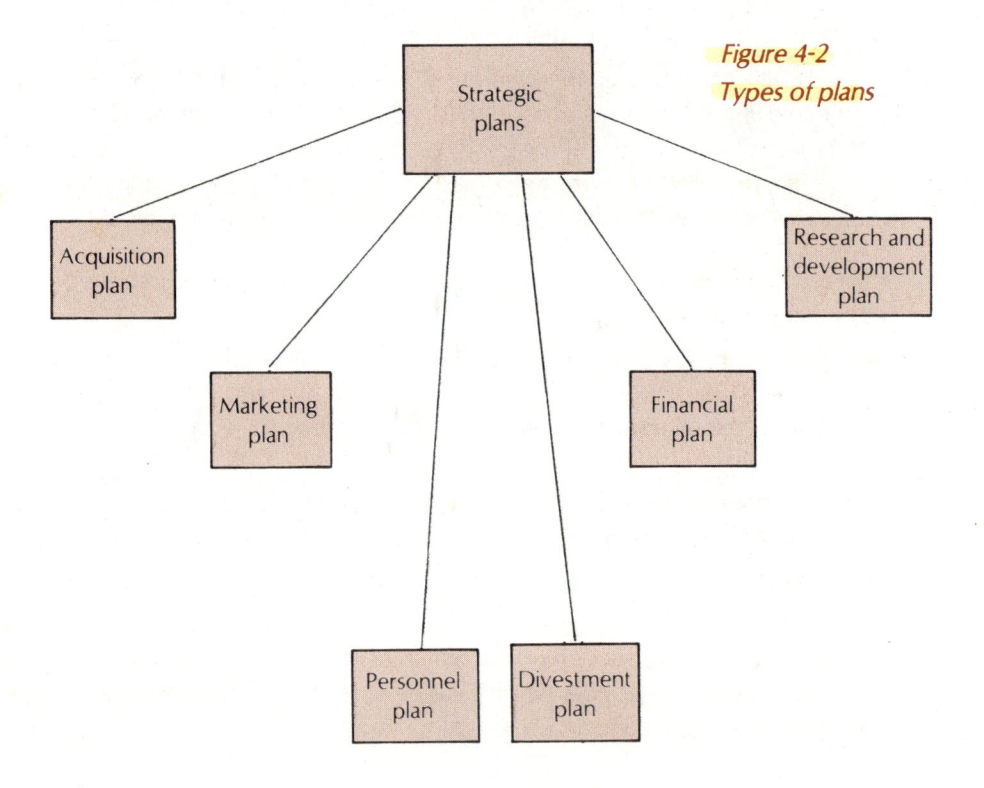

**Figure 4-2 Types of plans**

A diagram showing Strategic plans at the center, connected to: Acquisition plan, Marketing plan, Personnel plan, Divestment plan, Financial plan, and Research and development plan.

CHAPTER FOUR    FUNDAMENTALS OF PLANNING    91

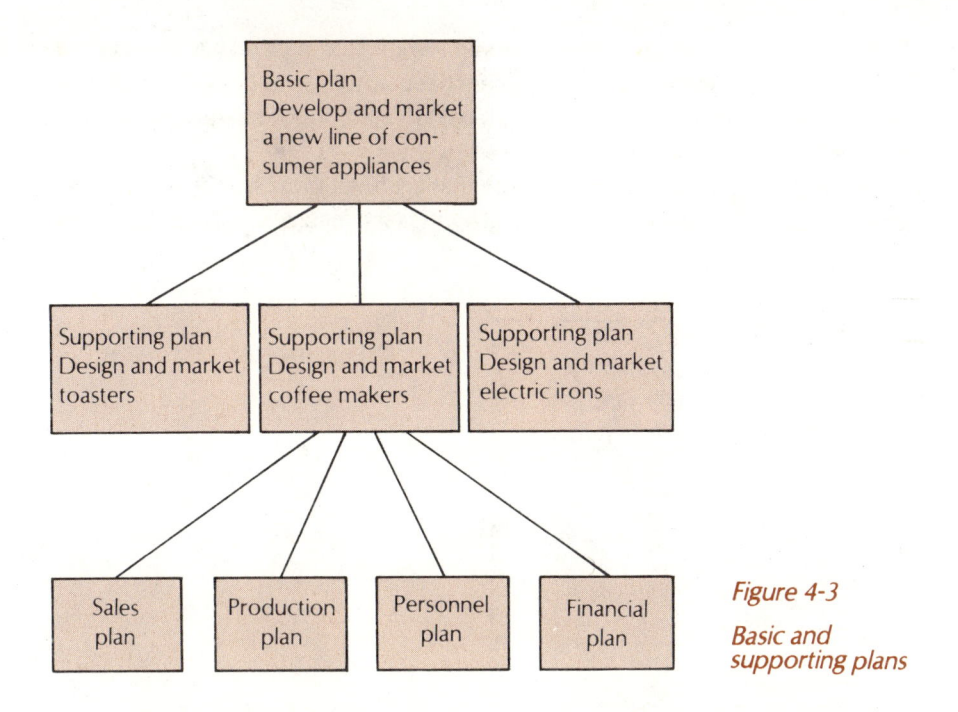

```
                    ┌─────────────────┐
                    │ Basic plan      │
                    │ Develop and     │
                    │ market a new    │
                    │ line of con-    │
                    │ sumer appliances│
                    └─────────────────┘
                ┌───────────┼───────────┐
    ┌───────────────┐ ┌───────────────┐ ┌───────────────┐
    │Supporting plan│ │Supporting plan│ │Supporting plan│
    │Design and     │ │Design and     │ │Design and     │
    │market toasters│ │market coffee  │ │market electric│
    │               │ │makers         │ │irons          │
    └───────────────┘ └───────────────┘ └───────────────┘
           ┌──────────┬──────────┬──────────┐
        ┌─────┐   ┌─────────┐ ┌─────────┐ ┌─────────┐
        │Sales│   │Production│ │Personnel│ │Financial│
        │plan │   │plan      │ │plan     │ │plan     │
        └─────┘   └─────────┘ └─────────┘ └─────────┘
```

*Figure 4-3*

*Basic and supporting plans*

**Basic (strategic) plans.** A basic plan is a fundamental strategy or plan of attack which will direct the organization toward a long-range goal. Basic plans outline major steps that will lead to the achievement of the goals. They often call for the preparation of additional (supporting) plans, which can be carried out on a day-to-day basis. (See figure 4-2.)

**Supporting (operational) plans.** Supporting plans are shorter range than basic plans. Supporting plans fill out and implement the broader aspects of the organization's basic plans. They deal with shorter time periods and greater details, and they relate to specific courses of action.

A supporting plan may spell out in detail a method or procedure, or it may list activities, timetables, and conditions which must be met. Figure 4-3 describes the plans required in order to develop and market a new line of small appliances. The basic plan involves the major decision to develop and market the new products. The supporting plans give the details of the marketing, design, personnel, and manufacturing efforts. Obviously, the basic plan must be prepared before the supporting plans can be implemented.

## Steps in Developing and Implementing Plans

The development of a successful plan requires that management follow a series of steps, from the determination of its goals to the final development of supporting plans and the evaluation of results. (See figure 4-4.) Let us consider the major phases in the planning process.

1. *Determination of goals.* The first step management must take is the selection of the goals it seeks to attain. Management has many courses of action open to it. However, until the desired results are clearly defined, subordinates cannot begin to achieve those results.

One of the major objectives which management must specify is whether it wishes to encourage slow or rapid growth. (See figure 4-5.) It must decide

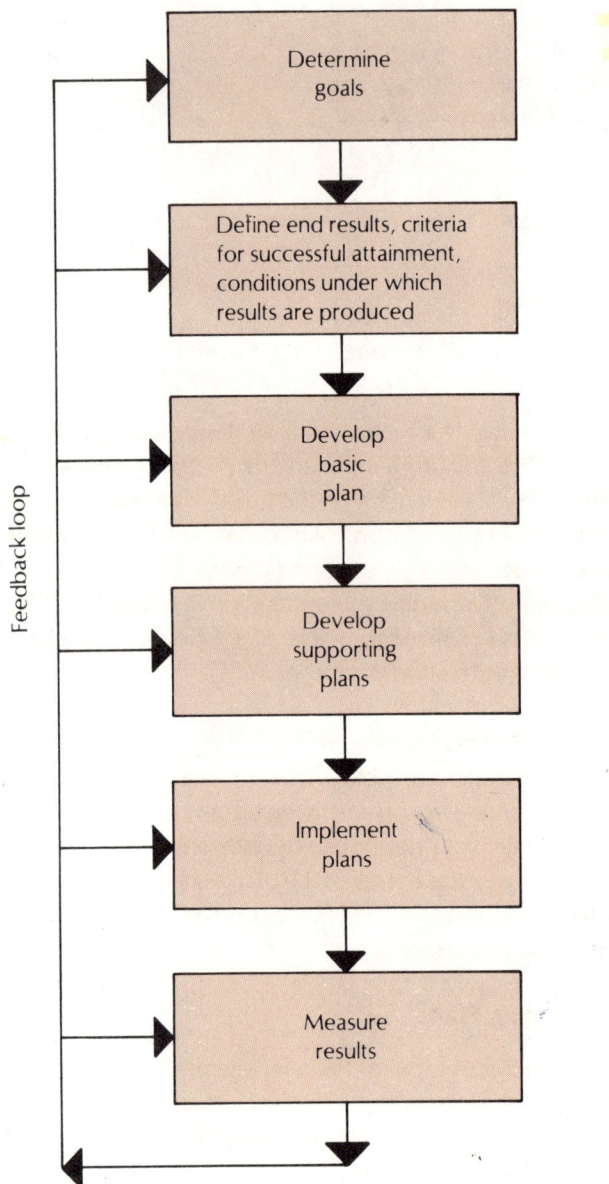

*Figure 4-4*
*Planning cycle*

Determine goals

↓

Define end results, criteria for successful attainment, conditions under which results are produced

↓

Develop basic plan

↓

Develop supporting plans

↓

Implement plans

↓

Measure results

Feedback loop

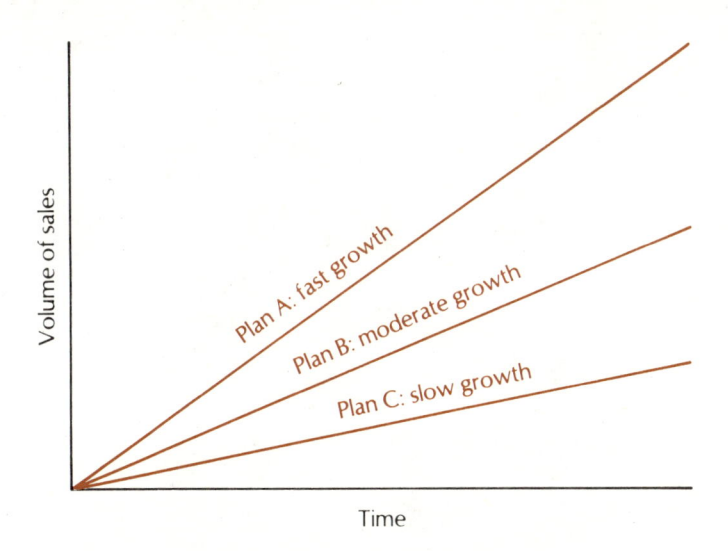

*Figure 4-5
Slow, moderate, and fast growth plans*

[Graph: Volume of sales vs. Time, showing Plan A: fast growth, Plan B: moderate growth, Plan C: slow growth]

whether to introduce many new products or just a few. Management must decide whether it wishes to maximize its profit quickly or over a long period of time. It must determine whether a major share of profits is to be paid to investors or reinvested in the development of new products or new facilities. There are many questions which must be resolved in this first phase of planning.

2. *Definition of criteria, conditions, and acceptable performance.* Management must define the conditions under which it will reach its goals, the criteria by which its progress will be measured, and finally what will be considered as acceptable performance or attainment of its goals. Unless management and subordinates are aware of what is considered an acceptable result, they cannot work effectively. For example, table tennis players agree on what constitutes winning the game. Without defining twenty-one points as winning, neither participant will know when the game is over.

3. *Development of basic plan.* A basic plan is now developed which makes clear the overall goal. The plan gives a broad direction to subordinates, laying out major deadlines, products, and profit bench marks. This basic plan should be thorough enough to be used as a foundation for developing detailed supporting plans.

4. *Development of supporting plans.* Once the basic strategy for reaching the goal has been defined, supporting plans map out details. Supporting plans are developed which describe specific procedures, week-to-week objectives, short-range programs, and courses of action. Supporting plans may require the hiring of personnel, installation of new equipment, and ordering of advertising and promotional materials. They may focus on many aspects of the basic plan.

5. *Implementation of plans.* In this phase, the organization carries out its programs by putting the plans into action. Personnel are hired and new equipment is ordered and installed. Implementation is always guided by the supporting plans.

> **REAL WORLD**
>
> ## P & G's New New-Product Onslaught
>
> The new-product managers at Procter and Gamble are on a merry-go-round that they can't stop. The success of P & G is built upon a continual introduction of new products. P & G's $9.3 billion a year sales in 1979 was principally made up of laundry and cleaning agents, soaps, shampoos, and some traditional foods. P & G managers plan to introduce a wide range of new products, including drugs, synthetic foods, and supplies for hospitals and nursing homes. They expect nonsupermarket items to account for twenty percent of the company's business by the mid 1980s.
>
> For the future, managers are considering soft drinks and agricultural chemicals for the P & G line. Chairman Edward G. Harness says that many of the new products are based on technology related to the soap-making industry. While P & G doesn't plan to become a conglomerate, it does seek to wash, feed, diaper, and deodorize the American public.
>
> Adapted from *Business Week*, 1 October, 1979

They leave little doubt as to what is to be done. The supporting plans serve as road maps guiding day-to-day decisions.

6. *Measurement of results*. The evaluation process begins after a period of time. In this phase, management compares the results achieved against the goals established in the earlier planning phase. It has clearly defined tools for measuring what constitutes acceptable performance.

Sometimes the results may fall short of or exceed those anticipated in the earlier planning phases. The basic plan may call for rapid growth and high profit, but the firm may find that it can only sustain a minimum growth and minimum profit. This leads to the last phase of the process, modification.

7. *Modification of plans*. The last phase involves the redevelopment of plans, or readjustment of existing plans to attain the desired goals. Perhaps the basic plan was unrealistic or unattainable in light of the current marketplace. Management's task is now to either readjust its goals and aspirations, or to form new basic and supporting plans to help it reach its goals. Modification may involve changing the measurement criteria, supporting plans, timetables, or policies and rules to bring them into line with the major goals of the organization.

This final phase is sometimes called a feedback loop. It is an essential part of

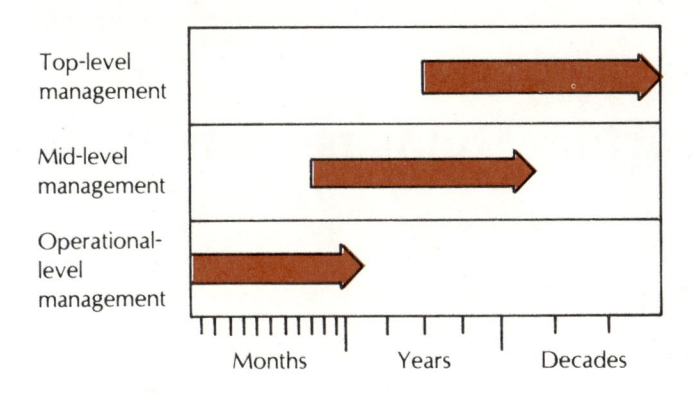

*Figure 4-6 Management planning time span*

the planning process. The feedback loop involves the systematic evaluation of a phenomenon and the adjustment of the process to bring about the desired ends. It regulates what is done by subordinates to assure that the results are within the desired range and expectation of management.

## PLANNING AT VARIOUS LEVELS OF MANAGEMENT

Each level of management is concerned with a different time span of planning. Figure 4-6 illustrates the different lengths of time which concern management. Generally, the higher the level of manager, the longer the planning time span.

Top-level managers are often concerned with long-range plans which may extend up to five or more years in the future. Mid-level managers tend to concentrate their planning efforts on periods of time ranging from less than one year to three or four years. Operational-level managers are concerned with an even shorter time span. Generally, operational-level managers concern themselves with plans which can be executed within a few days, weeks, or months.

This allows for specialization in the planning process. Operational-level managers may concentrate on plans which affect immediate needs. Top management may concentrate on long-range effects, freed from the task of day-to-day details.

## SUMMARY

As organizations grow larger, there is an increasing need for effective planning. Rational approaches to planning have many advantages, including providing better efficiency, control, and measurement of organization progress.

Goals are long-range statements of ends, while objectives are more precise and specify the time frame. Strategies, rules, and policies are used in planning. The major goals of organization include maximizing profit, sales, or return to investors. Major goals of nonprofit organizations may include noneconomic outputs, such

## POSTSCRIPT
# Soviet Factory Outmaneuvers Planners

MOSCOW — Every idler's dream has become reality for workers at the Belgorod asbestos factory in southern Russia.

Output at their plant nose-dived last year, most of their original production goals were not met, and yet the bonuses in their pay envelopes rose sharply.

To make them feel even prouder, the Belgorod workers were declared the winners of three production contests against other asbestos factories.

The secret lies in the curious working of the Soviet economic planning system, which issues directives for everything from industrial growth to the number of eggs to be laid by hens.

Theoretically, yearly and five-year plans are meant to translate the Communist party's economic policy into production targets, required growth rates and the like. But in practice, few treat planning figures as they should.

Belgorod's economic miracle, described by the government newspaper Izvestia, was just one example of the way production targets and actual results are juggled, fudged, and blurred.

The method used by the asbestos factory was relatively simple. When its production of asbestos pipes and roofing fell below requirements in the second quarter of 1977, the factory persuaded industrial planners to lower the quarterly target figure.

In return, management pledged to compensate by producing still more in the following three months. Thus they were able to claim bonuses for meeting the revised production goal.

The same thing happened at the end of the third quarter, so that in December the factory faced the impossible task of producing the equivalent of one-fifth of its entire 1976 output.

But failure to meet this last goal had no effect on wages for the other nine months of the year. The bonuses had already been paid.

Output slumped nearly fifteen percent in 1976, yet production premiums added $39,000 to the payroll.

Reprinted with the permission of Reuters Wire Service. Copyright© 1978.

as services rendered to citizens or clients.

There is a need for management to measure the progress of an organization in quantitative terms, rather than qualitative terms alone. Organization progress is measured in terms of end results, the conditions under which the results are achieved, and the criteria of acceptable performance.

# CHAPTER FOUR  FUNDAMENTALS OF PLANNING

Other methods of fooling the planners abound. Some involve huge wastes of effort just to keep up appearances.

A moving picture equipment enterprise was censured by the official press for inflating its production figures with vehicles produced elsewhere.

All the enterprise did was to buy vehicles in one town, send them hundreds of miles by rail to its workshops in two other towns, and fit them with plywood boxes — apparently for transporting films and equipment — which cost just over $68.

When it came to adding up the value of everything the enterprise produced, the whole "specially equipped" vehicle was included.

Then there was the building organization near Baku, on the Caspian Sea, that found it had not done enough work to justify its payroll. Off the builders went to a patch of wasteland, to build a large and useless fence from the most expensive materials they could find.

Soviet planners are not above playing the statistics game themselves.

The first clue to the size of the 1975 grain harvest, the worst for a decade, was given by a senior planning official who announced that production since 1971 had surpassed that of the previous five years by eight percent.

The result sounded good until calculations showed a 1975 total of some 137 million tons — 80 million below target.

It was the same this year when production figures for 1977 were published in the Soviet press. Only two industrial ministries, those responsible for ferrous metallurgy and the production of meat and dairy products, were officially reported to have missed their production goals.

But a comparison of results with targets published earlier showed that the output of oil, coal, electricity, most chemicals, and numerous other items had fallen short of expectations. The targets had evidently been revised in mid year, observers concluded.

Some Western experts believe that Soviet economic plans are intended not so much as a statement of expectations, but more as a stimulus for use in constant exhortations to work harder.

But Soviet leaders, among them President Leonid I. Brezhnev, seem to be growing increasingly impatient with those who fulfill their plan only on paper.

Brezhnev said last December that tighter checks were needed on the way output obligations were met. He also urged tougher attitudes toward red tape and those who tried to shift the blame for economic failures to others.

What he had in mind was probably the kind of cover-up cited by the newspaper Sotsialisticheskaya Industriya in a front-page editorial reprimanding several government ministries, including those responsible for heavy machinery and the chemical industry.

Basic plans lay out the fundamental strategy and long-range goals, while supporting plans are shorter in duration. The planning process includes determining goals, defining criteria, conditions, and acceptable performance, developing basic and supporting plans, implementing plans, measuring results, and modifying plans.

## KEY TERMS

Goal  81
Objective  81
Plan  82
Strategy  82
Policy  83
Procedure  83
Rule  84
Standard  84
Basic plans  91
Supporting plans  91

## REVIEW QUESTIONS

1. Why do organizations need rational planning? List the benefits.
2. Contrast the difference between a goal and an objective.
3. Contrast the difference between a policy, a rule, and a standard.
4. Explain the purpose of a procedure.
5. Describe some major goals of profit-making firms.
6. Describe some major goals of nonprofit organizations.
7. Contrast the difference between a qualitative and quantitative measure of performance.
8. Discuss the need for measurement criteria.
9. Describe the three major aspects of measuring organization performance.
10. How do the goals of profit-making and nonprofit organizations differ?
11. Why is it necessary to specify conditions of performance when evaluating progress toward goals?
12. List the steps in the planning cycle.

## Case Incident

The Municipal Harbor Department Board of Commissioners has approved a general program to expand the city's harbor. The program has been carefully researched and calls for the installation of modern containerized shipping facilities and cargo handling equipment. This would significantly increase the amount of cargo that could be handled and would be a big economic boon to the city. Jim Arnell, harbor department manager, has called together his planning staff to discuss the new expansion program.

One of the key members of Arnell's staff is Keith Roberts, who has been with the harbor department since its inception over twenty-six years ago. Roberts has been in charge of all the physical plant facilities. Much of the success of the current development of the harbor operations is due to him. Roberts' basic working style is intuitive. He avoids putting plans in an inflexible written form. Instead, he relies upon personal contacts and verbal communications with his subordinates.

Arnell has told Roberts that the harbor commissioners want a carefully drawn timetable and plan for the harbor expansion project. They need as much empirical detail as possible so that they can make a reasonable decision regarding expansion. Roberts has pointed out that he has developed much of the present harbor facility without the detailed written plans, specifications, or lengthy reports now being demanded by the commissioners. "If we've been so successful expanding and developing the harbor facilities up until now, why do we need to change?"

Roberts says that there is no need to put in writing what we all know needs to be done. In fact, Roberts feels so strongly about this that he flatly refuses to do so because it will interfere with getting the job done. To some degree, Arnell understands Roberts' position, but he knows that he must insist on detailed plans since he is under pressure from the harbor commissioners who are demanding everything in writing. The primary reason is that the harbor commissioners want to be sure plans are not based on emotional decisions and need the documentation to prove it.

## PROBLEMS:

1. Is the Harbor Commission reasonable in expecting written detailed plans in light of the department's successful operations in the past?
2. How should Arnell handle Roberts' refusal to prepare written plans?
3. Would written plans improve Roberts' operations?

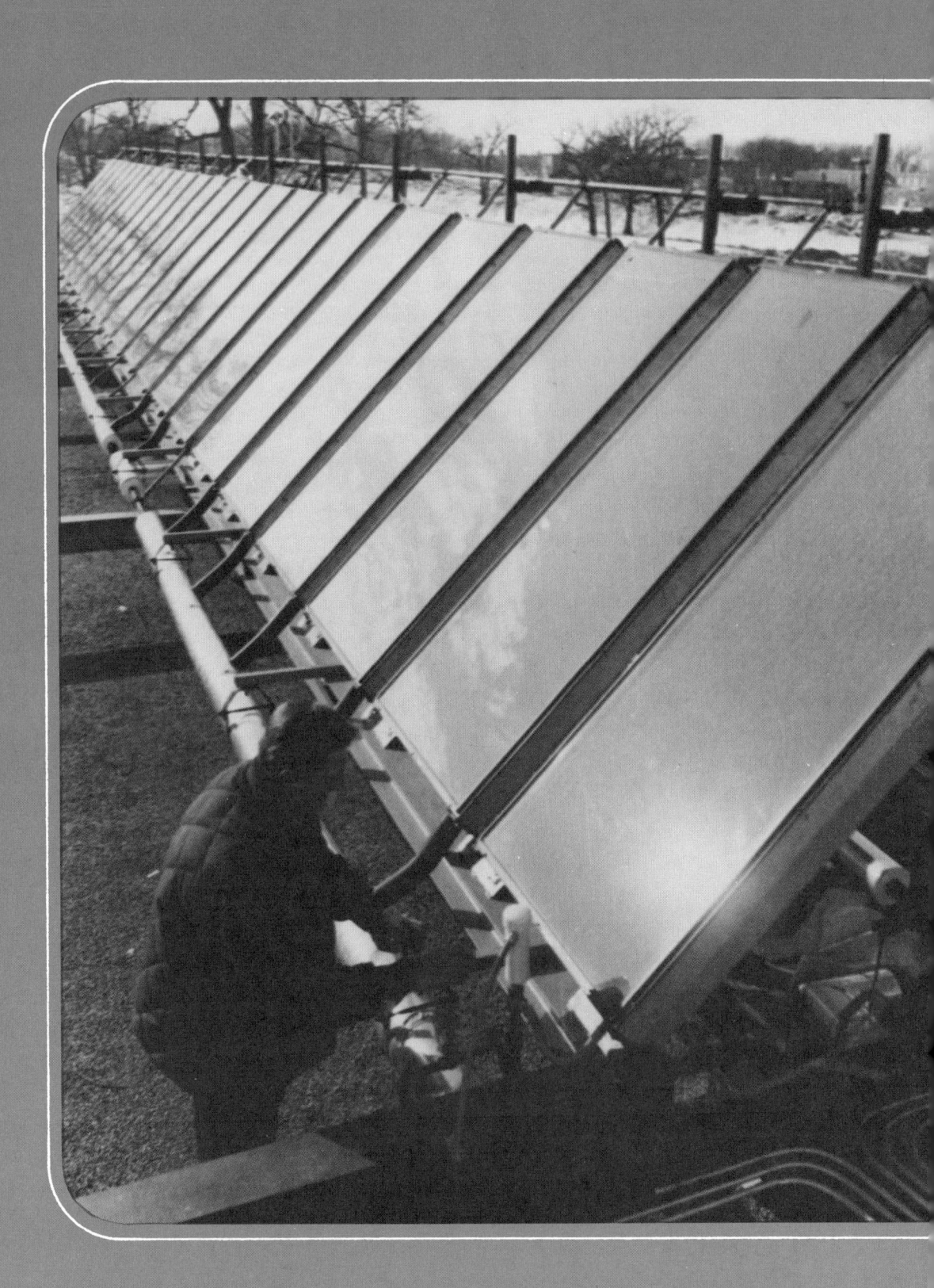

# 5
# Applied Planning

**LEARNING OBJECTIVES**

After studying this chapter, you should be able to:
1. Contrast the differences between long-range, short-range, standing, and one-time plans.
2. Summarize the four major management plans.
3. Describe the interrelationship and hierarchy of plans.
4. Identify the basic characteristics of good plan design.
5. Describe three approaches to staffing the planning effort.
6. List the basic planning tools.
7. Contrast four types of ratios used in planning.
8. Describe management by objectives (MBO) and how it relates to planning.
9. Explain how forecasting is used in the planning process.
10. List some major sources of external data available to the manager.

In this chapter, we look at the practical and applied aspects of the planning process. Previously we discussed the need for planning, definitions, goals, and objectives and how plans are evaluated. Now we look at the specifics of good plan design, staffing the planning group, and basic planning tools. This chapter concludes with a discussion of management by objectives (MBO).

## TIME ELEMENT

Managers use a variety of plans, including long-range, short-range, standing, and one-time plans. The time factor is the distinguishing feature between these plans. Time plays an important role in plan development and implementation. The very nature of a plan implies a relationship of events occurring over a span of time.

1. *Long-range plans.* A long-range plan may extend over a period of five or ten years or more. Long-range plans are designed to coordinate the organization's activities over many years, often under changing management conditions. Plans guide the long-range financial, marketing, personnel, and service-producing efforts of the organization. (See figure 5-1.)

The most commonly used long-range planning period is five years. A five-year period is sufficiently long to allow management to see an event on the horizon and take steps to deal with it.

Several five-year plans may be linked together. Each is built on the progress gained from the previous plan. Plans of ten or more years rely upon predictions and forecasts which are difficult to make with any degree of certainty. Plans of this length are of less use to management, since they do not provide the level of reliability necessary to make major decisions.

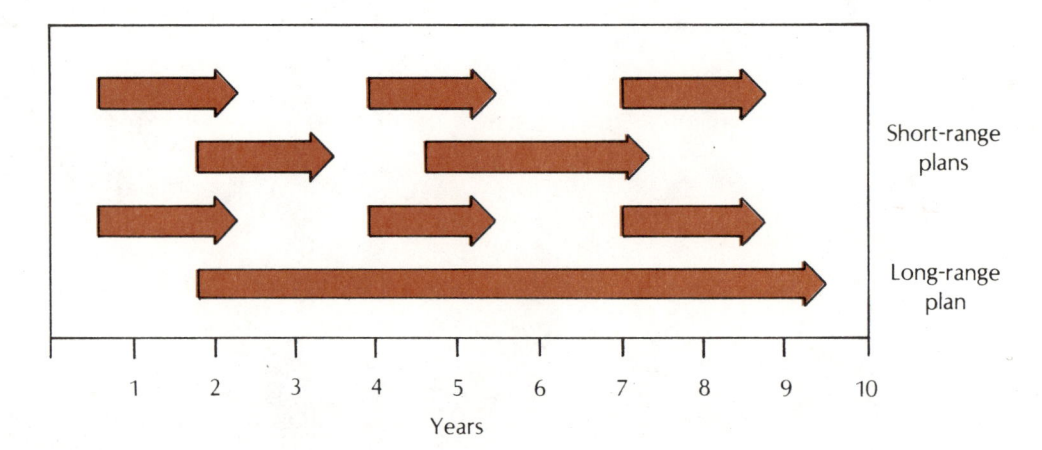

*Figure 5-1 Long- and short-range planning*

CHAPTER FIVE    APPLIED PLANNING                                              103

Long-range plans often involve the research and development of new products.

Long-range plans focus on the development of new markets, products, or plant facilities, or the acquisition and development of personnel. Long-range plans give an organization a continuity of effort. This continuity extends through the leadership of many managers. It gives direction and consistency to organizational growth and development.

2. *Short-range plans.* Short-range plans involve a time span ranging from a few months to several years. Short-range plans are supporting in nature and are directed to current conditions, while long-range plans focus on more distant problems.

3. *Standing plans.* A standing plan is one which has no termination date and remains in effect until revoked by management. A standing plan, for example, may outline methods of acquiring and training new personnel, improvements in public relations, or continuing efforts to raise capital or finance expansion.

To illustrate, a standing plan may be developed to improve safety conditions in the shop. The plan may call for periodic inspection of work stations, tools, and methods. It may require safety meetings and the regular inspection of guards, tools, and safety devices. The plan remains in effect as long as the shop is in operation, or until it is replaced by an updated plan.

Some examples of standing plans follow:
— plant safety plan;

— equipment maintenance plan;

— employee training and development plan;

— acquisition of new capital plan;

— new product development plan;

— new market development plan.

4. *One-time plans.* A one-time plan is designed for a single, one-time application. It is used to resolve a specific, nonrecurring problem or organizational objective. A one-time plan may be prepared to install a new assembly line, develop a new product, or raise capital for a new building or warehouse. Once the goal has been achieved, the plan terminates.

For instance, a one-time plan may be developed to relocate a firm's headquarters from one city to another. The single use plan may include a detailed timetable of events, from the acquisition of the new building to the removal of equipment and relocation of personnel. Once the move is accomplished, the need for the plan ceases, and it is terminated.

Further examples of one-time plans follow:

— build new cafeteria;

— relocate offices to new quarters;

— correct environmentally deficient production equipment;

— correct safety defects in existing production equipment;

— upgrade staff in preparation for new communications system.

## MAJOR MANAGEMENT PLANS

Management planning efforts generally focus on the preparation of four major plans. These basic plans include marketing, production, financial, and personnel plans. The nature of the enterprise often affects the plan selection. Obviously, a production plan would be minor, if it existed at all, in a hospital, school, or government agency. Let us consider the purpose and scope of plans often used by manufacturing organizations.

1. *Marketing plan.* One of the key plans used by management is the marketing plan. This is usually developed first, since production, personnel, and financial plans are all dependent upon a firm's sales and marketing efforts. The marketing plan is designed to predict the number of units of goods which will be demanded and sold over a given period of time.

The marketing plan includes supporting plans detailing the expenditures to be made for advertising, promotion, and personal selling efforts. The total marketing plan includes an assessment of consumer demand, costs of selling and advertising the goods, the type of products to be sold, and the competition. It considers the marketing mix (combination of products offered), price structure, and distribution methods.

Figure 5-2 shows a graph of a typical product life cycle. It is useful in planning the sales probability of a product. Products move through a life cycle, as shown in the figure. When a new product is first introduced, few people are aware of it. Sales and profits are predictably low. This calls for a large investment in advertising and promotional efforts. When the product moves into the growth stage, more units are demanded and profits begin to rise. In the maturity and saturation stages, sales volume falls off, as do profits. If the company is to remain successful, it must introduce a new product.

With charts and tables such as these, related to a specific product, a marketing plan is developed spelling out how much money is to be spent on advertising the original product, and how much will be spent on developing new products. The marketing plan indicates how many units will be demanded in the future in any given period. Sales estimates must precede planning efforts involving the production of the product, the employment of personnel, and the acquisition of capital.

2. *Production plan.* Once a marketing plan has been developed, the firm assembles a production plan to provide the marketing department with the goods. The supporting production plan depends upon the number and type of units which the marketing department estimates can be sold. Once these figures are known, management can plan new equipment and expansion of plant facilities.

The production plan concentrates on producing the designated goods in the quantity required, at a price which the marketing department feels is competitive. Production plans define how the units are to be produced, the types of raw materials required, and how the finished goods are processed.

The production plan considers methods of handling, warehousing, and ship-

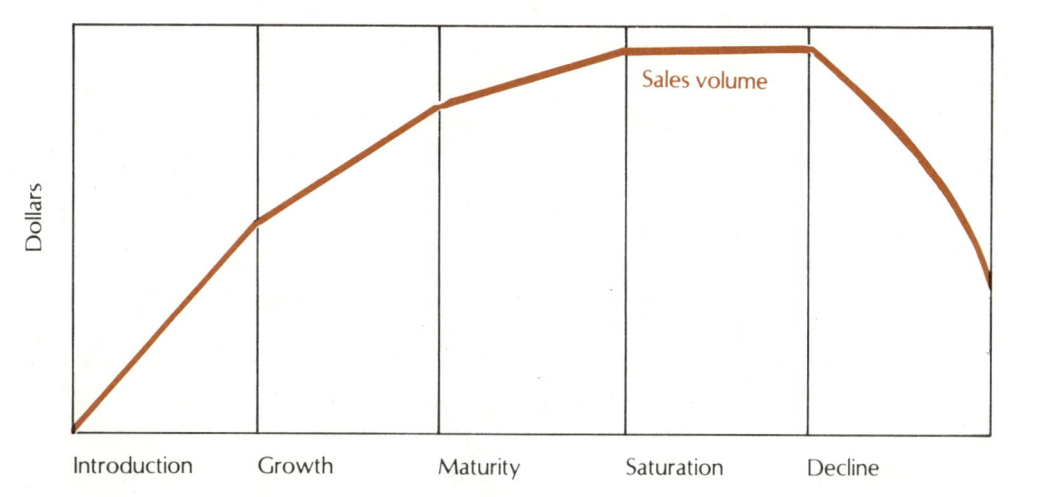

*Figure 5-2 Product life cycle (Single product)*

ping raw materials and finished goods. It selects suppliers of raw materials, establishes delivery dates, and estimates wholesale prices for raw materials.

3. *Personnel plan.* A personnel plan details the program which acquires and trains the staff. Personnel plans are dependent upon the size and scope of production facilities, which in turn depend on the marketing plans.

Supporting personnel plans detail how applicants will be interviewed and hired. Planning begins with an analysis of work force needs, and includes a description of the various jobs to be performed. This includes grading the jobs and establishing a wage structure.

Once the staff is acquired, the personnel plan considers performance appraisal, salary increases, and employee training. The personnel plan includes details on how on-the-job training is provided, and how off-the-job training is used in developing the staff.

Personnel plans are very extensive in nature and include bargaining with unions, means of handling employee grievances, and fringe benefits. In many industries, labor costs equal or exceed the material and fabricating costs of goods. Therefore, a sound personnel plan may be the key to producing a product at a price at which it can be marketed successfully.

4. *Financial plan.* The financial plan defines how capital is acquired and used. Financial plans detail how much money is needed, how it is obtained, and how surplus capital and profit is to be distributed.

Financial plans have two components: short and long-term financing. The short-term aspect of the financial plan deals with the immediate cash flow situation, and how funds are acquired and distributed for relatively short periods, usually less than two years. The short-term financial plan details how funds are obtained to buy raw materials, pay labor costs, and ship finished goods. It deals with financing seasonal needs and goods in production.

Long-term financial plans generally involve the acquisition of major capital items, such as real estate, buildings, and major pieces of equipment. A long-term plan considers financing such items for periods of ten years or more. Plans to finance buildings and acquire capital through the issuance of bonds and sale of stocks is considered. Retirement of bonds, payment of interest on borrowed money, and investment in other industries is part of the financial plan.

## Plans Based upon Scope of Task

Another means of classifying plans is by their range or depth of coverage. Some organizations develop a variety of plans which vary in scope. These deal with the establishment of policies, procedures, standards, or practices. In chapter 4 we defined how these are used in the planning function.

Thus, the planning phase may cover great depth and precisely defined policies, rules of behavior or employee conduct, or procedures for implementing various goals. Short- or long-range plans and major management plans such as marketing or personnel often include extensive statements of policy and procedures.

### Interrelationship of Plans

The plans described here are interrelated. The organization's major planning efforts for marketing, production, personnel, and finance must be undertaken in a systematic fashion. It is rare that an organization can develop a marketing plan which does not consider production and personnel, for example. Since the personnel plan and production plans affect how much goods will cost, the marketing plan must be interrelated with other basic plans of the organization.

If the organization is viewed as a system, a change in one supporting plan affects one or more of the other supporting plans. The manager must consider the overall impact of each plan on the total organization. This requires close cooperation and communication between managers in different departments in the organization.

### Hierarchy of Plans

Most organization resources are limited. If an organization had infinite sources of money, personnel, and time, it could achieve all goals it chose to undertake. But

---

**REAL WORLD**
# Looking for Longer Horizons

The profit and promise of multinationals in developing countries is gone, according to J. Peter Grace. Grace heads a $5 billion per year empire of chemical, retailing, energy, and restaurant firms. He feels that the big money made by the multinationals is over because the countries in which they do business are heavily in debt, and these debts are now coming due.

According to Grace, a firm's success is based upon its ability to do long-term planning, and there just isn't enough of it being done today. Poor planning is visible in our own government. Grace believes the four-year presidential terms aren't long enough to allow for long-range planning. Private industry places chief executives in charge for equally short tenures. Most research and development programs take eight to ten years to pay off. The short stint of most organization presidents forces them to look to immediate results at the expense of long-term benefits.

Adapted from *Time*, 4 February 1980, p. 72.

limitations on time, money, equipment, physical plant, and other resources require management to define which plans are most important. The placing of plans in a system of priorities is called a hierarchy of plans. It involves placing a list of plans in ranking order of importance (table 5-1).

A hierarchy of plans may place certain plans higher on the list than others so that these will be achieved first. A time-based hierarchy is developed which places certain plans above others. Once the subordinates understand the priorities, they can work effectively toward their implementation. Failure to establish a hierarchy causes confusion and a dissipation of organization resources.

## Good Plan Design

Sound plans possess certain basic characteristics. Plans should be readily understood by management and subordinates and encourage motivation and acceptance. Here is a list of major characteristics of good plan design.

1. *Measurable performance.* Plans should be prepared in a way which produces measurable results. Vaguely structured plans do not lend themselves to evaluation. Plans should specify desired results in clear, measurable, quantitative terms.

2. *Employee motivation.* Plans should develop enthusiasm and motivation. Good plans provide rewards and benefits for both the organization and the subordinates.

3. *Consistency.* Plans should be consistent with established policies and rules of organization. Plans which are inconsistent create conflict and will not be carried out.

4. *Attainable goals.* The results which are expected should be attainable. They should be high enough to achieve management's objectives, but realistic in terms

### Table 5-1. Hierarchy of plans

| Before Establishing Priorities: | After Establishing Priorities: |
|---|---|
| 1. Plan to repave parking lot. | 1. Plan to replace worn-out delivery equipment |
| 2. Plan to replace worn-out delivery equipment | 2. Plan to develop new product |
| 3. Plan to develop new product | 3. Plan to automate assembly process |
| 4. Plan to increase fringe benefits to employees | 4. Plan to increase fringe benefits to employees |
| 5. Plan to relocate plant nearer to markets | 5. Plan to repave parking lot. |
| 6. Plan to automate assembly process | 6. Plan to relocate plant nearer markets |

of what can be accomplished by employees and subordinates. Unreachable goals and plans cause anxiety and frustration.

5. *Flexibility.* Plans should be flexible. They should allow for change and modification as demanded by unforeseen events. Subordinates who are aware that plans are modifiable are more likely to accept them and work toward their success.

6. *Clarity and fairness.* Plans should be comprehensible to the manager and subordinate. Since plans are designed to be followed, they should be stated in terms which leave little room for misinterpretation. This calls for concise language and clearly defined terms. Finally, plans should be reasonable. They should, on their face, appear fair and equitable, and not be arbitrary.

7. *Consideration of social consequences.* Plans should consider social consequences, in addition to achievement of organizational goals. There is mounting pressure on many organizations to frame plans which take into account not only the impact upon the firm, but also the effect upon society. A plan which fails to weigh the social impact upon employment, demographics, or the community may not be acceptable to government agencies or to the public.

## THE PLANNERS

### Planning Departments

Some organizations centralize the planning function into a single department. This department is responsible for the development and implementation of various plans. The advantage of consolidating major planning activities into a single department is that it gives consistency and continuity to the planning effort. Plans can be coordinated and developed in a more logical manner where the responsibility is centralized. Centralized planning allows the assembly of a skilled and experienced planning staff.

The limitation of centralized planning is that it removes the planning function from close proximity to operating management. Decentralized planning, particularly where planning is done in different geographic territories, tends to create a patchwork of inconsistent rules, policies, and procedures throughout the organization.

### Selecting Planning Personnel

Individuals from many levels of the organization may be called upon to assist in the development, design, and implementation of a new plan. Top-level management personnel participates in long-range, basic, and strategic planning efforts. Mid-level management concentrates its efforts on short-range, supporting planning efforts. Operational-level managers take part in developing and implementing short-range plans. This is consistent with the manager's level of responsibility and position in the organization's hierarchy.

There are a variety of methods of selecting and staffing planning projects. Major planning efforts are usually handled by a project manager, task force, or planning committee. Let us consider the merits of each of these approaches to planning.

1. *Project manager planning.* In this approach, one individual is selected to manage the planning effort. The project manager is given full staff authority over subordinates to develop and implement the plan. The project manager may, of course, rely upon many individuals in the organization for assistance.

The project manager approach has several advantages. First, it places a single individual in charge of the entire planning effort. This facilitates quicker decision making and an integrated planning effort. The project manager may have many subordinates, but the manager shoulders the burden of the ultimate success or failure of the effort.

The limitations of the project manager approach are that one person is given full staff authority for the entire project. One individual is faced with making the final decisions which cannot be delegated to a group for a consensus.

The project manager approach to planning is widely used in the aerospace and electronics industries. One person is given the authority to plan a project for the development of a new system, including its research, planning, marketing, and all production efforts.

2. *Task force planning.* Another alternative to staffing the planning effort is the task force. A task force is a group of individuals drawn from many levels of the organization's management to develop and implement a plan. Once the plan has been implemented and the objective reached, the task force is disbanded.

The task force may be made up of supervisors, lead persons, or top-level managers. The group works together to develop a plan, pooling its capabilities and efforts.

The advantage of a task force is that it draws from many levels of management, thereby including many people with differing expertise. A task force tends to be broadly based; hence, its plans consider the total organization. It has a wider planning outlook than the project manager approach. However, task force planning may suffer from indecision and lack of direction, since many people are given the planning responsibility.

For example, a firm may assign a task force the project of planning a new company cafeteria. Members from many levels of management serve on the team. It includes supervisors, workers, department managers, and top management representatives. The group meets and plans the details of the new cafeteria, including the room layout, facilities, and selection of personnel.

3. *On-going committee planning.* An on-going committee is a group of individuals charged with the planning effort. Members of the on-going committee are

CHAPTER FIVE    APPLIED PLANNING                                            111

drawn from various levels of management. In contrast to the task force, the committee remains in existence until terminated by a directive from management, rather than disbanding once the objectives have been reached.

On-going committees may be charged with planning safety programs, new product development, marketing strategies, or financial planning. The advantage of the on-going committee is that it makes decisions based on a consensus and is responsive to different interests and points of view. However, committees often fail to reach decisions, or make decisions slowly, because the responsibility for planning is vested in many individuals, and compromises may often be necessary.

Much of the planning effort in Japanese organizations is through committees. These committees represent wide-based interests in the organizations. Thus, there is a tendency for decisions to be accepted by subordinates. This process takes more time than project manager planning, and the responsibility rests in many hands.

## BASIC PLANNING TOOLS

Management planners use a group of planning tools to assist them in their work. These include the use of accounting information, statistical methods, financial ratios, forecasting techniques, and lead and lag indicators.

### Budgets

A basic planning and control tool is the budget. A budget is a statement of position for a definite period of time, based upon estimates of expenditures during the period and proposals for financing them. A budget sets aside amounts of money or other resources available for a particular period. Budgets are both planning and control tools and provide a means of controlling and anticipating future behavior.

There are many types of budgets other than financial. These include production, human resources, materials, and marketing budgets. These budgets state the amount of funds or resources available during a future period for use in production, advertising, or marketing efforts. They may also specify output or anticipated results.

### Statistics and Descriptive Data

An important planning tool is statistics and descriptive data. Many organizations gather and report information which is useful in the planning process. Data is a historical record of past performance and a predictor of future behavior. Generally, data involved in an organization can be categorized as either internal or external.

1. *Internal data.* Internal data is gathered and reported from within the organization. It is information on the production, financial, and personnel conditions within a firm. Examples of internal data include the number of units produced in one week, number of hours worked by employees, cash in bank, annual profit, and cost of advertising. This type of information is obtained from the accounting, marketing, or production departments. It is rarely made available to anyone outside the firm, except government agencies where required.

2. *External data.* External data is gathered and reported outside an organization. Examples of external data include the prevailing interest rates in the community, median income of residents, and average investment in family dwellings. External data is useful since it defines the environment and community in which an organization exists.

The government provides organizations with much useful external data on population, income, and employment. This data is available from public records, the census bureau, the Department of Commerce, and other sources.

## Ratios

A ratio is a numerical expression of the relationship between two quantities. It is the quotient, or result of one number divided by another. It provides a convenient means of illustrating relationships and of making comparisons. A ratio is used to compare one firm's performance with that of another, or of an entire industry. Table 5-2 shows some ratios for a group of large industrial corporations. It compares earnings per share and sales data. The ratios can be used by a firm to compare its own progress over a number of years.

"Okay.. but except for that, when have I ever made a bad mistake?"

*Reprinted from* Datamation, *December 1973.*

**Table 5-2. Large industrial corporation ratios**

| Rank 1979 | Company | Sales ($000) | Earnings Per Share Growth Rate 1969-79 Percent | Rank | 1979 Percent | Rank | Total Return to Investors 1969-79 Average Percent | Rank |
|---|---|---|---|---|---|---|---|---|
| 1 | Exxon (New York) | 79,106,471 | 14.85 | 129 | 20.15 | 249 | 12.10 | 118 |
| 2 | General Motors (Detroit) | 66,311,200 | 5.37 | 375 | 2.89 | 383 | 4.53 | 289 |
| 3 | Mobil (New York) | 44,720,908 | 16.02 | 101 | 65.91 | 68 | 15.22 | 68 |
| 4 | Ford Motor (Dearborn, Mich.) | 43,513,700 | 9.26 | 295 | (14.78) | 460 | 6.30 | 237 |
| 5 | Texaco (Harrison, N.Y.) | 38,350,370 | 8.64 | 318 | 29.81 | 190 | 6.19 | 240 |
| 6 | Standard Oil of California (San Francisco) | 29,947,554 | 14.57 | 137 | 26.46 | 211 | 14.22 | 82 |
| 7 | Gulf Oil (Pittsburgh) | 23,910,000 | 8.71 | 315 | 56.97 | 87 | 7.77 | 206 |
| 8 | International Business Machines (Armonk, N.Y) | 22,862,776 | 12.08 | 212 | (9.12) | 441 | 1.54 | 355 |
| 9 | General Electric (Fairfield, Conn.) | 22,460,600 | 14.94 | 125 | 13.16 | 308 | 6.28 | 238 |
| 10 | Standard Oil (Ind.) (Chicago) | 18,610,347 | 16.25 | 96 | 44.59 | 124 | 17.05 | 49 |
| 11 | International Telephone & Telegraph (New York) | 17,197,423 | (0.90) | 423 | 2.58 | 390 | (3.19) | 418 |
| 12 | Atlantic Richfield (Los Angeles) | 16,233,959 | 16.55 | 93 | 45.59 | 121 | 9.49 | 169 |
| 13 | Shell Oil (Houston) | 14,431,211 | 12.98 | 184 | 75.41 | 51 | 14.46 | 79 |
| 14 | U.S. Steel (Pittsburgh) | 12,929,100 | — | — | (10.12) | 446 | 3.50 | 318 |
| 15 | Conoco (Stamford, Conn.) | 12,647,998 | 18.49 | 67 | 74.04 | 54 | 18.07 | 42 |
| 16 | E.I. du Pont de Nemours (Wilmington, Del.) | 12,571,800 | 10.11 | 273 | 2.68 | 388 | 5.94 | 251 |
| 17 | Chrysler (Highland Park, Mich) | 12,001,900 | — | — | (19.45) | 468 | (10.43) | 452 |
| 18 | Tenneco (Houston) | 11,209,000 | 8.66 | 317 | 35.53 | 158 | 11.40 | 128 |
| 19 | Western Electric (New York) | 10,964,075 | — | — | — | — | — | — |
| 20 | Sun (Radnor, Pa.) | 10,666,000 | 15.82 | 108 | 71.34 | 61 | 12.27 | 112 |

Reprinted from the May 5 issue of *Fortune* Magazine, p. 276 © 1980 Time Inc.

A thorough discussion of ratios and their analysis is beyond the scope of this book. However, a brief discussion of some of the major ratios used in organizational planning follows. (See also table 5-3.)

1. *Debt ratio.* A firm's debt ratio is an expression of its use of debt or borrowed financing. The debt ratio is found by dividing the firm's total debts by its total assets. The higher the debt ratio, the more the firm's assets have been acquired through debt financing.

The debt ratio provides a quick means of determining how much of the firm's assets are purchased on credit. Thus it is a measure of the firm's financial stability. When debts are reduced, the debt ratio is lessened or eliminated.

*Example:*

$$\frac{\$1{,}000{,}000 \text{ (Total debt)}}{\$5{,}000{,}000 \text{ (Total assets)}} \quad \text{Ratio: }.20$$

2. *Profit ratio.* A firm's profit ratio is an expression of the owner's return on investment. The profit ratio is found by dividing the net profit by the net worth. The higher the profit ratio, the greater the returns.

*Example:*

$$\frac{\$600{,}000 \text{ (Net profit)}}{\$6{,}000{,}000 \text{ (Net worth)}} \quad \text{Ratio: }.10$$

In this illustration, the investors receive a ten percent return on their investment. The profit ratio provides a quick means of measuring and comparing profitability. The greater the profit and the less net worth invested to make that profit, the better the condition of the organization.

3. *Current (liquidity) ratio.* The current ratio is an expression of a firm's ability to pay off its short-term debts and liabilities. The current ratio is found by dividing current assets by current liabilities. The higher the current ratio, the better able a firm is to meet its current expenses and liabilities.

*Example:*

$$\frac{\$2{,}000{,}000 \text{ (Current assets)}}{\$500{,}000 \text{ (Current liabilities)}} \quad \text{Ratio: } 4.0$$

In this instance the firm has four hundred percent greater current assets than it has liabilities. Obviously, a firm with a continually declining current ratio is building up liabilities over assets in an unsound manner. If the process continues, the firm could fail, since it could not meet its current liabilities.

4. *Activity ratio.* The activity ratio is an expression of a firm's use of its assets. It measures how intensively assets are used. The activity ratio is found by dividing total sales by total assets. The greater the ratio, the more intensively it is using its assets to produce sales. A variety of assets can be used to measure activity,

including fixed assets, equipment, and buildings.

*Example:*

$$\frac{\$2{,}000{,}000 \text{ (Total sales)}}{\$1{,}000{,}000 \text{ (Total assets)}} \quad \text{Ratio: 2.0}$$

In this case a firm's sales are double its investment in assets. If a competing firm produces $2,000,000 total sales, but has invested $2,000,000 to produce the same sales, then its activity ratio would be 1.0. That is, it would require twice the investment in assets for the same sales results, and hence, would not be using its assets as intensively.

5. *Other ratios.* A variety of other ratios are used in business management. These include short-term debt ratios, advertising expense to sales ratios, and sales to returned merchandise ratios. These and other ratios provide a convenient means of quantifying organizational performance. They give numerical values to performance, which are used in planning.

---

**REAL WORLD**

# Billionaire Ludwig's Brazilian Gamble

An aide once said of Daniel Keith Ludwig, "He just sits in his office and thinks three to five years down the road." Ludwig's philosophy epitomizes the planning concept. He amassed a fortune after World War II building supertankers in Japan and devising means of financing them. Ludwig is a shipbuilder and industrialist whose net worth is estimated at over $3 billion.

Ludwig operates dozens of global enterprises, including National Bulk Carriers, from his offices in Manhattan. He is probably the richest living American man. Foresight seems to be his greatest asset.

In the early 1950s, Ludwig saw the increased use of pulp and timber in the face of a dwindling supply. He bought land in Brazil in the 1960s for less than $1 an acre. His planning produced what is now the Jari Forestry and Agricultural Enterprises, in which he has invested over $520 million. He has turned the rain forests into towns, and built hospitals, schools, and roads. A few of his lesser enterprises include Mexico's Princess Hotel chain, some oil refineries, and a handful of savings and loan associations.

Adapted from *Time*, 10 December, 1979 p.76.

**Table 5-3 Major financial ratios**

| Ratio | Formula for calculating |
|---|---|
| Debt | Total debts / Total assets |
| Profit | Net profit / Net worth |
| Current | Current assets / Current liabilities |
| Activity | Total sales / Total assets |

## Forecasting

Forecasting is a major planning tool. It involves making predictions of future behavior based upon present behavior. Forecasting techniques are valuable since they enable managers to look ahead with a degree of certainty, based upon predictable trends or directions. Forecasts require making the assumption that present trends will continue in the future. While there is no certainty that a particular trend will continue, it does offer the planner some degree of predictability.

Figure 5-3 illustrates the historical and forecast figures for the age of the population in the United States. It reports the number of people in each age category from 1950 and is projected to 1990. Forecasts such as these are useful to management in preparing marketing, budgeting, expansion, and research programs.

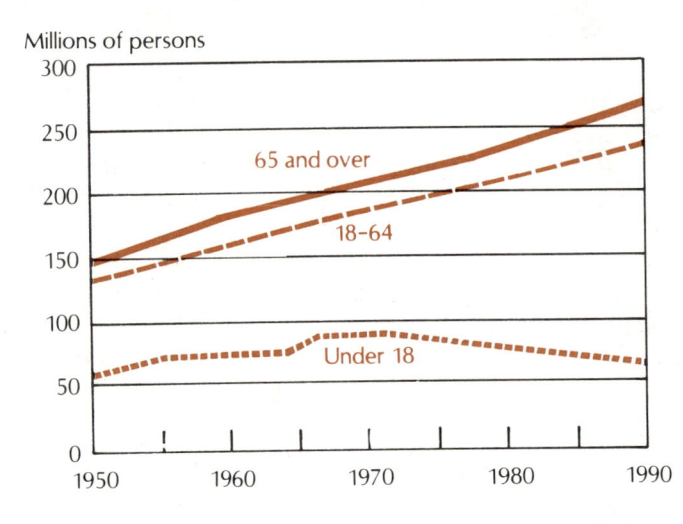

*Figure 5-3 Age of the population*

Reprinted from "A Look at Business in 1990," Government Printing Office, November 1972, p. 51.

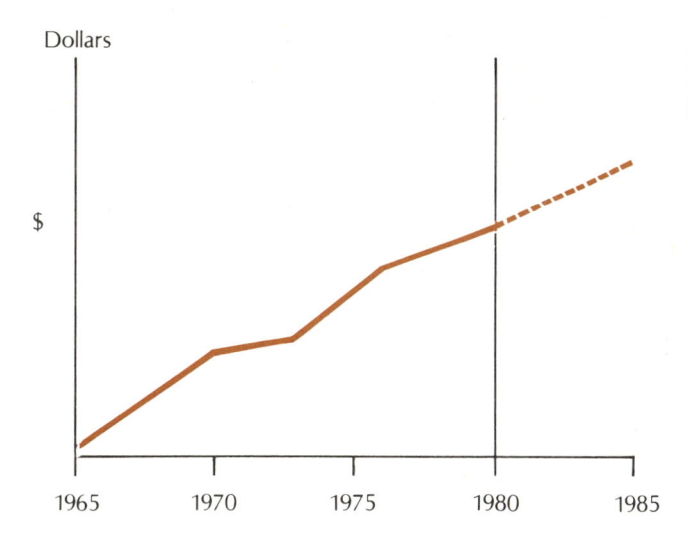

*Figure 5-4*
*Total operating expenses*
*(Five-year projection)*

Following are brief descriptions of a variety of statistical and mathematical forecasting techniques which may be used.

1. *Computers.* The computer is a useful tool in forecasting. A mathematical model is constructed which shows the relationships of the elements which are to be forecast. For instance, a manager may know that an increase in sales generally results from an increase in advertising and promotional expenditures. He may then construct a mathematical model in which the computer prints out expected sales based upon a finite series of advertising and promotional expenditures.

2. *Time series analysis.* Time series analysis uses charts or graphs which delineate a trend over time. Figure 5-4 shows a time series analysis of a firm's total operating expenses. The period from 1965 to 1980 indicates a historical increase in operating expenses. The period from 1980 to 1985 shows a projected forecast. Given the growth assumptions of the previous decade, it may reasonably be assumed that the operating expenditures will increase accordingly.

A variety of factors may influence forecasting. For instance, a firm's consumption of electrical energy may be plotted by time series analysis. (See figure 5-5.) If the firm chooses to operate its plant in the same fashion as it has in the past, it can forecast the growth pattern shown in trend line A. If it chooses to install new energy saving equipment and facilities, it can then forecast energy consumption along trend line B.

3. *Quantitative techniques.* Mathematics is a powerful quantitative tool for forecasting. Mathematical formulas, such as linear regression analysis, are useful in extrapolating trends and projections. Given a set of numerical data representing a firm's historical performance, regression analysis can forecast future performance with a high degree of certainty.

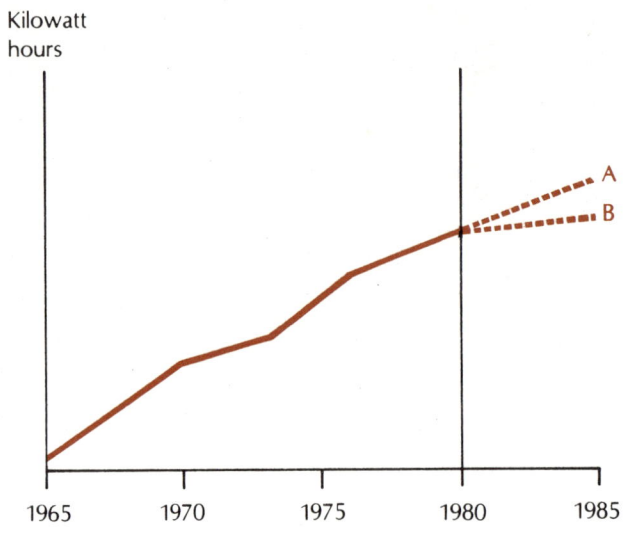

Figure 5-5
Electrical energy consumption
(Five-year projection)

For example, a manager may gather numeric information and data on sales performance of several retail outlets. They can then use a mathematical technique which can project future sales, based upon past performance. Thus they may find that the addition of four more sales representatives may increase sales by forty percent, but the addition of six representatives may increase sales by only fifty percent.

4. *Lead and lag indicators.* Lead and lag indicators are forecasting tools which rely upon reporting data from indicators which historically lead or lag present trends. A lead indicator shows a change or lead in a trend before other more widely based indicators. A lag indicator shows a change after an occurrence or trend is reported by other indicators. Some of the key consumer indicators are the disposable personal income of families, real growth in disposable income, rate of savings, and housing starts. An upturn in a lead indicator, such as housing starts, is a reasonably sure predictor that other, housing-related spending will follow. Once the homes are built, it can be expected that real estate sales will increase, as will sales of furniture, garden equipment, fencing, and other related items.

Managers follow lead indicators in their industries to look for trends. An analysis of lead indicators is used as the foundation for planning. For example, figure 5-6 illustrates two important lead indicators.

Large outlays by industry for new plant and equipment generally results in increased sales and production of goods later. Suppliers of raw materials can anticipate increased sales when plant and equipment spending indicators are rising. Conversely, a reduction in this lead indicator points to a downturn in the demand for raw materials.

CHAPTER FIVE    APPLIED PLANNING

## MANAGEMENT BY OBJECTIVES

Management by objectives (MBO) is one of the major planning tools to emerge in the last several decades. It is used in conjunction with the other planning tools described in this chapter.

In the 1950s Peter Drucker, a noted management theorist, outlined a concept of management which stressed the mutual involvement of the subordinate and the manager in setting goals and in the planning process. Drucker's concepts

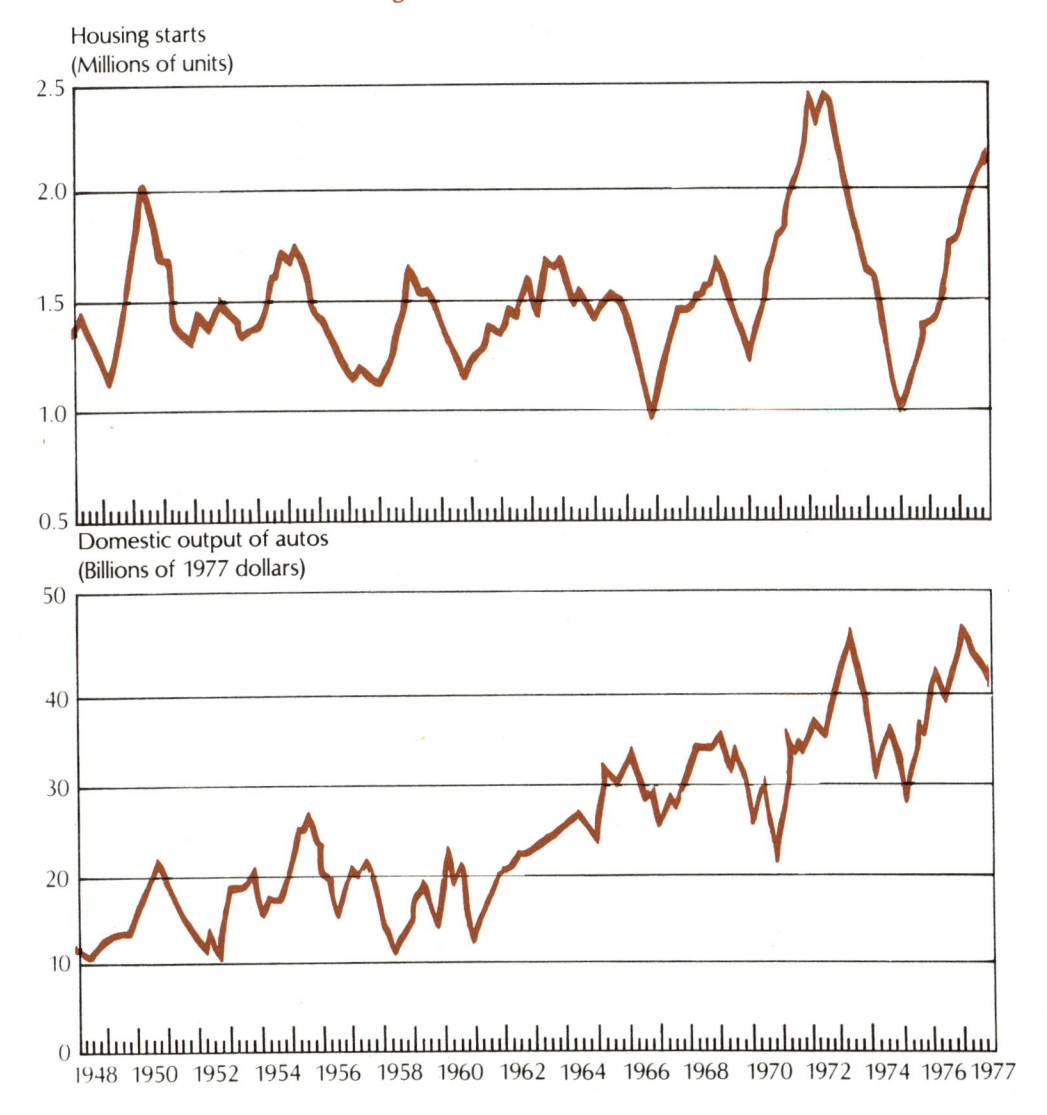

*Figure 5-6  Lead indicators*

Reprinted from The Conference Board, *Road Maps of Industry*, no. 1827.

Figure 5-7
Management by objectives (MBO)

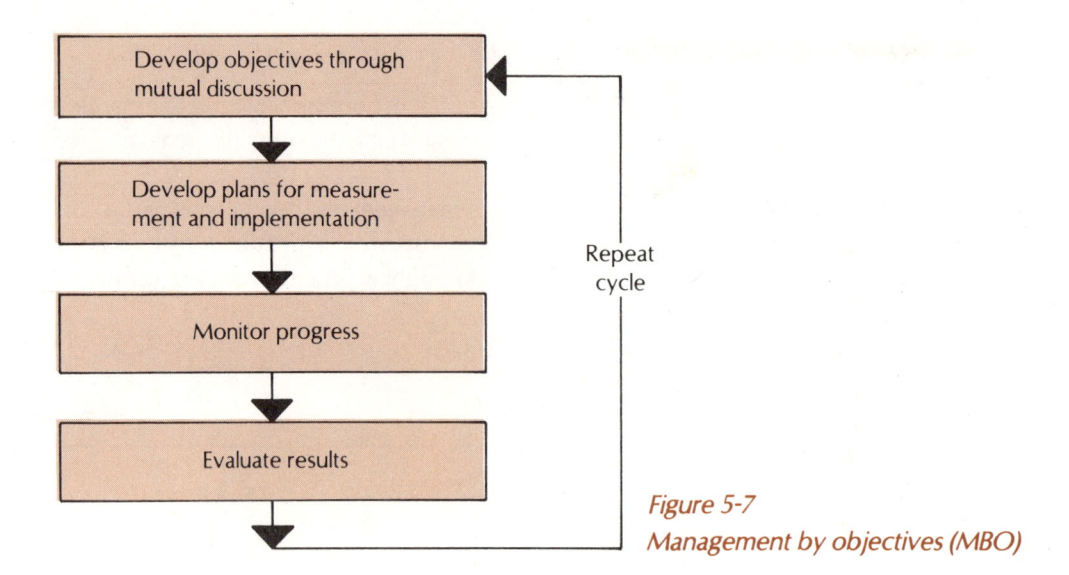

led to the development of a major philosophy of management, management by objectives (MBO).

MBO is the process of mutually establishing goals and plans involving both management and subordinates. Instead of management unilaterally establishing plans and objectives, which are then thrust upon subordinates, a mutual acceptance and development of plans and goals is fostered.

The process of MBO involves several steps. (See figure 5-7.) The process must be sanctioned by management, and accepted both in concept and application. The major phases of the MBO process are the following.

1. *Meeting to discuss plans and key results.* The manager and subordinates meet and discuss plans which hopefully will lead to the desired result. The plans must be results-oriented and measurable. They must include sufficient benefits for the subordinates so that they will accept the objectives and support their achievement.

2. *Development of detailed plans for achievement.* Once the end results are agreed upon, the subordinates develop a clear-cut plan of action which produces the desired results. As in the first step, the subordinates are involved in the formulation of the plan as well as in the development of the objectives. The plan must include a definition of how the end results will be measured.

3. *Monitoring of progress.* Both the subordinates and the manager are involved in the process of monitoring progress toward achieving the objectives. Since clear-cut progress bench marks and measurable results are expected, both can monitor the development of the plan. If progress is not as expected, the subordinates can alter their behavior and efforts to see that the objectives are achieved.

4. *Final evaluation of results.* The last phase of MBO involves an assessment of the end results. Since clear-cut plans have been agreed upon, the manager and subordinates assess the success of the effort for the period. Once the objectives are reached, the process begins anew. A new set of objectives is mutually agreed upon for a forthcoming period, a plan for achievement is developed, the progress is monitored, and the results evaluated.

## Advantages of MBO

MBO has many advantages over management by directive, including the following key benefits.

1. *Increased motivation.* Subordinates are part of the decision-making process and are involved in evaluating their own work. Thus they become more motivated since they have a stake in the plan they helped create.

2. *Increased output.* Since subordinates understand what is expected of them, they are more likely to produce at the desired level.

3. *Verifiable goals.* A distinct benefit of MBO is that it encourages quantitative and verifiable results. The process relies on use of defined goals stated in terms of dollars, time, or other verifiable elements. Thus, subordinate behavior in terms of

The British Aircraft Corporation and Air France missed the mark when they decided to pool resources and manufacture the Concorde, a supersonic passenger jet. Passengers have preferred the slower Boeing 747 and McDonnell Douglas DC-10 and the cheaper fares over the Concorde.

**POSTSCRIPT**

# 'Tinker Toy' Approach to Plant Design Saves Costly Errors

### By Ron S. Heinzel

Herb Wanderman is in the model business. But model manufacturers such as Mattel and Revell have nothing to fear—he'll never compete with them.

For unlike the $5.95 kits that can be built in a couple of hours, Wanderman's one-of-a-kind models sometimes take five years or more to complete and often are valued at $1.5 million or more.

His models aren't toys, they're tools—used by nearly every top engineering and construction company in the country, including Bechtel Corp., Fluor Corp., Ralph M. Parsons Co., C. F. Braun & Co. and Jacobs Engineering Co.

In the 1950s, plant models were something contractors built for clients, using working drawings as a guide. The "after the fact" models usually ended up on display at the client's headquarters.

Wanderman says he realized that if models were used "from Day One" of a project, costly errors could be discovered and quickly corrected, resulting in huge cost savings. "Drawings are two-dimensional and you have to refer to many drawings when checking a plant's design," he says, "while models are three-dimensional and you can see immediately how the design is."

In the mid 1950s, Wanderman set up a one-man operation in a garage where he designed and produced scale model plastic components. Today his firm has one hundred employees and five overseas offices, and sells in thirty-five countries.

Sales are approaching $5 million a year and the company has plans to consolidate and expand its Southland facilities, which include a manufacturing plant in Glendale and another in Whittier. EMA produces components and provides consulting services to

Reprinted from the *Los Angeles Times*, 21 October 1979.

observable and measurable output is encouraged. The process discourages qualitative or other vague measures of performance.

4. *Establishment of priorities.* A key advantage of MBO is its stress on priorities. The system forces both manager and subordinates to rank objectives and goals in a system of priorities. This forces a careful look at performance and tends to assure that the activities of subordinates will be more closely in line with organizational goals.

engineering and construction firms; it does not build models itself.

When Wanderman formed his firm, he discovered that selling his concept to builders was much tougher than producing model parts. Engineers had always designed plants on paper and they were reluctant to change.

"In the beginning the prime effort was with the oil companies," Wanderman says. "I went to Texaco and Shell and sold them on the concept and they fostered it on the engineering companies. Now the engineering companies back it because of the time and money it saves and because usually a client just gets a stack of binders full of drawings for his money. With a model he can look at what he's getting."

Design models originally were used exclusively by the oil and chemical industries, but the market has since been expanded to the power, pulp and paper, food processing, shipbuilding, atomic energy, and aerospace industries.

EMA currently produces more than 6,000 parts, but if a new design calls for a component not in stock, the firm customizes it. "We had to do that when we began nuclear plant components," Wanderman says.

He recalls one project—a one-table model—in which the plant engineer was allotted two weeks to check the drawings and approve the design. "He looked at the model instead and accomplished the job in a matter of hours. His time saved paid for the model several times over."

Wanderman says a design model costs from 0.1 percent to 1 percent of the entire cost of a plant, but the average is 0.5 percent. "Nobody is willing to admit what the savings are but they wouldn't have ongoing model programs if they weren't economically justified. We estimate average savings at 15 percent of total plant cost."

The firm also maintains a consulting service and produces manuals and training kits. One client, the University of Pennsylvania, asked Wanderman to draw up an aptitude test for model builders.

"I found they have to be dexterous, have a spatial sense, and like to play the devil's advocate. Their job is to try to prove the engineers are wrong. When they can't, you know you've got a good design," he says.

It's easy to assume that Wanderman was an avid model builder as a youth and has found a way to make a good living out of what he once did for free. Asked if this is true, he says:

"I'm not a model builder. I never was a hobbyist—my main interest has always been engineering."

## Limitations of MBO

As with many management tools and techniques, MBO has been accepted by some and rejected by others. Following is a list of some weaknesses or limitations of the MBO process.

1. *Demands on time.* The process can be time-consuming and draw heavily upon organizational resources. Managers and subordinates must often spend a

substantial amount of time in conference resolving differences and establishing priorities.

2. *Increased frustration.* A necessity of MBO is the meshing of individual and organization goals. This may not always be possible and thus may lead to frustration on the part of the manager and the subordinates.

3. *Difficulties in quantifying goals.* Many goals, while worthy, may not be quantifiable.

4. *Difficulties in communication or acceptance of MBO philosophy.* Some subordinates refuse to think in verifiable terms and thus may not work well in an organization which relies heavily upon MBO. MBO requires solid communication between manager and subordinate. Organizations which do not have sound communication channels may find MBO unworkable in their environment.

### Example of MBO

Let us consider two situations which contrast MBO with more conventional management philosophy. In Plant A, the manager holds a meeting with the supervisor of the service department. His top-down directive style demands that the supervisor improve the output of the department, give faster service, and reduce customer complaints. These goals are difficult to obtain since they are not stated in verifiable terms to the supervisor.

In Plant B, the manager relies upon an MBO philosophy. He discusses the goals of the service department with the supervisor and together they develop a priority list of goals stated in verifiable terms, such as numbers of units serviced per week, numbers of complaints handled, and specific dollar operating costs. The manager, aware of what is expected of her, and having output stated in verifiable terms, is better able to reach the goals than the manager of Plant A.

## SUMMARY

Time plays an important role in planning. Some plans are long-range in nature, extending over many years, while others are short-range, covering only a few months. Some management plans remain in effect until revoked, while others are instituted for a specific, one-time function.

The four major management plans are the marketing plan covering sales and promotion efforts, the production plan dealing with manufacture, the personnel plan relating to staffing, and the financial plan dealing with the economic aspects of the organization.

Plans are interrelated and are often placed in a hierarchy. Good plan design delivers measurable performance, encourages motivation, is consistent, attainable, and flexible. It is also understandable and reasonable and considers the social consequences.

The three major approaches to staffing the planning effort include the project manager, task force, and on-going committee. The basic planning tools include the use of budgets, statistics and data, ratios, and forecasting.

Management by objectives (MBO) has become a major planning tool. It involves the subordinates in the planning and evaluation effort.

## KEY TERMS

Long-range plan    102
Short-range plan   103
Standing plan   103
One-time plan   104
Project manager   110
Task force   110
Budget   111

Debt ratio   114
Current ratio   114
Activity ratio   114
Profit ratio   114
Forecasting   116
Management by objectives (MBO)   119

## REVIEW QUESTIONS

1. How do long- and short-range plans differ?
2. How do standing and one-time plans differ?
3. Discuss the function of the four major management plans.
4. What are the basic characteristics of good plan design?
5. What are the differences in the three approaches to staffing the planning effort?
6. Describe how budgets are used in the planning effort.
7. In what ways are statistics and descriptive data of value in the planning effort?
8. Summarize four planning ratios and how they are used.
9. What information is gained from lead and lag indicators?
10. Describe how management by objectives (MBO) differs from management by directive.
11. Determine your own debt ratio. Calculate your total debts and total assets and compute the ratio according to the formula.
12. Discuss some impacts of social trends on shareholders, employees, consumers, government, and the public.

# Case Incident

Glaser Construction Corporation is one of the largest building and construction firms in the United States and is based in a large western city. They specialize in the construction of high-rise office buildings. Because of the cost of construction financing, there's great pressure to complete each project on time. Olan Bergson, construction division head, has been informed several times by their insurance carrier that Glaser's industrial accident rate is well above the industry average. This will force their carrier to make a substantial increase in their accident insurance rates. To further compound Glaser's problem, OSHA (Occupational Safety and Health ACT inspectors have indicated that numerous safety violations have been observed on various Glaser construction projects.

Bergson knows that they must not only comply with OSHA's regulations, but that they must also greatly improve the safety on Glaser construction projects. Bill Gleason, a new construction supervisor, has suggested that the company put together an on-going safety committee to listen to reports of various safety violations and consider improvements in the firm's operations. He believes that the committee should consist of construction supervisors, managers, and line employees on the construction site. They should all get together and hold weekly meetings to discuss safety problems and solutions.

Don King, a veteran supervisor of fifteen years, feels that the on-going committee would be costly and unnecessary. He has suggested a get tough policy regarding safety and working condition violators. "Tell them the company is simply not going to stand for a big hike in insurance premiums because a handful of our employees are unnecessarily careless. We don't need a lot of meetings and talk to cure our problem with these violators. Let's get rid of the people who have violated safety rules after one warning."

## PROBLEMS

1. What weaknesses are there in the on-going committee approach?
2. What problems does the get tough policy present?
3. What approach would you favor to solve the problem? Explain.

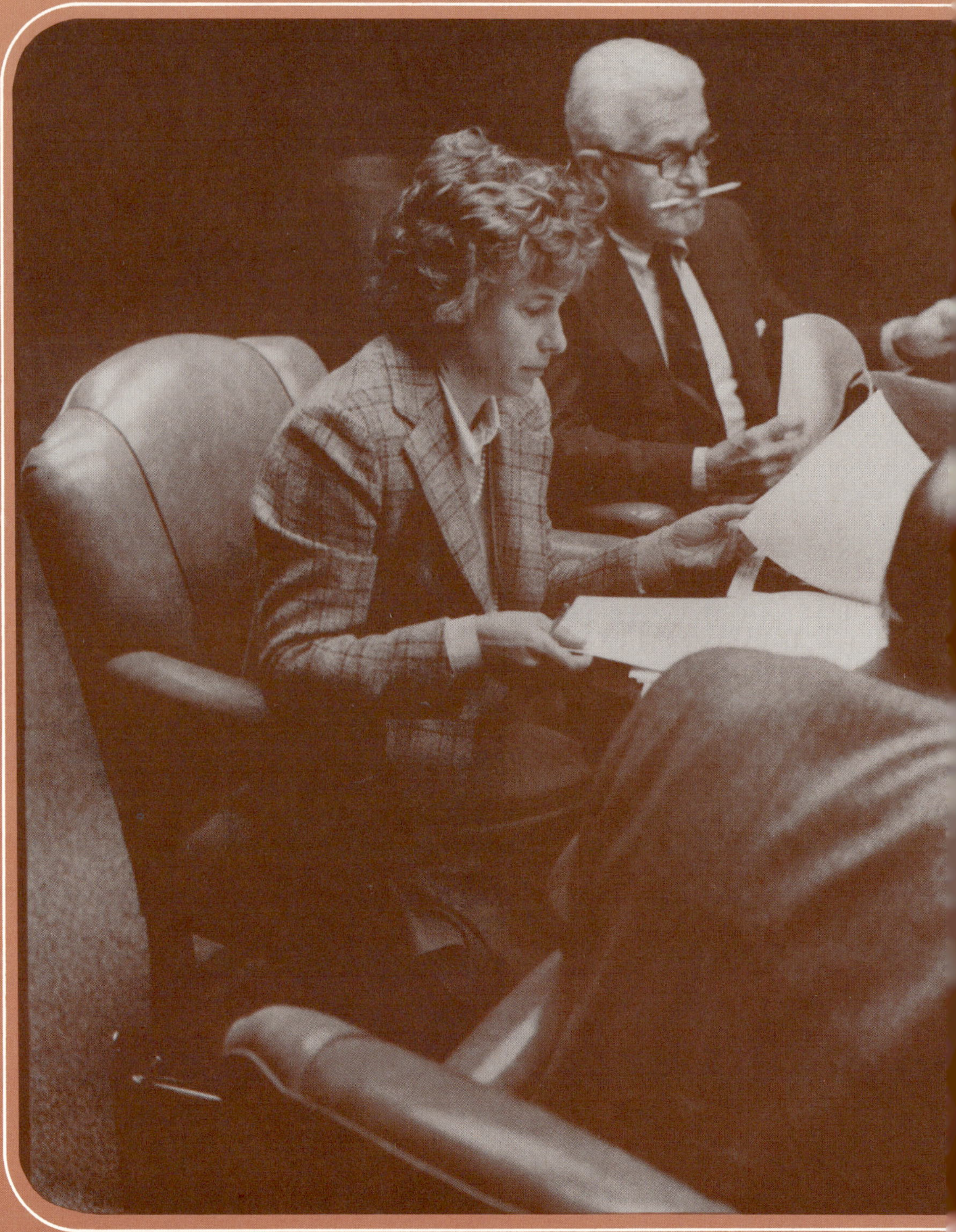

# 6

# The Decision-Making Process

**LEARNING OBJECTIVES**

After studying this chapter, you should be able to:
1. Define the decision-making process.
2. Contrast quantitative and qualitative decision making.
3. Describe the steps in the scientific method of decision making.
4. Explain how programmed decisions are made.
5. Explain how nonprogrammed decisions are made.
6. Discuss the contingency aspects of decision making.
7. Contrast group versus individual decision making.
8. Summarize how decision trees are used.
9. Summarize how decision tables are used.
10. Prepare a decision table.

In chapter 4 we considered the planning process and how organizations use basic and supporting plans to reach goals. The making of decisions is inherent in the planning process. This chapter considers the fundamentals of the decision-making process. Chapter 7 reviews some of the major quantitative decision-making tools used by managers.

The decision-making process is a demanding mental activity, which carries with it the risk of error and loss. People in all phases of life are continually faced with making decisions. Whether one is a student, government employee, small business owner, or president of a large corporation, decisions must be made. It is an essential part of the manager's task, and cannot be avoided, ignored, or deferred.

## DECISION MAKING AS A PROCESS

Many people believe that decision making is a one-step, single event. To them, decisions are made in single bursts of insight. This stereotyped view clouds the real process and focuses only on the end results. Decision making should be viewed as an ongoing process.

## DECISION MAKING DEFINED

Decision making is the process by which one systematically studies a problem, analyzes it, and selects the most appropriate alternative to reach a desired end. The heart of the decision-making process is the systematic search for alternatives and the analytical selection of the most promising course.

The decision-making process is analogous to a fork in the road. When a traveller comes to the fork in the road, he is forced to take one path or the other. He is at the point of decision. If he is to reach his destination, he must analyze alternative courses and make a choice.

## APPROACHES TO DECISION MAKING

Managers use a variety of approaches to decision making. These range on a continuum from unstructured and highly unscientific means to systematic, sophisticated computer-assisted decision-making techniques (figure 6-1). On one end of the scale are such unstructured techniques as hunches, guesses, and intuition. On the other end are such systematic techniques as mathematics, statistics, and computer-assisted decision making.

It is helpful to view all methods of decision making as falling into either of two categories: qualitative or quantitative method. (See table 6-1.) In the qualitative method, decisions are reached through rather general techniques which deal with qualities. In the quantitative method, variables are quantified and the

Least systematic ← Continuum → Most systematic

| Hunch | Intuition | Guess | Experience | Trial and error | Mathematics, statistics, laws of probability | Computer-assisted decision making |

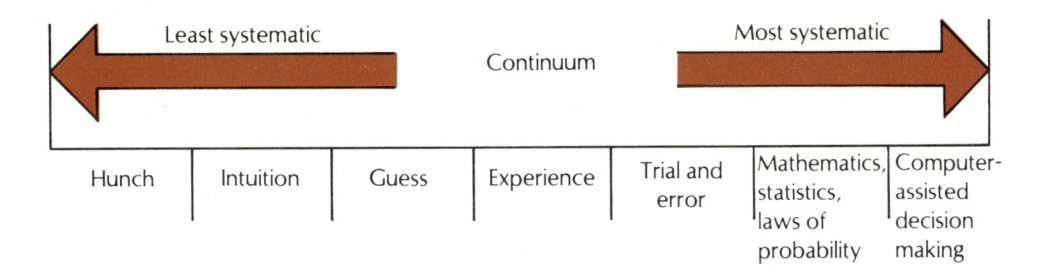

*Figure 6-1 Systematic and unsystematic decisions*

decision is reduced to numerical terms. Descriptions of both these general approaches follow.

## Qualitative Decision Making

In this approach, decisions are reached through an intuitive process. People, particularly experienced managers, are continually weighing alternatives and making decisions. They use the "computer of the mind," which relies upon less quantifiable and more subjective factors. For example, a manager may rely upon intuition or inner feelings to reach a decision regarding the introduction of a new product.

This method is sometimes called intuitive decision making. There is less emphasis on system or structure, and more on experience and subjective factors. It is based upon past performance and previous experience with similar problems. The assumption is that a decision can be made based upon historical patterns. However, the current problem may have little resemblance to previous situations, or there may be no historical experience on which to base a decision.

Trial and error is another method of making decisions. In this unscientific method, many alternatives to solving a problem are attempted. A given course of action is followed for a period: when it fails, another is selected. Trial-and-error decision makers hope to find the correct course by a process of elimination.

**Table 6-1  Types of decision making**

| *Qualitative* | *Quantitative* |
|---|---|
| Based on experience | Precise definition of problem |
| Methodology vague and not definable | Use of logic and scientific method |
| Use of hunch and guess | Systematic gathering of data |
| Reliance on trial and error | Reliable results |
| Results not reproducible | Reproducible results |

For example, a bad tube in a television set can be found by trial and error. One tube at a time is removed and substituted with a known good tube until the bad one is isolated. This approach takes time and requires a complete set of duplicate, functioning tubes. A better approach is to isolate the bad tube by analyzing the problem and using logic and the scientific method. A skilled repairperson studies the problem, analyzes the fault on the screen, tests voltages, and replaces only the faulty tube, based on logic and reasoning.

Business organizations which have heavy investments in personnel, equipment, and plants cannot afford to rely upon unscientific means to make decisions. Decision-making methodology should be specific and reproducible. Errors and wrong decisions could be expensive. Therefore, most managers approach decision making in a quantitative and scientific manner.

## Quantitative Decision Making

In this process, the decision maker uses the scientific method. The method requires quantifying the problem, and uses logic or mathematics to reach a decision.

Some managers reject the emphasis put on quantitative decision making. They believe it does not give adequate credit to human experience, opinions, and feelings. Many problems cannot be reduced to quantitative terms, and yet decisions must still be made.

The scientific method is characterized by close attention to detail. The decision maker must be objective and use precision in analyzing data and reporting results. The scientific method may use mathematics and statistical techniques and a systematic plan of attack. Finally, it requires an objective evaluation of results and an attempt to readjust a system to bring the output in line with the objectives.

## SCIENTIFIC APPROACH TO DECISION MAKING

Around the turn of the century John Dewey, a noted educator, outlined a series of steps for problem solving. This procedure has had a profound influence on management decision making. Dewey's work underlies much of the quantitative decision making now used by managers.

Dewey believed that most problems were solvable through a rigorous, systematic approach. (See figure 6-2.) The steps led from a recognition of the problem, through selecting alternatives and, finally, to evaluation of results. Before considering specific quantitative decision-making tools, let us review the fundamental steps in this method.

1. *Recognize the problem.* The first step in the scientific problem-solving method is to become aware of the problem. Unless a manager is aware that a

CHAPTER SIX   THE DECISION MAKING PROCESS                                        133

```
    ┌─────────────┐
    │  Recognize  │◄──────────────┐
    │   problem   │               │
    └──────┬──────┘               │
           ▼                      │
    ┌─────────────┐               │
    │   Define    │               │
    │   problem   │               │
    └──────┬──────┘               │
           ▼                      │
    ┌─────────────┐    ┌─────────────┐
    │  Develop    │    │ Evaluation  │
    │alternatives │    │    and      │
    └──────┬──────┘    │readjustment │
           ▼           └──────▲──────┘
    ┌─────────────┐           │
    │ Select best │           │
    │  course of  │           │
    │   action    │           │
    └──────┬──────┘           │
           ▼                  │
    ┌─────────────┐           │
    │ Implement   │           │
    │ best course │           │
    │  of action  │           │
    └──────┬──────┘           │
           └──────────────────┘
```

*Figure 6-2*
*Scientific decision making process*

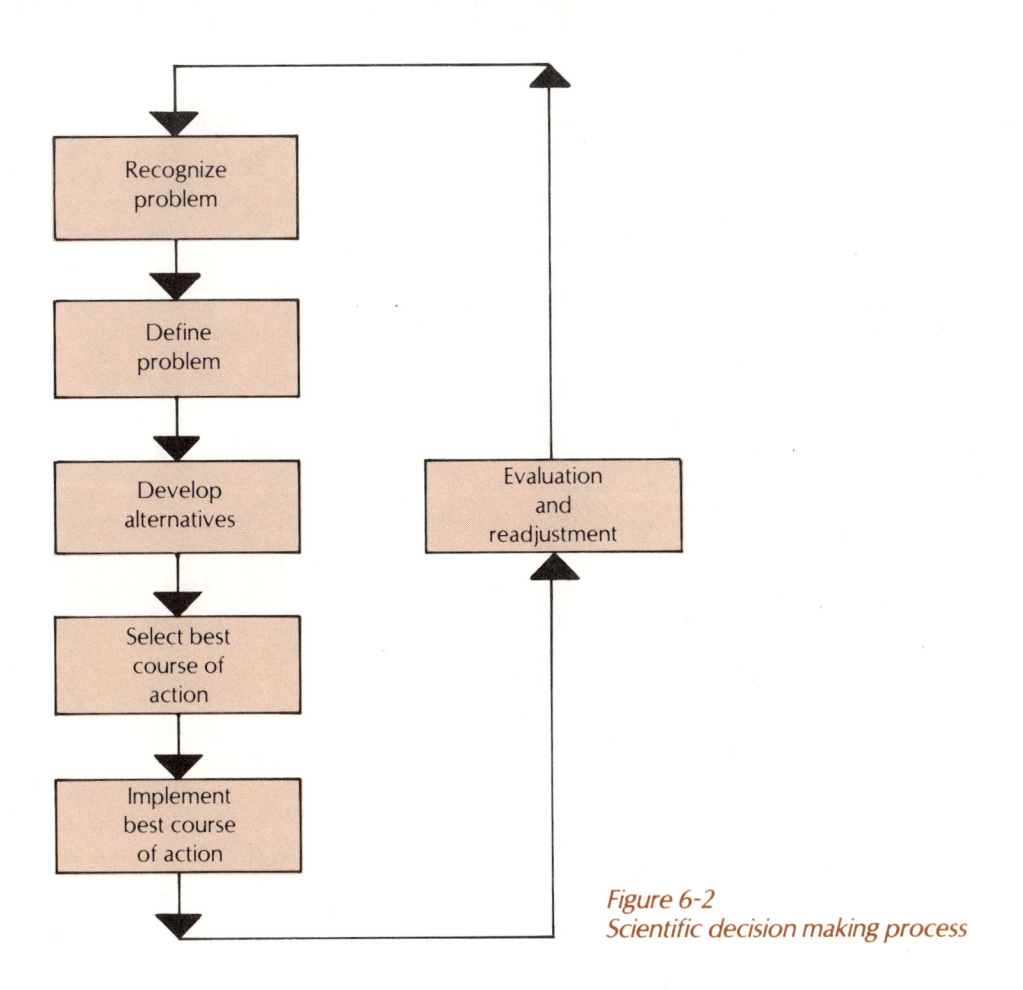

problem exists, he or she cannot solve it. In this first step, the manager undertakes a careful investigation of the facts to determine the exact nature of the problem and its causes.

For the manager this means actively seeking out problems in an organization and discovering their causes. This allows solutions to be found and decisions made before the problems grow in scope and difficulty.

To illustrate, suppose a large firm operates several punch presses in the production department. Suppose these machines have a useful life of five years and hundreds of thousands of cycles. After a certain number of stamping operations, the machines fail, even with proper maintenance. Should the production manager wait until a machine breaks down and cannot be repaired before it is replaced? Using the scientific method, the manager determines the approximate remaining life of the machine. The machine is replaced just before it is expected to fail. This eliminates the chance that the failure will occur during a busy period or when replacement equipment is not readily available.

> **REAL WORLD**
>
> # Paperwork and Regulations
>
> A lot of managers feel that government regulations and the deluge of paperwork are literally inundating and strangling business operations. One bank executive estimates that government regulations cost the American public more than $100 billion a year. This comes out to $470 per person.
>
> James K. Dobby, chairman of Wells Fargo Bank, puts it this way: "The problem is just as ominous as it can be. We have hired thirty-five to forty persons in the last ninety days to check up on the checkers, to make sure all our documents meet all the regulatory requirements. Now we would like to spend more of our time developing business, developing people." Leonard Weil, chairman of Manufacturers Bank, says that the problem is going to get worse until the public realizes that it is paying for it and demands something be done, for one regulation seems to breed another.
>
> Adapted from *The Executive,* April 1979, p. 57LA.

2. *Define the problem in quantitative terms.* In this step, the decision maker defines the problem in numerical or specific terms. A statement of the problem is made which reduces variables to measurable quantities. Unless this is done, one cannot measure performance and results. A quantitative statement is necessary to determine if the problem has been completely solved.

Suppose a marketing manager describes a problem relating to poor performance by the sales force. During the months of January through June, the average salesperson sells an average of $25,000 per month. During July through August, the salesperson sells an average of $18,000 per month. Stated in these quantitative (dollar) terms, the sales manager can measure changes in performance by the sales staff. On the other hand, such qualitative descriptions as "sales are up substantially" or "sales fell off sharply during the summer" are of less use.

3. *Develop alternatives.* During this phase of the decision-making process, the manager systematically discovers as many alternative courses of action as possible. This may be done by brainstorming, observing others, reading, or study.

Suppose, for example, a problem has been diagnosed as low productivity in the shop. The average monthly output is five hundred units below normal. During this phase, the manager develops alternative solutions to the problem. These may include pay increases to stimulate output, replacement of tools and machines, improvements such as the installation of air conditioning, or perhaps implementation of a rule limiting visiting while on duty.

An alternative frequently considered is to do nothing. This is part of the selection of alternatives and should not be overlooked. For some kinds of problems, doing nothing may be the best alternative.

4. *Select the best course of action.* During this phase, the manager looks carefully at each alternative and selects the one which promises to solve the problems. "If-then" reasoning is applied: **If** I do this, **then** this will result; **if** I do that, **then** that will result. After careful scrutiny, the best alternative is selected for implementation.

5. *Implement the chosen course of action.* Next, the manager puts into action the chosen alternative. This may require weeks or months of effort, installation of machines, hiring of people, or modification of the plant. The method chosen may or may not solve the problem. This leads to the last step.

6. *Evaluate and readjust.* In this step, the decision maker measures the results to see if the alternative selected has in fact solved the problem. If it has not, then other solutions are tried or perhaps a redefinition of the problem is made. A problem is not solved until there has been an objective evaluation. It is this last step which is often overlooked by management. Some managers carefully define a problem, and analyze and implement an alternative. But they do not evaluate results. Thus, they have no assurance that the problem is solved.

Purchasing raw materials in large volumes is a decision which cannot be made through intuition or trial and error.

*"He liked the idea so much he's going to promote me — I got so excited I forgot to mention it was your idea."*

Illustration furnished courtesy of *Modern Machine Shop* Magazine, © 1979.

## ADVANTAGES OF THE SCIENTIFIC APPROACH TO DECISION MAKING

The scientific method produces better decisions and improves the accuracy and reliability of results. Here is a summary of the major advantages of the scientific method and quantitative approach to decision making.

1. *Accuracy.* Scientifically based decisions result in greater accuracy and precision. Since the approach relies upon quantitative methods, decisions are more precise and specific than qualitative methods or guesswork.

2. *Predictability.* The scientific method lends a greater degree of predictability and certainty to decisions. Where the problem is stated in a clear, scientific manner, the resulting decision is more easily foreseen.

3. *Greater reliability.* Decisions reached through the scientific method are more reliable and less subject to error. Less faith and reliance can be placed in decisions reached through hunch or intuition.

4. *Reproducibility of results.* Decisions reached through the scientific method

can be reproduced and duplicated. The decision method is stated and defined and can be copied or followed by others.

5. *Ability to document results.* Since the scientific method relies upon objectivity and stating facts in a precise manner, the results of the process can be documented and put in writing.

There are, of course, costs and time expended in using the scientific method over less systematic means. It requires that facts be gathered and analyzed objectively and conclusions reached through an orderly process. This takes hours of work and close attention to detail and may involve expense.

## PROGRAMMED AND NONPROGRAMMED DECISIONS

In the mid 1960s, Herbert A. Simon[1] analyzed the decision-making process and defined two forms of decisions: programmed and nonprogrammed. (See table 6-2.) Simon's work influenced the development of an important school of management philosophy called decision theory.

**Table 6-2   Programmed and nonprogrammed decisions**

| Types of Decisions | Decision-Making Techniques | |
|---|---|---|
| | Traditional | Modern |
| *Programmed:* <br><br> Routine, repetitive decisions <br> Organization develops specific processes for handling them | 1. Habit <br> 2. Clerical routine: Standard operating procedures <br> 3. Organization structure: Common expectations A system of subgoals Well-defined informational channels | 1. *Operations research:* Mathematical analysis Models Computer simulation <br> 2. Electronic data processing |
| *Nonprogrammed:* <br><br> One-shot, ill-structured, novel, policy decisions <br><br> Handled by general problem-solving processes | 1. Judgment, intuition, and creativity <br> 2. Rules of thumb <br> 3. Selection and training of executives | Heuristic problem-solving technique applied to: <br> (a) Training human decision makers <br> (b) Constructing heuristic computer programs |

Reprinted from Herbert A. Simon, *The Shape of Automation,* revised edition, Prentice-Hall, 1977, p. 48.

---

[1] Herbert A. Simon, *The Shape of Automation* (New York: Torchbooks, 1965).

Selecting a new building site is an example of a nonprogrammed decision.

## Programmed Decisions

Programmed decisions are the repetitive and routine decisions made by managers. As a rule, there is a predefined procedure worked out for making these decisions. Each decision is not treated as a new situation.

The preparation of a company's payroll is a good example of a programmed decision. Suppose a firm must issue ten paychecks at the end of each week. A number of decisions must be made. A payroll clerk must determine the number of hours each employee worked, the pay rate, and the deductions in order to draft the paychecks. These decisions may be made by habit, clerical routine, or organizational structure.

Programmed decisions allow for orderly decision making. They result in consistent, routine decisions, which can be made by low-level employees. The guidelines for programmed decisions are stated in company policy manuals, rules, and regulations. They are worked out in advance and show how each decision will be handled.

## Nonprogrammed Decisions

The second category is decisions of the nonprogrammed, nonroutine type. In this kind of decision, there are no predefined rules or guidelines. Instead, the manager must rely upon basic scientific problem-solving techniques.

Nonprogrammed decisions require the ability to work in an unstructured capacity. Each problem is new, and no guidelines or rules exist for solving it. A problem such as selecting the site to locate a new office building or freight yard is an example of a nonprogrammed decision.

## DECISION TREES

A decision tree is a useful technique which illustrates programmed decision making (fig. 6-4). It enables management to structure the decision-making process along predetermined lines. Decision trees clarify the sequence in which decisions will be made and provide a degree of predictability.

A decision tree can be used whenever a manager wishes to make a series of decisions or anticipate a series of chance events which may occur over a period of

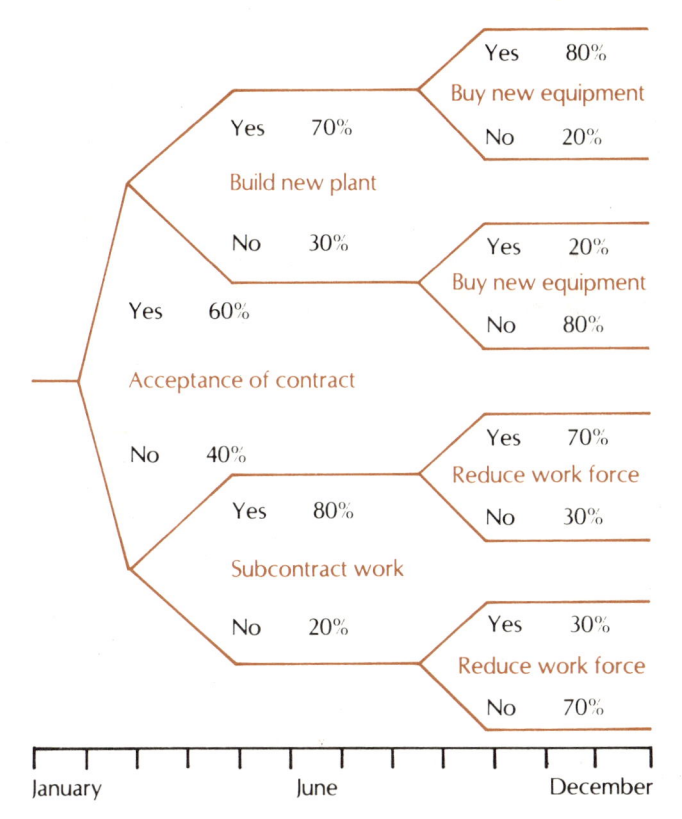

*Figure 6-4 Decision tree*

| Acceptance of contract | | Next decision | | Outcome | |
|---|---|---|---|---|---|
| Yes | 60% | Build new plant — Yes | 70% | Buy new equipment — Yes | 80% |
| | | | | No | 20% |
| | | Build new plant — No | 30% | Buy new equipment — Yes | 20% |
| | | | | No | 80% |
| No | 40% | Subcontract work — Yes | 80% | Reduce work force — Yes | 70% |
| | | | | No | 30% |
| | | Subcontract work — No | 20% | Reduce work force — Yes | 30% |
| | | | | No | 70% |

January — June — December

time. Decisions, such as whether to acquire new plant facilities, tools or equipment, or personnel can be drawn on a decision tree. Frequently, monetary values which have been carefully calculated for each branch are assigned. This enables the manager to calculate the total monetary value for each alternative considered.

In figure 6-4, a decision tree is diagrammed and several key decisions are shown, along with the percentage of their probability of occurrence. These deal with the decisions of a firm bidding on a new contract. The first major branch is the acceptance of the contract. If the contract is accepted, a decision is made to build a new plant. If the contract is rejected, the work is subcontracted out. If a new plant is to be built to handle the new contract, then the question of buying new equipment must be resolved. If the firm loses the contract and must subcontract the work, it must decide whether to reduce the work force.

The decision tree diagrams the possible alternatives in a logical, systematic way. It enables management to view each decision in sequence and in relation to each other. Use of a decision tree reduces the chances of being faced with unexpected decisions. Probability values are sometimes assigned to the occurrence of each event, and further add to the usefulness of this type of chart.

## DECISION TABLES

Another useful decision-making tool is the decision table, borrowed from the computer programmer and systems analyst. Decision tables are used by management to guide programmed decisions.

Decision tables are divided into four major parts, called *stubs*. (See table 6-3.) The condition stub (upper left-hand corner) lists all identifiable conditions which might be encountered in a given situation. The lower left-hand corner (action stub) lists all identifiable actions which might be taken in response to these conditions.

The upper right-hand corner of the decision table includes a group of rules. Here the term *rule* differs from its more common use. These rules are combinations of various conditions which may occur. A rule is devised for each group of conditions. This is usually shown by drawing a *Y* or *N*(yes-no) in line with each of the expected conditions.

In the lower right-hand corner are the action entries. These are the actions to

### Table 6-3 Decision table stubs

| **Condition Stub**<br>Lists all identifiable conditions. | **Rules**<br>Lists various combinations of conditions which may occur. |
|---|---|
| **Action Stub**<br>Lists all identifiable actions which may be taken. | **Action Entries**<br>Lists what actions may be taken in light of various conditions above. |

### Table 6-4 Decision Table

| Condition Stub | Rules | | | | | | |
|---|---|---|---|---|---|---|---|
| | 1 | 2 | 3 | 4 | 5 | 6 | 7 |
| Insubordination | Y | Y | Y | Y | N | N | N |
| High productivity | N | Y | Y | N | Y | N | N |
| Low absenteeism | Y | N | Y | N | N | Y | N |
| **Action Stub** | **Action Entry Stub** | | | | | | |
| Verbal reprimand | | | | | X | | |
| Written reprimand | | | | | | X | |
| Letter threatening termination | | | | | | | X |
| Letter ordering termination | | | | X | | | |
| One-week layoff, no pay | | | X | | | | |
| Two-week layoff, no pay | X | X | | | | | |

be taken for each rule. These are shown as an *X* drawn in the lower right-hand corner of the decision table. This portion of the table is completed last by programming the actions to be taken when a given rule occurs.

For example, suppose a manager wishes to program decisions for handling disciplinary matters with respect to employees. Table 6-4 lists in the upper left-hand corner (condition stub) identifiable conditions, including insubordination, level of productivity, and absenteeism. (In practice, many more entries are made, such as cooperation with other employees, dishonesty, and tardiness.)

In the lower left-hand corner (action stub), all identifiable actions are listed. These include a verbal reprimand, a written reprimand, a letter threatening termination, a letter ordering termination, and periods of layoff without pay. In the upper right-hand corner are listed the various rules or combinations of situations. Cases may arise where an insubordinate employee has low productivity and poor attendance. This must be dealt with firmly. There may be cases of high productivity and high absenteeism, or low absenteeism and low productivity by employees who show no insubordination. This will be treated less severely.

Below each rule, the manager programs which course of action is to be taken. In the case of the employee with high absenteeism, low productivity, and insubordination, a letter ordering termination is sent. Each case is dealt with logically, based on its merits.

Decision tables enable the manager to define which courses of action shall be taken in each situation. They also allow documentation of what must be done in various circumstances, so that others may assist with the assurance that a uniform decision-making policy will be followed.

Unfortunately, structures such as decision tables may be used by managers to avoid making decisions or to hide behind poor decisions. For instance, a man-

> **REAL WORLD**
>
> # Blue Collar in the Board Room
>
> It may seem an interesting twist of fate to have the chief of a major union serve on the board of directors of a major American corporation. But that is exactly what happened when Douglas A. Fraser, president of United Auto Workers Union, was asked to join the board of directors of Chrysler Corporation.
>
> There are mixed feelings about these strange bedfellows. The chairman of General Motors, Thomas A. Murphy, says, "It makes as much sense as having a member of General Motor's management sitting on the board of an international union." Some Chrysler workers believe that it is a sellout, convinced Fraser cannot keep his loyalty to his union while serving on the board of directors of an automobile manufacturing firm. Fraser believes that his appointment will be in the best interests of the entire Chrysler community, including the workers, dealers, stockholders, and the public.
>
> This is not a unique situation. In West Germany and other foreign countries, it is common to have union representatives and labor represented in the decision-making process of large corporations.
>
> Adapted from *Time*, 19 May 1980, p. 78.

ager may follow a poor course of action and justify it because it was the correct choice on a decision table.

## DECISION-MAKING FACTORS

The quality of a business decision is as important as the making of the decision itself. Not only must decisions be made on time, but they must consider the personnel involved and the situation in which they are made. Let us look at several contingency aspects of good decision making.

1. *Timeliness.* A decision must be made at a time in the business cycle when it will be of the greatest value to the enterprise. Decisions, no matter how well made, are of little value to an organization if they are reached too late.

For example, suppose a firm wishes to launch a large, seasonal advertising promotion effort. It requires many decisions, such as selection of advertising media, products to feature, and sale prices. These decisions must be made in advance of the holiday season so the firm can take advantage of the market. A late decision regarding selection of advertising media, no matter how good, is of no value.

2. *Economics.* The costs of reaching a decision must be reasonable. It is obviously fruitless to spend thousands of dollars and hours of time gathering information to reach a decision on an issue involving only a few hundred dollars. On the other hand, expenditure of a large sum of money to make a decision may be justified if the size of the problem warrants it. Managers have been known to ponder for weeks over decisions involving only a few dollars, and then make a snap judgment on problems involving hundreds of thousands of dollars.

3. *Consideration of the situation.* A good decision is one which is made in light of the situation. A decision should be based upon facts and figures relating to the current state of the organization, not its historical position or future expectations. Contingency management emphasizes the need to begin with an observation of the present financial, personnel, and production situation before making decisions.

4. *Consideration of all alternatives.* Good decisions are made when all practical courses of action have been considered. A good decision does not limit or rule out alternatives before they have been carefully evaluated. Bias, preconceived notions, or personnel stereotypes should be put aside before making decisions.

5. *Acceptability to participants.* A good decision is one which will be accepted by the organization participants. The best decisions are of little value if they do not consider the human element. Failure to consider the effect on personnel may mean employees will frustrate the implementation of a decision or undermine its operation.

## GROUP VERSUS INDIVIDUAL DECISIONS

The decision-making process may be carried out by a single individual or by a group. Figure 6-3 illustrates a continuum, with decision making by one individual on one end and large groups on the other. Let us consider the impact on the organization of this range of decision making.

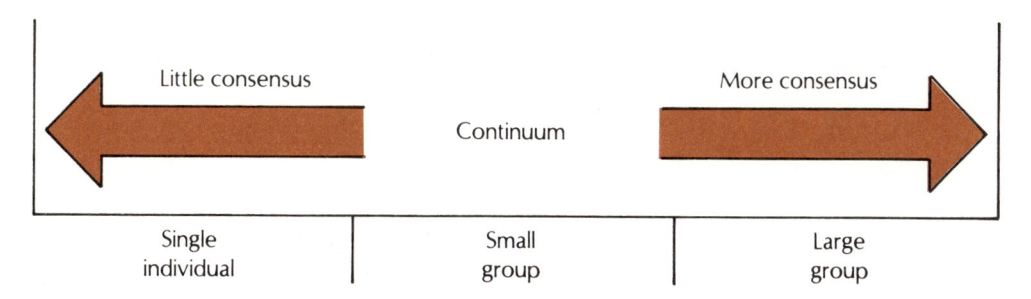

*Figure 6-3 Individual and group decision making*

## POSTSCRIPT
# Notable & Quotable

A. W. Clausen president and Chief executive of BankAmerica says . . . there is the idea of *stockholder democracy*, which would drastically change the present system under which stockholders have a voice in corporate affairs in proportion to their stakes in the business.

What a few propose now is that each investor have only one vote on stockholder matters, regardless of individual holdings in the firm. In addition to its other obvious flaws, this concept would, if it took hold, seriously undermine the investment process.

Another proposal would, in effect, subject the governing process of large, publicly owned firms to so-called public directors or the representatives of special interest groups by seating them as directors. The trouble with this idea, on top of its in-

Reprinted with permission of *Chief Executive Magazine*, Inc. © 1980 *Chief Executive Magazine.*

---

1. *Individual decision making.* It is said that a committee of one gets things done. This is often the case with a lone decision maker. One person in charge of making a decision can act quickly and responsively, since there is no need to consult others or gain the consensus of a group.

However, single individuals do not draw upon the resources of others. Decisions reached by one person lack the depth and broad character of those made by groups or committees. Further, these decisions are not so readily accepted by subordinates because they reflect one individual's thinking rather than the ideas of the peer group.

2. *Group decision making.* Large and small groups and committees make decisions. As a rule, these decisions are arrived at by a consensus. They draw upon the resources of many people. Group decision making may be time-consuming, expensive, and require compromise. Many people must be given the facts to study and alternatives to review, and must be involved in the selection process.

## SUMMARY

A variety of approaches to decision making are used by managers. These range from unscientific and unstructured techniques to sophisticated quantitative and computer-assisted decision-making techniques.

The qualitative approach to decision making uses a vague, undocumentable

herent unfairness to investors, is that it just is not practical, as anyone familiar with business realities knows. Directors, whatever their expertise, must have the breadth of experience and proven ability to deal with a wide range of complex corporate matters, not just those in which they have a personal interest. Moreover, directors must be free of obligations to outside groups so they can act independently.

As usual, the ultimate solution, a few have proposed, is to place all corporations under direct government control through a system of federal chartering.

None of these concepts has gained any significant degree of public support, even after being around in one form or another for some time. But insofar as they represent a pattern of hostility toward business, these proposals add to investor uncertainty, which is detrimental to our national interests. And statements by representatives of important regulatory agencies, appearing to support these notions, often make matters worse and work against the government's avowed goal to increase investor confidence.

methodology. The quantitative approach reduces the decision-making process to numbers and precise quantities.

Among the advantages of the scientific method are greater accuracy, predictability, reliability, and reproducibility of results. The scientific approach begins with an awareness of the problem and definition of problem, then considers alternatives, and finally evaluates results.

Nonprogrammed decisions are one-shot and nonrepetitive in nature. Programmed decisions, on the other hand, follow a prescribed, routine procedure for solution. Other factors of problem solving include an analysis of timeliness, economics, situational factors, alternatives, and acceptability to participants.

Decision trees and decision tables are two programmed decision-making techniques used by managers to lay out alternatives and define courses of action. These tools organize the decision-making process, but may sometimes be used to justify poor decisions.

## REVIEW QUESTIONS

1. Define decision making.
2. How does the quantitative method of decision making differ from the qualitative method?
3. List the advantages of the scientific method.

4. What are the major steps in the scientific method of problem solving?
5. What kinds of decisions are best made by a nonprogrammed approach?
6. What kinds of decisions are best made by a programmed approach?
7. What situational factors should be considered when making decisions?
8. What advantages does the group decision-making process have?
9. Draw a decision tree illustrating some upcoming decisions which you are about to make regarding your college career.
10. Draw a decision table outlining a group of alternatives faced by someone about to buy a new car.
11. Which situations are best analyzed with a decision tree, and which are best analyzed with decision tables?
12. How is a fork in the road analogous to a management decision?

## KEY TERMS

Qualitative decision making   131
Quantitative decision making   132
Scientific method   132
Reliability   136
Predictability   136
Alternatives   134
Problem definition   134

Programmed decisions   138
Nonprogrammed decisions   139
Timeliness   142
Group decisions   144
Decision tree   139
Decision table   140

# Case Incident

Timson Aircraft, Inc. employs 22,000 workers in its commercial aircraft division. One of many major benefits provided employees is a recreation center. This center includes a cafeteria, bowling alley, poolroom, picnic area, and several hobby and craft rooms. This facility has always been a cornerstone of the firm's employee relations philosophy. The facility itself is available to employees and their families throughout the year.

However, during the past year some employees have abused the privileges of the recreation center. Several groups in particular have begun to dominate the use of certain areas. They have also failed to clean up or maintain rooms after using them. Both management and employees are in general agreement that something must be done about those employees who abuse the facility and its rights and privileges.

Corporate vice president Russ Gibbons believes strongly that the firm should hire a full-time professional manager to take charge of the employee recreation center. This manager would have the power to make all decisions regarding the use and maintenance of the employee center, as well as establishing rules for the recreation center, subject to the approval of corporate management. Based on these rules, the manager would take final action on all disciplinary matters.

On the other hand, Victoria Bradley from the testing division is convinced that Gibbons' approach will not work. Instead, she would like to have a committee composed of four employees and one company manager which would establish rules for the use of the center. This would give the employees real decision-making power over how their own center is administered. In addition, the enforcement and handling of disciplinary matters would be up to the committee itself.

## PROBLEMS

1. What advantages does Gibbons' plan have?
2. What advantages does Bradley's plan have?
3. Discuss problems both plans present.

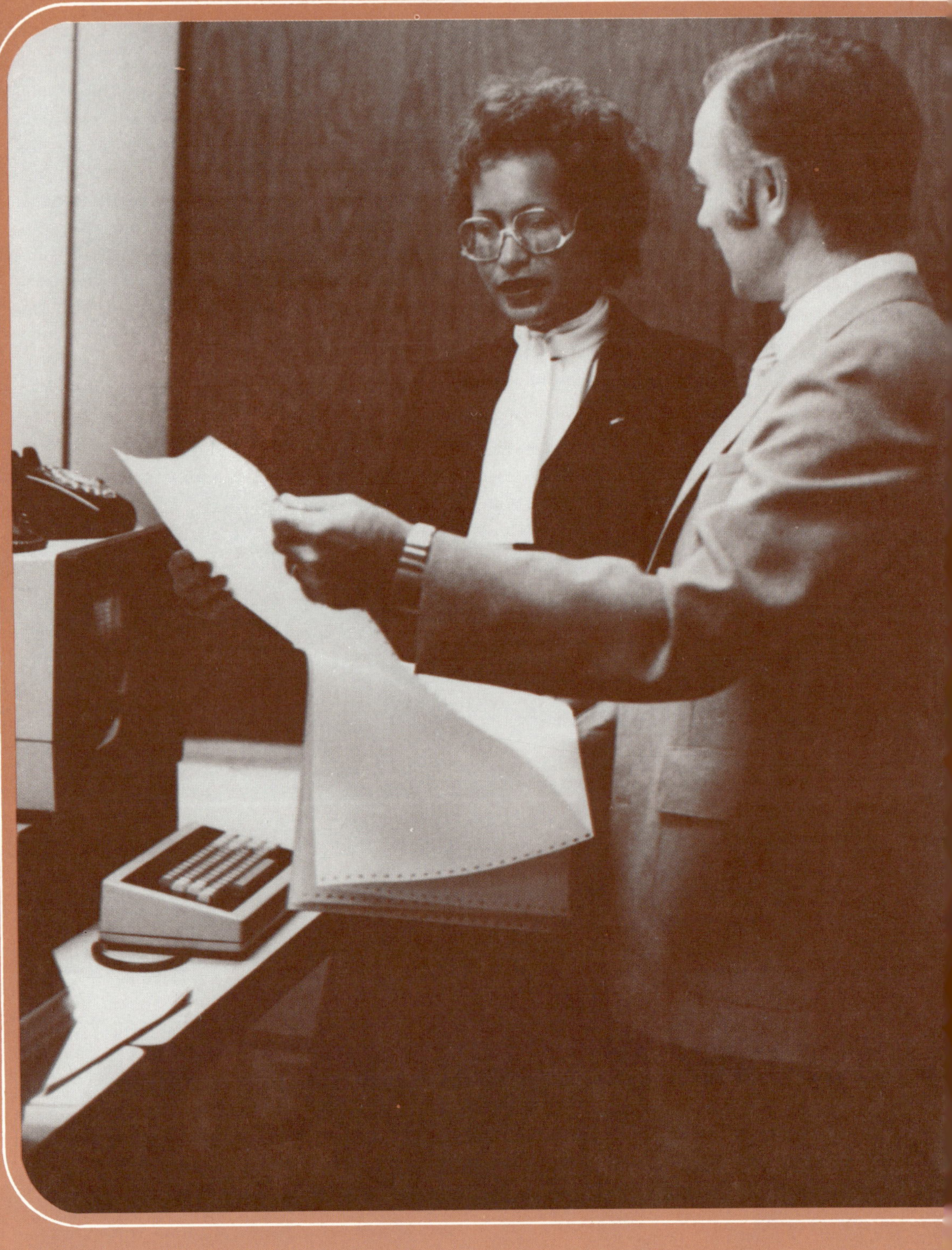

# 7

# Quantitative Tools of Management

**LEARNING OBJECTIVES**

After studying this chapter, you should be able to:
1. Define basic terms referring to quantitative tools of management.
2. Contrast differences between deterministic and stochastic systems.
3. Describe how modeling and simulations are used in management.
4. Describe the critical-path method (CPM) of project management.
5. Summarize how linear programming is used.
6. Describe how probability theory is used in management.
7. Describe queuing theory and its application.
8. Summarize how game theory is used in decision making.
9. Summarize how break-even-point analysis is used in decision making.

This chapter discusses the applied tools of decision making. It emphasizes the quantitative aspects of management including use of probability, mathematical modeling, critical-path method (CPM), program evaluation and review technique (PERT), linear programming (LP), break-even-point analysis, and other techniques.

The computer has greatly enhanced the manager's ability to make decisions in a quantitative way. Many of the problem-solving techniques discussed in this chapter would not be possible without the computer, discussed in chapter 8. The tools discussed in this chapter, together with the computer and electronic data processing, give managers a new magnitude of decision quality and speed.

## KEY TERMS

Before we consider the quantitative tools used in management, here are some of the fundamental terms used.

—*Quantitative decision making.* Quantitative decision making involves the use of computers, statistics, logic, and mathematics to arrive at decisions. In quantitative decision making, a problem is reduced to numerical quantities, and the laws of mathematics, reason, and logic are applied to solve it. Quantitative decision making differs from the traditional qualitative methods which rely upon intuition, experience, or other nonscientific methods.

—*Deterministic system.* A deterministic system is one in which the output or results of a process or activity can be predicted with a degree of certainty and reliability. The assessment of the costs of producing and distributing a magazine such as *Time* or *Newsweek* is an example of a relatively deterministic system. The publisher can predict the per magazine cost for editorial, printing, and distribution with some degree of certainty. He can anticipate costs based on a given number of pages and subscribers. Newsstand sales can also be anticipated. Deterministic systems are generally easier for managers to manipulate than those which are not predictable.

—*Stochastic system.* A stochastic system is one which behaves according to the laws of probability or chance. In stochastic systems, events occur in a random order. The manager is never sure what the results or output will be. They are not predictable.

For example, the number of customers who will line up for service at a given teller's window at a bank at any hour behaves in a stochastic manner. There is no way of knowing with certainty the exact number of customers who will demand service at any given time.

As a practical matter, most systems have elements of both chance and predictability. That is, they behave according to a combination of stochastic

CHAPTER SEVEN    QUANTITATIVE TOOLS OF MANAGEMENT                                151

A business system may involve both deterministic and stochastic elements.

and deterministic laws. The greater the degree of determinism, the more predictable the organization behavior and the easier it is to manage and control.

— *Systems analysis.* Systems analysis studies how systems function in order to improve their performance. Systems analysis involves the use of many tools and techniques including operations research (OR), questionnaires, investigative studies, time and motion studies, and audits.

— *Operations research (OR).* Operations research is the application of quantitative scientific tools to understand, predict, and manage the operation of an organization. It applies the laws of mathematics and statistics to the solution of problems. Operations research is used extensively in the allocation of resources, quality control, scheduling output, and planning and forecasting future events.

## QUANTITATIVE TECHNIQUES

The remainder of this chapter surveys quantitative decision-making tools. Many of these have been developed since World War II and rely heavily upon the computer and electronic data processing. The tools described are presented in basic, nonmathematical terms. In practice, these involve complex computer programs and mathematical techniques and formulas. Many are explored in courses in operations research, systems analysis, and quantitative methods.

## Modeling and Simulations

A useful quantitative planning and problem-solving tool is mathematical model and computer simulation. In this technique, real-life problems are reduced to mathematical formulas which are programmed into a computer. The manager runs test data through the model to determine how real-life conditions may actually respond. This technique allows the manager to experiment. Testing is done using the computer rather than the physical organization.

In the simulation and modeling technique, real-life conditions are observed and relationships are established and described. Upon observation, a restaurant manager may discover, for example, that under certain weather conditions sales go down. Given other conditions, there is a substantial increase in sales. Fluctuating prices of gasoline and holiday travel may also influence business. These situations are reduced to mathematical models which are programmed into the computer. Once the computer is programmed, the manager may experiment with various test data to determine what effect varying conditions will have on sales.

The following steps are used in developing and running a simulation and model (fig. 7-1).

1. *Observation and establishment of relationships.* Real-life conditions are observed, and mathematical relationships are established.

2. *Preparation of mathematical model.* A mathematical model is constructed which functions in a manner similar to real-life conditions.

3. *Preparation of computer program.* A program is written and placed on a computer to run against trial data.

4. *Running and testing.* Once the program has been placed on the computer, it is tested to be sure that the results conform to actual real-life conditions. If they do not, then the model or the program is modified so that the results reflect actual conditions.

5. *Problem solving.* The last step is to run various sets of experimental data to solve or understand a specific problem. The manager wishing to experiment with modifications in the real world uses modeling and simulations. For instance, to determine the effects of adding delivery trucks, opening additional teller windows, or adding tables in a restaurant, a set of experimental data describing these variables is assembled. The data is run through the computer to determine the effects of these changed conditions.

The advantage of mathematical modeling and simulation is the reduction in the need to test under actual field conditions. It is less troublesome and costly for a manager to test conditions on a computer than to make experimental changes in business operations. Once a solution has been worked out on the computer, it can be implemented in the business. Trial and error testing and experimenting on a computer is done quickly and with no inconvenience to the customer.

CHAPTER SEVEN    QUANTITATIVE TOOLS OF MANAGEMENT                                153

*Figure 7-1
Simulation
and modeling*

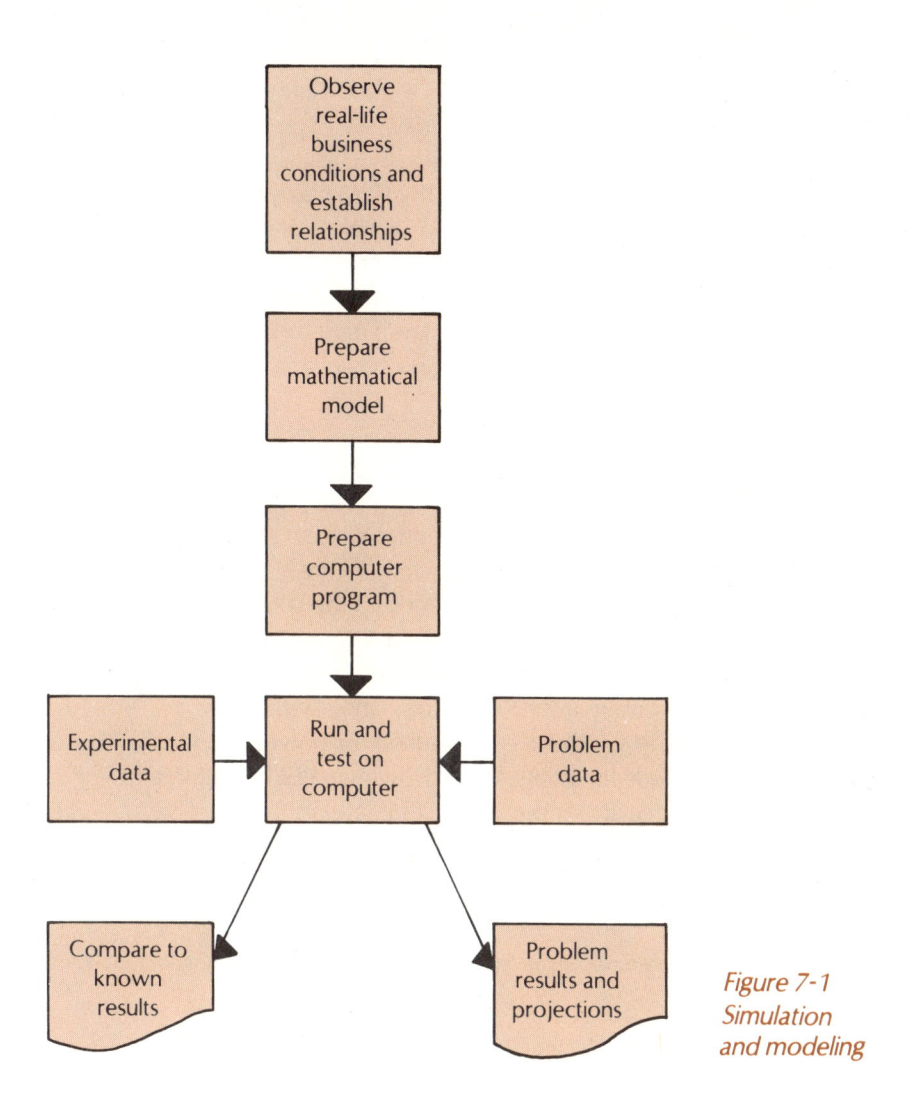

## Critical-Path Method (CPM)

The CPM technique is used in planning and in locating bottlenecks in output and scheduling operations. CPM alerts managers to critical events which must be watched carefully. It specifies which events and activities must occur in sequence in order to achieve the objective in the desired time.

The CPM technique was developed by the Navy in 1959. Their initial work dealt with finding and eliminating bottlenecks and reducing down time in maintaining equipment. CPM is now used to schedule complex jobs where the manager wishes to find the most efficient method of scheduling.

CPM uses a network chart which lists all the activities and beginning and ending events which must take place to reach a goal. Figure 7-2 describes the sequence of steps in planning and installing a new system such as a computer. It sequences such activities as preliminary design, mechanical construction, preparation of manuals, and training of personnel. The CPM makes a single or *best estimate* of the time which each task will take to complete and defines the critical path. The critical path is the sequence of key events and activities which must be done on schedule in order to complete the job in the allotted time. It gives the manager a diagram for those critical activities which must be monitored. CPM lays out a job in a network form. Since it relies upon a single time estimate of each activity, it is deterministic in nature.

## Program Evaluation and Review Technique (PERT)

The PERT technique is similar to CPM in that it is designed to eliminate bottlenecks and find the most efficient path to completing a job. Figure 7-3 shows a PERT chart which schedules activities. The heavy arrow denotes the critical path. Each major event is shown as a numbered circle. An activity always precedes an event. PERT was developed by Booz, Allen, Hamilton under a project for the U.S. Navy in 1959 to coordinate scheduling of the Polaris submarine system.

PERT differs from CPM in that it is best suited for one-of-a-kind jobs. It also uses the network technique for listing events. However, PERT uses three different time estimates for each activity. These include estimates of the best time, average time, and worst time in which each activity can be completed. This adds a stochastic element to the process.

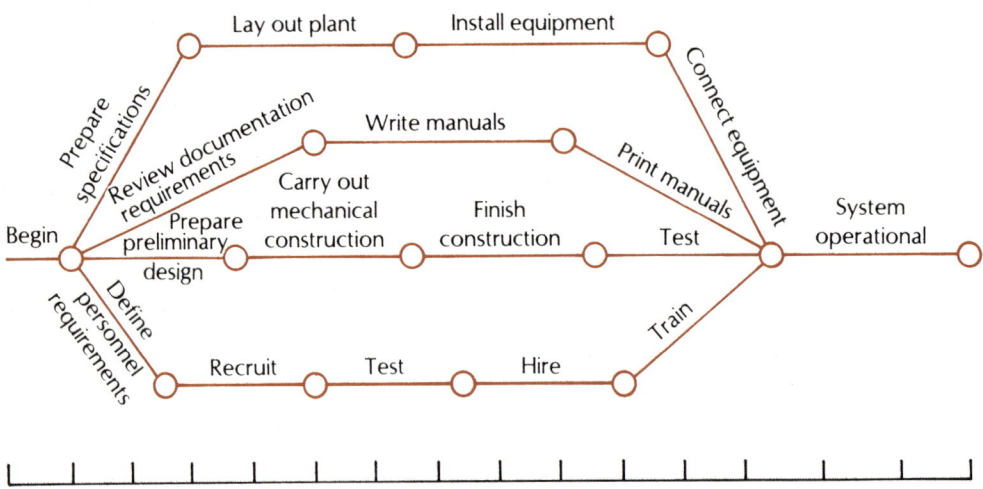

*Figure 7-2    Critical-path-method (CPM) chart*

*Figure 7-3
Program
evaluation and review
technique (PERT) chart*

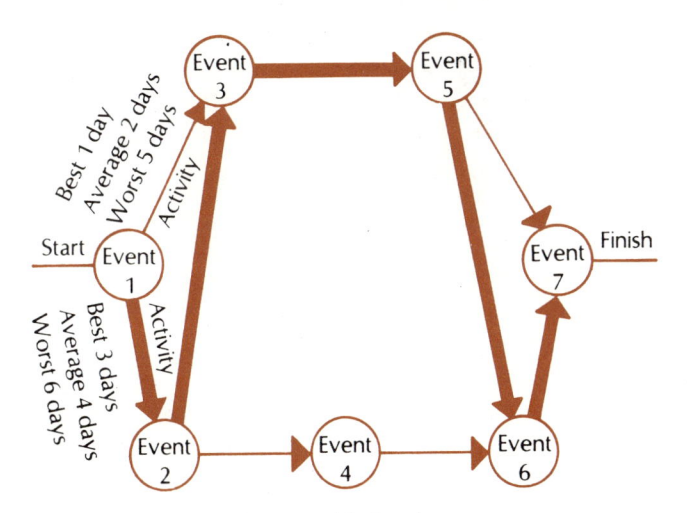

Heavy arrow denotes critical path.
Numbered circles are events.
Arrows denote activities which precede an event.
A *best, average,* and *worst* case time is shown for each activity on chart.

Both PERT and CPM are widely used by managers who schedule complex tasks which must be completed in the shortest possible time. For example, they can be used in the construction of a large building or the manufacture of a ship or airplane. All these jobs require careful schedule sequencing and attention to critical events. The failure to see that a required preliminary step is completed on time could set a project back months.

## Linear Programming (LP)

The LP technique is used to find the best mix or combination of elements when given a limited amount of resources. It is used principally for allocating resources when a job or task has many components. Many managers face a problem of finding the best combination of elements to achieve the maximum output. For example, they must decide how many machines, personnel, work stations, and dollars to assign to a task.

Suppose a small manufacturer assigns a manager the task of establishing an assembly line to produce electrical appliances. The manager is given a limited amount of money, personnel, work space, and other resources with which to produce small appliances. Many decisions must be made in setting up the line, including the number of machines to buy, operators to assign, and work stations to assemble and test the finished goods. LP can be used for this job. It produces a report, prepared by computer, which lists the most effective combination of machines, personnel, and work stations.

LP is often used in allocating resources in the transportation industry. (See figure 7-4.) In this example, a fruit grower seeks to ship the maximum amount of product between the home port and the market. There are limited resources of ships, loading and unloading personnel, and routes. The major product may be shipped from a nearby primary port or an alternate port reached by rail. The product may be received near its market at several primary receiving ports, or at an alternate port and then shipped by rail to the primary market. Major and alternate shipping routes vary in distance and affect transportation costs. Should more ships be added to the line, or should the unloading or loading facilities be improved to gain the maximum tonnage shipped? Should they buy faster or larger ships, or rely on alternate ports and rail lines, or a combination of these? If hundreds of ships, personnel, and routes are involved, the task of finding the best mix is complex.

*Figure 7-4   Linear programming problem*

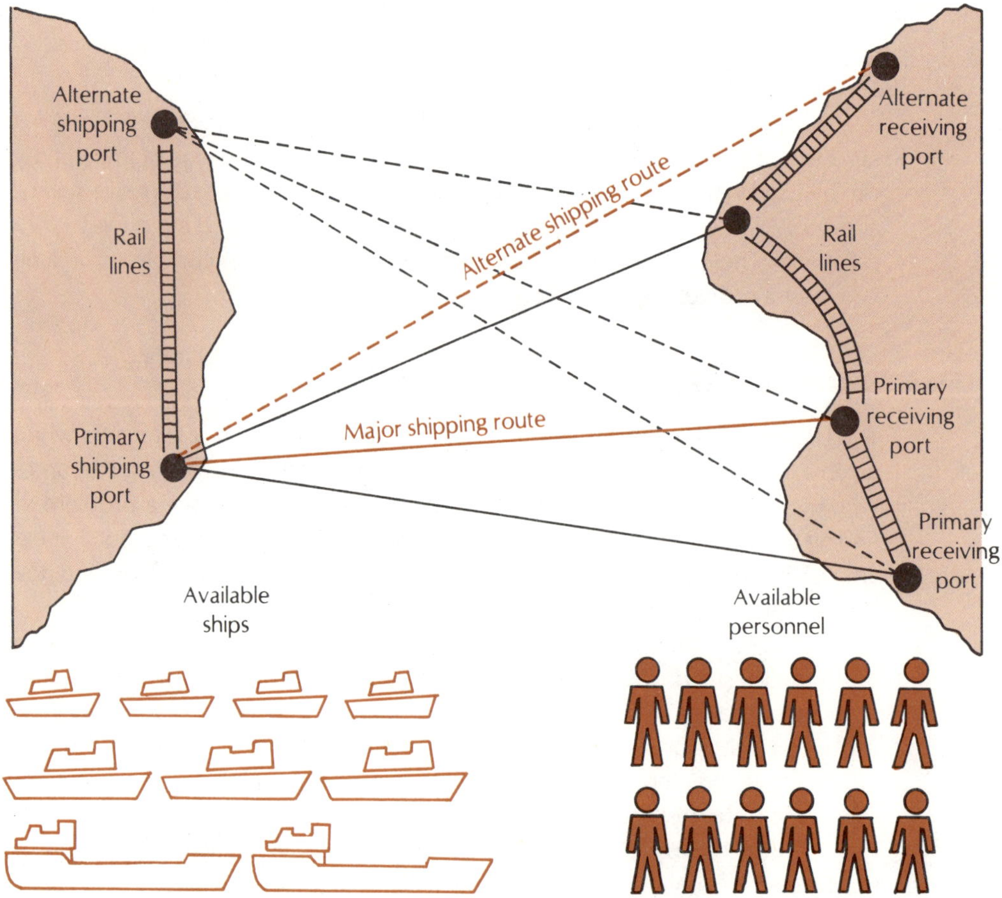

## Probability Theory

Many events occur in an orderly, predictable fashion. As defined, these are *deterministic* occurrences. For example, a coin tossed in the air will land on its face half the time and on its tail the other half. There is no way of knowing for certain how a particular coin toss will turn out. But one can predict the behavior of the coin toss percentage with some certainty over many occurrences.

Applying the law of averages to predict future events is part of the study of probability. Probability theory is one of the quantitative tools of management and is used to predict future events by observing current events.

Probability theory can be used to estimate the number of delinquent accounts which will occur in any given month, the percentage of goods which will be returned due to misrouting, or the number of days employees will lose due to illness. Probability theory attempts to reduce the chance occurrences to known quantities which can be dealt with in the present.

One of the most common manifestations of probability theory is the bell-shaped curve (fig. 7-5). A bell-shaped distribution is found when chance occurrences are plotted. In the figure, IQ scores are plotted for a group of students selected at random. Placing each score on a chart creates the bell-shaped curve. There will be a larger number of scores which cluster at or near the mean. There are fewer scores at each end of the curve. This is readily apparent from the grade distribution after a test. Many business, sales, marketing, and production phenomena exhibit similar patterns. Thus, the manager can apply the laws of probability to predicting the number of customers who will demand a given product, or the number of users who will place orders on a given day.

## Queuing Theory

Queuing theory is a quantitative tool for decision making which is used to eliminate bottlenecks in providing services. Queuing theory is based upon waiting lines of people, vehicular traffic or airplanes. It is used to balance demand upon a system and to maximize returns.

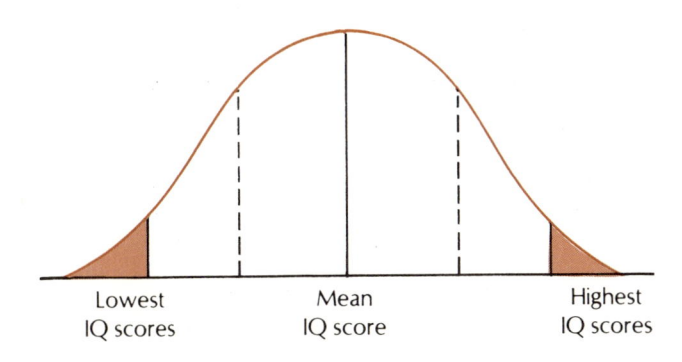

*Figure 7-5*
*Bell-shaped curve*

It is known that in any given waiting line situation, some people become discouraged and leave the line. Others who might buy a service refuse to wait in line if a long delay is expected. Others, not in line, might join a waiting line if the line is short and service can be expected momentarily. A close study of waiting-line behavior can provide management with much useful information.

Consider the problem of providing checkout services to customers at a supermarket. If there is an unlimited number of checkout stands and personnel available, a supermarket manager can simply open and staff as many checkout stations as needed to serve customers. This creates few dissatisfied customers since waiting time is held to a minimum.

This approach, while shortening waiting time, substantially increases labor costs. The other extreme is to permit only one station to remain open and to assign the checkout clerks to stocking shelves or performing other services. This reduces labor cost to a minimum but creates long checkout lines. Long lines discourage many customers, who leave the lines or just don't buy, and sales revenue drops.

Using the queuing theory, the manager can experiment with finding an optimum point where the fewest checkout stations produce the shortest lines, while maximizing revenue.

Understanding how people behave in waiting lines is important in industries which sell services over-the-counter.

CHAPTER SEVEN    QUANTITATIVE TOOLS OF MANAGEMENT                                159

## REAL WORLD

# There's Big Business in All That Garbage

Thousands of firms around the country are struggling to find ways to dispose of the vast amount of refuse and garbage they generate each year. This has proven to be a golden opportunity for Waste Management, Inc., of Chicago, which turns garbage into money. For years garbage collection was a dirty and uninspiring job, made more difficult by new rules and government regulations. Today collecting and disposing of industrial garbage and waste products is a complex scientific problem.

Dean L. Buntrock, chairman of Waste Management, uses engineers, geologists, hydrologists, and others to work out ways of disposing of thousands of pounds of industrial rubbish and trash. They have found ways to cope with the complexities of the various rules and government regulations.

Waste management is big business. Some of the contracts involve hundreds of millions of dollars and thousands of trucks and personnel to move and properly dispose of waste materials. This is done by precise routing and scheduling, efficient equipment, and small work crews.

Adapted from *Fortune*, 7 April, 1980, p. 106.

## Game Theory

A variety of approaches to game theory have been used in decision making. Strictly speaking, game theory is not a quantitative tool. However, it is often used with other tools described in this chapter to solve management problems.

Game theory is based upon the principle of using games to simulate real-life management situations. Games are structured which pit individuals against each other to anticipate how they would act under actual conditions. Game theory is often used in management-labor relations, in training managers, clerks, or line personnel. It allows a speeding up of decision making.

For example, suppose several employees are assigned the task of negotiating a labor contract. Management games could prepare them for actual negotiations. One group representing labor, the other management, is placed in a game situation. Each side is given bargaining points which must be won, and points which may be bargained away as follows.

"According to our research department, our public opinion polls, our sampling of potential users, our forecasts of marketing trends, our estimates of consumer reaction, and our statistical model manipulations, we overcooked the vegetables."

Reprinted from *Datamation*, November 1972.

Points you may concede or bargain away:

1. free parking spaces;
2. additional rest periods;
3. expanded dental coverage;
4. maternity leave.

Points you may *not* concede or bargain away:

1. pay raise of $1.10 per hour;
2. use of company automobile;
3. seniority privileges;
4. retirement benefits.

During the game session, each side attempts to gain the upper hand in the negotiations. The object is to win the most points or concessions from the other side.

Game strategy is a useful tool in situational management because it deals with the present situation, personnel, and problems. It can be used to give managers and subordinates an understanding of human relations problems. For instance, a manager may be assigned to play the role of a line employee. Another manager must reprimand the employee. Conflicts are created which the manager must learn to handle.

## Break-Even-Point Analysis

A useful quantitative tool is break-even-point analysis. Break-even-point analysis concerns itself with charting total revenue and costs to find points where profit is made or losses occur. It may be made on a unit cost basis, or on the operation of an entire plant. The break-even point is that point in the volume of output at which the revenue just matches the cost of producing the goods or services. Any further sale of goods nets a profit. A reduction in sales of goods results in a loss.

Some managers prepare cost-analysis charts (fig. 7-6). These charts show the component costs of producing and marketing a given product at various levels of production. Most products incur several costs in their manufacture and sale. These include fixed, variable, and sales and advertising costs. They combine to make up the total manufacturing and marketing costs of the product. Generally, the more units produced, the lower the per unit cost to produce and market.

Let us define some of these key cost factors before we explore how they are used in break-even-point analysis.

1. *Fixed costs.* Fixed costs are those costs which do not change with the volume of goods produced. These costs, called *overhead* or *burden,* must be paid regardless of the amount of goods produced. The costs of insurance, heating, lighting, and building maintenance are examples of fixed costs.

2. *Variable costs.* Variable costs change with the volume of output. They rise or fall with the amount of goods produced. Raw materials and labor are examples of variable costs. As a firm produces more goods, more raw materials and labor will be required.

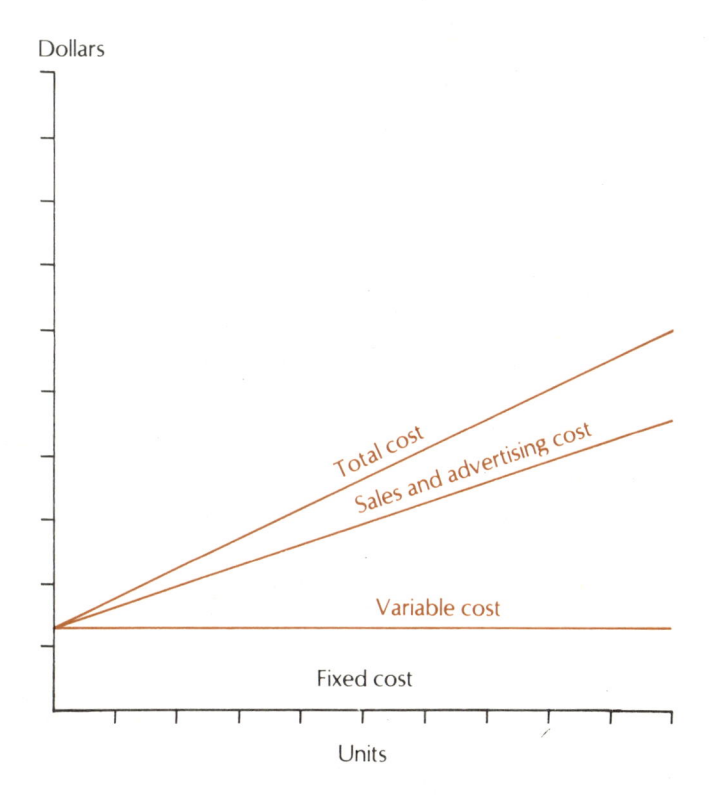

*Figure 7-6*
*Cost-analysis chart*

Generally, the larger the amount of raw materials purchased, the lower the unit cost. A firm buying a large volume of raw materials can take advantage of volume purchasing and subsequent price savings. While the net amount spent for raw materials increases as more goods are produced, the cost of raw materials on a per unit basis may decline.

3. *Sales costs.* Sales costs are those costs incurred in the sales and marketing of a product. Generally, the more money spent on sales and advertising, the greater the amount of goods sold.

4. *Total cost.* Total cost is the total amount of money expended in producing and marketing a product. It includes all fixed, variable, and sales costs. Generally, the more units a firm produces and sells, the lower the total per unit costs.

5. *Revenue.* Revenue is the amount of money received from the sale of goods and services. The greater the amount of goods and services sold, the greater the revenue they produce.

Figure 7-7 illustrates the total cost and revenue curves plotted on one chart to find the break-even point. Where only a few units are sold, the total cost is higher than total revenue. This results in a loss for operations before the break-even point.

At some point, total revenue just equals total cost. This is the break-even point. Any sales after that point result in a profit. By using break-even-point analysis, the manager analyzes the operation and establishes a sales and marketing level which assures that the firm will sell an adequate number of units to make a profit.

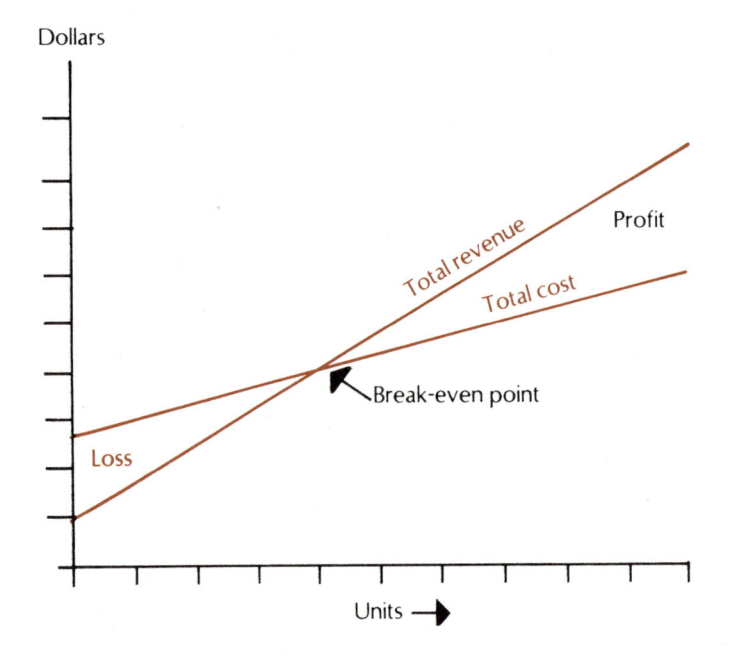

*Figure 7-7 Break-even-point analysis*

> **REAL WORLD**
>
> ## A Ride to Golconda in a Wavy Sole Shoe
>
> Everybody laughed when Joseph P. Famolare, Jr., president of Famolare, Inc., proposed the new shoe design. It was a wedge high heel with a funny, wavy sole. Surely no one would buy this product. His sales managers almost walked out in force when they saw the new design. The wholesalers thought it was doomed to failure from the start. But Famolare was right. The only people who liked the shoes were the customers. What the country had been waiting for was a comfortable walking shoe. And it didn't matter what it looked like.
>
> In 1979 Famolare expects to sell nearly $100 million worth of shoes. And the profit margin is substantially above that of domestic shoe manufacturers. Famolare believes this proves a point. An imaginative and optimistic entrepreneur can enter the market and make money. He must be right. His shoes are being worn in corporate offices all over the country.
>
> Adapted from *Fortune*, 30 July 1979, p. 104.

Break-even-point analysis shows the amount of profit to be made at each point on the curve. If sales do not produce profit, then the manager must reduce costs or raise prices to increase revenue.

Break-even-point analysis provides the manager with an effective quantitative tool for making decisions regarding the purchase of raw materials, advertising, and overhead expense items. It can be applied to analyzing total operations or per unit costs. Break-even-point analysis can be used in assessing labor, transportation, and distribution costs. It is a general purpose tool widely used to fine tune production and output levels.

## SUMMARY

The computer has greatly enhanced the manager's ability to make decisions. Systems either exhibit elements of certainty or behave according to chance (deterministic or stochastic). Many systems have elements of both.

Operations research (OR) is an important tool to understand and manage systems. OR uses laws of mathematics and statistics to solve problems. Modeling and simulation is a tool which reduces real-life problems to mathematical models for solution by computer.

## POSTSCRIPT
# Could Computers Have Kept Chrysler Healthy?

If the top executives of stricken Chrysler Corp. had relied on analysis of a unique data base of *business strategy experiences,* could they have avoided their current trauma — and made a taxpayer-burdening, hand-extended plea to Washington unnecessary?

This is the claim of Dr. Sidney Shoeffler, executive director of the Strategic Planning Institute. SPI is a nonprofit organization with 240 member companies, mostly in the U.S. but also in Canada and Europe. Spun off from General Electric Company seven years ago, SPI maintains a computerized database of some 1,900 real-life business strategy situations supplied by its members, who meet twice a year. (The number of situations is climbing at the rate of 300 to 400 a year.)

Chrysler's big mistake, according to Dr. Shoeffler, is that it tried to compete in all vehicle markets with its two immense rivals, both of whom have far greater resources. Instead, Chrysler's bosses should have studied the business strategies of other "No. 3s," both winners and losers. Dr. Shoeffler

Reprinted from *Computer Decisions,* Oct., 1979, p.4, copyright© 1979, Hayden Publishing Co.

Networking techniques locate bottlenecks in scheduling and output operations. The critical-path method (CPM) uses a single best estimate of time, while programming evaluation and review technique (PERT) uses three different estimates for each activity. Linear programming (LP) finds the best combination of elements when given a limited amount of resources.

Probability theory uses the law of averages to predict future events. In queuing theory the study and behavior of waiting lines is used to balance demand upon systems. Game theory uses role playing and situational episodes to provide managers with experiences which simulate real-life management situations.

Break-even-point analysis charts total revenue and costs to find the point at which profits or losses occur.

## REVIEW QUESTIONS

1. Define *deterministic* and *stochastic* systems.
2. List the major tools used in operations research.
3. List the steps in developing and running a simulation or model on the computer.
4. What is the critical path and why is is important to managers?

claims that his data bank contains many examples of low-share-of-market contenders in mature manufacturing industries from whom Chrysler could have gained invaluable insights.

One strategy for Chrysler might have been concentration on niche markets of either a product or a geographic nature. Dr. Shoeffler also would have recommended avoidance of heavy R&D expenditures for the stricken automaker.

Here are some of the questions that member companies often try to answer by tapping SPI's data bank: "How do we go about increasing our share of market, yet holding down cash drain?" "Given limited resources, which of three alternative growth plans do we pursue?" "What return will we obtain by growing in a certain direction?"

Most of SPI's member companies are manufacturers in the Fortune 1,000 and use remote terminals to tap the data bank, which is maintained on a DECsystem 10. However, smaller and smaller organizations down to $15 million in annual sales and increasingly of a service nature, are becoming members. The latter tend to obtain their data more slowly by mail. (SPI's annual charges, which range from $12,000 to $20,000 per member, depending on size, include ten free days of consulting, after which the charge per PhD runs up to $800/day.

The development of this unique data bank, which began at GE about twenty years ago, demonstrates again that the computer can play a powerful role in helping direct the fortunes of companies.

5. Describe the three different time estimates used in PERT.
6. What kinds of problems is linear programming best suited to solve?
7. What is the significance of the bell-shaped curve?
8. How does the queuing theory help management balance demand upon a system?
9. Explain why game theory is not strictly a quantitative tool.
10. Explain how a break-even point is found.
11. Define fixed costs and give several examples.
12. Define variable costs and give several examples.

## KEY TERMS

Deterministic system   150
Stochastic system   150
Systems analysis   151
Operations research (OR)   151
Modeling and simulations   152
Critical-path method (CPM)   153
Program evaluation and review technique (PERT)   154

Linear programming (LP)   155
Probability theory   157
Queuing theory   157
Game theory   159
Break-even-point analysis   160

# Case Incident

Wellington Parcel Delivery operates a very successful local package and parcel service in a medium-size eastern city. Wellington's fleet of trucks delivers packages for an increasing number of the local retailers in the community. Most of the parcels are picked up directly at the larger retailers for delivery to their customers. In addition, four separate pick-up centers are operated throughout the city for small and occasional customers who have only a few packages to handle at any one time.

The total volume of packages handled per week by the midtown pick-up station has continued to decline. This is due to the fact that most of the midtown retailers have slowly moved out to the suburbs and shopping malls. Wellington's management is seriously considering closing down the midtown pick-up station and shifting its responsibility to the other three centers.

Jennifer Barr, general manager of Wellington's data center, says that she can help solve the problem of whether to close down the midtown pick-up station and shift the load to other centers by using a mathematical model to simulate the closure. Since Wellington has extensive records of parcel delivery and pick-ups, she believes this would be the best way to make the decision on empirical evidence, since it would not jeopardize customer relations. After a thorough look at the basic data, Barr already feels that the mid-city operation should be closed down as soon as possible.

Tom Lawson, supervisor for the mid-city pick-up station, does not approve of the modeling simulation idea, thinking it rather foolish to use such a theoretical method for making such an important decision. Needless to say, Lawson is not eager to see his station closed down. He says, "Let's take a wait and see attitude on this matter. We should wait until volume falls off and we actually begin to lose money before we consider closing the pick-up station. One of the problems with the computer model is that it could tell us to close down the unit when in fact we can still make money on a slowly decreasing volume."

## PROBLEMS

1. What problems does Barr face in developing a mathematical model of the situation?
2. What problems does Lawson's wait and see attitude present?
3. Which solution to the problem do you prefer? Explain.

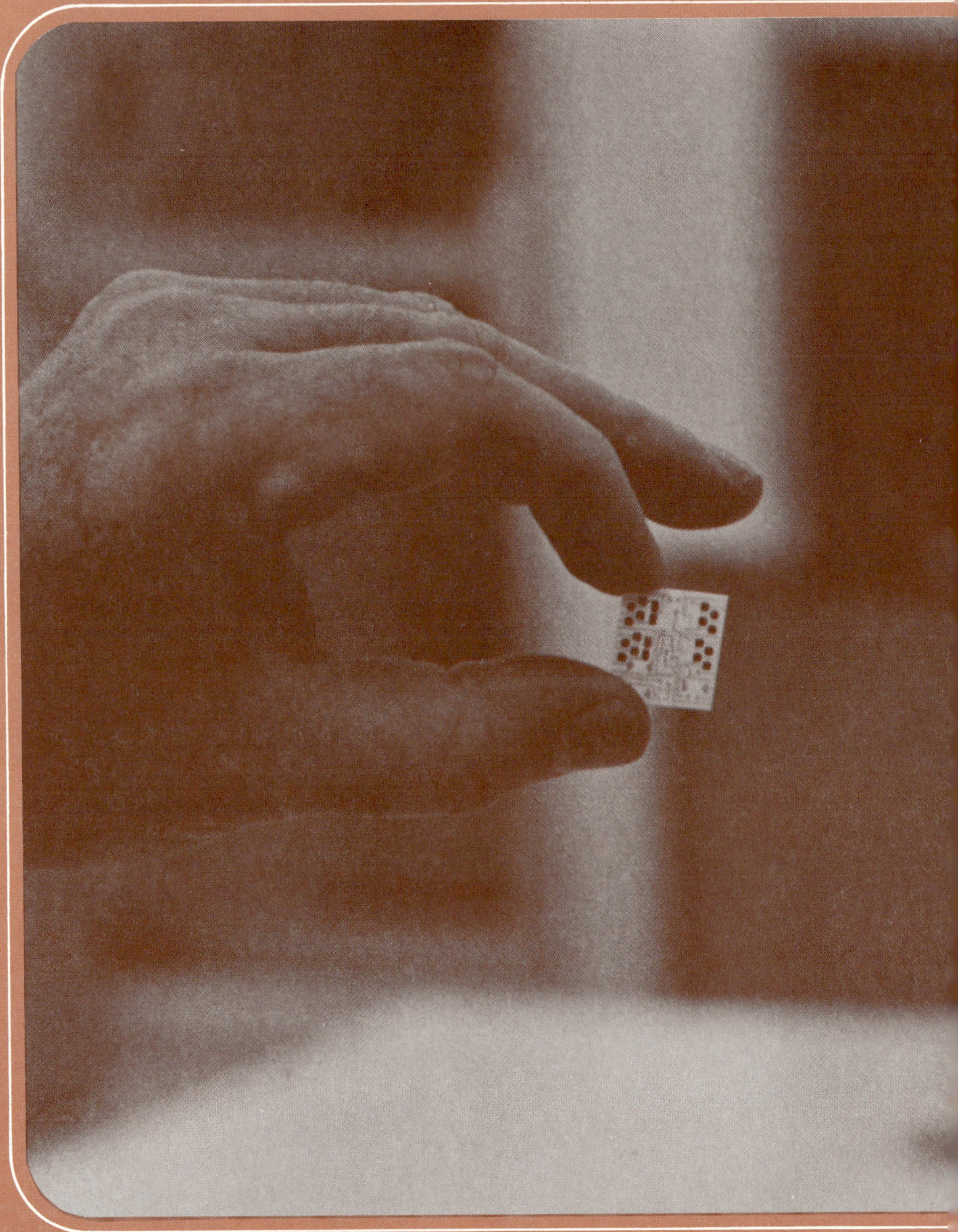

# 8

# Management Information Systems (MIS)

**LEARNING OBJECTIVES**

After studying this chapter, you should be able to:
1. Define basic terms used in information systems.
2. List the pressures on business which have brought about the reliance upon computers and information systems.
3. Describe some trends in the number of computers in use.
4. Summarize how computers are used in management.
5. List the advantages of computers.
6. Describe the major elements of management information systems.
7. Summarize the history of computers and data processing.
8. Describe the major components of a computer system.
9. Summarize the major elements which are considered when evaluating a new computer system.
10. Identify the problems of access, security, and cost control which management resolves regarding computer installations.

This chapter describes one of the most significant and innovative developments in management: computers and information systems. The computer has enhanced the manager's ability to plan, control, organize, and direct organizations. Computers add speed, accuracy, and a quantitative characteristic to management methods and the decision-making process.

We will consider the pressures on business which brought about reliance on computers and management information systems (MIS). The fundamentals of computers and their advantages will be presented.

A thorough discussion of computers and data processing is beyond the scope of an introductory course in management. However, future managers are urged to take courses in electronic computers, data processing, and programming in order to understand and be able to use this powerful new tool.

## KEY TERMS

Before proceeding with a discussion of management information systems and computers, let us define some fundamental terms.

—*Information (data).* Information is any knowledge which is useful in the operation, control, planning, or management of organizations. Managers rely upon accurate information to make good decisions. Good decisions make good management, and good management leads an organization towards its goals (fig. 8-1).

—*System.* A system is a regularly interacting or interdependent group of elements which form a unified whole. A system possesses capabilities which are greater than the sum of its parts. Organizations are systems composed of subsystems. A subsystem is a smaller system which forms a part of a larger system.

—*Real-time system.* A real-time system is one which processes transactions as they occur. According to the American National Standards Institute (ANSI), *real time* is defined as the actual time during which a physical process transpires. It pertains to the performance of a computation during the actual time that the related physical process transpires in order that results of the computer can be used in guiding the physical process.

For example, a bank teller terminal, connected on-line to a computer, processes transactions in real time (at the same time the physical process tran-

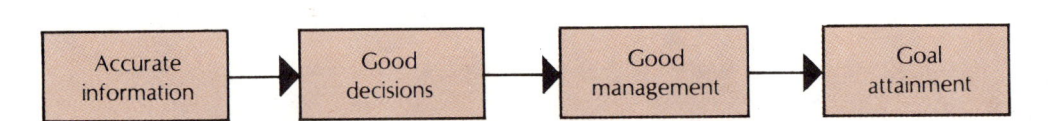

*Figure 8-1 Goal attainment and information*

Accurate information → Good decisions → Good management → Goal attainment

spires.) This is in contrast to a *batch system,* which processes the transaction at some time after the physical transaction occurs.

— *Timesharing.* This is a computer arrangement in which two or more terminals are connected to a single computer and process data simultaneously. Timesharing is the sharing of a single computer by many users at one time. Generally, this is done by allocating small slices of time to each user.

— *Computer.* A computer is an electronic device which processes data, is capable of input and output, and possesses such characteristics as high speed, accuracy, and the ability to store a set of instructions for solving a problem. Computers are electronic devices constructed from wires, transistors, and integrated circuits and able to execute a set of instructions, called a *program.*

— *Program.* A program is a set of instructions which is stored in a computer and which directs data processing. A program is the series of actions which will achieve a certain end. Thus, a program may tell the computer how to process information in a series of steps, such as in the preparation of a payroll.

— *Computer hardware.* Hardware is the machines, devices, mechanisms, and physical equipment used to process data. Hardware is the mechanical and electronic equipment such as line printers, terminals, and the central computer, as contrasted to software.

— *Computer software.* Software is the programs, computer languages, procedures, instructions, and documentation used in processing data. Software includes the library routines, manuals, diagrams, and programming instructions, as contrasted to hardware.

## PRESSURES ON BUSINESS ORGANIZATIONS

To appreciate fully how computers have come into widespread use in management, we must understand certain pressures on business organizations. These pressures have greatly stimulated the use of computers in management.

1. *Growing volume of transactions and paperwork.* Most business organizations have experienced a huge increase in the number of transactions which must be processed. This has generated a vast amount of paperwork, calculations, records, and related reports.

2. *Need for more timely information.* The sheer pace of modern business demands that organizations be more responsive to the people with whom it interacts. Employees, customers, vendors, and all levels of management require faster processing of information.

3. *Need for greater accuracy.* Customers, employees, government, and other organizations are insisting on more accurate information. There is a growing demand for information reported in a more precise, carefully analyzed form.

**4. *Rising costs.*** Inflation and the rising cost of labor and raw materials have brought about increasingly high prices. This has forced management to find more economical methods of operating, processing data, and preparing reports.

**5. *Social and consumer pressures.*** The growth of the consumer movement and a recognition of management's social responsibilities for protecting the environment have placed new pressures on organizations. Organizations must now report to government on air, water, and noise pollution and waste disposal. They must gather and report information concerning product safety and minorities and women in the labor force. This requires a closer observation of operations and the collecting and reporting of many new kinds of data.

## TRENDS IN THE NUMBER OF COMPUTERS IN USE

There is a continuing trend among organizations to rely upon computers. In 1977, $12.2 billion of general purpose computers were shipped. By 1982 it is expected that the annual shipment volume will reach $30 billion. In the United States alone 10,000 general purpose computers will be shipped by 1982. This figure is an increase of twenty percent over those shipped in 1977. Small computer shipments will reach 50,000 per year by 1982, and the even smaller minicomputer will reach 150,000 by 1982. This is up from 60,000 in 1977 (fig. 8-2).[1]

*Figure 8-2 Market for general purpose computers built by U.S. manufacturers*

Shipments And Retirements At Original Purchase Value

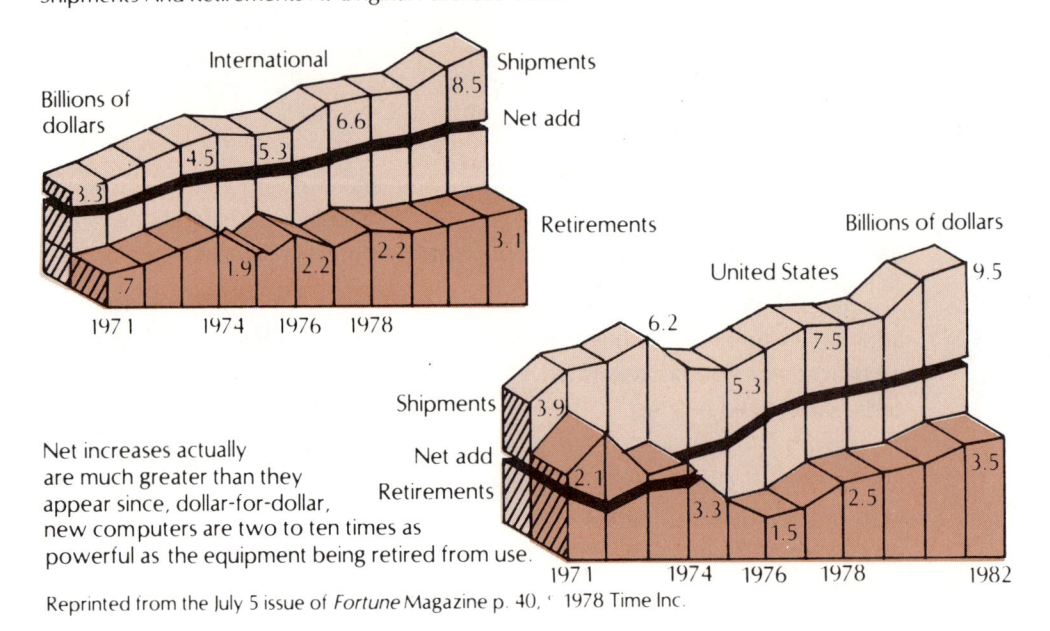

Net increases actually are much greater than they appear since, dollar-for-dollar, new computers are two to ten times as powerful as the equipment being retired from use.

Reprinted from the July 5 issue of *Fortune* Magazine p. 40, © 1978 Time Inc.

---

[1]*Fortune*, 5 July 1978, p. 40.

CHAPTER EIGHT   MANAGEMENT INFORMATION SYSTEMS (MSI)

> **REAL WORLD**
> # Managing the Unmanageable
>
> Russell E. Palmer, the chief executive officer of the accounting firm of Touche Ross and Company, believes that large corporations that try to handle thousands of accounting problems in complex companies around the world are facing a literally impossible task.
>
> Multinational business firms must account for thousands of people in many different localities. They face differences in language, varying qualities of workmanship, and different management philosophies. Standards of work ethics vary widely around the globe. Government regulations create a complexity of laws and rules with which the accountant must deal.
>
> Today's manager must be a lot smarter and stress long-range planning. The manager must lead rather than command others and be a master of the art of diplomacy and persuasion.
>
> Adapted from *Chief Executive Magazine*, No. 9 (Fall 1979), p. 6.

## HOW COMPUTERS ARE USED IN MANAGEMENT

As organizations grow larger and more complex, more data is produced. This places heavy demands upon managers who must read, digest, and interpret this mass of information. Traditional methods of storing, retrieving, and reporting data are not adequate today. As a result, computers have a wide range of applications in management planning, organizing, directing, and controlling functions. Following are some of the more common ways computers are used by managers.

1. *Decision making.* Computers are used to simulate business conditions, make projections, and anticipate trends. Computers can correlate data, condense information, and prepare reports upon which key decisions are made.

2. *Marketing.* Computers are widely used to assist in making management decisions related to the marketing of goods and services. The computer can forecast sales, handle inventory and marketing information, and assist in planning and budgeting.

3. *Personnel.* The computer is a valuable tool in personnel planning and management. It is used for processing payroll and maintaining data on employees. It com-

putes commissions, schedules work loads, provides work force profiles, and processes employment applications, promotions, and terminations.

4. *Finance.* The computer has many uses in financial planning and management. It is used to prepare and maintain ledgers, journals, depreciation and inventory records, profit and loss statements, and balance sheets. The computer prepares a variety of ratios and reports for financial analysis.

5. *Manufacturing.* The computer has many applications in manufacturing and production. It is a valuable tool in cost accounting and in scheduling manufacturing operations. It is widely used to produce reports for management on raw materials, inventory, warehousing, shipping, and plant operation and maintenance.

6. *Other applications.* Computers are used for registration at colleges and universities and produce accurate enrollment figures and class rosters. Hospitals, government agencies, and charitable institutions use the computer in many service capacities.

## ADVANTAGES OF COMPUTERS

The preceding applications are the result of the high speed and accuracy of computers. In summary, here are the major advantages of computers.

1. *Accuracy.* The computer is able to process information with a level of accuracy far above any other device yet invented. It can perform millions of calculations without a single error. Computer systems have built-in redundancy and error checks. This enables the computer to discover and diagnose its own failures. Of course, inaccurate information fed into the computer will produce inaccurate reports.

2. *Speed.* The computer can process data faster than any other device. This is because information is converted into electrical pulses for processing within the computer itself. As a result, the computer can manipulate data at the rate of millions of characters per second. There are some computing tasks which would take so long without the computer that they would not be practical.

3. *Cost efficiency.* While the initial cost of a large computer system is high, the net cost per calculation is low. Computer systems process a high volume of data at a minimum cost. Data processing, using computers, costs much less than other methods, such as manual or punch card.

4. *Reliability.* The modern computer is a marvel of electronic engineering. It has almost no moving parts to break down or wear out. Computations are done in solid-state circuitry, such as transistors and integrated circuits (ICs). These devices are highly reliable and rarely break down.

## MANAGEMENT INFORMATION SYSTEMS (MIS)

The introduction of computers and modern electronic data processing has brought about the development of the management information system (MIS). A MIS is designed to handle and process management information in a systematic way. Figure 8-3 diagrams a simplified management information system. Systems such as these store data which is immediately available when needed.

## MAJOR ELEMENTS OF THE MIS

MIS consists of a central data bank, which stores the master files of information, and terminals. Through the terminals, data is input to this data bank, updated, and retrieved as the need arises. Let us review the major elements of the MIS.

1. *Storing information in the data bank.* The heart of the MIS is a data bank which contains the master files of the organization. The information placed in a typical business data bank includes sales data, budget and cost information, transporta-

*Figure 8-3 Management information system (MIS) (Input and output)*

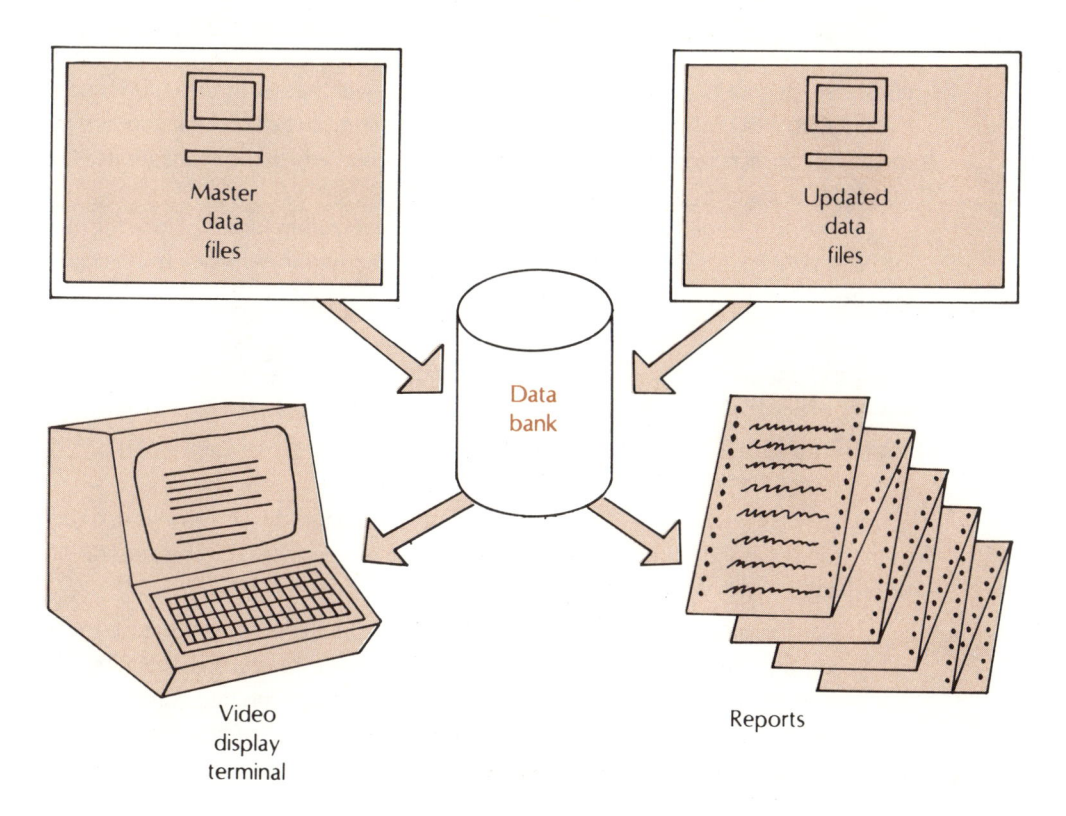

> **REAL WORLD**
>
> # How Detroit Got Stuck with All Those Cars
>
> Nobody understands the problems of inventory management better than General Motors chairman Thomas Murphy. In 1979 General Motors inventory managers set a new record — the wrong kind. General Motors wound up with a fat inventory of 2.15 million unsold cars and trucks. Murphy, who had predicted that the industry would sell over 15.5 million cars and trucks in 1979, was wrong.
>
> The stockpile of cars built up. Unsold vehicles sat in dealers' showrooms, proving that even experts can be wrong. The most sophisticated and efficient forecasting and inventory systems go awry. One of the big problems was that sales managers were using past experience as their measure for future inventory. The moral is that any inventory management system, no matter how well conceived, is only as good as the sales forecasts upon which it is based.
>
> Adapted from *Fortune*, 22 October 1979, p. 54.

tion rates, accounts payable and receivable data, purchasing information, financial data, cost of materials, and personnel information. The data bank contains information on all important aspects of the organization which the manager uses to make decisions.

In the first stages of implementation, the organization inputs all master files into the data bank. This provides the core of information which is revised and updated as business conditions change.

2. *Updating the data bank.* Information in a data bank must be periodically revised and updated if it is to be of use to management. Revised data come from a variety of sources, including field reports, invoices, raw material inventories, and sales receipts. Updating adds new data, changes existing data, or deletes data which is no longer needed in the data bank.

3. *Accessing the data bank.* Information in the data bank can be retrieved, or *accessed,* in several different ways. These include on-line access or the generation of reports:

   a. *On-line access.* In this mode, information stored in the data bank is made available through on-line terminals. Cathode ray terminals (CRTs) are placed in managers' offices and connected directly to the data bank. This allows managers to display information in the data bank on a real-time basis. This means information can be displayed as the transactions occur. Managers can retrieve information throughout the day without waiting for reports to be physically delivered. CRT terminals provide a fast, low-cost means of accessing large amounts of data. CRT terminals allow information to be displayed on the screen. Contents of the data bank may also be changed by inputting new information from the keyboard of the terminal.

    b. *Preparation of reports.* In some instances, a hard copy (paper) report may be desirable. These can be produced from the information stored in the data bank. A line printer is used to print out reports, individual records, or entire files from the data bank. These reports are given to various managers for decision-making purposes, or are used in the field. (See table 8-1.)

## ADVANTAGES OF MIS

MIS have a variety of advantages for management. A systematic means of handling and processing data improves the quality of decisions. MIS make data available at the time and place where it will be of greatest use to the manager. MIS which operate in a real-time mode provide information at the time a transaction is processed. Computerized systems process data at a low cost and with a high level of accuracy. This gives the decision maker greater flexibility. The manager can respond quickly to problems and make decisions which are more accurate and relevant. Finally, MIS provide data for decision making early enough in the business cycle so that management can take advantage of opportunities that arise. Late delivery of information could mean the loss of an important sale or contract.

**Table 8-1 Management report**

| Capital Ratios | Actual Current Year | Projected |
|---|---|---|
| Long-term debt | 25.6 | 26.7 |
| Liability to equity | 87.5 | 78.5 |
| **Operating Ratios** | | |
| Operating cost to sales | 4.5 | 4.5 |
| Earnings to sales | 20.1 | 20.0 |
| Pre-tax to sales | 30.2 | 34.5 |
| **Working Capital Ratios** | | |
| Current ratio | 3.5 | 3.4 |
| Sales to accounts receivable | 5.3 | 5.3 |
| Inventory | 6.2 | |
| Sales to working capital | 18.5 | 20.5 |
| **Other Ratios** | | |
| Depreciation to plant | 4.3 | 4.6 |
| Current rate of tax | 44.7 | 45.0 |
| Dividend to net income | 22.3 | 25.0 |

**Table 8-2  Data processing eras**

| Manual | Unit Record | Electronic Data Processing (EDP) Computers ||||
|---|---|---|---|---|---|
| Pencil, paper, and simple mechanical devices | Punch cards — electrical accounting machines (EAM) | 1st | 2nd | 3rd | 4th |
| | | | Generation |||
| 1890 | 1946 | | | | |

## HISTORY OF COMPUTERS AND DATA PROCESSING

Data processing has moved through three major eras of development: manual, unit record, and electronic data processing. (See table 8-2.) Prior to 1890 virtually all computations and data processing were done by hand using relatively simple mechanical devices. Pencil, paper, the slide rule, abacus, and mechanical wheel calculator were used to process numerical data.

In 1833 Charles Babbage, an English mathematician, designed several machines which laid the foundation for the development of computers. His *difference engine,* and later his *analytic engine,* were designed to perform arithmetic functions from data read into the mechanism. However, Babbage never built these machines, and it wasn't until 1890 that Herman Hollerith, working for the U. S. Census Department, perfected punch-card accounting machines.

The machines designed and built by Hollerith were capable of receiving data from punch cards and tallying the results on counters. These devices, called electrical accounting machines (EAM), became widely used for processing data between 1890 and the advent of the first electronic computers in 1946. While unit record or EAM were more efficient than manual methods, they still did not possess the accuracy and reliability needed for modern business data processing.

## EARLY COMPUTERS

In 1944, a physicist at Harvard University devised the Automatic Sequence Control Calculator called the Mark I. This early computing device used vacuum tubes and relays to perform calculations. Shortly thereafter, a Princeton mathematician, John von Neumann, conceived the idea of a computing device which could receive and store a set of instructions. This freed the operator from having to control each step of the operation manually. As a result, in 1946 the Electronic Discrete Variable Automatic Computer (EDVAC) was built. This early device was constructed of vacuum tubes and relays and could store and follow a set of instructions (program).

This, and other machines built during the late 1940s, led to the development of modern electronic computers. The early first-generation computers proliferated during the mid 1950s. These devices were later improved by substituting transistors for vacuum tubes and relays. The transistor heralded the advent of the second-generation machines. Second-generation computers were lower in cost and more reliable than earlier machines.

In the 1960s the invention of the microtransistor and later integrated circuits (ICs) led the way toward the development of third-generation computers. These machines were smaller, more reliable, and lower in cost. During the third generation, managers began to rely heavily upon computers.

The fourth generation of computer development came in the early 1970s, with the advent of large-scale integrated circuits (LSIs).

Further reductions in the size of electronic components, and new microelectronic circuitry, led to the production of an entire central processor for a computer on a small chip of silicon. These devices made computers even smaller, lower in cost, and more readily available.

## WHAT IS A COMPUTER?

A computer is an electronic device capable of receiving input, processing data, outputting results, and following a stored program. Electronic computers are characterized by high speed, accuracy, and the ability to follow a stored set of instructions (program). Figure 8-4 diagrams the basic elements of a computer system. These include input, processing, secondary storage, and output systems. Here is a brief summary of each of these major elements.

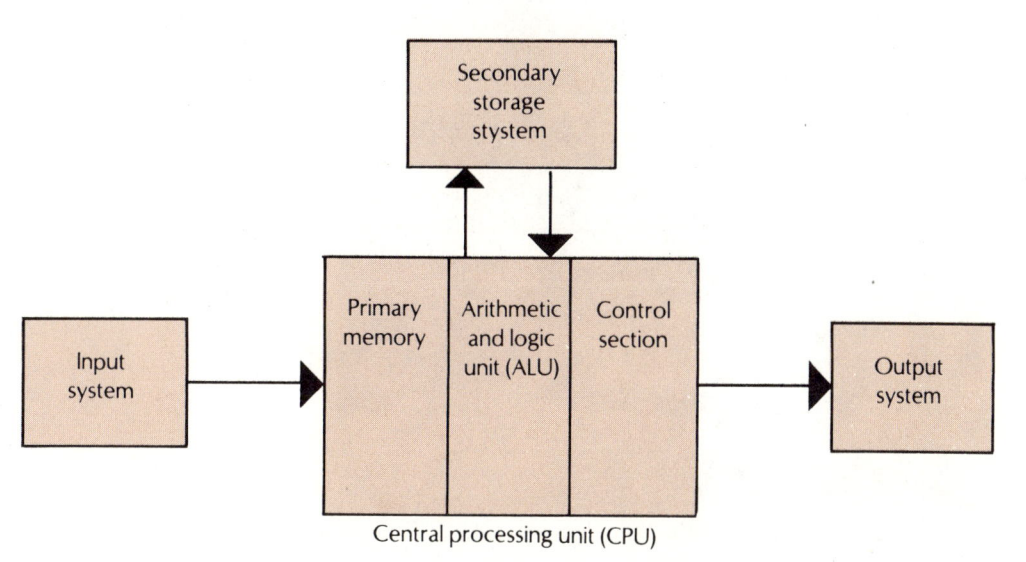

*Figure 8-4 Computer system*

### Input System

The computer's input system is designed to receive data for processing. It converts information into electrical pulses, which are sent to the central processor for manipulation. A variety of devices are used for inputting information to the central processing unit. The most common devices are the card reader, paper and magnetic tape readers, console typewriter, and, in the newer computers, desk devices. Optical character recognition (OCR) and magnetic ink character recognition (MICR) devices are also used.

### Central Processing Unit (CPU)

The heart of the computer system is the central processing unit (CPU) (fig. 8-5). The CPU performs three main functions: arithmetic and logic, control, and data storage (primary memory). These functions control and coordinate the overall operation of the entire system.

1. *Arithmetic and logic unit (ALU).* The ALU portion of the CPU performs mathe-

*Figure 8-5
Central processing
unit (CPU)*

CHAPTER EIGHT   MANAGEMENT INFORMATION SYSTEMS (MSI)

*Figure 8-6 Magnetic disk secondary storage devices*

matical calculations, comparisons, and computations.

2. *Control unit.* This portion of the CPU is designed to coordinate the operation of the CPU. It switches in and out devices and controls the timing and movement of data in the CPU.

3. *Primary memory.* The primary memory portion of the CPU stores the program and data to be processed. The primary memory unit is composed of tiny ferrite cores, or semiconductor devices, which electronically store thousands of characters or numbers in the memory for further processing.

### Secondary Storage System

In addition to the primary memory system, many computers contain an additional memory system called secondary storage. This system of magnetic tape or disk devices is capable of storing large amounts of data which can be read in and out of the CPU. It serves as a giant electronic scratch pad to hold files, records, and data which cannot be conveniently stored in the CPU's primary memory. Figure 8-6 illustrates disk storage devices which can store millions of characters of data for instantaneous retrieval.

### Output System

After data has been processed, it must be reported, or output, in a convenient form. The output system converts the electrical pulses to a readable form. Common output devices include line printers, teletypewriters, cathode ray tube displays, paper and card punches, and audio response units. These and other devices are able to print out reports, paychecks, punch cards, documents, and records or display them on the face of a cathode ray tube.

## COMPUTER SYSTEMS

Computer systems come in many sizes and configurations. They range from relatively low cost, limited capacity systems such as the minicomputer and microcomputer costing a few hundred dollars to several thousand dollars (fig. 8-7), to very large systems (fig. 8-8). A large computer system may cost millions of dollars and support dozens of input and output devices, including line printers and terminals.

Figures 8-9 and 8-10 illustrate small and medium-size computing systems. Machines such as these range in price from $10,000 to over $100,000. They are used to process a large amount of data and for preparing management reports, documents, and files.

## COMPUTER PROGRAMMING

A computer must be given a detailed set of instructions (program) before it can solve a problem. The program is written by a programmer who prepares a de-

*Figure 8-7 Minicomputer system*

CHAPTER EIGHT    MANAGEMENT INFORMATION SYSTEMS (MSI)                    183

*Figure 8-8
Large-size computer system*

tailed, step-by-step list of the operations the computer must perform. Programming costs can often exceed the cost of the computer hardware itself.

Programs are available for immediate use for handling various tasks such as payroll and management and financial reports. In other instances, the user must prepare the programs. It may require hundreds of hours of time and effort to write and correct errors (debug) in a complex program.

Programming may be done in a variety of languages. The most widely used language is COBOL (COmmon Business Oriented Language). FORTRAN (FORmula TRANslating System) is often used for programming mathematical and scientific work. Other languages, such as BASIC (Beginners All-Purpose Symbolic Instruction Code), Assembler, and Report Program Generator (RPG) are used for various special applications. At present there is no single universal computer language in use. The specific language selected for programming depends upon the characteristics of the computer used, the application or problem to be solved, and the skill of the programmer.

## EVALUATING COMPUTER SYSTEMS

Managers must evaluate the effectiveness and impact of the computer on the total organization. Computer installations may cost many thousands of dollars and affect the number and types of employees needed in the organization. Here are some of the major elements which must be considered when evaluating computer systems.

1. *Cost.* The full cost of a system must be carefully analyzed. This requires estimating the one-time cost, installation, and purchase price of new equipment.

*Figure 8-9
A small computer system*

The impact upon operating cost, labor, maintenance, and support personnel must be evaluated. It is not uncommon for an organization to install a new computer system intending to reduce costs, only to find that costs are higher than before. This may be due to the organization's increasing reliance on computers. Managers may come to expect more information and reports than before the installation of the new system.

2. *Personnel.* Computer systems may have great impact on the number and types of jobs held by employees. A system may require hiring skilled computer operators, programmers, systems analysts, and technicians. On the other hand, there may be reduced need for manual and clerical help. Personnel may require special training to prepare them to handle the new system.

3. *Indirect effects.* A new computer system may have many indirect and unforeseen effects upon the organization. For instance, how will the system affect the attitudes of customers, vendors, and employees? Will it have an adverse affect upon sales volume or labor turnover?

A system must be evaluated for its reliability and expandability. Will the new system perform reliably over a long period of time? Will the system increase the firm's ability to handle a larger work load and more customers? These questions are difficult to answer and require a careful analysis of many tangible and intangible factors.

## PROBLEMS OF SECURITY, ACCESS, AND COST CONTROL

When a new computer system is installed, management must resolve a number of issues regarding access to the computer, security, and cost control. Here are some of the issues which must be resolved before a new computer system can perform effectively.

1. *Security.* Managers must design systems which will protect valuable records and files stored in computers. An organization faces many threats to its valuable data bank. There may be internal threats from dishonest or disgruntled employees. Methods and procedures must be established to screen employees and control access to confidential and irreplaceable records. Managers must also protect their computerized data from external dangers, such as fires, floods, earthquakes, and other natural disasters.

A variety of security measures are employed to guard against these threats. Only selected employees are permitted to have access to the computer. Back-up files and duplicate hardware may be built into a system to enable an organization to rebuild its files if they are lost or destroyed.

2. *Access to the system.* A major issue which must be resolved is, who shall have access to the data and records stored in the computer. If too many people are permitted access, unauthorized use of data may occur. Valuable records may be removed, stolen, or misused. The problem of access becomes even more difficult to control where the computer supports many remote terminals in hundreds of locations in many cities.

*Figure 8-10 A medium-size computer system*

## POSTSCRIPT
# Computer May Be Wonder or Thief

### By Alexander Auerbach

A computer can do wonders for a small business — provided it isn't used to rob the company blind and the decision to buy a computer is made after some careful thought and not just to keep up with Jones Inc.

That's the gist of the advice two panelists will be giving at a conference on small business computer systems.

Jay Becker, a Los Angeles deputy district attorney and director of the National Computer Crime Data Center, said in an interview that computer-related crimes can be devastating to a small company, yet often are difficult to prosecute under existing laws.

"One problem that is affecting both large and small companies is controlling access to the data in a computer system that uses distributed data processing," which is a network of computers and terminals in different locations linked by phone lines.

"There are more chances for people to snoop at information, change their own records — such as payroll information — or to enter false information," Becker said.

The average computer crime involves $400,000, he adds, but that figure includes everything from students using unauthorized time on a university computer to the Equity Funding scandal, in which — to inflate profits — millions of phony life insurance policies were created in the company's computerized files.

Dishonest employees can use a system to order delivery of merchandise to a confederate which the computer will indicate is paid for, or even issue checks to pay nonexistent bills, he says.

A disgruntled employee who deliberately wipes out information in a computer, or who messes up a program so that the machine produces incorrect data, may escape with little more than a slap on the wrist

Reprinted from *Los Angeles Times,* 13 November 1979.

Elaborate systems of codes, user numbers, and passwords are employed to limit the access to only selected users. Managers must decide who will be given user numbers and allowed access to computer facilities.

3. *Cost control.* Computer time can be very expensive. A system must be established to manage and control data processing costs and computer usage. If employees are allowed unlimited access to the system, costs may rise because of

CHAPTER EIGHT    MANAGEMENT INFORMATION SYSTEMS (MSI)

if caught, Becker says.

"California has a new statute which creates the category of 'felony malicious mischief,' but in some states that kind of activity can only be prosecuted as a misdemeanor (meaning milder penalties) even if it causes $1 million in damages," he adds.

Prosecutors also have trouble with employees who steal company computer time (for their own projects), which in larger computer systems is valued at many dollars per second. "The business community itself has not sufficiently addressed the problem of employees who steal time, and there are wide variations in what is considered acceptable," he says.

"Some firms think of it in the same category as taking pencils home from the office. But very few people who take a pencil are likely to steal a typewriter, yet the potential of a person who steals one hour of computer time to then steal one hundred is very real."

Few judges understand computer systems, Becker says, and prosecutions for theft of computer time are difficult. Florida is the only state with a law specifically making it a crime. A bill now before Congress—S 1776—would make this and other computer crimes federal offenses.

Most small companies don't think much about security problems when considering the purchase of a computer, said Ira Gottfried, president of Gottfried Consultants Inc., Los Angeles. "They may worry about payroll records, and perhaps a list of clients, but they just don't realize that a fire could put them out of business by wiping out the computer and its records."

Security is just one item that should be on the shopping list of a small business owner thinking about a computer, says Gottfried, whose management consulting firm does much of its work in helping firms design and select computer systems.

The first step, however, is not to go shopping for a computer, but to analyze current operations. "Every business has some kind of system to handle the flow of paper work. It may be manual or computer, but it's the flow of information that's important. Break the business down into its parts, by function or by organization, and look at what information comes into each part, what is done with it, and what the needed output is—checks, reports, shipping orders, whatever.

"Figure out the volume of work that must be handled, and the costs. Then, when you know what's going on and what it costs, talk to a computer salesman."

As with other purchases, he says, managers looking at computers should do some comparison shopping by talking to salesmen for several different machines.

"Pick a company that is going to be around in a few years, and remember that software (programming) can be more expensive in the long run than the hardware itself," he warns.

uncontrolled usage. Some firms use an authorization system which allows only those jobs which have approval and whose cost will be charged to specific departments to be run on the computer.

4. *Distributive data processing.* Another major issue is whether the firm wishes to use a centralized or decentralized data processing system. Is it better to buy one large computer and make it available throughout the organization from a

*"You certainly come well-recommended. Did they want to get you off their hands?"*

Reprinted from *American Machinist,* February 1977.

single point? This may mean that one large system can be purchased and operated by carefully screened personnel. However, this could make access difficult and delay the return of valuable management information.

An alternative to centralization is distributive data processing. In this approach, many small computers are distributed throughout the organization and linked by a communications network. This brings computer power closer to the managers and users. However, it raises problems of coordination and control. Distributed data processing systems are becoming widely used in organizations because they reduce the overhead associated with large central systems.

## SUMMARY

A variety of pressures on organizations have brought about the greater use of computers. The pressures include growing volume of transactions, need for more timely information and greater accuracy, rising costs, and social and consumer pressures.

There has been a steady increase in the number of large and small computers in use. The computer is used in management for decision making, marketing, per-

CHAPTER EIGHT    MANAGEMENT INFORMATION SYSTEMS (MSI)

sonnel management, finance, and manufacturing.

Among the advantages of computers are its ability to process data at high speed and accuracy, with low cost for large volumes of data. The computer is also highly reliable.

Management information systems (MIS) include a data bank and means of inputting, updating and outputting information. The advantages of MIS include availability of on-line information and faster preparation of reports.

Computers have moved through four generations of development, beginning with early machines using vacuum tubes and relays to modern computers using large-scale integrated circuits (LSIs). Modern computers are programmed in a variety of languages.

## REVIEW QUESTIONS

1. Define the term *system*.
2. How do real-time systems differ from batch processing systems?
3. How does computer hardware differ from computer software?
4. Describe four specific applications for the computer in management.
5. List four major characteristics of the computer.
6. Describe how data is input and output from information systems using terminals.
7. Briefly trace the development of data processing through its three major eras.
8. Explain how the stored program is used.
9. Draw a diagram of the computer system, label each part, and give an example of the devices associated with each part.
10. Describe some of the computer languages in use. How do they differ?
11. List several factors which managers should consider when evaluating a new computer system.
12. What efforts can be made to protect computer files?

## KEY TERMS

System    170
Real-time system    170
Timesharing    171
Program    171
Computer hardware    171
Computer software    171
Data bank    175

On-line access    176
Input system    180
Output system    181
Secondary storage system    181
Central processing unit (CPU)    180
Distributive data processing    187

# Case Incident

Chief Glenn Davidson heads a large municipal police force of 820 officers. Within the police force there is a central criminal records division which contains files of data on criminal activity within the community. This master file includes records of auto thefts, stolen goods, and the names and descriptions of known criminal violators. It is also tied to the federal National Crime Information Center (NCIC).

In an attempt to make this information more useful and practical to the on-the-beat officer, Chief Davidson has appointed a study team to analyze the record retrieval and data base of the entire police department. After considerable study, this team has recommended that more computer terminals be installed in the police department's various substations. In this way, the information can be relayed to the field much more efficiently. The direct access to the data base is made through terminals by keying in the complete name, Social Security number, or other identifying information on the suspect. The computer is programmed to use this key as a means of going through an extensive file search. It then displays the results of the search of the data base, giving all pertinent information on the suspect.

While the study team has indicated the overwhelming need for more terminals within the department, it has also severely criticized police lieutenants who have allowed the system to be abused. Only recently several people within the department obtained unauthorized access to the data and leaked critical information concerning suspects to the press, which nearly resulted in a mistrial. (Unauthorized release of the data base could further subject department individuals to legal liability.) In fact, several members of the city council have already put pressure on the department to ensure that such situations do not occur in the future.

## PROBLEMS

1. What security problems does a proliferation of terminals pose for the police department?
2. What means should be used to control access to the information on the system?
3. What advantages does an on-line record-keeping system have for the police department?

PART THREE

# The Organizing Function

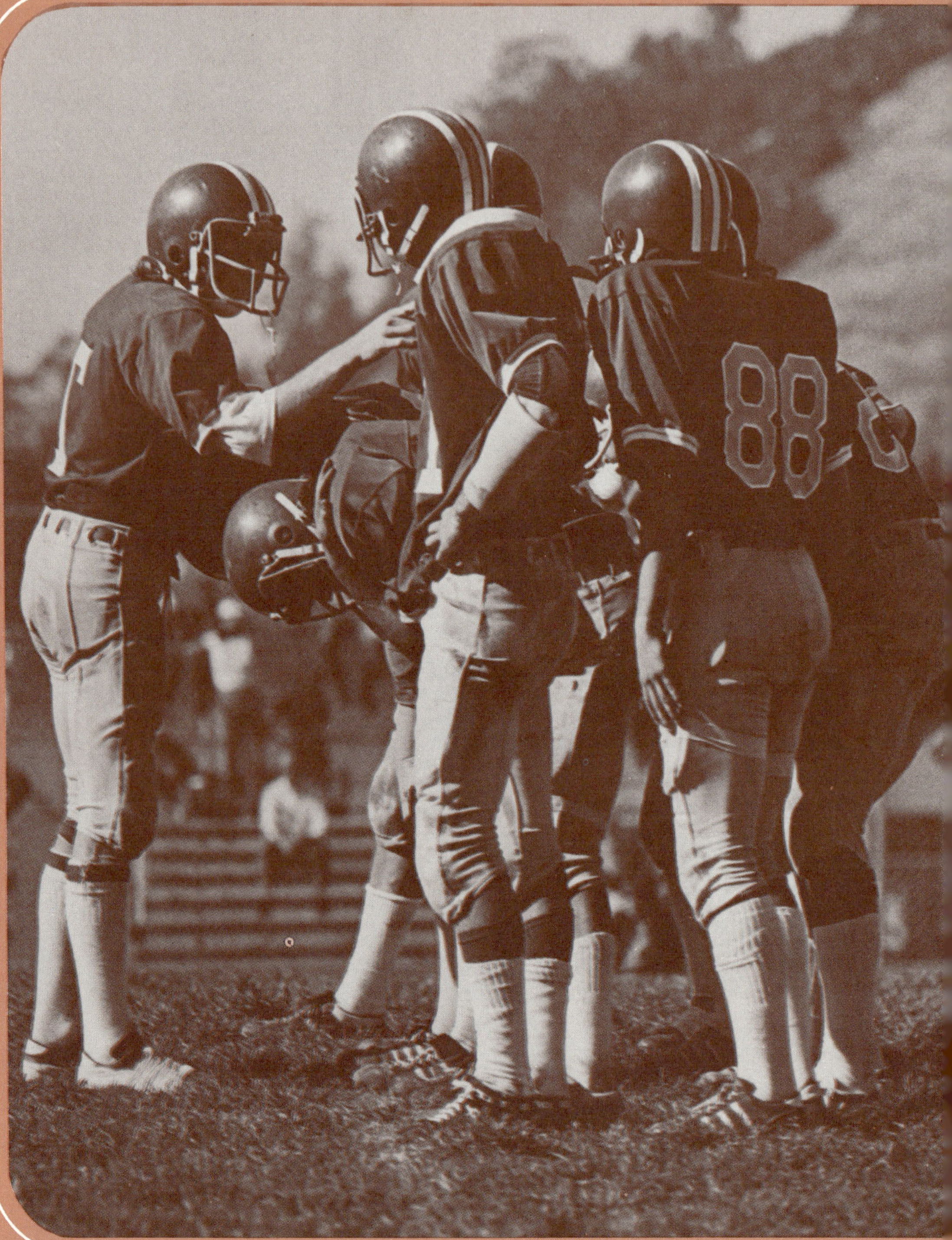

# 9
# Fundamental Organizational Principles

**LEARNING OBJECTIVES**

After studying this chapter, you should be able to:
1. Describe the organizing process.
2. Define key terms including *authority, responsibility,* and *accountability*.
3. List the basic steps in organizing.
4. Explain the concept of the division of labor.
5. Contrast the difference between accountability and responsibility.
6. Explain the unity of command principle and how it relates to organizational structure.
7. Explain the process of departmentalizing.
8. List several bases upon which the organization may structure departments.
9. List some sources of authority and how it is delegated.
10. Contrast the difference between *flat* and *tall* organizations.

This chapter describes the basic theory of organizational structure and departmentalization. It considers the methods and processes by which managers assess the organization's work tasks and activities and divide them into departments or areas. Lines of authority, responsibility, and accountability and documenting organizational structure are discussed. Chapter 10 considers the applied aspects of organizational structure.

## WHAT IS ORGANIZING?

Organizing is the process by which an organization is formally structured into departments or working units, based upon lines of authority or tasks to be accomplished. This should be done by design. It is one of the major responsibilities of the manager, who is responsible for assessing tasks and functions, and developing a practical organization with lines of responsibility defined and documented.

Before an organization can move toward its goals, it must be structured in a way which will enable it to function efficiently. A small enterprise, such as a sole proprietorship with only a couple of employees, needs relatively little organization and structure. The owner, acting as manager, considers tasks to be done and delegates jobs to subordinates. There is little need to formalize the process, document relationships, or prepare organizational charts.

In a large organization which employs hundreds or even thousands of people, workers must be grouped by functions, duties, product lines, or other criteria. They must know their assignments and to whom they are responsible. Their work must be arranged in a manner which establishes authority and responsibility and eliminates conflicts regarding whose directive they must follow.

## ORGANIZING EXISTING OR NEW STRUCTURES

An existing organization may already have a structure with which management must deal. Lines of authority, responsibility, manager-subordinate relationships, and departments are already established. An existing organization presents managers with many constraints, including personnel commitments, union contracts, marketing agreements, and other already defined terms.

A new organization has fewer constraints. But there may be less data and experience to draw upon when making judgments. In structuring a new organization, the manager must define each work task, establish a working relationship between managers and subordinates, departmentalize the work load, then document the structure. Both new and existing organizations require analysis of what is to be done, when, where, how, and by whom. Once structured, the plan must be communicated by the manager to all concerned.

CHAPTER NINE   FUNDAMENTAL ORGANIZATIONAL PRINCIPLES        195

> **REAL WORLD**
> # The Right Mood
>
> For a long time government has been telling big business what to do and how to do it. Now the tables have turned, and government is turning to business people for advice. Mayor George V. Voinovich of Cleveland, Ohio, realized that the city was in the red and sinking fast. More government bureaucracy was not the answer.
>
> Voinovich put together a task force of business people, including E. Mandell De Windt of Eaton Corporation, and executives from Sohio, Republic Steel, and Reliance Electric, all of whom donated their time and resources to the city. This task force examined the operation of all the city's departments and came up with a series of recommendations.
>
> Private industry personnel, such as data processing, purchasing, accounting, and personnel managers, are helping Cleveland out of a hole. Perhaps other cities, or even the federal government, can benefit from this approach.
>
> Adapted from *Fortune*, 11 February 1980, p. 32.

## KEY TERMS

Listed below are key terms which relate to organizational structure. After defining these terms, we shall consider the steps in organizing and various methods of departmentalizing functions.

— *Formal organization*. The formal organization is the agreed upon, stated, or documented structure of an organization. It shows the established, officially recognized relationships between managers and subordinates. The formal organization follows defined rules which are communicated by organizational charts, memos, policy manuals, and position descriptions. In effect, it is the organizational blueprint of the company.

— *Informal organization*. The informal organization is the undocumented structure in an organization which may be separate and apart from the formal organization. Informal organizations are not formally recognized. Nevertheless, they have influence on the organization. Informal organizations operate via the *grapevine* and are composed of key individuals who exercise power. These undocumented managers are often looked to by subordinates for help, advice, and information.

— *Authority*. Authority is the delegated right to plan, direct, or control the efforts of others. It is the right to perform a task or make a judgment or decision. It may involve the discretionary power to do or not to do something.

— *Responsibility.* Responsibility is an accepted obligation to perform the tasks related to an assignment.

— *Accountability.* A person who is accountable must answer to a superior for the results of his or her actions. The subordinate bears the consequences if the job is not done correctly. Accountability cannot be delegated.

— *Department.* A department is a division, section, or portion of a larger entity. Departments are major administrative sections of organizations which are usually headed by managers. *Departmentalizing* is the task of dividing a large group of activities or functions into small units, called *departments.* (See figure 9-1.) A department is an area or territory over which a manager has authority.

— *Span of control.* Span of control refers to the number of individuals reporting to one manager. It is the number of people who are directly responsible to a manager and under the manager's direction. For example, the manager in figure 9-2 has three employees who answer directly to him, and therefore a span of control of three. The wider the span of control, the more individuals who report to a manager. A narrow span of control means few subordinates answer to one manager.

— *Chain of command.* The chain of command is the linking of authority in an organization. It is the formal relationship between individuals and provides a channel for the flow of authority and responsibility. (fig. 9-3). The chain of command provides the pathways by which information, accountability, and authority are communicated between managers, and between managers and subordinates, in an unbroken line. This is sometimes known as the scalar principle.

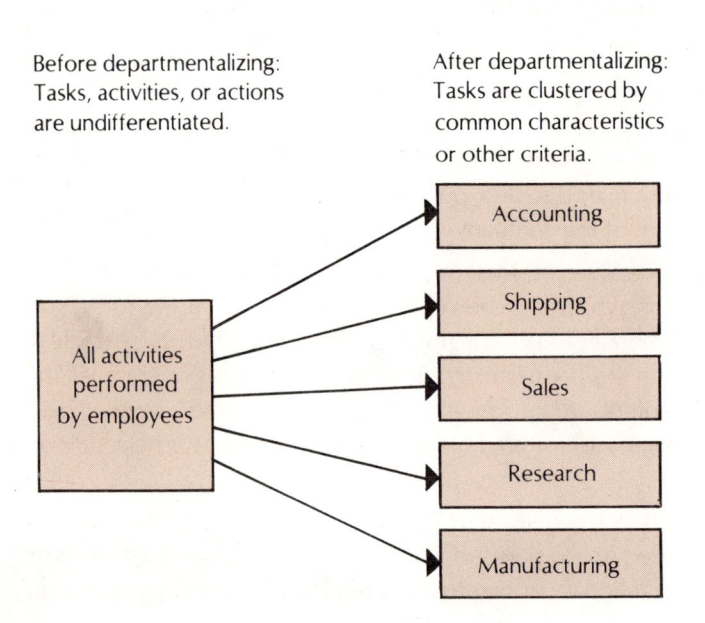

Before departmentalizing: Tasks, activities, or actions are undifferentiated.

After departmentalizing: Tasks are clustered by common characteristics or other criteria.

*Figure 9-1 Organizational structure before and after departmentalizing*

All activities performed by employees → Accounting, Shipping, Sales, Research, Manufacturing

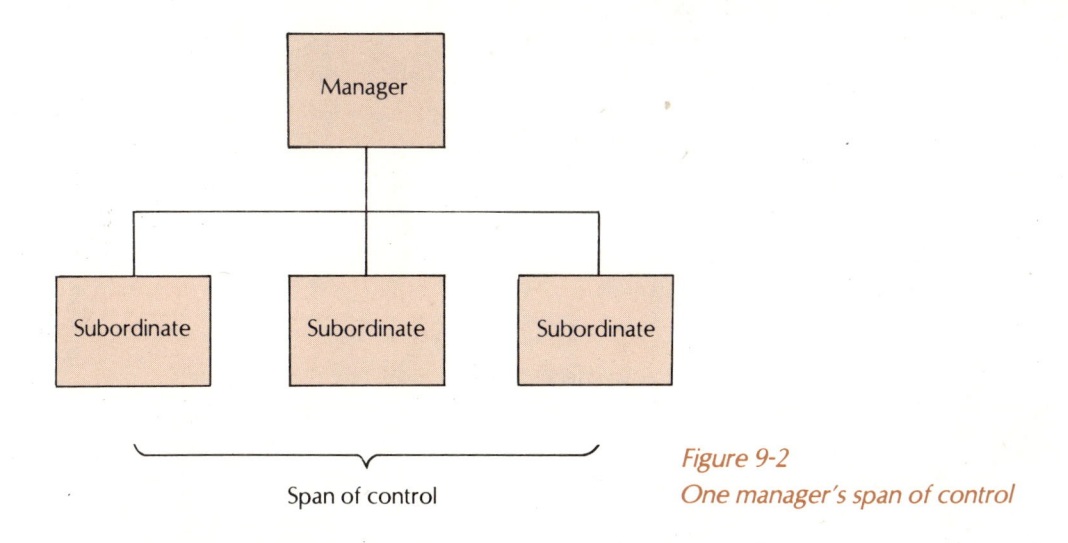

CHAPTER NINE    FUNDAMENTAL ORGANIZATIONAL PRINCIPLES    197

*Figure 9-2*
*One manager's span of control*

## BASIC PRINCIPLES OF ORGANIZING

In discussing the fundamentals of organizing, we must consider the steps in organizing and the concepts of division of labor, authority and delegation, accountability and responsibility, organizational shape, levels of management, unity of command, staff function, and departmentalizing.

### Steps in Organizing

Organizing is the process by which management analyzes its goals and objectives, then designs and builds a means to reach that end. Figure 9-4 illustrates the steps which are generally followed in structuring a new organization. Obviously, an existing organization requires an approach which begins with the present structure and existing situation and builds from there. Let us review these steps in detail.

1. *Define goals and objectives.* The first phase in building an organization involves identifying the goals and end results desired by management. End results vary from organization to organization. A charitable group seeking to raise money to build and operate a new hospital may have a different organizational structure than a profit-making firm, such as a manufacturer of automobile tires.

2. *Develop a plan or vehicle to reach the specified ends.* This step involves preparation of a plan of action and the allocation of resources to reach that end. Limits are established on the time, money, and human resources available for the operation of the organization.

3. *Identify specific tasks and skills needed.* Management defines specific job skills and abilities needed by the organization's personnel. For example, an esti-

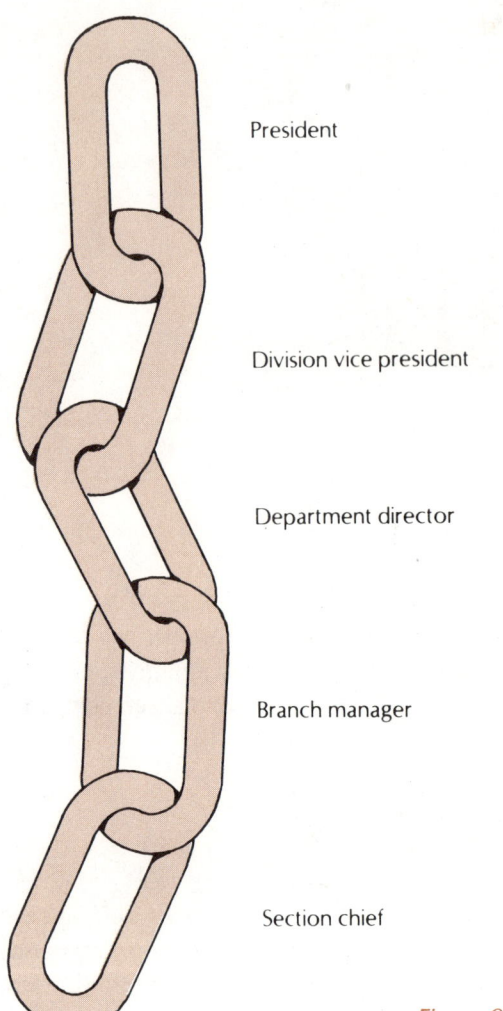

*Figure 9-3   Chain of command*

mate is made of the number and type of accounting, marketing, clerical, and other workers needed to provide the required output.

4. *Departmentalize.* In this phase, the manager groups similar activities into departments or areas. Activities may be grouped into departments on a variety of bases, including common functions, activities associated with a given product, or activities carried on in a given geographic area. Once the number and type of personnel for each department is specified, the management and supervision requirements are defined.

As a result of this step, for example, all accounting functions in a company may be assigned to one department and the responsibility to manage it given to a manager.

CHAPTER NINE   FUNDAMENTAL ORGANIZATIONAL PRINCIPLES                                199

5. *Formalize and document the structure.* Formal relationships between managers and subordinates are developed and documented. Organizational charts and manuals are prepared to record and communicate the formal structure to others. This results in a clear-cut statement of responsibility, authority, and lines of communication. Figure 9-5 illustrates an organizational chart for a large company, showing the lines of authority and the formalized relationships between managers and subordinates.

6. *Select staff.* The last step in organizing is the selection of personnel to staff each position. Staffing is an organizing function and involves finding the right number and type of people to fill each management and subordinate position. Some management authorities prefer to list staffing as a function separate from organizing.

*Figure 9-4   Steps in structuring a new organization*

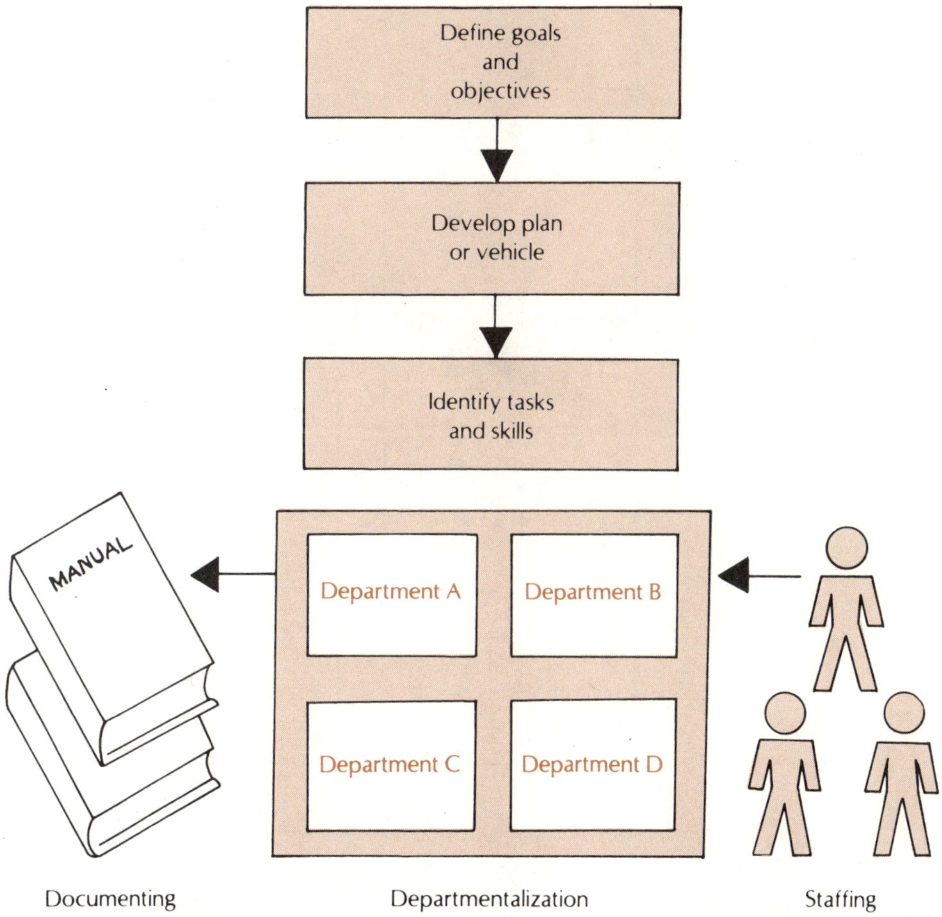

Figure 9-5  Documenting an organization

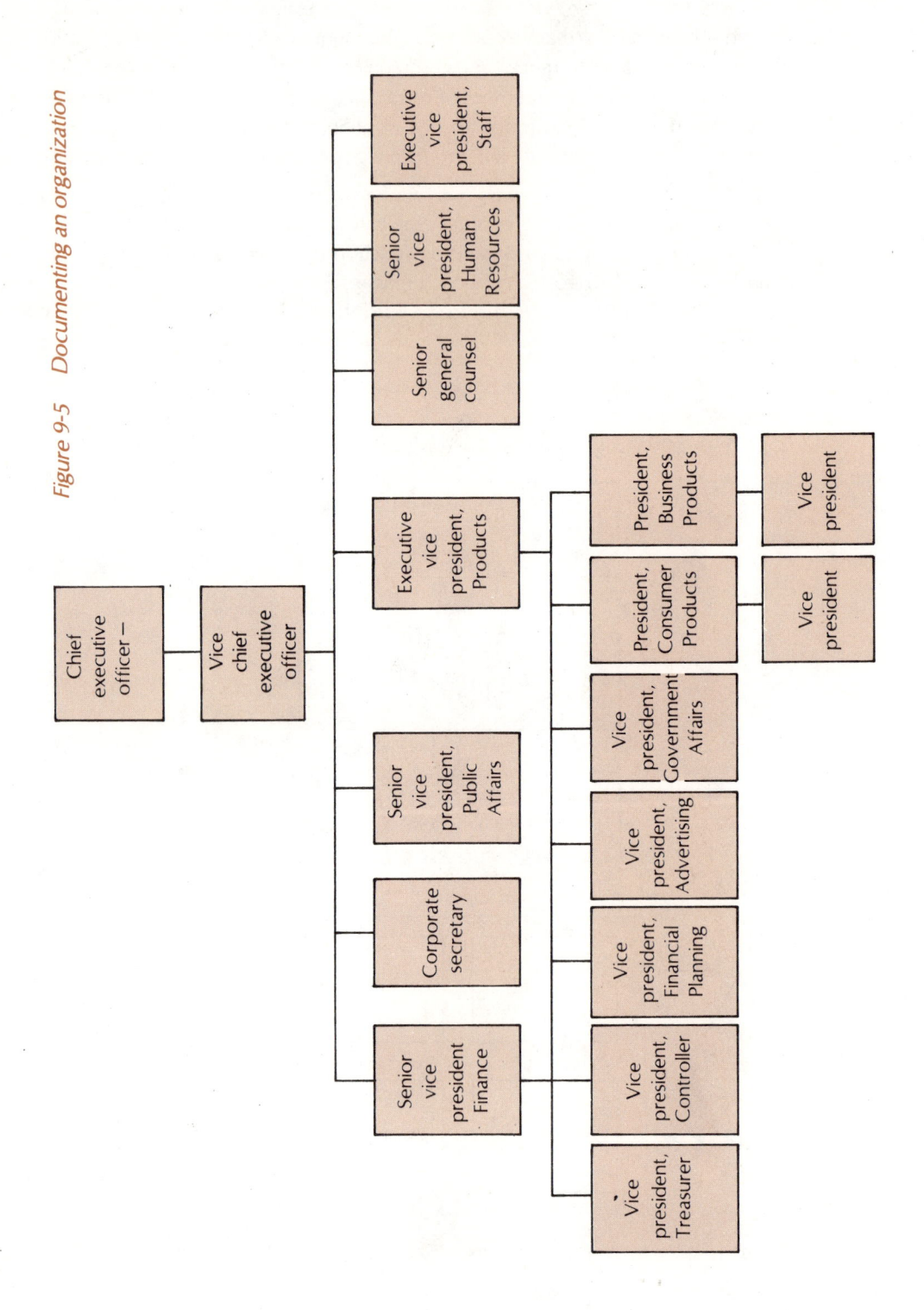

- Chief executive officer
  - Vice chief executive officer
    - Senior vice president, Finance
      - Vice president, Treasurer
      - Vice president, Controller
      - Vice president, Financial Planning
    - Corporate secretary
    - Senior vice president, Public Affairs
      - Vice president, Advertising
      - Vice president, Government Affairs
    - Executive vice president, Products
      - President, Consumer Products
        - Vice president
      - President, Business Products
        - Vice president
    - Senior general counsel
    - Senior vice president, Human Resources
    - Executive vice president, Staff

## Division of Labor

In organizing departments, the manager attempts to assign the optimum number of individuals to each department. He or she staffs each unit with the most efficient and productive number of people. Overstaffing costs money and raises overhead. Understaffing slows output and reduces capacity.

If too few workers are assigned to a task, it takes longer to complete and may not be done as well. The nature of some jobs requires two or more people if the jobs are to be done properly. For example, it requires two people, one at each end, to test a telephone line.

On the other hand, if too many people are assigned to a job, they may get in each others' way, slowing down output. There is no simple formula for allocating the optimum number of people to a job. It requires an understanding of output, productivity, and worker performance.

*Division of labor* involves breaking down large, complex tasks into smaller parcels and assigning these to various individuals. Figure 9-6 illustrates a division of labor. The complex job requires three workers to jointly assemble, finish, and test each unit produced. Under the division of labor and reassignment of workers, the complex task is broken down into three separate and distinct jobs, each of which is assigned to a different person, who becomes expert at the task.

The benefit from this reassignment may not be obvious until one looks at the results. Figure 9-7 illustrates the benefits derived from a division of labor.

For example, suppose a task, such as the installation of an office telephone system, can be completed in 1½ days if three people are assigned to work together. In all, there is a total labor requirement of 4½ days. However, if only one

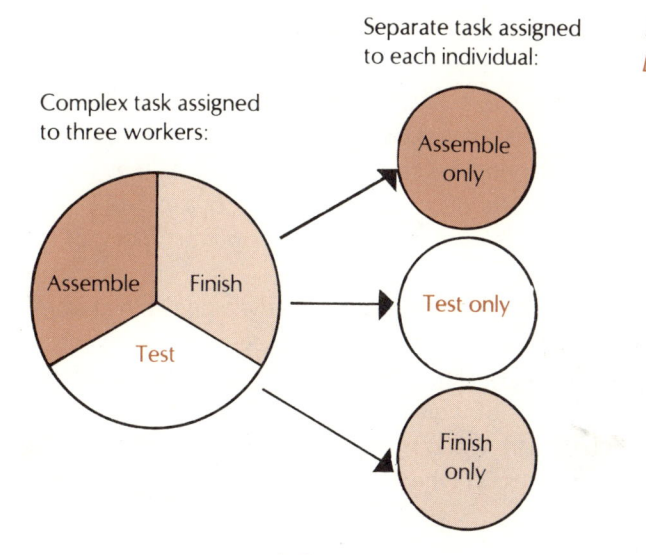

*Figure 9-6*
*Division of labor*

Required days to complete task

| Number assigned | Lapsed days | Total days |
|---|---|---|
| 1 | 6 | 6 |
| 2 | 2.5 | 5 |
| 3 | 1.5 | 4.5 |
| 4 | 1.25 | 5 |
| 5 | 1.2 | 6 |
| 6 | 1.1 | 6.6 |

Figure 9-7
Division of labor

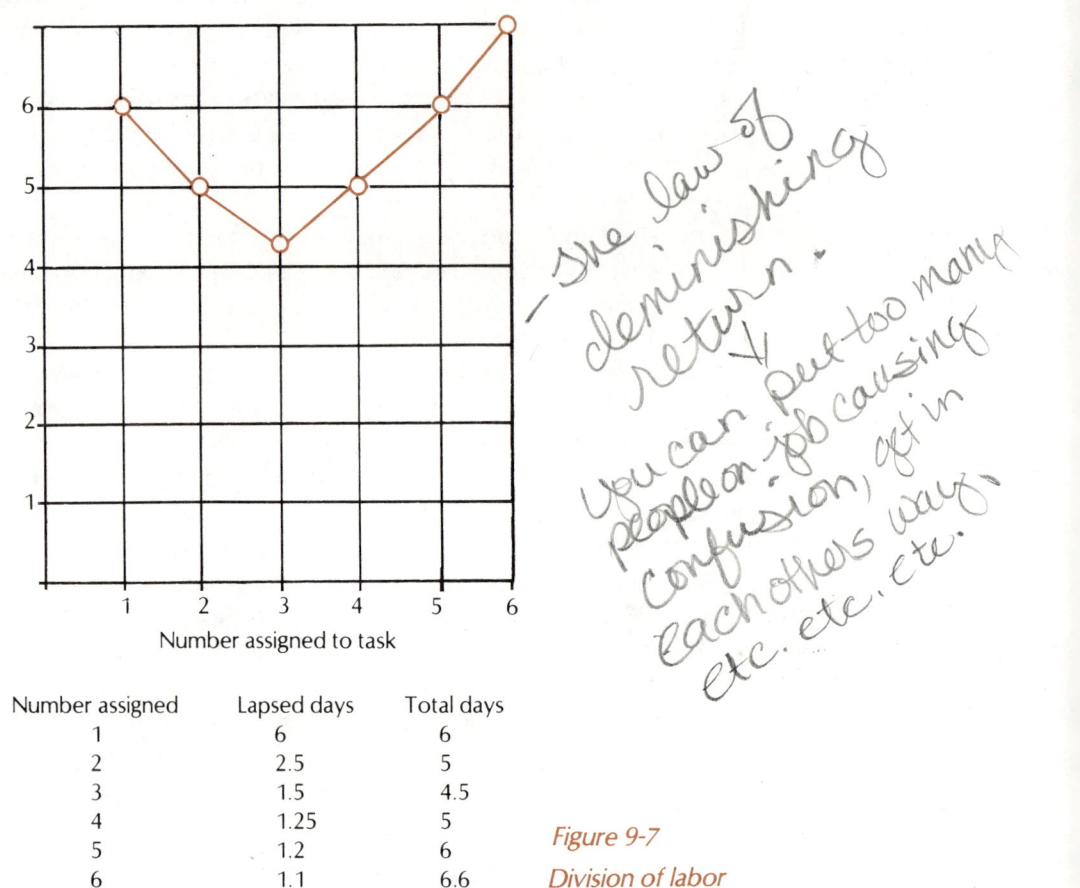

person were assigned to the entire job, it could take 6 full days of labor. This is because of the inefficiency of one person working alone, who cannot benefit from the assistance of others. But if six people were assigned to the task, they would become so inefficient that it would require 1 1/10 days apiece, or a total of 6 6/10 days of labor, to complete. It can be seen that there is an optimum point of returns, in this case three employees.

Henry Ford understood this principle and used it to advantage at the turn of the century. Ford implemented an assembly line to produce automobiles which used specialization and the division of labor. Prior to the assembly line, automobiles were manufactured by groups of workers who jointly shared all aspects of the assembly job. Under Ford's plan, workers were each assigned a specific task on the line. One would mount tires on wheels, another tightened lug nuts, and so on.

The result was an immediate reduction in total labor costs per unit manufactured. Other benefits included the need for less skilled, more easily trained workers. Single individuals became more expendable, since each job required only a limited amount of skill and knowledge.

## Authority and Delegation

Authority is the delegated right to plan, direct, or control others to achieve organization objectives. One of the major tasks of management is to define lines of authority in an organization and provide ways by which it can be delegated. Authority is vested in the manager by the upper echelons of the organization. The manager, in turn, may delegate authority to others, but cannot delegate her responsibility for their acts. A manager always remains responsible for subordinates. By accepting a position, a subordinate acknowledges the authority given him by the manager.

Authority may come from many sources. It may come from the ownership of property, money, or possession of knowledge. It may also be delegated to another. The shareholders of a corporation have authority or control by virtue of their ownership of property. They can exercise this power directly or delegate it

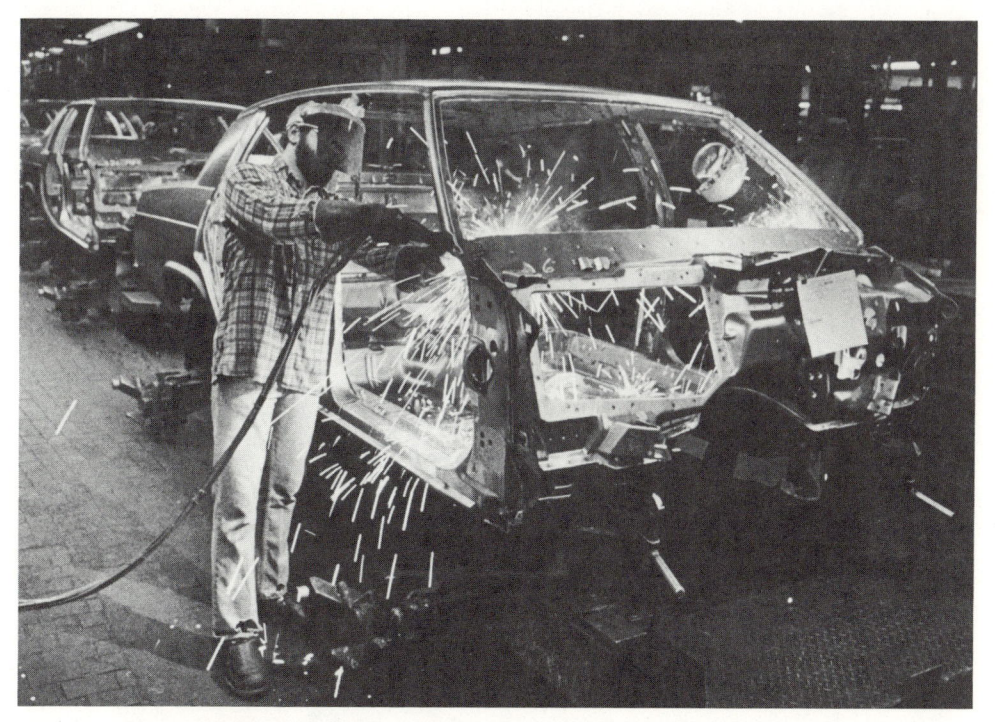

The automobile assembly line is a good example of how the division of labor can dramatically cut costs and increase output.

> **REAL WORLD**
>
> # Producers in Revolt
>
> Organizational structure problems are as prevalent in the television industry as in government and private business. In 1979 not one of the twenty new television shows introduced made the top ten list. William Froung, chairman of the Caucus for Producers, Writers, and Directors, has some ideas on the reasons for this. He thinks the problems are structural. Artistic control is taken from the hands of the people who actually create the product.
>
> In the old days each television network maintained a single department that had full control over its programming. This was headed by experienced executives. Under the present system, there is a maze of departments. For instance, there are departments for comedy, drama, miniseries, daytime, movies, children's shows, and so on. These departments are staffed by layers of executives in a top heavy bureaucracy. This reduces the ability of the producer and writer to exercise creative influence. Froung is horrified when five television executives file into a room for a meeting, when only one of them has any authority but all of them have something to say.
>
> Adapted from *Newsweek*, 10 December 1979.

to others. This is done when shareholders delegate authority by use of proxy votes. They are free to profit from their investment without the need to exercise direct control.

## Accountability and Responsibility

Accountability is the state of being answerable to another and is created as a result of the manager-subordinate relationship. When a subordinate is assigned a task, he becomes answerable or accountable to the manager for his actions. The manager can delegate authority as she chooses. The subordinate, in turn, is free to redelegate authority to successively lower levels, and this is the essence of effective delegation.

Authority flows downward in the organization while accountability flows upward. (See figure 9-8.) Managers rely upon delegating authority to free themselves for more important activities. But managers must bear the full responsibility for their subordinates and take the blame for faulty decisions.

CHAPTER NINE   FUNDAMENTAL ORGANIZATIONAL PRINCIPLES                                205

*Figure 9-8   Authority and accountability*

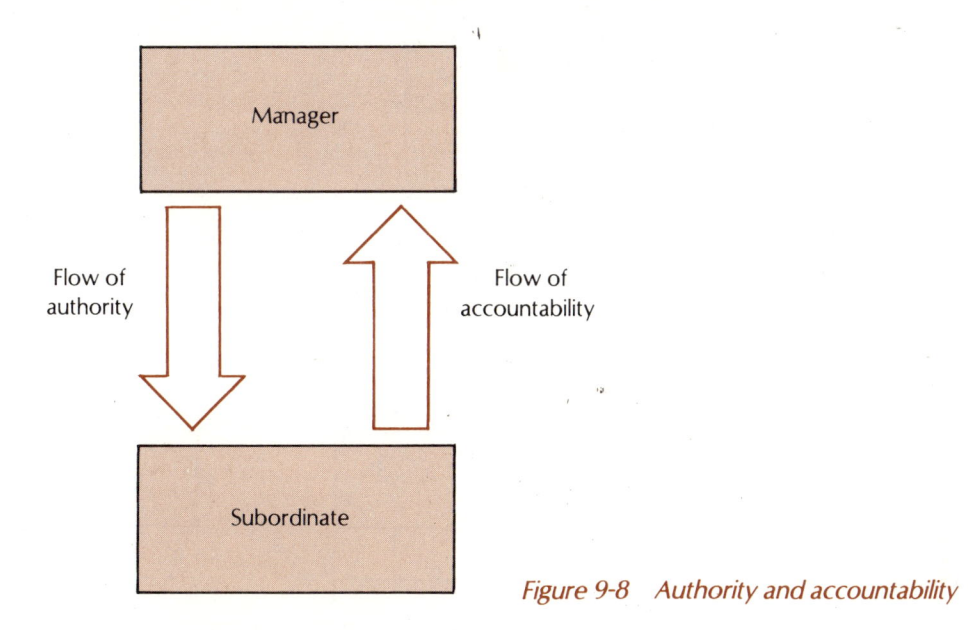

## Organizational Shape

*Span of control,* the number of individuals reporting directly to one manager, affects the *shape* of an organization. Organizations are described as being *flat* or *tall* in design.

Figure 9-9 illustrates a *flat* organization. In this example, there are many subordinates reporting directly to one manager. This results in an organizational chart with a wide, low profile.

A *tall* organization is built on a narrow span of control. In this type of organizational structure, a few subordinates report to each manager. (See figure 9-10.) This results in an organizational chart with a tall, narrow base.

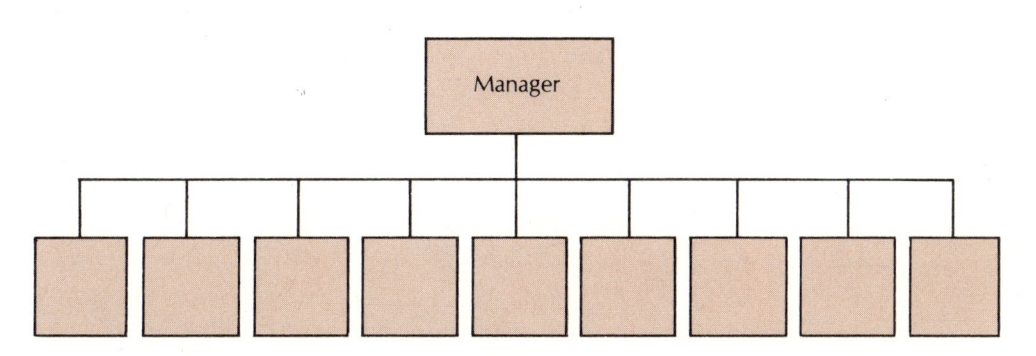

*Figure 9-9   Flat organization*

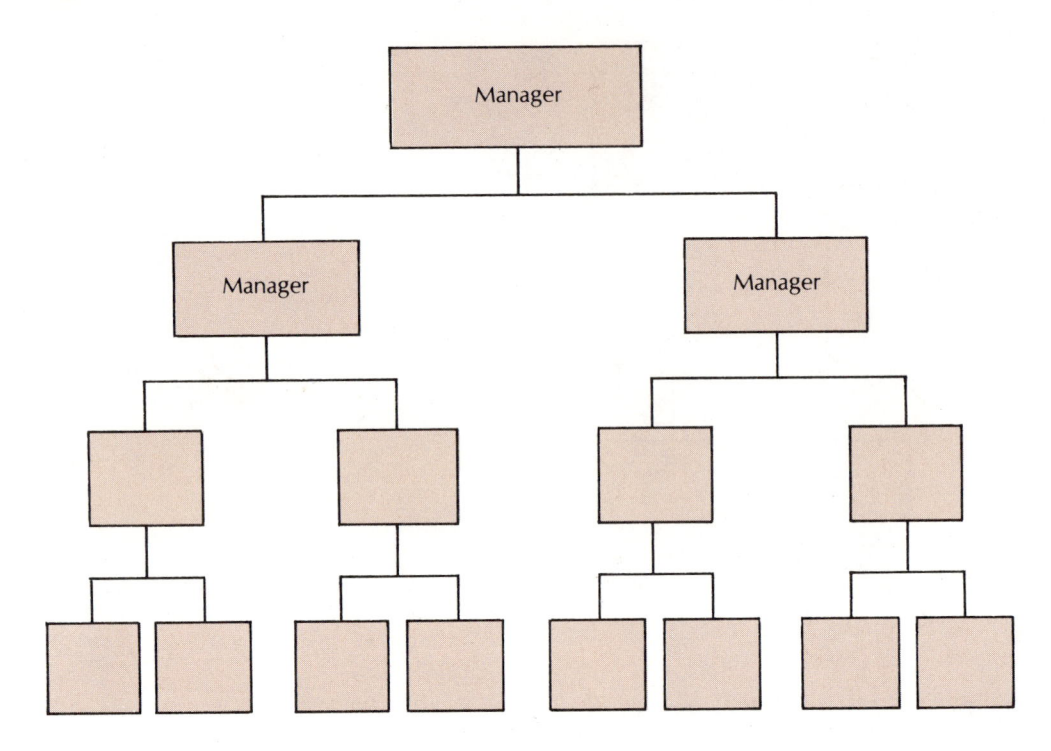

*Figure 9-10    Tall organization*

## Levels of Management

Each time a manager is interposed between another manager and a subordinate, a level of management is created. The number of levels of management is a function of the structure of the organization. Flat organizations have many subordinates reporting to one manager, resulting in few levels of management. Tall organizations have many levels of management.

There is no ideal number of subordinates who must answer to one manager. The subject has been studied and written upon extensively. Some management authorities believe the optimum number of subordinates reporting to one manager should be between six and fifteen. Others consider three to nine or ten to thirty best. While there is no consensus, most organizations have between one and twenty four.

The argument for a narrow span of control is that it improves the flow of directives in the organization, since a manager need interact with only a few subordinates. However, this creates many levels of management and hence increases overhead and management costs.

On the other hand, a flat organization is more economical since fewer managers are needed. However, subordinates may find it difficult to share the manager's time, since they must compete with many others for attention.

A key factor in determining how many subordinates should report to one manager is the type of job to be performed and the skill and ability of the subordinates. Jobs which are not complex and require little supervision can be managed best with a flat organization. Organizations with subordinates who are skilled and trained also require less supervision. Conversely, tasks which require close supervision and which involve employees who lack skill and training require a tall structure to provide adequate management.

## Unity of Command   "one Boss"

A basic principle of organization structure is that a subordinate should not report to more than one manager at a time. There must be a unity of command. There are many reasons for this simple principle. With only one manager to report to, there is little doubt in the subordinate's mind about whose direction to follow. The subordinate can ignore conflicting demands from other managers, since the lines of responsibility are clear-cut and flow from only one individual.

Figure 9-11 illustrates the differences between unity of command and a divided command. In figure 9-11(a), there is a divided command; the subordinate is subject to the direction of two managers. In figure 9-11(b) the subordinate is responsible to only one manager.

There is, however, a major weakness in the principle of unity of command. The subordinate must turn to one manager for all guidance, direction, and decision making. While this is clear-cut, it is not always practical, particularly where the subordinate's job encompasses many areas of expertise.

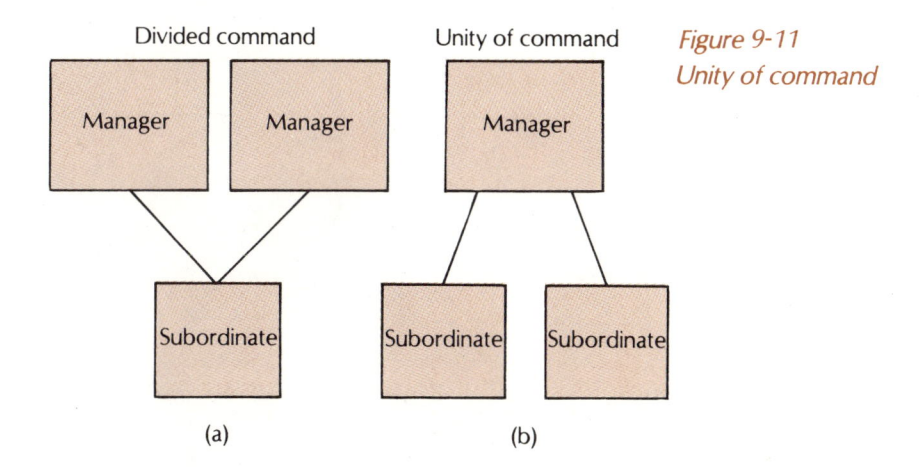

*Figure 9-11*
*Unity of command*

## Staff Function

Figure 9-12 illustrates a means of resolving the dilemma between a single manager and the resources of several managers. This figure shows two relationships, line and staff. There is a single line of authority between each manager and subordinate. This arrangement allows the marketing manager to turn to the promotion and advertising staff for consultation. Thus, the principle of unity of command is met. The staff managers give guidance, support, and assistance to the subordinate. However, they do not directly supervise others or displace the manager's line authority.

A broken line is usually drawn on the organizational chart to show a staff relationship, while a solid line is drawn to denote a direct line authority. With this arrangement, one subordinate may look to two or more staff managers for help and guidance without confusing the lines of authority.

Most large business organizations use the line and staff form of organization. Chapter 10 discusses this and other forms of organization in more detail.

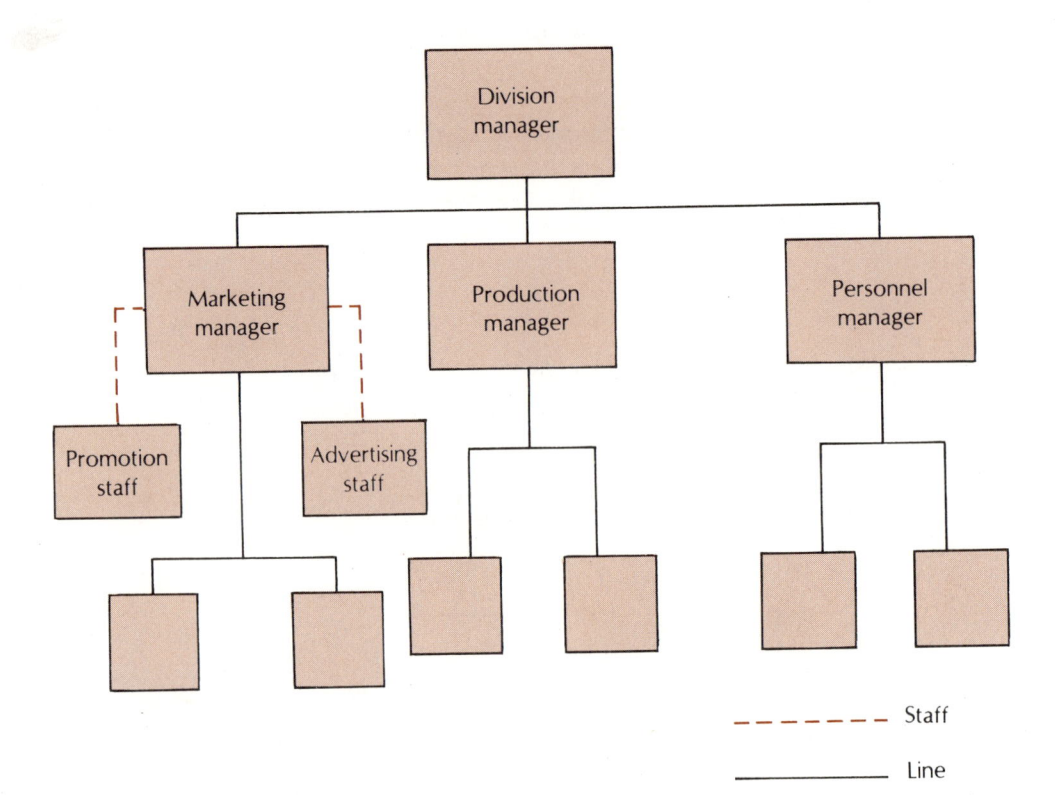

*Figure 9-12 Support staff function*

- - - - - - Staff

_____ Line

CHAPTER NINE   FUNDAMENTAL ORGANIZATIONAL PRINCIPLES                209

Newspapers usually are flat organizations. Many reporters will report back to the same editor.

## Departmentalizing

*Departmentalizing,* sometimes called *functionalizing,* is the task of analyzing, categorizing, and combining functions into departments or clusters. Each area or department is assigned one or more managers. Without departmentalizing, large organizations would be little more than large collections of people and uncoordinated activities which would be difficult to direct and manage.

Departmentalizing improves organization efficiency, communication, and responsiveness. There are many reasons that organizations are departmentalized. Similar jobs can be performed in one area and under one supervisor. Those tasks requiring special skills can be clustered into a single specialized department. Special hiring, training, and supervision policies can be implemented where the staff is organized into departments.

There are a variety of approaches to departmentalizing an organization. One approach is simply to analyze the activities to be performed, then categorize them into departments. All like tasks are grouped together. For example, all accounting functions from all parts of the organization may be combined into an accounting department. This department handles cost accounting, payroll, tax accounting, and so on.

Another approach is to analyze the makeup and characteristics of the personnel within the organization and to structure departments based upon their skills, knowledge, or experience.

The following discussion describes some of the most common criteria for organizing departments. Many considerations enter into the decision, including

*"I thought the policy around here was not to make any waves."*

Reprinted from *American Machinist,* January 1978.

the skill of employees, type of product, experience of managers, and transportation and communication costs.

1. *Function.* Functional job organization is the most common form of departmentalization. In this form of structure (fig. 9-13), jobs are categorized and departments formed based upon function, or the nature of work performed. Functional organization clusters like jobs into a common department.

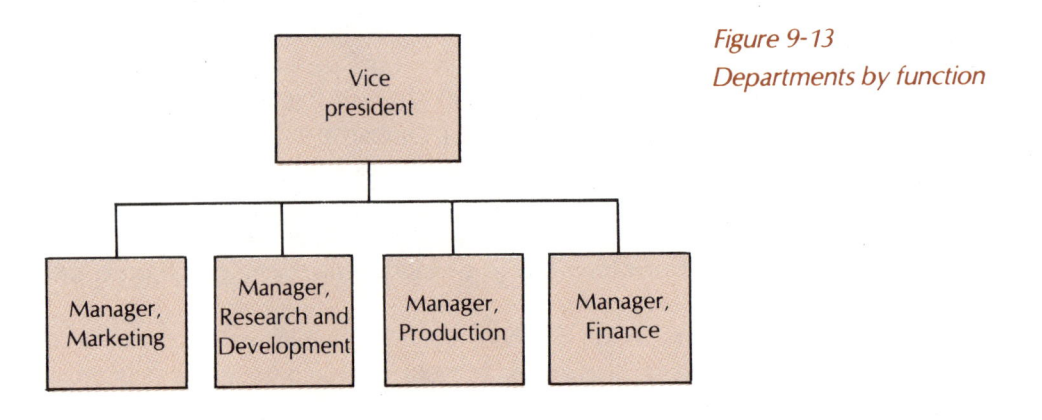

*Figure 9-13
Departments by function*

```
                    ┌─────────────┐
                    │    Vice     │
                    │  president  │
                    └──────┬──────┘
         ┌─────────────────┼─────────────────┐
   ┌─────┴─────┐     ┌─────┴─────┐     ┌─────┴─────┐
   │  Manager, │     │  Manager, │     │  Manager, │
   │Frozen Foods│    │Canned Foods│    │Packaged Foods│
   │  Division │     │  Division │     │  Division │
   └───────────┘     └───────────┘     └───────────┘
```

*Figure 9-14*
*Departments by product*

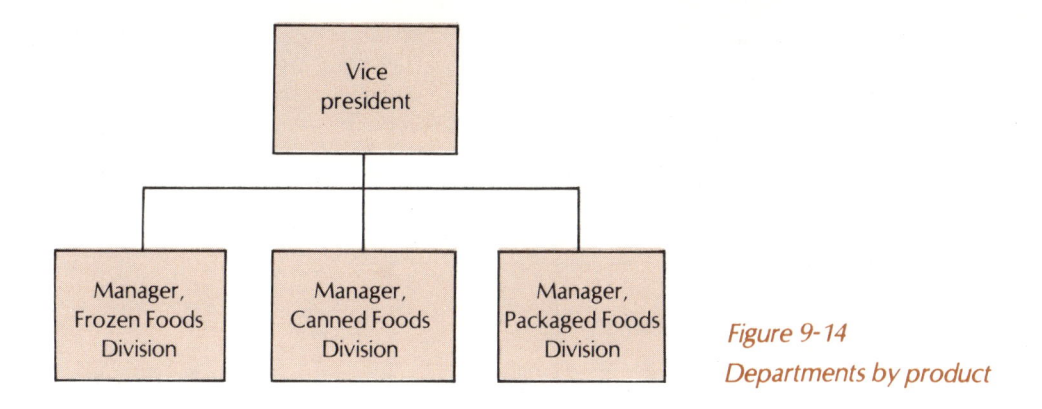

Examples include accounting departments (clustering all accounting functions), research departments (clustering all research and development work), and marketing departments (clustering all sales and distribution efforts).

These departments may transcend geographic boundaries, product lines, or differences in types of consumers or buying patterns. The functional approach has many advantages, including simplicity of organization, logical clustering, and convenient grouping of trainees. It also has major limitations. Functional departments are oriented toward the tasks done by employees, not toward products sold, physical logistics, or channels of distribution.

2. *Product line.* Another form of departmentalization involves grouping all tasks into a single department based upon products produced by a firm. (See figure 9-14.) In this form of organization, all activities are clustered about particular products manufactured or services provided. For example, a large food processing plant might be organized into frozen food, canned food, and packaged food departments. Within each of these departments are clustered all activities which relate to the production, marketing, and distribution of that product.

3. *Territory.* Another common form of departmentalization involves grouping activities according to geographic territory. (See figure 9-15.) In this form of organ-

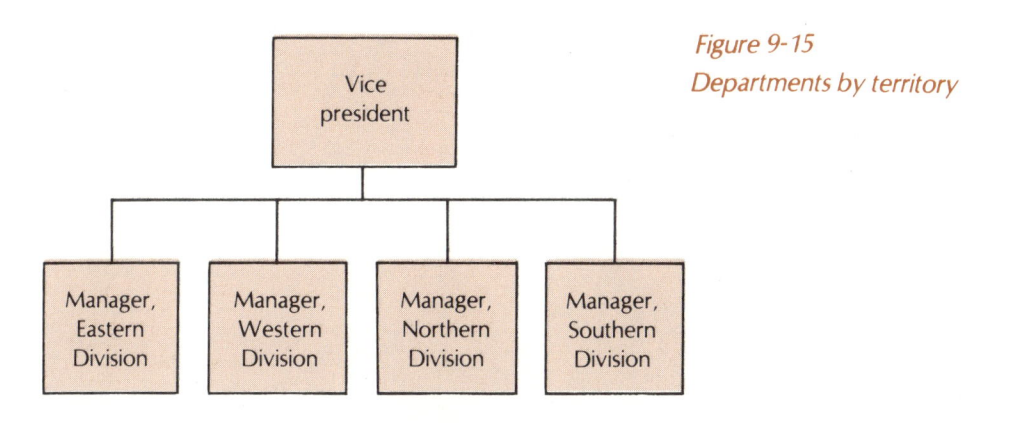

*Figure 9-15*
*Departments by territory*

```
                        ┌─────────────┐
                        │    Vice     │
                        │  president  │
                        └──────┬──────┘
         ┌──────────────┬──────┴───────┬──────────────┐
   ┌─────┴─────┐  ┌─────┴─────┐  ┌─────┴─────┐  ┌─────┴─────┐
   │  Manager, │  │  Manager, │  │  Manager, │  │  Manager, │
   │  Eastern  │  │  Western  │  │  Northern │  │  Southern │
   │  Division │  │  Division │  │  Division │  │  Division │
   └───────────┘  └───────────┘  └───────────┘  └───────────┘
```

*Figure 9-16
Departments by time factor*

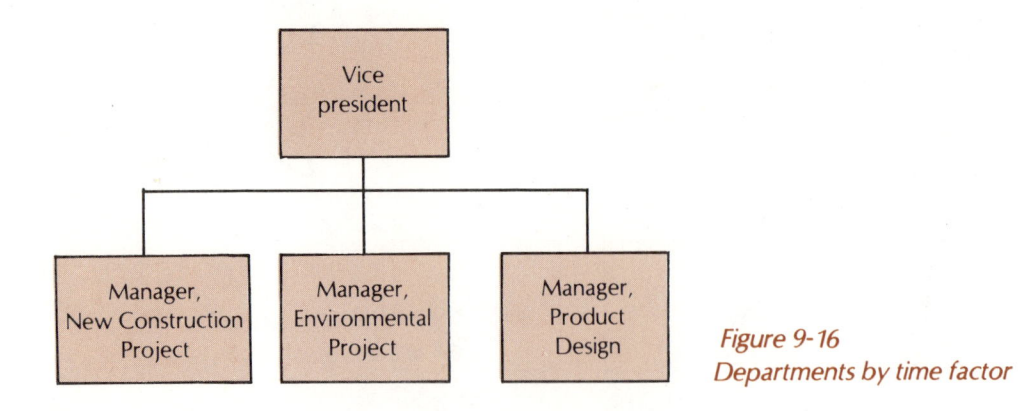

ization, all tasks common to a given geographic boundary are clustered into a single department. The boundaries may be city wide, statewide, or even national. Within each geographic boundary, all tasks are handled in one department.

For example, all sales, accounting, finance, production, and distribution efforts for all products sold and manufactured by a company may be clustered by states. The advantage of this form of organization is that it can be responsive to local consumer needs and to local laws and ordinances.

4. *Time factor.* Activities may also be clustered on the basis of time. (See figure 9-16.) In this instance, departments are organized based upon a particular time period. For example, a department may be set up to operate for six months to handle the design of a new product. Once the product is designed, the department is phased out.

Departments can be set up for various periods of time and assigned such tasks as facilitating the move of a plant from one city to another, preparing a one-time government report, or even bringing about a change in the ethnic balance of the firm's work force.

5. *Distribution channel.* The channels by which goods are sold or distributed may be used as the basis for a department. (See figure 9-17.) In this instance, a de-

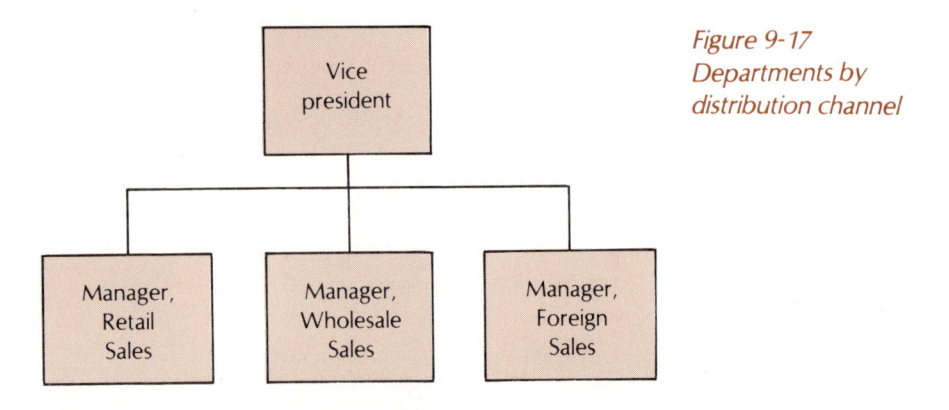

*Figure 9-17
Departments by distribution channel*

CHAPTER NINE    FUNDAMENTAL ORGANIZATIONAL PRINCIPLES    213

*Figure 9-18 Departments by manufacturing process*

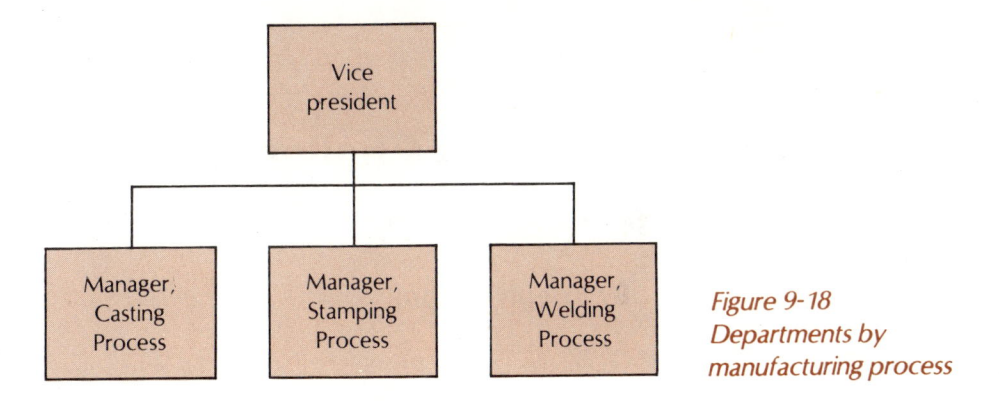

partment is established to handle all activities for goods distributed through a given channel, such as wholesale sales. Other departments may be established to handle retail sales, and still another may be set up to handle goods distributed to foreign markets. This form of departmentalization recognizes the different channels which move goods from manufacturer to the ultimate consumer.

6. *Manufacturing process.* A manufacturing process may be used as the basis for organizing departments. (See figure 9-18.) A firm may set up departments on the basis of manufacturing operations with all related activities clustered in the one department. For instance, all casting, stamping, or welding operations may be assigned to separate departments. Within each department all payroll, accounting, shipping, personnel, and other functions are handled.

The advantage of this form of organization is that it can be responsive to changes in manufacturing technology. As new manufacturing methods are uncovered, new departments are set up. As manufacturing processes become obsolete, departments can be closed down.

7. *Consumer needs.* The special and differing needs of consumers can be used as the basis for departmentalizing. (See figure 9-19.) In this instance, all functions and activities are clustered on the basis of the unique needs of a given class of users.

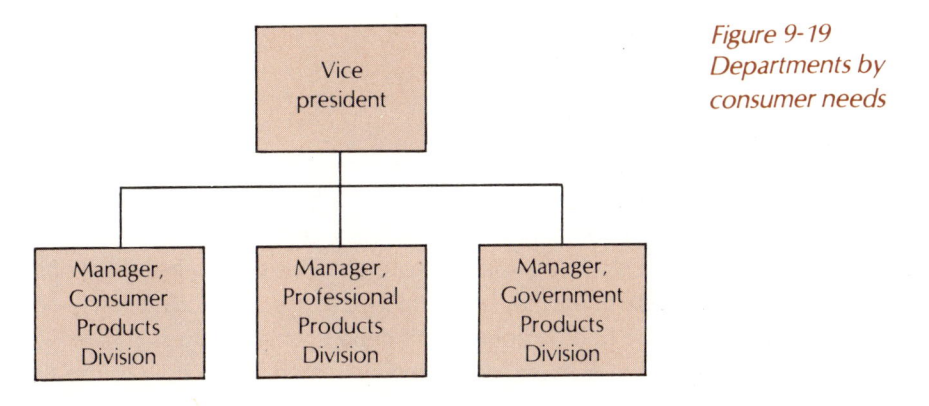

*Figure 9-19 Departments by consumer needs*

## POSTSCRIPT
# Family Businesses Challenge to Managers

### By Joseph Egelhof

NEW YORK — There are corporations that have sons and daughters, brothers and sisters, aunts and uncles, and cousins.

They are called family companies, and many professional managers are afraid to work for them. The fear is that the manager's decisions may be overturned by words whispered in the ear of the boss at the family picnic.

Rene Plessner, president of Rene Plessner Associates Inc., concedes that such things happen in family firms, and some fear is justified.

Yet Plessner is a great booster of the opportunities to be found by taking an executive job with a family business. Being such a booster is in the nature of Plessner's occupation. He is a professional recruiter who has made a specialty out of getting outside executives into family companies.

"I mean they've had ten people in the last five years in that job," a person Plessner contacts might object.

Depending on what he knows about the company, Plessner may respond that they have been hiring "the wrong people."

"The reason I'm talking to you is that I think I understand the mentality of the family," Plessner will say. "And in checking I've found that you probably are better than any of the others and could get along. If I'm right you probably will have a fantastic career because now you're No. 21 in your company's organizational chart, and if you go to work for this family you're going to deal with the president and chairman every day."

Plessner says there are more than 2,500 family-owned firms with an individual net worth of $5 million or more in the United States.

They're obviously a major element in the employment picture, and yet when he surveyed some 360 executives in non-family companies he found thirty-one percent "very reluctant" to join a family firm.

Permission granted by the Chicago Tribune - New York News Syndicate, Inc. ©1979.

---

For instance, a manufacturer of photographic equipment may set up departments based upon its customers' needs. One department may produce and sell goods to the amateur photographer, the ordinary consumer. This department places stress on simple operating instructions and novice training in the use of its products. Another department may be established to produce and market goods sold only to professional photographers. This department may stress consistency of product and speed of delivery, and place less emphasis on how to use the

Another twenty-six percent said their decision would be contingent on the company and management's attitude toward outsiders. The other forty-three percent said they would join a family firm if the salary were high and there were good fringe benefits.

It may take more tact and sensitivity to work for such a firm, but if the recruited manager has these qualities, he actually may be in a position to have more impact on the family business than in a nonfamily firm. He is a professional manager, and the family has already decided that his skill is just what they need.

Having a larger impact on the business is a source of satisfaction, but, according to Plessner, that's not all. He said many family firms, because they usually aren't in a position to offer stock and options, make up for it by paying higher salaries with good contracts.

And that's not all. There are other economic and social benefits, such as Uncle John's having a home in Acapulco that you can use on vacation.

Plessner said he advises prospects to "take a lot of time" on the interview.

"You have to understand the personalities, and if you conclude that they are never going to let you have the authority that goes with the responsibility, then don't go," he bluntly tells them.

It may be that the outsider will get the authority but has to use it flexibly, as in the case where the founding entrepreneur wanted chains of command but insisted that they shouldn't curb a star salesman who had a habit of calling the president with his problems because the star salesman would quit if he couldn't do that.

The aging founder may well be a sort of genius who makes decisions by the seat of his pants and who probably likes in others the ability to decide by personal judgment.

Plessner was reminded of a family firm that was supplied two market men from the outside. After two weeks he called them in and asked what they needed. One said he wanted to hire a market research firm for $100,000, which might have been a good answer elsewhere.

The second responded, "shelves." He explained he wanted to put all the company's and competition's products on the shelves and ponder them to determine who was really meeting the customer's needs.

The old founder liked the second guy best because his was the "hands dirty" approach.

Plessner sometimes feels like a marriage broker. He tries to understand both sides before bringing family and executive together.

Couldn't recruiting be done better by using psychiatrists, he was asked.

"No," Plessner said. "And the reason is that entrepreneurs are pretty eccentric and don't believe in psychiatrists."

products. Still another department may deal with products sold to government agencies.

Within any organization one might find any number of different kinds of departmentalization. For example, a bank may be departmentalized according to function, but the loan department may in turn be departmentalized on the basis of customer needs (real estate loans, consumer loans, commercial loans, and so on.) A manufacturing company may be departmentalized functionally. But its production department may in turn contain units departmentalized on the basis of equipment (lathes and drill presses) and process (assembly line and job order).

## SUMMARY

Both large and small organizations require carefully planned organizational structures. These place managers and subordinates in defined relationships. New organizations have fewer constraints than existing organizations when developing a new structure.

In organizing, a manager considers goals and objectives, develops a plan, identifies specific tasks and skills, and structures departments. Then the formal structure is documented and staffed.

The division of labor concept is important because it allows a smoother functioning organization by breaking down large complex tasks into smaller units.

Authority is the right to influence others and may be derived from many sources. Once authority has been acquired it may be delegated, but responsibility may not be. Accountability is the state of being answerable to another and flows upward in an organization.

The span of control is the number of individuals reporting to one manager. Some organizations have a tall shape, while others have a flat shape, indicating the number of levels of management necessary to operate.

Departmentalizing is the task of categorizing and combining functions. Departments may be built around functions performed, products sold, territories, time factor, distribution channels, manufacturing process, or consumer needs.

## REVIEW QUESTIONS

1. Describe the process of organizing.
2. Contrast the difference between organizing existing and new structures.
3. How do formal and informal organizations differ?
4. Explain the steps in organizing.
5. What effect does the division of labor have on efficiency and productivity?
6. Describe authority and the sources from which it is derived.
7. How does accountability differ from responsibility?
8. Explain the differences between a *tall* and a *flat* organization.
9. What is meant by the term *span of control?*
10. How does the unity of command principle affect organizational structure?
11. Explain why departmentalizing is necessary in large organizations.
12. Discuss some criteria or bases for forming departments in organizations.

## KEY TERMS

Formal organization   195
Informal organization   195
Authority   195
Responsibility   196

## CHAPTER NINE  FUNDAMENTAL ORGANIZATIONAL PRINCIPLES

Accountability   196
Department   196
Span of control   196
Chain of command   196
Division of labor   201
Unity of command   207
Staff function   208
Distribution channel   212 *(movement from manufacturer to consumer.)*

# Case Incident

Skokie Manufacturing produces expensive electronic guidance equipment for the aerospace industry. Housed within their main assembly plant are a large number of expensive electronic components and guidance parts. Because of their critical nature in the guidance systems, these parts are both top secret and extremely expensive. They are kept locked in a steel cage near the receiving entrance of the plant. On numerous occasions Ralph Kelly, manager of the assembly department, has emphasized to Betty Garretson, night shift supervisor, the extreme importance of seeing that the steel cages are locked at the end of her shift. Ralph has stated on several occasions that if anything happened to those parts, it would set their production schedule back nearly a full month.

On the day in question, Betty Garretson had to leave early because of illness. However, before Betty left she told Bill Alexander, one of her most responsible subordinates, to lock the steel cage at the end of the shift. She made it a point to tell Bill how important this was and that it must be done properly. After giving Bill clear instructions, Betty left the plant.

Before the end of the night shift, Bill Alexander was called out of the plant on an emergency service call. Since the call took much longer than expected, Bill did not have a chance to get back to the plant and lock the steel cage. The next morning it was discovered that a substantial number of critical parts had mysteriously disappeared.

Ralph Kelly called Garretson into his office. He reminded her that he had frequently emphasized the importance of making sure that the steel cage was always locked, and he put the blame for the loss directly on her. She explained that, because of illness, she had had to leave early, and that, in turn she had assigned the task to Bill Alexander, one of Skokie's most reliable employees. She said that if Kelly wants to hold anyone responsible, it should be Alexander and not her, since he knew the importance of locking the cage before leaving at the end of the shift.

**PROBLEMS**

1. Who should take responsibility for the incident?
2. Could Kelly legitimately delegate responsibility to Garretson?
3. Could Garretson reasonably delegate responsibility to Alexander?

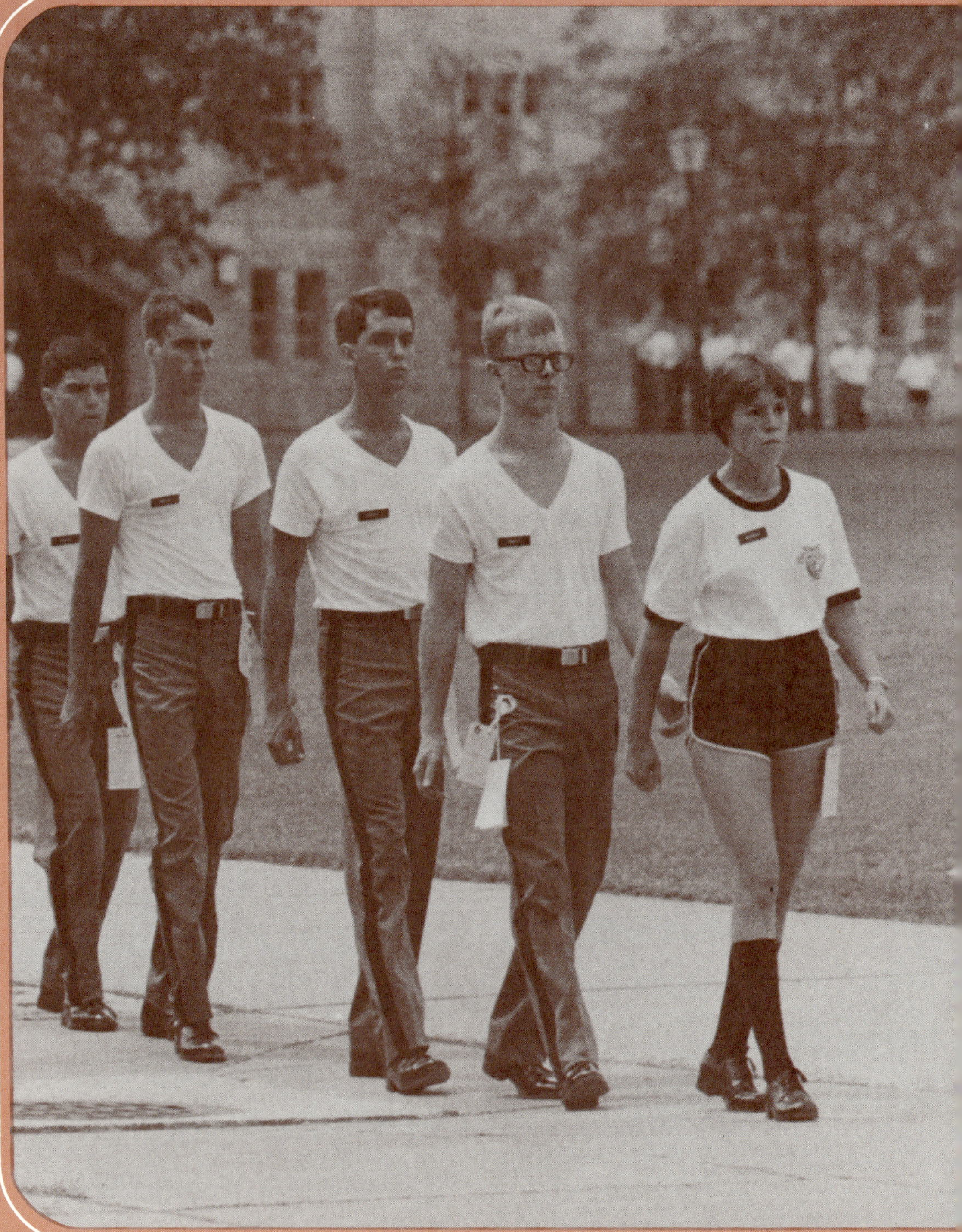

# 10

# Applied Organizational Principles

**LEARNING OBJECTIVES**

After studying this chapter, you should be able to:
1. List five major forms of organization structure in use.
2. Describe the situational factors which must be considered when designing an organizational structure.
3. Contrast centralized versus decentralized structure.
4. Summarize the influence of the computer on organizational structure.
5. Describe how organizational structure is documented.
6. Contrast the difference between vertical, horizontal, and circular organizational charts.
7. Summarize the effects of over- or under-organizing a structure.
8. Describe some major mistakes made by managers when implementing organizational designs.
9. Contrast the differences between central and supporting services.
10. Explain the structure of the matrix organization.

This chapter considers the practical aspects of organizational design, including line, line and staff, committee, task force (project), and matrix structures. The chapter surveys the issue of centralization versus decentralization and documenting organizational structure. It concludes with a discussion of common problems and failures in organizational design.

## CENTRAL AND SUPPORTING FUNCTIONS

To understand organizational structure, we must consider the distinction between central and supporting functions. A central function is the primary or major job performed by an individual or department. For example, the central function of the transportation department of a large firm is to provide transportation and vehicles for company use. This is their central task or duty.

However, for this central function to be carried out efficiently, the department requires service or support functions. Support functions reinforce central functions. The central function (transportation) requires hiring of personnel, purchasing of supplies, contracting for outside services, and so on. These are ancillary in nature. (See figure 10-1.)

Support or service functions may be carried out wholly within a department or they may be delegated to other departments. When delegated to other departments, the support function is shown as a broken line on the organizational chart.

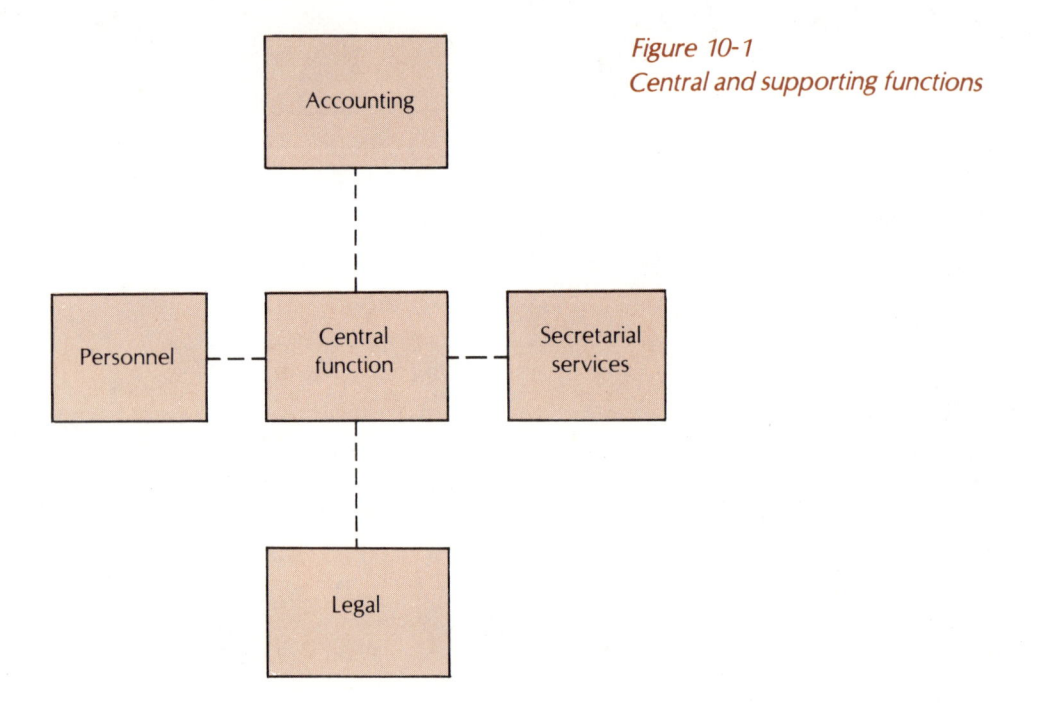

*Figure 10-1*
*Central and supporting functions*

Table 10-1  Organizational structure comparison chart

| Type of Organization | Lines of Authority Clearly Defined? | Speed of Decision Making | Draws on Consensus? | Application |
|---|---|---|---|---|
| Line | Yes | Fast | No | Military and small organizations |
| Line and staff | Yes | Moderate | Small degree | Large organizations |
| Committee | No | Slow | High degree | Large organizations |
| Task force | Clouded | Moderate | Moderate | Single projects |
| Matrix | Clouded | Moderate | Moderate | Multiple projects |

Some typical support or service functions are legal services, personnel (hiring, promotions, and dismissal), secretarial services, and planning and design. A clear-cut relationship between the line functions (direct authority) and support (consulting) functions is established.

## BASIC ORGANIZATIONAL STRUCTURES

Let us consider the five major forms of organization structures in use. These are contrasted in table 10-1. They include the line, line and staff, committee, task force (project), and matrix structures. Each has unique characteristics, advantages, and limitations. All are used in varying degrees by organizations. These structures delineate the relationships and roles of individuals or departments in an organization.

### Line Organization

A simple and basic form of structure is the line organization. (See figure 10-2.) This form of organization places all departments in a strict line relationship. There is a direct flow of authority from departments on the top of the hierarchy to those on the bottom. Each department or position is answerable directly to those above. Line structure is typical in the military, with a few exceptions such as quartermaster and auditor-general, which are staff services. Generally those in command are at the top and in a direct line of authority over those below.

*Figure 10-2
Line organization*

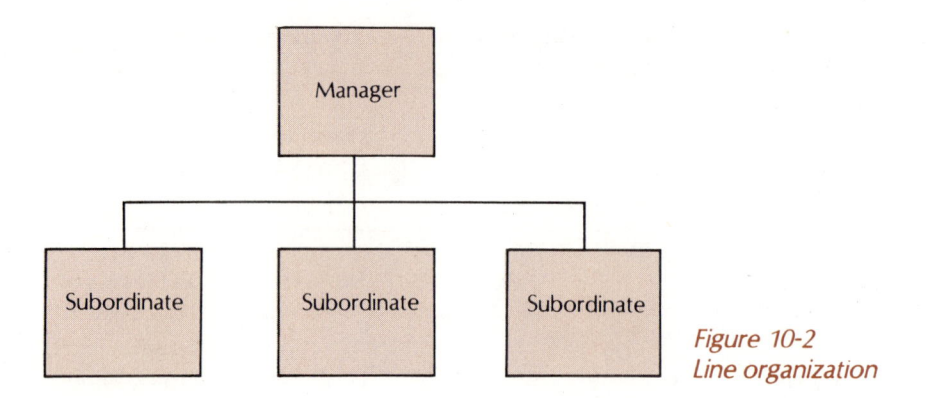

The advantage of this form of structure is its simplicity and clarity of relationships. The structure leaves little doubt regarding who reports to whom. An employee need only look at the chart to locate his direct and immediate manager or his subordinates. There are no supporting functions to confuse lines of authority.

The weakness of the line organization is that it makes no provision for support, staff, or consulting functions. Since there are no support functions, each manager is expected to be an expert in all forms of the job. The subordinate has no one to turn to for consultation except the person directly above him in line. While the military uses essentially a line organization, it is not practical for large organizations where complex tasks are performed or complex products manufactured.

## Line and Staff Organization

Figure 10-3 illustrates the most widely used form of structure, the line and staff organization. It possesses the benefits of the pure line organization, showing clear-cut lines of authority from top to bottom of the hierarchy. In addition, it provides staff or support functions. These are shown as dotted lines on the chart. Subordinates are expected to turn to others, shown in dotted lines on figure 10-3, for staff, consultation, or support.

While there are clear-cut lines of authority, subordinates also have clearly defined lines of consultation and staff assistance. They may turn to these people to support their primary task. Some common staff functions provided to central departments are hiring, promotion, payroll and accounting, purchasing, and secretarial services.

The consulting staff has limited authority. In well-structured organizations, functional authority is granted to them, thus giving them the right to direct the activities of individuals in other departments.

The line and staff organization has three aspects of authority: line, staff, and function. *Line authority* is a direct right to command a subordinate. *Staff authority* is an advisory or consulting relationship. *Functional authority* is the exercise of a limited amount of control in a specific functional activity.

The line and staff organization is suited to large firms. It provides clear-cut authority, yet allows for additional support resources. The limitation on the line and staff organization is that it may become complex, especially where many lines of support cross one another. For instance, it is not practical to draw several dozen support functions (broken lines) to one subordinate position. This is best provided through another form of organization, the committee.

While line and staff is widely used, several weaknesses are often found in its implementation. Responsibility is often not clearly delegated; thus, relationships between line authority and staff function may become clouded. This creates inefficiency and duplication of effort. Line and staff organizations may contain serious imbalances. Thus, they may rely too heavily on a line structure and provide inadequate staff support. Conversely, they may overstress staff support, which creates confusion and overlapping of responsibilities.

## Committee Organization

The committee organization is a widely used structure. It is often found in conjunction with the line and staff structure. Figure 10-4 illustrates the use of committees on an organizational chart.

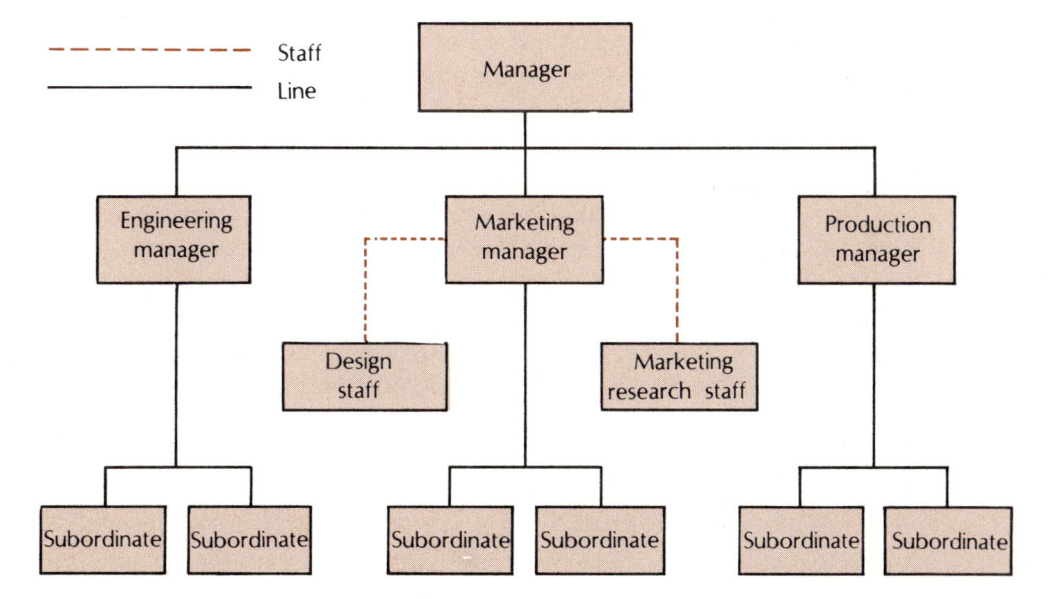

*Figure 10-3 Line and staff organization*

*Figure 10-4
Committee organization*

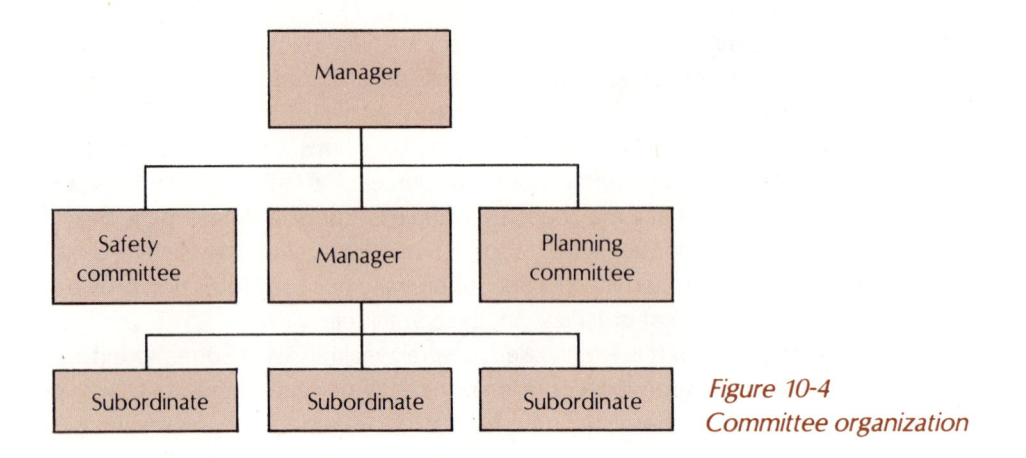

The authority and power of a given manager is delegated to a committee. The committee assumes the full responsibility to study a problem and render a decision. The committee may be composed of individuals from many levels of an organization.

Committees may be given many tasks or responsibilities. For example, committees may be charged with hiring, promotions, plant safety, operation of company cafeterias, employee facilities, and so on. The committee is often given the authority to act just as though the power were vested in a single individual, although sometimes it is empowered only to make recommendations.

The major advantage of a committee is that it draws from a wide base of human resources. It utilizes the mental capabilities of many people, who interact in reaching a decision or making a rule or policy. Thus, the committee benefits from combined judgment, experience, and skill of all members.

Decisions made by a committee are more likely to be accepted by subordinates than decisions made by a single individual. The committee structure facilitates communication, since many individuals meet to discuss a problem and work out solutions.

There are several limitations to committee structure. A committee may be very slow to act, since many people may be involved. It may never reach a decision if a consensus of members cannot be obtained. Committees may be costly if many individuals are asked to serve and time is taken away from regular jobs.

Committees are sometimes improperly used to avoid making decisions or to diffuse responsibility for poor decisions. A poor decision can be blamed on the committee; thus, individuals are absolved of bad decisions.

There is no set number of individuals who may serve on a committee. A committee should be large enough to bring together the varied experiences and resources of key people. It should not, however, be so large that it becomes unwieldy to manage.

CHAPTER TEN  APPLIED ORGANIZATIONAL PRINCIPLES 225

Task forces are frequently used in the aerospace industry.

## Task Force (Project) Organization

The task force, or project, form of organization has become popular during recent years. (See figure 10-5.) A task force consists of a group of individuals assembled for a one-time effort designed to complete a project or task.

Task force organization is used in the electronics and aerospace industries. It is charged with a one-time assignment. Upon completion of the task, the group

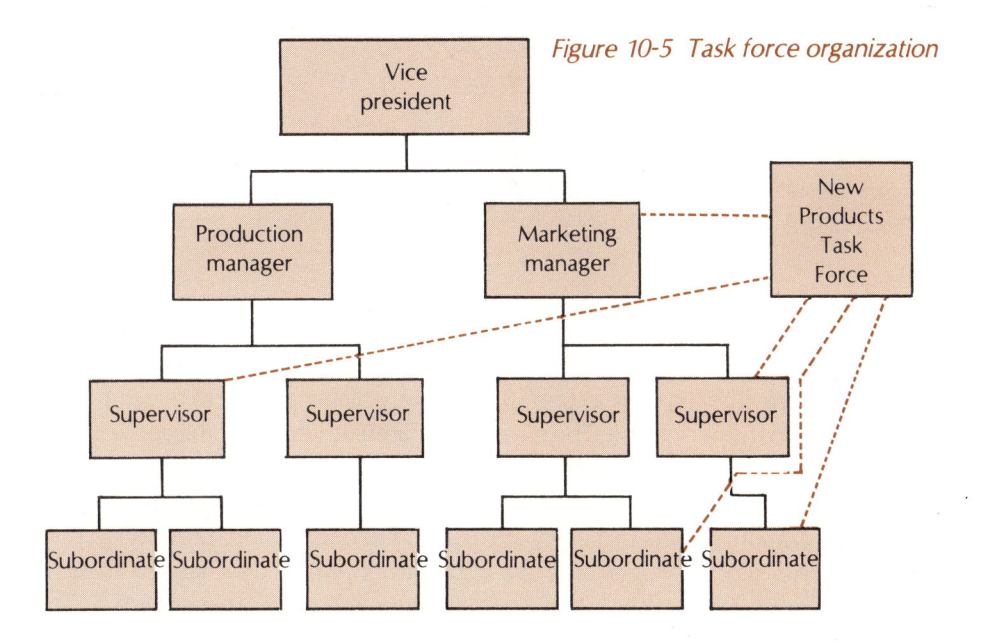

*Figure 10-5  Task force organization*

> **REAL WORLD**
>
> ## Learning to Do It All
>
> Some managers think that the grass is greener on the other side of the fence. They stress sales abroad and overlook the home market, at a great loss in profits. Chairman William H. Kilkenny of Hyster Co., a manufacturer of forklift trucks, discovered that the grass is considerably greener in his own back yard.
>
> In 1974 Hyster was doing a lot of things wrong. Earnings slid from $2.80 to $1.22 per share of its stock. Hyster was so involved in expanding abroad and building new products that it had lost sight of its forklift customers at home. Kilkenny quickly assembled a nine-person task force to turn things around. The first thing the task force did was to cut middle management by one-third. Then they instituted tough financial and inventory controls. They began cultivating lost accounts and unhappy customers. All these efforts paid off for Kilkenny and his staff. While Caterpillar and Allis-Chalmers' earnings slid, Hyster's earnings rose twenty percent in 1977.
>
> Adapted from *Forbes,* 26 November 1979, p. 158.

disbands. Members of the task force are usually drawn from a variety of departments in the organization and assigned to one project leader. The project leader has the broad responsibility for the group.

There are many advantages of the task force organization. It can be assembled from existing personnel in an organization. It can be broad based and responsive. Upon completion of its mission it can be disbanded and the personnel reassigned to their old departments.

One of the difficulties with task force organization is that personnel may maintain allegiance to their former department or boss rather than to their project manager. They may wish to preserve their old positions, and hence make decisions based upon vested interests rather than the merits of the project.

### Matrix Organization

The matrix organization is a variation of the task force. This is sometimes called a grid structure. The matrix is a form of structure which attempts to match the organization to the people in it. The matrix may combine several of the above forms into a task-oriented organization.

The matrix is useful for structuring project-oriented organizations. In the matrix organization, project managers are assigned to one or more products or projects. Each project manager will have a staff group assigned to her and charged with the project responsibility. At the same time, these subordinates will be answerable to their functional line manager. Where the task force structure seeks to solve one problem or deal with one project, the matrix organization deals with many. The matrix structure places all departments (manufacturing, research, personnel) down one side of the chart, and all projects or product lines across the top. Each project intersects many departments and each department intersects many projects.

Each project manager draws upon the assistance and resources of all departments in the company. In turn each department manager is answerable to many project managers. There are many intersecting points of authority on this chart.

The advantage of the matrix organization is that many complex projects (or product lines) may be undertaken, drawing from existing departments in the firm. In effect, each project has the full resources of all functional departments in the company. The disadvantage is that many conflicting lines of authority are set up. Departmental managers must answer to many project leaders.

## CONTINGENCY ORGANIZATIONAL STRUCTURE

How should the best form of organizational structure be selected? According to contingency theorists, there is no ideal form suitable to all organizations under all circumstances. The contingency manager begins with an assessment of the local management problems and the characteristics of the organization, and designs a structure from there. This requires an investigation of many factors, including the history of the firm, its personnel, physical and financial resources, and so on.

The following list describes some of the important situational factors which the manager must consider when designing an organizational structure.

1. *Characteristics of employees.* The age, number, type, experience, turnover, and training of employees bears heavily upon organizational design.

2. *Services and products manufactured or sold.* The kinds of products produced and services offered influence organizational design. Complex services and goods require complex marketing and manufacturing operations. These in turn require more specialized management.

3. *Characteristics of customers.* The kind and type of customers served influences organizational design. Management and marketing efforts vary with the customer's sophistication and understanding of the product and its usage.

4. *Size of organization.* The physical and economic size of the organization has a heavy influence on the kind of organizational structure selected. Small firms may operate successfully with limited management, while larger organizations require a carefully planned and implemented management structure.

5. *Existing practices.* The existing industrywide manufacturing, marketing, and distribution methods play a part in the design of the structure.

6. *Related factors.* A variety of other factors influence organizational design, including prevailing wage rates, labor supply, competition, government controls and regulations, and financial factors. These and the nature of the work itself influence the number and type of managers and the amount of consulting and staff services required.

## CENTRALIZED VERSUS DECENTRALIZED STRUCTURE

One of the major questions to consider in organizational design is the degree of centralization of management. In a highly centralized management structure, virtually all major organizational decisions are made at the top of the hierarchy (See figure 10-6.) Key decisions regarding such matters as finances, personnel, and marketing are made by a few managers who hold the maximum power in the organization.

In a highly decentralized management structure, virtually all decisions are made by those down in the organizational hierarchy. Key decisions are made by staff, apart from the individuals with the maximum authority in the organization. Centralization is a matter of degree. No large organization is totally centralized or decentralized. Centralization affects the speed at which decisions are made and how responsive they are to local conditions.

### Influence of the Computer

The modern electronic computer has an influence on the issue of centralization. Modern computers and advances in communication technology enable firms to operate with a greater degree of centralization or decentralization. Large amounts of management information can be processed quickly and economically at a central point. Conversely, large files of information, located at central offices, can be made available quickly and economically at decentralized locations.

A major trend is toward *distributive* management information processing. Instead of installing a large central computer system, many firms use a group of small computers tied together into a network. Each small computer can access management data from the network and place information into the network. This arrangement provides more data at branch offices more quickly than large central systems.

### Factors Affecting a Decision to Centralize

—*Advantages.* The major advantage of centralization is the close control which can be maintained from the top of the management hierarchy. Managers can keep a close watch on organizations where all purchasing, personnel, policy making, financial, and marketing operations are centralized.

Centralization offers greater opportunity for security of information and pro-

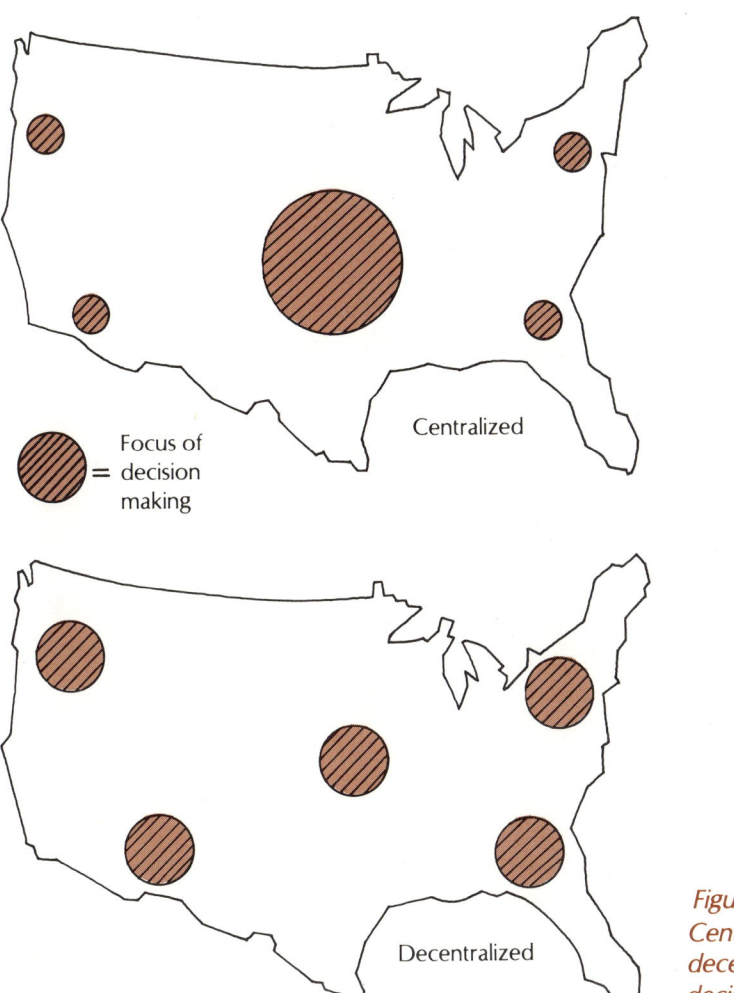

CHAPTER TEN    APPLIED ORGANIZATIONAL PRINCIPLES                          229

*Figure 10-6
Centralized and decentralized decision making*

prietary data. Where all important or sensitive information is kept at one point, it can be maintained securely.

Organizations sometimes obtain cost benefits from centralizing all purchasing, personnel acquisition, and training efforts in one place. The benefit of sheer volume often justifies and dictates heavy centralization.

— *Limitations.* The major weakness of a highly centralized organization is that decisions are made at the top, away from the points affected by those decisions. Decisions made in highly centralized organizations tend to be made slowly and with less consideration for local issues and personnel. Centralized management structure leaves little room for local creativity and innovation. This may frustrate mid-level managers, who will not stay long in an organization which does not give them latitude to function.

> **REAL WORLD**
> # Sidetracked Sisters Tackle Success
>
> They read the right books and then proceeded to ignore them. Two sisters, Pam Brace and Peggy Jones, founded Sidetracked Home Executives (SHE), with almost no money but a great will to succeed. They also wrote a book about how to reorganize and make the best use of time, aimed at disorganized homemakers and working women. Their book sold over thirty thousand copies and they were off on the lecture and seminar circuit. They reduced their system to a set of 3" x 5" cards and some simple rules. Pam and Peggy discovered that once you systematize what you need to do you are able to get a lot more done in a lot less time. Their book teaches homemakers how to run their homes efficiently and still have time to enjoy life.
>
> Pam and Peggy advocate going into business with other family members, ignoring qualifications, and hiring people on the basis of qualities they possess. They advise mixing business and pleasure. "Talk like normal people and forget professional jargon." It's working just fine for them.
>
> Adapted from the *Los Angeles Times,* 20 May 1980.

— *Situational considerations.* The contingency manager looks very closely at many local factors before deciding upon the degree of centralization to be implemented. Contingency-oriented managers study cost, time factors, and local resources and personnel before making a decision regarding the degree of centralization. A full assessment is made of the cost benefits before implementing any plan which provides a specific degree of centralization or decentralization.

## DOCUMENTING THE ORGANIZATION

An important part of the manager's task is documenting the organization's structure. An organizational chart is frequently used together with manuals and other graphic devices to describe the structure of an organization. An organizational chart is a diagram or drawing which places each manager and subordinate in his or her respective position in the organizational hierarchy.

A variety of organizational charts are used to describe lines of authority, responsibility, and support functions. Horizontal, vertical, and circular organizational charts, as well as organizational manuals, are important documenting tools.

Organizational charts may be prepared showing only specific management-subordinate positions in the organizational structure, or they may include the name of the individual filling the position as well. (See figure 10-7.) The advantage of including individuals' names is that it relates people to positions of authority. On the other hand, this type of chart becomes outdated quickly. New charts must be prepared whenever individuals change positions or enter or leave the organization.

Organizational charts are prepared following a few basic rules. A position in the hierarchy is drawn as a rectangle. Rectangles are connected with lines which show the flow of authority. The flow is from top to bottom or left to right, depending upon the type of chart.

Solid lines show direct lines of authority or line responsibility, while broken lines show staff or support functions.

Organizational manuals are often prepared to further document organizational structure. (See figure 10-8.) These may describe positions, names of individuals filling specific jobs, and a list of subordinates reporting to each manager. Detailed descriptions of each manager or subordinate position are often included.

1. *Vertical organizational charts.* The most common form of organizational chart is the vertical chart, shown in figure 10-9. This chart takes the form of a pyramid. Individuals with the greatest power in the organization are shown at the top, and those with the least power are at the base of the pyramid. There is increasing authority as one moves up in the hierarchy. Vertical organizational charts focus on the hierarchical relationship of the positions.

2. *Horizontal organizational charts.* Another form of organizational chart is the horizontal diagram (fig. 10-10). This chart uses a branching form which lays out the hierarchy in a horizontal fashion. Those with greatest power in the organization are shown on the left, and those with the least power are on the right.

This form of chart is used where the designer wishes to deemphasize the hi-

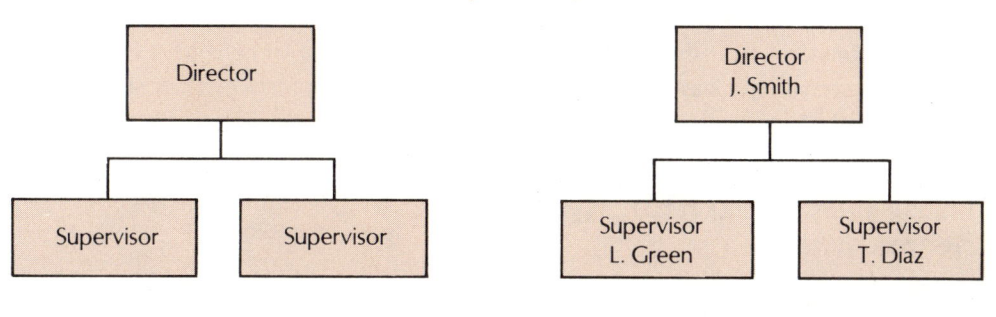

*Figure 10-7 Types of organizational charts*

Positions only

Position and individual names

```
                        JOB TITLE
              COMPUTER OPERATOR (Category I)

JOB DESCRIPTION:
    Responsibilities include hands-on operation
    of company computers, including logging
    jobs, scheduling work, and diagnosing
    system problems.
POSITION IN ORGANIZATION:
    Position reports directly to day-shift
    supervisor. Responsible for activities
    of two assistants assigned during normal
    shift operation.
IMMEDIATE SUPERVISOR:
    R.F. Jackson, day-shift supervisor


DUTIES:
    Initial program loading, load tape drives,
    card readers and line printers. Break-apart
    jobs, and route to appropriate departments.
SALARY RATE:
    Category I, Starting salary $18,000 per year.
    Advancement and salary increases as per
    Category I employees.
```

*Figure 10-8
Page from
organizational manual*

erarchical relationship of positions. Since all rectangles are drawn on approximately the same horizontal level, there is less stress on the manager-subordinates relationship and more on the flow of authority.

3. *Circular organizational charts.* Another form of organizational chart is the circular design (fig. 10-11). This chart places the position with the greatest power at the hub of a wheel. Positions with less responsibility are drawn in a concentric fashion, out from the center. Those with the greatest power are in the center, and those with the least power are at the periphery. This form of chart stresses the central functions of key positions and individuals.

## MAJOR PROBLEMS AND FAILURES IN ORGANIZATIONAL DESIGN

Mistakes or failures are sometimes made when planning and designing an organization. These are often due to lack of consideration for local needs or situational

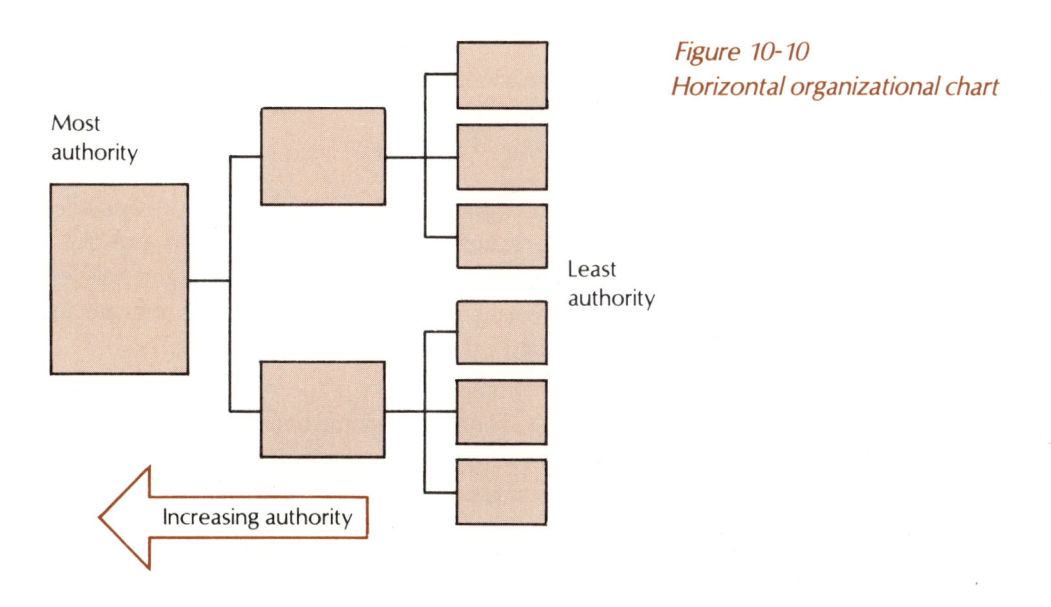

CHAPTER TEN   APPLIED ORGANIZATIONAL PRINCIPLES    233

*Figure 10-9*
*Vertical organizational chart*

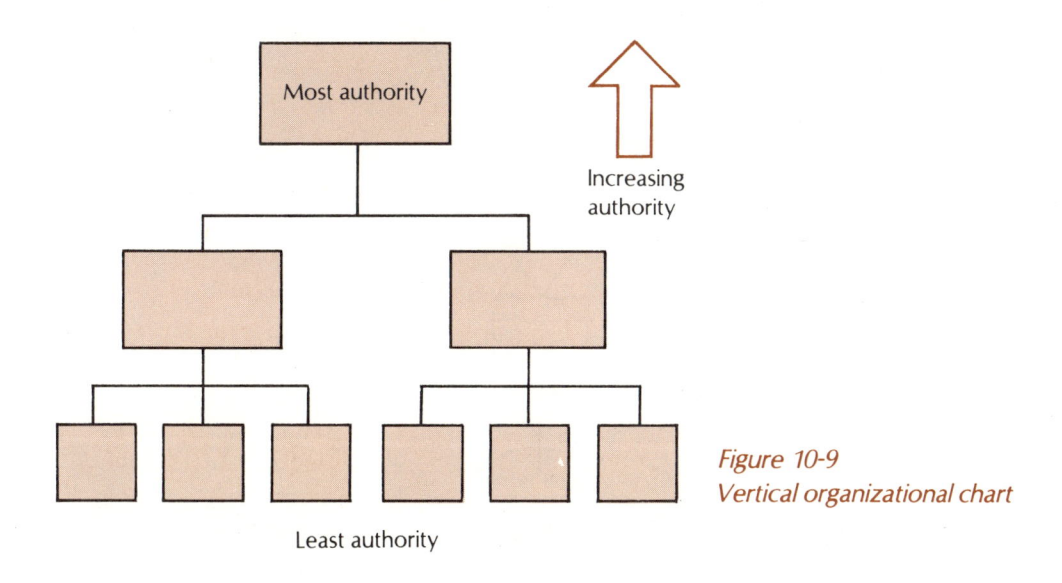

factors. Failure to consider personnel needs, costs, attitudes, or the demands of customers or suppliers can result in faulty organizational planning.

Let us look at some of the common faults made by managers when implementing organizational designs.

1. *Overorganized structure.* A common mistake of managers is to create an overorganized structure. This results in excessive management, overhead, and policies. Overorganization requires that too many people be consulted and too many rules followed, which creates inefficiency.

*Figure 10-10*
*Horizontal organizational chart*

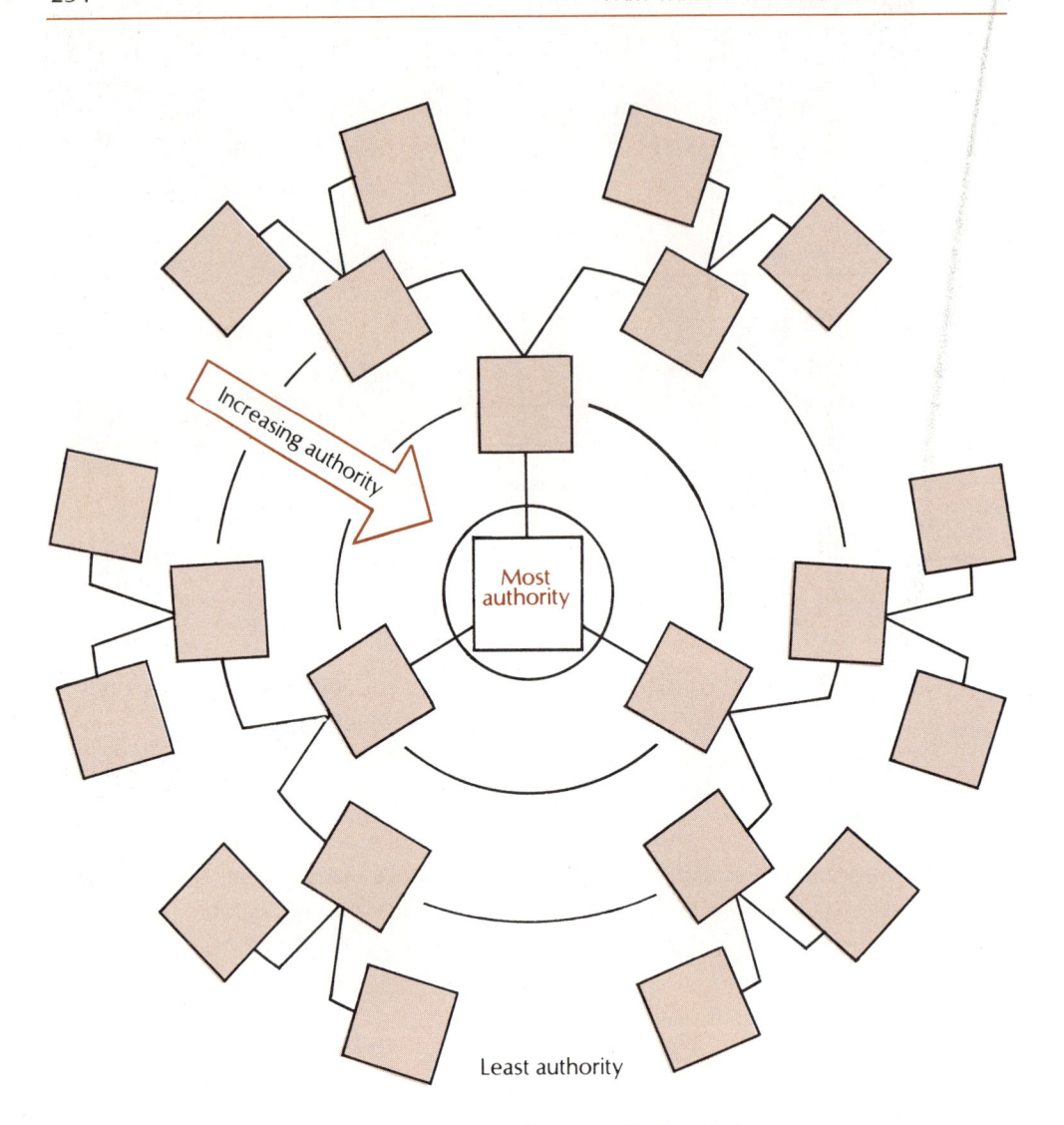

*Figure 10-11 Circular organizational chart*

2. *Underorganized structure.* In this instance, the designer fails to provide adequate structure to enable the organization to function efficiently. As a result of lack of structure, little control is exercised over decisions, personnel, and policies. Subordinates are never quite sure what must be done and to whom they are answerable. Underorganizing is as much a weakness as overorganizing.

3. *Failure to delegate authority.* A common mistake made by managers is the failure to delegate authority. As a result, managers become overburdened with tasks which should be done by others. These managers run one man shows, which may work in small organizations, but are not successful where large numbers of subordinates are involved. The key to successful management is the ability to delegate work to others.

CHAPTER TEN     APPLIED ORGANIZATIONAL PRINCIPLES                                      235

4. *Failure to document organizational design.* A sound organizational structure should be fully documented. This requires clear organizational charts and manuals. The failure to document a system, no matter how well conceived in design, results in confusing lines of authority and unclear responsibility for organization participants.

5. *Failure to communicate organizational structure.* It sometimes happens that even though a well-planned and well-executed organizational structure is implemented and documented, no effort is made to communicate this design to other managers or to the subordinates involved. This failure undermines even the most carefully designed system. Each manager and subordinate must understand his or her role and relationship to others in the organization.

6. *Failure to consider situational factors.* Some management structures are designed in a vacuum. These systems fail to consider the local needs, attitudes, and characteristics of the personnel and resources involved. It is a case of a well-designed shoe which doesn't fit the foot.

7. *Failure to change.* Even the best structure must be flexible and able to change. As new technology, personnel, and resources are brought into organizations, the structure must change to accommodate these new factors. Good organizational designs which are cast in concrete may solve a problem today but become a liability tomorrow.

"It's been a drawback all through his career . . . the inability to delegate. . . ."

Reprinted from *Graphic Arts Monthly*, November 1979.

## POSTSCRIPT
# Papering According to Form
### Art Buchwald

They've been trying to keep it a secret, but there is a serious paper shortage in Washington. A strike of Western paper workers, which is expected to be taken up by workers on the East Coast, has caused a paper deficit in Washington. The reason the government has been keeping it a secret is it fears that if the word gets out, panic will set in and different departments and agencies will start hoarding paper, while others might resort to some very dirty tricks to ensure that its memo flow is not turned off.

One department, which shall remain anonymous, got wind of the shortage and has already held twenty-seven meetings on the crisis.

At the last meeting it was decided to alert all employees to the situation.

In a memo, which was sent to the agency's 27,500 workers, a deputy director wrote: "It has been brought to my attention that we can expect a serious paper shortage in the next few months, which could affect productivity and the morale of this agency. Therefore, I am asking everyone to conserve every sheet of paper possible, even if it involves such dire emergencies as using both sides of the paper. I am also requesting all employees to submit to me in writing how the agency can conserve paper. These suggestions should be made out in triplicate with one copy for me, one for your supervisors, and one to keep for yourself in case any action is taken.

"Supervisors are requested to submit weekly reports to the Administrative Supply Office as to how many employees are fol-

Reprinted with the permission of the author. Copyright © 1979 Art Buchwald.

---

8. *Assignment of responsibility without authority.* One of the most frustrating positions for a manager to be in is to be assigned a responsibility without the authority to do the job. Good management practice requires that authority be commensurate with responsibility.

9. *Inadequate staff and support functions.* A common mistake is to rely too heavily upon line authority without providing adequate staff consultation and support. A subordinate must have resources and support in order to do a job well. In a complex organization, subordinates must be able to turn to others for assistance and support. The failure to provide adequate staff support places too heavy a burden upon the manager who is directly in line.

10. *Over- or undercentralization.* There is an optimum degree of centralization

lowing this directive, and if this memorandum has increased or decreased the use of present supplies. If an employee does not send in a suggestion, his or her supervisor must put in writing to the personnel director why he or she failed to do so. The personnel director will evaluate and report on Form 2-D to his superior whether or not the excuse is valid.

"What we plan to do with the suggestions is have the public affairs division compile a collection of the most interesting ones, which will then be distributed to all personnel — not only from this agency but from corresponding agencies, which find themselves in the same shortfall position.

"It is my hope that this compilation can be published by the General Printing Office and sold to the public. A steering committee has been appointed to study the best methods of distribution, as well as costs, and the report should be on my desk by the early part of next month. Each department head will receive a copy of the report comments as well as additional thoughts.

"To facilitate matters on the book project, it is suggested that all departmental correspondence concerning conservation be submitted on yellow 8x10 memorandum sheets (G-234 forms), while those regarding distribution be written on the blue double carbon pads (K-677). If you do not have these colors in stock, you can obtain them from the supply room by filling out Form 2323.

"It goes without saying that this agency will be out of business if it is unable to supply the documentation to justify the written decisions it makes. Therefore, everyone from the top agency officials to the mailroom personnel must comply with all regulations regarding the conservation of our paper supply.

"The first of these regulations is now being distributed. If you do not receive it in a week, please notify this office on Green Form 1456, using the White No. 10 envelope.

"Anyone who does not have a Green Form 1456 may apply for a written waiver by using the manila folder 10-DC in which this memo is being distributed."

— A. Clancy,
Acting Chief Deputy Counsel,
Paper Conservation Committee

for any given organization under a given set of circumstances. Too little or too much centralization can cause delays in making decisions or decisions which do not take into account local conditions.

11. *Failure to view the organization as a system.* Some organizational designers view the structure as a group of disassociated elements. They overlook the interactive and interdependent nature of organizational components. Good design suggests that organizations be viewed as a whole. The most successful organizations are those which are constructed with a systematic view. It has long been said that the whole is greater than the sum of its parts. This is especially true when considering organizational structure.

## SUMMARY

Most tasks in an organization are either central or supporting in nature. A variety of forms of organizational structures are used, including line, line and staff, committee, task force, and matrix forms. Important situational factors considered by managers are the characteristics of employees, products manufactured or sold, characteristics of customers, size of organization, existing practice, and related factors.

In highly decentralized structures most decisions are made at lower levels in the hierarchy, while in highly centralized organizations decisions are made at the top of the structure. The computer has had a great influence on the ability of management to distribute or decentralize its decision-making authority.

Organizational structure is documented using manuals, position descriptions, and organizational charts. The principle organizational charts include the vertical, horizontal, and circular forms.

Some of the major problems and failures in organizational design include overorganized structure, underorganized structure, failure to delegate authority, failure to document, failure to communicate structure, and failure to consider situational factors.

Other problems include failure to cope with change, or the assignment of responsibility without authority. Inadequate staff and support functions, over- or undercentralization, and failure to view the organization as a whole are also problems.

## REVIEW QUESTIONS

1. What is the difference between a central and a supporting function?
2. What are the advantages of line organizational structure?
3. What is the advantage of the line and staff organizational structure?
4. What kinds of projects is the task force organization best suited for?
5. Explain how the matrix organization is constructed.
6. What contingency factors must be considered when developing an organizational structure?
7. What influence has the computer had on organizational structure?
8. What are the advantages of a highly centralized organization?
9. What are the advantages of a highly decentralized organization?
10. Describe the purpose of documenting an organization.
11. How do vertical organizational charts differ from horizontal organizational charts?
12. Discuss some of the major problems and failures frequently found in organizational design.

# CHAPTER TEN  APPLIED ORGANIZATIONAL PRINCIPLES

## KEY TERMS

Central function   220
Supporting (service) function   220
Line organization   221
Line and staff organization   222
Committee organization   223
Matrix organization   226

Centralized structure   228
Decentralized structure   228
Vertical organizational chart   231
Horizontal organizational chart   231
Circular organizational chart   232
Delegation of authority   234

## Case Incident

East Bay Gas and Electric Company is one of several major public utilities in the state. It provides both gas and electric service to hundreds of thousands of customers. East Bay Gas and Electric is made up of nine separate and distinct distribution and billing centers which provide services for cities throughout the state.

Due to the real concern about energy shortages, the management of East Bay Gas and Electric has decided to embark on a program of energy conservation. This program will include a public relations effort designed to encourage energy conservation on the part of residential and business customers. The program calls for printing and distributing various forms of literature, posters, and interviews with local radio and TV stations, in addition to the usual advertisements. Tony Brill was one of the senior staff members in the company's marketing department. He has recently been appointed to the position of manager of the energy conservation program. Among several people on Brill's staff is Elaine Hawkins, a public relations manager.

In setting up and organizing the master plan for the energy conservation program, Brill believes that the project should be managed from the utility's home office. From this location, they would handle all news media contacts, public relations, and advertising for the entire state. Brill says this is the procedure that has been used so effectively in the marketing for other programs. The biggest benefit would be that it would give them a uniformly acceptable program. It would also allow them to put their full budget into some very high-quality media campaigns. It would have a maximum impact on their service area and would help them to ensure that they achieve their goal of energy conservation.

Elaine Hawkins believes instead that the energy conservation program should be implemented on a decentralized, regional basis. She suggests that each of the nine separate distribution and billing centers implement their own media programs based upon some general guidelines distributed by Brill's office. By working on a decentralized basis, each of the distribution billing centers would be able to tailor its own campaign to suit its residential and business customers. Also, it would enable them to allow for other regional variations which could make a big difference in the methods they would employ in achieving reduced energy consumption.

## PROBLEMS

1. What problems and advantages does Brill's approach have?
2. What are the advantages and limitations of Hawkins' approach?
3. Which approach do you favor? Explain.

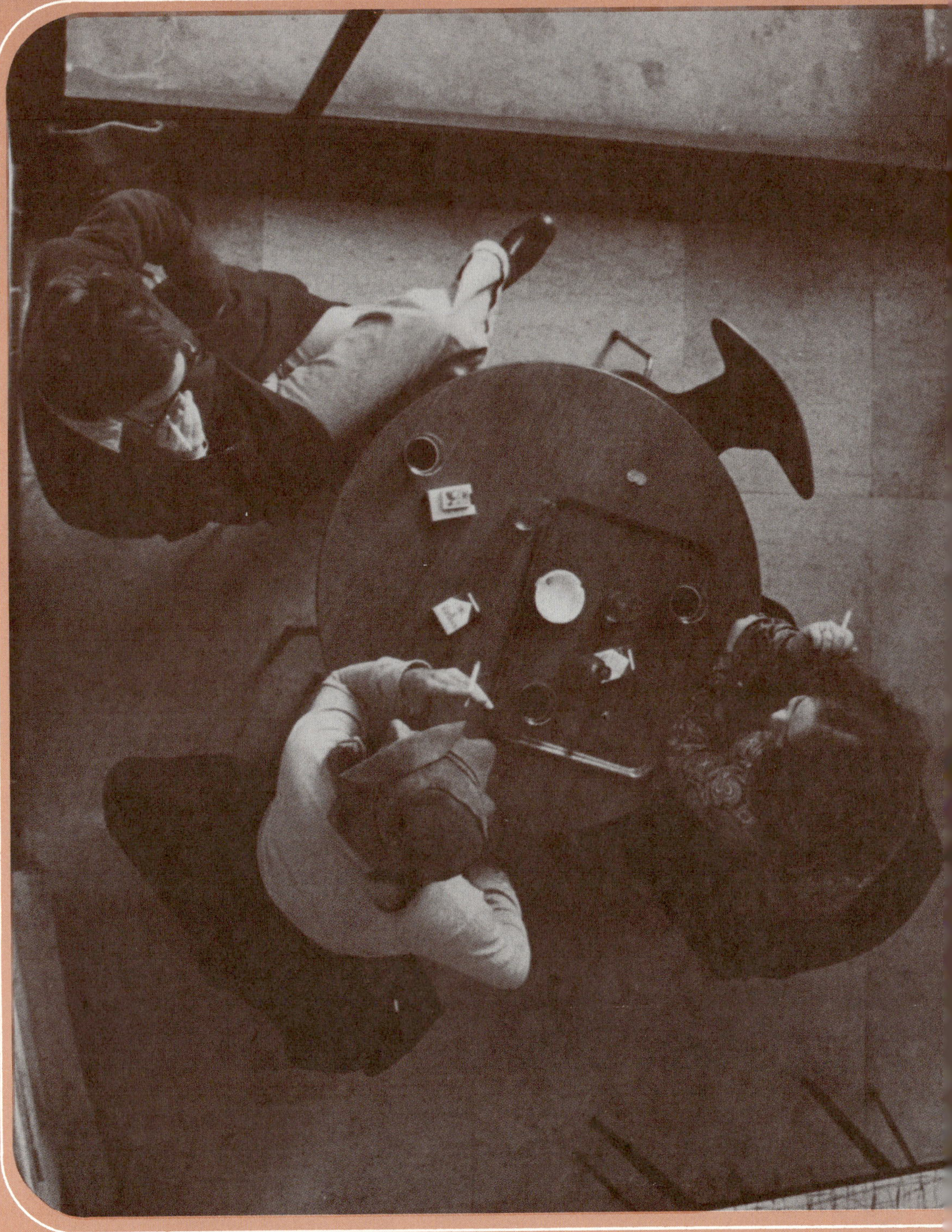

# 11
# Group Dynamics and Informal Organizations

**LEARNING OBJECTIVES**

After studying this chapter, you should be able to:
1. Define key terms used in the study of group dynamics.
2. Explain why informal organizations exist and grow.
3. Contrast and compare four types of groups which evolve in informal organizations.
4. Contrast three methods of studying groups.
5. Describe the grapevine and how it influences communications in an organization.
6. Contrast four different types of communication networks.
7. Discuss group norms and their influence on the organization.
8. Describe group sanctions, disciplines, and rewards.
9. Explain how informal leaders emerge in an organization.
10. Discuss how the informal group can be used to the manager's advantage.

In chapter 10 we reviewed the principles of formal organizational structure. The unit described the documented and official structures found in organizations. Now we look at group dynamics and the informal organizational structure. Informal organizations develop spontaneously and are a dynamic and changing part of organizations. This chapter considers the nature of groups, cliques, face-to-face relationships, and the influence of the informal structure on the formal structure.

An understanding of the principles of group dynamics is necessary for managers. To work with people effectively the manager must be aware of role models, status, emergent leaders, communications channels, group norms, rewards, and sanctions.

## KEY TERMS

Informal organizations are present in virtually all formal organizations. They may have a positive or negative influence on the attainment of organizational goals. Before looking at group dynamics and at how the informal organization influences the formal structure, let us review some basic definitions.

— *Group dynamics.* Group dynamics is the study of how people interact in groups. Group dynamics is concerned with such things as role, role conflict, status, power, group decision making, and control. This subject has been researched extensively by sociologists. Much of their work has value to managers who must work with individuals as part of groups.

— *Group.* A group is a collection of individuals with like interests or tasks, or under common command. Groups form as a result of face-to-face contact. They may emerge from clustering of individuals in like departments, work teams, offices, or common jobs and work stations.

Groups range in size from a couple of people to several hundred. They emerge whenever people are placed in close proximity to each other. Individuals under common managers, job categories, or with similar interests interact with each other and influence the behavior and attitudes of other members.

— *Role.* A role is the expected pattern of behavior associated with a job or position. A role consists of the characteristics and behavioral phenomena related to a given station or position in an organizational hierarchy. Managers, for example, are expected to fill a role of leadership by directing others. Subordinates, on the other hand, are expected to fill the role of followers by accepting orders.

An individual may fulfill many roles in life simultaneously. One may be a parent, employee, and spouse, all at the same time. Roles sometimes come into conflict. The role one fills as a sales manager may conflict with the role one fills as a consumer. The handling of role conflicts of organization participants is one of the responsibilities of management.

— *Status*. Status is the social position of an individual in the eyes of other people. Status consists of one's rank or position compared to others. Ownership status, for instance, places a business proprietor in a position of authority over subordinates.

An individual's social status is often based upon her peer group's assessment of her occupation, education, source of income, or kind of home. Table 11-1 illustrates a ranking showing how others associate status with occupation.

Status among coworkers may be different from one's official status in the organizational hierarchy. An individual may be held in high esteem by fellow workers, but occupy a low-status position on the organizational chart. The converse may also be true.

**Table 11-1  Status by determinants**

| Status Level | Occupation |
|---|---|
| 1. | Major executives of large firms or successful licensed professionals with advanced degrees. |
| 2. | Major executives of small firms; middle management executives of large firms; moderately thriving licensed professionals; faculty members of the better colleges; editors, critics, commentators, and other opinion molders. |
| 3. | Minor-responsibility business jobs; white-collar supervisors; professionals without licensing protection; high-school teachers. |
| 4. | Supervisors of manual workers; skilled white-collar workers; technicians; high-responsibility blue-collar employees. |
| 5. | Salaried manual workers; semi-skilled white-collar workers; semi-professionalized service workers. |
| 6. | Semi-skilled manual workers; white-collar machine attendants. |
| 7. | Casual laborers, domestic servants. |

| Status Level | Education |
|---|---|
| 1. | Professional- or graduate-school attainment. |
| 2. | Graduate of a four-year college. |
| 3. | Graduate of a two-year college or at least one and one half years of college (but without a degree). |
| 4. | High-school graduate plus "trade school" or "business school" education or attendance for a year or less at a regular college. |
| 5. | High-school graduate. |
| 6. | Attended high school but did not graduate. |
| 7. | No more than eight grades of schooling. |

**(Table 11-1 continued)**

| Status Level | Source of Income |
|---|---|
| 1. | Most of income from inherited wealth. |
| 2. | Most of annual income from investments and savings gained by earner. |
| 3. | Most of income from profits of business or fees from practice of profession. |
| 4. | Most of income from salary of job or commissions on sales. |
| 5. | Most of income from hourly wages from job or piecework. |
| 6. | Most of income from private assistance (friends, relatives, etc.) plus part-time work. |
| 7. | Most of income from public relief or nonrespectable sources such as bootlegging. |

| Status Level | Kind of Home |
|---|---|
| 1. | Own two homes, both with fashionable addresses. |
| 2. | Fine, large, well-kept home in "nicest" part of town; or live in high-status apartment building with doorman and tastefully decorated foyer. |
| 3. | A good, roomy house in one of the better sections of town or countryside; or live in a modern, well-kept apartment building. |
| 4. | A small, modern development house costing less than $15,000; or a plain, nonfashionable larger one in a nice but nonfashionable neighborhood; or live in an adequate but rather plain apartment building. |
| 5. | A double house or row house or an old walk-up apartment building where cooking odors and garbage are likely to be noticed in the hallways. |
| 6. | A small, plain, run-down house or apartment, badly in need of paint or redecoration, in one of poorer sections of town. |
| 7. | A dilapidated house or apartment in the poorest section of town. |

Reprinted by permission of David McKay Co., Inc., from the book *The Status Seekers,* copyright 1959 by Vance Packard.

— *Status symbols.* Symbols are key factors in identifying status. Organizations often provide symbols, or clues, which associate an individual with status or position in the hierarchy. For instance, a reserved parking space may be given to selected people and be seen as a status symbol by other employees. Status symbols in the work place include private secretaries, private offices, names lettered on doors, private telephones, or air-conditioned suites.

In our personal lives, status symbols play a role in identifying our position and station in life. Possession of an expensive automobile, jewelry, or certain brands of clothing provide status identification. A manager must understand the implications of status to subordinates.

— *Norm.* A norm is an authoritative standard or model. Organizational norms may be defined by management. Managers establish the limits of behavior, volume of output, dress code, or language used by subordinates. Norms are used to limit, control, and modify behavior.

Norms are also unofficially established by groups within an organization. For example, a group of clerical typists may informally establish a norm of twenty reports per day. This is the expected and group accepted output from each worker. Employees who outproduce the norm may be subject to criticism or sanction by the group.

Informal group norms sometimes come into conflict with established organizational norms. For instance, a manager may state thirty reports as the acceptable minimum output for one day. But the work group may allow only twenty. This places the individual in conflict between the group norm and the organizational norm. The manager should understand the implications of norms and how they affect and control the behavior of individuals.

---

**REAL WORLD**

# Stockholders' Meetings—Assured Calm

Most Japanese firms try to run their shareholders' meetings in a quiet, low-key manner. But in these highly controversial times Japanese consumers and activists are asking a lot of questions in board meetings. The directors are continually faced with the problem of questioning shareholders who put them on the spot.

This sets the stage for Seigo Matsushima, a full-time expert on managing shareholders' meeting. He is paid over $200,000 a year by Japanese corporations. His job is to see that no embarrassing questions are asked or controversial issues raised in stockholders' meetings. It is not uncommon for a Japanese stockholders' meeting to last less than half an hour with not one question raised from the floor.

Matsushima's arsenal includes a group of intimidating loudmouth shareholders who shout down objections. He also does research on individuals and their expense accounts and is not above using this information to see that challenges are kept to a minimum.

Adapted from the *Los Angeles Times*, 20 February, 1980.

— *Clique.* A clique is a narrow, exclusive group of persons. Cliques consist of small groups of people who share a common interest, goal, purpose, or command. A characteristic of cliques is their small size and exclusivity. Usually, only a select few are accepted into a clique. Cliques are still part of the larger work group and several cliques may simultaneously form in one office or department. Each may be distinct from the other and have exclusive membership and norms.

— *Subclique.* A subclique is a subset, or smaller group, which is part of a larger clique. A subclique may consist of only two or three members who themselves may be part of a clique. An understanding of cliques is important to the manager since these small groups establish norms and attitudes and control behavior.

— *Cohesiveness.* Cohesiveness is a measure of the degree to which members of a group stick together. In highly cohesive groups, members are bound closely to one another. In groups with low cohesion, there is little affinity for the group. Members may drift in and out freely. Some groups have little common bonding while others have high cohesion. The manager should be aware of this element in group dynamics and how it influences group interaction.

— *Locomotion.* Locomotion is the movement of a group toward a common goal. Groups, much like individuals, are capable of reaching goals. If all members of a group have a common goal, the group is more likely to reach it. They exhibit a high degree of locomotion. If many individuals in a group are in disagreement, the group cannot reach its goals and thus exhibits low locomotion.

## WHY DO INFORMAL ORGANIZATIONS EXIST AND GROW?

Informal groups are part of virtually all organizations. They form whenever individuals meet on the job in face-to-face situations. Informal groups emerge during lunch and rest periods, union meetings, and in off-the-job social activities.

### Job Dissatisfaction and Boredom

To fully understand why informal groups emerge, it is necessary to consider the nature and makeup of many jobs. In the modern industrial society, many jobs provide little satisfaction or reward. Many assembly line tasks involve repetitive work with little personal contact between employees. These jobs are dull and often involve hours standing at one place or next to a production line.

The pace and specialized nature of other jobs forces workers to perform alone or in surroundings which provide little social and personal contact. Many jobs are devoid of creativity and interest. Thus the worker finds himself dissatisfied, alienated, and alone. He may harbor feelings of frustration and anxiety toward his job, supervisor, or even the entire organization.

It is accepted that each individual has a need for satisfaction and reward for work well done. The nature of many jobs precludes self-satisfaction and creative outlets and in fact forces conformity and regimentation on employees.

## Need for Rewards, Security, and Social Outlets

Since many jobs do not provide intrinsic rewards and opportunity for self-satisfaction, workers look for it in informal groups on the job. Spontaneous groups and cliques which flourish in offices and shops provide the workers with needed rewards, status, and prestige.

The informal organization also provides employees with a communication channel and source of information. (See figure 11-1.) A degree of job security can also be found in the informal group. When an employee becomes a friend of the personnel clerk, he knows that he will be favored for choice assignments.

The informal group establishes norms which provide economic security to group members. For example, informal work groups often establish the maximum acceptable output for each employee. Thus, workers in a department are assured of work, since overproducers are pressured into slowing down.

The informal group, by providing camaraderie, personal friendships, and peer recognition, gives members a feeling of belonging. These elements are gained from the informal group and thus reduce work fatigue and frustration.

## TYPES OF GROUPS

Four types of groups have been defined by Sayles.[1] An understanding of these categories helps the manager view the informal structure more clearly. They focus on the patterns by which groups form.

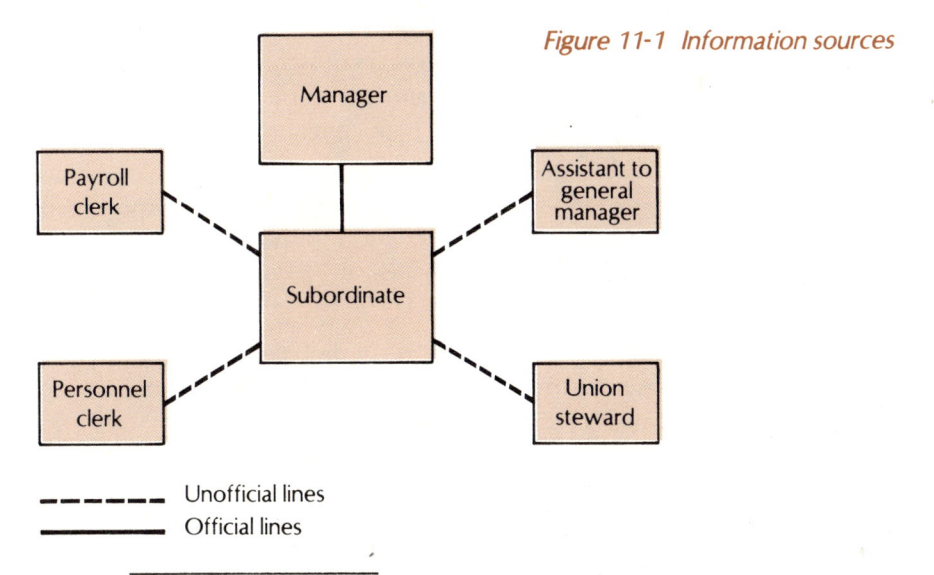

Figure 11-1 Information sources

---

[1]Leonard R. Sayles, *Research in Industrial Human Relations* (New York: Harper and Row, 1957).

Cohesiveness usually develops when group members work together as a team.

1. *Command group.* The command group is made up of individuals who are under a common command. This relationship is established when subordinates are subject to the same manager. Thus all line employees under a given department manager belong to a common command group.

2. *Task groups.* Task groups form when individuals cluster together to perform a common job or task. Workers in one department or on the same shift, performing like duties, soon form task groups. Their common bond is in their job-related functions.

3. *Interest groups.* Interest groups form when employees have common interests and face similar problems. For instance, newly hired employees, minority employees, or those with many years of seniority form groups to protect their common interests.

4. *Friendship groups.* Employees with like interests, hobbies, recreational activities, and political leanings form friendship groups. These employees look to one another for support, companionship, and friendship.

## INTERRELATIONSHIP OF GROUPS

While groups may exist in organizations, the manager should not view groups in isolation. Managers are in effect links which tie together various groups. (See figure 11-2.) A given manager will link a higher-level group to a lower-level group by

CHAPTER ELEVEN GROUP DYNAMICS AND INFORMAL ORGANIZATIONS 251

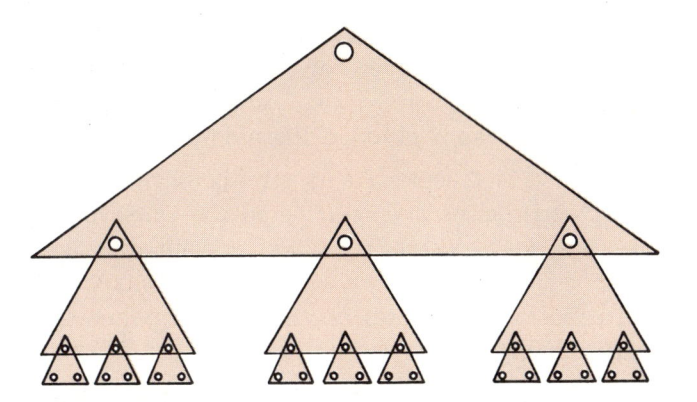

*Figure 11-2
Interrelationship of groups*

Reprinted from Rensis Likert, *New Patterns of Management* (New York: McGraw-Hill Book Co., 1961), p. 105.

providing a communication link, thus forming a chain. The entire organization is in reality many related and interacting parts.

## METHODS OF STUDYING GROUPS

Sociologists and managers have analyzed many useful techniques for studying people in groups. They have developed methods for documenting group formation and behavior. The following three methods are illustrative of how group dynamics are studied and documented. They give the manager useful insights into the workings of informal organizations.

1. *Contact chart.* A contact chart (fig. 11-3) shows the actual physical contacts

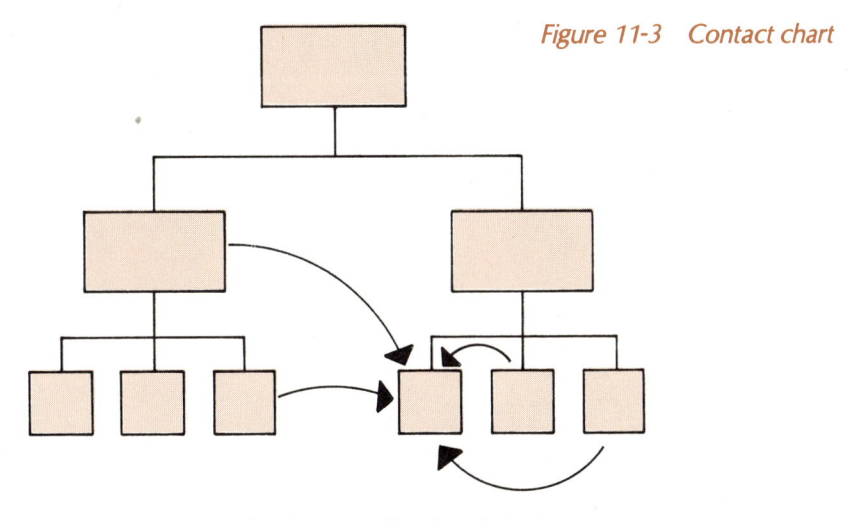

*Figure 11-3   Contact chart*

(Arrows point to individual with special skills or knowledge.)

made between individuals as they work throughout the day. This chart depicts the communication lines that take place between coworkers. It gives the manager a clue to the kinds and types of groups which form. Charts such as these enable the manager to piece together a graphic picture of the informal structure.

2. *Sociogram.* The sociogram (fig. 11-4) depicts the social relationships between members in a group. It is prepared from information gathered from employees or group members. Employees are asked to identify fellow workers with whom they prefer to associate, those they prefer not to work with, or those about whom they have no opinion. This sociogram focuses on the friendships between coworkers and how they pair up on the job.

3. *Power center chart.* This chart (fig. 11-5) illustrates the power relationships in an organization. It identifies various individuals and the power and personal influence they wield. These powerful individuals influence the thoughts and actions of others. There is often a difference between the official power structure and the actual power structure in many organizations. These differences are delineated in a power center chart in order to gain insights into on-the-job politics and pressures.

## THE GRAPEVINE

Informal communication channels exist in all organizations. News, gossip, information, rumors, and opinions flow through these channels. Employees learn

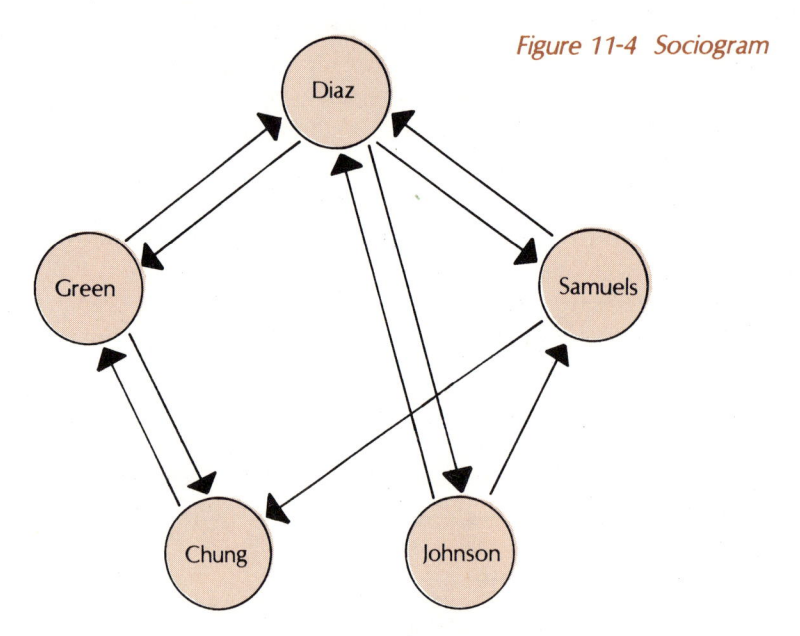

*Figure 11-4  Sociogram*

Reprinted from J. L. Moreno, "Contributions of Sociometry to Research Methodology in Sociology," *American Sociological Review* (1947): p. 287-292.

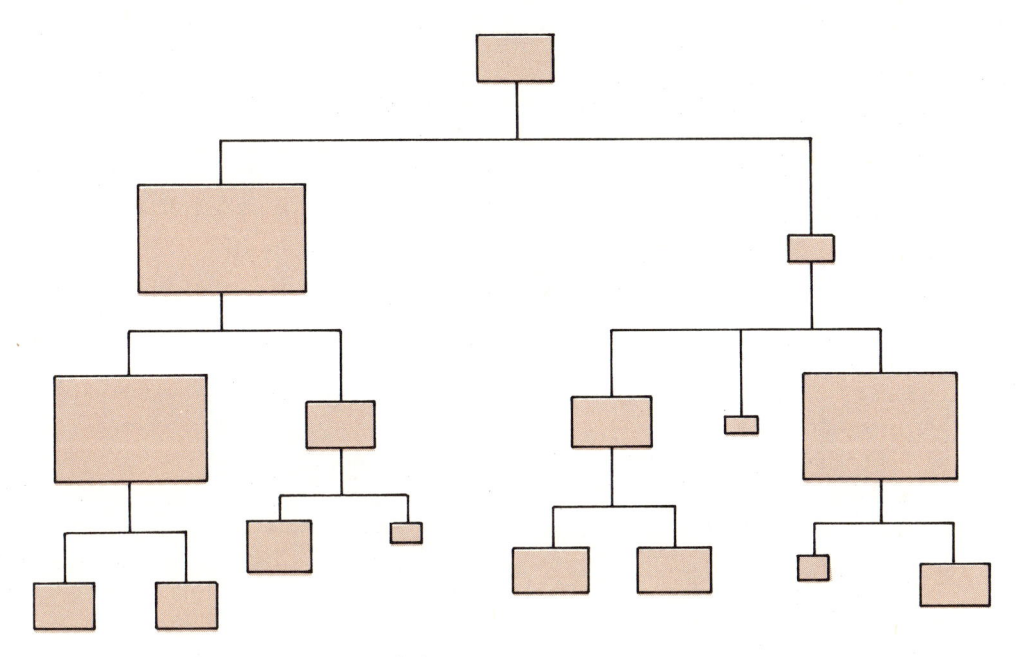

CHAPTER ELEVEN    GROUP DYNAMICS AND INFORMAL ORGANIZATIONS    253

(Size of positions drawn to scale of power held in organization.)

*Figure 11-5    Power center chart*

about events and people that affect their jobs via the grapevine. News of layoffs, promotions, and pay raises travels very quickly through the grapevine. Information, not always factual, may reach the ears of workers long before it is officially announced.

The grapevine may work in a positive or negative way for management. If misinformation and rumors proliferate, it may take months of effort and personal meetings to correct the resulting misconceptions. On the other hand, the speed with which information flows through the grapevine can be put to good use by management. They may become aware of situations and problems by means of the grapevine, which they would never hear about through formal channels. Managers can use the grapevine to test concepts and get reactions before they make an official announcement.

Figure 11-6 illustrates the flow of information through a typical grapevine. Information flows around certain individuals who are not in the informal network. The grapevine uses face-to-face communications, letters, memos, telephone calls, and so on.

## BAVELAS' COMMUNICATION NETWORK

Communications networks in formal and informal organizations have been studied in great depth. The work of Bavelas stands out because it provides many in-

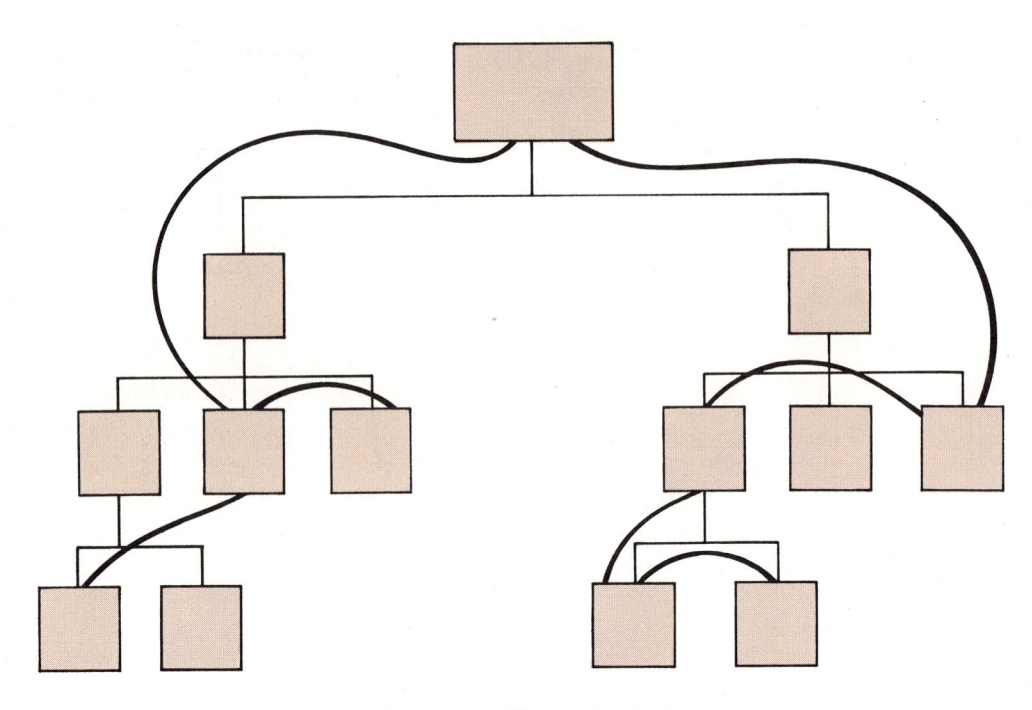

*Figure 11-6 The grapevine*

sights for managers.[2] Bavelas conceived all information as flowing through one of four different networks (fig. 11-7). In the middle of each network is a key individual. The communication process begins with this key person and flows in various directions.

— *Circle channel.* Information originates at one point in the circle and flows around the circle. In practice, an employee may pick up a piece of gossip or hear a rumor of a policy change. The employee relays this to a coworker, who in turn passes the information around to others in a circular fashion.

— *Y channel.* Information originates at the fork in the *Y* and flows out through several branches. In practice, the individual at the branch of the *Y* passes a piece of information along to others, radiating out from that position.

— *Line or chain channel.* Information flows in a linear or direct line in this channel. A person who has a piece of information passes it along to someone else and it moves down the line. Frequently this channel of communication follows a direct line of authority, as indicated on the formal organizational chart.

— *Wheel or hub channel.* A key or central figure who possesses information transmits this data to others, radiating out from the center of a wheel. In practice,

---

[2]Alex Bavelas, "Communication Patterns in Task-Oriented Groups," *Journal of Acoustical Society of America,* Vol. 22, pp. 725-730 (1950):

one person comes into contact with others and serves as the focal point of the information network. Fellow workers turn to this person for news, gossip and opinion. Bavelas concluded that power and satisfaction gravitate to key people in the communications chain. He found that speed and accuracy varied among the various networks, and that they all tended to move toward effective patterns of communications over time.

## GROUP NORMS AND GOALS

Informal groups establish goals, norms, and standards of performance for their members, much as formal management. These goals and norms determine the attitudes, work output, speed, and performance of each member. Group norms, however, are not formalized or documented, but they do play a significant role in controlling and setting the limits of employee behavior.

A common norm established by informal groups is the acceptable volume of output per day per worker. Employees may informally agree to do only a given

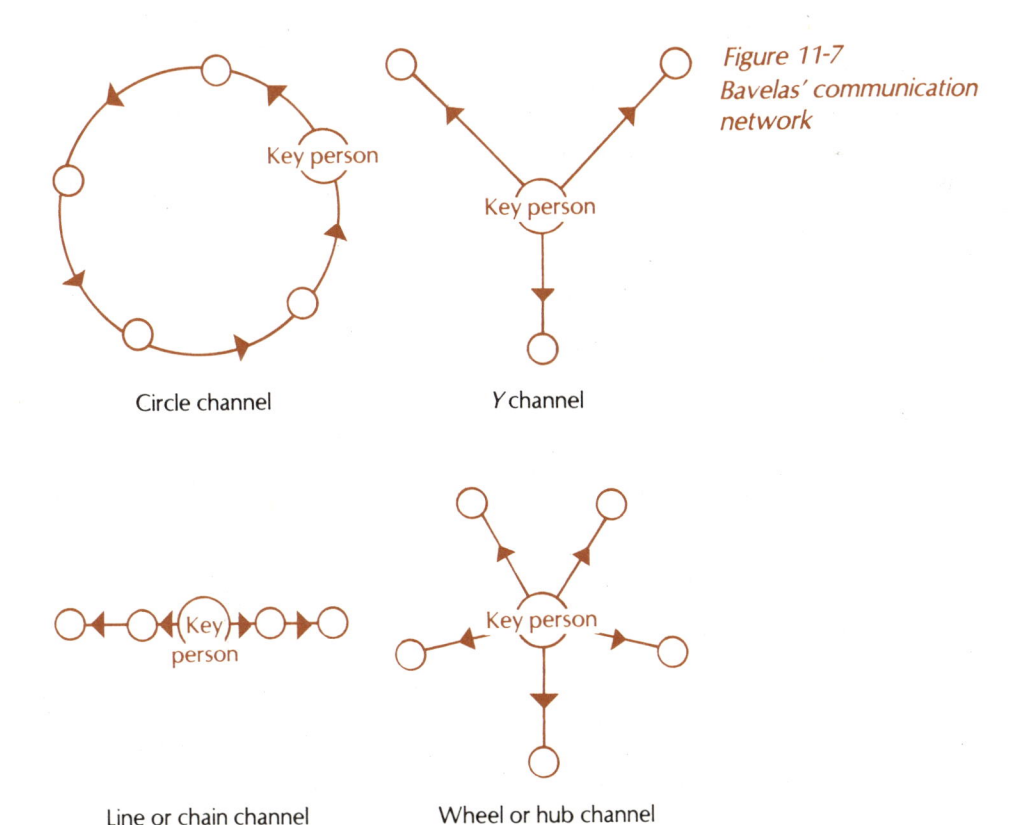

*Figure 11-7
Bavelas' communication network*

Circle channel

Y channel

Line or chain channel

Wheel or hub channel

Informal groups often set their own standards of performance.

amount of work and no more. This may be at variance with official output norms.

Any group member who attempts to outproduce others is firmly told to slow down, or, "that's not the way it's done around here." The employee must then choose to conform to either the group norm or the formal management norm. This creates conflicts. If she overproduces, she is subject to criticism and discipline by the group. If she fails to overproduce, she may not get the manager's attention and the desired promotion or pay raise.

Informal groups exert a great deal of pressure on their members to conform. Managers must be aware of these pressures and peer group influences when handling management problems.

## GROUP SANCTIONS, DISCIPLINE, AND REWARDS

When an individual violates a group norm or standard, she is subject to discipline. The group may shun or avoid the overproducer during lunch breaks, or ostracize her from the car pool or company baseball team. The group can discipline by verbal pressure, by withdrawing friendship and support, or by thrusting unpleasant tasks on her.

Groups provide rewards and bonuses to members who follow group norms. Cooperative individuals receive the friendship, support, and confidence of fellow workers as long as they conform.

Informal rewards, such as assignment to easy jobs and covering up for tardiness or absence, are given to fellow workers. These group influences and rewards are powerful forces at work on the job.

## INFORMAL LEADERSHIP

Informal leaders emerge to control, direct, and set norms for the informal organization. These informal managers and leaders may wield as much power in the organization as those who are officially sanctioned.

Individuals who have dominant personalities, or who possess exclusive knowledge, skill, or ability, may become group leaders. For instance, a line subordinate with a particular skill at repairing a troublesome machine quickly learns that he can exercise control in his department. Managers and subordinates soon turn to him whenever problems arise. They may look to him for direction and counseling long before employees turn to their official manager.

Groups may have several leaders emerge to exercise control. The larger the group, the more likely the chance of several informal leaders emerging. These leaders may have differing values and goals and create conflicts. This may force

---

**REAL WORLD**

# Firms Allow Employees to Set Their Own Hours

More and more companies are realizing that it is efficient to allow workers to set their own time and working schedule. *Flex-time* has been experimented with by companies all around the country.

One of the leading proponents of flex-time is Metropolitan Life Insurance Co. Its workers may arrive anywhere between 7:00 and 10:00 A.M. and leave when they have completed their 7 hour 45 minute day. Setting their own schedules allows employees to come to work at convenient times. About half the 1,300 workers for Metropolitan Life are able to save ten minutes by avoiding the rush hour traffic. They can also arrange car pools and use mass transit more easily. Employees are more punctual and relaxed on the job. This creates a happier situation for both employees and management.

Adapted from the *Los Angeles Times*, 18 April, 1980.

## POSTSCRIPT
# How to Boost Power in 'Brainstorming'

### By Martin Rossman

*Brainstorming — A group problem-solving technique that involves spontaneous contribution of ideas from all members of the group.*

Brainstorming has become a rather common management technique when a company needs a new idea, product concept, or marketing strategy.

Last week in New York, the head of a firm called Strategic Innovations Inc. outlined before an Association of National Advertisers workshop a refinement which he believes goes "beyond brainstorming."

In the typical brainstorming session, F. D. Buggie said, the person with responsibility for solving the problem usually picks the ten "smartest" people in the department and informs them when to meet in the conference room down the hall.

"Everybody files into the room and sits next to his pal, or in the same chair he sat in at the last meeting, at the long, rectangular conference table."

The meeting starts. "We want to do a little brainstorming here," the person in charge says, "and you remember the rule: Anything goes . . . no criticizing or putting down anyone else's idea . . . and just say anything that comes into your head. Now here's the problem . . ."

The session drones on, the recording secretary takes notes, and after a few hours everyone goes home. Next day, the recording secretary types up the notes, which may yield "a few new ideas which have potential merit." They are turned over to a subor-

Reprinted from the *Los Angeles Times,* 20 November 1978.

---

subordinates to take sides or play politics to survive in the informal organization.

Failure to side with the right person, the one who is in line for promotion to department manager, can have a devastating effect on employees later. Those who did not support the one who gets promoted soon find they are subject to criticism and punitive action when she becomes the manager.

### USING INFORMAL GROUPS TO ADVANTAGE

Successful managers are aware of the influence and power of the informal organization and its leaders. They have learned to channel these forces for the good of the organization.

dinate for "further investigation."

"And that," Buggie said, "is how it goes."

Well, he told the group, it could go better. A few changes, some mechanical, some psychological, can convert that session into what he calls a highly productive "innovation session."

The mechanical changes:

—"Hold the session offpremises, not inside the walls of the corporation, which seems to be organized to prevent creativity. Certainly don't conduct this creative session in the same room where other kinds of meetings . . . are commonly held.

—"Get yourself a *round* table. No head, no foot, no respective positions. Round!

—"Provide facilities for visual exposition: flip charts, blackboard, places to hang and mount things.

—"Wire the room so you can tape record the session. . . . Catch everything.

—"Hold the session in the morning, first thing. That's important. Don't use Mondays.

—The leader should be skilled and experienced in running such a session, and it should not be the person with the problem-solving responsibility unless he possesses these skills.

—The leader should have "a sidekick, an assistant leader, or 'facilitator.' "

—"Friends should not sit beside each other. The leader sits nearest the door. The facilitator sits opposite him, at the other side of the table."

—There should be six participants, give or take one. "Fewer than five is below critical mass; more than seven and you begin to change the character of the group. Also you 'lose' some contributors."

—The leader introduces each participant, citing his relevant background. "Everyone there is equally (and very) important."

—The leader opens the session by instructing them how to behave and what is expected of them.

As for the psychological side, Buggie urges, among other things, that everyone contribute, that there is no "right" answer, and that a wide range of ideas—some of them "way out"—be striven for.

How well does it work?

Buggie, whose firm organizes such sessions and has access to 2,000 outside experts in a wide variety of fields, maintains that "the process *always* delivers a number of useful new ideas."

One of the most difficult problems is to handle the informal leader whose attitudes and goals differ from those of the formal organization. One approach is to single out this individual and use personal persuasion to encourage her to accept the organization norms. Another approach may involve bargaining and trade-offs. A manager may offer a raise or bonus to the informal leader, provided she accepts the organizational norms and is willing to go along with company policy. This must be done carefully in order not to offend the informal leader.

The subtleties and nuances of managing and controlling the informal structure are very complex. Managers who fail to understand the workings of this structure may find that their best efforts and plans are sabotaged from within. Conversely, managers who understand and influence informal leaders and groups find that they get jobs done more quickly and that they are able to take on complex plans with a greater degree of success.

## SUMMARY

Group dynamics play an important role in the study of management. Managers are concerned with role, role conflicts, status, power, and the group decision-making process.

Status symbols, norms, and small informal groups have great influence on the output of work groups. Informal organizations form because of job dissatisfaction and boredom often found in the work place. Employees have a need for rewards, security, and social outlets which are fulfilled by informal associations on the job.

Several types of groups have been defined including command, task, interest, and friendship groups. The contact chart, sociogram, and power center chart are often used to study group behavior and communication.

The grapevine is an informal communication channel found in many organizations. Bavelas defined the circle, *Y*, line or chain, and wheel or hub channels as patterns in which information flows through the informal organization.

Informal group leaders often emerge to direct and set norms in an organization. Groups offer rewards and benefits to cooperative members, while sanctions and disciplines are meted out to uncooperative members of the group.

"You don't have to stay tonight, but how will you explain 'uncooperative' after your name in this report?"

Reprinted from *American Machinist,* January 1978.

## REVIEW QUESTIONS

1. Explain what is meant by the term *group dynamics*.
2. Describe some common status symbols and how they influence organization participant behavior.
3. What is the difference between a clique and a subclique?
4. How do groups differ in their degree of locomotion?
5. Explain how job dissatisfaction and boredom influences the role of informal groups.
6. How do command and task groups differ?
7. How do interest and friendship groups differ?
8. What useful information is shown in the sociogram?
9. Explain how information travels within an organization.
10. Explain how informal group norms may come into conflict with formal organizational norms.
11. Can you give some reasons that informal leaders emerge?
12. Explain how managers can channel informal leaders into positive directions in the organization.

## KEY TERMS

| | | | |
|---|---|---|---|
| Group dynamics | 244 | Job dissatisfaction | 248 |
| Status | 245 | Rewards | 249 |
| Status symbol | 246 | Contact chart | 251 |
| Norm | 247 | Sociogram | 252 |
| Clique | 248 | Power center chart | 252 |
| Cohesiveness | 248 | Grapevine | 252 |
| Locomotion | 248 | Informal leader | 257 |

## Case Incident

Adele Sportswear is one of a group of shops located in the heart of the garment district of a major east coast city. The firm is owned and operated by Robert Adele, who employs eighteen needle operators in the shop. The operators assemble and sew individual garments which are, in turn, resold to local garment jobbers. Ellen Rivera, who is the lead lady, knows from experience that her operators can easily produce an average of ninety-eight garments per day. Each of her operators is paid a basic guaranteed salary with a small piece work supplement included as an incentive.

Mary Luiz, who has been with Adele for several years, was very disappointed to see Sue Chin, a new employee, come to work at the shop. Almost as soon as Sue Chin began work, she was easily able to average 120 units per day. This was particularly troublesome during the warm weather of the summer when most of the other operators would slow down and reduce their output.

Quite predictably, within a short time conflict arose between Sue Chin and Mary Luiz. Mary took the opportunity of taking Sue aside to tell her, "Look, hotshot, I know you're a new employee here and you want to impress people that you're doing a good job, but that's not the way we do it around here! If you don't stop overproducing, you're going to make the rest of us look bad." Sue Chin was visibly shaken by this warning of peer group pressure. Because of a large family to feed at home, she was only interested in making the most of the small piecework supplement that was paid. This concerned Sue so much that she complained about Mary's warning to her lead lady, Ellen Rivera.

## PROBLEMS

1. How should Ellen Rivera handle the situation?
2. Describe the pressures at work on Sue Chin.
3. Describe the pressures at work on Mary Luiz.

# PART FOUR
# Staffing

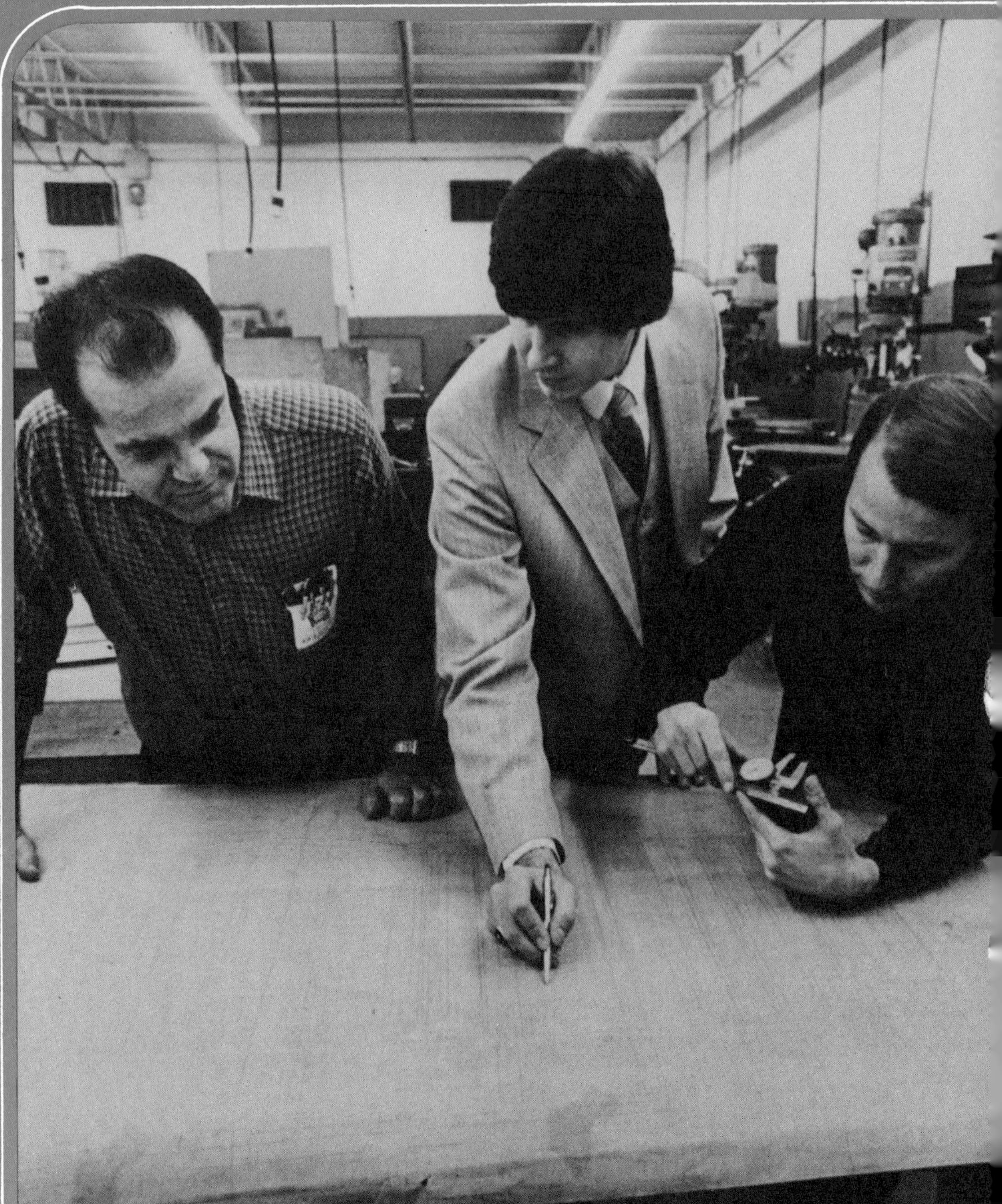

# 12

# Human Resources Management

**LEARNING OBJECTIVES**

After studying this chapter, you should be able to:
1. Describe several differing approaches to human resources planning.
2. Contrast the key difference between job simplification and job enrichment.
3. List the major steps in developing a compensation program.
4. Describe the major objectives of human resources inventories.
5. Summarize how computers are used in human resources inventories.
6. List the major steps in the acquisition of human resources.
7. Describe the elements considered in the selection process.
8. Summarize some of the techniques management uses to orient new employees to the job.
9. Discuss the evaluation process.
10. Summarize management's role in the termination of employees.

S taffing is a major function of management. Frequently it is handled by line managers. At other times this function is turned over to the personnel or industrial relations department. Regardless of which approach is chosen, the task of adequately staffing the organization remains a key element in successful management.

The purpose of staffing is to provide the organization with an adequate number of employees who possess the right skills, training, and knowledge. Labor cost is an important element in most operations.

In this chapter we discuss a rational approach to human resources planning and acquisition. It describes the fundamentals of job design, wage administration, employee recruitment, selection, training, and job orientation. The chapter reviews performance evaluation and the role of management in labor-union negotiations.

## HUMAN RESOURCES MANAGEMENT

Most managers readily recognize that the most valuable asset in any organization is its human resources. They know that the success or failure of the enterprise depends upon the quality of people in the organization as much as any physical asset. Human resources must be acquired, managed, and developed carefully.

Human resources management is a part of every manager's responsibility. It is principally concerned with a systematic approach to labor planning, job design, establishing wages for executives and subordinates, and promotion and termination of personnel. In addition, affirmative action programs, stress on equal opportunities, and a new awareness of social responsibility have further

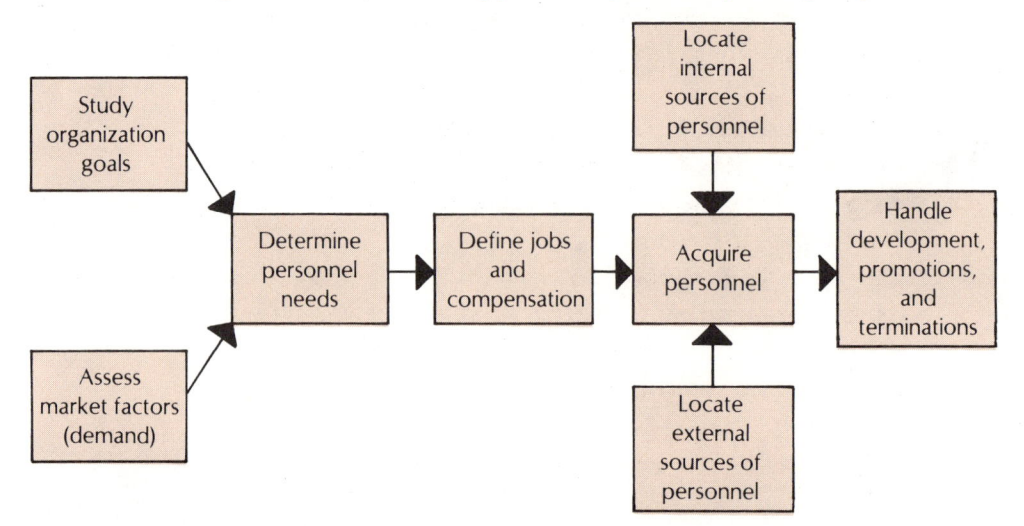

*Figure 12-1   Systematic approach to personnel planning*

CHAPTER TWELVE    HUMAN RESOURCES MANAGEMENT    267

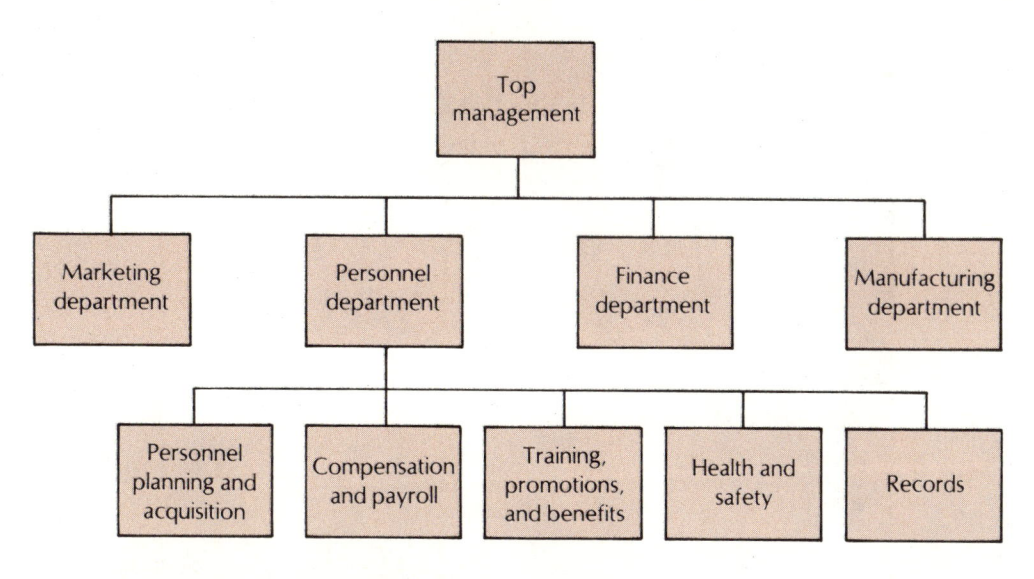

*Figure 12-2  Personnel departments in organization*

expanded the demands on human resources management. Figure 12-1 illustrates a systematic approach to these responsibilities.

## THE STAFFING FUNCTION

Many large organizations delegate the management of human resources to the personnel department, sometimes called the industrial relations department. It may be charged with the task of assessing future labor needs, acquiring and developing personnel, processing payroll, handling promotions and terminations, among other things. The modern personnel department is an outgrowth of the earlier hiring offices, which performed only the limited function of acquiring new personnel.

In some organizations, the personnel department is on an equal level with other major departments such as finance and marketing (fig. 12-2). The personnel department is generally a service department which supports other departments and services their needs.

Some of the important staffing considerations are administering the salary and wages program, human resources planning, affirmative action programs, medical and dental insurance, credit union functions, and collection of union dues.

## OVERVIEW OF HUMAN RESOURCES PLANNING

Most large organizations approach the acquisition and management of human resources in a systematic manner. Very few leave this important function to an

> **REAL WORLD**
>
> ## Court Upholds Ruling on Bias of Dress Code at Chicago S & L
>
> The management of Talman Federal Savings and Loan has enforced a dress code for many years. Since the early 1940s it has required female employees to wear a career ensemble that consisted of a two-piece coordinated outfit. These outfits were given to the employees by Talman. They were also considered income by the IRS and taxable to the female employees.
>
> The male members of Talman, however, were expected to dress in business apparel of their choice. Unhappy because of this blatant discrimination, Mary M. Carroll decided to take it to court. She lost the first round at the trial court level, but the United States Seventh Circuit Court of Appeals reversed the verdict and overturned the dress code. The court ruled that it was discriminatory to require that women wear a uniform while the males could wear ordinary business attire. They also said that it is discriminatory to require the women to pay for cleaning and repairing their clothing and for only women to pay income taxes on their uniforms.
>
> Adapted from the *San Fernando* (California) *Valley News,* 18 March 1980.

unplanned, unsystematic approach. The personnel function can be divided into three major phases: planning, inventory, and acquisition.

1. *Planning.* Determining what human resources are needed in the long and short term. The definition of the various jobs to be performed and administration of a consistent and equitable wage and salary scale.

2. *Inventory.* An assessment of personnel already employed, including a profile of the size and makeup of the work force. An assessment of future promotions, layoffs, resignations, and retirements.

3. *Acquisition.* The acquisition of personnel to fill positions which are required and which cannot be filled from within the organization. This involves recruiting, testing, and selection of prospective employees.

Let us consider each of these major elements of human resources management in more detail.

## HUMAN RESOURCES PLANNING

The first phase in the acquisition and staffing process is the development of a plan specifying the number and types of people that will be needed in the organization. This requires an assessment of the number and types of jobs to be done and projections of the volume of goods and services to be offered and the available capital. Estimates of these elements hinge upon projected sales and demand for goods and services to be produced or marketed by the enterprise.

A basic personnel plan is prepared which specifies the number of individuals assigned to each department and the amount of management staff required. Often a detailed report is prepared listing the number of jobs and work stations, together with expected turnover, promotions, and terminations.

### Differing Approaches

Human resources planning may be done from several different perspectives. One approach involves structuring the personnel plan around available people in the organization. Existing managers are assigned new or different positions. Another approach involves developing a human resources plan without assessing the presently employed work force. After the plan is completed, personnel are acquired. If the required people are already on the payroll, they are assigned to various units. Unfilled openings are then staffed from outside.

Human resources planning involves a look at both the short- and long-range picture. The planning effort determines how many new people will be needed each week or month and for the years ahead. This necessitates an analysis of turnover rates, resignations, promotions, and retirements.

### Job Design

A major element in the personnel plan is the definition and description of each job in the organization. It is up to line management to specify which activities and responsibilities are assigned to each employee. Two useful tools for preparing job descriptions are the *Dictionary of Occupational Titles* (DOT) and the *Standard Industrial Classification* (SIC) *Indexes*. These manuals list various standard job classifications used by business and government in rating personnel and classifying employees.

Once a standard job title has been assigned to a position, then a detailed specification is written. This documents the precise nature of the work, the skills, aptitudes, and abilities necessary to perform it, and other pertinent details. Figure 12-3 illustrates a job specification sheet typical of those prepared by firms for each of their positions.

A major consideration in job design and the preparation of the job specification sheet is the content of each position. If jobs are too limited in scope, they are

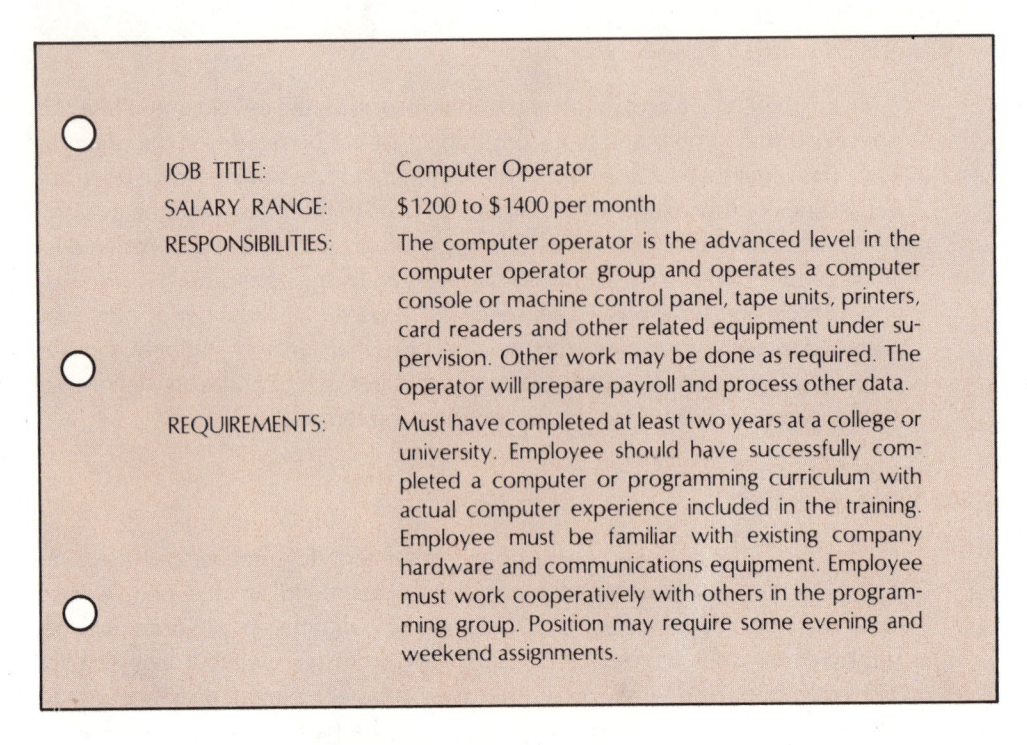

| | |
|---|---|
| JOB TITLE: | Computer Operator |
| SALARY RANGE: | $1200 to $1400 per month |
| RESPONSIBILITIES: | The computer operator is the advanced level in the computer operator group and operates a computer console or machine control panel, tape units, printers, card readers and other related equipment under supervision. Other work may be done as required. The operator will prepare payroll and process other data. |
| REQUIREMENTS: | Must have completed at least two years at a college or university. Employee should have successfully completed a computer or programming curriculum with actual computer experience included in the training. Employee must be familiar with existing company hardware and communications equipment. Employee must work cooperatively with others in the programming group. Position may require some evening and weekend assignments. |

*Figure 12-3   Job specification sheet*

dull and uninteresting. If jobs are too broad in scope, they require persons with wide knowledge and ability who may be difficult to find. Therefore, the manager must balance two aspects of job design: job simplification and job enrichment.

The objective is to create positions that are interesting and challenging, yet at the same time easily filled. For example, it is easier to find people to operate the assembly line in an automobile factory than to locate people with skills in engine or transmission design.

1. *Job simplification.* Job simplification involves reducing complex jobs to small units or components which are assigned to several people. The objective of job simplification is to make each job less complex, thus broadening the number of persons capable of performing the task. As jobs are made less complicated, they require less skill and training and thus command a lower salary in the job market. However, oversimplification creates jobs which are limited and dull. These positions may not hold the interest of talented people, and thereby create high turnover rates.

2. *Job enrichment.* Job enrichment involves combining several elements into one position and expanding the tasks, responsibilities, or activities performed. Job enrichment draws many activities and duties under a single job classification. This results in a more challenging position with greater responsibility. It also demands

CHAPTER TWELVE   HUMAN RESOURCES MANAGEMENT                                271

If a job is too simple, there will usually be a high turnover rate.

greater skill and knowledge on the part of the employee. The effect of job enrichment is to reduce turnover rates. However, the wider range of skills and knowledge required for the position demands individuals be paid higher salaries. When a job cannot be made more meaningful by enlarging it, it can sometimes be made less routine. Through job rotation or short interval scheduling, a more challenging job can be created.

## Compensation

A major task of management is to establish compensation for each management and subordinate position in the organization. This complex job is influenced by the supply and demand of labor in a given community, the skills and experience required for the position, union rules and regulations, and the financial condition of the organization.

Table 12-1 illustrates a typical list of salary schedules for one firm. It lists each position with a range of salaries. Preparation of these tables requires consideration of many factors. The final table must be internally consistent and must also be

### Table 12-1  Salary schedules ABC Corporation

| Position | Range (annual) |
| --- | --- |
| President | $46,000 to $60,000 |
| Vice president | $36,000 to $38,000 |
| General managers | $30,000 to $32,000 |
| Supervisors | $22,000 to $24,000 |
| Leadpersons | $16,000 to $18,000 |
| Line employees | |
|     Class 1 | $12,000 to $13,000 |
|     Class 2 | $10,000 to $11,000 |
|     Class 3 | $8,000 to $9,000 |
| Trainees | $6,500 to $7,000 |

competitive with other organizations. Let us look at some of the factors and methodology used in establishing salary schedules.

1. *Ranking and grading.* The first step in the establishment of salary schedules is ranking and grading each position. This is done in several ways. One approach is to assign a point system to each element of the job. The total number of points scored determines the salary for that position. Table 12-2 illustrates a point system used for assigning a pay value to positions.

Once each position has been graded, it is ranked or placed in a hierarchy. A list of all positions in the firm is prepared, with those commanding the highest salary on top of the list and those with the least on the bottom. This list must be internally consistent. That is, jobs demanding lesser skills or knowledge should not be placed higher on the list than those demanding greater skill.

2. *Establishing compensation.* Once each job is defined, graded, and ranked, the personnel department must assign a specific dollar amount to each position. Assignment of compensation is dependent upon many factors, including the labor supply and demand, union rules, and contractual agreements.

Another factor considered is the compensation base. Payments are based upon an hourly rate or a fixed salary. If a fixed salary is selected, the base pay period must be determined. Common base pay periods are the weekly, biweekly, and monthly periods.

3. *Direct and indirect pay.* Employee compensation is not always made by cash or check. Compensation may be in many forms, including bonuses, stock options,

and fringe benefits. Common fringe benefits which are part of an employee's compensation are use of company automobile, medical and dental plans, pension and retirement programs, paid vacations, educational benefits, and credit union services.

Some managers do not label these as fringe benefits because they in fact cost the firm money and are part of the employee's compensation. Under some contracts, fringe benefits amount to a substantial portion of the employee's salary.

4. *Executive compensation.* A task of management is the establishment of executive compensation. Key personnel in the firm deserve special consideration when establishing direct and indirect pay. Firms that want to keep talented executives must offer them attractive benefits. These may include stock options, profit sharing, retirement and pension plans, fully paid health and medical coverage, and liberal expense accounts.

**Table 12-2  Point evaluation form: Characteristics required for job**

| Point Value | Training and Education | Supervision Required | Responsibility Required | Ingenuity and Creativity Needed | Ability to Relate to Others |
|---|---|---|---|---|---|
| 5 | Less than high school; no training | Continual supervision | Minimal responsibility | No imagination needed | Very slight contact with others |
| 10 | High school graduate; minimal training | Work must be checked at regular intervals | Some responsibility | Low level of creativity required | Must be able to work in a group |
| 15 | Two years college; moderate training | Routine work; some supervision | Handles some cash; moderate responsibility | Some self-starting ability necessary | Moderate public contact; must work with other employees |
| 20 | College graduate; advanced training | Spot checking at infrequent intervals | Need high level of trustworthiness | High level of inventiveness required | Great deal of contact with public and other employees |
| 25 | Graduate school; extensive training | Works unsupervised | Must be bonded; failures result in costly delays or shutdowns | Extremely innovative free-thinker needed | Must have likable personality; very visible as company image |

## HUMAN RESOURCES INVENTORY

Once the manager has established job descriptions, graded and ranked each one, and established compensation, an inventory must be made of current staff. The purpose of a human resources inventory is to determine the exact number and types of individuals already employed by age, years of service, promotability, and the like. This human resources pool is used for staffing future positions and promotions. A thorough inventory avoids hiring and training outside individuals where adequate human resources are already available in the organization.

### Computer-Based Personnel Inventories

Computers are an indispensable tool for preparing human resources inventories. Computers print out reports listing the number and types of people already on the staff. These reports are categorized by the employee's skills, training, or experience. Computerized inventories provide a profile of the work force, including the average age of employees, number of years worked, health, education, and sex distribution. The computer inventory can also make projections as to the number of individuals expected to retire or leave service in a given year, and keep track of promotions, special training acquired by employees, and so on.

## HUMAN RESOURCES ACQUISITION

A large amount of time is spent acquiring new personnel. The personnel acquisition process involves recruitment activities, testing, screening, selection, and orientation procedures. Most large organizations follow a systematic procedure from recruitment of new personnel to orientation on the job. (See figure 12-4.) Let us consider these in more detail.

### Recruitment

The recruitment function consists of locating candidates for potential employment with the organization. Recruitment is conducted in a variety of ways. Prospective employees can be reached through newspaper advertising, help

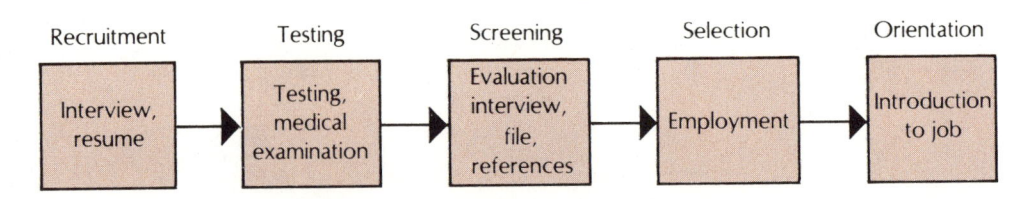

*Figure 12-4 Employment sequence*

| Recruitment | Testing | Screening | Selection | Orientation |
|---|---|---|---|---|
| Interview, resume | Testing, medical examination | Evaluation interview, file, references | Employment | Introduction to job |

CHAPTER TWELVE    HUMAN RESOURCES MANAGEMENT

> **REAL WORLD**
>
> ## Sexual Harassment Lands Company in Court
>
> Mary K. Heelan wasn't happy about the demands placed on her by her boss, Joseph Consigli, vice president of Johns-Manville Corporation. He pressured her to have an affair with him. His demands became insistent as she continually refused. Things got so bad that he threatened to dismiss her if she did not submit to his advances. Heelan decided to do two things: she changed jobs and took her ex-boss to court.
>
> In a decision handed down in April 1978 by the Denver District Court, Judge Sherman G. Finesilver laid down the rules regarding sexual discrimination on the job. Under Title 7 of the 1964 Civil Rights Act, the boss is liable when refusal of a supervisor's unsolicited sexual advances is the basis for an employee's termination. The whole matter was settled out of court for an estimated $100,000. Consigli still has his job with Johns-Manville, but feminist groups are trying to change that.
>
> Adapted from *Business Week*, 1 October 1979, p. 120.

wanted signs, employment agencies, radio and TV ads, college campus recruiting drives, personal contact, and state departments of employment.

The purpose of recruitment activity is to develop a stream of candidates seeking employment. These potential employees are given information about the firm and its hiring and promotion activities. Recruiters attempt to locate individuals who have the ability, aptitude, and experience to fill various openings.

A steady stream of unsolicited applicants for employment reaches many personnel departments. The mere presence of a large firm in a community generates employment inquiries. However, the recruiting staff may have to expand upon this supply by travelling to other cities and attending conventions or meetings to encourage applicants.

### Sources of Applicants

Applicants for employment come from a variety of sources, both solicited and unsolicited. Of major concern to many managers is the acquisition of an ethnically and minority balanced staff. This may require extensive recruitment in the local community to find individuals from minority backgrounds, women, or others to fill existing positions.

The pressure on management to provide equal opportunities has forced personnel departments to seek out individuals who were previously considered unqualified. Senior citizens, hard-core unemployed, and younger people are now sought.

## Testing and Screening

The testing and screening process in most companies begins with the employment application and the resume. Prospective job applicants complete a questionnaire on their first visit. (See figure 12-5.) The applicant is asked many questions concerning background, training, and experience. This provides information upon which to make judgments regarding the applicant's suitability for the job.

*Figure 12-5 Employment application*

| FOR OFFICE USE ONLY | |
|---|---|
| Possible Work Locations | Possible Positions |
| | |

**EMPLOYMENT APPLICATION**

**(Short Form)**

(PLEASE PRINT PLAINLY)

| FOR OFFICE USE ONLY | |
|---|---|
| Work Location ______ | Rate ______ |
| Position ______ | Date ______ |

To Applicant: We deeply appreciate your interest in our organization and assure you that we are sincerely interested in your qualifications. A clear understanding of your background and work history will aid us in placing you in the position that best meets your qualifications *and* may assist us in possible future upgrading.

Position(s) applied for ______ Rate of pay expected $______ per week

Would you work Full-Time ______ Part-Time ______ Specify days and hours if part-time ______

Were you previously employed by us? ______ If yes, when? ______

If your application is considered favorably, on what date will you be available for work? ______ 19 ______

**PERSONAL** Date ______

Name ______ (Last) (First) (Middle) Social Security No. ______

Present address ______ (No.) (Street) (City) (State) (Zip) Telephone No. ______

Do you have any physical condition which may limit your ability to perform the particular job for which you are applying? ______ If yes, describe such condition ______

**List below all present and past employment, beginning with your most recent**

| Name and Address of Company and Type of Business | From Mo | From Yr | To Mo | To Yr | Describe the work you did | Weekly Starting Salary | Weekly Last Salary | Reason for Leaving | Name of Supervisor |
|---|---|---|---|---|---|---|---|---|---|
| | | | | | | | | | |
| Telephone | | | | | | | | | |

| Name and Address of Company and Type of Business | From Mo | From Yr | To Mo | To Yr | Describe the work you did | Weekly Starting Salary | Weekly Last Salary | Reason for Leaving | Name of Supervisor |
|---|---|---|---|---|---|---|---|---|---|
| | | | | | | | | | |
| Telephone | | | | | | | | | |

| Name and Address of Company and Type of Business | From Mo | From Yr | To Mo | To Yr | Describe the work you did | Weekly Starting Salary | Weekly Last Salary | Reason for Leaving | Name of Supervisor |
|---|---|---|---|---|---|---|---|---|---|
| | | | | | | | | | |
| Telephone | | | | | | | | | |

May we contact the employers listed above? ______ If not, indicate which one(s) you do not wish us to contact ______



Courtesy of Eimicke Associates, Inc. © copyright 1977 — V.W. Eimicke Associates, Inc., Bronxville, NY.

The personal interview is an important tool in the screening process.

1. *Employment application.* The employment application lists education, previous employment, training, and so on. The application is generally reviewed by both the personnel department and operating department managers to determine whether the individual is qualified for employment.

In the past, the employment application was used as a negative screening device to preclude the hiring of certain types of employees. However, most states have passed legislation mandating fair employment practices.

2. *Resume.* Another useful screening device is the resume. A resume is a short written summary prepared by the applicant, outlining background, education, and experience. Usually one or two pages in length, it summarizes the applicant's experience, education, interests, and personal data.

Prospective applicants leave resumes with employers with whom they seek employment. The resume provides a convenient means of reviewing a candidate's background and may be kept on file for staffing present or future positions.

A good resume is one which includes a fair assessment of a candidate's background and abilities. It should not exaggerate or oversell the applicant's ability. Applicants often follow up their first contact with a second visit to the employment office.

3. *Interview.* The personal interview is an important tool in the testing and screening process. During the personal interview the prospective employee is asked many questions about himself, his background, and his interests.

It gives the manager an opportunity to talk to applicants in person and assess their poise, confidence, verbal ability, and personal mannerisms. For many job openings these are very important considerations. Some personnel interviewers complete an evaluation form either during or after the interview to document their findings and conclusions. (See figure 12-6.)

4. *Testing.* Tests form an important part of the information upon which the judgment to hire the applicant is made. A variety of mental and physical tests may be administered to the prospective employee, particularly at the operating employee level. These may include typing and manual dexterity tests and assessments of writing ability. Psychological testing may be done, as well as personality inventories and aptitude tests.

*Figure 12-6*
*Interview report*

### INTERVIEW REPORT

NAME OF APPLICANT: _____  DATE OF THIS INTERVIEW: _____
ADDRESS: _____ PHONE: _____
CANDIDATE FOR: _____ (Job Title)   THIS IS: ☐ 1st INTERVIEW  ☐ 2nd INTERVIEW  ☐ 3rd INTERVIEW
INTERVIEWER: _____

PLEASE REPORT YOUR INTERVIEW IMPRESSIONS BY CHECKING THE ONE MOST APPROPRIATE BOX IN EACH AREA.

| | ☐ | ☐ | ☐ | ☐ | ☐ |
|---|---|---|---|---|---|
| **1. APPEARANCE** | Very untidy; poor taste in dress. | Somewhat careless about personal appearance. | Satisfactory personal appearance. | Good taste in dress; better than average appearance. | Unusually well groomed; very neat; excellent taste in dress. |
| **2. FRIENDLINESS** | Appears very distant and aloof. | Approachable; fairly friendly. | Warm; friendly; sociable. | Very sociable and outgoing. | Extremely friendly and sociable. |
| **3. POISE-STABILITY** | Ill at ease; is "jumpy" and appears nervous. | Somewhat tense; is easily irritated. | About as poised as the average applicant. | Sure of himself; appears to like crises more than average person. | Extremely well composed; apparently thrives under pressure. |
| **4. PERSONALITY** | Unsatisfactory for this job. | Questionable for this job. | Satisfactory for this job. | Very desirable for this job. | Outstanding for this job. |
| **5. CONVERSATIONAL ABILITY** | Talks very little; expresses himself poorly. | Tries to express himself but does fair job at best. | Average fluency and expression. | Talks well and "to the point." | Excellent expression; extremely fluent; forceful. |
| **6. ALERTNESS** | Slow to "catch on." | Rather slow; requires more than average explanation. | Grasps ideas with average ability. | Quick to understand; perceives very well. | Exceptionally keen and alert. |
| **7. INFORMATION ABOUT GENERAL WORK FIELD** | Poor knowledge of field. | Fair knowledge of field. | Is as informed as the average applicant. | Fairly well informed; knows more than average applicant. | Has excellent knowledge of the field. |
| **8. EXPERIENCE** | No relationship between applicant's background and job requirements. | Fair relationship between applicant's background and job requirements. | Average amount of meaningful background and experience. | Background very good; considerable experience. | Excellent background and experience. |
| **9. DRIVE** | Has poorly defined goals and appears to act without purpose. | Appears to set goals too low and to put forth little effort to achieve these. | Appears to have average goals; puts forth average effort to reach these. | Appears to strive hard; has high desire to achieve. | Appears to set high goals and to strive incessantly to achieve these. |
| **10. OVERALL** | Definitely unsatisfactory. | Substandard. | Average. | Definitely above average. | Outstanding. |

Courtesy of Eimicke Associates, Inc. © copyright 1963 — V.W. Eimicke Associates, Inc., Bronxville, NY.

*"You have a great future ahead of you, Higby... unfortunately, this company has no place for people like that."*

Reprinted from *Graphic Arts Monthly,* May 1978.

5. *Medical examination.* Many organizations require prospective employees to take a medical examination. This may include dental and psychological examinations as well as sight and hearing tests. Medical examinations are taking on increasing significance as more organizations offer extensive medical and dental coverage to employees. The employment of people with medical problems can raise the organization's insurance premiums substantially.

## Selection Process

The last step in the preemployment sequence is the actual selection of applicants. The line manager reviews each applicant's test results, references, and letters of recommendation (fig. 12-7) in order to reach a decision. The objective is to hire the most qualified person from the pool of available applicants. Acquiring employees who lack the necessary skills or ability can be costly. Unqualified people may require extensive training to prepare them for the job or may make expensive mistakes. Applicants who are overqualified can also be costly because the candidate may not remain on the job for any length of time or may job hop to improve income.

Once the selection has been made, the manager communicates with the candidates by phone or letter. The applicants are asked to come in for further testing and additional processing.

In some instances, qualified candidates may be informed that they are ac-

**TELEPHONE REFERENCE CHECK GUIDE**

APPLICANT _____ Name _____ Soc. Sec. Number _____ DATE OF REF. CHECK _____

CANDIDATE FOR _____ Job Title _____ CHECKED BY _____

PREVIOUS EMPLOYER
- COMPANY NAME _____
- ADDRESS _____ No. Street City State Telephone
- PERSON TALKED TO _____ Name Title

INTRODUCE YOURSELF BY NAME, TITLE AND COMPANY

Mr.* (name of applicant) has applied for employment with us and has told us that he previously worked for your Company. I should like to verify some information he has given us. Do you have time to answer a few questions? (If not, get a definite time to recall.)

1. Was he employed by your Company? YES _____ NO _____

2. He states that he worked for your Company from _____ to _____
   Is that correct? YES _____ NO _____ If not, show correct dates: from _____ to _____

3. What was his job when he began to work for you? _____

4. What was his job when he left your Company? _____

5. He states he was earning $ _____ per _____. Is that correct? YES _____ NO _____
   If not, show actual rate $ _____ per _____

6. What did you think of the quality of his work? _____

*If applicant is female, use appropriate title and change pronouns throughout GUIDE.

*Figure 12-7 Telephone reference check guide*

Courtesy of Eimicke Associates, Inc. © copyright 1963 — V.W. Eimicke Associates, Inc., Bronxville, NY.

cepted for employment but are not needed at the present time. They may be asked to remain in an available pool for employment when openings occur because of terminations or promotions.

## Orientation to Job

After being hired, the new employee is generally assigned to a supervisor or manager who will orient her to the new job. Job orientation involves informing the employee of duties and responsibilities. The employee may be given literature or presentations on company policy, fringe benefits, medical and health plan options, the credit union, and other available benefits.

Orientation to the job may be conducted in a small group with other new employees. The new employees may be given lectures and company manuals to study, or they may be shown slide, video tape, or motion picture presentations. Orientation to the job may take a few hours or as long as several months, depending upon the organization and the complexity of the job.

Training for the new position may be given directly on the job by a supervisor, training manager, or lead person. In some instances a peer employee may be assigned the task of breaking in the new member. Orientation training is given in a classroom or in evening programs. In other instances employees are sent to private or industry-sponsored schools for training.

## OTHER PERSONNEL FUNCTIONS

### Evaluating Employee Performance

Once settled on the job, the employee's progress must be monitored. This involves periodic evaluation of performance on the job as well as acceptance by fellow workers. Postemployment evaluation is performed after a few days on the job or at periods ranging from several weeks to many months after hiring. Let us examine the evaluation process in more detail.

—*Purpose of evaluation.* The purpose of postemployment evaluation is to assure that the employee is suited for the job and is a productive member of the work force. The evaluation may measure progress over months and provides management with information on candidates for future promotions and development.

—*What is evaluated?* The manager evaluates a new employee's progress in accepting responsibility. The employee may be evaluated on ability to learn new procedures, to operate new machines, and so on. Since it is important for new employees to become part of a team, the evaluation may measure peer group acceptance.

A key reason for evaluation is to move employees up in responsibility and salary. Most firms have a systematic program for promoting employees who show merit and superior performance on the job.

—*Evaluation methods.* Performance may be evaluated by a variety of methods. For instance, a new employee's performance may be measured by output, speed, or willingness to accept responsibility. It may be measured in quantitative terms, such as reject rate, time lost away from job, and so on.

Evaluations may be conducted by subordinates, supervisors, or by peer groups. Evaluations may be written or verbal. Figure 12-8 illustrates a typical employee evaluation form. It assesses such characteristics as accuracy, alertness, creativity, attendance, physical fitness, and courtesy. These evaluation forms become part of the employee's permanent personnel file and are used as the basis for promotions and raises.

## Termination of Employees

The personnel department or line manager is charged with the task of processing terminations, resignations, and retirements. (See figure 12-9.) Employees termi-

*Figure 12-8 Employee evaluation form*

**EMPLOYEE EVALUATION FORM**

NAME: _____ DATE: _____

DEPARTMENT: _____ JOB TITLE: _____

**Purposes of this Employee Evaluation:**
To take a personal inventory, to pin-point weaknesses and strengths and to outline and agree upon a practical improvement program. Periodically conducted, these Evaluations will provide a history of development and progress.

**Instructions:**
Listed below are a number of traits, abilities and characteristics that are important for success in business. Place an "X" mark on each rating scale, over the descriptive phrase which most nearly describes the person being rated. (If this form is being used for self-evaluation, you will be describing yourself.)

*Carefully evaluate each of the qualities separately.*

Two common mistakes in rating are: (1) A tendency to rate nearly everyone as "average" on every trait instead of being more critical in judgment. The rater should use the ends of the scale as well as the middle, and (2) The "Halo Effect," i.e., a tendency to rate the same individual "excellent" on every trait or "poor" on every trait based on the *overall* picture one has of the person being rated. However, each person has strong points and weak points and these should be indicated on the rating scale.

**ACCURACY** is the correctness of work duties performed.

| Makes frequent errors. | Careless; makes recurrent errors. | Usually accurate; makes only average number of mistakes. | Requires little supervision; is exact and precise most of the time. | Requires absolute minimum of supervision; is almost always accurate. |

**ALERTNESS** is the ability to grasp instructions, to meet changing conditions and to solve novel or problem situations.

| Slow to "catch on." | Requires more than average instructions and explanations. | Grasps instructions with average ability. | Usually quick to understand and learn. | Exceptionally keen and alert. |

**CREATIVITY** is talent for having new ideas, for finding new and better ways of doing things and for being imaginative.

| Rarely has a new idea; is unimaginative. | Occasionally comes up with a new idea. | Has average imagination; has reasonable number of new ideas. | Frequently suggests new ways of doing things; is very imaginative. | Continually seeks new and better ways of doing things; is extremely imaginative. |

Courtesy of Eimicke Associates, Inc. copyright 1962 — V.W. Eimicke Associates, Inc., Bronxville, NY.

## EMPLOYEE EXIT INTERVIEW

Date _____

Name _____ Department _____
Social Security No. _____ Job Title _____
Supervisor's Name _____ Date Hired _____ Date Separated _____

TYPE OF TERMINATION: Retirement _____ Resignation _____ Discharge _____ Layoff _____

### I. STATED REASON FOR SEPARATION
(Please check the reason that applies)

**RESIGNATION**
- Physical Condition
- Family
- Returning to School
- Secured Better Position
- Going into Business for Self

Disliked:
- Hours
- Supervisor
- Type of Work
- Wages
- Working Conditions

Other Reason: _____

**DISCHARGE**
Inadequate:
- Ability
- Personality
- Drive
- Efficiency
- Cooperation
- Dishonesty
- Rules Violation
- Absenteeism
- Tardiness
- Accident Prone

Other Reason: _____

**LAYOFF**
- Temporary Work
- Reduction of Staff
- Other Reason: _____

**RETIREMENT**
- Age
- Medical

Complete when employee has RESIGNED:
New Employer _____ Location _____
Nature of new work _____ Pay _____ Hours _____

Complete in DISCHARGE cases:
When was employee notified _____ How was employee notified _____

Complete in LAYOFF cases:
Was employee offered transfer? Yes _____ No _____
To which department? _____ To which job? _____
Why was transfer refused? _____

*Figure 12-9 Employee exit interview*

Courtesy of Eimicke Associates, Inc. © copyright 1967 — V.W. Eimicke Associates, Inc., Bronxville, NY.

nate employment for many reasons. They may be dismissed because of inferior work, poor evaluations, insubordination, or high absenteeism. They may also be terminated because of rollbacks in the firm's output and diminished personnel needs. Employees also may quit to seek work elsewhere.

Disciplinary matters related to termination are generally initiated by the employee's supervisor, then turned over to the personnel department. Unsatisfactory employees may be given personal or written reprimands. (See figure 12-10.) Employees who fail to improve or who refuse to follow company rules may be dismissed. The personnel department must process the paperwork for these employees, including closing paychecks and severance pay when appropriate.

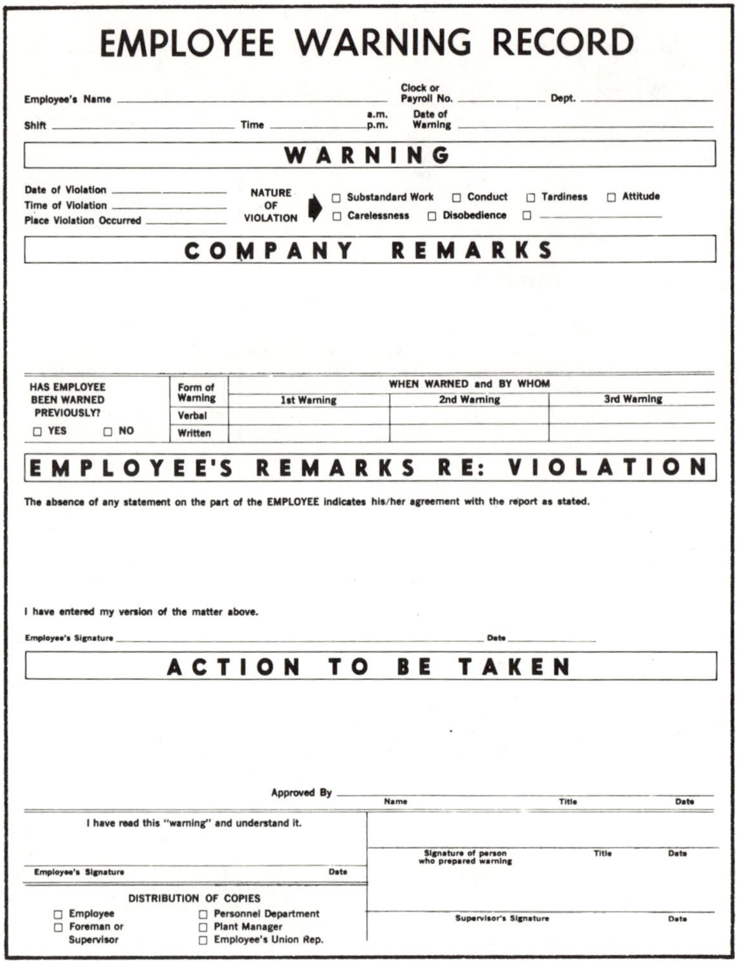

EMPLOYEE WARNING RECORD

Employee's Name ______ Clock or Payroll No. ______ Dept. ______

Shift ______ Time ______ a.m. p.m. Date of Warning ______

WARNING

Date of Violation ______
Time of Violation ______
Place Violation Occurred ______

NATURE OF VIOLATION ☐ Substandard Work ☐ Conduct ☐ Tardiness ☐ Attitude ☐ Carelessness ☐ Disobedience ☐ ______

COMPANY REMARKS

| HAS EMPLOYEE BEEN WARNED PREVIOUSLY? ☐ YES ☐ NO | Form of Warning | WHEN WARNED and BY WHOM 1st Warning | 2nd Warning | 3rd Warning |
|---|---|---|---|---|
| | Verbal | | | |
| | Written | | | |

EMPLOYEE'S REMARKS RE: VIOLATION

The absence of any statement on the part of the EMPLOYEE indicates his/her agreement with the report as stated.

I have entered my version of the matter above.

Employee's Signature ______ Date ______

ACTION TO BE TAKEN

Approved By ______ Name Title Date

I have read this "warning" and understand it.

Employee's Signature Date

Signature of person who prepared warning Title Date

DISTRIBUTION OF COPIES
☐ Employee ☐ Foreman or Supervisor ☐ Personnel Department ☐ Plant Manager ☐ Employee's Union Rep.

Supervisor's Signature Date

*Figure 12-10 Employee warning record*

Courtesy of Eimicke Associates, Inc. © copyright 1970 — V.W. Eimicke Associates, Inc., Bronxville, NY.

## UNION-MANAGEMENT RELATIONS

Some of management's time is spent dealing with unions, negotiating contracts, and participating in collective bargaining efforts. It is the manager's responsibility to work with unions in matters relating to wage rates, promotions, and seniority rights.

### Collective Bargaining

Collective bargaining is the process by which management and labor reach agreement on contract terms. The collective bargaining process requires that management and labor sit down at the conference table and bargain in good faith on matters related to working conditions, wages, and employee benefits. The collective bargaining process usually results in the signing of an agreement, called a labor contract.

## Labor Contract

The labor contract, signed by both management and union, puts in writing the terms and agreements between the parties. Some of the clauses generally included in labor contracts are the following:

— compensation rates;
— mediation and arbitration procedures;
— payment of union dues and withholdings;
— dismissal and suspensions;
— medical and health benefits;
— retirement and pensions;
— working hours and conditions;
— seniority rules;
— strike and lockout provisions;
— union steward agreement and duties.

Once the contract has been signed, both management and labor are expected to live by the terms of the agreement. It sometimes happens that misunderstandings or disagreements arise concerning the terms of a labor contract. The resolution of these difficulties often falls into the hands of the manager.

## Resolving Disputes

A variety of tools have been worked out to assist management and labor in ironing out difficulties in labor relations. The most important of these include mediation, arbitration, and fact finding.

1. *Mediation.* Mediation is the process of resolving a labor dispute by a third person or committee, using personal influence and persuasion to bring the parties together. The mediator has no decision-making authority, but simply attempts to bring both parties together to resolve the conflict by discussion. Mediators may be professionals trained in mediation, such as those available from the American Arbitration Association, or respected members from the business or professional community.

2. *Arbitration.* Arbitration involves placing a matter in dispute in the hands of a

## POSTSCRIPT

# 'Loaning' Workers Assures Japanese of Lifetime Jobs

### By William Chapman

FUJISAWA, Japan — If he were an American steelworker, Tatsuo Fujisaka would find his life traumatic these days.

Kawasaki Steel, for which he has worked twenty seven years, is short of orders and running far below capacity. It has more workers than it can use and needs to trim its payroll until business picks up.

In Youngstown or Pittsburgh, U.S. steelmakers solve that problem by laying off employees by the thousands.

Fortunately for Fujisaka, things work differently in Japan. He has been "loaned" for six months to the Isuzu Motors Ltd., and is busily turning out cars at that company's plant here south of Tokyo.

Fujisaka suffers no loss of pay: Kawasaki guarantees him the same wage he earned with them. Next spring, he'll return to Kawasaki Steel with seniority intact and enjoy that company's annual pay raise.

He and thirty one other Kawasaki workers transplanted to Isuzu have only one worry, he says. They fear they may make a mistake or cause a careless accident in the auto factory that would reflect badly on their training at Kawasaki Steel. It would be a terrible thing, he says, to bring "dishonor" on Kawasaki.

Fujisaka is a case history in Japan's unusual industrial system, which guarantees employees lifetime jobs, through thick and thin, and earns their unwavering loyalty in return. Firings are rare and massive layoffs unthinkable. When Fujisaka joined Kawasaki Steel twenty seven years ago, both he and the company expected he'd be there for life.

During most of Japan's postwar history, the economy has been strong and assembly lines busy. Keeping the permanent-employment bargain was no problem while the good times rolled.

But Japan in now mired in a four-year-old recession, and major industries are in trouble. The steel industry is running at only

Reprinted with the permission of the publisher. Copyright © 1978 *The Washington Post*.

---

third person or committee which is given decision-making power. This third party has the power to render a decision binding on both parties. In arbitration, both sides present their positions and the arbitrator renders a decision. Arbitration is frequently used in resolving labor disputes.

*3. Fact finding.* Fact finding involves giving a third party investigatory power to analyze issues and present the facts or prepare a report. After the fact finder pre-

seventy percent of capacity. But most of the bargains have been honored so far.

How well the pledges have been met is illustrated by Japan's low unemployment rate, which has remained phenomenally steady through the years. It is now 1.9 percent, just what it was in 1957. In the last twenty years, there has never been a variation of more than 1 percent in the monthly unemployment rate. Even today, it is far below that in the United States.

"In the United States, four percent unemployment is considered acceptable," observed one Western economist. "In Japan they worry if it hits two percent."

The government helps out by subsidizing salaries in companies forced to suspend business because of a recession. Since 1975, the Labor Ministry has been authorized to subsidize half the salary of an employee in a large enterprise and two-thirds of the wage paid someone in a small and medium-sized company. Nearly 70,000 companies spanning twenty five industries are keeping workers on their payrolls with the help of subsidies now.

Since last October, Kawasaki Steel has sent thirty one workers to the Isuzu auto plant here. Mitsubishi Heavy Industries transferred 600 employees to other companies within the Mitsubishi Group. Some companies don't like to talk about such transfers because they constitute a loss of face in business circles. One executive acknowledged that forty workers had been transferred to an auto plant but asked that his company name not be printed because it was not an "honorable" practice.

Isuzu, with its passenger car and pickup truck orders booming, is a natural place to farm out excess labor. It has accepted a total of 520 workers from eleven other companies—five of them part of the Nippon Steel Group of enterprises.

Elaborate arrangements are made to assure the workers that they are only temporarily relocated and to preserve their basic company loyalties.

Isuzu also created the title of "intern" for the Kawasaki employees who came to work in Fujisawa so that their special status would be recognized. Special badges bearing the word "intern" are on their jackets.

The salaries paid at Isuzu are lower than at Kawasaki. To assure the men their status remained unchanged, despite the change in factories, Kawasaki pays the difference between their old and new wages.

To ease any lingering anxiety about leaving Kawasaki Steel, the men were also given a pep talk by their bosses. They should think of their time at Isuzu, they were told, as an opportunity to study car-making and develop new ideas for making steel that goes into autos. When they return to Kawasaki in the spring, they were informed, their ideas may help their company make better steel products when times are better.

sents the facts in an objective way, it is hoped that a resolution of the dispute will be reached.

4. *Grievance hearing.* Another means of resolving disputes between union and management is the grievance hearing. In this procedure a panel of employees and representatives from management are empowered to hear a grievance and render a decision. The grievance procedure attempts to resolve disputes by

discussion and informal investigation. It avoids the time and expense of litigating disputes in the courts. This method of resolving conflicts is growing in importance.

5. *Unresolved disputes.* It sometimes happens that the proceding methods do not resolve the conflict or disagreement. Management and labor then turn to other means of bringing pressure on one another. The common means that management uses to force labor into agreement include public pressure and the injunction. Extensive public relations campaigns, lobbying efforts, and use of the news media are often employed. Management can also obtain a court order, called an *injunction,* which forces unions to abide by the terms of an agreement.

Union's methods of bringing pressure on management include the strike and the boycott. Striking employees pressure management into agreement by refusing to work. Picket lines are thrown up around the plant. These lines are usually respected by other unions, whose members will not cross the lines. The boycott involves economic pressure by unions, who seek to discourage people from buying goods or services from the organization being boycotted. Through this economic pressure, the union attempts to force management to meet its demands.

## Other Issues

A variety of other issues are within the domain of the manager. These deal with union shop agreements, agency agreements, exclusive representation agreements, and so on. This area of management is very complex and is delegated to managers with many years of experience in union-management relations.

## SUMMARY

Staffing, a major function of management, provides the organization with its necessary complement of employees. The manager is concerned with planning, inventorying, and acquiring human resources. Human resources planning involves defining and describing each job in the organization. A balance must be reached between job simplification and job enrichment.

Management must establish compensation for each position in the organization. First, all jobs are ranked and graded according to predefined criteria. Then a specific dollar compensation is assigned to each position. Other considerations which enter into the decision include direct and indirect pay elements and unique characteristics of executive positions.

Computers are useful in human resources inventorying. The steps in acquiring human resources involve recruiting, testing, screening, selecting, and finally, orienting new employees. Once acquired, the employee is periodically evaluated.

The manager is also concerned with the termination of employees and dealing with labor and unions. Collective bargaining, labor contracts, and the resolution of disputes between management and labor are part of the tasks of the manager.

## REVIEW QUESTIONS

1. What are the major functions of the personnel manager?
2. Describe the major functions of human resources planning.
3. Summarize the objectives of human assets inventorying.
4. Describe the major steps in the acquisition of human resources.
5. What is the purpose of job design?
6. Why is it necessary to rank and grade jobs before assigning compensation?
7. How do direct and indirect pay differ?
8. What is the major function of recruitment?
9. List several major sources of applicants.
10. What function does the interview play in the acquisition process?
11. List some criteria by which an employee's performance is evaluated.
12. List several reasons that employees may be terminated.

## KEY TERMS

| | |
|---|---|
| Job design   269 | Recruitment   274 |
| Job simplification   270 | Resume   277 |
| Job enrichment   270 | Orientation to job   280 |
| Compensation   271 | Termination   282 |
| Ranking and grading   272 | Collective bargaining   284 |

## Case Incident

The Ferris Corporation is a large fastener manufacturing firm which employs about twelve hundred men and women. Because of some recent contracts which have been awarded, President David Moore has approved a plan to open a completely new assembly department which requires about one hundred additional workers.

Because of his outstanding work record in another department, Brian Carter has recently been transferred and promoted to head of the personnel program at Ferris. Carter believes very strongly in the policy of promotion from within, but in developing some detailed manpower projections, he has found that his predecessor's personnel records are terribly incomplete. Thus, Carter is not entirely sure of the exact number of employees possessing key skills which would be required in order to transfer to the new department. Since Carter is so unsure of the personnel profile of the company, he is forced to advertise for experienced personnel in the local newspaper.

In talking with Carter, Wilma Williams, a well-liked five year employee at Ferris, has said that several of her friends would like to be employed at the firm if there are job openings available. Since Williams is the local union steward, she said her friends should be given some special preference in hiring. However, there are a number of present employees who have outstanding work records who wish to transfer to the new department. Many of them claim to have the work skills and training necessary to qualify for the new department.

## PROBLEMS

1. What information should be included in personnel records in the future?
2. How should Carter handle Williams' suggestion regarding employment of her friends?
3. What approach should Carter employ to ensure that the problem will not arise again?

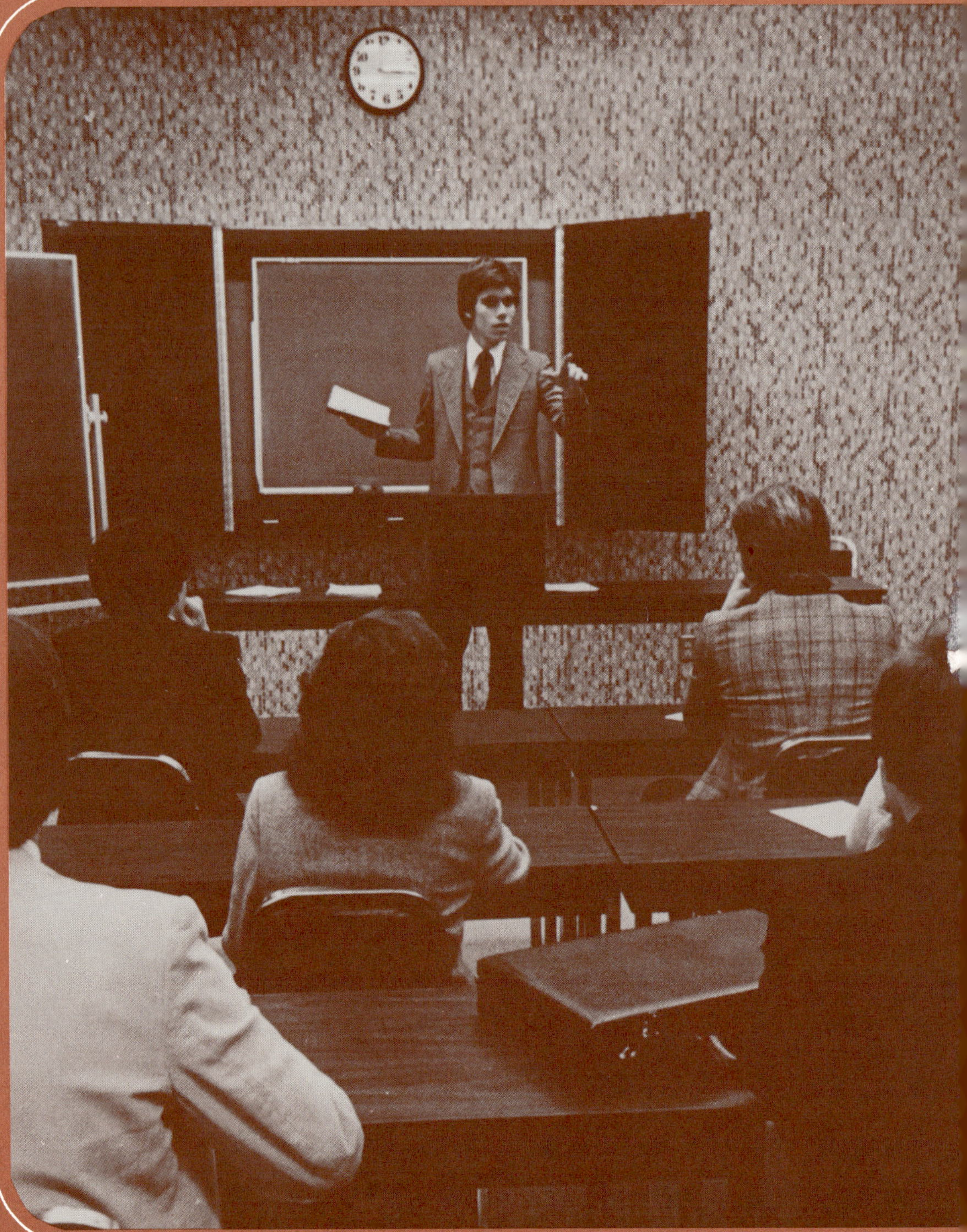

# 13

# Management Development and Training

**LEARNING OBJECTIVES**

After studying this chapter, you should be able to:
1. Define basic terms related to management development and training.
2. Contrast management development and training and organizational development.
3. Summarize the need for management development and training.
4. List the major benefits from management development and training.
5. Summarize desirable traits developed by training programs.
6. List the steps in the process of staff development.
7. Describe some ways in which people learn.
8. Summarize some applied training techniques.
9. Describe the objectives of executive development.
10. Discuss how *assistant to* positions are used in training programs.

In this chapter we look at management development and training. One of the major responsibilities of management is to maximize productivity of its work force through in-service training and management development programs. The staffing function includes the development of executives, managers, and line employees to do a better job through day-to-day coaching and training.

This chapter reviews the basic approaches to training, including such techniques as on-the-job training (OJT), vestibule training, and self-study training courses. It also describes simulations, management games, encounter and T group training, and other management development techniques. The chapter concludes with a survey of job rotation, *assistant to* positions, and the role of outside consultants.

The focus in this chapter is on the individual, and how he or she can be improved and developed on the job. Executives, managers, and line employees are discussed as subjects of training. In chapter 14 we shall review a broader approach to training, organizational development (OD). Organizational development (OD) focuses upon total staff improvement and how organizations are developed as a totality. This chapter sets the foundation by describing many of the training techniques which are employed in organizational development. (See figure 13-1.)

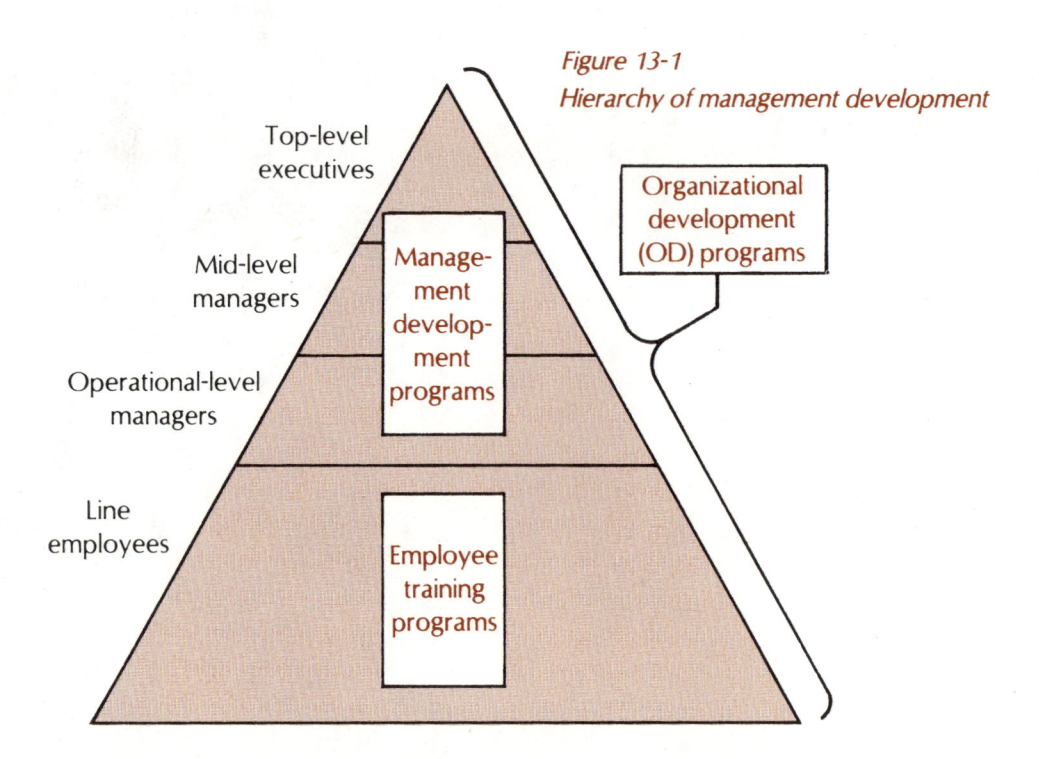

*Figure 13-1*
*Hierarchy of management development*

> **REAL WORLD**
>
> ## How the Japanese Do It
>
> It has been reported that in one forty-hour week a typical Japanese steelworker can produce 4.8 tons of steel, while an American produces only 4.6 tons, and a West German produces 3.8 tons. Japanese steel manufacturers such as Nippon Kokan (NKK) are models of management efficiency.
>
> Nothing makes Japanese productivity shine more than the new NKK plant built near Tokyo Bay at a cost of $3 billion. The new nonpolluting plant employs only eight thousand people to produce six million tons of steel per year. The old plant required eighteen thousand workers, who only produced 5.5 million tons annually. Managers pulled out all stops for the new plant. It has modern automated material handling equipment, efficient blast furnaces, and a computerized central system. Adding to the payoff is the fact that NKK's workers receive only about half as much in wages and benefits as their American counterparts.
>
> Adapted from *Time*, 17 March 1980, p. 67.

## KEY TERMS

— *Training*. Training is the process of growth, achieved through instruction, discussion, or drill. It is the preparation for a task, duty, or activity. Training seeks to prepare an individual to understand and perform a job in the most efficient way. Examples of training include instruction in how to operate a new machine, ways of handling customer complaints, or improving written and oral communication skills.

— *Management development (Executive development)*. Management development, sometimes called executive development, is the process of improving the skills and knowledge of managers or other executives. In the broadest sense, management development is aimed at making managers better able to function in their jobs. In a limited sense, management development is an ongoing program which teaches managers and executives how to make better decisions, plan more effectively, or work as members of a team.

— *Organizational development (OD)*. Organizational development (OD) is the application of the behavioral sciences to the improvement of the overall health, productivity, and efficiency of the total organization. Organizational development encompasses executive and management development, individual training, and all techniques which seek to improve the quality of the staff. Organizational development is a total program of growth which considers the broadest aspects of improving both individuals and the organization.

In recent years, top management has become aware of the need to view training and development of individuals as part of a total program involving the entire organization. Organizational development is gaining in importance as organizations seek to apply systematic and team approaches to executive and staff training.

## MANAGEMENT DEVELOPMENT AND TRAINING

### Need for Management Development

As organizations grow, they must manage more human and physical resources. The approaches to training executives and line employees used by a small organization cannot simply be copied by a large organization. A small firm may use informal, on-the-job training or coaching effectively. However, large organizations, employing thousands of people, with long-term commitments to executives and managers, must use a more comprehensive and systematic approach. Two major factors are causing more organizations to use a systematic approach to organizational development and training.

1. *Technical obsolescence.* Industry, business, government, and all other types of organizations, are continually undergoing change. New methods, machines, and procedures come into use almost daily. New office systems, word processing machines, computers, and communications systems force change on employees at all levels.

Many employees must learn to use new technology. They require instruction to solve problems with new systems. In order to provide this training, organizations use a variety of programs.

Only two decades ago an office manager would have been hard pressed to manage a modern office using computers, new communication, reproduction, and copying equipment. Employees who cannot adjust to new technology are inefficient and costly to organizations.

2. *Executive obsolescence.* Another factor which affects management development is executive obsolescence. Not only do machines and the physical environment change, but so do management methods and concepts. Managers who do not keep up with new methods of communication or who ignore advances in understanding of human behavior and psychology become ineffective.

It is, therefore, imperative that organizations undertake on-going programs to improve management skills. These include training in human sensitivity, group process, and industrial psychology.

CHAPTER THIRTEEN    MANAGEMENT DEVELOPMENT AND TRAINING    297

Computer technology has revolutionized the typesetting industry. Hot metal typesetting (left) has been made obsolete by photocomposition (right).

## Benefits of Management Development

Little is obtained by organizations without paying a price. Managers spend millions of dollars each year providing in-service training to their employees. This expenditure is made with the objective of improving efficiency, accuracy, and output. Here is a list of major benefits gained from a systematic approach to management development programs.

1. *Reduction in cost.* As management competency increases, performance on the job improves and this reduces costs. Trained managers make better decisions and fewer mistakes. These show up in reduced operating costs.

2. *Reduced turnover.* Management development programs result in better employee morale. Happier and better adjusted employees are less likely to change jobs and are absent less often. Employees with high morale are more likely to want to support organization goals.

3. *Improved management.* Training results in better organizational management. Trained managers are better able to conceptualize problems and carry out their duties more efficiently. Executives and line personnel make better decisions more promptly when they have been properly trained.

4. *Human resources reserve.* A major benefit of management development is the human resources pool which accrues in an organization. The systematic exposure to new ideas, concepts, and positions provides management with a rich resource of individuals to staff the organization.

5. *Faster decision making.* Decisions are made more quickly and the organization is generally more responsive where managers have a higher degree of training.

6. *Continuity of effort.* Management development gives an organization continuity. Where long-range training programs are in effect, managers emerge with a clear grasp of goals and management philosophy. Management development tends to reduce costly midstream changes in leadership and organization direction.

## Desirable Abilities Developed by Management Training Programs

Management development and training programs are aimed at fostering, nurturing, and encouraging a variety of management and subordinate abilities. Table 13-1 lists some of the desirable abilities which training programs develop. Let us consider these in more detail.

1. *Subordinate characteristics.* Good subordinate characteristics include the ability to follow directions, dependability, and reliability. Some tasks require subordinates to meet the public; and thus neatness, courtesy, and personal appearance are important. A good subordinate knows when a problem should be brought to his superior, and when he should resolve it alone. Desirable subordinate characteristics include the ability to work well with others and to accept and carry out organizational goals.

2. *Executive abilities.* Key executive characteristics include the ability to lead and direct others, and to plan and conceptualize long-range goals. Executives must possess a high degree of creativity and decision-making ability. Successful managers should have drive and ambition and instill these characteristics in others.

**Table 13-1 Desirable manager and subordinate characteristics**

| *Executive Characteristics* | *Common Characteristics* | *Subordinate Characteristics* |
|---|---|---|
| Creativity | Personality, work well with others | Ability to follow directions |
| Decision-making ability | Physical fitness | Alertness, neat work habits |
| Drive, ambition | Job knowledge | Good personal appearance |
| Communication skills | High quantity and quality of work | Good attendance |
| Leadership ability | Oriented toward organizational goals | Dependability |
| Planning ability | | Stability |
| Conceptual perspective | | Courtesy |

CHAPTER THIRTEEN   MANAGEMENT DEVELOPMENT AND TRAINING

*"Your aptitude tests indicate your best opportunities lie in a position in which your father holds an influential position."*

Reprinted from *Modern Machine Shop* Magazine, ©1978.

Executives must be people-oriented. They must understand human nature and encourage others to do their best work. In addition, the manager must be knowledgeable in the technical aspects of her work and that of her subordinates.

There are other desirable characteristics common to both executives and subordinates which are developed by training. The ability to work well with peers, physical fitness, and orientation toward company goals are important. Personnel must produce a high volume of output, and the quality of the work must be good. Lacking these characteristics, individuals, whether in positions of leadership or subordinates, are liabilities to an organization.

The purpose of management development and training is to bring out the desired attributes in employees. Many of the desired skills can be learned through practice, study, example, or by various training exercises.

## STAFF DEVELOPMENT

Most organizations approach staff development in a systematic manner. (See figure 13-2.) The process begins with a definition of goals for training and develop-

```
┌─────────────┐
│ Define goals,│
│  long-term  │
│  objectives │
└──────┬──────┘
       ↓
┌─────────────┐
│ Assess staff│
│  weaknesses │
│and strengths│
└──────┬──────┘
       ↓
┌─────────────┐
│   Develop   │
│  long-range │
│     plan    │
└──────┬──────┘
       ↓
┌─────────────┐
│   Develop   │
│   specific  │
│ short-range │
│training programs│
└──────┬──────┘
       ↓
┌──────────────┐   ┌─────────────┐   ┌──────────────┐
│ Use outside  │→  │  Implement  │ ← │  Use inside  │
│resources and │   │   training  │   │resources, key│
│ consultants  │   │   programs  │   │people on staff│
└──────────────┘   └──────┬──────┘   └──────────────┘
                          ↓
                   ┌─────────────┐
                   │  Evaluate   │
                   │   program   │
                   │effectiveness│
                   └─────────────┘
```

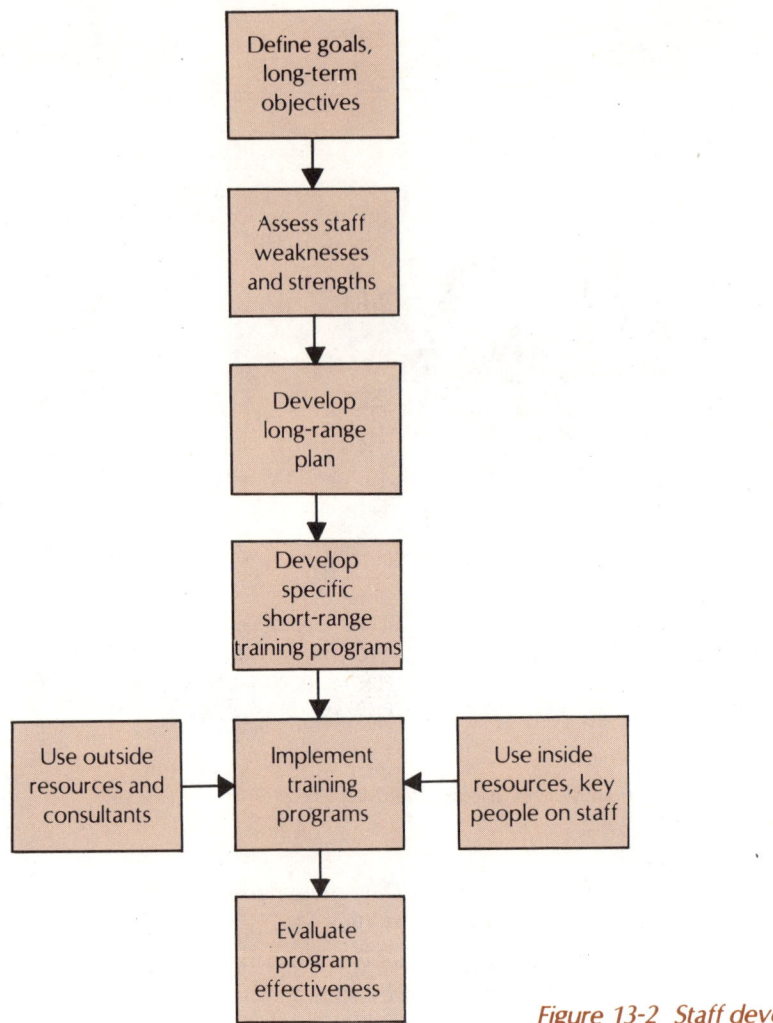

*Figure 13-2 Staff development process*

ment and concludes with an evaluation of program effectiveness. Let us consider the major steps in the staff development process.

1. *Define goals.* The first step in a systematic program of staff development is a definition of goals and long-term objectives. Management must define what it seeks to achieve through its development program. Long-range goals may include development of a large pool of qualified individuals ready for promotions, a staff possessing skills and knowledge well above the industry average, or a staff which has a high level of academic excellence, creativity, or innovativeness.

2. *Assess staff weaknesses and strengths.* Before a training program is undertaken, management must assess the strengths and weaknesses of its pres-

ent complement of personnel. An analysis is made of unique abilities and characteristics of those already employed and of gaps and omissions in their training. This information will be helpful in developing long-range plans and specific training programs.

3. *Develop long-range plan.* In this phase, management develops a long-range plan. It outlines major milestones such as annual training goals, numbers of individuals who are to receive specific kinds of training, and the approximate annual cost of providing such training. The long-range plan defines the organization's commitment of economic and personnel resources over months or years.

4. *Develop specific short-range training programs.* Detailed training programs are now undertaken. This involves acquiring text and training materials, preparing teaching aids, selecting instructors, and so on. The purpose is to reduce the long-range goals to practical units which can be implemented.

5. *Implement training programs.* In this step, the manager puts the training programs into operation. This may require the use of outside consultants, executive trainers, or assistants. In other instances, personnel in the organization are assigned to the training task. Classrooms are provided and individuals are released from regular work assignments or placed in outside training programs.

6. *Evaluate program effectiveness.* The last step in the process is the assessment of effectiveness. Evaluation efforts focus on measurable improvement of executive performance. If programs do not achieve their goals, they must be modified. Improved training techniques are developed or additional time and resources are devoted to classroom instruction. New learning materials may be prepared or additional consultants assigned.

## HOW PEOPLE LEARN

Managers should understand educational theory and practice and learning behavior. Figure 13-3 shows some of the common means of learning new jobs and skills. These range from direct personal experience to the intellectual process of restructuring knowledge. The following list shows approaches used individually or in conjunction with each other to develop desirable management characteristics.

1. *Experience.* A common means of learning is trial and error and personal experience. Through contact with people and the environment, employees gain skill in their work. However, unstructured learning and trial and error are not ideal learning methods. Few managers would simply assign a new employee to a complex, costly machine without instruction. There are some kinds of jobs where it is more economical to allow an employee to learn by experience, but on the whole it is not desirable.

2. *Lecture/discussion.* Another means of gaining knowledge is through lecture

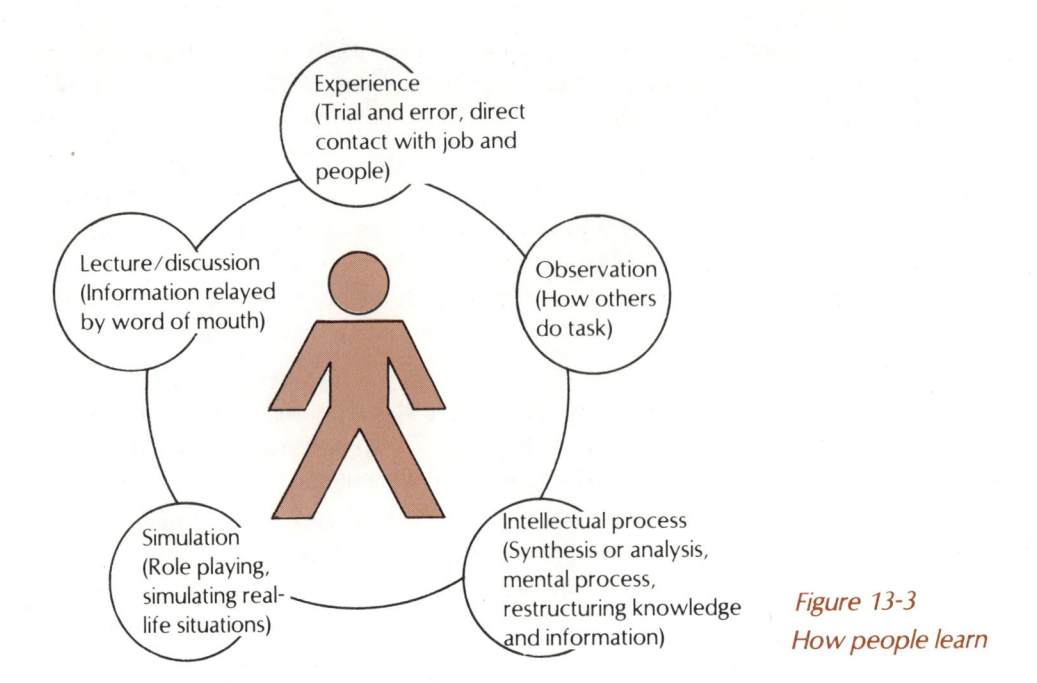

Figure 13-3 How people learn

- Experience (Trial and error, direct contact with job and people)
- Observation (How others do task)
- Intellectual process (Synthesis or analysis, mental process, restructuring knowledge and information)
- Simulation (Role playing, simulating real-life situations)
- Lecture/discussion (Information relayed by word of mouth)

and discussion. This approach is used in some job training situations. Managers or subordinates are placed in classroom settings and given lectures or presentations. Discussions enable trainees to share their experience and knowledge with others. This form of learning removes the employee from the job to a classroom or other training facility.

3. *Observation.* People learn by simply observing others. Using observation training, managers or line employees can see how other people do a job. Through watching others they learn how to perform tasks and avoid pitfalls.

4. *Simulation.* People learn in many ways besides trial and error, lecture, or observation. A significant learning technique is the process of acquiring knowledge through simulation. In this mode, people are placed in situations which simulate real-life problems. Thus knowledge and insights may be gained without trial and error or other costly methods.

5. *Intellectual process.* The mental process of restructuring knowledge and information to gain new knowledge is a form of learning. Knowledge may be gained intellectually through the processes of synthesis and analysis. In learning through synthesis, isolated elements are restructured into wholes. In analytical learning, knowledge is gained through the process of breaking down complex structures into component parts. For example, a sales manager may gain useful insights into the organization through careful study of the manufacturing process. Conversely, a production manager may gain useful knowledge by analyzing the complex process of marketing a new product. A manager who studies a business

CHAPTER THIRTEEN    MANAGEMENT DEVELOPMENT AND TRAINING                303

problem at length, then proceeds to develop a solution by combining existing knowledge and information, is using the intellectual learning process.

## APPLIED TRAINING TECHNIQUES

A variety of specialized training techniques are used in organizations to instruct employees. These tools range from the case study to coaching and vestibule training. Figure 13-4 illustrates some of the training techniques used at various levels in the organization. Let us consider some training techniques used for line employees and operational-level management.

1. *On-the-job training (OJT).* On-the-job training involves training a manager or subordinate while actually on the job. The employee is given instruction in various aspects of the work. The employee learns while being supervised and assisted by the trainer. No formal training program is set up and no special classrooms or lectures are needed. A variety of management skills can be imparted by direct contact on the job.

The advantage of on-the-job training is its flexibility and economy. The trainee is given instruction while actually producing, thus remaining as part of the productive work force during instruction. This form of training is sometimes called *coaching,* and is similar to coaching in the sports world. Training can be geared to the immediate needs of the individual trainee, who is thus brought into the productive work force quickly.

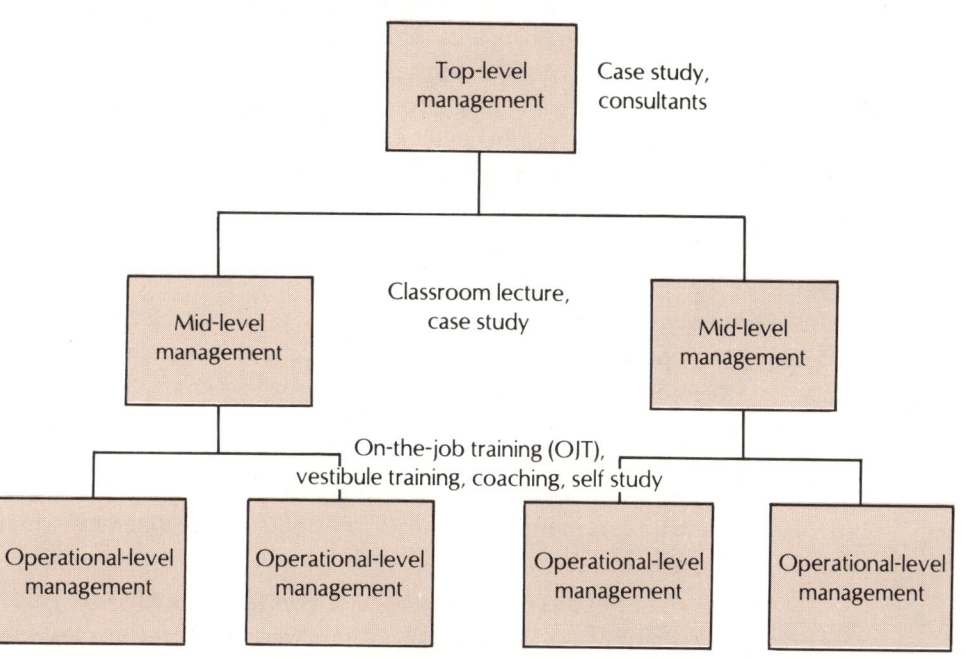

*Figure 13-4 Typical training methods at various organization levels*

American Airlines is using Control Data's PLATO computer to train pilots through simulation.

2. *Vestibule training.* In vestibule training, the trainee is placed in a training area or vestibule to receive instruction in various aspects of the job. Vestibule training requires an instructor and a training area set aside. The methods and procedures are less formal than the classroom or lecture method.

The vestibule approach is flexible and can be tailored to the needs of the specific trainees. Individuals may be given detailed instructions on specific management skills, or gaps in their knowledge may be rounded out. The limitation of vestibule training is that the employee is not productive during the training period. However, training is more efficient since the employee is removed from the distractions of the job.

3. *Classroom/lecture method.* Another commonly used training technique is the lecture. This approach, similar to that used in schools and colleges, places trainees in a classroom environment. There they are given group instruction in various aspects of their work.

Large numbers of trainees can be moved rapidly through classroom training programs. Trainees are not given individualized attention as they are in the vestibule or on-the-job training methods. However, the approach is economical when large numbers of trainees are involved.

4. *Case study, in-basket, case history methods.* Other training methods include case histories, case studies, and in-basket problem solving. These techniques vary

in application and approach. The common element is the case, which deals with actual or hypothetical problems. The trainee analyzes the problem and facts in the case and proposes solutions. The trainee's conclusions and methods of handling the problem are compared with those of other trainees or with the solutions found by actual experienced managers.

The advantage of case study, in-basket, and similar techniques is that the trainee is systematically exposed to problems and faced with actual job situations. Cases may range from relatively simple problems to complex problems found in large organizations. The case approach teaches the trainee to define a problem, gather relevant data, and solve it in a logical way.

5. *Self-study.* The self-study course is widely used as a training tool. A variety of self-study courses are used which cover many aspects of training. In the self-study technique, the student is given training manuals, textbooks, readings, periodicals, programmed instruction texts, or other materials for study.

These are read at leisure or during assigned training periods. The trainee sets his own pace and progress through the course. Self-study training is economical to prepare and distribute. Outlines, reading materials, and other items may already be available for purchase by the training departments. A weakness of self-study is that low-motivated employees may not complete the prescribed course of study.

6. *Electronic teaching media.* A wide variety of electronic teaching media are used in training courses. These include videotapes and audio tapes, motion picture films, slides, transparencies, teaching machines, and computers.

The advantage of electronic media is that they reduce the need for instructors and classrooms. Trainees assigned to learning programs using videotapes or computers, for example, proceed at their own best pace without the cost of an instructor. Electronic media can be replayed many times to reinforce concepts. Enrichment and remedial learning units may be given to the trainee as needed.

7. *Simulations, games, and role playing.* A diverse group of training techniques including simulations, management games, and role play situations are in use. All these techniques place trainees in situations which simulate real-life problems. The trainee learns to deal with actual problems which may arise on the job.

Trainees may be assigned roles to act out, such as union negotiators, supervisors, line employees, and so on. They may work in teams or as individuals.

Banks and savings and loan associations, for example, use role play as an effective tool in training tellers. Trainees are assigned roles, such as irate customers, branch managers, and so on. The trainee learns to deal with problems in the classroom before being exposed directly to the public.

8. *T groups, encounter groups, and sensitivity training.* A diverse array of training techniques fall into this category. These draw from the knowledge gained from group psychology and behavioral sciences. Various forms of group encoun-

> **REAL WORLD**
>
> ## Sears Searches for Success
>
> Sales at Sears, Roebuck, the nation's leading retailer, have plummeted 12 percent over the last year. Sears' corporate bonds have been downgraded in status by Standard and Poor, and they seem to be losing the war against K Mart and other discounters. With this writing on the wall, Sears management recognized the need for aggressive new leadership at the top.
>
> Sears Chairman Edward Telling decided to bring in one of the most promising young executives in the Sears chain. Telling picked Edward Brennan to serve as president. Brennan previously headed 150 stores in the southern United States for Sears.
>
> Brennan faces a difficult task — how to implement change. The company has layers of rules and policies to govern its 864 stores. It follows traditions dating back many decades. Sears is heavily encrusted with a bureaucracy that seems intractable. Managers are watching closely to see whether Brennan can turn this aging monolith around and bring it into the 1980s.
>
> Adapted from *Time* 5 May 1980, p. 88.

ter are used in training. For example, a group of supervisors may take part in an encounter group and be asked to give honest, frank evaluations and criticisms of each other. This helps individuals see themselves as others see them.

Encounter groups uncover personal hostilities, biases, and prejudices which may affect an employee on the job. Employees learn to understand themselves and others through intensive, probing group sessions.

9. *Schools and outside seminars.* Other training resources are outside schools and training seminars. Many public and private schools and organizations provide training programs which are used in business and industry.

These programs are diverse in nature and avoid the need for establishing in-house programs. Community colleges, evening adult schools, and university extension classes offer training programs.

10. *Consultants and special training.* Consultants and seminar programs are often used for training. Private research and training organizations offer industry and business training programs for a fee.

Seminars, short courses, and one- and two-day training sessions are given by organizations in many parts of the country. Trainees are either sent to centers for instruction, or seminars may be conducted on the premises with actual instruction provided by outside consultants for a fee.

## EXECUTIVE DEVELOPMENT

Executive development deals with training for upper-level management and executive positions. It deserves special consideration because executive development programs provide the human resources pool for filling top-level vacancies. Executive development and training programs use many of the teaching techniques discussed for line employees and operational-level management. In addition, several other techniques including job rotation, *assistant to* positions, and trial promotions are used. Here is a list of some common executive development techniques.

1. *Job rotation.* Job rotation involves the systematic shifting of a manager through several positions in the organization to develop various skills and abilities. (See figure 13-5.) The manager is moved through several positions in sequence to round out her knowledge and skill and prepare her for advancement.

    Job rotation is based upon a planned progression of positions, increasing in responsibility. Thus, the manager is systematically exposed to the problems and decisions which occur at higher levels. Once the manager has served in various job capacities, her broadened background prepares her for advancement.

2. *Assistant to positions.* This form of executive development involves assigning individuals to serve as assistants to other executives. In this capacity, they work under the supervision of seasoned and experienced executives. This is a different

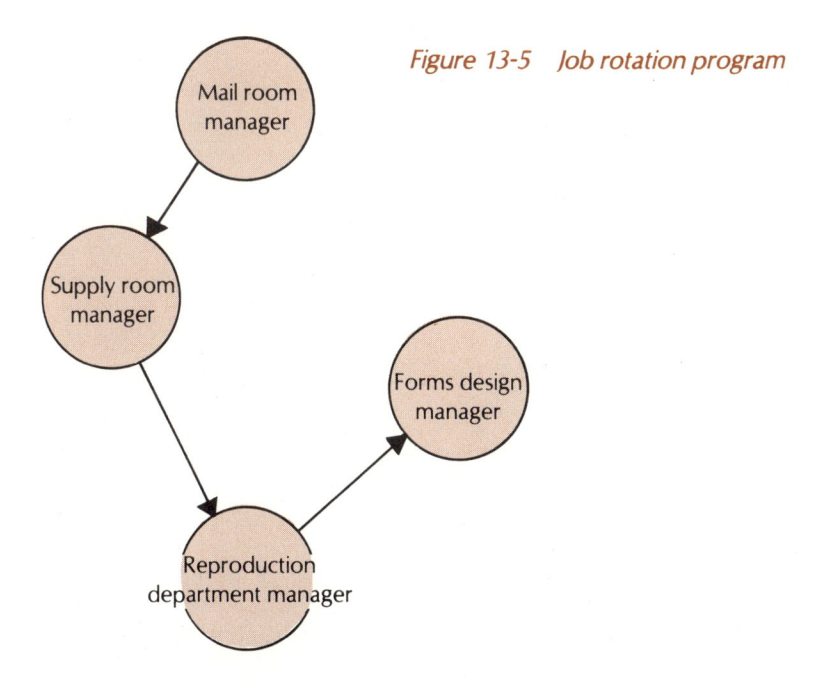

*Figure 13-5 Job rotation program*

## POSTSCRIPT
# Firm's Goal Is to Make Training Cost-Effective

### By Loretta Kuklinsky Huerta

Everyone wants to know how to do it better, to borrow a phrase from Carly Simon's popular song.

Even major corporations such as IBM, Coca Cola, and Alcoa have been discovering small firms such as National Training Systems, Inc., one of a new breed of training companies that uses space age systems analysis to streamline learning and doing.

Yet the three principals of NTS admit that their industry's battle for recognition hasn't been won. "Training is still treated as a cottage industry," admits Jay M. Sedlik, executive vice president of the six-year-old Marina del Rey firm.

While working on his doctorate in instructional technology and cinema at USC twenty years ago, his colleagues were sure that the training industry would come of age within five years, he says. Two decades later, he finds, "It is still breaking ground."

"It isn't the same as with an advertising agency," says Ronald S. Posner, president of NTS. "Companies aren't accustomed to going to an outside agency."

Then how does the firm, which expects gross revenues of $2 million in this fiscal year, even get past the plush front desk of a giant corporation? Sedlik says the answer is "to show them a more cost effective package. We package the program, deliver it, and they have it when they need it."

NTS uses a variety of media, including videotape, cassette audio tapes, brochures, printed guidelines, reports, and even a hand-held video viewer on one occasion.

None is cheap, and the NTS principals make no bones about the cost of their services. "Packages," says Posner, "have ranged from $25,000 to $750,000, depending on the scope of the project. Usually a project means three to four months of work."

Leonard J. Kapner Jr., senior vice president, is in charge of the custom training division of NTS, which is responsible for seventy-five percent of the firm's income. He claims that "inflation and foreign competition have forced companies to look inside and ask, 'How can I make these people more productive?'"

The growth of new technology also

Reprinted from the *Los Angeles Times*, 19 November 1979.

---

assignment than an assistant manager, who carries out routine assignments and whose position is shown on the organizational chart.

*Assistant to* positions enable managers to learn first hand the problems and

has helped NTS. "One reason we have experienced a surge in activity is that companies are spending a lot more time making sure that machinery is easy to use," Posner says.

NTS was contracted to produce videotapes for Sony's Betamax videotape recorder to teach both customers and sales people how to use the new video recording device. The Lexicon Videotype machine for typists was explained by NTS via a portable cassette tape recorder and a stand-up binder with instructions.

Kapner says that most clients usually assign a small project initially to find out how well NTS techniques work. Larger projects generally follow.

The background of the three principals has assisted in getting even small contracts, they say. "I was executive producer of Air Force films for Air Training Command and for the Secretary of the Air Force Office of Information," Sedlik says.

In addition, he was an associate professor at the U.S. Air Force Academy where he taught in the psychology and fine arts departments and helped manage the eighty-five-member instructional technology directorate.

It was Sedlik's doctoral thesis, in fact, that brought him to Posner's attention. Posner and Kapner were working for another company, and were preparing to form their own organization. Sedlik was brought into the firm by Posner and eventually all three formed NTS.

"There were some trial-and-error approaches," Posner admits. "When we perfected them, we left to form our own company."

Part of the trick in making the new business work, Posner says, was to operate as much like a large corporation as possible. He pulls out elaborate brochures that are used to introduce NTS.

"We have planning as well-developed as a major corporation. We have a board of directors, the three of us in this privately owned corporation, and we involve others. We have an attorney and an accountant.

"You tend to get involved in your own mystique. It's easy. When you're writing your own story, you tend to believe it. You tend to want to validate it.

"Anything new we test very carefully . . . and we tend to avoid the typical problems of a small business . . . which usually doesn't have tight financial controls of money available for capital development."

Sedlik adds, "When we instituted these controls, it became easier for us to interact. We knew what to expect (from each other.)"

Employees — there are thirty full-time staff members — also find their work carefully monitored. "We can't allow the company or an individual to fail on individual projects," Sedlik says. "Therefore, we closely monitor everyone with a series of checkpoints. For instance, they are asked, 'Why use video instead of audio, which is less expensive for clients?' It is very tightly controlled."

Kapner claims it takes NTS 1½ to 2 years to train one instructional designer. They look for individuals with advanced degrees and teach them the specifics of the training business.

responsibilities faced by managers. The *assistant to* is sometimes asked to fill in for executives while they are away. This gives the *assistant to* an opportunity to experience firing line decision making.

3. *Outside industry experience.* Another development technique designed to broaden executive ability is outside industry experience. Some firms allow executives a leave during which they may work in positions with other firms or agencies. While they are away from the parent company, the executives have the opportunity to learn new skills. These new skills will hopefully be put to use when they return. Government, public, and private agencies, schools and universities provide opportunities for private sector employees to serve training periods.

4. *Trial promotion.* The trial promotion is another useful executive training tool. Trial promotions move lower-level executives into higher-level positions for trial periods. They provide both the executive and the organization an opportunity to evaluate one another in the new relationship. If the employee does well, she may be assigned to the new position permanently.

5. *Internship programs.* A variety of cooperative university and industry programs are used for executive development. These programs provide a combination of on-the-job training and academic study. Executive interns carry out their academic work while assigned to executive training positions. Promising young interns are often assigned full-time executive positions once they complete their academic training. Thus the organization is assured of a steady flow of new executive talent.

## SUMMARY

Organizations use a variety of training techniques to develop management and staff. On-the-job, vestibule, and self-study training are often used for line employees. Simulation, management games, encounter and T groups are frequently used in management development.

Technical and executive obsolescence are major factors which cause organizations to use a systematic approach to training. Reductions in cost, reduced turnover, improved management, and human resources reserves accrue from management training programs.

Staff development begins by defining goals, assessing staff weaknesses and strengths, and developing a long-range plan. Then training programs are established and implemented, and finally they are evaluated for effectiveness.

People learn through experience, lecture, discussion, observation, simulation, and the intellectual process. Classroom, lecture, case study, and in-basket techniques are used in the field to train executives and line employees.

Executive development deals with special considerations of improving upper-level management positions. These include *assistant to* positions, trial promotions, and internship programs.

## REVIEW QUESTIONS

1. How does management development differ from organizational development?
2. How does technical obsolescence influence management training?
3. List several benefits from management development and training programs.
4. List some good subordinate characteristics.
5. List some good executive characteristics.
6. List the steps in the process of management development.
7. Contrast the difference between learning by experience and by observation.
8. Describe the process of on-the-job training.
9. Describe the process of vestibule training.
10. What are the advantages of a self-study course?
11. Describe how T groups and encounter groups are used in training.
12. What is an *assistant to* position?

## KEY TERMS

Training   295
Management development   295
   (Executive development)
Organizational development (OD)   295
Simulation   302
On-the-job training (OJT)   303
Vestibule training   304

Case study   304
Role play   305
T groups   305
Job rotation   307
*Assistant to* positions   307
Internship program   310

## Case Incident

The Burgess Manufacturing Co. has been in operation for sixteen years. The firm was originally founded by Tom Burgess, and it now manufactures a complete line of office machines and dictation equipment. Because of the rapid growth of the office machine market and due to some technological breakthroughs, Burgess is going through a major boom period, and the outlook is extremely bright.

Both Carmen Bond and Irma Hoffman have been with Burgess almost since the inception of the company. They originally began as regular line employees. Because of their hard work and ability to learn new skills and take on responsibilities, they have both worked up to positions as managers of key departments.

Because of the firm's rapid growth, Burgess has decided to install some complicated new computer equipment that will make their operation more efficient. However, by installing this equipment, Burgess will require special training for many of the employees, including the department managers. Managers must be able to run and maintain the new machine. Part of this training will include a visit to the vendor's out-of-town training school and a period of orientation to the new machine at the vendor's local sales office.

When informed about the new computer equipment, Bond told Mr. Burgess, "I'll be more than willing to take courses in the operation of the new machine, since I can see how important it will be in my department. However, I'll do so only on company time, with Burgess paying all the expenses. Since this is a change in my job and responsibilities brought on by the company, it really seems only fair since I am willing to travel and take time away from my department to learn about the operation of the new computer."

On the other hand, Hoffman told Burgess that she will not take any of the training courses, but that she is willing to read the various operator's manuals that are provided by the vendor on the new equipment. Part of the problem is that she is unwilling to travel out-of-town because of her family at home. "It's really unfair to expect one of your best and most loyal employees to have to go through a complete change in a job definition. I really don't have any background or skills with computers, and I don't know why the company expects me to go on a crash course to become an expert."

Burgess knows that in the past both Bond and Hoffman have proven to be fast learners, and that they have shown the ability to pick up new skills on their own. This is a big part of the reason they have risen to such key managerial positions, and is also why the company has shown such great trust and confidence in their abilities.

## PROBLEMS

1. What kind of training and management development does Burgess face?
2. How should Burgess handle the responses of Bond and Hoffman to his request to take training?
3. Discuss long-range plans that will prevent similar problems from developing in the future.

# PART FIVE

# The Directing Function

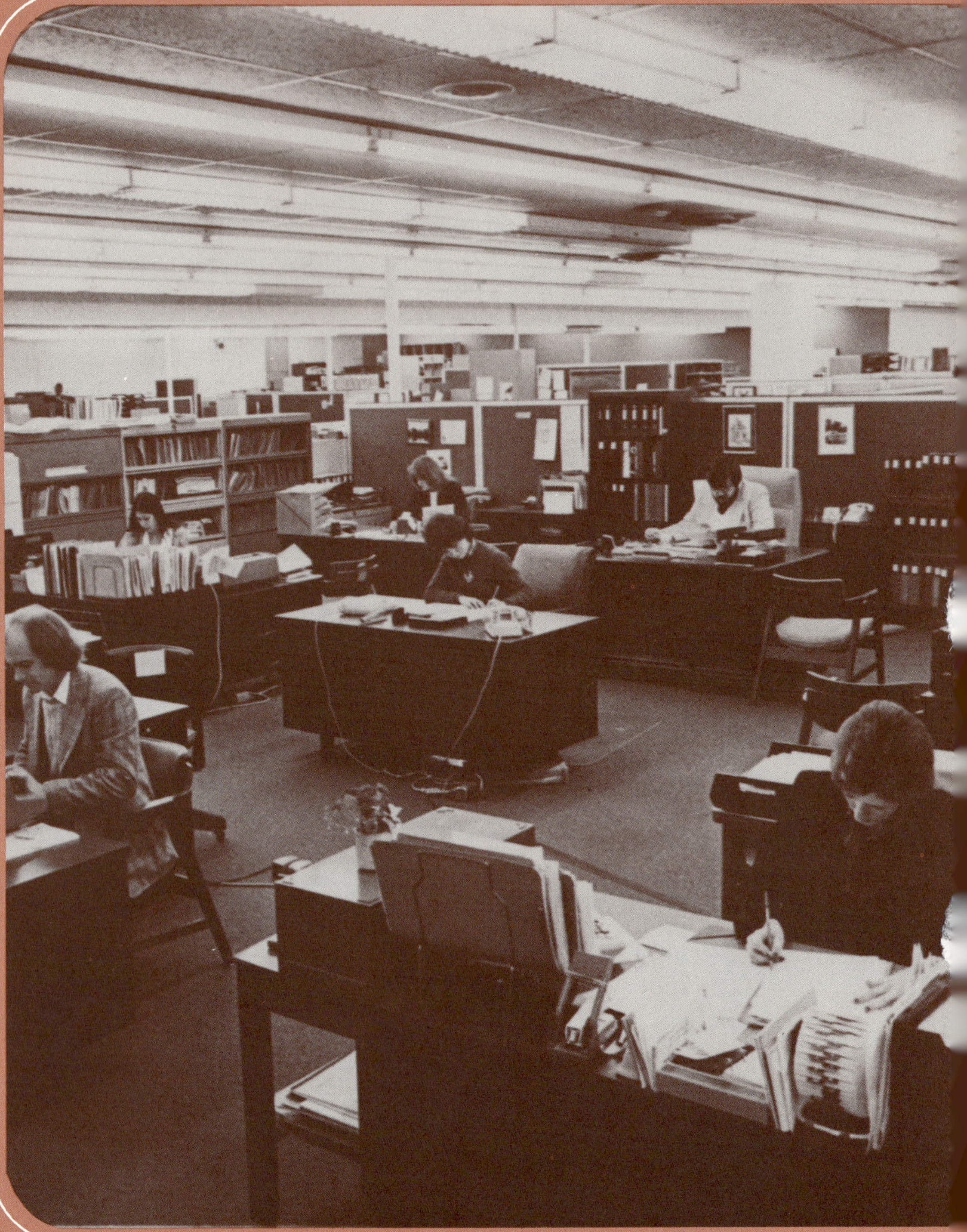

# 14

# Organizational Development and Change

**LEARNING OBJECTIVES**

After studying this chapter, you should be able to:
1. Describe the impact of change on organizations.
2. Contrast the differences between internal and external change forces.
3. Describe the influences of the rate of change on organizations.
4. List reasons individuals and organizations resist change.
5. Summarize the major kinds of conflicts experienced in organizations.
6. Define organizational development and contrast it with management and executive training and development.
7. Describe the unfreezing, change, and refreezing process.
8. Summarize Greiner's view of change.
9. Summarize Leavitt's change model.
10. List the major tools of organizational development.

In this chapter, we look at the ways managers cope with change and the ever present conflicts which are part of organizational life. We shall look at the change process, conflict management, resistance to change, and organizational development (OD). It is important that the manager understand these factors.

In chapter 13, we studied management and executive training and development of the individual. Now we consider development and training in a total organizational context. Organizational development has been defined as the application of the behavioral sciences to the improvement of the overall health, productivity, and efficiency of the total organization. This rapidly growing area of management deals with a systematic view of growth and development.

Organizations are continually in a state of change. They move through a life cycle, much as any living organism. Figure 14-1 traces the life cycle of one organization from entry into the market, through expansion and maturity, to its eventual decline. This process can be controlled and moderated by management.

The manager should be aware of where the organization is on the life cycle continuum. New growth and vitality can be encouraged through proper management.

## CHANGE

### Impact on Organizations

Webster defines *change* as "giving a different position, course of direction to; the undergoing of a transformation, transition, or substitution." Change, rather

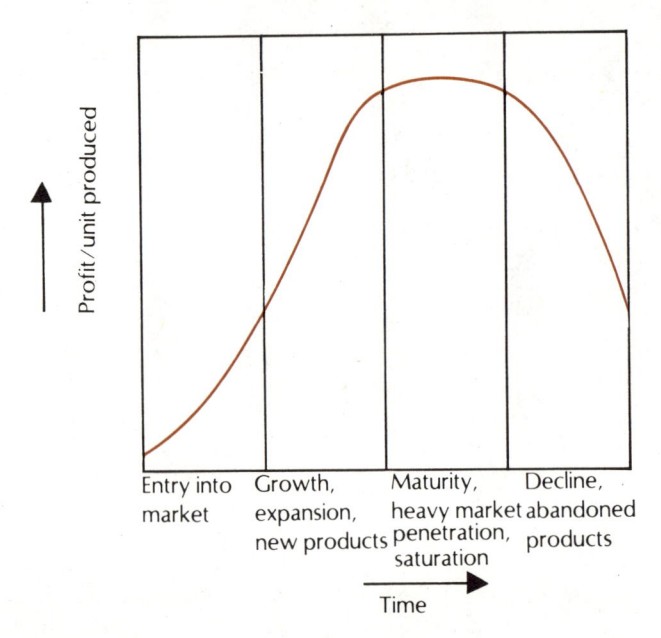

*Figure 14-1*
*Life cycle XYZ corporation*

# CHAPTER FOURTEEN  ORGANIZATIONAL DEVELOPMENT AND CHANGE

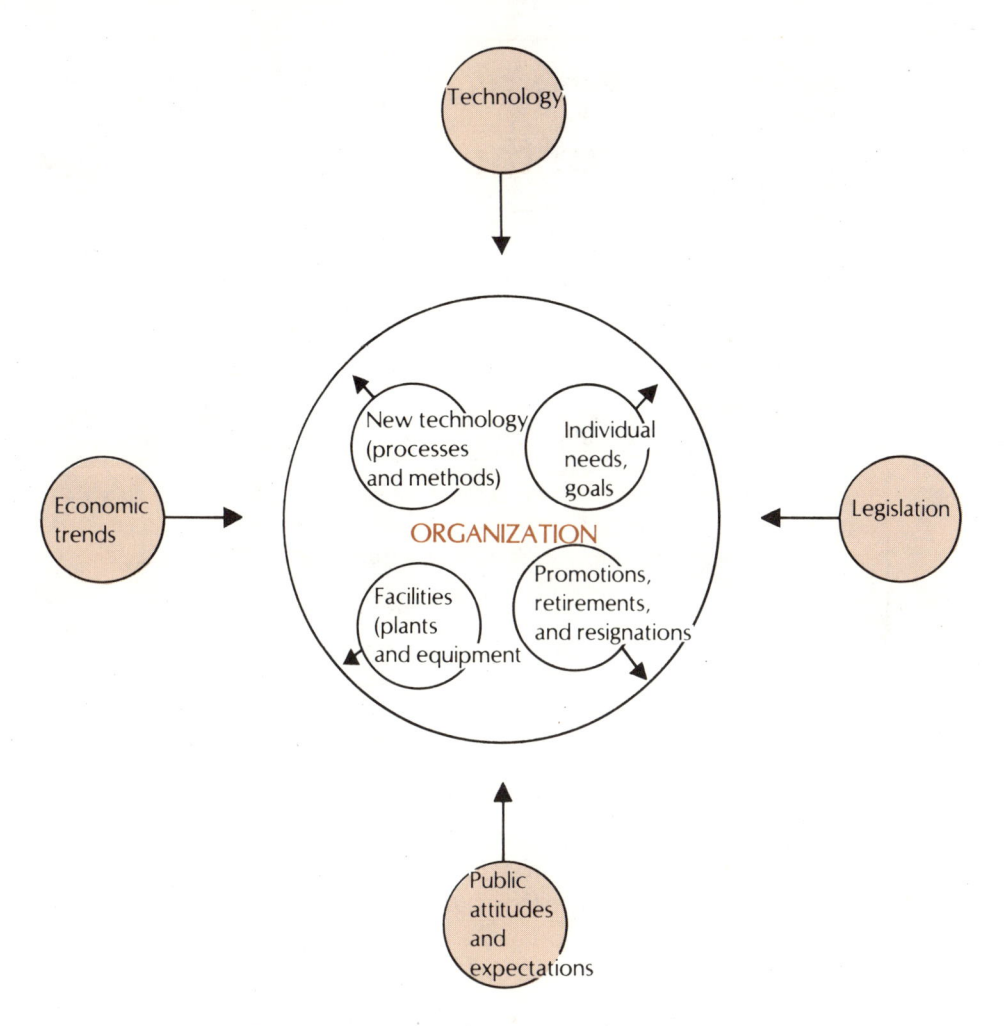

*Figure 14-2  Internal and external change forces*

than permanence, is the norm in organizational life.

Managers, subordinates, groups of employees, shareholders, customers, and suppliers are continually undergoing substitution and transition. It is therefore essential that managers be aware of the anatomy and physiology of the change process. They must be able to anticipate change and understand its roots and causes. Successful managers view themselves as directors of the change process, rather than as merely reactors to it.

## Internal and External Change Forces

Organizations experience change forces that come from outside as well as within. These internal and external forces are illustrated in figure 14-2. From

> **REAL WORLD**
>
> ## Now for the Greening of Pillsbury
>
> For most corporations, the goal is profit. But for William H. Spoor, chairman and chief executive of Pillsbury Co., it is "greatness." Spoor believes in expansion. He plays at business with a seriousness found among few executives. He buys and sells companies, moves managers about, and deploys resources like a general.
>
> In the six years that Spoor has been associated with Pillsbury, he has brought many new businesses to the Pillsbury group, including the Green Giant Co. Spoor's concept of greatness involves doubling the company's size by 1983, hopefully with sales of $5 billion. He expects much of this to come from acquisitions. So far, sales have increased 18 percent per year, with sales topping $2.2 billion and earnings of over $83 million in 1979.
>
> Adapted from *Fortune*, 5 November 1979, p. 126.

within, organizations experience change brought about by new processes and methods, new physical equipment and plant facilities, and a turnover or reshuffling of employees. Not only does the physical mix of employees change over a period of time, but so do individual needs, goals, and attributes.

Many external forces also have an effect on organizations. Changes are brought about by new consumer needs, wants, and buying patterns. Legislation, economic trends, shifting public attitudes, expectations, and new technology bring pressure on organizations.

Consider the transformation mass electronic communications, computers, and jet air transportation have brought to operating methods in the last twenty years. New plastics, materials, manufacturing processes, methods of distributing goods, and changes in retailing, education, and health care, all demand that organizations devise new ways of responding if they wish to remain competitive.

The attitude of the public has changed enormously over the past several decades. Society's attitude toward the use of nuclear power, the environment, consumer rights, and openness in government is markedly different today than it was only a few years ago.

Managers who fail to recognize the changing ecology in which organizations grow and exist are not successful. A manager's job is as much concerned with managing the intangible forces of change as with managing people and physical resources.

## Rate of Change

The rate of change in organizational life is not a constant. While the manifestations of change are often obvious to managers, the rate by which these changes occur is more subtle. Some managers assume that change occurs at a relatively fixed rate. This misunderstanding about the nature of change creates many problems in organizations.

Alvin Toffler, in his incisive book, *Future Shock,* comments very clearly on the fact that change is occurring in society at a rapidly accelerating rate. He notes that society is in the throes of an increase in the rate of change which has radically altered our perception of reality and the way we feel and respond to the world. Toffler points out that ninety percent of all scientists who ever lived are alive today. These change agents are thrusting society headlong into a new world of technology, values, and life styles.

Figure 14-3 graphically illustrates the rate of change and generation of new knowledge. There has been a spiraling increase in the amount of human knowledge and information produced. In all of Europe in the 1500s, only about 1000 book titles were in existence. By the mid 1960s the number had risen to over

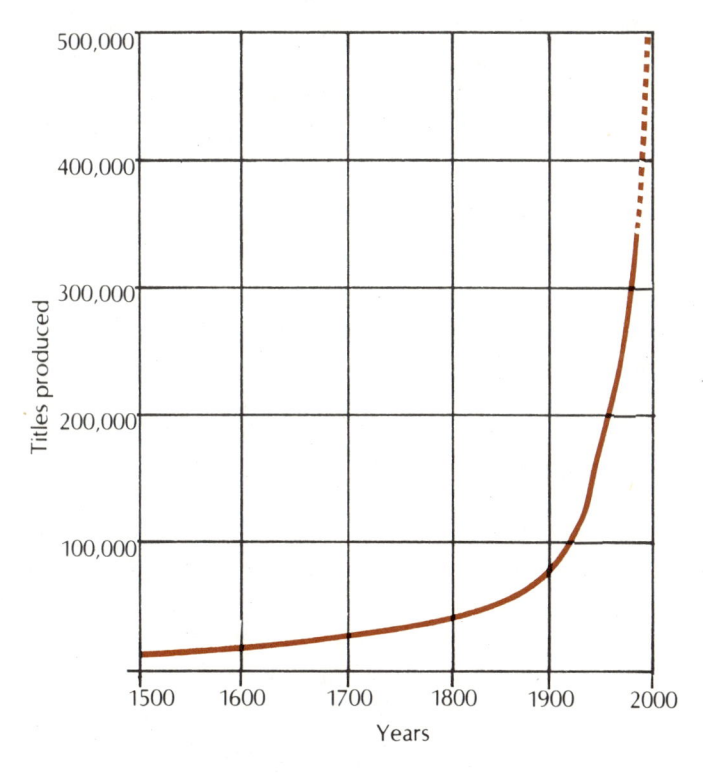

*Figure 14-3*
*Books in print*

Adapted from Alvin Toffler,
*Future Shock* (New York: Bantam Books, 1970), p. 30.

"We all make mistakes, Jones. And I hope you won't let this one destroy the confidence you'll need to find another job . . ."

Reprinted from *Graphic Arts Monthly,* August 1978.

365,000. This represents an exponential increase in the documented knowledge which managers must deal with. It is almost impossible to predict the vast amount of new knowledge and information which the manager will have to assimilate and cope with in the next several decades. Certainly old ways of collecting, disseminating, retrieving, and cataloguing knowledge will give way to new methods and systems.

## Attitudes toward Change

People have very different ways of dealing with this headlong rush into new technology and values. A common response is simply to ignore the accelerating rate of change and assume that the same rules, standards, technology, and values of the past exist today. This denial of reality is exhibited by managers who cling to the status quo and refuse to accept change and growth. The history of American business organizations is full of examples of corporations that failed to accept and adapt to change. Whole industries have succumbed to new industries structured by managers who acknowledge change and have adapted to it.

Some very successful enterprises have been built on the very acceleration of change. The growth of the computer and data processing industries is largely due to their ability to manipulate information more quickly and effectively than previous manual methods. There are some tasks that computers and machines can do that can be done equally well by human beings. However, the speed, lower cost, and greater accuracy by which electronic computers operate is the reason they are replacing people.

A positive attitude toward change, and an understanding of the process, has enabled many organizations to flourish and grow in the face of new attitudes and technology. Change-oriented managers look forward to different methods, technology, and structures, knowing that they can be used to the advantage of the organization.

## Resisting Change

Resistance to change may be found at many levels in an organization. Forces may be at work which militate against a sound, planned approach to handling change. The manager should understand these forces and be able to manage them for the health of the organization.

1. *Resistance by individuals.* Single individuals may resist change, while the organization may encourage it. People resist change because they fear loss of income or job security, or a deterioration in their working conditions. Managers or subordinates may refuse to go along with badly needed changes for fear that their own personal status, power, or value will be diminished.

Habit is another major reason people resist change. It is easier to follow the old, comfortable patterns than to adapt to new and different ways of doing things. At the root of this habit is the diminished need for decision making. Habit frees us from this demanding task.

2. *Resistance by organization.* Organizations as entities may resist change, while individuals within the organization may seek it. People, systems, physical plant, policies, and regulations as a total organization entity may resist change violently. Established business firms, governmental agencies, educational institutions, and financial institutions may grow in size and complexity to the point where change would be more costly and difficult than perpetuating established ways. At the root of this resistance is the unwillingness of an organization to accept reduced control, authority, or power.

There are many governmental agencies which have come into existence during the last fifty years and have now outlived their usefulness. These agencies violently resist any changes which may threaten their existence. Labor unions, associations, trade, and industry groups resist changes which diminish their control, power, or authority.

3. *Resistance by industry.* Entire industries may collectively resist change. For many of the same reasons that individuals and organizations fear change, so do entire industries. The airline, railroad, petroleum, radio, and television industries have vested interests in the economy. Changes in laws, tariffs, regulations, governing bodies, and institutions may be fought vigorously by these industries because they wish to preserve their economic position, status, independence, or power.

Chrysler resisted the trend toward smaller cars and they almost went bankrupt. Their new K cars represent an acceptance of change.

## CONFLICT IN ORGANIZATIONS

Conflict inevitably brings about change. The subject of conflict and conflict resolution has been widely recognized and studied by managers. The deliberate generation and management of conflict are often used by managers to force change upon organizations and their participants. Conversely, change attempts very often lead to conflicts within the organization.

In the past, conflict was viewed in a negative way by many managers. They believed that conflict had an adverse effect on organizational life and growth. However, this view is changing, and many managers believe that a controlled and managed level of conflict is actually healthy for organizations. Let us consider two views of conflict widely held by managers.

1. *Avoid and deemphasize conflict.* Some managers take a traditional bureaucratic view that conflict is harmful in organizations and therefore should be reduced or eliminated. They view avoiding confrontations and smoothing over differences as a key role of managers. They see the lessening of conflict as desirable, and the mark of a healthy organization as one which exhibits minimal conflict.

2. *Introduce controlled conflict.* A counter view of conflict is held by many managers. This dynamic approach holds that conflict is a healthy force, present in most organizations, and one which is to be acknowledged and fostered. These

managers believe that conflict forces people and organizations to take a close look at themselves and their methods and goals, and to seek alternatives. A healthier, more effective and viable organization results from this scrutiny.

## Introduction of Conflict

Managers who hold the belief that a controlled amount of conflict is healthy in an organization may use many tools and techniques to foster it. The following describes some of the commonly used techniques which introduce conflict and ultimately bring about solutions to problems.

1. *Introduction of outsiders.* Managers may introduce outside consultants as change agents into the organization to deliberately create conflict. These individuals may hold different views and beliefs and thus force the organization's participants to look at their own positions more critically.

2. *Introduction of rules or policies which create conflict.* The implementation of

---

**REAL WORLD**

# Women Rise as Entrepreneurs

Beatrice Fitzpatrick, chief executive office of the American Woman's Economic Development Corporation (AWED), is convinced that there are an increasing number of women moving into positions as entrepreneurs, and that women are dramatically changing the face and complexion of business and management. In the past women were confined to such female-related industries as cosmetics or clothing. However, today women are finding positions as executives and leaders in a wide variety of industries. For example, Redactron Corporation, founded by Evelyn Berezin, is a firm which entered the word processing equipment market and has now reached sales of $16 million.

All over America women are moving into key management positions in large corporations. For example, Lore Harp and Carole Ely head Vector Graphic, Inc., a firm they started which employs over 125 people. ASK Computer Services, Inc., with $12 million annual sales, is headed by Sandra L. Kurtzig. Shirley Collins formed Sur la Table, a restaurant supply business in Seattle, which is now expanding into the mail order catalog sales of gourmet cookware. These women are examples of what may turn out to be the decade of women managers in the 1980s.

Adapted from *Business Week*, 25 February 1980, p. 85.

a new set of rules, policies, or regulations can often force conflicts on organization participants. Changes in work rules, levels of output, dress standards, and so on force individuals to make reevaluations of themselves and others.

3. *Introduction of "play it by the book" policy.* Organizations may often have carefully prescribed sets of rules and regulations for the conduct and behavior of individuals and departments. These rules may sometimes be on the books, but rarely enforced by managers and subordinates. The sudden demand by an organization that its participants "follow the book" may create a substantial amount of conflict. This in turn forces participants to take a close look at the rules, policies, and procedures they are using and recommend improvements.

4. *Reorganization.* Another common means of creating controlled conflict is to vary the mix of people in a given department or unit. A reorganization of people, shifting of employees, and the changed juxtaposition of individuals with differing views may create conflict. This in turn may force managers and subordinates alike to assess their own behavior and productivity.

## Kinds of Conflicts

Conflicts may exist at many levels in an organization. Managers should be aware of the interplay between individuals and the organization. The understanding of this interplay is important to managers who must use it to benefit the organization. The following summarizes some of the major conflicting elements present in organizations.

1. *Conflict between the organization and society.* The goals and objectives of an organization may be incompatible with social values and standards. Organizations sometimes find themselves in conflict with the collective needs and demands of society. For example, a power company may be pressured to generate increasing amounts of electrical energy. But it may also face environmental laws or pressure groups which make burning coal or nuclear generation socially unacceptable.

2. *Conflict between the organization and groups.* An organization may be in conflict with one or more groups in society or within the organization. For example, an oil refinery may experience conflicts with environmental groups or certain governmental agencies over air pollution. Yet their goals may be consistent with other groups who demand a large supply of low-cost fuel. Sometimes organizations may conflict with groups within the structure, such as safety committees or unions.

3. *Conflict between groups.* Many conflicting groups may exist within one organization. Members of union groups, management, trainees, or high seniority employees, may be at variance with one another. Differences in attitudes, needs, and wants between groups may create substantial discord.

4. *Conflict between individuals.* Frequently, individuals in an organization may be incompatible. Specific employees, managers, or subordinates may have differing personalities and life styles which are in conflict. Sometimes these may be conflicts between an individual and the organization. For example, an employee may demand special privileges or benefits at the expense of the organization.

5. *Conflict within people.* People are not always integrated psychological entities. It is not uncommon for managers and subordinates to have conflicting wishes and attitudes within themselves. For instance, an employee may want to complete a job by the prescribed time, but also want to get home and spend time with his family.

## ORGANIZATIONAL DEVELOPMENT

A new and somewhat controversial approach to dealing with change and conflict in organizations is the study of organizational development (OD). Organizational development deals with the ramifications of conflict, change, and growth on the total organization. It is an effort by management to gain the maximum output and efficiency through a planned and managed effort at change. Organizational development draws from the behavioral sciences and has gained widespread attention in recent years.

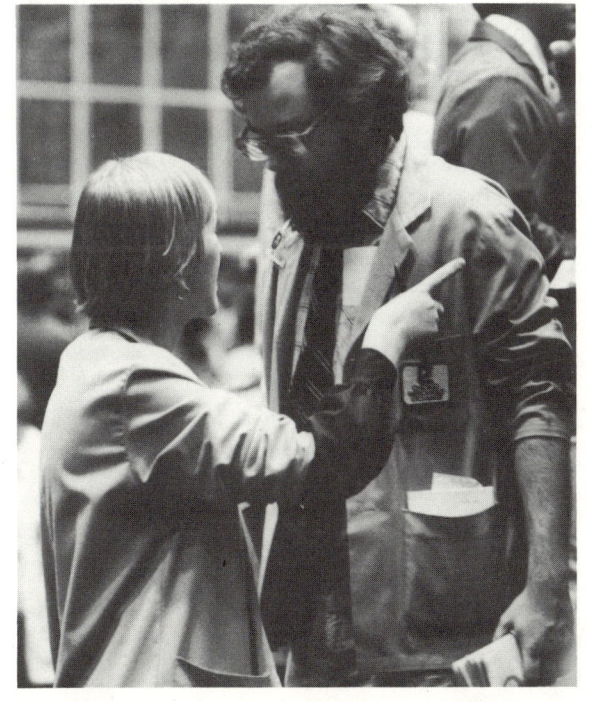

Conflict between individuals is a common problem in organizations.

Let us look at this growing field of study and how managers use the behavioral sciences to improve the overall health and productivity of the organization. Organizational development began in the 1940s, with efforts of behavioral scientists seeking to understand organizational behavior through an analysis of the needs and wants of individuals. Participants learn to function in cohesive teams. Over the years, organizational development has emerged as a broad group of strategies for handling change. It now includes team building, behavior modification, action studies, use of consultants, interviews, and other techniques.

## CHARACTERISTICS OF ORGANIZATIONAL DEVELOPMENT

Management and executive training programs tend to focus on people as individuals and not as members of a team. Organizational development builds a team spirit among managers and subordinates, and views the organization as a whole entity.

To better understand organizational development, we must look at some of the major concepts and theories which have influenced its growth. The work of Kurt Lewin dealing with group dynamics and human relations, and the efforts of Larry Greiner and Harold J. Leavitt, have molded much of today's organizational development thinking. Let us now look at the concepts of unfreezing, change, and refreezing, force field analysis, multiphase change process, grid design, and Leavitt's change model to see organizational development in perspective.

### Unfreezing, Change, Refreezing

In the mid 1940s, Kurt Lewin described the dynamics by which managers are able to make change in organizations. According to Lewin,[1] change is brought about in organizations in a three-phase process (fig. 14-4).

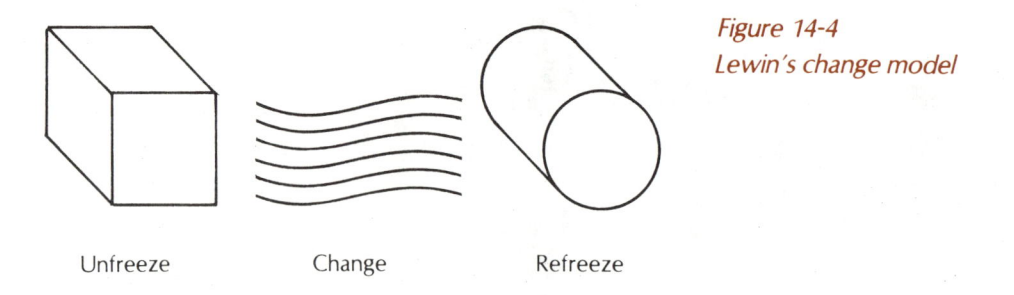

*Figure 14-4*
*Lewin's change model*

Unfreeze   Change   Refreeze

---

[1] Kurt Lewin, "Frontiers in Group Dynamics," *Human Relations* 1, no. 1 (1947): 5.

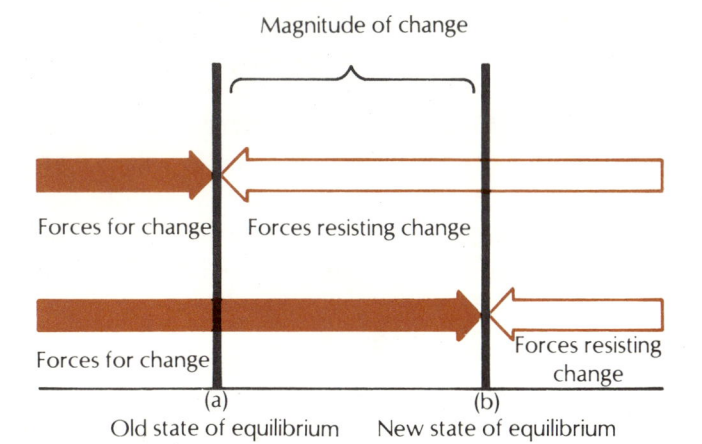

*Figure 14-5*
*Force field analysis*

1. *Unfreezing.* In this phase, managers seek to break old habits, routines, and patterns. An attempt is made to force change by questioning existing attitudes and practices. Using Lewin's model, managers may vary the rules, policies, or procedures in the organization. This results in an unbalance. Dissent, conflict, and dissatisfaction arise, and with them an unfreezing of attitudes and behavior patterns. This uncovers and defines problems.

2. *Change.* In the second phase, Lewin suggests that the individuals find solutions and new ways of dealing with problems. The conflicts, dissensions, and problems which result from the unfreezing require new ways of thinking and a critical look at existing methods. What ultimately emerges from this phase is more efficient and productive ways of dealing with and solving problems. But changes, no matter how effective, are only temporary unless an effort is made to make them a permanent and on-going part of the organization.

3. *Refreezing.* The last step in the process is the refreezing or solidifying of the new behavior patterns. Once improved ways of dealing with problems have been developed, these improvements must become a permanent part of the organization. This involves documenting and reporting the changes which have taken place. Acceptable changes are acknowledged and rewarded and thus become the new norm of behavior.

## Force Field Analysis

Kurt Lewin has expanded on our knowledge of organization change with his force field analysis concepts. These concepts are useful to managers because they focus on the ways changes occur in institutions, and on the forces which militate for or resist change.

According to Lewin, organizations exist in a state of balance or equilibrium (fig. 14-5). There is a balance between the pressure for change and the pressure against change. Since these forces are of equal magnitude, the organization remains in a state of equilibrium. The forces for change equal the forces resisting it, and thus a balance exists.

However, if one of these forces exerts more pressure than the other, the organization becomes unbalanced and changes occur. Finally, a new state of equilibrium develops between forces, and the organization is again stable.

The forces which press for change may range from the introduction of new machines and technology to the reduction of threats and penalties against new ideas. Variations in the demand for goods and services, the technology for producing them, or competition cause imbalance.

The forces which militate against change in an organization may be the fears or insecurities of the participants regarding new ideas, methods, or technology. Existing rules, regulations, policies, or habit may form a solid barrier against which few changes can occur.

## Greiner's View of Change

Another theorist who had an impact on organizational development is Larry Greiner.[2] Greiner studied the change process and saw it as resulting from the actions of a change agent, who introduces a multiphase transition from the present state to the acceptance of a new practice. (See figure 14-6.)

Greiner described the change process as moving through six phases. Change begins when pressure is applied from the top of an organization by its management. This results in an arousal to take action. In turn, a reorientation takes place which forces a recognition and diagnosis of existing problems. Once the problems are recognized, pressure mounts for the discovery of solutions and a commitment to a new course of action.

In the last phases of the change process, Greiner observed that subordinates experiment with new solutions and search for results. Finally, when satisfactory solutions have been discovered, management reinforces the positive behavior, and this in turn leads to the acceptance of the new practice.

There is a parallel between the force field analysis of Lewin and the six phases of Greiner. In both views, a force for change brings about an unstable condition, which results in solving problems and finally acceptance of the improved condition.

## The Management Grid

Another useful tool of organizational development was developed by Blake and Mouton.[3] Blake and Mouton observed that managers may be described by their

---

[2]Larry E. Greiner, "Patterns in Organization Change," *Harvard Business Review* (May-June 1967): p. 126.
[3]R. R. Blake and J. S. Mouton, *The New Managerial Grid®* (Houston: Gulf Publishing Co., 1978).

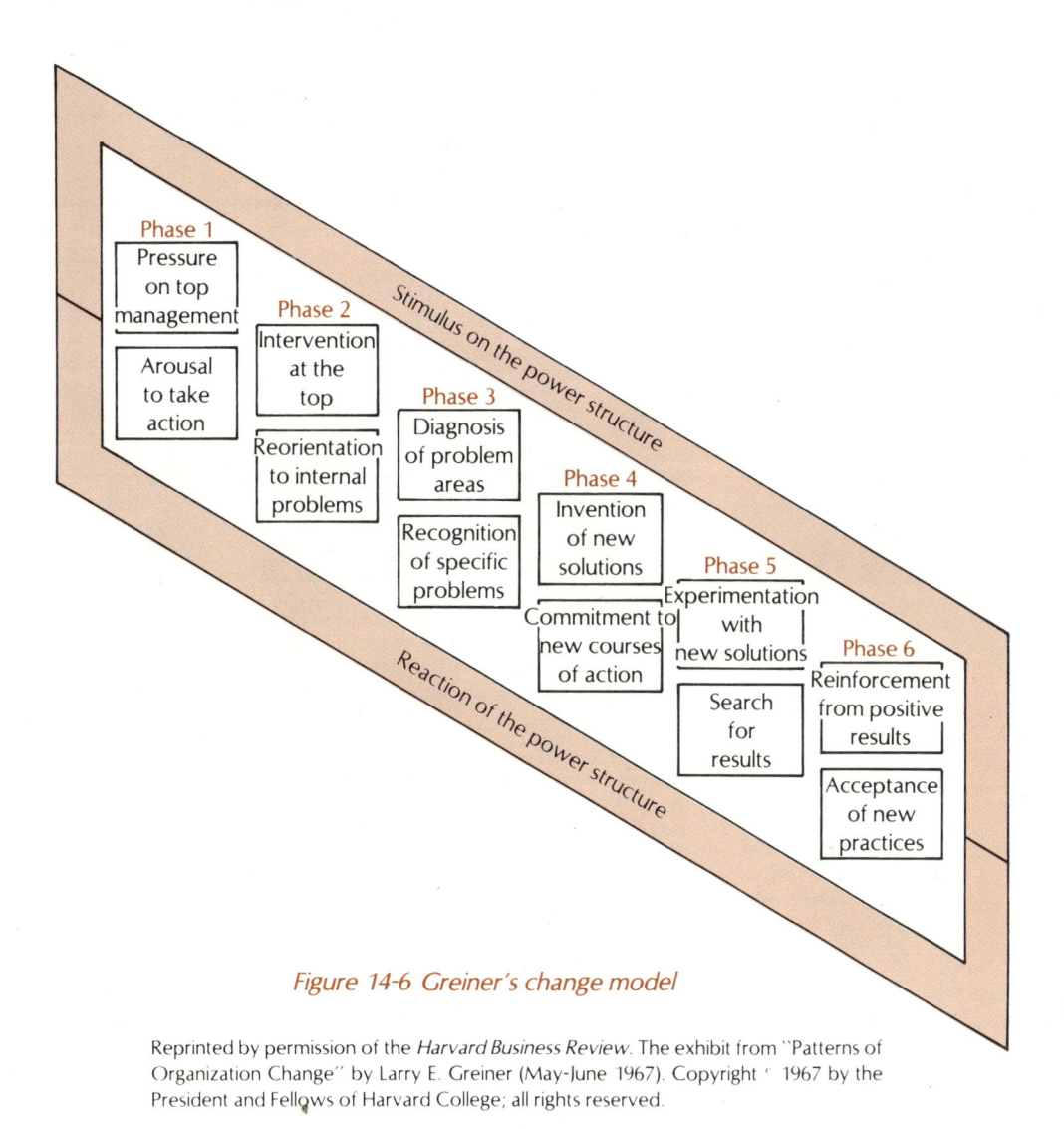

CHAPTER FOURTEEN  ORGANIZATIONAL DEVELOPMENT AND CHANGE                    329

**Phase 1**
Pressure on top management

Arousal to take action

**Phase 2**
Intervention at the top

Reorientation to internal problems

**Phase 3**
Diagnosis of problem areas

Recognition of specific problems

**Phase 4**
Invention of new solutions

Commitment to new courses of action

**Phase 5**
Experimentation with new solutions

Search for results

**Phase 6**
Reinforcement from positive results

Acceptance of new practices

*Stimulus on the power structure*

*Reaction of the power structure*

*Figure 14-6 Greiner's change model*

Reprinted by permission of the *Harvard Business Review*. The exhibit from "Patterns of Organization Change" by Larry E. Greiner (May-June 1967). Copyright © 1967 by the President and Fellows of Harvard College; all rights reserved.

position on a Grid® (See figure 14-7.) Through training, team development, group interaction, and goal setting, managers may be repositioned.

Two major influences are at work on managers: concerns for people and concerns for production. Each of these forces is delineated along the side and bottom of the Grid®. The matrix allows us to position individuals or organizations on a checkerboard and plot changes that take place as a result of development.

Managers who have a high regard for people are placed on the top of the Grid.® These managers foster a comfortable, friendly working environment. At the bottom of the Grid® are managers who deemphasize concerns for people.

At the right of the Grid® are managers who have a high concern for produc-

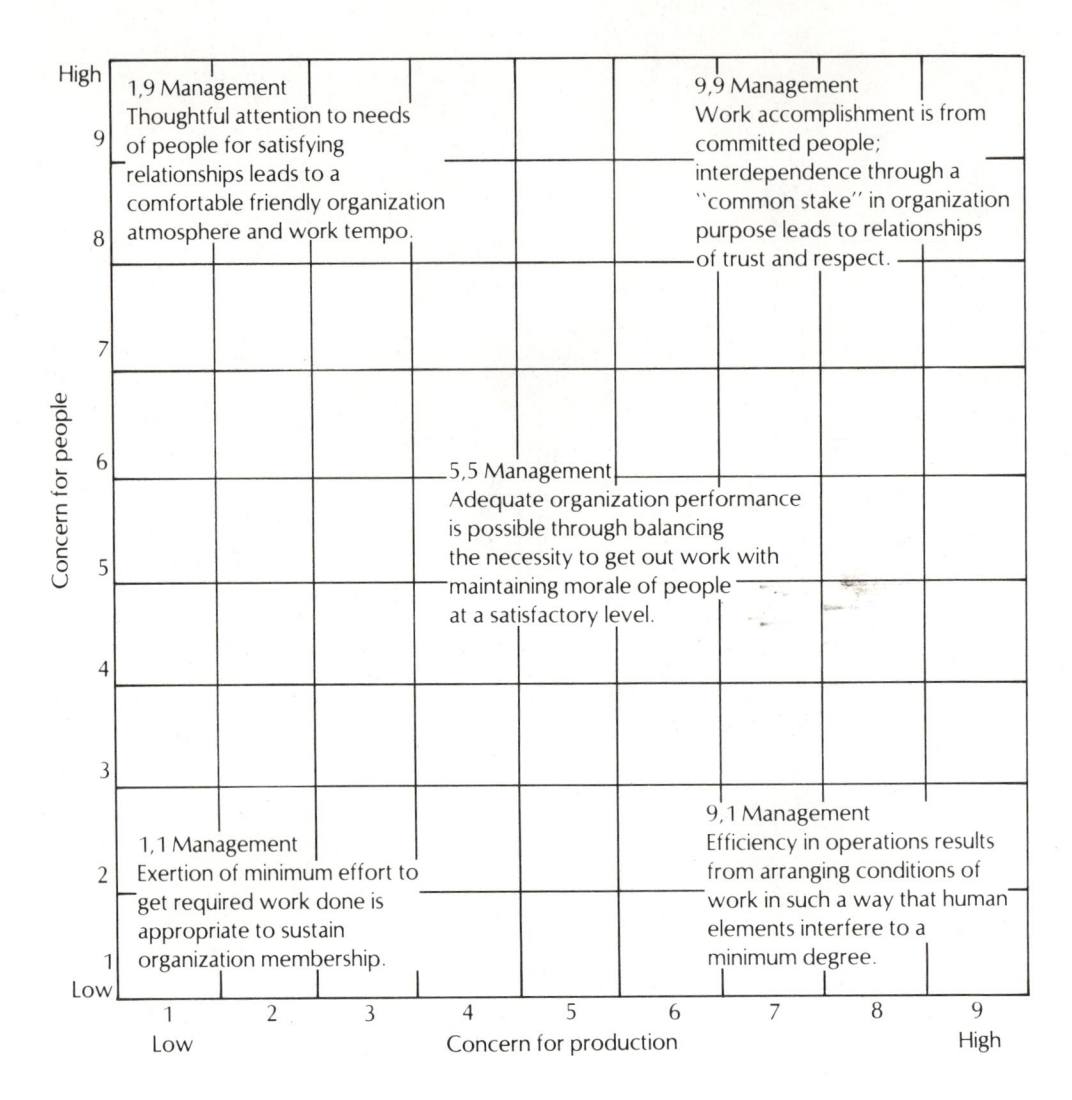

## Figure 14-7 The managerial Grid®

**1,9 Management** — Thoughtful attention to needs of people for satisfying relationships leads to a comfortable friendly organization atmosphere and work tempo.

**9,9 Management** — Work accomplishment is from committed people; interdependence through a "common stake" in organization purpose leads to relationships of trust and respect.

**5,5 Management** — Adequate organization performance is possible through balancing the necessity to get out work with maintaining morale of people at a satisfactory level.

**1,1 Management** — Exertion of minimum effort to get required work done is appropriate to sustain organization membership.

**9,1 Management** — Efficiency in operations results from arranging conditions of work in such a way that human elements interfere to a minimum degree.

*Axes: Concern for people (vertical, 1 Low – 9 High); Concern for production (horizontal, 1 Low – 9 High)*

The Grid® reprinted from R.R. Blake and J.S. Mouton, *The New Managerial Grid* (Houston: Gulf Publishing Co., 1978).

tion. They stress output, productivity, and efficiency. At the left of the Grid® are managers who have a low concern for production.

For example, we may have a manager who, early in his career, is positioned as 1, 1 due to his low concern for production and for people. However, as he gains skills in management through organizational development, he may move to position 9,9 on the Grid®. He evolves into a manager with high regard for production and deep concern for people.

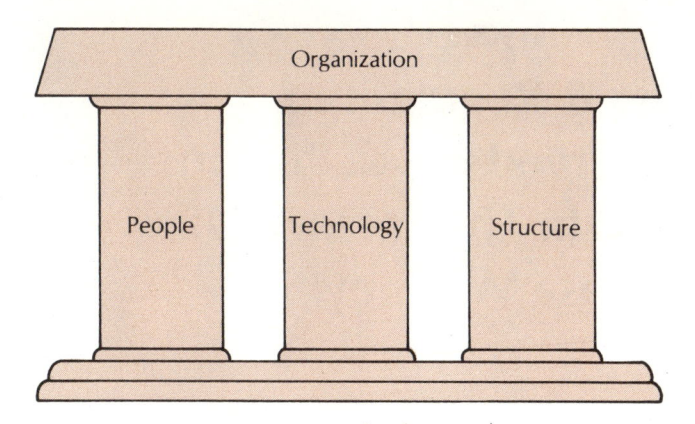

*Figure 14-8*
*Leavitt's change model*

## Leavitt's Change Model

The last major change model we shall look at is the work of Leavitt.[4] In Leavitt's view, there are three ways to bring about change in organizations: changes in people, technology, and structure. (See figure 14-8.) An alteration in any one of these factors has a major influence on the course of an organization. Managers can use each of these three interrelated factors to induce organizational transformation.

1. *Changes in structure.* Managers can bring about a change in the organization by instituting alterations in the formal structure. (See figure 14-9.) For instance, a realignment of departments or of manager-subordinate relationships greatly changes the organization.

2. *Changes in technology.* The introduction of new materials, processes, machinery, equipment, or methods will force change on an organization. New technology influences the structure of an organization and its staffing and personnel requirements.

3. *Changes in people.* The human element is a third major factor in organizational change. Variations in the human element have profound repercus-

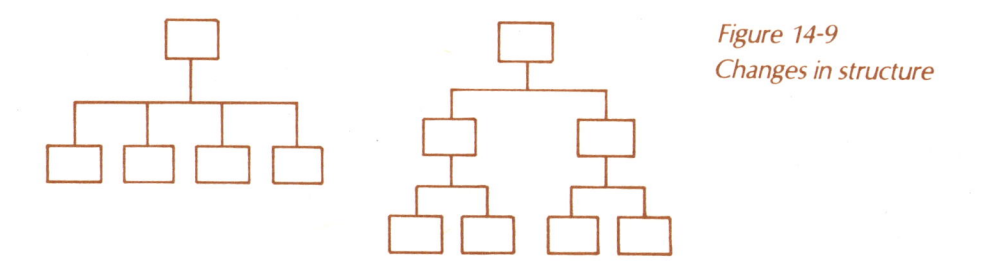

*Figure 14-9*
*Changes in structure*

---

[4]Harold J. Leavitt, "Applied Organization Change in Industry," *New Perspectives in Organizational Research* (New York: John Wiley & Sons, 1964), p. 56.

## POSTSCRIPT
# Rules & Regulations To Be Observed By All Persons Employed In The Factory Of Amasa Whitney

FIRST: The Mill will be put into operation 10 minutes before sunrise at all seasons of the year. The gate will be shut 10 minutes past sunset from the 20th of March to the 20th of September, at 30 minutes past 8 from the 20th of September to the 20th of March. Saturdays at sunset.

SECOND: It will be required of every person employed, that they be in the room in which they are employed, at the time mentioned above for the mill to be in operation.

THIRD: Hands are not allowed to leave the factory in working hours without the consent of their Overseer. If they do, they will be liable to have their time set off.

FOURTH: Anyone who by negligence or misconduct causes damage to the machinery, or impedes the progress of the work, will be liable to make good the damage for the same.

FIFTH: Anyone employed for a certain

Figure 6-1, "Factory Rules in 1830," reprinted from Samuel H. Adams, *Sunrise to Sunset* (New York: Random House, 1950).

---

sions on the structure. The introduction of a change-oriented manager, for example, can influence the technology used in the organization and, in turn, its structure. Differences in the attitudes, skills, and abilities of managers or subordinates are obvious factors in the selection of manufacturing, processing, and distribution methods.

## TOOLS OF ORGANIZATIONAL DEVELOPMENT(OD)

To this point, we have discussed a variety of methods which managers use to describe the change phenomenon in organizations. While these are useful in planning and implementing an overall strategy, specific tools are needed. Managers use many of the following tools to implement desired changes on an operational level.

1. *Consultants.* Consultants are frequently brought into organizations as change

length of time, will be expected to make up their lost time, if required, before they will be entitled to their pay.

SIXTH: Any person employed for no certain length of time, will be required to give at least 4 weeks notice of their intention to leave (sickness excepted) or forfeit 4 weeks pay, unless by particular agreement.

SEVENTH: Anyone wishing to be absent any length of time, must get permission of the Overseer.

EIGHTH: All who have leave of absence for any length of time will be expected to return in that time; and, in case they do not return in that time and do not give satisfactory reason, they will be liable to forfeit one week's work or less, if they commence work again. If they do not, they will be considered as one who leaves without giving any notice.

NINTH: Anything tending to impede the progress of manufacturing in working hours, such as unnecessary conversation, reading, eating fruit, &c.&c., must be avoided.

TENTH: While I shall endeavor to employ a judicious Overseer, the help will follow his direction in all cases.

ELEVENTH: No smoking will be allowed in the factory, as it is considered very unsafe, and particularly specified in the Insurance.

TWELFTH: In order to forward the work, job hands will follow the above regulations as well as those otherwise employed.

THIRTEENTH: It is intended that the bell be rung 5 minutes before the gate is hoisted, so that all persons may be ready to start their machines precisely at the time mentioned.

FOURTEENTH: All persons who cause damage to the machinery, break glass out of the windows, &c., will immediately inform the Overseer of the same.

agents. These individuals possess unique skills and abilities. They should have a firm foundation in the behavioral sciences and thus be able to influence human behavior. Consultants may be called in from the outside, or existing staff members may be shifted from department to department. In either case, it is the presence of a skilled individual who influences the change process.

2. *Field interviews.* Extensive field interviews may be conducted by managers who seek to bring about change. These interviews enable them to collect data on the attitudes, abilities, and interests of the participants. Armed with this information, the manager may implement a sound change strategy.

3. *Action studies.* Managers may undertake a variety of action studies. They may wish to gain knowledge about specific local problems in an organization. For example, a study may focus on low output or productivity, employee attitudes, or weaknesses in employee training and knowledge.

4. *Behavior modification.* Once a new pattern has been developed, managers

must make it a permanent part of the participants' behavior. Through positive reinforcement, managers may make certain kinds of behavior permanent. Conversely, unacceptable behavior can be discouraged by the use of negative reinforcement such as withholding bonuses or extra privileges. A thorough understanding of human behavior is essential in managing the growth and development of organizations.

5. *T groups.* T groups are small, informal encounters of participants which are useful in organizational development. These groups allow managers and subordinates to gain understanding and insights into the behavior and attitudes of other members of the organization and themselves. T groups foster frank, honest communication between people. Individuals who participate in T groups develop common bonds of understanding which can be transferred to their day-to-day activities.

6. *Conferencing.* The use of conferences is a valuable tool which brings together individuals in an organization and develops understanding and positive attitudes. Conferences foster intergroup awareness and common goal aspirations.

7. *Team building.* A variety of team building efforts are used in organizational development. The purpose is to encourage people to think of themselves as members of a team rather than as isolated individuals. They are encouraged to place the interests of the total organization over their own. Team building also develops a spirit of interdependence and reliance upon others. Members of a team draw upon a wide base of personal contacts to solve problems, rather than relying on a limited number of people, or only on their own resources.

## SUMMARY

Organizational development (OD) deals with change in a total organizational context. Organizations experience change from both internal and external forces. Change occurs at differing rates. Attitudes toward change differ between managers. Some resist change while others encourage it.

Change occurs in organizations as a result of conflict. Some managers try to avoid or deemphasize conflict, while others introduce a controlled amount. Conflict is introduced by bringing in outsiders, changing rules, playing it "by the book," or changing the mix of participants.

Conflicts exist between organizations and society, between organizations and groups, between groups within organizations, between individuals in organizations, and within individuals themselves.

Several change models have been developed to describe how organizations change. Lewin's force field analysis and Greiner's model describe organizational change. The management Grid® is another useful tool in describing change in two

CHAPTER FOURTEEN    ORGANIZATIONAL DEVELOPMENT AND CHANGE            335

dimensions. Leavitt's model focuses on three sources of change: people, technology, and structure.

The common tools of organizational development are consultants, field interviews, action studies, behavior modification, T groups, conferencing, and team building.

## REVIEW QUESTIONS

1. What internal and external forces are at work changing organizations?
2. Does change occur at a relatively fixed rate? Explain.
3. Describe different attitudes managers may have toward change.
4. Give some reasons individuals resist change.
5. Give some reasons organizations resist change.
6. Contrast two views of conflict which are held by managers.
7. List some ways managers deliberately introduce conflict.
8. Describe Kurt Lewin's force field analysis concept.
9. Summarize the six phases of Greiner's view of change.
10. What are the two influences at work on the management Grid®?
11. According to Leavitt, what are the three sources of change in an organization?
12. Explain how consultants [People skilled in business] are used as change agents.

## KEY TERMS

Organizational development (OD)   316
Rate of change   319
Conflict   322
Force field analysis   327
Management Grid®   328
Field interview   333

Action study   333
Behavior modification   333
T group   334
Conferencing   334
Team building   334

## Case Incident

General Hospital is located in a small community where there is a serious shortage of skilled nurses. The 363-bed hospital has three separate shifts, each headed by a nursing supervisor. Recently, an opening has developed in the highly desirable first shift because of the retirement of the current nursing supervisor. Carrie Colton and Helen Rice are supervisors of the second and third shifts. Both women have expressed a clear preference for the first shift because of the desirable working hours.

Each has approached Robert Phalen, the senior hospital administrator, and indicated her strong desire to be considered as the new first-shift supervisor.

As a result, much dissension has arisen between the two supervisors. Over the years both Colton and Rice have developed very close friendships with employees on their respective shifts. Because both supervisors and some of their close friends have been involved in the competition for this position, it has created a great deal of conflict between individuals on the nursing staff. Since the question of who will become first-shift supervisor has become so intensely competitive, both women have threatened to leave the employment of General Hospital if they are not given the first-shift opening.

In the meantime, a new hospital has opened in the community, and, in order to recruit new staff, it has offered employment to both Colton and Rice. Since there is such a shortage of skilled nurses in the community, the new hospital has made very attractive offers to both supervisors. Although both would prefer to stay with General Hospital, each has threatened to take several of her close friends and nurses with her to the new hospital it she is not given the first-shift supervisor's position. Mr. Phalen clearly realizes that he will have to take some definite action soon. He knows that whichever supervisor he appoints to the first shift, he will have to contend with the other's threat to leave General Hospital and take several other nurses with her.

## PROBLEMS

1. What organizational development problems exist at the hospital?
2. Discuss the conflicts present within the organization and how these can be resolved.
3. How can similar conflicts be avoided in the future?

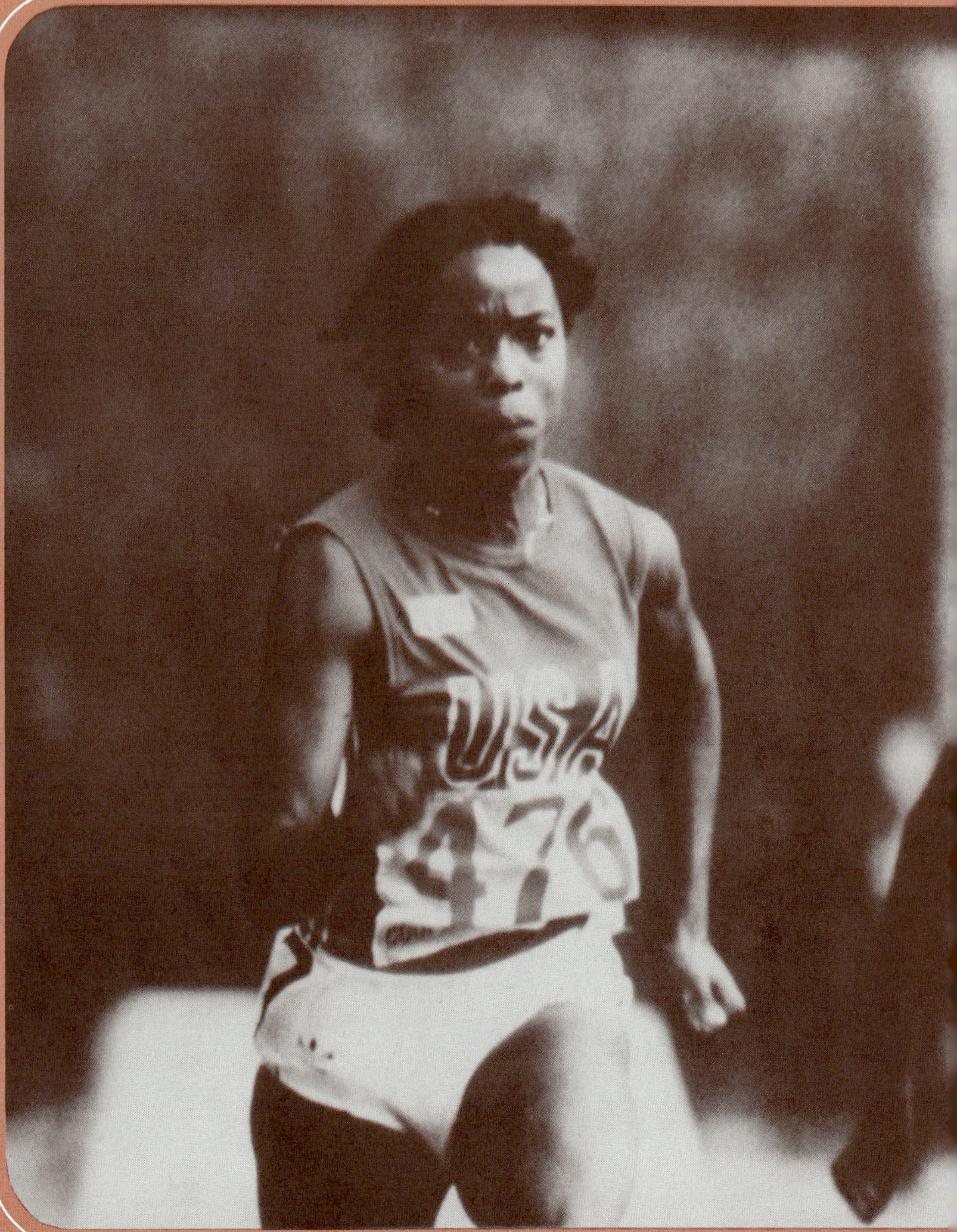
USA
476

# 15

# Motivation

**LEARNING OBJECTIVES**

After studying this chapter, you should be able to:
1. Define the key terms related to motivational theory.
2. Summarize the classical view of motivation.
3. Describe the influence the human relations approach had on motivation.
4. Summarize how money is used as a reward.
5. Describe how the design of the job influences motivation.
6. Summarize the behavioral reinforcement theory.
7. Describe several widely accepted need theories.
8. Summarize the equity theory of motivation.
9. Summarize the expectancy theory of motivation.
10. Describe the effects of morale on output and productivity.

An understanding of human motivation is crucial to effective management. A knowledge of basic human needs, wants, and motivational factors is the key to understanding why people work and expend energy. In this chapter we look at motivation, drives, incentives, rewards, and underlying reasons for people's acting as they do. The chapter summarizes a variety of basic theories of motivation, including early classical views, the behavioral, need, equity, and expectancy theories.

Motivation and why people work has been studied extensively by psychologists, behavioralists, and managers. There is no universally accepted motivation theory. However, the manager should have a grasp of various theories since these are important in understanding human behavior, and in turn maximizing output and productivity of subordinates.

Table 15-1 contrasts several common theories of motivation. These include theories which view motivation as stemming entirely from outside influences, and those which place it entirely within the psychological makeup of the individual.

## KEY TERMS

Motives, needs, and incentives are considered fundamental to goal attainment. Before exploring some of the common theories of motivation, let us define some key terms.

—*Motive.* A motive is a need or desire that causes a person to act. Motives are needs or drives which spring from within and which cause an outward manifestation, action, or behavior. Motives supply the energy or driving force which causes people to act as they do. They are internal forces, as opposed to incentives which are external forces.

—*Motivation.* Motivation is a total system or view of human behavior which analyzes the forces, drives, and motives which cause people to act in a particu-

**Figure 15-1  Comparative motivation theories**

| Theory | Fundamental view of motivation |
|---|---|
| Classic theory | External system of rewards; carrot and stick |
| Human relations theory | Interaction with others; human side of behavior emphasized |
| Behavioral/reinforcement theory | Stimulus-response (S-R bonds); reward and punishment; reconditioning |
| Need theory | Need is perceived; pressure to act; satisfaction of need |
| Equity theory | Perception of fairness and equity in situation |
| Expectancy theory | Result of value placed on a goal and chances of achieving it |

lar way. It is the collective forces and stimuli which act upon the will.

— *Need.* A need is a want or condition which requires satisfaction. A need is manifested as a lack of something which can be satisfied by the attainment of that thing. Human needs range from physical necessities, such as food and shelter, to psychological needs, such as the desire to be accepted by others or the wish for personal growth and development.

— *Incentive.* An incentive is an external influence such as financial reward or other benefit which incites one to act. Incentives are inducements which work on the individual externally and cause him to complete an action. They differ from motives, which are internal forces.

## HISTORICAL VIEWS OF MOTIVATION

### Classical Theory: Carrot and Stick

The classical theory of motivation was characterized by an external system of rewards. Frederick W. Taylor's studies of productivity and output framed much of the early theories on motivation. These views held that the expenditure of effort was directly tied to financial rewards and incentives. Under Taylor's *economic man* theory, motivation and the attainment of a goal was primarily a function of the amount of money or financial reward given upon completion of the task.

Early theorists viewed motivation in terms of a carrot and stick. People are compelled to action by two forces, a stick (punishment) and a carrot (reward). This early view stems from the work of behavioralists. Money was considered the most effective form of reward, and punishment was meted out in the form of verbal reprimands or withdrawal of privileges.

For some kinds of human endeavors the carrot and stick is effective. People do exhibit motivation and desire to attain goals when given economic rewards, and are pressured into action by such punitive measures as verbal threats and reprimands. However, this early view of motivation did not consider the internal needs, desires, and drives of people. The human personality and potential were overlooked, and only external factors were weighed.

In the 1930s this rigid view of motivation gave way to a more liberal position. Partly as a result of the Hawthorne studies (see chapter 2) and more enlightened information about human behavior, emphasis was placed upon the interaction between people. This led to the development of a human relations theory of motivation.

### Human Relations

The human relations view of motivation held that people interact with and are influenced by their environment and other people. The attitudes of superiors, sub-

> **REAL WORLD**
>
> # One Dollar a Year?
>
> In 1979, Chrysler Corporation was faced with the problem of economic survival in an increasingly competitive world of imported automobiles. Chairman John Riccardo and President Lee Iacocca waived their annual salaries of $360,000 in exchange for cash or credit, to be paid at a later date, which is to be tied to the value of Chrysler stock. They also reduced by about fifteen percent the salaries of the more than seventeen hundred executives employed by the firm.
>
> Chrysler now faces a deficit of $700 million. The reduction in salaries should help the organization reduce this shortfall. Business leaders have commented that the plan should be watched carefully.
>
> Adapted from *Time*, 10 September 1979, p. 73.

ordinates, and peer groups become important factors in motivation.

According to the human relations approach, high motivation is achieved when an individual sees herself as part of a team or family in the work place. High motivation results where workers feel they are wanted and needed by their employer and peer group. During the 1930s many employers stressed human relations and company-related activities.

The human relations approach to management and motivation has fallen into disfavor in the past several decades, largely because it oversimplified the problem. It assumed a direct bond between happiness and productivity. However, it has been established that a cause and effect relationship does not exist. Human beings are complex, and their interaction with the environment and other people is based upon many factors, both internal and external. The importance of the human relations school of thought is that it opened the eyes of managers to the internal human qualities and needs of the worker. This in turn led managers and psychologists to make more indepth, thorough studies of motivation.

## Money as a Reward

Money has long been viewed as a reward which causes people to expend effort. It has little or no intrinsic value. Money is sought because of what it will buy. It provides the necessities of life, freedom from want, the ability to travel, social outlets, and many other things. Money is essentially an external and indirect force which motivates people to work.

It was logical for managers to use money as an incentive to increase output and productivity. Table 15-2 lists some common pay bases which are associated with money as a reward. The basic rationale is that output will increase when greater productivity is rewarded by an increase in pay. Thus, wage incentives are part of many current pay programs.

However, money does not always increase output and productivity. Behavioralists know that other factors motivate employees to produce work. Social factors on the job, the nature of the job itself, personal interactions between manager and subordinate, job security, and psychological benefits play major parts in an employee's output.

## Job Rewards

Much of the compensation from a job is not in the pay envelope, but in the secondary benefits it gives employees. Many occupations provide face-to-face contact and social and emotional releases. Individuals working on the same team or crew, or in the same office develop friendships and form cliques and social groups. People working together often travel in the same social circles, attend the same church, and spend their leisure time in similar activities.

An individual's occupation or job serves many purposes in addition to providing money for food, shelter, clothing, education, and entertainment. A job gives people a sense of belonging and being accepted. It gives a person a place to go each day and provides for a regulated and structured existence. A job offers relief from boredom and a chance to meet people and make friends.

## Design of the Job

Job content should be designed to consider the human element. Sound job design calls for maximum output from the employee, but it also gives her a chance

**Table 15-2 Money as a reward**

| Payable to: | Performance Basis: |
|---|---|
| Individuals | Quantity of goods produced |
| Departments | Quality of goods produced |
| Divisions | Quantity of goods sold |
| Entire organizations | Profit |
|  | Cooperation, attitude |
| Pay Basis: | Reduction in waste, defects, returns |
| Hourly | Cost savings to organization |
| Salary, fixed base |  |
| Salary, variable base |  |
| Bonus |  |
| Fringe benefits |  |

for human interaction and contact. Employees who are isolated from others because of their work feel alienated and frustrated. Bringing these workers into closer interaction with other employees often results in greater productivity and less frustration.

Conversely, job design which allows excessive interaction between employees can lessen performance and output. Excessive talking and personal distractions on some jobs create other problems. Managers seek to provide a balance between the social interactions and the need to perform the job in the most efficient manner.

## Morale

Morale is a measure of the contentment experienced by individuals in an organization. High morale is associated with high output, reduced friction between employees, and lower absenteeism. Employees with high morale tend to support organization goals and be more willing to work with management to attain them.

Low morale may cause high absenteeism, employee dissatisfaction, friction, and sometimes low productivity. An important task of management is to foster high morale and a cooperative spirit among employees. Team effort, worker cooperation, and esprit de corps are usually indicators of a well-run organization.

Sound job design allows for interaction with other people.

Morale is generally increased by providing employee benefits, fair compensation, vacations, health and medical plans, and so on. Recognition of superior performance by management and fair treatment of employees leads to improved morale. A flexible, supportive organization climate is preferable to one which is rigid and nonhumanistic.

## CONTEMPORARY VIEWS OF MOTIVATION

Motivation has been studied and widely researched. A variety of basic theories of motivation have evolved from this research. These include the behavioral view, need theories, equity theory, and expectancy theory.

### Behavioral/Reinforcement Theory

One of the earliest theories of motivation grew out of the work of Pavlov and later Edward Thorndike and B. F. Skinner. These researchers studied animal and human behavior and formulated theories based upon a stimulus and response, and conditioning. (See figure 15-1.)

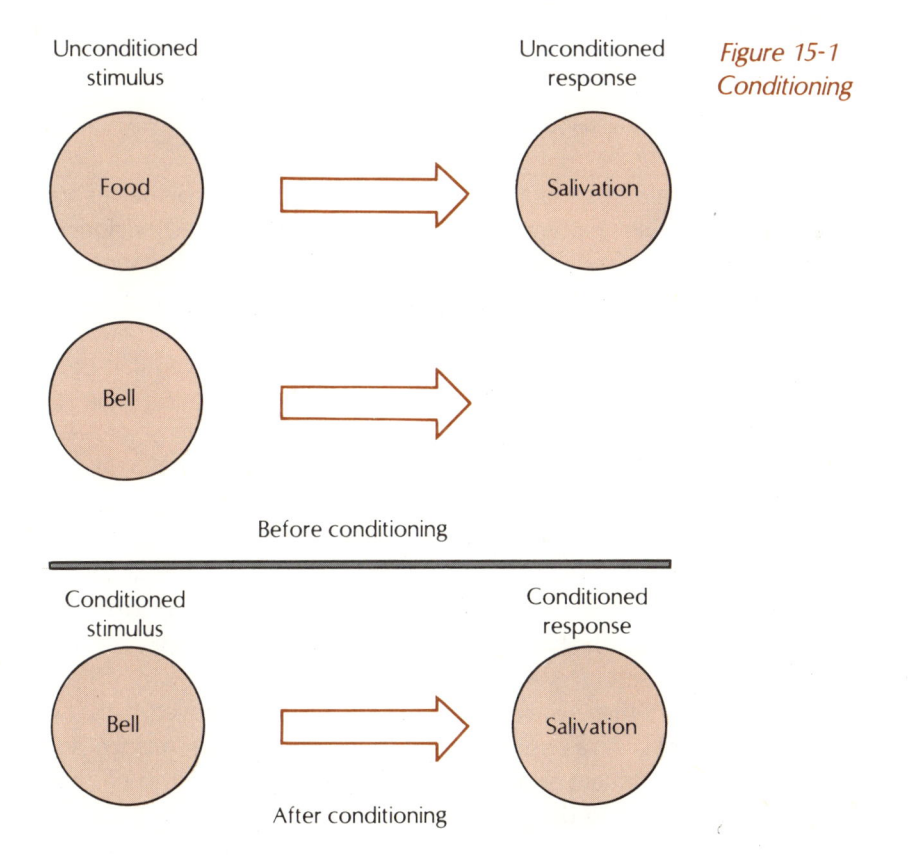

*Figure 15-1 Conditioning*

"Yes, we can use a man with drive, ambition, and talent. How's your shorthand?"

Reprinted from *Graphic Arts Monthly*, January 1979.

A principle premise of this theory is that both animals and human beings are born with certain behavior patterns which can be changed or reconditioned. Pavlov called this conditioning a response. It involves setting up new stimulus-response patterns, or new S-R bonds.

In his famous studies of animal behavior, Pavlov experimented with salivation in dogs and the stimulus which caused them to salivate. He observed that dogs began to salivate upon the appearance of the animal trainer at feeding time. He experimented with ringing a bell just before feeding time to change or recondition the dogs' response. After repeatedly ringing the bell at feeding time, Pavlov found that the dogs associated the bell with eating and began salivating at the ringing of the bell, even though food was not present.

Thus, a conditioned response or new S-R bond was established in which the learned behavior became the new behavior for the dogs. Motivation theories based upon the operant conditioning or reinforcement theory involve conditioning responses.

Under this theory, human behavior can be conditioned or changed. If, for example, subordinates are given a positive reward for acceptable performance, and negative treatment (punishment or criticism) for unacceptable performance, their behavior on the job can be modified.

Thus, according to behavioral/reinforcement theorists, high output is achieved through a system of rewards and punishment. Bonuses, compliments, special favors, and privileges are given to reinforce desired behavior. Withdrawal of privileges, criticism, or verbal reprimands are used to discourage undesirable behavior.

Theories such as this are widely held by managers. However, this approach to understanding human behavior does not deal with the complex, inner needs and personalities of human beings. It tends to relate human behavior closely to animal behavior and does not stress the more complex intellectual nature of people.

## Need Theories

Another approach to understanding motivation is the need theory. A number of behavioralists, psychologists, and managers believe that the roots of motivation are in an assessment of innate human needs, which must be satisfied.

Figure 15-2 illustrates the need-satisfaction process. First a person perceives a need, is pressured to action by it, and finally attains satisfaction and reward through some action. Virtually all need theories are based upon this basic premise. Need theories include those of Maslow, Berne, and McGregor.

**Maslow's Need Theory** According to Maslow, every individual is born with five

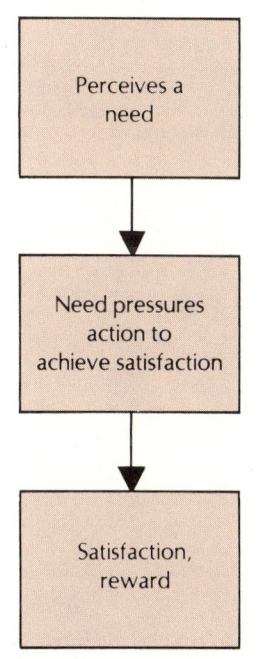

*Figure 15-2   Need theory*

basic, innate needs.[1] (See figure 15-3.) These five basic needs must be met if we are to function as fully productive human beings.

1. *Physiological needs.* The need exists in all human organisms for food, shelter, water, rest, sex, and other basic physical requirements. These are primary to our very existence.

2. *Safety needs.* All organisms have a need for self-preservation and safety. There is a need to be free from harm and secure and stable in our lives and our work. A need exists to be free of pain and other destructive forces.

3. *Social needs.* There is a need for love, affection, peer acceptance, and belonging in all human organisms. This manifests itself as a need for social interaction and acceptance.

4. *Ego needs.* A higher level need in people is to be recognized by others and to command respect and status. We all have a desire to be competent in what we are doing and to be acknowledged by others.

5. *Self-actualization.* The highest level of need in the human organism relates to personal growth and achievement. There exists a need to achieve the maximum potential that we are capable of as human beings.

Maslow places these five needs on a hierarchy, suggesting that the desire to

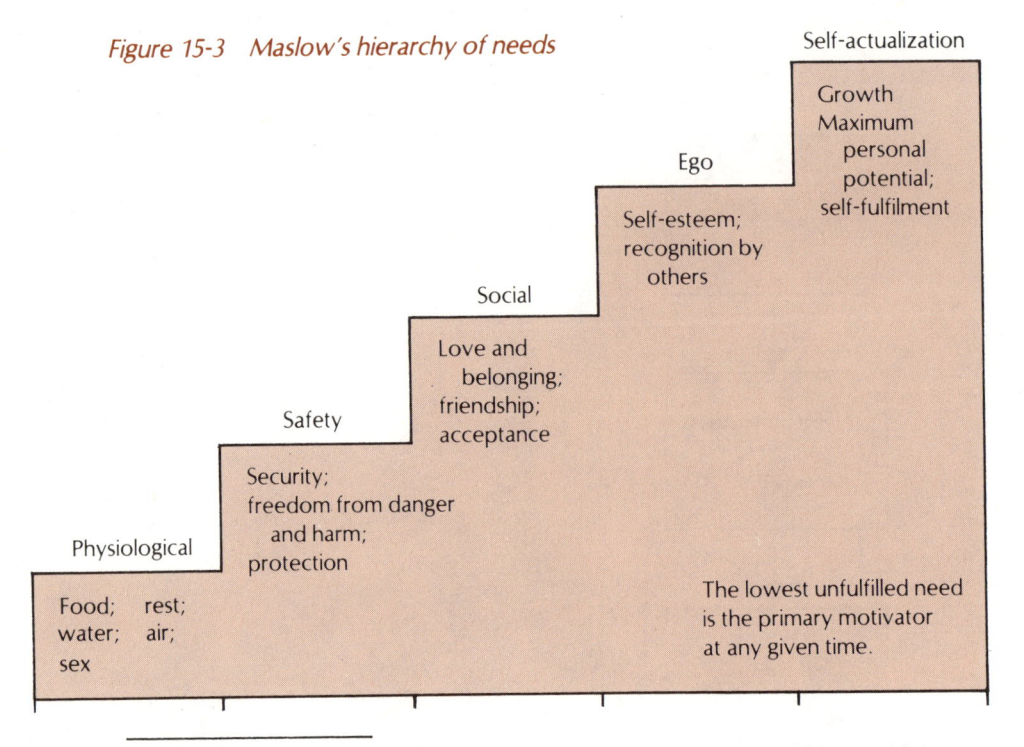

*Figure 15-3  Maslow's hierarchy of needs*

Physiological
Food; rest; water; air; sex

Safety
Security; freedom from danger and harm; protection

Social
Love and belonging; friendship; acceptance

Ego
Self-esteem; recognition by others

Self-actualization
Growth Maximum personal potential; self-fulfilment

The lowest unfulfilled need is the primary motivator at any given time.

---

[1]Abraham Maslow, *Motivation and Personality* (New York: Harper and Row, 1954).

achieve the higher level needs does not manifest itself until we have attained those on a lower level. Thus, one does not exhibit a need for personal growth or self-fulfillment until the primary needs for food, water, rest, security have been satisfied.

Maslow views motivation to achieve human needs as the principle driving force behind people's actions. All efforts to achieve a goal are directed at satisfying these five needs in the hierarchy.

**Berne's Need Theory.** A more recent and slightly different view of needs is Berne's need theory.[2] Berne's theory is based upon hungers (need) and strokes (satisfactions). According to Berne, each human organism is born with certain innate hungers. These include the hunger for touching, recognition, time structuring, and acceptance. These needs are inborn and develop as we mature.

Berne sees human beings as having needs which are satisfied by stroking. Strokes or satisfaction may be verbal or nonverbal conduct toward others. A stroke is recognition by others of one's merit, worth, and presence as a human being. Berne views strokes as being either positive or negative. (See table 15-3.)

—*Positive strokes.* Positive strokes are in the form of a compliment, a pat on the back, or personal recognition. Positive strokes recognize the whole person and validate what we are and who we are. An example of a positive stroke is any statement of affection or appreciation, such as a sincere ''thank you'' or ''you look nice today.'' Just listening to and understanding another person's feelings, concerns, or wishes is a form of positive stroking.

—*Negative strokes and discounting.* A negative stroke is a form of behavior in which a person's presence, existence, or worth is denied. In negative stroking we discount or ignore the feelings and desires of another person. Common forms of negative stroking include not talking to another person, denying that he is capable of solving a problem, not recognizing his solution, or denigrating the importance of his problem to him.

**Table 15-3  Strokes in organizations**

| Positive | Negative |
|---|---|
| ''You have a good solution.'' | ''We don't think your plan will work.'' |
| ''We are confident you can do a good job.'' | ''Are you sure you can handle this account?'' |
| ''That was very well done.'' | ''Try to do a better job next time.'' |
| ''We're glad you are here.'' | ''We're not able to see you now.'' |
| ''We know the Jones job is important to you.'' | ''Put the Jones job aside and help on the Smith account.'' |

[2] Eric Berne, *Transactional Analysis* (New York: Ballantine Books, 1961).

> **REAL WORLD**
> # Compensation Woe: How to Pay?
>
> Many managers know that when they give their employees a raise it really doesn't mean more money. With inflation and taxes, raises often wind up going to the government instead of the employee's pocketbook. So managers are beginning to look at other forms of compensation. Bruce Ellig, a compensation expert at Pfizer, Inc., says that the results of many compensation systems are simply to reward mediocrity and stifle improvement of performance.
>
> Previously, many employers increased the nontaxable benefits given employees, such as health and education programs. But this trend has been declining. A better approach is to use the *cafeteria plan*. This arrangement allows employees to select the benefits that they prefer. It is up to them to decide whether they want improvements in medical, pension, or life insurance coverage, or whether they want cash. Thus, a high-salaried, unmarried employee might be better off plowing more money into a pension plan at the expense of a medical plan, since the employee has no dependents.
>
> Adapted from *Time*, 15 October 1979, p. 110.

Berne's need theory also encompasses a need for structured time. Every human organism has a need to escape boredom. We need a period when we can withdraw from contact with others, and we also need intimacy and closeness. The human desire for games, rituals, activities, and pastimes is indicative of our need for structured time.

Berne's theory is of value to managers because it stresses positive, supportive behavior. Most motivational theories overlap and parallel one another.

## McGregor's X and Y Theories

Douglas McGregor's theory of motivation is based upon attitudes of managers. According to McGregor, two assumptions of human motivation are found among managers. These are opposing views which provide insights into motivation because they challenge accepted assumptions of human behavior.[3]

— *X theory.* Under this assumption, human beings exhibit a basic dislike for work and the expenditure of effort. People must be coerced, controlled, and threatened into producing. Under the X theory, subordinates must continually be pres-

---
[3]Douglas McGregor, *The Human Side of Enterprise* (New York: McGraw-Hill, 1960).

sured into working. Further, it is assumed that the average human being does not want to be self-directed and prefers to be directed by others, and that more value is placed upon security than upon taking responsibility.

— *Y theory.* Under this assumption, work is as natural as play. The human organism not only accepts the need to work, but actually seeks it. Thus, people do not need to be controlled or coerced into action. Instead, they prefer self-direction and, under the proper conditions, seek responsibility. The need for achievement in most people is greater than their need for security. A high degree of imagination and creativity is found in most people and is not limited to a gifted few.

Thus, under McGregor's assumptions, managers take two different approaches to motivation based upon their view of subordinates. In one case, the manager pressures and coerces employees to produce, while in the other the manager provides the environment which allows the internal force within people to work.

## Herzberg's Two Factor Theory

Frederick Herzberg studied groups of several hundred engineers and people in other occupations to determine which elements motivated people to high output and performance. His research indicated that two important factors were at work. These were labeled motivation factors and hygiene factors.[4] The motivation factors relate to the content of the job and are sources of worker satisfaction. Hygiene factors relate to conditions of work and are sources of dissatisfaction. (See figure 15-4.)

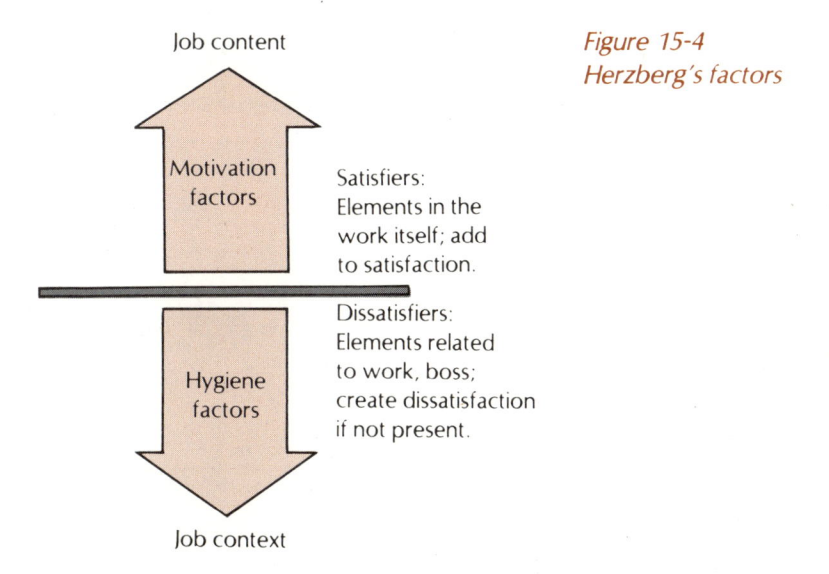

*Figure 15-4*
*Herzberg's factors*

Job content

Motivation factors

Satisfiers: Elements in the work itself; add to satisfaction.

Hygiene factors

Dissatisfiers: Elements related to work, boss; create dissatisfaction if not present.

Job context

---

[4]Frederick Herzberg and B. Snyderman, *The Motivation to Work* (New York: John Wiley & Sons, 1959).

—*Motivation factors.* In every job there are elements which are motivational in nature. These elements are intrinsic to many jobs and produce feelings of achievement, satisfaction, self-worth, and responsibility. Herzberg's motivation factors, if present in the work, increase motivation. However, their absence does not create dissatisfaction.

—*Hygiene factors.* For every job there is a group of related factors which deal with the context or conditions under which the job is done. According to Herzberg, these are important elements, since they can have a negative effect on the performance. Examples of hygiene factors are job security and benefits, company policies, the attitude of the supervisor, and pay.

Maximum output and performance can be expected from workers when strong motivational factors are present on the job and when the hygiene factors do not detract from the job. High motivation and output are a result of the job itself and the context which surrounds it. The manager's task is to increase the motivational factors (job design) and eliminate those hygiene factors which lessen performance.

## McClelland/Atkinson Need Theory

A more complex need theory of motivation has been developed by Atkinson and applied to management by McClelland.[5] According to these theorists, motivation springs from a well of potential energy within each person. They perceive all people as having a potential for achievement. It is the situation and conditions present in one's life which cause this potential to emerge as useful work and output.

In their view, motivation is based upon three distinct needs (table 15-4): need for power, need for affiliation, and need for achievement.

1. *Need for power.* According to this theory, people have a need for power. It is manifested as a basic drive to control and direct others. People possess an innate desire to supervise others or command their attention.

2. *Need for affiliation.* Another basic need is to affiliate with others. The need for friendship, personal relationships, and social interaction is present in all people. This is the force which causes us to join social clubs, groups, and fraternities.

3. *Need for achievement.* A third need is the need to attain a goal. The need to

Table 15-4 McClelland/Atkinson theory

| | Needs | |
| Power | Affiliation | Achievement |
| --- | --- | --- |
| Control and direct others | Friendship; social interaction | Goal achievement; creative efforts |

---

[5]David C. McClelland, *The Achieving Society* (Princeton, N.J.: Van Nostrand, 1961); and John W. Atkinson, *An Introduction to Motivation* (New York: Van Nostrand, 1964).

CHAPTER FIFTEEN    MOTIVATION

*The need to achieve something of personal value is inborn in many people.*

achieve something of personal value is inborn in many people, though it is not universally distributed in the population. It is this internal need which causes people to build organizations, gather personal wealth, or indulge in creative efforts.

These three needs sometimes conflict. A manager with a high need for affiliation may sacrifice organizational goals to gain personal favor. He may place friendship with others or acceptance by his peer group ahead of organizational rules or policies.

Similarly, a manager with a high need for power may seek to dominate others and be overly directive simply to fill this need. Further, a manager with a strong need for achievement may place a high degree of pressure on subordinates, even if it means losing friends on the job.

### Equity Theory

Another school of motivation theory centers on the principle of balance or equity. According to this viewpoint, the level of motivation in an individual is a direct result of her perception of the fairness or equity in her relationship with the manager or the organization. The greater the degree of fairness she perceives, the greater her motivation. Conversely, people who see themselves as being treated unfairly exhibit low motivation.

For example, an employee who feels that her contribution is of greater

## POSTSCRIPT
# Well Pay:
# Bonuses For Just Showing Up

Sick pay is one of those necessary and sensible corporate institutions that are often abused. If an employee is hung over or simply does not feel like working because it is a lovely day, he can call in with a feigned case of the blahs. That escape hatch from the workaday world is being mildly threatened by a newfangled idea aimed at throwing dedicated malingerers into a dilemma: well pay.

Now being tried in several small and medium-size companies on the West Coast, well pay rewards people for doing what they are supposed to do: go to work regu-

Reprinted by permission from *Time*, 7 August 1978, p. 67; Copyright © Time Inc. 1978.

---

worth than a more highly paid coworker senses an inequity. That sense may exist even if the favoritism is only suspected. Therefore, the individual should be reprimanded or rewarded the same as others for similar actions. Otherwise this sense of inequity will affect the individual's behavior. Figure 15-5 illustrates this. Subordinates who see themselves as being treated with fairness and equity are highly motivated to achieve organizational goals. Essentially, the motivation level is a function of perceived fairness.

The equity balance may be achieved in different ways. Fair treatment may be manifested in financial terms, such as money or bonuses. Or it may be perceived in psychological terms. Employees who feel their manager or organization treats them fairly exhibit high motivation, even though the financial rewards may be low.

The problem with the equity theory is in determining what is fair. Fairness to one person may seem unfair to another. A manager may feel he is giving fair pay or fair treatment to subordinates, but it may not be perceived that way by the employees. The equity theory tends to oversimplify motivation, placing it in terms of weighing equities. It overlooks the complex psychological underpinnings and drives which constitute a large part of human behavior.

### Expectancy Theory

Another theory which has greatly influenced thinking on motivation is the expectancy theory, articulated by Victor Vroom. According to Vroom, there is a direct relationship between the level of motivation, the importance of a goal, and the

larly and on time. Some results have been impressive. Reports James Parsons, 59, president of Parsons Pine Products of Ashland, Ore., maker of nearly eighty percent of the nation's wooden mousetrap bases: "Our absenteeism has dropped thirty percent, and our tardiness is almost zero." Parsons' incentive: an extra day's pay at the end of every month to workers who are punctual. Reichhold Chemicals' fiberglass manufacturing division in Irwindale, California, offers half an hour's extra pay for each week a worker completes a full shift without illness or absence. The bonuses are called "sweet pay" (for Stay at Work, Earn Extra Pay).

Most employees like the idea, but some workers and union leaders seem skeptical. Says Mildred Corriveau, a vocational nurse at one of the 151 nursing homes owned by Pasadena's Beverly Enterprises, whose employees get five percent bonuses each month for showing up on time: "It's not enough money to persuade a person to come to work. I think we will still have as much diarrhea as we used to." For some folks, no reward can match the luxury of loafing.

expectation of achieving it.[6] Vroom stated this relationship in a basic formula:

$$\text{Motivation} = \Sigma \text{ Expectancy} \times \text{Valence}.$$

Expectancy is a person's estimate of the chances that a desired goal can be achieved. Valence is the value or worth that a person places upon that goal.

The motivational force exhibited by a person is the summation of the value or importance placed on the goal multiplied by the expectation of achieving it. People exhibit a high degree of motivation when the goal sought is of great personal value and at the same time is very achievable. Conversely, if there is little chance of achieving a goal, and if it has little personal value, the individual exhibits low motivation.

*Figure 15-5
Equity theory*

---

[6]Victor Vroom, *Work and Motivation* (New York: John Wiley & Sons, 1964).

In management terms, one can expect a high level of motivation from subordinates where organizational goals are closely in line with their personal goals. High motivation results where there is a good possibility that the goal can be achieved. Where there are vast differences between expectations and goal importance between subordinates and organizations, motivational problems arise.

The expectancy theory places a high degree of rationality on the motivation process and deemphasizes needs and inner psychological drives. It reduces motivation to a logical analysis of value and expectation. Unfortunately, people do not always assess situations in wholly rational terms.

Individuals vary greatly in their commitment to organizational goals. Even given equal commitment, the range of human wants and needs is enormous. This places a burden on the manager, who must deal with great diversity while seeking fairly uniform and widely applicable motivational techniques.

## SUMMARY

There is no universally accepted motivational theory. The classical view of motivation is characterized by an external system of reward. The development of the human relations theory later led to emphasis being placed on the human element.

Job content and job rewards, including money, play an important part in motivation. Morale can be increased by meeting the employee's economic needs and providing sound job design. Team effort and esprit de corps are important to a well-run organization.

There are several contemporary views of motivation. The behavioral/reinforcement theory stresses the stimulus-response bond and conditioning. Various theories have been put forth by Maslow, Berne, McGregor, Herzberg, McClelland/Atkinson, and others. These theories describe motivation from the context of human needs.

The equity theory of motivation is based upon the principle of fairness as perceived by the subordinate. The expectancy theory of motivation is based upon a person's estimate of the chances of a goal's being achieved and the valence or value placed on that goal.

## REVIEW QUESTIONS

1. Contrast the classical view of motivation with the human relations view.
2. Discuss some ways in which morale can be improved on the job.
3. What is the basic premise of the behavioral theory of motivation?
4. According to Maslow, what are the five basic needs?
5. How do positive strokes differ from negative?
6. Contrast McGregor's X and Y theories.

7. Contrast Herzberg's motivation factors and hygiene factors.
8. Describe the three needs outlined by McClelland/Atkinson.
9. What role does fairness play in the equity theory?
10. Explain the basic relationship of expectance and valence on motivation.
11. Describe some common ways that money is used as a motivational factor.
12. What is meant by *reconditioning* behavior?

## KEY TERMS

Motive   340
Motivation   340
Need   341
Incentive   341
Human relations   341
Rewards   342
Morale   344
Behavioral/reinforcement theory   345
Strokes   349
Motivation factors   351
Hygiene factors   352
Equity   353
Expectancy   354

# Case Incident

Lonnie Johnson is senior vice president of the Osborne Advertising Agency, which employs over three hundred people in its creative services department. Johnson has just recently called a meeting with two of his supervisors, Victoria Shepard and Marvin Chumley. The agency is faced with two serious, but related, problems of high turnover and declining output. Employee morale is very low and several of their most creative and valuable employees have recently gone to work for competing agencies, with little or no increase in pay.

In talking with several friends at other advertising agencies, Johnson has found that the employees left Osborne because of excessive job pressure, unreasonable deadlines, and inflexible management. After hearing this and thinking about the matter for some time, Shepard believes that the solution to the problem lies in providing more nonmonetary incentives for the employees. She thinks that improving working conditions, including private offices, free parking, and additional clerical and support staff will help relieve the pressures and improve employee morale.

Chumley, too, has given the situation considerable thought. He has decided that Osborne employees can work under the pressures and the deadlines if they are paid well enough. "They really don't need any additional fancy offices or secretaries. The environment that we provide for them is more than acceptable. What they really need is more money to make them feel appreciated. Even though Osborne employees are well known as being the highest paid in the industry, they need to know that we are aware that they are under a great deal of pressure and strain. They must know that we don't take them for granted."

**PROBLEMS**

1. How effective do you believe monetary incentives will be in improving morale in the department? Explain.
2. Will the free parking privileges and private offices improve morale? Explain.
3. What other forces are at work which affect morale and output in the department?

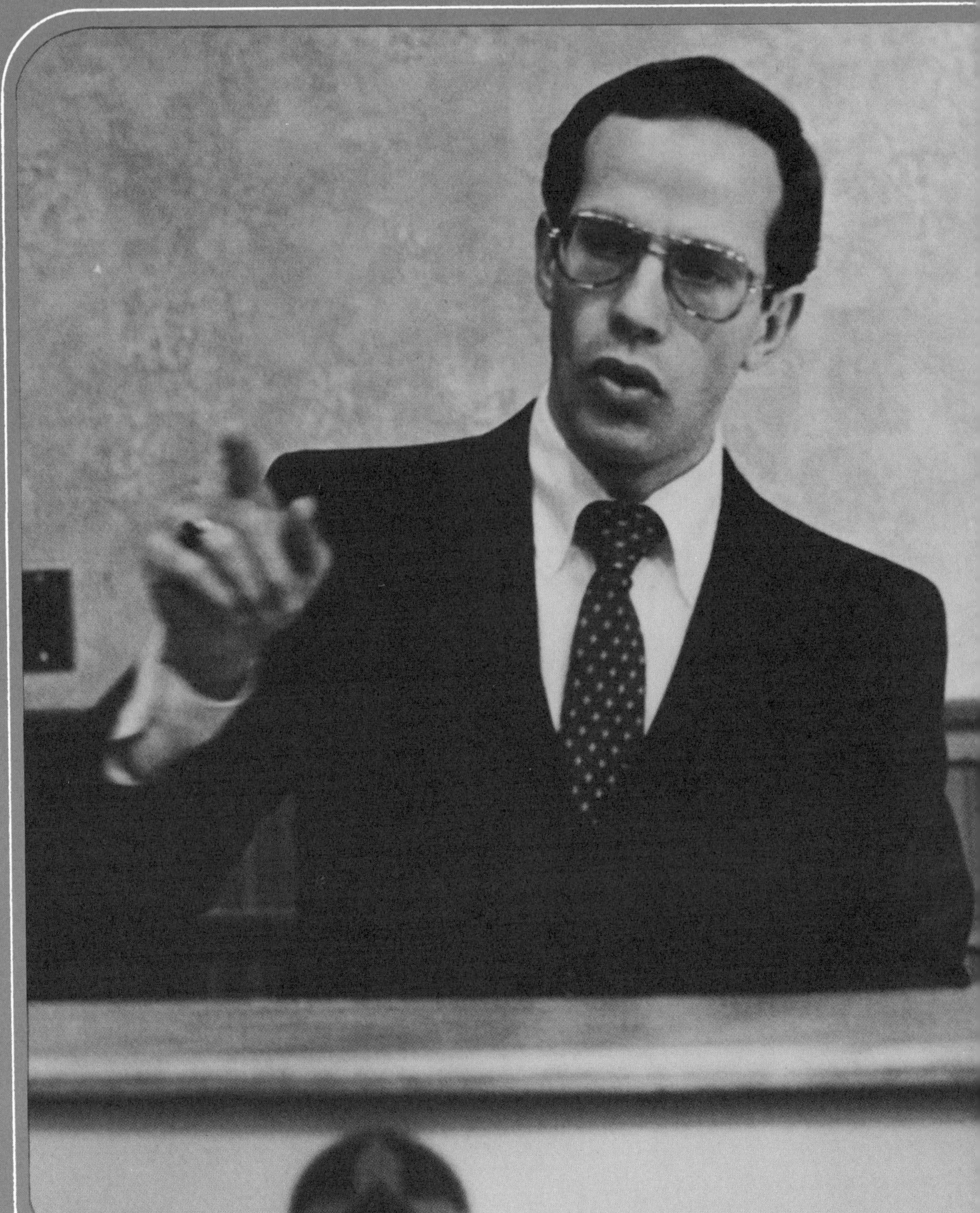

# 16

# Leadership in Organizations

**LEARNING OBJECTIVES**

After studying this chapter, you should be able to:
1. Define key terms related to leadership in organizations.
2. Describe sources of power and their influence on leadership.
3. Summarize the major attributes of the trait theory of leadership.
4. Summarize the major attributes of the behavioral theory of leadership.
5. Summarize the major attributes of the contingency theory of leadership.
6. Contrast Lewin's three styles of leadership behavior.
7. Summarize Likert's four systems.
8. Describe the influence of the Ohio State studies on leadership.
9. Describe Tannenbaum and Schmidt's contribution to leadership behavior.
10. Summarize Fiedler's research on leadership.

Leading is one of the most important functions of the manager. In this chapter we review the key aspects of leadership. We consider the roots of leadership and the environment in which it is exercised.

Three major theories of leadership have evolved: the trait, behavior, and contingency theories. To understand the nature of leadership, the student should have a grasp of these major theories. They are discussed in this chapter, along with descriptions of several models developed by leadership theorists, including Rensis Likert, Fred Fiedler, Victor Vroom, and others.

The manager faces many major tasks: these include leading people, guiding the physical growth and development of the organization, and directing its financial growth. Of these three tasks, leading people is viewed by many as the most important, since all other aspects of the organization are dependent upon the best utilization of personnel.

## KEY TERMS

The field of leadership theory has been studied and researched widely. There are dozens of views on how and why people lead other people. To focus on this important management function, let us review some key definitions.

—*Leadership*. Leadership is the process by which an individual influences and guides others toward a goal. Inherent in the definition of leadership is the ability to influence others to attain a goal. Leadership deals with guiding and showing the way. It relies upon influence rather than upon force and authority.

—*Leader*. A leader is anyone able to exert influence or control over others. Leaders may be those formally delegated by the hierarchy, or individuals who accept leadership informally and exercise it without the sanction of the formal organization. A leader exercises this ability either through the possession of personal traits, the display of leadership conduct and behavior, or through position or status in an organization.

—*Power*. Power is the possession of influence, control, or authority over others. The possession of power gives an individual the tools with which to influence or control others. Power is a key element in the exercise of leadership.

## THE ENVIRONMENT OF LEADERSHIP

Leadership does not function in a vacuum. To understand the nature of leadership we must look at the characteristics of both the leader and the follower. We must also examine the conditions or circumstances under which leadership is exercised.

As we shall see, the environment and conditions in which the leader functions have great influence. There are three forces at work when leadership is

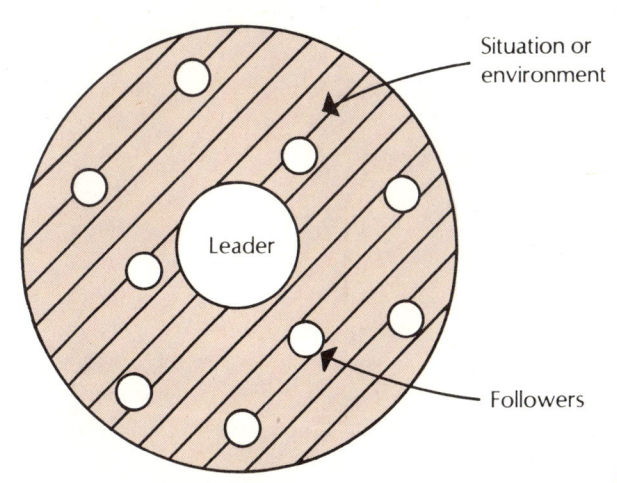

CHAPTER SIXTEEN   LEADERSHIP IN ORGANIZATIONS   363

*Figure 16-1   Leadership forces*

exercised: conditions within the leader, conditions within the individuals being led, and environmental forces. (See figure 16-1.)

The process of leadership cannot be fully understood if we look only at the characteristics of the leader. While personal traits are important, the behavior of the leader and the expectations, experience, and attitudes of the follower are also relevant. Let us explore the sources of power before looking at the three major theories of leadership in more detail.

## SOURCES OF POWER

Some useful insights into the sources of power and its influences on leadership come from John French and Bertram Raven.[1]

French and Raven outlined five major bases by which one acquires and exerts power. Their study, which is one of many which focus on the sources of power, gives the manager a good foundation in the etiology of power. Table 16-1 contrasts their five sources of power.

**Table 16-1   Sources of power**

| Power | Characterized by: |
| --- | --- |
| Reward | Monetary and nonmonetary rewards, compliments |
| Coercive | Threats, fear, punishment |
| Legitimate | Position in organizational hierarchy |
| Expert | Possession of knowledge, skill, information |
| Referent | Taking on traits or identification with those in power |

[1] John French and Bertram Raven, *The Bases of Social Power,* ed. D. Cartwright (Ann Arbor, Mich.: Institute for Social Research, 1959), p. 150.

> **REAL WORLD**
>
> # A Movie Mogul Eats Her Words
>
> Once a model, actress, and mathematics teacher, Sherry Lansing now heads Twentieth Century-Fox Studios. Lansing, 35, was recently appointed to head productions at the major studio. She is the first woman to head a major studio.
>
> Lansing will earn at least $300,000 a year and have a production budget of over $100 million. She breaks up a clique of all male managers that has dominated the motion picture industry since its inception.
>
> Lansing is aware of the fact that the job will not be easy and will require aggressiveness, strength, and toughness. But she doesn't plan to be tough. She looks forward to running the big company with "human decency, kindness, and respect for people." Is there room for an ambitious, hard-working, intelligent ex-model in the rapacious world of Hollywood yes-men? It is anyone's guess.
>
> Adapted from the *Los Angeles Times,* 4 January 1980.

1. *Reward power.* This form of power comes from the granting of a reward or gift for a job well done. Rewards may be in monetary (money or economic elements) or nonmonetary (special favors) form. Monetary rewards include cash bonuses, discounts, or things of financial worth. The granting of special privileges, or personal praise and compliments, are nonmonetary rewards.

2. *Coercive power.* In this form, the base of power arises from the individual's ability to punish or coerce. Fear of punishment is the principal motivation which causes a subordinate to follow a manager's directives. Coercive power may be very effective where substantial punitive threats are exercised.

3. *Legitimate power.* Legitimate power is derived from one's position in the formal power structure in the organization. It is vested in individuals as a result of the accepted or official position they occupy in the hierarchy. The higher the individual is on the hierarchy, the greater that person's legitimate power.

4. *Expert power.* People in possession of exclusive knowledge, skills, or ability wield power. Their power is derived from the fact that they possess expertise or information not readily available to others. For example, a manager who has knowledge of the special characteristics of a particular machine which is not understood by others can exercise power. As the only individual with the knowledge or skill to keep the machine running, the manager can dictate many of the conditions under which he works.

5. *Referent power.* Power is acquired by taking on the attitudes, behavior, language, or dress of someone in power. In this instance, power is based upon a transference or association with someone who has power gained by one of the other bases.

An example of referent power is a supervisor who takes on the dress, attitudes, and language of top-level managers in the company. He gains a degree of power by simple transference.

## MAJOR LEADERSHIP THEORIES

An extensive amount of analysis and research has gone into the study of leadership theory. Great political leaders, social reformers, politicians, and labor organizers have been studied to ascertain what characteristics or leadership traits they possess. Business organizations have also been studied and the actions of managers observed closely to isolate leadership behavior. For instance, McGregor's X and Y theories, discussed in chapter 15, are among the many important attempts to describe leadership behavior. The interaction among the leader, the follower, and the situation have been scrutinized carefully.

Three distinct approaches to leadership have evolved: the trait, behavior, and contingency theories. (See figure 16-2.) Each of these approaches places a different emphasis and perspective on the nature of leadership. No one theory is universally accepted by managers, and each has its adherents.

The trait theory emphasizes the forces present in the leader. It stresses the traits and attributes of the leader and deemphasizes the leader's behavior or the environment. The behavioral theory stresses the learned behavior and actions of the leader, rather than innate traits. Finally, the contingency theory, which has gained much attention, stresses the interrelationship among the leader, the follower, and the situation.

## TRAIT THEORY

The earliest attempts to define leadership centered about the traits possessed by successful leaders. The trait theory holds that leadership springs from the internal attributes possessed by leaders. According to this view, leadership is a function of

| Trait theory | Behavioral theory | Contingency theory |
|---|---|---|
| Forces in leader | Learned behavior or actions of leader | Interrelationship of leader, follower, and situation |

*Figure 16-2*

*Acquiring expert knowledge can be a source of power.*

a cluster of distinguishing qualities within the leader. These traits are seen as inborn and natural to some people. They are unique to individuals, unlike behavior which is learned. This theory supports the *born leader* philosophy, but most academicians and managers do not accept its basic premise.

Among the traits possessed by leaders are high intelligence, maturity, an understanding of human relations, motivation, and the ability to work well with people. Charisma and self-confidence are other traits found in successful leaders. Charisma is defined as a personal, somewhat magical quality which elicits a popular loyalty and enthusiasm. There is some validity to this theory, since great leaders have emerged in business and society with little management training, but with personal traits that contributed much to their success.

Attempts have been made to define traits possessed by nonleaders. There do not appear to be any clearly defined characteristics held by either leaders or nonleaders. Thus, most management theorists support the behavioral and contingency theories.

## BEHAVIORAL THEORY

A second major theory of leadership is the behavioral school. According to this rationale, leadership is a function of the behavior of the individual, rather than any internal traits. This behavior consists of attitudes and actions which result in other individuals' becoming followers. In essence, a person who acts like a leader becomes a leader.

One of the earliest behavioral theorists was Kurt Lewin.[2] His work, expanded upon by others, described a group of leadership styles. In his writings, Lewin noted that leaders exhibit democratic, authoritarian, or laissez-faire leadership styles.

To understand the leadership behavior philosophy, we must also look at the work of Robert Tannenbaum, Warren Schmidt, Rensis Likert, and the researchers who conducted the Ohio State studies.

### Lewin's View of Leadership Styles.

The work of Kurt Lewin contains one of the earliest descriptions of leadership behavior. Lewin studied a group of children in a classroom. After careful observation, he noted that leadership behavior exists on a continuum, ranging from authoritarian behavior on the one hand to laissez-faire on the other. (See figure 16-3.)

1. *Authoritarian leadership style.* Authoritarian leaders exhibit behavior which places the major decision-making power in the hands of the leader. There is little or no participation by followers. For some kinds of groups, authoritarian leadership style is preferable. Groups which expect to be directed will function best with this type of leadership style. Obviously those who expect great freedom, or who wish to participate in the leadership process, will not function well under an authoritarian leader.

2. *Democratic style.* This leadership style evokes participation from followers. The decision-making responsibility is shared between the leader and subordinates. Groups which expect to participate in the decision-making process fare better under this style of leadership than under authoritarian or laissez-faire leadership.

3. *Laissez-faire style.* Under this style of leadership, the responsibility for decision

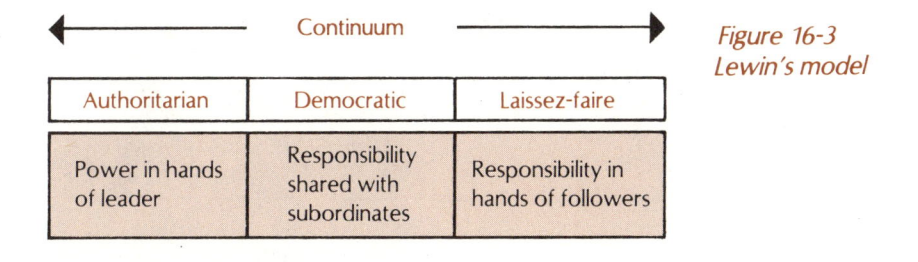

| Authoritarian | Democratic | Laissez-faire |
|---|---|---|
| Power in hands of leader | Responsibility shared with subordinates | Responsibility in hands of followers |

← Continuum →

*Figure 16-3 Lewin's model*

---

[2] K. Lewin, R. Lippit, and Ralph K. White, "Patterns of Aggressive Behavior in Experimentally Created Social Climate," *Journal of Social Psychology,* p. 10.

making is shifted to followers. Laissez-faire leaders do not take a strong stand on rules, nor do they insist that subordinates follow their direction. A "hands off" style is exhibited where the leader goes along with the group. Laissez-faire behavior is best suited for groups of highly professional individuals who desire to exercise the maximum degree of self-control. Placing these individuals under a democratic or authoritarian leader would be frustrating to both the manager and subordinates.

## Likert's Systems

Rensis Likert explored leadership behavior and developed a model describing leadership as a continuum with four major styles. (See figure 16-4.) Likert studied hundreds of leadership styles in organizations and observed four common systems.[3]

According to Likert, System 1 leadership is very job-centered, while System 4 is very democratic and employee-centered. Let us look at each system in detail.

1. *Exploitive-authoritative.* The System 1 leader uses an exploitive and authoritative style. All decisions are made by the leader without consulting subordinates. The manager makes choices with little or no input expected or accepted from others. Threats and coercion are used to get the task done. It is best described as heavy-handed management, applied from the top.

2. *Benevolent-authoritative.* In this style, the manager uses a benevolent and sometimes condescending attitude toward subordinates. While the manager may listen to subordinates, their input has little effect on decisions and policies.

3. *Consultative-democratic.* In this system, the manager consults with subordi-

*Figure 16-4 Likert's Systems*

← Continuum →

| System 1 | System 2 | System 3 | System 4 |
|---|---|---|---|
| Exploitive-authoritative<br><br>Decision making by leader | Benevolent-authoritative<br><br>Accepts decision in name only | Consultative-democratic:<br><br>Subordinate input used in decision-making process | Participative-democratic:<br><br>Decision making by subordinate, relied on by manager |

← Job-centered          Employee-centered →

---

[3]Rensis Likert, *New Patterns of Management* (New York: McGraw-Hill, 1961); also *The Human Organization* (New York: McGraw-Hill, 1967).

"The top item on the agenda today is the problem of how best to inform our stockholders that we poured another 11 million dollars down the rat hole in the first half of '75."

Reprinted from *Datamation,* July 1975.

nates and uses their input in the decision-making process. However, the manager remains in control and makes the ultimate decisions. The real power remains with the leader, who uses the subordinates as a sounding board.

4. *Participative-democratic.* This system is illustrative of the true democratic process. Subordinates are involved in the decision-making process and their wishes are relied upon by the manager. This system uses true interaction between manager and subordinates with open lines of communication. Decisions are made at a grass roots level rather than from the top down, as in System 1. It involves the highest level of participation and employee involvement.

## Ohio State Studies

Another important leadership model was developed by the Bureau of Business Research at Ohio State University in 1945. Researchers were looking for key leadership behavior characteristics. They found that leadership behavior could be described according to two major elements: consideration and initiating structures. These studies show two distinctly different leadership approaches. In one, the emphasis is on participation, trust, cooperation, and friendship between manager and subordinate. In the other, the managers emphasize the task. They stress getting the job done, maintaining a timetable, and following carefully prescribed rules and regulations. These studies narrowed down the three- and four-element systems of Lewin and Likert to two dimensions.

1. *Initiating structures.* Leaders who exhibit this style of leadership stress the task to be done over individuals. Leaders with high initiating orientation focus on work output, with little emphasis upon the human aspects of the job. They create a working environment in which subordinates are watched closely. High levels of frustration are often present, and the managers tend to be very directive.

2. *Consideration structure.* Leaders who fall into this category place high emphasis upon the employees and the human aspects of the task. They frequently involve the subordinate in the decision-making process. As a result, the subordinate is under less pressure and is more productive. The consideration structure encourages motivation from within the subordinate and relies less upon outside directive force.

Managers may fall into any of four quadrants in figure 16-5. They may exhibit low consideration and initiating structure. In this instance, they place little emphasis on getting the task done or on people. At the other extreme are managers who emphasize the human aspects of the work as well as getting the job done. These managers foster high productivity and a warm, friendly working environment.

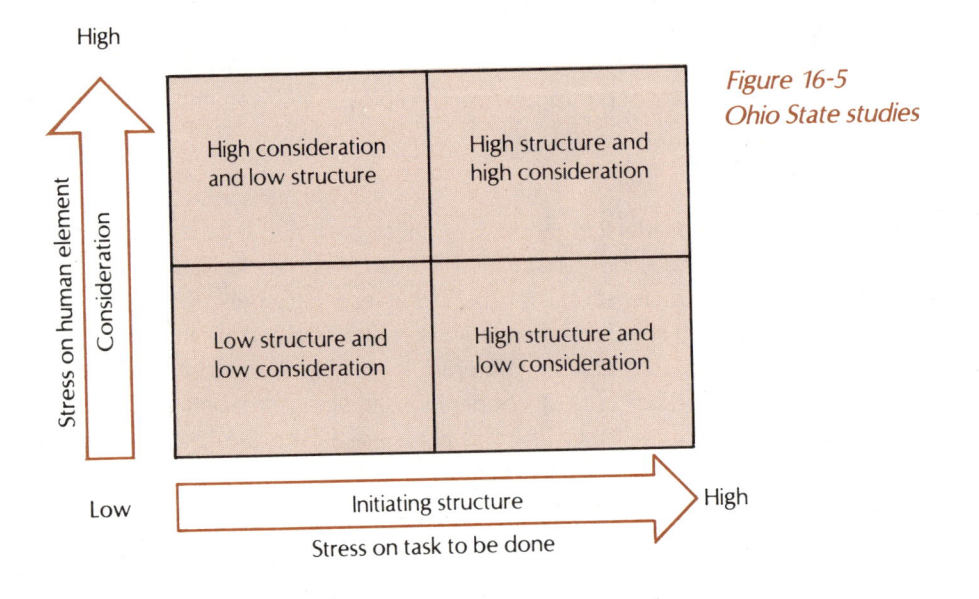

## Tannenbaum and Schmidt's Contribution

Robert Tannenbaum and Warren Schmidt studied a variety of leadership behavior characteristics and developed another continuum. (See figure 16-6.) At one end of the continuum are leaders who exhibit a highly boss-centered style of leadership. At the other end are leaders who use a highly subordinate-centered style.

*Figure 16-5*
*Ohio State studies*

|  | | |
|---|---|---|
| | High consideration and low structure | High structure and high consideration |
| | Low structure and low consideration | High structure and low consideration |

Stress on human element / Consideration (High ↑ Low)

Initiating structure / Stress on task to be done (Low → High)

CHAPTER SIXTEEN    LEADERSHIP IN ORGANIZATIONS    371

```
Boss-centered                              Subordinate-centered
leadership                                         leadership
```

Use of authority by the manager

Area of freedom for subordinates

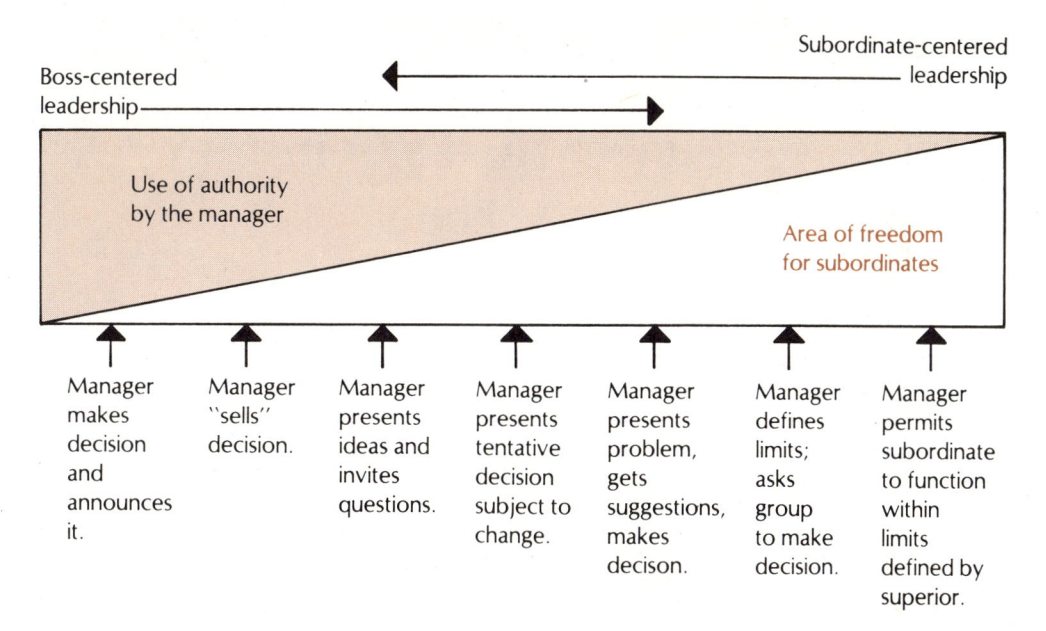

| Manager makes decision and announces it. | Manager "sells" decision. | Manager presents ideas and invites questions. | Manager presents tentative decision subject to change. | Manager presents problem, gets suggestions, makes decison. | Manager defines limits; asks group to make decision. | Manager permits subordinate to function within limits defined by superior. |

*Figure 16-6    Tannenbaum and Schmidt continuum*

Reprinted by permission of the *Harvard Business Review*. The exhibit from "How to Choose a Leadership Pattern" by Robert Tannenbaum and Warren H. Schmidt (May-June 1973). Copyright © 1973 by the President and Fellows of Harvard College, all rights reserved.

The boss-centered leader is characterized as one who studies a problem, makes a decision, then announces it to subordinates. The subordinate-centered leader permits subordinates to function within defined limits. This type of leadership grants a much higher degree of freedom to the subordinates.

Leadership between these two extremes includes managers who sell their decisions to subordinates, and those who rely upon subordinates for decisions, subject to change. Other managers may present a problem to subordinates, seeking their suggestions before making a decision. Still others set a limit and ask subordinates to make a decision within this carefully prescribed limit.

The exact placement of a leader on the continuum is seen by Tannenbaum and Schmidt as a function of three major factors: the situation, the forces within the subordinate, and the forces within the manager. Thus, there are no absolutes or best styles of leadership, but only styles based upon the characteristics of the given situation and personalities.

1. *The situation.* A major factor in leadership style is the situation in which the manager and subordinate function. The specific tasks, available time and money, and the nature of the job to be done are major determinants in leadership style. Thus, the conditions which foster one kind of leadership style might not work well with another style.

> **REAL WORLD**
>
> # Bunker Hunt's Comstock Lode
>
> People say that Bunker Hunt looks like "Burl Ives in a Tennessee Williams play." Bunker Hunt, or "Bunkie," set out to use his unconventional management style to corner the entire silver market. He bought vast amounts of silver and watched it rise in value as the market for precious metals skyrocketed.
>
> Along with his speculation in precious metals, Hunt directs the family-owned business of Hunt International and owns the Shakey's Pizza chain. It is said that Bunkie can spend hours on a menu item for the Shakey's chain, then turn around and make an instant decision involving millions of dollars. He is sometimes accused of making these decisions based upon prejudice rather than financial facts.
>
> But Bunkie's methods almost brought the Bache Group, Inc., to its knees when the sales of silver dropped from $20 to a little over $10 per ounce in only four days.
>
> Bunkie, who wins some and loses some, is among the wealthiest people in America.
>
> Adapted from *Time*, 14 January 1980, p. 61 and 80.

2. *The subordinates.* The attributes, experience attitudes, and aspirations of the subordinates are major determinants in leadership style. Some subordinates require a high degree of boss-centered leadership to function effectively. They require a great deal of direction, with little freedom of choice. Others need a high degree of freedom and a subordinate-centered leadership style to function effectively.

3. *The leader.* The forces within the manager are another major determinant of leadership style. The leader's abilities, interest, experience, and training are important factors in selecting a leadership style. Managers with a high degree of education, training, and experience are suited for a leadership style with great freedom. On the other hand, a manager with less experience and knowledge functions better with a more limited style of leadership.

To illustrate these three factors at work, consider the differences between leadership needs of a group of medical doctors in a community hospital, and the needs of a group of day laborers hired to do road repair work. One group consists of highly skilled people, each with extensive training and professional knowledge.

The members of the other group have little education and training, and are expected to be closely supervised.

The leadership style which would be the most effective for the medical doctors would be one which gives them the greatest freedom and latitude to select treatments, procedures, and working standards. The leadership most effective for the road repair crew would be the one which limits their freedom of choice. Their leader is expected to define each step of the task, assigning rest periods, and so on.

Reversing the leadership styles for these two groups would result in a substantial decrease in output and an increase in frustration and dissatisfaction for both groups. Given too much freedom, the road crew might fail to complete their work properly, while the doctors would rebel against excessive control.

## CONTINGENCY LEADERSHIP

The third major school in leadership theory is the contingency school of thought. This view of leadership emerged from the work of Tannenbaum and Schmidt, and was brought sharply into focus by Fred Fiedler.[4] Prior to Fiedler's research,

Construction workers typically need a high degree of boss-centered leadership.

---

[4]. Fred E. Fiedler, *A Theory of Leadership Effectiveness* (New York: McGraw-Hill, 1967).

most management theorists assumed that leadership was either a function of the traits within the leader, or the result of the leader's behavior. Fiedler's work suggested that the situational factors played a much more important role than had previously been realized.

For Fiedler and his followers, the appropriate style of leadership is a function of the nature of the individuals being led, the characteristics of the leader, and the conditions surrounding the task to be done. Thus, there is no right or wrong style of leader, merely leaders in the right or wrong place in an organization. Further, Fiedler's research pointed out a basic fact: it is easier to change the organization's mix of subordinates and managers by relocating individuals than to change behavior patterns or personal traits in people.

Fiedler found that any leadership style can be effective given the right set of subordinates and conditions. The task of effective management is to place managers in the right situations.

According to Fiedler, there are three major elements which affect the favorableness of a situation and the ability of the manager to work well. These include the task structure, the leader-member relations, and the leader's position power.

1. *Nature of task.* The task structure bears heavily upon leadership style. Routine and repetitive tasks require less freedom, and subordinates may be expected to follow directives very closely. The amount of task structure affects the degree of influence needed by the leader. Obviously, a clearly defined task requires a very different kind of leadership than tasks which are ill defined.

2. *Nature of leader-member relations.* The suitability of a leader for a given situation is a function of the relations between the manager and subordinates. The better this relationship, the less the manager must rely upon formal power. Poor manager-subordinate relations require a greater reliance upon formal power, coercion, and threats to get the job done.

3. *Nature of the leader's position power.* The higher the leader is in the organizational hierarchy, the greater is the leader's formal power. Thus, a more favorable leadership condition exists.

Figure 16-7 illustrates the effects of these three elements on the favorableness of the situation. Along the bottom of the chart is a table listing eight sets of conditions. There are various combinations of factors, ranging from good to poor leader-member relations and from strong to weak leader position power. Tasks range from structured to unstructured. For each given set of conditions, a degree of favorability exists for various styles of leadership.

According to Fiedler, task-oriented leaders are more effective when tasks are structured and leader-member relations are good. On the other hand, the leader's performance is poorest when the task is unstructured and poor leader-member relations exist.

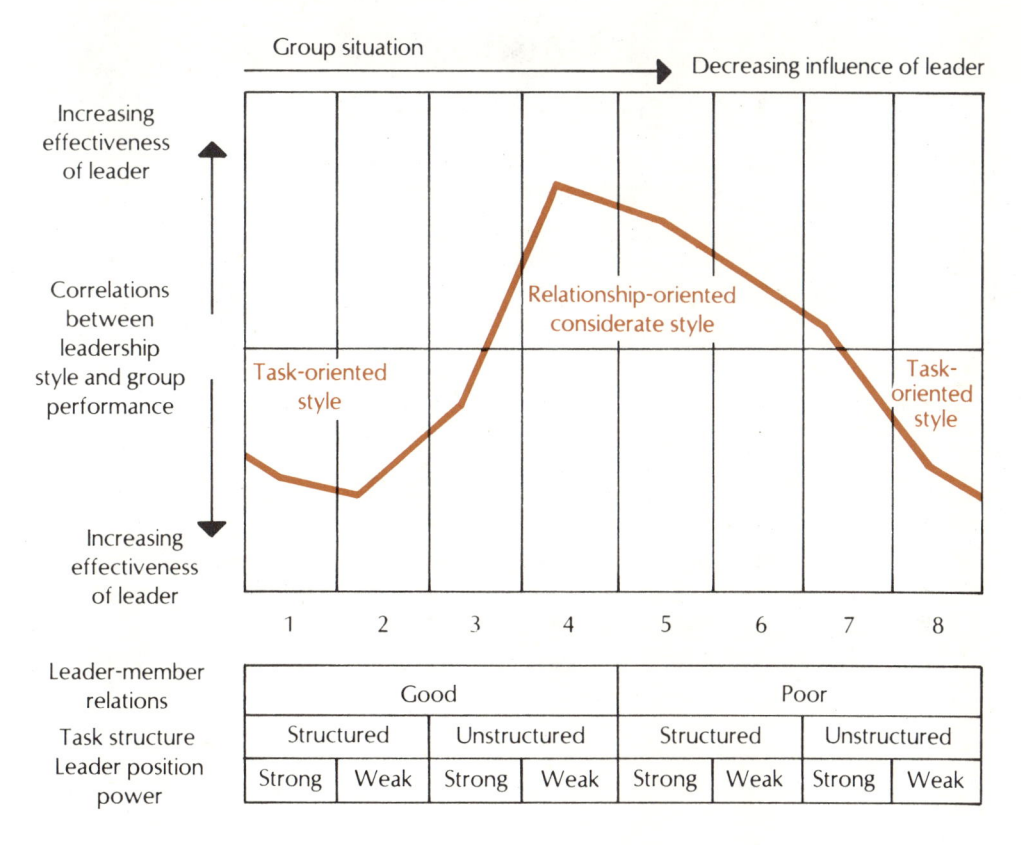

CHAPTER SIXTEEN    LEADERSHIP IN ORGANIZATIONS    375

| Leader-member relations | Good | | | | Poor | | | |
|---|---|---|---|---|---|---|---|---|
| Task structure | Structured | | Unstructured | | Structured | | Unstructured | |
| Leader position power | Strong | Weak | Strong | Weak | Strong | Weak | Strong | Weak |

Reprinted by permission of the *Harvard Business Review*. The exhibit from "Engineer the Job to Fit the Manager" by Fred E. Fielder (September-October 1965). Copyright © 1965 by the President and Fellows of Harvard College, all rights reserved.

*Figure 16-7    Fiedler's model*

## Vroom and Yetton

In 1973, an important leadership theory was published. Victor Vroom and Philip Yetton described leadership styles according to key decision making present in an organization.[5] Five degrees of decision making are present.

1. Problems are solved and decisions are reached by the manager working alone and only with the information available at the moment. This is effectively decision making in isolation.

2. In this situation, the manager seeks some information and a limited amount of input from subordinates, then ultimately reaches a decision unilaterally. Subordi-

---
[5]Victor Vroom and Philip Yetton, *Leadership and Decision Making* (Pittsburgh: University of Pittsburgh Press, 1973).

## POSTSCRIPT
# Wistful View From the Corporate Heights

### By Lynn Darling

ALEXANDRIA, Va. — At night, she has a recurrent dream, and in the dream she is driving her car in darkness when suddenly a fog closes in out of nowhere and she can no longer see. And the terror of it is that she is no longer in control.

In the morning, the sunlight spills into the office of one of the most powerful executives in publishing. Joan Manley is on the phone, elegant fingers beating a steady tattoo as she talks in a voice as clear as the sky.

"You'll simply have to accept the fact that you're to be divided up neatly and programmed to a fare-thee-well," she says. "April first, that's in Hong Kong? . . . That's in Tokyo . . . You're only in the country one day, so we might as well get it straight . . . We've probably bought ourselves two weeks of uncertainty with this weather."

Sooner or later there will be no need to totemize the women who have made it, but that time isn't this time and, for now, Joan Manley is the consummate success story. She is the $54-a-week secretary who got to the top of a publishing business that did more than $350 million in sales last year, that includes ten separate companies and that has her ensconced in a gleaming, book-encased, wood-paneled office with a number of secretaries of her own outside the door.

She looks rather wistfully out her window across the way into another window, where two young women are bent to their work. "I've had both their jobs at one time or another," she says, fingering the gray ultrasuede dress rather absentmindedly. "It's hard sometimes to keep my hands off those parts of the business I used to do and used to love to do."

As the head of Time Inc.'s book division, as a group vice president of the giant corporation, at a salary of more than $203,000, as a onetime prospect for Cabinet office, Joan Manley, 46, knows something about success, and the shades of sacrifice with which it can be tinged as well.

"I know I'm used quite a lot to convince young women not to eschew the role of secretary as a way to the top," she says, but talk of herself as any sort of role model does not come easily. She tends to dismiss her success as "a matter of luck, I didn't have a plan or a plot," she says. "It was just a great accident of timing. How clever of me to be born in 1932."

She was a legatee, she says, of the women's movement and the pressure on corporations to make room for female executives at the time when she was ready to take on executive responsibilities.

Her predecessor at Time-Life Books,

Reprinted with the permission of the publisher. Copyright © 1979 *The Washington Post*.

Jerome S. Hardy, disagrees with so modest an assessment. "I never dreamed the foreign operation could be as successful as it has been," he says. "That was her doing. It was her decision to buy the Book of the Month Club. She has a natural instinct for knowing what kind of things will be both salable and tasteful, and an uncanny ability for picking the right people for the right jobs. She's a superbly talented, gifted executive."

More than twenty years ago, Manley was Hardy's secretary at Doubleday Books in New York. When he came to Time to begin its venture into mass-market books, she followed as his assistant. Since the division began in 1961, Time-Life Books has put out more than 250 million books with more than six hundred different titles, ranging in subject matter from human behavior to gardening and home repair. More than one thousand seven hundred employees in offices around the world put together the books, eighty percent of which are sold through the mail. It has been estimated that at least one in ten American readers owns a volume.

She loved the selling, the marketing of books. In her office now is a large statue of a straight-backed peddler who seems to confer a silent benediction on her words. "Selling," she says, "is the final step of the creative process — since I didn't have the ability to be in on the beginning of a book, the writing of it, then I wanted to be in on the end.

"I really got a belt out of it," she says now. "It seemed like more of a game sometimes than a business. It meant spending all your time on tiptoe, being measured every day. It's like the way some people enjoy gambling — I guess I got the same sort of satisfaction."

She glances again across the atrium of the office building in Alexandria at the two young women. The measurements come less frequently now, the yardsticks constantly shifting. "Now I'm measured on what my companies do," she says, the possessive adjective coming rather naturally. Now she "gets a belt when somebody who works for me does something terrific."

### Corporate Milestones

She ticks off the benchmarks of her rise through the corporate ranks — circulation director in 1966, director of sales in 1968, publisher of Time-Life Books in 1970, a Time Inc. vice president in 1971, group vice president in 1975, a member of the board of directors in 1978.

The most telling milestone was the promotion to publisher. "It was a complete surprise," she maintains. "My boss just called me in one day and said, 'I'm leaving. You're in charge.'" She makes it sound so easy. "I never really planned the next step."

### Now the Future

Now there is the future to consider. Since she was named publisher, there has been public speculation over whether she might eventually become the first female head of the vast corporation.

Hardy, her former boss, believes "she would have to begin to associate herself with corporate activities other than book publishing to put herself in the running."

Manley herself turns the question of the future modestly, if not convincingly, aside. "My father still puts in a full day at the office, and he's 77," she says. "I can retire someday. Before I'm 65. Maybe even before I'm 60."

nates are not involved in an explanation or an understanding of the problem.

3. Problems are shared with subordinates individually, and an effort is made to solicit input. Then the manager makes a decision which may or may not be influenced by subordinates. Solutions may often be at odds with the subordinates' wishes or desires.

4. In this process, the manager may state the problem to the subordinates as a group, and solicit their input and ideas. The manager's final decision will not necessarily reflect the wishes of the group.

5. Decisions are reached after a careful sharing of the problem by the group and their involvement in its resolution. The manager solicits group interaction, comments, and a thorough discussion of alternatives. Only after the subordinates' input has been listened to and evaluated thoroughly is a decision reached. This is a group process involving consensus, and the results may be at odds with the leader's personal feelings.

Thus the Vroom-Yetton model provides managers with a structure or model for decision making. Using this model, together with key questions which analyze the situation, the manager is equipped to exercise more effective leadership.

### Reddin's Three-Dimensional Model

Another contribution to leadership theory is the work of William J. Reddin.[6] According to Reddin, leadership can be described according to a three-dimensional model. (See figure 16-8.)

The basic leadership style is described as *relationship-oriented* or *task-oriented.* Reddin believes there are eight distinct patterns which emerge. Less effective leaders are described as missionary, compromiser, deserter, or autocrat. More effective leadership styles are characterized as the developer, executive, bureaucrat, and benevolent autocrat. The effective manager employs the optimum combination of these characteristics to do the job.

The advantage of the Reddin model, as some managers view it, is that it places leadership in many dimensions and adds many descriptive terms to define leadership styles. Other managers feel that the model is only descriptive and adds little to the leadership theories already described in this chapter.

### SUMMARY

Leadership is an important management function. Many theories of leadership have evolved. Power is an important basis of leadership. It may be derived from a

---

[6]William J. Reddin, "Managing Organization Change," *Personnel Journal* (July 1969): 503.

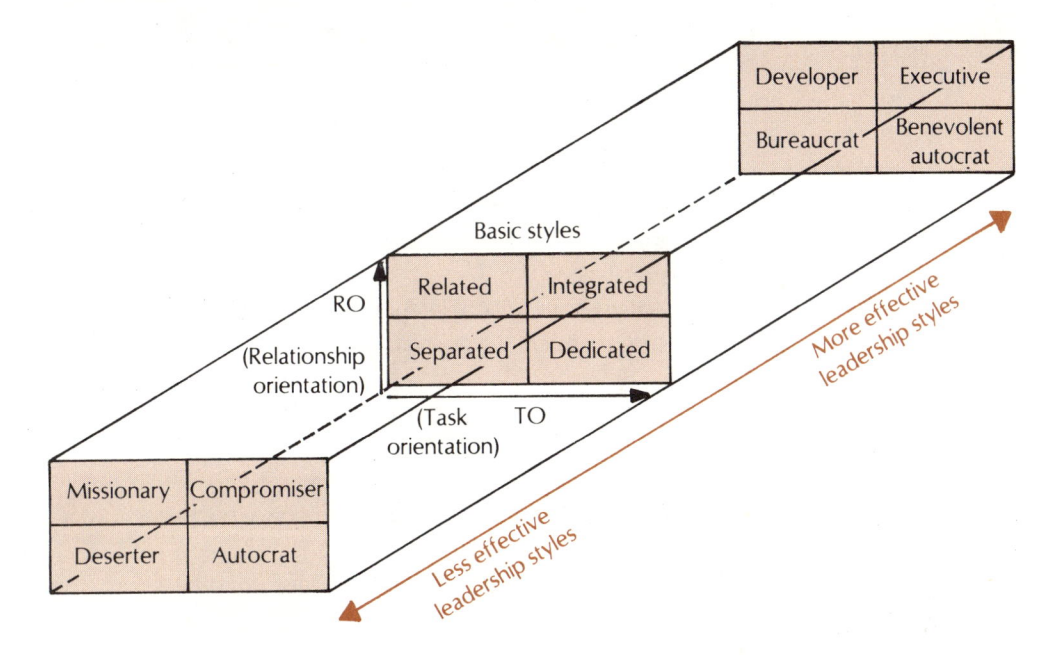

CHAPTER SIXTEEN    LEADERSHIP IN ORGANIZATIONS    379

*Figure 16-8    Reddin's three-dimensional model*

Reprinted from William J. Reddin, Managerial Effectiveness (New York: McGraw-Hill Book Co., 1970), p. 230.

variety of sources. There is reward power, coercive power, legitimate power, expert power, and referent power.

The trait theory describes leadership behavior according to personal traits. Thus, leadership springs from the internal attributes possessed by the leader.

Another theory of leadership is the behavioral school. This school holds that the external attributes and actions of the leader and the leader's style are key considerations. Lewin describes three important leadership styles, including authoritarian, democratic, and laissez-faire behavior.

The Ohio State studies showed that two distinct approaches to leadership exist. One emphasizes participation and trust, while the other stresses getting the job done and following a timetable.

Contingency leadership theories stress the interrelationship of the situation, subordinate, and leader. Situational factors play a more important role than had previously been realized. There were no right or wrong styles but merely leaders in right or wrong places. Vroom and Yetton have described leadership styles according to key decision making, while Reddin has described leadership in a three-dimensional model.

## REVIEW QUESTIONS

1. Why is power important to the understanding of leadership?
2. How does reward power differ from coercive power?
3. What are some common traits possessed by leaders?
4. Contrast Lewin's authoritarian leadership style with the democratic leader.
5. Contrast Likert's participative-democratic System 4 with his System 1, the exploitive-authoritative leader.
6. Contrast initiating structure with consideration structure.
7. How do boss-centered leaders differ from subordinate-centered styles of leadership?
8. Describe important influences the situation has on leadership.
9. Describe important influences subordinates have on leadership.
10. Describe important influences the leader has on leadership.
11. According to Fiedler, what are the three major elements which affect favorableness of a situation?
12. How does Reddin's model of leadership theory differ from others?

## KEY TERMS

| | |
|---|---|
| Reward power 364 | Laissez-faire leader 367 |
| Coercive power 364 | Initiating structure 370 |
| Legitimate power 364 | Consideration structure 370 |
| Expert power 364 | Contingency leadership 373 |
| Referent power 365 | Relationship-oriented 378 |
| Authoritarian leader 367 | Task-oriented 378 |
| Democratic leader 367 | |

## Case Incident

Allied Insurance Agency operates three separate branch offices in a major southern city. Allied sells a complete line of insurance packages, everything from personal life to business, hospitalization, and major medical insurance programs. Because of vacations, periodic changes in sales volume, and employee turnover, sales people are often transferred among the three branches. Over a period of time, it has been discovered that a successful sales agent in one office may do very poorly after being transferred to one of the other offices. After eliminating all other variables, Allied's management has decided that the problem appears to be in the different styles of leadership practiced in the three offices.

David Lui, manager of branch office no. 1, insists that his sales people have always worked best under a system of self-direction. Lui says, "I don't want to run these people with a heavy hand. I try to allow my sales agents to set their own schedules, working hours, and methods of obtaining new insurance leads. Everyone who has ever worked in this business knows that top sales agents are all self-starters and self-motivated. As far as I'm concerned, they're on their own."

Joyce Skiffer, manager of branch no. 2, follows a different managerial approach. "I tell all my people right from the start how I want things done. I set very precise guidelines regarding their work reports and their working hours, as well as specific procedures to follow in new client prospecting. I monitor each lead to see that my agents are following them up properly. I also require a careful reporting system, and I want all sales agents to use form letters which I know work. I want them to use the specific systems and procedures that have been proven successful over time."

The manager of branch no. 3, Ben Mata, has a completely different managerial style. He holds weekly meetings with his sales agents and allows basic decisions regarding working hours, reports, and prospecting techniques to be made by them. Rather than try to set hard and fast rules that are rigid and inflexible, he tries to implement only those policies agreed on by the sales agents as a whole. In this way, specific rules and guidelines are set up, but since each individual has some real say in the final decision, they also feel a much stronger commitment to work hard to make them work.

Because of the clearly different styles of leadership between each of the three offices, there has been a substantial amount of conflict when individuals have been transferred to other offices. The management of Allied Insurance Agency is concerned about this and is considering various methods of resolving this problem.

## PROBLEMS

1. Describe the leadership style of each of the three managers.
2. Should a single method of leadership be espoused for all three offices?
3. Why have conflicts and dissension developed when salespeople transfer between offices? Explain.

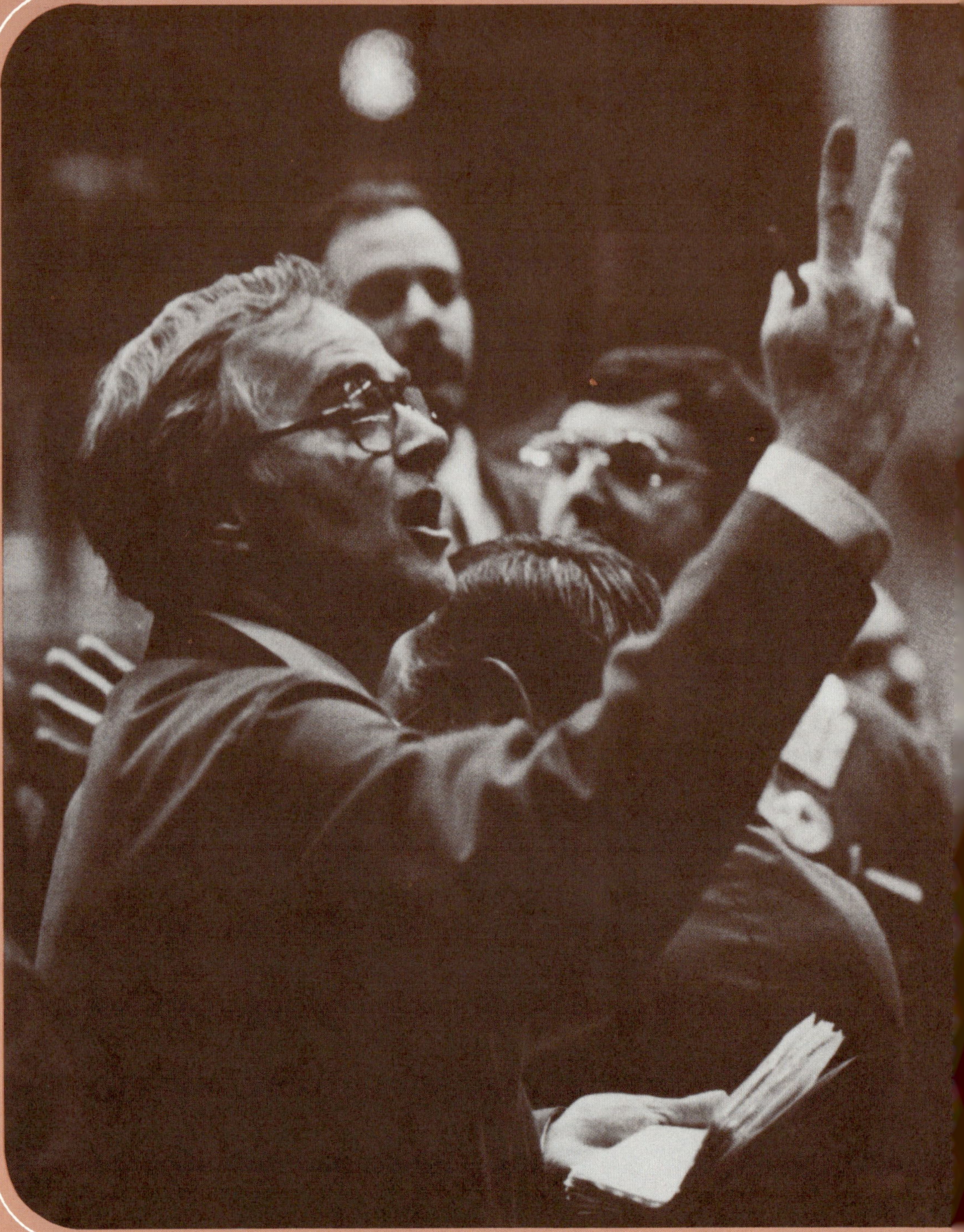

# 17
# Principles of Communication

**LEARNING OBJECTIVES**

After studying this chapter, you should be able to:
1. Define key terms related to communications.
2. Summarize the communications process.
3. Contrast one-way and two-way communications.
4. Contrast internal and external communications flow.
5. Describe formal and informal communications networks.
6. Summarize the basic principles of semantics.
7. Describe some characteristics of language.
8. Contrast major communications media.
9. Describe barriers to good communication.
10. Describe ways to improve communications.

Throughout each business day managers, supervisors, and subordinates actively engage in communication. Communication is vital to effective management and commands a substantial portion of the manager's time and energy.

In this chapter we look at the principles of semantics and the communication process. The chapter explores internal and external communications, informal and formal communications, and the grapevine. The chapter concludes with a discussion of communications media, both verbal and nonverbal. Suggestions for improving written and oral communications are also outlined.

## IMPORTANCE OF COMMUNICATIONS

Communications is the nervous system which ties together all elements of the organization. It serves as a link between management and subordinates. Without structured communications, organizations would be little more than collections of people, resources, and money unable to achieve goals.

Communications serve many functions. Through communications, the manager alters organizational and individual behavior. Communications provide the pathways by which data and information flow throughout the organization. Communications is vital to the decision-making process, giving the manager access to accurate information at the optimum time and place in the business cycle.

## KEY TERMS

Communication relies upon words, symbols, and signs in both verbal and nonverbal forms. Let us define some key terms which relate to the art of communication.

— *Communication.* *Communication* is the process by which information is exchanged between individuals through a common system of symbols. *Communications* encompasses the technology for the transmission of data and deals with the written and verbal exchange of information.

— *Semantics.* Semantics is the study of words and their meanings. It is the study of the historical and psychological classification of changes in the significance of words. Semantics is the branch of knowledge which deals with the relationship between symbols and what they mean.

— *Communications network.* A communications network is the pathways by which information flows through an organization. Networks may be formally or informally structured. They include flow of information between individuals at various levels within the organization and between members of an organization and the outside world.

— *Symbol.* A symbol is a sign which stands for something else by reason of relationship, association, convention, or accidental resemblance. Symbols are arbitrary or conventional signs used in writing or printing to represent operations, quantities, elements, or relationships of quantities. A symbol may also be an object or an act that represents an unconscious association or a culturally significant occurrence.

— *Message.* A message is a communication, either written or oral or by signals. Messages are encoded concepts and ideas transmitted from one person to another.

— *Channel.* A channel is a pathway or conduit by which information, meaning, or ideas are transmitted from one individual to another. A channel may be spoken or written, such as a telephone line or postal communication.

— *Kinesics.* Kinesics is the study of body language. Body language is a form of nonverbal communication based upon conscious and unconscious movements of all or part of the body which communicate a message to the outside world.

## THE COMMUNICATION PROCESS

Managers should view communication as a process rather than a single event. Figure 17-1 illustrates the fundamental communication process. Basically, communication involves converting an idea into a message or symbols transmitting

Messages can also be non-verbal.

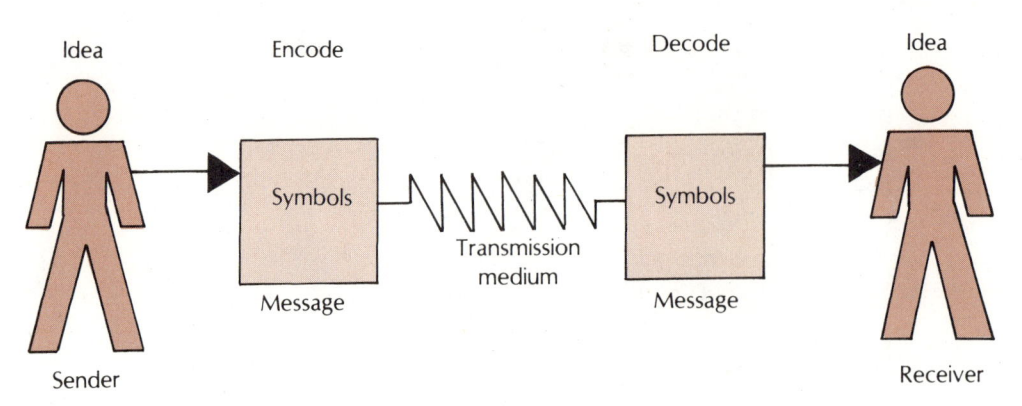

*Figure 17-1 Communication process*

the message, then finally converting the message back into an idea in the mind of the receiver.

Messages rely upon symbols, which stand for ideas, concepts, or actions. Messages are communicated from one person to another through a medium, such as written or oral words, pictures, gestures, diagrams, or photographs.

An important part of the communication process consists of encoding concepts in symbols, then later reconverting those symbols into ideas. The process moves from idea, through encoding, to transmission, decoding, and finally back to idea.

— *Sender.* A sender is anyone who wishes to communicate an idea, action, concept, or thought to another person. The sender must translate the idea into a symbol or sign which stands for the idea or action. The process involves the use of language, signs, or actions. The sender may have many choices of symbols or signs in which to encode the message.

The selection of the appropriate medium and words, symbols, or signs to carry the message is very important. High quality communication relies upon skillful selection of medium and careful encoding.

— *Encoding.* Encoding is the process of converting an idea, thought, or action into words, symbols, facial gestures, or body movements which stand for or represent the idea being transmitted. Symbols or ideas have different meanings to different people and should be defined and selected carefully.

— *Medium.* The medium is the means by which a message is transmitted. Media include verbal and nonverbal communications such as letters or memos, signals, facial expressions, signs, and so on.

In some instances, the absence of a signal may have meaning. Pauses, silence, or refusal to answer letters or questions are often the medium selected to communicate a very specific message.

Sometimes a sender may choose to relay a message via several media at one

CHAPTER SEVENTEEN   PRINCIPLES OF COMMUNICATION   387

time. This concurrent transmission provides redundancy and helps assure that the message will get through. The policeman directing traffic on a corner often uses multiple media to convey the message. Blowing his whistle, raising his hand, and making an appropriate facial expression or body movement all indicate that traffic flow is to stop.

— *Decoding.*  Decoding is the process by which symbols are converted back into ideas, thoughts, or actions in the mind of the receiver. The decoding process is essential to communication and must be done with as much care as encoding if the accuracy of the initial message is to be preserved.

— *Receiver.*  The receiver is the recipient of the message. The receiver must convert the message and symbols into meaningful ideas which accurately reflect the concepts intended by the sender. The more accurate the decoding, the higher quality the final translation.

## ONE-WAY AND TWO-WAY COMMUNICATIONS

Up to this point it has been suggested that communication is a one-way process by which a sender transmits a message to the receiver. Many communications are

---

**REAL WORLD**

# Crocker National Bank's
# Thomas R. Wilcox

Flair and a family style epitomize the way Thomas R. Wilcox carries out his work as chairman of Crocker National Bank. Wilcox shares his role with his wife Jane. They entertain bank customers together because he feels that bringing his wife into the picture helps build a sounder and more permanent relationship with clients. He encourages other executives to follow his style. According to Wilcox, wives are emphasized at Crocker Bank and many of them know as much about banking as their husbands do. This is a distinct asset.

Wilcox deals with his employees in person rather than through written directives. He avoids memos. People working with Wilcox say that he is more like an old-fashioned sea captain than a top executive. He acknowledges that division and department heads know more about their phase of the business than he does. While some people may find his unorthodox style difficult, he does bring his staff together and gets them working toward a common goal.

Adapted from *The Executive,* September 1979, p. 11LA.

handled in this manner. However, there is no assurance that the message received accurately reflects the one sent. Further, there is no assurance that the message has in fact been received.

It is better to think of communication as a two-way transaction. In a two-way exchange of information (fig. 17-2), the message received is confirmed by the receiver. This is done by a return signal or message. Two-way communication consists of a feedback loop in which confirmation is relayed back. This confirmation may be in the form of a spoken or written word, facial expression, or body sign.

A statement transmitted over the radio is an example of a common one-way communication. There is no assurance that the speaker's message has been received and comprehended. A conversation between a clerk and a customer at an airline reservation desk is an example of a two-way communication. The customer asks questions and obtains responses. The clerk asks questions and engages in an exchange of information.

## COMMUNICATIONS NETWORKS

Communications in organizations should not be viewed as isolated, discrete events, but instead as part of a system or network. A network is an interlocking fabric through which flows data, information, news, gossip, and reports. It is helpful to view communications networks as a pyramid in which internal information flows horizontally (laterally) and vertically (up and down) in the organization. In addition to this internal flow, there is also an external data flow.

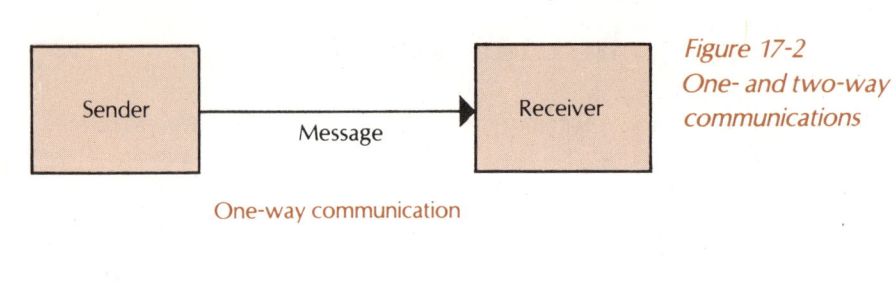

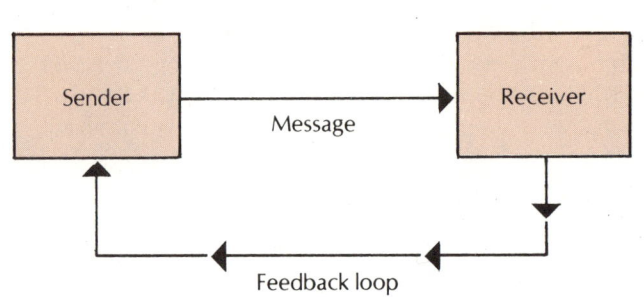

*Figure 17-2
One- and two-way communications*

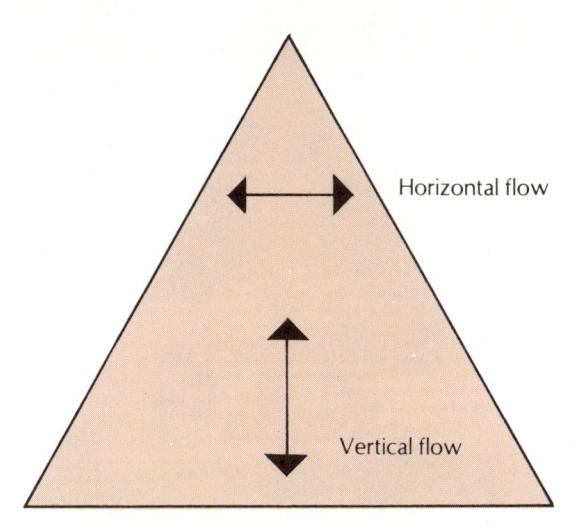

*Figure 17-3*
*Internal communications network*

## Internal Communications Flow

A large volume of information flows within most organizations. These communications consist of letters, memos, reports, phone conversations, and face-to-face exchanges. A major portion of the manager's time is spent handling internal communications. These can be categorized as horizontal and vertical (fig. 17-3).

1. *Horizontal (lateral) flow.* Data flow is horizontal when it flows between individuals at the same level on the organization's hierarchy. Examples of horizontal flow are phone calls between supervisors, memos sent between line employees, or reports sent back and forth between managers.

2. *Vertical flow.* In this mode, information flows up and down the hierarchy. Information exchanged between individuals at different levels on the organizational pyramid fall into this group. Examples include reports from a company president to subordinates, or a memo from a line employee to a supervisor.

## External Communications Flow

A vast amount of information flows in and out of organizations. These communications may be addressed to, or received from suppliers, customers, government agencies, the public, unions, and so on. Examples of external communications include tax reports to the government, statements from the bank, purchase orders to suppliers, and orders from customers.

Figure 17-4 illustrates some of the typical groups which form a major portion of the organization's external flow of data. These communications are important because they help form the public's image of a company and contribute to success in marketing.

*Figure 17-4*
*External communications network*

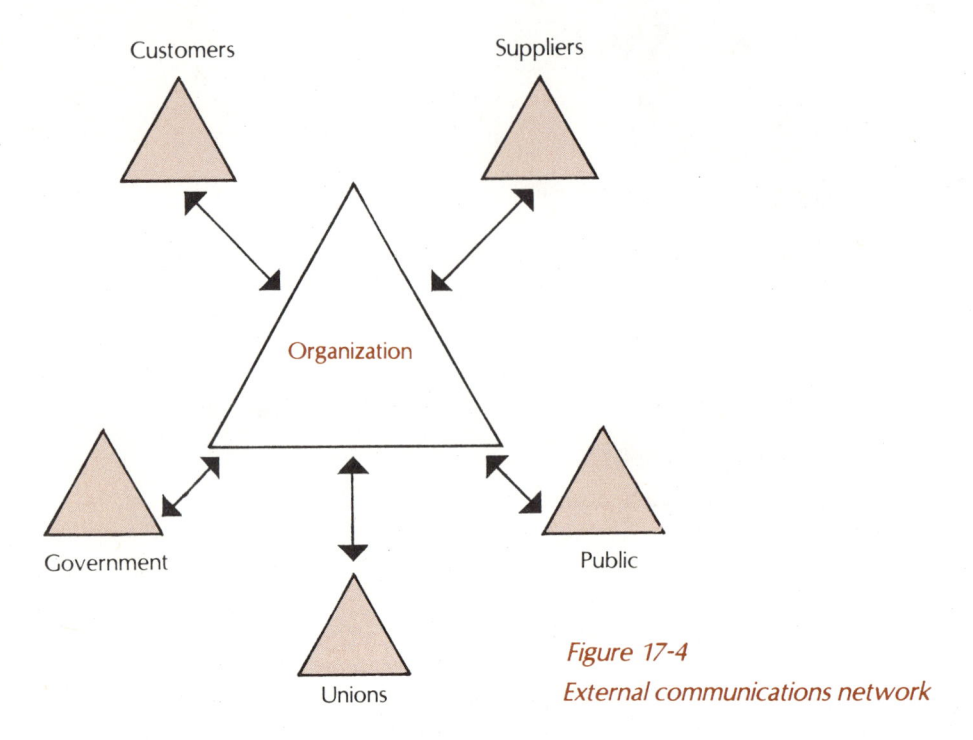

## FORMAL AND INFORMAL COMMUNICATIONS NETWORKS

Up to this point we have been discussing formally accepted communications. These flow through recognized channels between the organization and other agencies. A discussion of communication would be incomplete without reference to the informal organization and its channels, including the grapevine.

The formal organization is documented by most organizations on the organizational chart and in position (job) descriptions. These documents describe the accepted, formal, and recognized relationship between individuals in the organization. The organizational chart also describes the communications channels through which letters, memos, reports, and telephone calls flow. Formal communications tend to be slow and cumbersome. The informal channels tend to be faster and more responsive to the needs of the individuals within the organization.

### The Grapevine

Keith Davis has described some common pathways by which information flows through an organization's grapevine.[1] (See figure 17-5.) According to Davis, four

---

[1] Keith Davis, "Management Communication and the Grapevine," *Harvard Business Review* (Sept.–Oct. 1953): 45.

paths are frequently found: the single strand, gossip, probability, and cluster.

In the single strand mode, information moves along a chain from one person to another. Gossip, on the other hand, radiates out from one individual. In the probability mode, information moves throughout an organization in a chance or random occurrence. In the cluster mode, information held by selected individuals is simultaneously passed along to others. Thus, a piece of information acquired by a committee may spread throughout the organization from each member of the committee. All these forms of communication may occur simultaneously in an organization, along with the formal communications.

The grapevine serves a variety of purposes other than merely communicating information. It provides individuals within the organization with a social outlet and an opportunity to meet with each other and talk. The grapevine gives individuals a degree of security, since they know they will be among the first to hear important information.

The grapevine is fast and unstructured. News may travel much more quickly than through recognized formal channels. Studies have indicated that a large amount of information which flows through the grapevine is accurate. The manager should not stifle the grapevine but should recognize its presence.

People believe that which they hear first, whether it be fact or rumor. The grapevine is useful to managers as a means of getting feedback concerning ideas

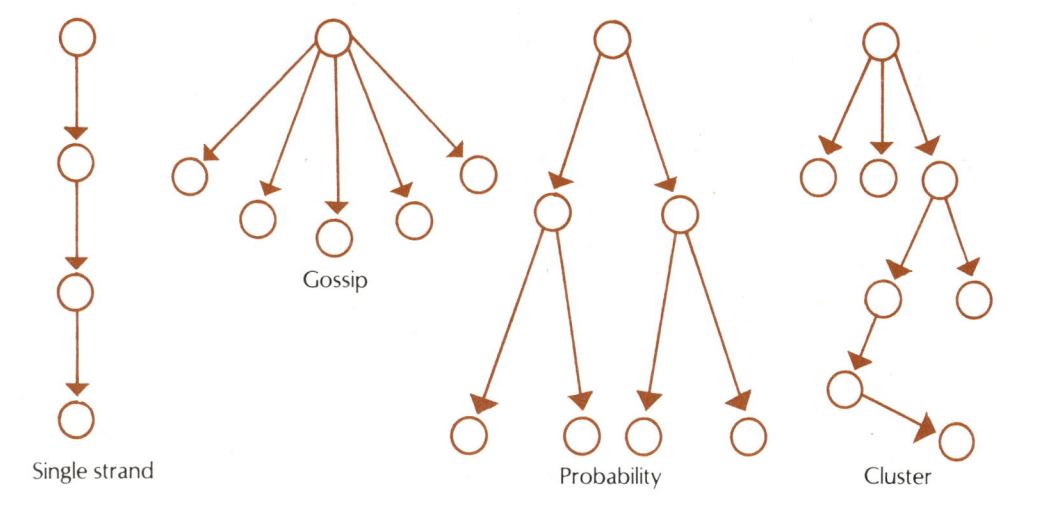

*Figure 17-5 Grapevine communication*

Single strand    Gossip    Probability    Cluster

Reprinted by permission of the *Harvard Business Review*. The exhibit from "Management Communication and the Grapevine," by Keith Davis II (September-October 1953). Copyright © 1953 by the President and Fellows of Harvard College, all rights reserved.

and learning about situations of which they are unaware. Managers can use the grapevine to get the facts out before rumors start.

## PRINCIPLES OF SEMANTICS

Semantics deals with the study of words and their meanings. The study of semantics shows that words are interpreted in various ways by the sender and the receiver. Managers should understand the basic principles of semantics and how they affect communication.

### Symbol Selection

Basic to all communication is the selection of symbols or words to communicate our ideas, thoughts, and actions. We rely heavily upon signs and symbols to stand for the thing we wish to communicate. The meaning of a symbol is influenced by the emotional and psychological attitudes and perceptions of the user. (See figure 17-6.) This figure shows the triangular relationship between the symbol (word), the referent (information being communicated), and the reference (emotional and psychological connotations). Appropriate symbol selection is a key to successful communication.

### Words as Holders of Meaning

A widely held belief is that the meaning of a word is contained within the word itself, much as a glass holds water (fig. 17-7). Many semanticists do not accept this

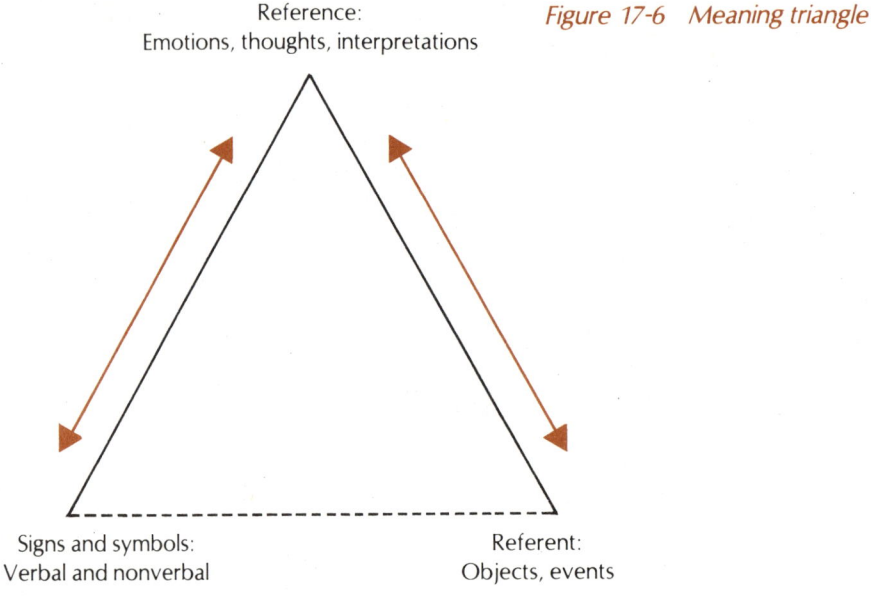

*Figure 17-6  Meaning triangle*

Reference:
Emotions, thoughts, interpretations

Signs and symbols:
Verbal and nonverbal

Referent:
Objects, events

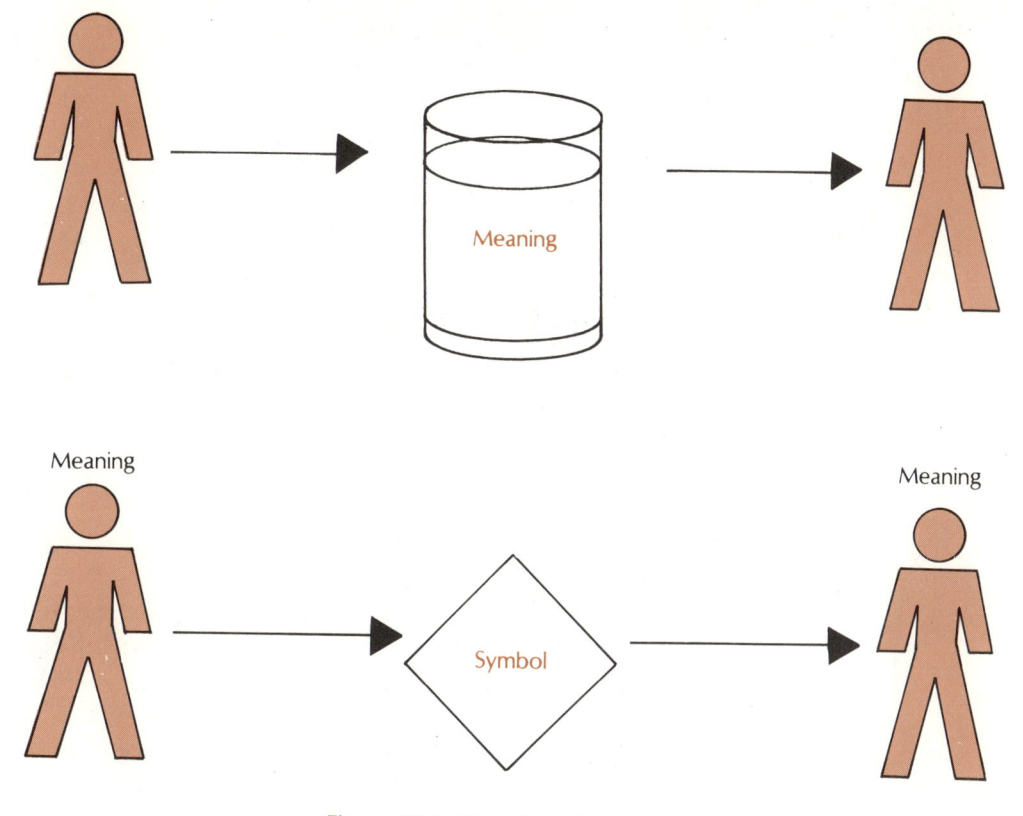

CHAPTER SEVENTEEN   PRINCIPLES OF COMMUNICATION   393

*Figure 17-7   Words and meaning*

premise. Instead they believe that the meaning of words is in the way they are interpreted by the sender or receiver.

According to semanticists, one must look to the attitudes, perceptions, and experiences of the sender and receiver for the meanings of words, rather than the dictionary. For example, how does your interpretation of words like *cool, neat,* or *black* differ from the dictionary definition or the interpretation of a classmate? This idea may be hard to accept for many people, since we are taught as children to look up meanings of words in the dictionary. The dictionary gives the formal, historical meaning of a word, which is not necessarily how either the sender or receiver perceives it. Those who are successful at communicating recognize the fact that words mean different things to different people. For instance, *cheap* may mean inexpensive to one person and shoddy to another.

**Language**

Language is the tool or vehicle used to convey ideas and thoughts. It is a powerful instrument which is ever changing and dynamic. Language influences the way we

"Actually I get four weeks vacation . . . the boss takes two, then I take two."

Reprinted from *Graphic Arts Monthly,* March 1978.

think and act. When considering language and semantics, the following three important points should be kept in mind.

1. *Range of meaning.* Words differ in their range of meaning. Some words have a narrow range, while others have a very wide range of meaning. For example, the words *drinking water* have a very limited range of meaning and are not subject to wide interpretation. They refer to a potable liquid which may be consumed by humans.

On the other hand, the word *profit* has a wide range of meaning. Profit is the amount of money left over after all expenses for the period have been met. However, the period has not been defined. Profit is the money left after expenses have been paid, but what items are considered expenses? Is profit the money remaining before or after taxes? Should depreciation, inventory, or accounts receivable be considered in the definition of profit?

2. *Changing language.* Language is always undergoing change. Words take on new meanings as social mores, attitudes, and values change.

3. *Cultural and social aspects of language.* The culture in which we live has great

influence upon our choice of words. Language exists in a complex social setting. Cultural stereotypes, national values, and perceptions affect the meaning of words.

## Personal Perceptions

A major determinant in an individual's understanding of meanings is personal perception. The ways in which we perceive ideas and meanings are greatly influenced by our attitudes and experiences. Our feelings toward other races, religions, and those on different social and economic levels or in different occupations affect our use of words. To communicate effectively, the manager must be aware of the complexities surrounding words and their meanings.

## COMMUNICATIONS MEDIA

The selection of media is important in the process of communications, since they provide the channel by which information is exchanged. The sender of the message often has a choice of media to facilitate communication.

Fundamentally there are several different means of communicating with others: written words, spoken words, symbols, and actions. Verbal and nonverbal media may be used to communicate a message, including body language, motions, gestures, and even the absence of action. Symbols such as a red light or hexagonal sign also convey meaning. Table 17-1 lists some common means of communicating.

## Written Communication

The printed word is a major communications medium used in organizations. Managers and subordinates rely upon letters, memos, reports, and correspondence to convey messages. Written media have several distinct advantages. A written message is permanent. Written messages can be copied, mailed, and distributed. They leave a record of the transaction which can be checked at a later date. The phrase, "avoid verbal orders" (AVO), is frequently used because written messages receive a higher level of treatment than verbal communications.

However, written communications have limitations. The written word lacks

**Table 17-1  Common forms of communication**

| Oral | Written | Nonverbal |
|---|---|---|
| Telephone conversations | Correspondence | Gestures |
| Face-to-face | Letters | Motions |
| Lectures | Memos | Facial expressions |
| Speeches | Reports | Silence or inaction |

> ## REAL WORLD
> # Black Beauty
>
> Johnson Products Co., Inc., has long been known for its line of cosmetics aimed at blacks. George E. Johnson's firm was one of the first to enter the market successfully and be listed on the American Stock Exchange. In 1965 he introduced Ultra Sheen No-Base, a hair relaxer. But before long competition moved in and he soon found himself competing with giants like Revlon in the marketplace. Pitted against Revlon, his share of the market dropped from 60 percent to 40 percent in 1975.
>
> Undaunted, Johnson moved ahead with other new products and new markets. His latest thrust into the market of hair care is Precise, a product that both straightens and conditions hair. He expects to make the most money in West Africa. He recently opened a $2 million factory in Lagos, Nigeria, and expects to be a major supplier of hair care products and cosmetics for the African continent.
>
> Adapted from *Time,* 28 April 1980, p.45.

the tone and inflection of the spoken word. Pictures or drawings often convey more than written words. Written communication takes more time to prepare than a similar verbal message.

## Oral Communication

The spoken word is a primary communications medium. The spoken word is relied upon for most face-to-face and telephone communication. The spoken word takes on color, intonation, and meaning as it is delivered. Good oral communication skills are essential for the manager.

The limitation of the spoken word is that it lacks the permanence and import of the written message. Spoken communications are ephemeral and transitory, and thus often lack the depth of the written word. Once uttered, the spoken word cannot be easily filed, accessed, mailed, or retrieved.

## Nonverbal Communication

Body language which uses signs, gestures, movements, and actions is another communication medium. E. T. Hall did much to explore this medium,[2] and much of Hall's work has been popularized by Julius Fast.[3] Fast describes how body posi-

---
[2] E. T. Hall, *The Hidden Dimension* (Garden City, N.Y.: Doubleday, 1969).
[3] Julius Fast, *Body Language* (New York: Pocket Books, 1970).

tions, winks, blinks, nods, and so on, are used in nonverbal communication to convey a message as effectively as either the written or spoken word. Messages are conveyed through body language and other media simultaneously.

The manager should have an understanding of how body language is used. A manager, for example, may say that she supports a subordinate's actions on a given matter, while at the same time shaking her head from side to side. While her words communicate positive acceptance, her motions state that she disagrees with the subordinate's position.

Much of our body language is associated with our body space. According to Fast, each person requires a certain body space or territory. When others intrude on this space, we become anxious and irritable. The science of kinesics explores these and other factors in communication.

## BARRIERS TO GOOD COMMUNICATION

Communications are subject to many problems. Often barriers arise to frustrate good communication. These include noise, poor selection of words or medium, filtering, empathy, status, overloading, perceptions and value judgments, and time limitations.

*—Noise.* Noise is any unwanted sound or interference with a transmission. (See figure 17-8.) It takes many forms. For the spoken word, noise can be planes flying overhead, phones ringing, people talking, or other unwanted sounds. For the broadcast word, electrical static is noise. For the written word, a blurred image or poor photocopy is noise. Noise results in poor transmission of a message.

*— Poor selection of words or medium.* The poor selection of words or media is a major barrier to good communication. Words should be carefully selected, keeping in mind the recipient of the message. Sometimes the right word delivered by the wrong medium can be a barrier to good communication. For example, a subordinate will be happy to see a compliment printed in the company newsletter. But a criticism should be given in a face-to-face communication.

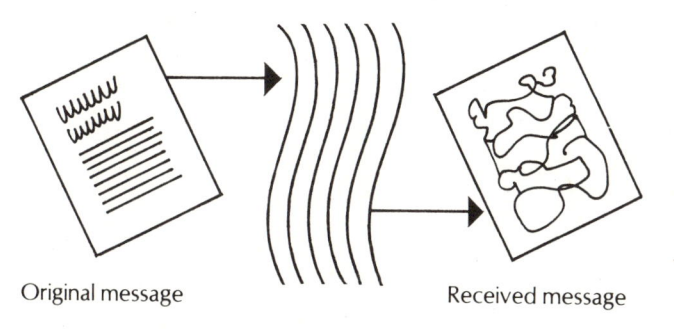

*Figure 17-8 Noise*

Original message

Received message

Unwanted sounds

— *Filtering*. Individuals sometimes sift information or place it in a more positive light as it passes through them in the communication chain. It is not uncommon for a subordinate to pass along only selected information to a superior if disclosure of the facts would hurt the employee's position in the organization. Filtering occurs all about us. The meanings of messages change because of our prejudices, prior relations with others, or the status of the one giving the message. The manager must continually be alert to problems of filtering. (See figure 17-9.)

— *Empathy*. Empathy is a feeling for others. A message may be distorted or changed in content as it passes from one to another because of empathy. A manager seeking to protect a subordinate may alter a communication because the manager empathizes with and wishes to protect a subordinate.

— *Status*. The status of the individual in a hierarchy determines how a message will be received. Messages from those higher on the organizational structure take on importance and significance. The economic and social status of the sender affects the interpretation of the message.

— *Overloading*. An individual is capable of receiving and absorbing only a limited amount of information at a given time. If we are given more information than we can handle, we overload and simply ignore or bypass some of the information. We become overloaded when we are given too much to read at once or when too many people speak to us at the same time.

— *Perceptions and value judgments*. Our personal feelings, prejudices, and perceptions of others affect our communications. People accept messages more positively from those with whom they agree politically or intellectually. People from the same social, ethnic, or economic background tend to respond in similar ways.

— *Time limitations*. Another barrier to good communication is time. It requires time to frame written and spoken messages so that they will be effective. Speaking too fast or writing important memos without adequate preparation can adversely affect the quality of the communication.

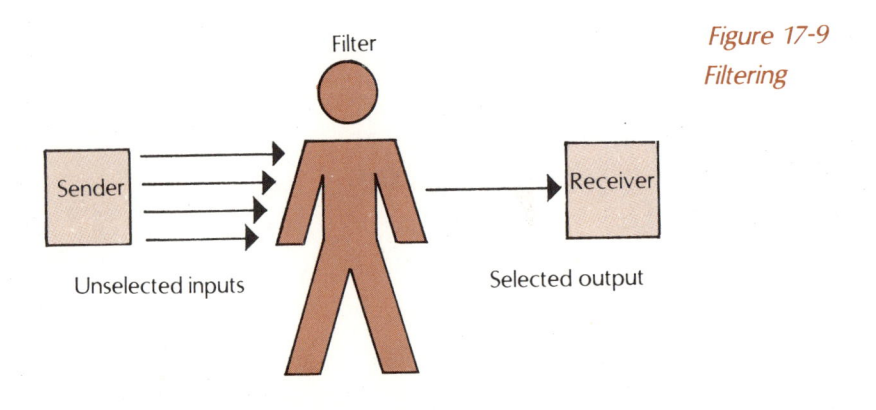

*Figure 17-9*
*Filtering*

CHAPTER SEVENTEEN   PRINCIPLES OF COMMUNICATION                             399

*A person's status within an organization determines how a message will be received.*

## HOW TO IMPROVE COMMUNICATIONS

Good communications follow proper planning. They are the result of care, effort, and an understanding of semantics and the communication process. Both the words and the medium must be carefully selected. Following are some basic rules for framing messages and other communications.

1. *Select words carefully.* Select words with an eye toward how they will be received and interpreted by the reader or listener.

2. *Use redundancy.* Deliver a message through several media. This helps assure the accuracy of the communication. There is an old redundancy rule that goes like this: (a) Tell them what you are about to tell them; (b) tell them; (c) tell them what you just told them.

3. *Use feedback.* Ask questions and solicit responses from the receiver of the message to be sure that the message is interpreted as intended.

4. *Don't form opinions until all the facts are in.* Wait until the entire message has been received before forming opinions, drawing conclusions, or taking action.

5. *Overview content at the beginning of the message.* Provide the receiver with a brief overview of what, when, and how the message is going to be transmitted.

6. *Summarize the content of the message.* Brief summaries should follow the transmission to recapitulate important points and underscore key topics.

7. *Use short, simple sentences and action words.* Write clearly and concisely. Select words which bring forth images and actions.

8. *Outline before you write.* Prepare an outline of the major points to be covered before you write.

9. *Edit and revise the message.* Go over your written communication several times to delete unnecessary words and sharpen the language.

10. *Present the body of the message in a logical way.* Generally, move from the simple to the complex. Gradually expand on points. Do not make quantum jumps in logic or content.

11. *Speak at an appropriate rate.* Speak at a rate which will enable the listener to understand and yet not become bored.

12. *Select an appropriate time and place for the spoken message.* Avoid noisy rooms or other conditions which interrupt the flow of conversation. Do not expect subordinates to respond effectively when they are fatigued.

## TRANSACTIONAL ANALYSIS

New insights into communications have been developed during the past several decades. The research into transactional analysis and body language now plays an important part in the study of communication. Eric Berne points out that whenever individuals meet in social intercourse, a transaction takes place. According to Berne, these transactions may be analyzed by a set of rules. Each transaction begins with a stimulus and ends with a response.[4]

The ego states present in individuals are important to communication and transactional analysis. These ego states consist of three components: the adult, child, and parent. (See figure 17-10.) Every personality is made up of these three elements, which provide the various stimuli we use to deal with others. In turn, people react to stimuli with transactional responses. These three states affect the way we relate and communicate with each other.

*Figure 17-10*

*Ego states*

[4]Eric Berne, *Transactional Analysis in Psychotherapy* (New York: Ballantine Books, 1961).

*Figure 17-11*

*Complementary transaction*

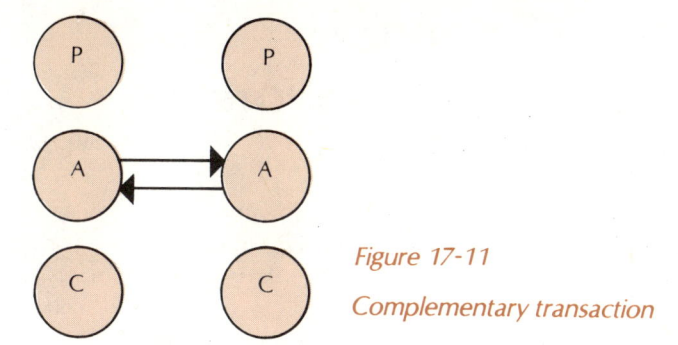

—*Parent.* During the early years of our lives, we are exposed to a large amount of information and stimuli provided by our parents. According to Berne and others, this results in a recording in our minds of all of the controls and constraints placed on us by our parents. All the scoldings and admonitions of childhood become unedited parts of our personality. The nonverbal communications we receive as children, such as cuddling or lack of it, facial expressions, and touching, also become part of a taped message. This influences our actions toward others later in life.

—*Child.* Another input to our personality takes place during our early years. This is a recording of the external events in our lives as children, which we carry around in our subconscious. Thus, every adult contains a relic of childhood.

—*Adult.* This phase of our personality is much akin to a computer. We absorb data, input information, and make judgments and evaluations. The adult in us sees that we respond in appropriate and mature ways to problems and conditions we face.

Transactional analysis deals with how we respond to the stimuli we receive from others. Communication proceeds smoothly as long as the stimulus we receive is responded to in the same way. This is called a complementary transaction. (See figure 17-11.) The adult personality responding to the adult personality generates little friction, as does the child part of our personality responding to the child part of another. Problems in communication arise where a crossed transaction occurs (fig. 17-12). A childlike response to an adult stimulus generates con-

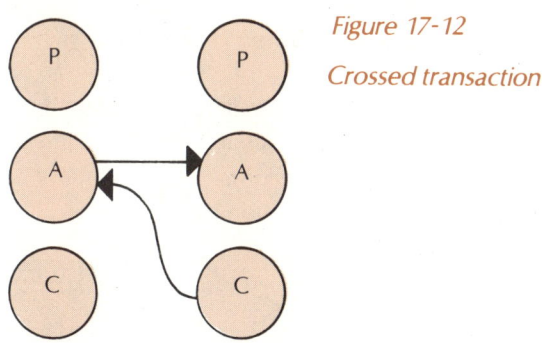

*Figure 17-12*

*Crossed transaction*

## POSTSCRIPT
# Firm Raps with Workers

A communication exposition affecting employees within corporations is taking place across the nation, and one large California company is helping lead the way.

General Telephone Co. of California, with more than twenty thousand employees, has increased its internal flow of information considerably within the past eighteen months and intends to continue with what it terms the "art of communications" in order to improve the "science of communications."

Much of the information flowing at General most recently has been in the form of upward communications. The employees seem to like it, judging from surveys indicating that seventy-three percent say they have a "better understanding of company plans, policies, and procedures," which is up twenty-eight percent from 1976.

General says it has two important upward channels of information introduced in 1976, which have proved of value to management as well as employees. The two programs are known as rap-around and question team.

Reprinted from the *San Fernando Valley News*, 9 July 1978.

flict. Following are a few specific examples of ego state communications.

Parent to parent exchange:
    P1: "Our sales managers are not happy with our budget."
    P2: "After we buy them lunch and tell them it's the best we can do, they will accept it."
Child to child exchange:
    C1: "I think it's fun working here."
    C2: "Yes, the boss never watches us too closely."
Adult to adult exchange:
    A1: "The Robinson report must be completed by Friday."
    A2: "I agree. You can count on our section to finish on time."
Parent to child exchange (crossed transaction):
    P1: "We are $1400 over budget this month."
    C2: "That's not my fault."

Thomas A. Harris also has explored transactional analysis and parent, adult,

> The rap-around program invites all of General's employees to meet in small groups with management employees three levels above in their line of organization. The purpose of the meeting is to afford all employees the opportunity to voice their concerns and ask questions about the company with a member of higher management responding.
>
> It was rap-around opinion cards from those attending meetings in 1977 that showed the increased understanding on the part of employees. Also, ninety-four percent of the cards said "yes" when asked if the atmosphere of rap-around is conducive to asking questions. This compares to eighty- eight percent the year before.
>
> Question team, or Q.T., is a confidential question-and-answer channel, using special postage-paid U.S. mail forms or a toll-free number for employees to call.
>
> Users of Q.T. receive an individual answer from a top General Telephone management source normally within ten working days. This acts as a safety valve for employees to express their concerns between rap-around meetings.
>
> Stewart W. Phillips, vice president, public affairs for General, said that rap-around and Q.T. do not replace the role of one-to-one communications with supervisors.
>
> They provide an authoritative source for answers to questions that supervisors may not be able to answer. He also said that the programs do not replace the company's employee suggestion plan, nor are they a means to bypass the company's agreement with the Communications Workers of America or its grievance procedures.

child (PAC) elements in our personalities.[5] Harris describes four distinctly different life positions in people. These life positions are entrenched attitudes accepted by people as they grow and mature. They become part of each of us and affect our lives and ability to communicate. Following are four basic life positions which affect our ability to communicate.

1. *I'm not OK — you're OK.* In this life position, we view ourselves in a negative context. It is based upon negative feelings gained as a child. In this state, we need a great deal of support from others. We feel ill-equipped to deal with life, but if positive support (called strokes) is present, we are able to cope.

2. *I'm not OK — you're not OK.* Individuals who adopt this life position feel inadequate and helpless. They feel there is no hope and live in despair. They do not draw upon their adult ability to reason and solve problems.

3. *I'm OK — you're not OK.* This life position is often found in children who were treated harshly by their parents. When they grow up, they are negative to others and reject them.

---

[5] Thomas A. Harris, *I'm OK, You're OK* (New York: Avon Books, 1967).

4. *I'm OK — you're OK.* The fourth life position represents the adult in us. Those who exhibit this behavior recognize and solve a problem in an open, rational way.

## SUMMARY

Communication is important to sound management. Communication is the linking element tying together all parts of the organization. The communication process involves a sender who encodes a message, the medium for transmitting the message, and the receiver who decodes the message.

Communication may be one-way or two-way. It may take place in a network in which information flows internally or externally. Internal data flow may be vertical or horizontal.

Both formal and informal communications are present in organizations. The grapevine is a major channel by which information flows through the informal organization.

An understanding of semantics, symbols, symbol selection, and language is important to good communication. Words have differing ranges of meaning. Meanings change and are influenced by cultural and social perceptions. People use verbal and nonverbal means and gestures, to convey messages. Noise, poor selection of medium, filtering, empathy, status, and overloading interfere with communications.

Transactional analysis and body language play a role in communication. A person's ego states and life positions affect how he communicates with others and how he will interpret and respond to a message.

## REVIEW QUESTIONS

1. Why is it important for the manager to understand the importance of communication?
2. How does the function of the sender differ from that of the receiver in the communication process?
3. What is the difference between a one-way and a two-way communication?
4. Describe several forms of internal communications flow.
5. How do formal and informal communications networks differ?
6. Describe how information moves through the grapevine.
7. Are words holders of meaning? Explain.
8. Describe some of the major characteristics of language.
9. How does personal perception influence communications?
10. How is body language used to communicate in a nonverbal form?
11. Contrast the parent, child, and adult ego states.
12. What are the four common life positions described by Harris?

## KEY TERMS

| | | | |
|---|---|---|---|
| Semantics | 384 | Oral communication | 396 |
| Symbol | 385 | Nonverbal communication | 396 |
| Channel | 385 | Filtering | 398 |
| Encoding | 386 | Empathy | 398 |
| Decoding | 387 | Status | 398 |
| Receiver | 387 | Overloading | 398 |
| Grapevine | 390 | Transactional analysis | 400 |

# Case Incident

Batton, Rust, and Claymore is one of the city's oldest and most well-respected investment brokers. A great deal of the success of Batton, Rust, and Claymore can be attributed to their reputation for service and business integrity. One of their employees is Ken Jones, vice president of finance. Among Jones' duties is the preparation of a monthly list of BR & C's accounts and customer activities. This special report contains a substantial amount of confidential information about various securities, as well as individual information on their major investors. If leaked to competitors, this information could be very costly to BR&C's competitive position.

This report has always been typed by Emily Gustoff, secretary to Jones. Gustoff is a valued career employee at BR&C. She has been with the company for over five years. Recently Gustoff has been dating Frank Powers, a young clerk at Baxter Green Investment Corporation, whose offices are in the same building. Although Baxter Green doesn't have nearly as many clients as BR&C, they have been making some rather aggressive steps to increase their share of the investment broker market. It has come to Jones' attention that periodically some confidential information from the report has appeared in the hands of various competitors. Jones is also aware that Gustoff has been seeing Powers.

## PROBLEMS

1. How should Jones handle the leak of confidential information to his competitors? Can he use it to his advantage?
2. Should Jones approach Gustoff and question her about the information leak? What problems would arise from a confrontation?
3. What means can be employed to prevent the flow of confidential information in the future?

# PART SIX

# The Controlling Function

SCALE
ABS
INCR
LINE
ARC CEN
ARC END CW
ARC END CCW
RTN
STOR X
7
8
9
ZERO SET
PLAY Y
4
5
6
KB CLR
READ R
1
2
3
C/C θ
0
BURN
+Y
STOP
GO
-Y

# 18

# Control Process Fundamentals

**LEARNING OBJECTIVES**

After studying this chapter, you should be able to:
1. Define key terms related to control process fundamentals.
2. Summarize the need for control in organizations.
3. Describe the basic control process.
4. Describe the basic control tools.
5. List the key areas of control.
6. Summarize some applied aspects of control.
7. Summarize some major issues in control.
8. Describe the influence of the Hawthorne effect on control.
9. Describe real-time control systems.
10. Describe how standards are used in control.

We now explore the last major function of management, control. Control is the observation of progress and the redirecting of efforts and activities to assure that planned goals are reached. The control process is vital to managers and is closely interwoven with the planning function.

This chapter defines basic terms and outlines the need for control. The chapter describes control tools and concepts, including the budget, audit, and reporting systems. Characteristics of a good control system are presented. The chapter concludes with a discussion of the Hawthorne effect and real-time control systems.

In this chapter, the emphasis is upon such fundamentals as control loops, feedback, measurement, and system correction. Chapters 19 and 20 expand upon these basic concepts by treating the applied aspects, including financial and nonfinancial control.

## KEY TERMS

The systematic study of control is a relatively new discipline. Before touching on the fundamentals, let us define some key terms dealing with the control process.

—*Control.* Control is the realigning or redirecting of efforts within predetermined standards to assure that planned goals are reached. As used in management, the control process is the systematic establishment of goals or plans, the measurement and comparison of results with plans, and the taking of corrective action when necessary to assure achievement of goals.

—*Corrective action.* A corrective action is any effort to adjust, redirect, or bring a phenomenon back in line with a predetermined result. Corrective action is an integral part of the control process.

—*Real-time control system.* A real-time control system exercises control over the system's variables while the events and transactions are still taking place. A system which controls the output of a papermaking machine while paper is being produced is an example of real-time control. This is contrasted with a *postdefect control system,* which adjusts a phenomenon some time after the events being monitored take place.

—*Cybernetics.* Cybernetics is the study of the automatic control process formed by the nervous system and brain or by mechanical-electrical systems. In the automatic control process, the output of a system is coupled back to the input. Thus the system automatically adjusts itself based upon the results produced. The study of cybernetics deals with any system that can be automatically controlled.

—*Throughput.* Throughput is the total volume of work produced by a system in a given amount of time. Throughput is a measure of an organization's or a

This automated assembly line is an example of cybernetics.

system's output and efficiency. The greater the throughput, the greater the volume of goods and services produced.

— *Turnaround time.* Turnaround time is a measure of the elapsed time between submitting a job or task and the return of results. Control systems are concerned with throughput and turnaround time. Systems with fast turnaround deliver results more quickly than those with slow turnaround.

— *Standard cost.* A standard cost is a predetermined cost needed to produce a given good or service. Standard costs are derived from studies of time and material costs over many observations. They provide a basis for comparing production and operating costs over time.

— *Time standard.* A time standard is a predetermined time allotment necessary to produce a given good or service. Time standards are derived from observation of many cycles in the production of a product or service. They provide a basis for comparing production time over a number of units produced.

## NEED FOR CONTROL

One might ask why there is a need for control if organization plans are carefully prepared and implemented by managers. The answer is that the real world is full of variables and influences which cannot be foreseen or incorporated into a plan.

It is this unexpected deviation from a plan which forces managers to redirect organizational behavior and take corrective action. Some organizations operate for many years without major outside or unexpected influences. An equilibrium or balanced condition exists, and the organization moves along a planned, expected path. In this instance a steady state is present [fig. 18-1(a)].

Imbalances can occur in organizations which cause variables to go out of control. Changes in the economy, the human factor, internal financial changes, regulations, or governmental controls cause organizations to deviate widely from expected plans [fig. 18-1(b)].

Without an adequate control system, costs, turnaround time, throughput, or quality of services could seriously deteriorate. The function of a control system is to assure that time, cost, quality, or other goals are achieved. A good control system is responsive and enables corrective action to be taken before serious problems occur.

For example, imagine the problems which could result if no effort were made to check the quality in the construction and operation of a modern jet airplane. These planes have thousands of parts, electronic components, devices, fasteners, and bolts, all of which are subject to breakdown. With quality control and maintenance there is a high degree of assurance that all elements will function properly.

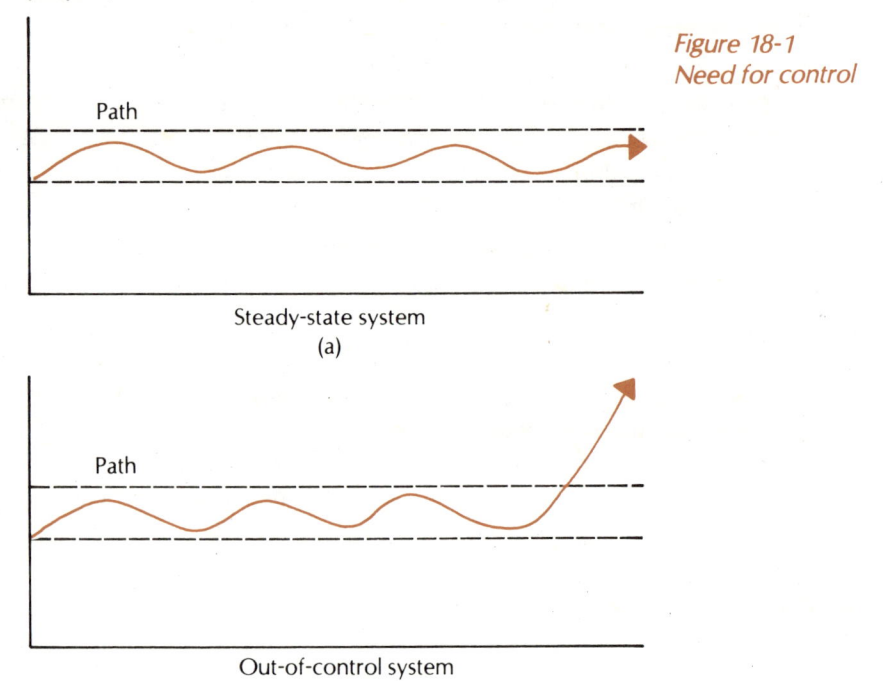

*Figure 18-1*
*Need for control*

Steady-state system
(a)

Out-of-control system
(b)

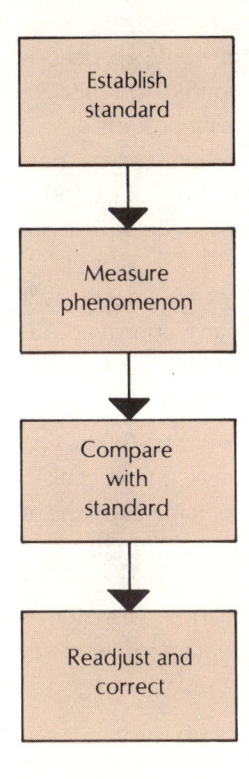

```
┌──────────┐
│Establish │
│standard  │
└────┬─────┘
     ▼
┌──────────┐
│ Measure  │
│phenomenon│
└────┬─────┘
     ▼
┌──────────┐
│ Compare  │
│  with    │
│ standard │
└────┬─────┘
     ▼
┌──────────┐
│Readjust and│
│ correct   │
└──────────┘
```

*Figure 18-2*
*Basic control process*

## THE BASIC CONTROL PROCESS

The basic control process is seen all around us. Control is found in human and animal organisms, in nature, business, industry, hospitals, schools, and other organizations. Wherever a group of variables interact or are subject to change, the control function is applied.

The control process may be manual or automatic. In a manual system, a human being observes an operation; if he sees a deviation he exerts a redirecting influence on the system. In an automatic control process the observation and redirecting takes place without human intervention.

The steering of an automobile is an example of a simple manual control process. The driver, observing that the vehicle is running off the road, steers the car back onto the right path. The process involves a standard (centerline), measurement of a phenomenon, comparison, and corrective action.

An example of the automatic control process is the domestic heating furnace and thermostat. The system involves a standard (thermostat set to a comfortable level), measurement of a phenomenon (sensing room temperature), comparison, and corrective action. The burner is lighted and room temperature adjusted without human intervention. Figure 18-2 lists these actions in sequence. Let us look at these steps in the control process more closely.

1. *Establish standards and measuring tools.* The first step in the control process is the establishment of standards by which events will be compared. This also involves selection of measurement tools and is part of the planning process.

In the case of a business system, standards may be established for personnel and financial performance or for quality of manufacture. Standards of performance may be established for selected individuals, entire departments, or even whole organizations.

Figure 18-3 illustrates a standard used by a bank in granting consumer loans. It lists standards or conditions which must be present before a loan is approved. Table 18-1 describes some measurement tools.

2. *Measure phenomenon.* The second phase involves measuring the phenomenon. Using standards and tools of measurement, an assessment is made of the system's performance. In organizations, costs, profit, return on investment, quality, throughput, and turnaround time are measured. For example, a manager might measure the productivity of the labor force by dividing their output into the total number of units produced.

In this phase, objective data about the real-world performance of a system is gathered. The number of hours worked, cash in bank, percentage of items re-

*Figure 18-3*

### CONSUMER LOAN EVALUATION REPORT

Add points

| | |
|---|---|
| Telephone | 5 points |
| Years on job | 1 point per year |
| Own own home | 10 points |
| Own own car | 5 points |

Deduct points

| | |
|---|---|
| On job less than 1 year | 5 points |
| Sued by collection agency | 5 points |
| No bank account | 5 points |
| Under 21 years of age | 5 points |

Income/payment ratio

Monthly payments $ _____

Ratio _____

Income, monthly $ _____

Loan officer: Deny consumer loan if plus points are less than 17; deny loan if deduct points are over 6. Deny loan if income/payment ratio is over 75 percent. Grant loan if plus points are over 18.

### Table 18-1 Measurement tools

| Phenomenon measured | Tool/criteria |
| --- | --- |
| Profit | Dollars |
| Return on investment | Ratio/dollars |
| Vendor performance | Average time to fill and ship order, in days |
| Employee performance | Days absent; reject rate, percentage |
| Sales staff performance | No. units sold, dollar volume |
| Service department performance | Percentage of call backs |

turned, number of items assembled or shipped, or services provided are measured.

3. *Compare with standard.* In this step, the results are compared with the standard. A comparison is made between what actually occurred and what was expected to occur. Actual profit for the period may be compared with planned profit, sales volume with planned volume, reject rate with expected reject rate, graduates with dropouts, and so on.

4. *Readjust and correct.* The last step in the process requires the correction and readjustment of the system to bring actual results in line with desired results, if necessary.

A variety of corrective actions may be taken, such as acquiring new equipment or personnel, changing budgets, reassigning personnel, or even opening or closing plants.

## FEEDBACK LOOP

In actuality, the automatic control process is an on-going, repetitive activity. It is implemented in a loop, or cycle, which continually monitors performance, takes corrective action if necessary, and adjusts inputs.

Figure 18-4 illustrates this feedback loop concept, which is present in all automatic control systems. Inputs to a system may be money, raw materials, personnel, facilities, or equipment. The process may be a manufacturing operation, assembly line, or system for delivering services. The outputs are the goods or services produced. This may be color television sets, automobiles, building materials, or hospital care or other services.

In the control cycle a process takes place which produces an output or result. If the output is beyond the desired range, the feedback loop adjusts the processing step. This brings the output into line with the standard. The cycle continues with output being measured and corrective action fed back to the system. The heart of the control process is the feedback loop linking the output of the system to the input.

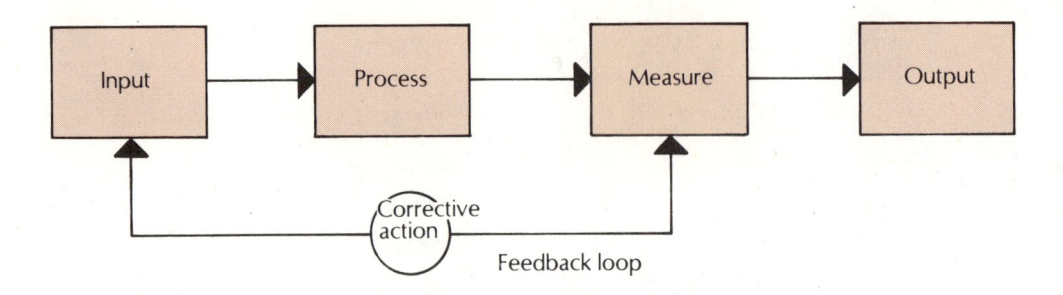

*Figure 18-4 Control cycle*

## BASIC CONTROL TOOLS

The manager has a variety of basic tools to control operations. These include the standard, data collection and reporting forms, audits, ratio analysis, budgets, and responsibility centers.

1. *Standard.* The standard is a fundamental tool of control. A standard is a predetermined time or cost allowance to produce a given good or service. Standards are prepared after many observations and a careful analysis of real-life occurrences to establish criteria and norms of behavior.

For example, the automobile repair industry uses standards. Manuals are available which give industrywide labor or repair time allowances. They provide the repair shops with a useful control tool. The performance of any given mechanic or group of employees can be compared with the industry norm. If local time allowances exceed the given norms, the manager can analyze and improve the operation.

2. *Data collection and reporting forms.* A variety of control forms and reports are used. They gather and report information on the number of hours worked and the number of units produced, shipped, sold, and returned in an organization. Data input forms provide a means of assembling information about an operation so that productivity can be analyzed. Forms such as that shown in figure 18-5 provide the manager with an efficient, consistent means of collecting data for decision making and control.

3. *Audits.* Audits are independent investigations of activities or operations. They are formal, official examinations of accounts or records with a methodical review to check their accuracy.

External audits may be conducted by outside agencies such as public accountants and examiners. They may also be conducted internally by organization personnel. Audits should be conducted by independent, experienced personnel to verify the truthfulness, accuracy, and completeness of data.

Audits are control tools, since they provide a means of obtaining information

CHAPTER EIGHTEEN    CONTROL PROCESS FUNDAMENTALS                                    417

for comparison. Audits which examine an organization's finances, personnel records, production, and inventory data insure better control.

*Figure 18-5    Personnel report*

| | | XYZ CORPORATION | | |
| | | PERSONNEL INVENTORY | | |

Department # _____    No. _____

Supervisor _____    Badge _____

Please complete the personnel inventory on available employees and return to Personnel Dept. each Friday.

| Total salary | | Total hourly | | |
|---|---|---|---|---|
| Dept. number | Available for work | On assignment | On leave | Hourly/ salary |
| | | | | |
| | | | | |
| | | | | |
| | | | | |
| | | | | |
| | | | | |
| | | | | |
| | | | | |
| | | | | |
| | | | | |
| Totals | | | | |

Complete this form in triplicate. Report only employees who have been assigned to your department. Consult Personnel Dept. policy no. 23-034 for details.

> ### REAL WORLD
> # Rent-a-Suit
>
> Haas Tailoring Co. is striking it rich in a relatively new field, rent-a-suit, for managers and executives. The firm, headed by Irving Neuman, can hardly keep up with the demand for renting $500 suits on a monthly lease. Haas provides executives and managers with natty, high-fashion clothing.
>
> Suit leasing helps managers beat inflation because they can trade in last season's model for this year's look without a lot of waste. As any leasing company, Haas begins with an analysis of the customer's needs and offers the usual tax benefits. A dozen $400 suits leased for two years costs the lessee about $5,000, and includes professional advice on how to dress properly as an executive.
>
> Business managers rent their plant facilities and automobiles, so Neuman believes they should be renting their clothes as well. He must be right because it is all they can do to keep up with their orders.
>
> Adapted from *Time*, 10 March, 1980, p. 71.

4. *Ratio analysis.* Ratios are mathematical statements which express a relationship between two variables. A variety of ratios are discussed in chapter 5. These include the profit, debt, activity, and current ratios. These ratios are used frequently by managers. They are important control tools since they allow managers to track an organization's progress over time or in comparison with other organizations.

Ratios can be used for both internal and external comparisons. For example, a firm's debt ratio may be compared with the industry average to determine how the organization compares to other firms in similar circumstances. This is an external comparison. An internal check may be made of the firm's debt ratio by comparing it to itself over time.

5. *Budgets.* Budgets are also major control tools. A budget is a statement of position for a definite time, based upon estimates of resources for the period. There are many kinds of budgets, including production, advertising, and marketing. Financial budgets show how much money is put aside for operations for a given period.

The budget is both a planning and a control device. Before the budget is adopted it is a planning tool. After it is adopted it is a control device.

6. *Responsibility centers.* Responsibility centers are relatively new control tools. The responsibility center is a concept which breaks down larger units into smaller entities, thereby allowing the exercise of better control. A center is a unit, respon-

sible for its own costs, operations, revenue, or profit. Responsibility centers are sometimes called cost centers.

A responsibility center may be structured around geography, product lines, technology, or type of customer. Centers may also be developed around profit, revenue, cost, or other bases. By reducing larger entities to smaller, discrete units, the manager can monitor progress more precisely and take more efficient corrective action. Without responsibility centers, the manager must deal with controlling an entire unit or organization.

For example, out-of-control labor costs are hard to correct if the manager only has total labor cost figures for the entire organization. But if labor cost figures are broken down by cost center, the manager can identify those units which need corrective action.

## KEY AREAS OF CONTROL

In most organizations there are strategic areas which require close control. These key elements must be watched carefully and corrective actions taken early if the organization is to function efficiently. Some common areas of strategic control include financial, production, marketing, personnel, and social and environmental impact.

1. *Financial.* Important areas of control are cash, capital, and debt. Financial controls are exercised on investments in equipment, real property, vehicles, and stocks and bonds.

A major amount of effort is spent on financial matters such as cash flow, reserves, return on investment, working capital, and credit and collections.

2. *Production.* The production of goods and services is another key area of control. Managers must control the quantity and quality of goods produced. This involves consideration of productivity, inventory, warehousing, and distribution.

The objective of production control is to provide customers or clients with the right amount of goods at the best price, delivered at the right time and place. This requires control of production lines, raw materials, purchasing, and warehouse facilities.

3. *Marketing.* Marketing is a strategic area of control. Most production operations are geared to expected sales levels. Once sales for the period have been established, resources are allocated for production, finance, and personnel. Control of the sales and marketing process is fundamental to the success of an organization.

If sales fall below plant capacity, the per unit cost of goods rises, since the plant is not operating at its maximum level. If sales demand exceeds plant capacity, unit costs may rise since production of the required volume must shift to outside suppliers or subcontractors. A key goal of control is to establish and maintain an optimum level of sales for a given plant size and capacity.

**4. *Personnel.*** Labor costs are often the largest single cost in the manufacture of goods or production of services. Out-of-control labor costs mean increases in the cost of goods sold, and higher selling prices in turn reduce sales volume.

There are many aspects to personnel control, including acquisition, training, benefits, funding of retirement programs, and health and vacation planning. The object of control in this area is to provide the organization with the right type and number of personnel at the lowest price to provide the needed staffing and services.

**5. *Social and environmental impact.*** During the last several decades there has been increased emphasis on social and environmental influences. In the past, organizations could operate successfully with little control over these elements. Today, government and the public are demanding an accounting of the effects of organizations on the physical environment.

This pressure requires that organizations control their pollution and emissions. The industrial use of waterways, oceans, air, and land is now monitored carefully. Failure to properly control environmental pollution can lead to fines, shutdowns, or greater governmental regulations.

In today's environmentally conscious world, corporations must control pollution.

"We've finally cut production costs to a minimum. We've removed all machines: they were costing us money to operate."

Reprinted from *American Machinist,* February 1978.

## APPLIED ASPECTS OF CONTROL

To this point we have discussed the general concepts of the control process. When an organization actually implements a control system, unexpected problems and difficulties may arise. These include high costs, inefficient or inflexible controls, or lack of controls where needed. The following list describes the attributes of effective control systems.

1. *Clear and comprehensible.* A control system should be clear and easily understood by managers and subordinates. Complicated systems do not produce effective results.

2. *Accurate.* The concept of control itself implies accuracy. Control systems should be designed to accurately measure and adjust business systems. Controls which are overly broad and do not collect or report information correctly lead to wide disparities in system output.

3. *Reliable.* A major feature of a sound control system is reliability. Control systems must be dependable. Those which are intermittent or unreliable will not be used by managers.

4. *Timely.* Information must be timely to be of value in the control process. Reports on the system should be delivered early enough in the cycle so that corrective action may be taken. For example, a credit report delivered to a sales manager after credit has been extended to a person with a poor rating has little or no control value.

5. *Economical.* Control systems should be economical to operate. There is little value in a control system if its cost of operation exceeds the costs it seeks to control.

6. *Easy to administer.* Control systems should be straightforward and easy to administer. They should not require extensive forms or an unreasonable amount of management time.

7. *Flexible.* Control systems should be responsive to the changing needs of the organization. Inflexible systems which do not change with the needs of the organization fall into disuse.

8. *Suitable for needs of the enterprise.* Control systems should be designed to fit the organization they seek to control. Systems should be built upon existing functional lines and conform to the needs of the specific enterprise.

9. *Based upon exceptions.* Effective control systems should report the exception, not the norm. Normal conditions should be assumed, and only deviations from the standard should be routinely reported.

## MAJOR ISSUES IN CONTROL

The design and implementation of a control system requires many subjective judgments. The determination of what is to be controlled, by whom, when, and what is acceptable performance, are major issues to be resolved. Following is a list of considerations which should be addressed in implementing an efficient control system.

1. *Who will be responsible for control?* The assignment of personnel to the control function is important. Those in control should have the training and experience to do their job properly. They should not have vested interests in protecting isolated areas of the enterprise. They should also be independent and not subject to veto by the controlled.

2. *What will be controlled?* A decision must be made regarding what is subject to control. It is virtually impossible to control all aspects of the organization. Priorities must be established so that control is given to the most important areas of the organization. Thus, bottlenecks or high cost operations should be watched carefully.

3. *How often should control be exercised?* Effective systems apply control in varying degrees. The quality control applied to the manufacture of a light bulb is very different from that applied to the manufacture of a pacemaker.

4. *What is acceptable performance?* A determination must be made regarding what are acceptable limits for the phenomenon under control. A sales manager may regard one level of sales acceptable, while the production manager may consider another level satisfactory.

5. *How much control is needed?* The level of control is an issue which must be resolved. Overcontrol results in rigidity, unnecessary paperwork, and increased costs. Undercontrol may result in poor quality.

6. *Should there be a backup system?* It is sometimes necessary to build in a backup control system to assure regulation of a system at all times. This second system increases costs but also results in greater reliability.

## THE HAWTHORNE EFFECT

An important consideration in system control is the Hawthorne effect, in which personnel sometimes alter their behavior when being observed. Whenever a system is being observed closely, the manager should be aware of the Hawthorne effect and the biased results that may occur. The Hawthorne effect was documented by Elton Mayo after a study of productivity at the Hawthorne plant of Western Electric. (See chapter 2.) In any control situation the manager must be aware of the complex human factors which surround measurement of performance. The failure to consider human factors could result in ineffective control systems.

---

**REAL WORLD**

# Federal's Nighthawks

According to Frederick W. Smith, founder of Federal Express, sound control is necessary to succeed in the air freight business. Smith's Federal Express guarantees overnight delivery.

Smith began with $4 million from a family trust and an idea. By owning the planes and the delivery service, the carrier can exercise full control. Thus it is not at the mercy of the commercial carrier. With $72 million of venture capital, and aided by the folding of Railway Express Agency, Smith's flying parcel service has earned $260 million a year in revenue. His control philosophy is all encompassing. Federal coordinates the efforts of 6,700 employees, shipping over 65,000 packages per night to eighty-nine different cities. And it all goes through their sorting center in Memphis. Smith calls it the KISS ("Keep it simple, Stupid") principle.

Adapted from *Fortune*, 31 December 1979, p. 31.

## POSTSCRIPT
# The Ten Worst Guesses of Experts

### By Henry Duval

Most of the wrong guesses involve the experts' inability to correctly envision the progress of science. And, many of the guesses were made recently—during the so-called Age of Science, when literate men have accepted the inevitability of change in technology:

1. In 1956 the Astronomer Royal of England (that's his title) said that space travel "is utter bilge" and that man may never get to the moon or other planets. (U.S. astronauts landed on the moon on July 20, 1969.)

2. Lord Rutherford, the great pioneer of atomic physics, maintained that it was impossible to harness nuclear energy. (Enrico Fermi ignored this learned opinion and in December 1942 achieved the first self-sustaining chain reaction. The atomic age was born.)

3. In 1880, the chief engineer of the British Patent Office solemnly told Parliament that "Americans have need of telephones, but we do not. England has plenty of messenger boys."

4. Nikola Tesla, the genius who developed the induction motor, wireless transmission of electric power, and the concept of wireless telegraphy that made Marconi famous,

Reprinted from *Management Digest*, May 1978.

## REAL-TIME CONTROL SYSTEMS

The modern electronic computer has made possible the real-time control system. Real-time systems control a phenomenon while the processing event or transaction is taking place. On the other hand, a *postdefect control process* exercises control *after* the event takes place. The processing of a weekly payroll illustrates this activity, since all transactions are carried out at the end of the week, after work has been performed. Real-time control systems have greatly improved the manager's ability to regulate systems.

With real-time control, the manager can gain control information while an event is taking place. For instance, using the computer terminal the manager can

did not have much faith in the future of alternating current, of which he was a major theoretician. He sold his patents to George Westinghouse for a million dollars. This was a relatively paltry sum when viewed against the fantastic future that these patents opened for the American electrical industry.

5. In 1926 Thomas Edison, who had a difficult time trying to perfect talking movies, declared that talking pictures were "a hopeless novelty the public will not support."

6. When the young George Westinghouse presented his ideas about a new air brake to Commodore Cornelius Vanderbilt, the railroad magnate, he laughed him off with, "If I understand you, young man, you propose to stop a railroad train with wind. I haven't the time to listen to such nonsense!" Within a few years all other railroads were replacing their hand brakes with air brakes made by Westinghouse.

7. A major financial-industrial blunder was made by the Dodge brothers—John and Horace—and several minority shareholders of the Ford Motor Company who agreed to accept Henry Ford's offer of $75 million for their 41½ percent interest in Ford stock in 1919. The company is now worth billions and their $75 million part would be worth about $2 billion.

8. Chauncey Depew, head of the New York Central Railroad, wouldn't buy any stock in auto firms and warned a relative not to invest $5,000 in Ford stock "because nothing has come along to beat the horse" (except his railroad, of course).

9. H. G. Wells, that futurist-optimist, sold science short when he said in 1902, as the first submarine was launched: "I must confess my imagination refuses to see any sort of submarine doing anything but suffocating its crew and foundering at sea."

10. In 1934 the British Under-Secretary of State for Air told gas-turbine (jet) engine inventor Frank Whittle that "scientific investigation into the possibilities has given no indication that this method can be a serious competitor to the airscrew-engine combination." (Have you seen a propeller-driven airliner lately?)

And, only thirty years ago, other experts similarly forecast no future for nuclear-powered submarines and missiles fired from them. Right now the experts are saying that sunpower will never become a major energy source.

monitor plant output throughout the day. Control can be exercised early enough to correct problems as they arise.

Real-time control systems operate with data bases or collections of information from many parts of the organization. Real-time control systems may be tied to strategic points in the business operation and provide information for decision making at critical times.

The advantage of real-time control systems is they are fast and responsive and provide a better level of information.

The disadvantages of real-time systems are the hardware costs and system failures. Real-time systems may involve expensive computer installations, terminals, and communication networks. Failure in the communication lines could mean a temporary loss of control. In spite of these problems, there is a continued trend toward real-time control systems.

## SUMMARY

Control is the observing and redirecting of efforts to assure planned goals are reached. Control corrects unexpected deviations from a plan. The basic control process involves a standard, measurement of phenomenon, comparison, and readjustment or corrective action.

The basic control tools used by managers include the standard, predetermined cost or time allowances, data collection and reporting forms, audits, ratio analysis, budgets, and responsibility centers. In most organizations strategic control is exercised on the areas of finance, production, marketing, personnel, and social and environmental impact.

A good control system should be understandable, comprehensible, accurate, reliable, and timely. It should be economical to operate, easy to administer, and flexible, and it should follow functional lines and be based upon exceptions.

Major issues in control include: who will be responsible for the systems, what will be controlled, and how often control should be exercised. Other issues include establishing acceptable performance, level of control, and backup systems.

Real-time control systems process events or transactions while they take place. They give managers greater control since they are fast and responsive. However, such systems are subject to hardware failures and communication costs.

## REVIEW QUESTIONS

1. Why is there a need for control in an organization?
2. List the major steps in the basic control process.
3. What is meant by the feedback loop?
4. How are standards used in control?
5. How is ratio analysis used in control?
6. List some strategic areas which require close control in organizations.
7. List some key attributes of effective control systems.
8. Summarize the problem regarding responsibility for control.
9. Discuss the level of control required in organizations.
10. Why are backup systems sometimes useful in a control system?
11. How does the Hawthorne effect bias results?
12. What advantages do real-time control systems have over batch control?

# CHAPTER EIGHTEEN  CONTROL PROCESS FUNDAMENTALS

## KEY TERMS

Control   410
Corrective action   410
Cybernetics   410
Throughput   410
Standard cost   411
Time standard   411
Feedback loop   415
Audit   416
Ratio analysis   418
Budget   418
Responsibility center   418
Hawthorne effect   423

## Case Incident

Benson Market Research performs market research and testing for a variety of retail firms. They use a great number of questionnaires and field surveys to gather market research information that is used in developing the reports they sell to their clients. These reports are filled with statistical data that is very important in validating the reports.

Benson Market Research employs a large staff of statistical typists in its clerical pool. These typists prepare a variety of tabulated forms and statistical reports where accuracy is extremely important. Supervisor Jane Stone has observed, through random samples, that some typists make many errors, while others do excellent, error-free work. In talking with her boss, Stone has considered a bonus system as an incentive for the typists. She also wishes to assess the output of various workers.

Stone has devised a plan in which each typist's output would be observed and recorded for a specific period of time, then compared to a norm or standard set by the company. Those typists who did not meet the standard would be given a two-week period to improve the quality of their work, or their employment with the firm would be terminated. They would receive training and other assistance to help them increase their quality and productivity in order to meet the standard.

Supervisor Ralph Macmillan believes that the employees should not be told when their output would be monitored. In this way, management would be able to get a true reading of the worker's average performance. He feels that if they knew when they were being monitored, they would certainly improve their work during the monitoring period but return to their old habits once the period had ended. On the other hand, Stone believes that the employees should be told when their work would be monitored by the supervisors. She feels that this would enable them to work with less strain and give them a fair chance to meet the standards.

The company, of course, must decide which system of monitoring output would be most effective. The company needs a testing program that is as representative of the workers' performance as possible, while at the same time giving the employees every opportunity to meet the standard. Since the employees perform a relatively routine and repetitive type of activity, it should be relatively simple to measure them with a great deal of accuracy.

## PROBLEMS

1. What methods should be used to monitor the output of the typists in the pool?
2. What factors are at play when workers know they are being monitored?
3. Should periodic, intermittent, or unexpected performance monitoring be used? Explain.

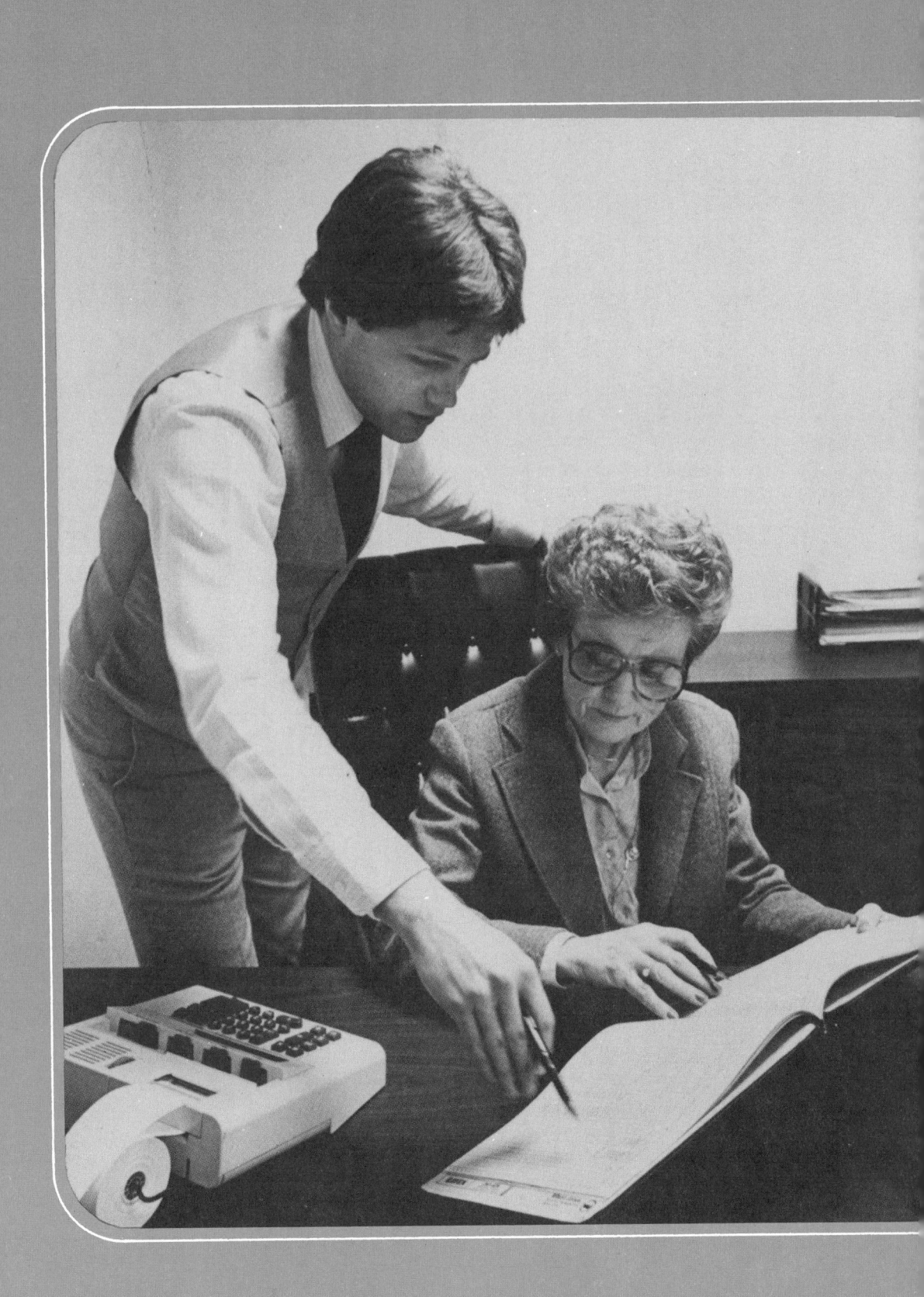

# 19

# The Financial Control Process

**LEARNING OBJECTIVES**

After studying this chapter, you should be able to:

1. Define key terms related to the financial control process.
2. Describe the basic accounting system.
3. Describe the major statements used in the accounting process.
4. Describe how ratios are calculated.
5. Summarize how ratios are used in the control process.
6. Describe the budgetary control process.
7. Discuss how the budgetary effort is staffed.
8. Contrast fixed and variable budgets.
9. Summarize the basic elements of zero-base budgeting.
10. Describe some of the human and psychological factors involved in actual budget implementation.

Managers use both financial and nonfinancial tools to control an enterprise. Financial controls deal with the flow of funds in the organization. Ratios, ratio analysis, and budgets are often used for this purpose. Nonfinancial control tools deal with the nonmonetary aspects of production, inventory, shipping, distribution, personnel, and the like.

This chapter discusses the financial side of control, while chapter 20 treats the nonfinancial. Both are essential to sound management. After defining key terms, we review the basic accounting process and statements. Ratios and ratio analysis are explained, followed by a discussion of various kinds of budgets and the applied aspects of budgeting.

## KEY TERMS

The financial manager is concerned with many economic elements of the organization, including cash, credit, investment, capital, dividends, and return on investment. Let us begin by defining some of the key terms dealing with this aspect of the control function.

—*Budget.* A budget is a statement of position, based upon estimates of expenditures or allocation of resources, including funds, for some future period. Financial budgets deal with the flow of money, investment, and capital for a future period. Nonfinancial budgets deal with allocating human and physical resources and production operations for a future period.

Budgets are often based on one year periods. Before they are adopted, they are planning tools. Once adopted, the budget becomes a control tool. It designates bench marks against which performances are measured.

—*Budgetary control.* Budgetary control is a system of control based upon the use of budgets. It involves planning and allocating resources for a future period and the comparing of results with anticipated performance.

—*Nonbudgetary control.* A system of nonbudgetary control is based upon the use of ratios, performance standards, or statistical control tools which do not include a budget. The system deals with such nonmonetary aspects as raw materials, production, distribution, and personnel.

—*Asset.* An asset is a tangible or intangible thing which is owned by an organization. Assets may include money, raw materials, goodwill, real and personal property, inventions, patents, and stocks and bonds.

—*Liability.* A liability is a claim against an organization. Liabilities may include unpaid bills, debts, and accounts payable. Money owed, notes, or stockholders' claims on assets are examples of liabilities.

—*Net worth.* Net worth is the net value of an organization after all liabilities have been met. It is the amount which accrues to the owner or proprietor after all bills, debts, and claims on assets have been paid.

— *Capital.* Capital includes money, goods, financial resources, or real and personal property placed at the disposal of an organization for operations. An owner invests capital in a business in hopes of making a return. The return paid to the investor is called *return on investment,* or just *ROI.*

— *Fixed cost.* A fixed cost is a cost associated with producing a good or service which does not change with the volume of output. Fixed costs can be calculated on the basis of a single unit or the total production of an operation. Examples of fixed costs include rent, insurance, heating, and building maintenance. These costs remain relatively constant whether a firm produces a large or small volume of output.

— *Variable cost.* A variable cost is one which changes with the level of output of a good or service. Variable costs may be calculated upon single units produced or on an entire operation. Examples of variable costs include raw materials, labor, supplies, or items which go into the manufacture or production of goods and services.

— *Total cost.* The total cost associated with the production of a good or service includes all costs of operations. It also may be calculated upon single units produced or on an entire operation. Total cost includes advertising, fixed and variable costs, and return on investment.

---

**REAL WORLD**

# The Solid-State Linguist Makes Its Debut

Ronald Gordon, head of Friends Amis, Inc., started with no plant, no inventory, and no long-term debts. But he had an idea—an electronic language translator about the size of a pocket calculator.

Gordon founded a firm which sells over 400,000 of these translators annually. At thirty-nine, Gordon is fully in command of his company. Although he prefers backpacking to business, his recreational activities take a back seat to his financial planning. Gordon built the success of his business on letters of credit instead of cash. In an involved but practical system of exchanging letters of credit from distributors with letters from the bank, he was able to generate the cash necessary to operate the business. Friends Amis expects to make $8 million profit on sales of more than $30 million in 1979.

Adapted from *Fortune,* 8 October 1979, p. 170.

"Just a minute, sir! Let's not spoil everything by starting out talking price."

Reprinted from *CARE Digest*, January 1979. © Fillers for Publications, 1979.

— *Revenue.* Revenue is the total income from all sources including sales of goods, real estate, interest, and return on investment.

— *Profit.* Profit is the amount of money left at the end of a period after all expenses for the period have been met. It is the funds left after payment of taxes, return on investment, depreciation, and overhead. Profit is that amount which the owner or proprietor can withdraw from a business.

## THE BASIC ACCOUNTING SYSTEM

Accounting is a basic tool of control and should be understood by managers. It deals with the gathering, collating, and reporting of financial data on a firm's operations. The accounting system summarizes information pertaining to all financial activities.

The accounting process deals largely with the reporting of historical data. That is, information collected and reported after the fact. It is distinguished from financial planning, which gathers and reports information on future events or conditions.

Accounting is important, since it provides the records and information used to control the direction of the organization. Accounting stresses how the information is gathered, while finance stresses how the information is used.

The basic accounting system is concerned with three distinct kinds of information: assets, liabilities, and net worth. An understanding of the relationship and conditions of these three elements is essential to sound management. There is a basic relationship between these elements:

$$\text{net worth} = \text{assets} - \text{liabilities}.$$

Net worth is the sum total of all assets, less any liabilities. That is, the worth of a business is what remains after all bills and expenses have been paid. For example, the net worth of an organization with $100,000 worth of assets and $25,000 worth of liabilities is $75,000.

The relationship above is sometimes described as:

$$\text{assets} = \text{liabilities} + \text{owner's equity}.$$

Thus, an organization's total assets should equal all of its liabilities plus the owner's equity.

## THE BASIC ACCOUNTING STATEMENTS

Accountants and controllers prepare and use a set of basic statements which describe the condition of the organization. The principal accounting documents are the balance sheet, income statement (profit and loss statement), and the statement of retained earnings. Variations of these forms are used by nonprofit organizations; however, measurement of their performance is based upon the amount of services rendered, rather than simply economic terms.

—*Balance sheet.* The balance sheet (table 19-1) is the basic accounting document. It states the relationship of a firm's net worth, assets, and liabilities. The balance sheet is prepared at the end of a specific period of time and shows the condition of these three items as of a given date.

The balance sheet is divided into two sections. On the left side are all assets, with the most liquid on top. On the right are all liabilities. The list of liabilities shows all debts, notes and accounts payable, and claims on the organization's assets. The

### Table 19-1  Balance sheet

| Assets | 12/31/80 | Liabilities | 12/31/80 |
|---|---|---|---|
| Cash | $ 200,000 | Accounts payable | $240,000 |
| Securities | 600,000 | Notes payable | 400,000 |
| Accounts receivable | 800,000 | Accruals | 40,000 |
| Inventories | 1,200,000 | Federal income tax reserve | 520,000 |
| Total current assets | $2,800,000 | Total current liabilities | 1,200,000 |
| Equipment and plant | $7,200,000 | Mortgage bonds | 2,000,000 |
| Less depreciation | 2,000,000 | Debenture bonds | 800,000 |
| Net equipment and plant | 5,200,000 | Total liabilities | 4,000,000 |
|  |  | OWNER'S EQUITY |  |
|  |  | Common stock $2,400,000 |  |
|  |  | Retained earnings $1,600,000 |  |
|  |  | $4,000,000 |  |
| Total assets | $8,000,000 | Total claims on assets | $8,000,000 |

amount remaining after liabilities have been met is the net worth or owner's equity.

A balance sheet must balance. That is, all assets must equal the total of all liabilities and net worth. The balance sheet reveals important information regarding the firm's assets, available cash, level of debt, and accounts receivable. It also places the assets in a hierarchy of liquidity. For instance, securities are placed ahead of inventories since they are more readily converted into cash. It provides the manager with the most basic information with which to make decisions.

— *Income statement.* The second major accounting document is the income statement (table 19-2). This statement, sometimes called the profit and loss sheet, or P & L statement, reflects the results of operations for a given period of time. It shows the amount received as revenue and all expenses paid out. It indicates the profit or loss for all operations during the period.

This document enables the manager to determine the total profit made for the period and in turn the amount of funds available for distribution to shareholders or owners of the organization. The income statement, however, does not show how the income was actually distributed. This is reserved for the retained earnings statement.

— *Retained earnings statement.* Another major accounting document is the statement of retained earnings (table 19-3). This report shows the total profit

### Table 19-2  Income statement
### (For year ended December 31, 1980)

| | | |
|---|---:|---:|
| Net sales | | $12,000,000 |
| Cost of goods sold | | 10,320,000 |
| Gross profit | | $ 1,680,000 |
| Less operating expenses | | |
|    Selling | $88,000 | |
|    Administrative and general | 160,000 | |
|    Lease on factory | 112,000 | 360,000 |
| Gross operating income | | $1,320,000 |
|    Depreciation | | 400,000 |
| Net operating income | | $ 920,000 |
|    Other income | | |
|    Royalties | | 60,000 |
| Gross income | | $ 980,000 |
| Less other expenses | | |
|    Interest on notes payable | $32,000 | |
|    Interest on debentures | 48,000 | |
|    Interest on first mortgage | 100,000 | 180,000 |
| Net income before income tax | | $ 800,000 |
| Federal income tax | | 320,000 |
| Net income after income tax | | $ 480,000 |
| Earnings per share | | $ .40 |

made for a given period and how it was distributed. It indicates what amounts have been distributed to owners or shareholders and what has been kept or retained in the organization.

Obviously, where large amounts of profits have been distributed to shareholders as dividends, the amount remaining in the organization will be reduced. Conversely, small distribution to shareholders or owners results in substantial amounts of profits being retained in the organization and available for investment or declaration of future dividends.

The three statements above, taken collectively, provide the manager with

### Table 19-3  Statement of retained earnings
### (For year ended December 31, 1980)

| | |
|---|---:|
| Balance of retained earnings, January 1, 1980 | $1,520,000 |
|    Add: Net income, 1980 | 480,000 |
| | $2,000,000 |
|    Less: Dividends to stockholders | 400,000 |
| Balance of retained earnings, December 31, 1980 | $1,600,000 |

important tools to scrutinize the changing financial condition of the organization. They provide data on which comparisons and analysis can easily be made.

## RATIO ANALYSIS

The basic accounting statements only report important financial data. However, these must be analyzed and compared to make them meaningful. A useful tool for making comparisons is the ratio and its analysis. Ratio analysis concerns itself with the comparative interpretation of ratios for control purposes.

A *ratio* is a statement of a relationship between two quantities. A ratio is the quotient, or the result of one number divided by another. Ratios can be used to compare changes in profit, return on investment, sales, use of assets, and other data.

### Developing Ratios

A variety of ratios are used for control purposes. Four of these have already been described in chapter 5. (See table 19-4.) Ratios are as important in the control function as they are in planning. The four major ratios focus on liquidity, debt, activity, and profitability. The *current (liquidity) ratio* is found by dividing current assets by current liabilities and indicates a firm's ability to meet its short-term liabilities. The *debt ratio* measures how effectively debt financing is used as leverage. The *activity ratio* indicates how intensively an organization is using its assets. And finally the *profit ratio* measures the organization's effectiveness in terms of return on investment.

Dozens of other ratios are used by managers. They include collection performance, fixed assets value, inventory levels, and sales and working capital relationships.

### Comparing Ratios

Ratios are extremely useful because they allow comparisons against other firms, entire industries, or by a firm over several years of performance. Let us focus on these three common applications of ratio analysis.

**Table 19-4  Some common ratios**

| Ratio | Formula | Indicates: |
| --- | --- | --- |
| Debt ratio | Total debt / Total assets | Use of debt financing |
| Profit ratio | Net profit / Net worth | Overall effectiveness and return on investment |
| Current ratio | Current assets / Current liabilities | Ability to meet short-term liabilities |
| Activity ratio | Total sales / Total assets | How intensively assets are used |

# CHAPTER NINETEEN   THE FINANCIAL CONTROL PROCESS

## Table 19-5   Examples of retailer ratios

| Line of Business (and number of concerns reporting) | Current assets to current debt | Net profits on net sales | Net profits on tangible worth | Net profits on net working capital | Net sales to tangible net worth | Net sales to net working capital |
|---|---|---|---|---|---|---|
| | Times | Percent | Percent | Percent | Times | Times |
| 5531 Auto & Home Supply Stores (54) | 3.81 / 2.24 / 1.66 | 3.33 / 1.58 / (0.17) | 13.73 / 7.29 / 0.00 | 18.62 / 8.66 / 2.03 | 8.76 / 3.84 / 2.39 | 9.22 / 5.39 / 2.76 |
| 5641 Children's & Infants' Wear Stores (39) | 4.30 / 2.93 / 2.26 | 11.11 / 3.95 / 0.43 | 23.33 / 10.71 / 0.48 | 34.29 / 13.51 / 1.44 | 5.45 / 4.26 / 1.77 | 6.15 / 4.51 / 2.29 |
| 5611 Clothing & Furnishings, Men's & Boys' (220) | 5.52 / 2.87 / 1.94 | 6.02 / 2.76 / 0.80 | 20.67 / 7.89 / 0.85 | 23.11 / 10.14 / 3.13 | 5.12 / 3.45 / 2.15 | 5.35 / 3.76 / 2.67 |
| 5311 Department Stores (333) | 5.36 / 3.06 / 2.02 | 3.91 / 2.12 / 0.86 | 15.37 / 8.18 / 2.87 | 19.53 / 10.97 / 4.21 | 6.01 / 4.03 / 2.65 | 7.12 / 4.59 / 3.20 |
| Discount Stores (98) | 2.97 / 2.21 / 1.71 | 2.33 / 1.26 / 0.59 | 18.52 / 11.22 / 3.46 | 22.31 / 12.88 / 6.08 | 9.62 / 7.03 / 4.21 | 11.75 / 8.53 / 5.63 |
| Discount Stores Leased Depts. (27) | 3.69 / 2.90 / 1.70 | 4.00 / 2.72 / 1.02 | 19.21 / 13.68 / 4.36 | 34.07 / 14.49 / 4.74 | 7.98 / 5.43 / 4.22 | 9.07 / 6.20 / 4.87 |
| 5651 Family Clothing Stores (97) | 10.43 / 3.86 / 2.41 | 10.21 / 3.27 / 0.50 | 16.45 / 8.26 / 0.87 | 25.78 / 12.79 / 2.96 | 3.39 / 2.59 / 1.69 | 4.31 / 2.99 / 2.18 |
| 5712 Furniture Stores (158) | 5.94 / 3.70 / 2.01 | 5.88 / 2.80 / 1.00 | 13.78 / 6.50 / 1.77 | 16.67 / 8.33 / 3.42 | 4.83 / 2.59 / 1.48 | 5.81 / 2.70 / 1.72 |
| 5541 Gasoline Service Stations (79) | 4.11 / 2.00 / 1.31 | 6.11 / 1.72 / 0.54 | 19.72 / 8.99 / 2.61 | 59.62 / 25.31 / 6.98 | 8.94 / 4.90 / 2.68 | 18.92 / 10.95 / 6.51 |
| 5541 Grocery Stores (138) | 2.20 / 1.70 / 1.36 | 1.77 / 1.12 / 0.57 | 16.78 / 12.35 / 8.04 | 44.95 / 29.48 / 17.77 | 15.56 / 12.25 / 8.41 | 40.24 / 25.12 / 16.25 |
| 5251 Hardware Stores (92) | 6.46 / 3.79 / 2.21 | 6.80 / 3.56 / 1.25 | 17.90 / 8.63 / 2.03 | 21.33 / 14.18 / 4.80 | 3.89 / 2.97 / 1.74 | 5.17 / 3.30 / 2.21 |

Reprinted from Dun and Bradstreet *Key Business Ratios*, 1978, p. 4

1. *Industry comparison.* Much useful control information can be developed by comparing an organization's performance with an entire industry, or one industry with another. Table 19-5 lists various lines of retailers and their industry ratios. For

> **REAL WORLD**
> # Autumn Binge
>
> Recently President Carter singled out year-end spending orgies as among the greatest abuses in government. Every year there is a last minute rush to spend every nickel of the agency's appropriations before the fiscal year runs out. Agency managers fear that money left unspent will cause a decreased appropriation the following year. In the last fiscal year government spending commitments ranged from $39.5 billion to $51.2 billion a month. At the end of the year the budget spree took root and spending jumped to $86.8 billion.
>
> Budget director James McIntyre feels that control of year-end spending is one of the biggest problems faced by government. Virginia Congressman Herbert Harris has even proposed a bill that would limit agencies to spending no more than twenty percent of their annual budget in the last two months of the year.
>
> Adapted from *Time,* 17 September 1979, p. 52.

example, it shows how the current assets to current debt ratio of discount stores compares to that of grocery stores. It can be seen that some retail businesses have substantially better debt leverage than others.

Information such as this is available from various trade and professional organizations, associations, and government agencies. Data on manufacturing, retailing, and wholesaling industries are published regularly and used in comparing ratios.

2. *Organization to organization comparisons.* Another useful comparison is that of assessing the performance of a specific firm against one or two others. A manager may wish to compare sales, debt, investment, or other performance against that of a major competitor.

3. *Internal comparisons.* A third important application of the ratio is to compare an organization's performance against itself over time. A manager may wish to know how activity or profit compares with past performance. This is easily done by use of the ratio.

The ratio also gives early warning signs of trouble. Difficulties may be avoided if a manager knows in time that debt or collection ratios are in trouble. The manager can slow down inventory growth or take more aggressive action on collections if the information is available.

CHAPTER NINETEEN   THE FINANCIAL CONTROL PROCESS

## BUDGETARY CONTROL

One of the most important tools of control is the budget. A budget reduces an organization's goals to fixed points in the future and states them in dollars and cents. The remainder of this chapter discusses the function of budgets and how they are prepared and used. Armed with a budget as well as such nonbudgetary means as ratio analysis and statistical tools, the manager can exert a strong control influence on the organization.

### Purpose of the Budget

The budget is both a planning and a control tool. Budgets are essential to the planning process since they indicate which resources are to be committed for some future period. Once the budget has been adopted, its function changes to that of control. The adopted budget now becomes binding upon management, and the organization must operate within these established constraints.

One of the most important aspects of the budget is in providing bench marks for comparisons. A budget such as that in table 19-6 indicates the allocation of re-

**Table 19-6  Budget with percent variance**

|  |  | Plan | Actual | Percent Variance |
|---|---|---|---|---|
| Net sales | | $12,000,000 | $15,000,000 | 25 |
| Cost of goods sold | | 10,320,000 | 13,000,000 | 26 |
| Gross profit | | 1,680,000 | 2,000,000 | 19 |
| Less operating expenses | | | | |
|   Selling | $ 88,000 | | | |
|   Administrative and general | 160,000 | | | |
|   Lease on factory | 112,000 | 360,000 | 400,000 | 11 |
| Gross operating income | | $ 1,320,000 | $ 1,600,000 | 21 |
| Depreciation | | 400,000 | 450,000 | 12 |
| Net operating income | | $ 920,000 | $ 1,150,000 | 25 |
| Other income | | | | |
|   Royalties | | 60,000 | 100,000 | 66 |
| Gross income | | $ 980,000 | $ 1,250,000 | 28 |
| Less other expenses | | | | |
|   Interest on notes payable | $ 32,000 | | | |
|   Interest on debentures | 48,000 | | | |
|   Interest on first mortgage | 100,000 | 180,000 | 240,000 | 33 |
| Net income before income tax | | $ 800,000 | $ 1,010,000 | 26 |
| Federal income tax | | 320,000 | 400,000 | 25 |
| Net income after income tax | | $ 480,000 | $ 610,000 | 27 |
| | | $ .40 | $ .50 | 25 |

sources for the coming period (plan). Actual performance is also shown. Performance can then be tracked against expectations. If a manager sees that current performance is out of line with expectations, efforts can be redirected to bring about the desired performance.

Budgets are generally constructed in monetary terms, stating how many dollars will be allocated for a given period. However, a budget may also be prepared in nonmonetary terms. This form of budget shows the number of people, units produced, and shipping or raw materials ordered for a future period. These nonmonetary controls are discussed more fully in chapter 20.

## Staffing the Budgetary Effort

A budget may often require subjective judgments and the assignment of priorities. This is particularly important where there are limited available resources. The effective use of budgets depends upon the proper assignment of personnel to this effort. It is important that skilled managers be assigned to budget control and that the goals of the budget be communicated effectively to all participants. The three most common approaches to staffing are line management, budget director, and budget committee.

1. *Line management.* An important group involved in the implementation of a

Marketing managers are periodically asked to prepare sales forecasts.

budget is line management. These are the individuals who are closest to the marketing department or production line and in touch with the immediate needs of the organization. Periodically, marketing managers are asked to prepare a sales forecast for a coming period of operation. This is given to the production department, and the managers prepare a one year personnel, equipment, and financial budget. Information is collected from all managers and used as the basis for developing the complete budget for the next year.

2. *Budget director.* One person is sometimes assigned the task of putting the budget together and presenting it to the board of directors or other appropriate authority. It is usually the budget director who gathers information from various managers. The budget director is in charge of seeing that necessary data is collected and reported in a consistent form. She then prepares a draft of the budget and submits it for review to the managers before submitting it to the board. She is in charge of the final draft, including its dissemination and implementation.

The budget director works closely with the accounting and data processing departments. It is her task to see that all relevant data is gathered, assembled, and submitted for approval.

3. *Budget committee.* A committee is sometimes used in budget preparation. This committee is composed of individuals from various departments or levels of the organization. It makes decisions and establishes priorities with the needs of the total organization in mind.

Once the budget has been prepared, it is given to the board of directors or other appropriate authority for approval. The board of directors holds the ultimate decision-making power and is responsible to the shareholders for the success of the organization.

The board of directors reviews major items in the budget and, after discussion and revision, approves the final document. This approved version becomes the controlling document which is binding on all managers for the coming budget period.

The actual administration of the budget is in the hands of the budget director, who sees that all departments and managers adhere to the budget. The budgetary process is usually on-going. Once the current year's budget has been approved, work begins on next year's budget. The current year often serves as a model upon which the following year's figures are developed. Thus, the budget director is closely involved in the planning efforts of the organization.

### Types of Budgets

Several common variations of the budget are found in management. A budget may be basically fixed or variable. That is, the budget may be unchanged for the coming period, regardless of the performance of the organization, or it may be adjusted depending upon operating conditions.

A budget may be developed from a previous year's experience. In this case, it may simply be an extension of a previous budget with only minor changes or deviations. Conversely, a new budget may be prepared each year, with little resemblance to the previous year's figures. Let us consider these possible budget variations.

1. *Fixed budget.* A fixed budget is based upon certain assumptions for a future period. The budget in table 19-7 assumes that 1,000 units will be produced for the period; thus all revenue and expense items are fixed. This budget includes labor costs, supplies, and overhead, all based on a certain level of output.

As long as the operations remain as expected, the fixed budget provides a useful control tool. However, the budget director must consider changes which might occur if demand increases. This could result in an increased level of operations and present a totally different cost picture for the period. The fixed budget is appropriate where the volume of output or distribution of services is known with some certainty. For example, a school with a maximum enrollment limit could use a fixed budget. Where this is not true, the variable budget may be more appropriate.

2. *Variable budget.* A variable, or flexible, budget allocates resources for a future period in differing amounts. Variable budgets are flexible and changing, depending upon the actual conditions which may be experienced in the coming period. Table 19-8 shows budgeted revenue and expenditures based upon 1,000, 2,000, and 3,000 units sold. This could also be applied to number of students enrolled, hospital beds occupied, or airline seats sold.

**Table 19-7   Fixed budget**

|  | Based on 1,000 units sold |
|---|---|
| Gross revenue | $1,000,000 |
| Less |  |
|     Labor cost | 200,000 |
|     Supplies | 100,000 |
|     Overhead | 200,000 |
| Cost of goods sold |  |
|  | $ 500,000 |
| Gross profit | $ 500,000 |
| Less |  |
|     Plant overhead | 200,000 |
|     Supervision | 100,000 |
|     Marketing expenses | $ 100,000 |
| Total expenses | $ 400,000 |
| Net income | $ 100,000 |

CHAPTER NINETEEN   THE FINANCIAL CONTROL PROCESS

Table 19-8  Variable budget

|  | Based on 1,000 units sold | Based on 2,000 units sold | Based on 3,000 units sold |
|---|---|---|---|
| Gross revenue | $1,000,000 | $2,000,000 | $3,000,000 |
| Less |  |  |  |
| Labor cost | 200,000 | 350,000 | 500,000 |
| Supplies | 100,000 | 150,000 | 200,000 |
| Overhead | 200,000 | 300,000 | 400,000 |
| Cost of goods sold | $ 500,000 | $ 800,000 | $1,100,00 0 |
| Gross profit | $ 500,000 | $1,200,000 | $1,900,000 |
| Less |  |  |  |
| Plant overhead | 200,000 | 350,000 | 500,000 |
| Supervision | 100,000 | 150,000 | 200,000 |
| Marketing | 100,000 | 125,000 | 150, 000 |
| Expenses |  |  |  |
| Total expenses | $ 400,000 | $ 625,000 | $ 850 ,000 |
| Net income | $ 100,000 | $ 575,000 | $1,050,000 |

To better understand the need for variable budgets, let us look more closely at the impact of changing output volume on the costs of goods manufactured. As was stated earlier, the total costs of producing goods include both fixed and variable costs. Variable costs are dependent upon volume of output. Thus, if output of the plant increases, often the variable costs per unit will drop. If output decreases, the variable costs per unit often increase. This is because an organization can take advantage of economies of scale and volume purchasing.

In figure 19-1, notice that as the volume increases, the unit cost to produce the goods drops. Fixed costs remain relatively constant regardless of the amount of goods produced. The variable budget is designed to take this important fact into consideration. It allocates costs for a future period on different assumptions of output. If output increases or decreases, the amount allocated changes. This is in line with the actual conditions which may be expected.

3. *Zero-base budgeting.* A relatively new concept in budgets is the zero-base budget.[1] To appreciate the application of this concept, we must consider the traditional means of establishing budgets. Generally, budgets are prepared on an annual basis, using information and figures influenced by the previous year. Allocations based on last year's figures are often used as the beginning point, or basic assumption for the coming year's performance.

---

[1]Peter A. Pyhrr, "Zero-Based Budgeting," *Harvard Business Review* (Nov-Dec. 1970): 111-121.

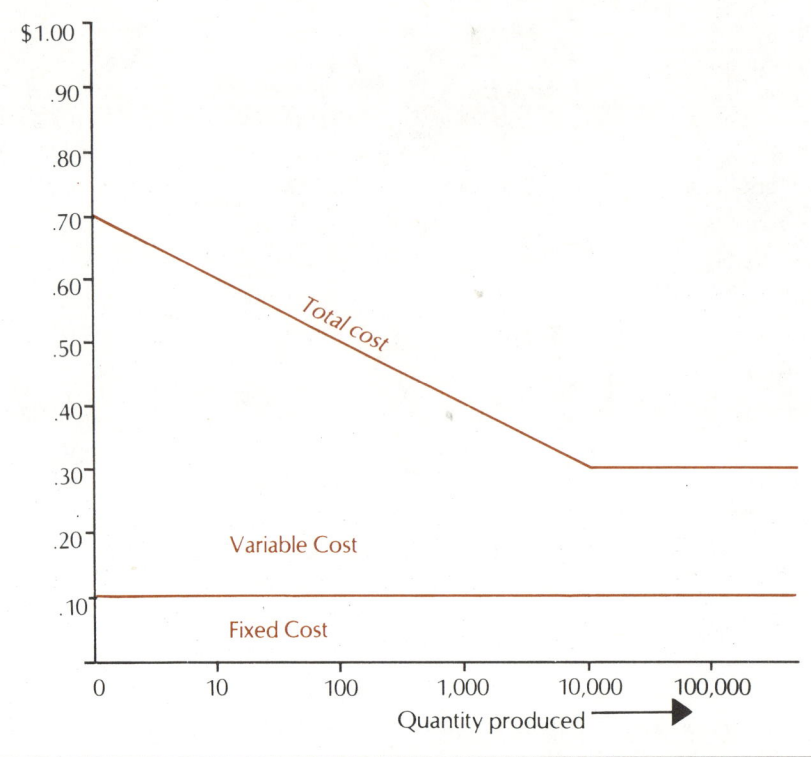

| Cost per unit ||||
| Quantity produced | Fixed cost | Variable cost | Total cost |
| --- | --- | --- | --- |
| 10 | .10 | .50 | .60 |
| 100 | .10 | .40 | .50 |
| 1,000 | .10 | .30 | .40 |
| 10,000 | .10 | .20 | .30 |
| 100,000 | .10 | .20 | .30 |

*Figure 19-1 Total cost per unit produced*

This traditional approach of beginning with last year's figures has several major limitations. First, it builds in an assumption that the coming period will behave the same as the previous year. Second, it does not stress a justification for all items in the budget, only that they were present in last year's budget. (See figure 19-2.)

In the zero-base budget, first used by Texas Instruments, no built-in assumptions are made. Funds are not allocated for the future period merely because they were included in the previous year's budget.

This forces managers to justify every item in the budget each year. It makes no assumptions, and it requires that items be included on a priority basis. The process generally begins with the development of *packages*. Packages are

CHAPTER NINETEEN   THE FINANCIAL CONTROL PROCESS   447

As volume increases, the unit cost to produce a certain item will drop.

subunits of the larger organizational goals and activities. After the packages have been isolated, each package is placed in ranking order of priority. That is, each item is listed in order of its greatest need. The most important may be approved promptly, while those down on the list may require more extensive justification.

*Figure 19-2   Zero-base budgeting*

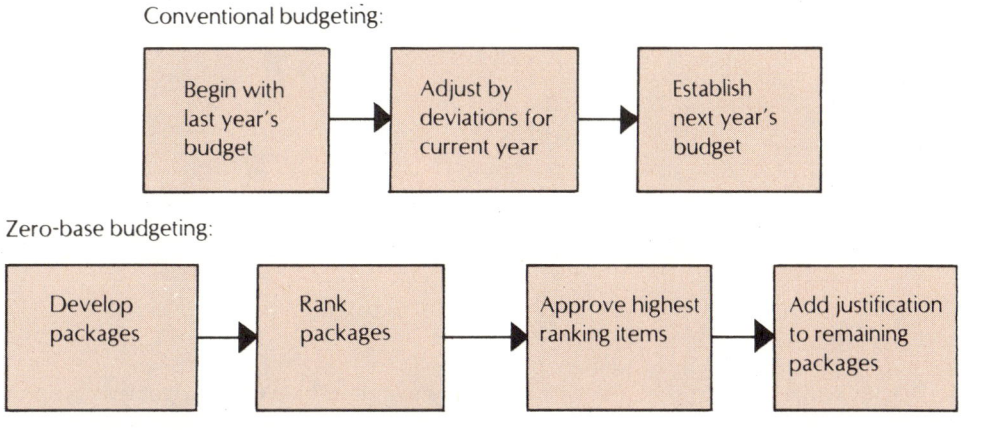

Conventional budgeting:

Begin with last year's budget → Adjust by deviations for current year → Establish next year's budget

Zero-base budgeting:

Develop packages → Rank packages → Approve highest ranking items → Add justification to remaining packages

**POSTSCRIPT**

# An Embarrassment of Riches: A Look At Big Oil's Big Profits in Third Period

### By Paul Blustein

Television news viewers this week are seeing a lot of old footage showing motorists lined up last summer at gasoline stations. That is TV's way of illustrating the news that profits of some major oil companies went skyhigh in the third quarter.

Earnings at Exxon Corp., the world's largest oil concern, jumped 118 percent, while Standard Oil Co. (Ohio) posted a 191 percent gain; Conoco Inc., 134 percent; Mobil Corp., 130 percent; Cities Service Co., 64 percent; Marathon Oil Co., 58 percent; Standard Oil Co. (Indiana) 49 percent, and Atlantic Richfield Co., 45 percent.

What caused the profit surge? And were the gains made at the expense of those fuming American motorists?

In brief, what happened is that the oil companies took advantage of a special market situation to raise their prices — and thus their profits. That situation included a temporary disruption in world oil supplies, accompanied by a sharp price boost by the Organization of Petroleum Exporting Countries.

The oil companies, anticipating an angry outcry this week, were quick to defend themselves. "People don't bother to see where our increase came from," grumbled Ulyesse LeGrange, Exxon's controller. Echoing the argument of most other oil executives, Mr. LeGrange said Exxon's latest profit rise came mainly from overseas rather than domestic operations.

To American motorists, who are paying an average of more than $1 a gallon for gasoline compared to about 67 cents a year ago, Mr. LeGrange's case sounds unbelievable. Yet most analysts confirm his position.

To be sure, U.S. oil operations didn't exactly suffer during the third quarter. Take

Reprinted by permission of the *Wall Street Journal*, 25 October 1979. © Dow Jones & Company, Inc. 1979. All Rights Reserved.

---

This approach to budgeting has resulted in better control and reduced operating costs.

## APPLIED BUDGET CONSIDERATIONS

In actual practice, the development and implementation of a budget is a complex matter. Many human and psychological factors may be involved, and changing

Exxon, for example. Its U.S. oil and gas profit expanded a healthy 19 percent in the period, to $447 million, or about 31 percent of total operating earnings. But that gain seems puny beside the 145 percent jump in Exxon's overseas petroleum profit, to $933 million.

The main reason for the difference in results overseas and at home is simple: U.S. price controls. While some of Exxon's U.S. oil and gas production is exempt from controls — primarily its Alaskan crude, whose price has doubled since last year — much of domestic production isn't. And gasoline is also subject to controls.

Still, the oil companies' defense can only be taken so far; they can't escape the relationship between their high profits and the motoring public's misery. The same market forces that contributed to the gasoline crisis — disrupted world supply and the OPEC price jump — helped inflate the bottom lines at oil companies.

Oil-industry critics contend that free-market forces aren't really working in the world petroleum market because it is controlled by OPEC, a cartel. The Carter administration has thus argued that the higher revenues the oil companies make on decontrolled U.S. production ought to be subject to extra taxes. The skyrocketing third quarter profits are further ammunition in the fight for a "windfall" profits tax.

Here's how Exxon, again as an example, benefited from the recent market crisis.

The revolution in Iran and the ensuing scramble for petroleum, which gave OPEC a golden opportunity to lift its prices 60 percent in the first half, also proved a boon to Exxon. The company, like others, raised its prices for production in non-OPEC foreign areas — like the North Sea and Malaysia — in line with the OPEC increase. And a new production there was turned on full blast.

Second, as panic oil buying developed in Europe, Exxon's big European refining and marketing network experienced a remarkable turnaround. It boosted prices for gasoline and other petroleum products strongly, and its output, which was well below capacity last year, surged.

Furthermore, the European operation's profit margins, which had been depressed, were bolstered by Exxon's crude oil buying advantage. As one of four oil companies that obtain crude from Saudi Arabia, Exxon pays $18 a barrel, a low rate compared with the $20 to $26 a barrel that other OPEC nations charge.

Mr. LeGrange hasn't any apology for the benefits Exxon has gained from the oil crisis. "I just fail to see how the public is being gouged by us," he says.

Oilmen in general contend that the laws of the free market are at work, that a shortage situation is supposed to lead to juicy profits for suppliers, the idea being that the profits will attract fresh supplies.

As for the argument that OPEC makes free-market principles obsolete in the oil business, Mr. LeGrange replies: "What you've got to do is question whether oil prices would fall if there were no OPEC."

business and economic conditions can have great influence on the success of the budget effort. Let us consider some of the problems and variables of which budget directors must be aware.

—*Human factors.* The budget has a major impact on the attitudes and motivation of personnel in the organization. If used properly, the budget can result in increased output, productivity, and motivation. The people who will be affected by the budget should be consulted when a budget is constructed. Failure to do so can cause feelings of alienation and frustration.

Budgets should include sound, realistic features and estimates. They should reflect the ability of those in the organization. Budgets which demand unrealistically high levels of output or impossibly low costs prove sources of dissatisfaction when they cannot be met in practice.

— *Over- and underestimating.* A common problem in budgeting is over- and underestimating. A manager may deliberately overestimate sales and underestimate costs to make the operation look more profitable. When the budget year is complete, the manager may blame external factors for the increased expenses.

— *Simplicity and clarity.* Budgets for large organizations are by their nature complex documents. However, they often become more complicated than necessary. Budgets should be clearly written and understandable to those who must implement them. Overly complex budgets will not be adhered to.

— *Flexibility.* A budget should be a flexible control device, tailored to the needs of the organization. Budgets which do not reflect changes in the marketplace or the internal economics of an organization are poor control tools. Budgets should not be used as punitive devices where conditions are beyond the control of the manager. Conversely, they should not be used to reward a selected department or individual for arbitrary reasons.

— *Power influences.* Budgets are often used as a basis for increasing a manager's power and influence in an organization. Some managers try to gain exclusive control of the budgets of profitable departments hoping to build power. Conversely, they may seek to remove unprofitable departments from their budgetary unit. The budget should be structured to be fair and reduce empire building in organizations.

— *Centers of responsibility.* A responsibility center is a smaller unit of a larger organization charged with its own responsibility for a share of the organization's revenue, cost, sales, or profit. Budgetary control may be applied to the total organization as a unit, or it may be applied to smaller units for better control. The responsibility center reduces large, complex budget operations to smaller, more easily managed and controlled units. Operating centers which shift responsibility to smaller, discrete units facilitate better control.

The design of responsibility centers should be based on a logical or functional division of the organization. An operating center may be constructed for all marketing, sales, production, and distribution of a particular good or service in a specific geographic area. Or an operating center may be built around common goods in a product line, or a common group of employees with like skills or experience.

# CHAPTER NINETEEN  THE FINANCIAL CONTROL PROCESS

## SUMMARY

The basic accounting system in an organization provides the information by which the control process is exercised. The balance sheet, profit and loss statement, and retained earnings statement provide important data by which comparisons are made. Similar statements are used by nonprofit organizations.

Ratio analysis is important to control since it allows comparisons to be made on an industrywide basis, organization to organization, or for internal comparison.

The debt ratio indicates the use of debt financing, while the profit ratio shows the overall effectiveness and return on investment. The current ratio indicates the ability of a firm to meet its short-term liabilities, and the activity ratio shows how intensively a firm uses its assets.

The budget is a major control tool. The budget process may be staffed by line management, a budget director, or a budget committee. A fixed budget is unchanging while a variable budget accounts for differences in output.

When a budget is being implemented, several human and psychological factors must be considered including over- and underestimating, simplicity, clarity, flexibility, power influences, and centers of responsibility.

## REVIEW QUESTIONS

1. What is the function of the balance sheet?
2. What is the function of the income statement?
3. What is the function of the retained earnings statement?
4. How are ratios calculated?
5. List three ways ratios are used in making comparisons.
6. Contrast budgetary and nonbudgetary control.
7. List three ways that the budgeting effort is staffed.
8. Contrast the fixed and variable budgets.
9. How does zero-base budgeting differ from traditional budgeting?
10. Describe some human factors involved in the budget process.
11. What is a responsibility center?
12. How is the budget related to power in an organization?

## KEY TERMS

Budgetary control   432
Nonbudgetary control   432
Fixed cost   433
Variable cost   433
Total cost   433
Profit   434
Balance sheet   435

Income statement   436
Retained earnings statement   436
Ratio analysis   438
Fixed budget   444
Variable budget   444
Zero-base budget   445

# Case Incident

Diane Albert is the head of the purchasing department in a large metropolitan school district. She has responsibility for purchasing all of the equipment, supplies, and materials for the district. Albert now has fourteen clerks and six purchasing agents who work for and report to her. The superintendent of schools, George Bowen, has asked Albert to prepare a detailed operating budget for the coming year. This budget is to include all operating expenses, salaries, overhead, and capital expenditures for her department.

Albert knows that preparing this budget will be one of the most important tasks that she will have to perform in the coming year, and that with the increasing concern for the cost of education the budget will have to be prepared very carefully. In discussing the coming year's budget with other people within the department, Albert finds that there are two distinctly different positions. Knowing that the budget will undergo considerable scrutiny by both the superintendent and the school board, she wants to make the best possible decision.

Sam Bell believes that next year's budget should be overestimated slightly and include some items of marginal nature. He feels that additional clerks' salaries should be included, and additional office furniture and copying equipment should be purchased. This is to protect the department's budget in the face of declining enrollment and pressures to cut costs and to justify their current level of expenditures. Also, he is worried that if the department budget is seriously cut, it may lead to the layoff or elimination of some of the employees.

Susan Chang thinks that Albert should turn in a far more conservative budget. This will show Bowen and the entire school district that the purchasing department has been operating cautiously and that there is no waste. She would like to show that money is being used wisely, and she believes that this will prevent budget cuts which could hurt the department. Building a case for the budgetary and fiscal responsibility of the department would shift the focus from cutting back on the purchasing budget to making sure that all expenditures are cost-effective.

The issue of school district expenditures is an important one. Both the school board and the public are very concerned about operating expenditures. This is especially true because school board and school district elections will be coming up in the coming year. Without doubt, the school budget will be one of the primary issues in these elections.

## PROBLEMS

1. What problems does Albert face if she overestimates the budget?
2. What problems does Albert face if she underestimates the budget?
3. Should Albert request a variable budget based upon the enrollment next year? Explain your answer.

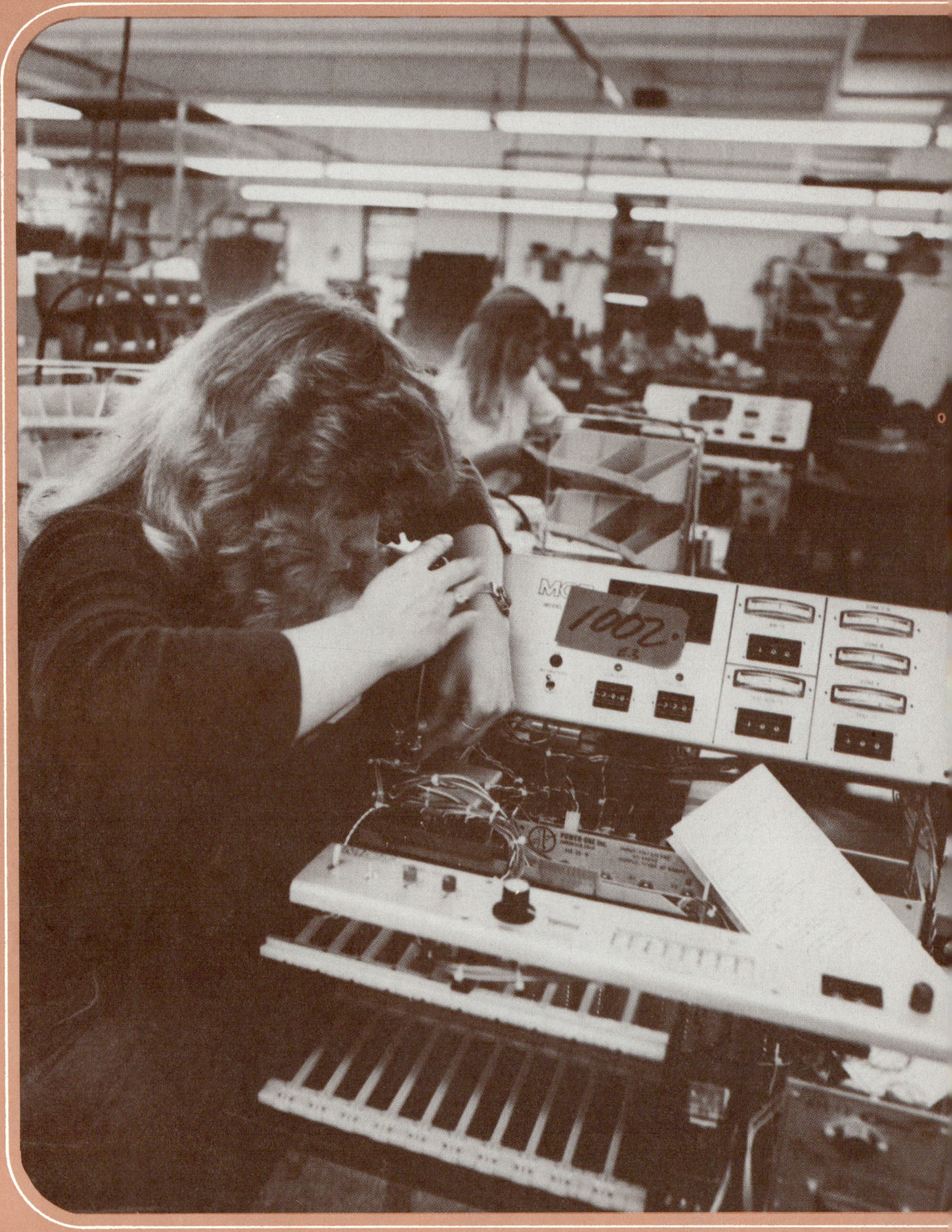
1002

# 20

# The Nonfinancial Control Process

**LEARNING OBJECTIVES**

After studying this chapter, you should be able to:

1. Define key terms related to nonfinancial control.
2. Present an overview of the nonfinancial control process.
3. Describe some major aspects of production control.
4. Describe the function of quality control.
5. Discuss the need for inventory control.
6. Contrast ordering and holding costs.
7. List three methods for determining the optimum size of order.
8. Describe how the economic order quantity (EOQ) is found.
9. Explain the need for lead time and safety stock in ordering.
10. List the major considerations in distribution control.

This chapter rounds out the discussion of the control process by discussing the nonfinancial aspects. Financial control regulates the performance of an organization from the perspective of accounting statements and economic considerations. This was described in chapter 19. Nonfinancial control focuses on the qualitative and quantitative aspects of marketing, production, inventory, personnel, or distribution of services.

This chapter describes management of the research and development effort, scheduling of work in progress, ordering and inventory of raw materials, statistical quality control, and acquisition and handling of personnel.

This chapter deals principally with manufacturing organizations. Nonfinancial control is also important to service organizations, such as schools, hospitals, and charitable groups. The specific nonfinancial control tools applied to such organizations depend upon their unique characteristics or operations.

## KEY TERMS

Several key terms are used in discussing nonfinancial control in organizations. They deal with the tracking and flow of raw materials, their inventory and distribution.

—*Operations management.* Operations management is the process of tracking the flow of raw materials from purchasing, production, and inventory to distribution of finished goods. Operations management concerns itself largely with the ordering, routing, holding, and storing of raw materials.

—*Production control.* Production control deals with the timing and path that goods follow as they move through the production process. Production control assures that raw materials are converted into the right kind and quality of goods to meet customers' needs.

—*Inventory control.* Inventory control manages the storage and inventory of raw materials and finished goods. Inventory control deals with the holding of goods, supplies, and materials during production, and warehousing of completed goods.

—*Quality control.* Quality control is the process of maintaining a specific quality of goods produced. It concerns itself with the physical attributes of goods produced, assuring that the finished goods meet specific characteristics. Quality control provides goods which fall within a defined range of quality, excluding those which are above or below the design standard.

## OVERVIEW OF NONFINANCIAL CONTROL

Financial control concerns itself primarily with the flow of cash and financial resources, while nonfinancial control treats the flow of physical goods and materials. Figure 20-1 illustrates an overview of the nonfinancial control process. This process monitors new product development, sales and marketing efforts, production of goods and services, and finally shipping and distribution. The nonfinancial control process is concerned with inventory of raw materials and finished goods, as well as human resources.

It should be noted that nonfinancial control is not exercised independently of financial control. In most organizations there is a close relationship between the control of physical, human, and financial resources. Excessive inventories, backlogs of orders, or excessive staffing show up as lost profit on financial statements.

Let us describe the major nonfinancial control efforts present in organizations. These range from new product design and innovation to distribution of finished goods and services.

## NEW PRODUCT DEVELOPMENT

New product development is concerned with the systematic identification and development of new products or services for manufacture and distribution by the organization. The object is to provide an on-going supply of new products designed to meet consumer demands and market trends. This effort is sometimes called research and development, or R & D.

Where would Ford Motor Company be if it had failed to develop new models after its highly successful Model T? What would 3M's diverse product line look like today if they had failed to develop products beyond cellulose tape and sandpaper?

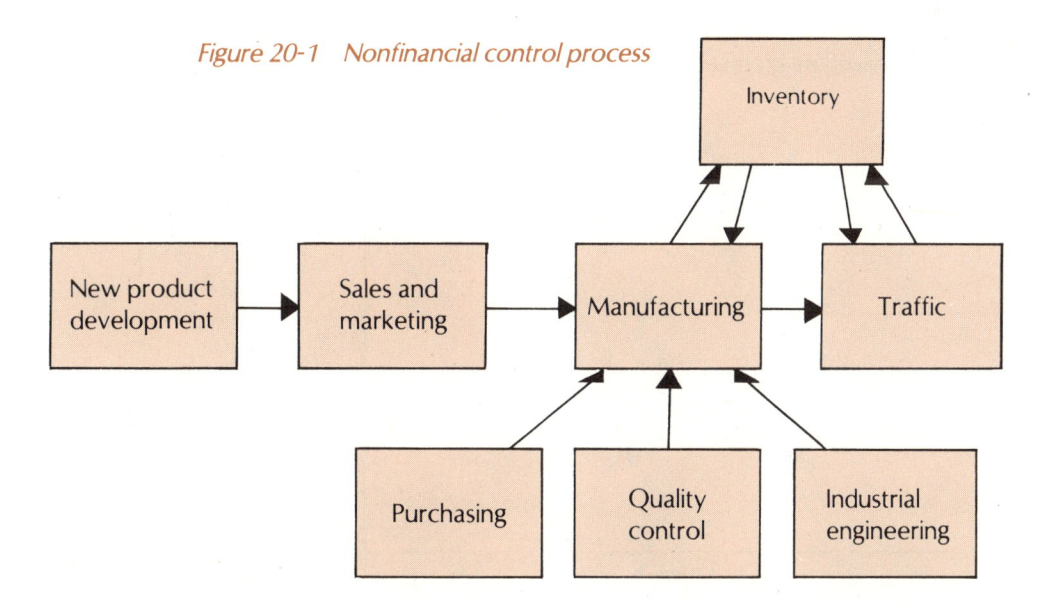

*Figure 20-1  Nonfinancial control process*

R & D efforts play an important role in the life of an organization because they provide a steady stream of new products. Without the introduction of new goods and services, an organization would find itself obsolete because of competition and changing consumer demands.

Products move through a life cycle, much as living organisms (fig. 20-2). When first introduced, a new product is unknown and has little demand. At this stage, the organization seeks to establish the product's identity and acceptance. Sales volume and profits are low.

After a product has gained initial acceptance, it moves into a mature phase of development. Consumers are aware of the product, sales volume increases, and profits rise. After some period of time, the product moves into a decaying phase. This may take many months or years. The sales volume drops, as does profit. The decay may be due to changing consumer demands, competition, or changes in taste. If no systematic effort is made to introduce a replacement product, the organization may find itself out of business.

New product development involves many decisions regarding the kind and type of products to be developed. For example, should a new product be priced high, thus earning a larger profit but a smaller volume of sales? Or should it be priced low, with profit built on a small margin and gained from many sales? Should the existing line of goods be expanded to include other related products? Or should the product line be limited to reduce warehousing and distribution costs? Should a new product go after an existing market or be aimed at a new market where few competitors exist?

## MARKET CONTROL

A major aspect of the organization's nonfinancial control deals with regulating sales and marketing efforts. Marketing is a key element in control, since most or-

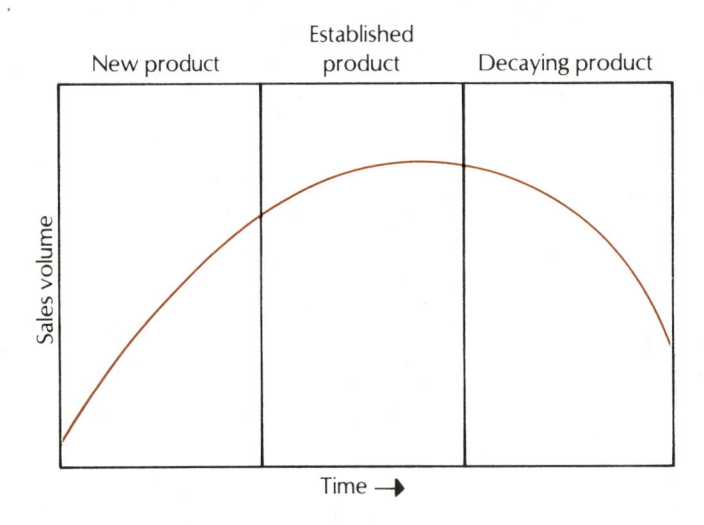

*Figure 20-2*
*Product life cycle*

*Without the research and development of new products, most organizations would eventually fail.*

ganizations base their personnel, manufacturing, and distribution efforts on sales or sales forecasts.

Market control deals with the design and definition of sales territories, product mix, type of customers, and pricing. Market control is the total effort of an organization to plan, advertise, sell, and distribute goods and services to satisfy the needs and wants of customers.

Market control begins with a close analysis of consumer demands, and attempts to provide goods and services at the time and place consumers need them. It involves many factors, such as competition, pricing, and changing social and consumer patterns.

Marketing managers generally seek to design sales territories to maximize sales and profits. They determine the mix of products offered for sale. Control is applied to the range of products offered, their price, and the promotions and advertising efforts to sell them.

Market share is important to an organization. Figure 20-3, illustrates a market shared by various companies. A goal of control may be to expand or just hold a given share of the market in a particular geographic area.

Company A 45%
Company B 25%
Company C 15%
Company D 10%
Company E 5%

Total market

*Figure 20-3 Share of market*

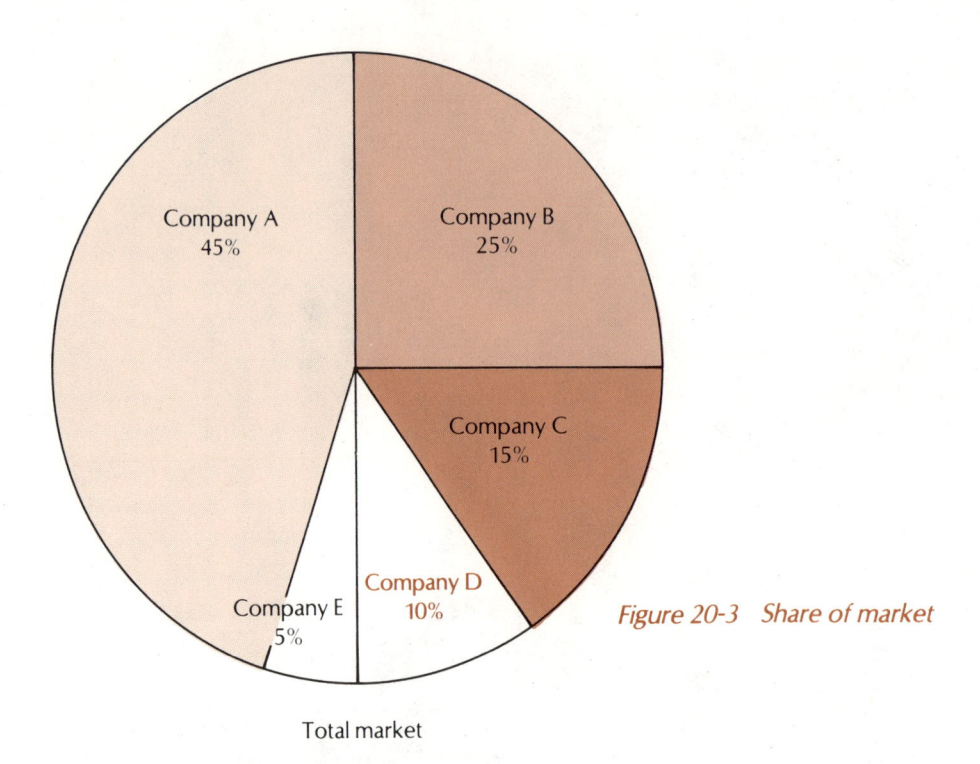

## PRODUCTION CONTROL

Production control is an important phase of nonfinancial management. It concerns itself with the flow of goods and services through the production and manufacturing cycle. Management of this aspect of the organization assures that the proper type and quality of goods is produced and made available for sale at the best possible price. Since production control is concerned with manufacturing, the orderly flow of raw materials, labor, and physical plant facilities is important. Control is aimed at both the path and timing of raw materials as they move from unfinished to finished goods.

Production operations may be categorized in several ways. One approach is to divide production into extracting, analytic processing, synthesizing, or fabricating processes. The manufacturing process may remove raw materials from nature, break down complex substances into smaller units, transform the basic nature of a substance, or assemble components into a finished product.

Another means of categorizing production is by the form of manufacture (fig. 20-4).

1. *One-of-a-kind production.* In this form of production, a single unit is produced. This unit may be a very complex and intricate system, such as a space shuttle or custom-built machine tool.

CHAPTER TWENTY    THE NONFINANCIAL CONTROL PROCESS    461

2. *Batch process.* In this form of production, goods are manufactured in small or large batches. The production plant is set up to produce a given lot of goods. The run may last several hours or many days. Then the shop is set up to produce a different batch of goods. Thus, the production cycle is broken into a series of operations, each producing a different lot of goods. A manufacturer who produces lots of chairs, tables, then dishes, does so in a batch process. A batch of 1,000 chairs is produced. Then the plant is retooled and a batch of 1,000 tables is produced. Printing establishments, cabinet shops, and sheet metal shops are other examples of batch operations.

3. *Continuous process.* In the continuous process, raw materials are converted into finished goods in a continuous, uninterrupted cycle. For example, a plant may manufacture a plastic or petroleum distillate and operate around the clock for months or years without interruption. Control of this operation involves adjusting the flow of raw materials or inputs to the continuous process to assure a steady stream of finished goods. The production of gasoline in a refinery illustrates the concept. Thousands of gallons of gasoline may be produced each month in an unending stream.

Whether the production operation is continuous or batch, there are certain basic control elements common to both. Production control focuses on the routing, scheduling, and timing of the manufacturing process. Let us consider the four major elements of production control.

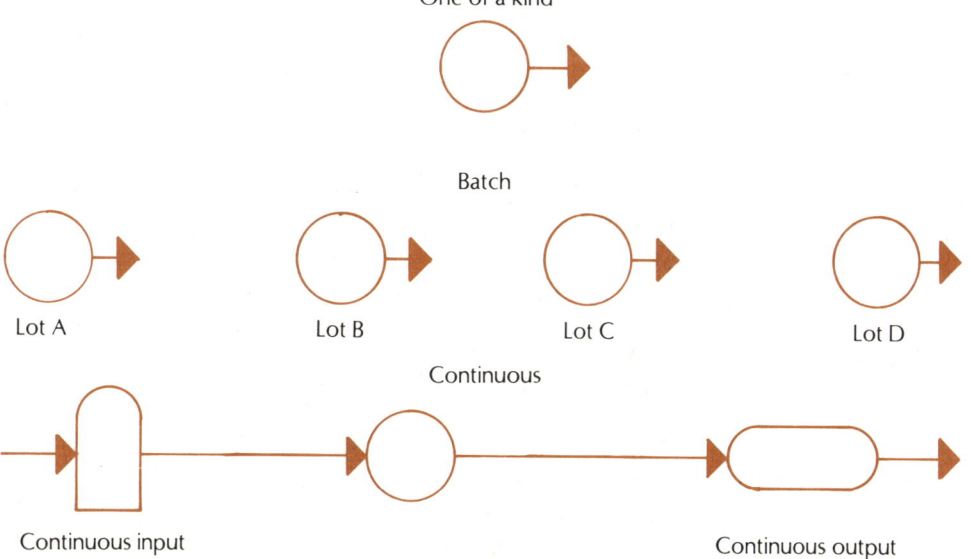

*Figure 20-4  Forms of manufacture*

One of a kind

Batch

Lot A     Lot B     Lot C     Lot D

Continuous

Continuous input                    Continuous output

> ### REAL WORLD
> # The Fast-Feeding of America
>
> Ray Kroc, senior chairman of McDonald's, is firmly committed to quality control. While other hamburger stands have folded, Kroc's belief in quality and service has built McDonald's into a giant. He believes hamburger stands should not only sell hamburgers, but must also provide quality, service, cleanliness, and value.
>
> It is essential for McDonald's to maintain control over quality, service, and cleanliness. They have built a special machine that produces 1.6-ounce precut hamburger patties, and a cybernetic deep fryer to produce fries of the proper crispiness. Employees are indoctrinated in Kroc's methods with an almost religious fanaticism. The stress Kroc places on quality control has built an empire for McDonald's which is now valued at over $1.6 billion.
>
> Adapted from *Fortune,* 31 December 1979, p. 34.

1. *Routing.* Routing is the process of selecting the best path or route goods will follow in manufacture. Routing guides the work through the shop and defines which operators and process will be employed. Figure 20-5 illustrates a routing schedule which specifies a sequence of operations in the manufacture of electronic circuit boards. Frequently a job control order, or job ticket, accompanies goods through the manufacturing operation.

2. *Scheduling.* Scheduling deals with the timing of operations in manufacture. It assures that the materials and labor are available at the place and time needed.

   A major consideration of scheduling deals with the ordering of raw materials so they will be delivered on time. This function is usually delegated to a specialized department concerned principally with purchasing raw materials and supplies. The failure to properly schedule raw materials could hold up an entire plant and cause substantial delays in the production of finished goods.

3. *Dispatching.* The dispatching function deals with the orderly release of materials and labor in accordance with the schedule. Dispatching involves assignment of employees to specific production operations. Dispatchers release the necessary raw materials, supplies, parts, or transportation already ordered, which are needed to complete the operation.

4. *Expediting.* Expediting is the follow-up activity which assures that goods, materials, or human resources are actually delivered on time. Production expediters monitor orders and shipments and keep them on schedule. In recent years expediting has changed to reflect more emphasis upon preventative measures.

Manufacture of electronic circuit boards

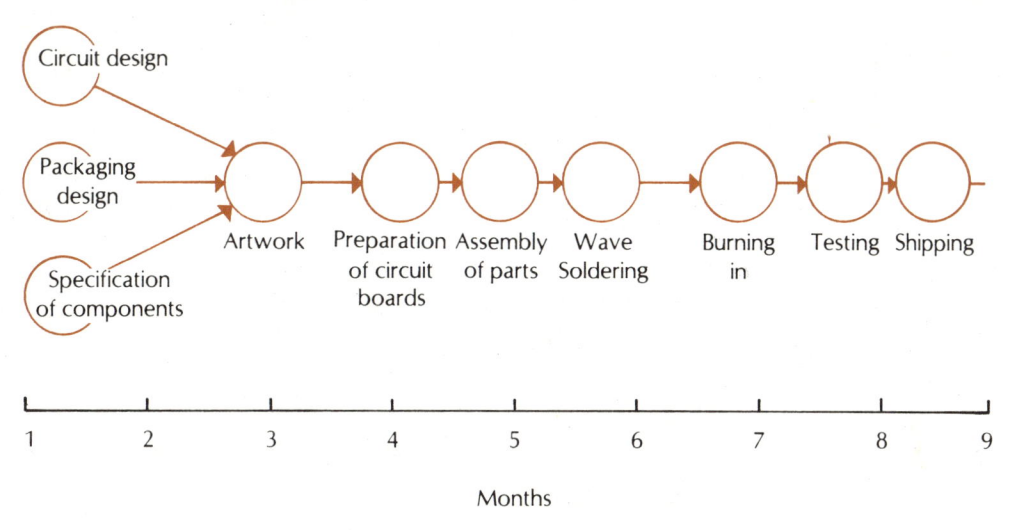

*Figure 20-5  Routing schedule*

Thus, good expediting consists of anticipating and avoiding delivery problems, rather than addressing them after the fact.

Production control involves many decisions which influence the manufacture of goods. Managers must decide whether it is best to lease or buy a new machine. The advantages of leasing include tax benefits and the ability to expand or reduce the manufacturing operation easily to meet changing needs. Advantages of ownership include title to equipment and continued use for many years without making payments. Assets which have been paid off may be used as collateral for loans.

## QUALITY CONTROL

Another aspect of production control is the maintenance of quality of finished goods. The purpose of quality control is to assure that finished goods meet predefined limits. Finished goods should not fall appreciably above or below established design limits. Goods which exceed design limits are more expensive to produce. Those below fail in the marketplace and must be recalled or replaced. Figure 20-6 illustrates the quality range which one manufacturer has defined for a particular product.

There are a variety of statistical and mathematical tools used in quality control. These include probability studies, sampling techniques, and inspection procedures. The quality control department is responsible for meeting the standards.

*Figure 20-6*
*Quality control design limit*

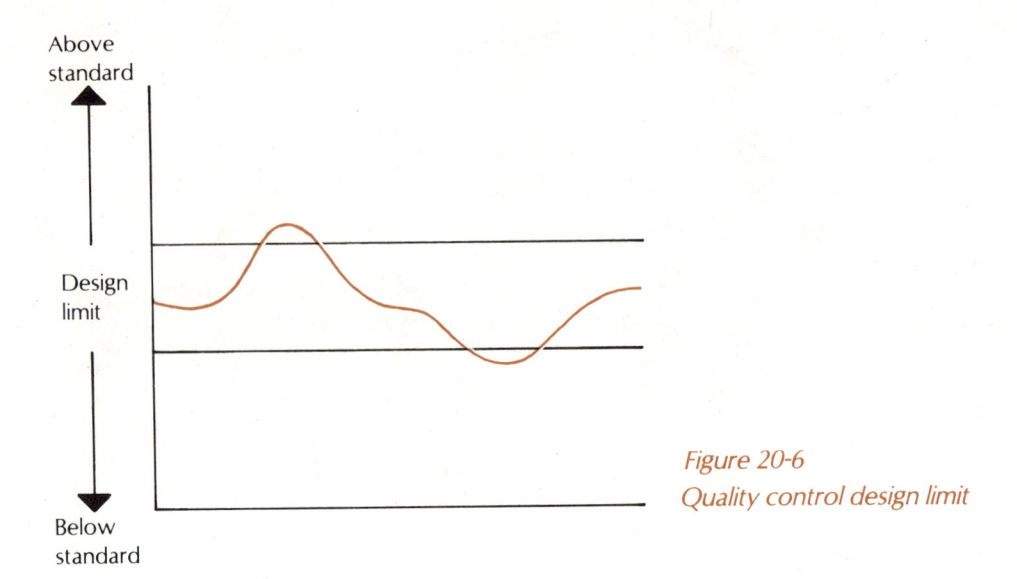

For example, during normal production operations, a quality control operator may sample every twenty-fifth unit produced. The unit is removed from the line and given extensive tests and measurements. As long as the tested unit falls within the established limits, the sampling and testing continues on every twenty-fifth unit produced.

If a sample fails to meet the test, corrective measures are instituted, and every fifth unit is removed from the line and tested. If faulty units still appear, more corrections are made, and all units are tested. After corrective measures show results, then sampling goes back to every fifth unit, and finally back to every twenty-fifth unit.

Quality control may be exercised on a variety of consumer product characteristics. These include taste, color, texture, or freshness. In manufactured items, quality control may be exercised over the durability, size, weight, strength, or performance of goods.

## INVENTORY CONTROL

Inventory control is an important part of the management of an enterprise. The purpose is to see that the proper level of inventory is maintained. Inventory control is concerned with the ordering and holding of raw materials, as well as the storage of finished goods. It sees that the right quality of goods are on hand for all phases of the production operation. Inventory control also assures that an adequate supply of finished goods is available to fill orders.

There are two major considerations involved in inventory control. One centers on the timing of orders, and the other on how much to order. Managers must decide how early goods should be ordered so that they will be available when needed, and how much should be ordered at a time. Inventory control answers both these questions by specifying how much and how often goods should be ordered.

In considering the quantity of goods to order, two elements must be evaluated: ordering costs and holding costs. These two factors work in opposition to each other (fig. 20-7).

1. *Ordering costs.* Each time a quantity of goods is ordered, an ordering cost is incurred. There is cost in specifying what is to be purchased, contacting suppliers, preparing orders, receiving and checking goods, and paying bills.

The larger the single order, the lower the ordering cost per unit of goods purchased. For example, it costs almost as much to order one typewriter as ten. Ideally, a manufacturer would order the largest amount of goods possible at one time. This reduces the order processing cost and obtains the best possible price from the suppliers. However, once the goods are placed in inventory, a holding cost is incurred.

2. *Holding costs.* Goods kept in a warehouse or storage area are subject to damage, spoilage, or pilferage, and they tie up capital. Inventories of goods become outdated because new products are brought on the market, changes are made in design, or changes occur in consumer buying patterns. Taxes are often assessed against goods held in inventory.

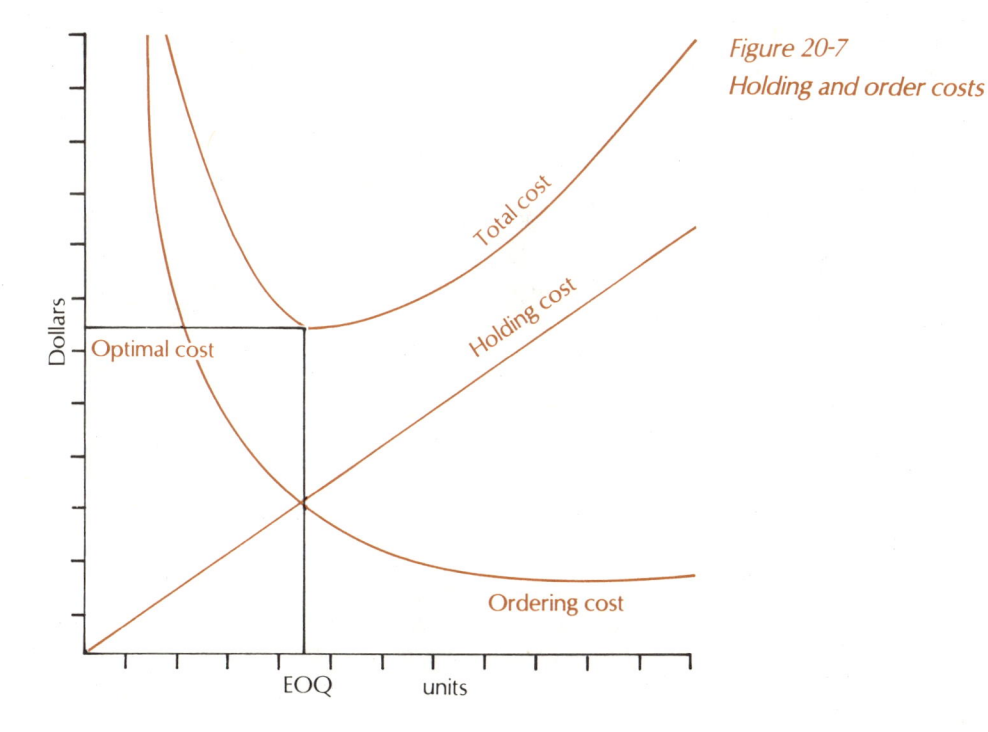

*Figure 20-7*
*Holding and order costs*

> **REAL WORLD**
>
> ## Camping It Up
>
> Some would think that Sheldon Coleman, 77, chairman of the board of Coleman Co., is eccentric. Instead of spending his time in well-lit, paneled corporate offices, he will likely be found shooting the rapids or driving a snowmobile or minibike. But there is method in his madness. Coleman believes that there is no reason the chairman of the board shouldn't test the company's products. Coleman's philosophy has helped manage the company's growth into one of the world's leading manufacturers of camping equipment.
>
> One of the advantages of being a principal shareholder in a large family-owned company is that you can retire and take it easy in your declining years. Coleman has firmly declared he will not work past his one hundredth birthday.
>
> Adapted from *Time*, 17 September 1979, p. 57.

Holding costs are kept to a minimum by purchasing the least amount of goods at one time. But this increases ordering costs. The manager in charge of inventory is faced with a major decision: What is the optimum amount of goods to order at one time?

## Optimum Size of Order

If the manager orders too large a supply, ordering costs are reduced but holding costs go up. Conversely, if the manager orders too small a supply, goods must be frequently reordered to avoid running out of stock. Holding costs are kept to a minimum, but ordering costs are increased because of the many small orders needed to keep goods in stock.

There are three common means of resolving the question of how much to order: trial and error, fixed order size, and economic order quantity (EOQ).

1. *Trial and error.* One means of establishing the size of order is simply by trial and error. A manager orders a given amount of goods, places it in stock, and observes the inventory. If he has underordered, he places a larger order next time. If he has overordered, he places a smaller order next time. The process is repeated with guesswork the principal means of determining how much to order. Trial and error is satisfactory if only a small amount of goods is involved.

2. *Fixed order.* Another means of establishing the size of an order is the fixed order. Under this arrangement, a fixed quantity of goods is ordered. The fixed order may be placed periodically, for example each month, or when stock falls to a low level.

Table 20-1 illustrates a fixed order buying pattern. A given amount of goods is ordered each month. The system is simple to administer, since a fixed quantity is purchased each cycle. This system works well where the consumption of the goods is predictable.

3. *Economic order quantity (EOQ).* A third method for determining the most appropriate quantity to order is the use of a mathematical formula. The economic order quantity (EOQ) method uses the following formula to find the optimum quantity to order to minimize costs:

$$EOQ = \sqrt{\frac{2\ A\ B}{C}}$$

Where,

2 = constant;
A = annual usage;
B = order cost per order;
C = carrying cost per unit.

For example, suppose a trucking firm wishes to determine the most economical quantity of spare parts to order to minimize their annual ordering cost. Assume they use one hundred of the parts per year, and it costs $50 in paperwork to process an order. Further assume a carrying cost of $10 per unit. This carrying cost is the expense to warehouse, inventory, and insure the parts in storage. The optimum size of the order can be determined by the formula:

A = annual usage = 100 units
B = order cost per order = $50;
C = carrying cost per unit = $10.

**Table 20-1  Fixed order schedule**

|  | Units Ordered | Units Sold |
|---|---|---|
| January | 100 | 100 |
| February | 100 | 105 |
| March | 100 | 110 |
| April | 100 | 100 |
| May | 100 | 95 |
| June | 100 | 90 |
| July | 100 | 80 |
| August | 100 | 70 |
| September | 100 | 90 |
| October | 100 | 110 |
| November | 100 | 120 |
| December | 100 | 130 |

The quality control department is responsible for making sure that the finished product meets pre-defined design limits.

Therefore:

$$EOQ = \sqrt{\frac{2 \times 100 \times 50}{10}} = \sqrt{\frac{10000}{10}} = \sqrt{1000} = 31.62.$$

The trucking firm should buy thirty-one or thirty-two spare parts in order to minimize the annual ordering cost.

## Optimum Time to Order

The second major question in inventory is when to place the order. Where the demand for a good is predictable and constant, the manager can order goods in advance without difficulty. Two problems, lead time and safety stock, are key considerations in placing orders.

1. *Lead time.* Lead time is the elapsed time between the placing of an order and the delivery of goods. This can vary from only a few hours to many months. Lead time must be considered when ordering goods.

CHAPTER TWENTY    THE NONFINANCIAL CONTROL PROCESS    469

"Engineering don't want to design it, and Production don't want to make it!"

Reprinted from *Industry Mart,* November-December 1977.

Figure 20-8 illustrates lead time and order points. The order point is shown as a broken line. The lead time is the period between placing the order and the arrival of the new shipment. The inventory level is shown along the left margin. As goods are consumed or removed from stock, the level falls. Reorders must be placed early enough to assure that the goods are delivered before the present supply is exhausted.

*2. Safety stock.* A safety stock is an excess of inventory to cover problems which might arise in delivery of the order. Safety stock is needed because usage is often

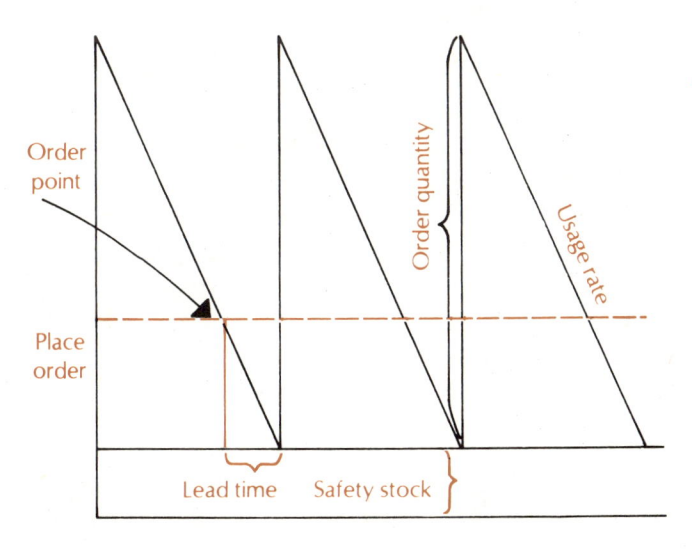

*Figure 20-8
Lead time and order points*

## POSTSCRIPT
# Productivity Is Key, Eastern Says
### By Ken Gepfert

Getting maximum performance out of employees—rather than picking the best flying machine—will determine which half of the nation's trunk airlines will survive during the 1980s, Eastern Airlines Chairman Frank Borman said Thursday.

"Productivity is what is going to make us or break us in the years ahead," the former astronaut told a meeting of the Los Angeles Society of Financial Analysts at the Biltmore.

In an interview later, Borman said he will emphasize subjects such as cost-effective management and "employee awareness" programs in his drive to assure Eastern is one of the survivors in the decade ahead.

He said such relatively mundane concerns—he compared them to "grind-it-out football"—would replace the more glamorous subjects which lately have captured much of the industry's attention: mergers and new-generation airplanes.

Borman told the analysts that Eastern had no plans "in the immediate future" to seek a merger partner in the wake of the Civil Aeronautics Board's rejection of the Miami-based airline's proposed consolidation with National Airlines.

He also predicted a "hiatus" in other

Reprinted from the *Los Angeles Times,* 7 December 1979.

---

unpredictable. The level of safety stock depends upon consumer buying patterns, changes in preferences, competing goods in the market, and other factors.

### Turnover of Inventory

Turnover is the rate at which goods in stock are replaced by new goods. High turnover rates are sometimes better than low, since goods do not remain in inventory for long periods of time. This reduces the incidence of spoilage and deterioration. High turnover rates mean goods are being sold promptly, and this enables the total inventory to be kept up-to-date as new models or designs come into use. Inventory is affected by interest rates and the cost of borrowing money. This also influences turnover.

## DISTRIBUTION CONTROL

Nonfinancial control is also concerned with the distribution system of an organization. Once goods and services are produced, they must be distributed to cus-

airlines' attempts to grow through consolidation, but he said he expected the trend to resume eventually—ultimately trimming the current eleven trunk carriers by one-half.

Purchases of new-technology aircraft won't be as important in the future, Borman added, because planes due for delivery in the 1980s won't produce as dramatic gains in technology and economy as previous innovations, such as the commercial jetliner and widebody aircraft.

For Eastern, he explained, equipment purchase decisions are no longer priority considerations because the airline already has chosen its primary two additions for the 1980s — the European Airbus consortium's A-300 and Boeing's new 757.

Instead, Borman said, the airline would continue to emphasize programs which encourage optimum performance by workers, such as profit sharing and earnings keyed to company profits.

In the interview, Borman said Eastern planned to announce another major "employee participation" program next year.

On other subjects, Borman told the analysts:

— He was puzzled why "anyone" would buy Boeing's new 767 when comparing the operating economics of an Airbus A-300. His remark was a not very veiled reference to Wednesday's decision by Trans World Airlines to buy ten 767s instead of a later Airbus model, the A-310.

— He is "ambivalent" about the rejected National merger because subsequent rapid rises in interest costs would have made a successful takeover much more expensive than anticipated.

— He was wrong when he argued against airline deregulation prior to its passage by Congress last year. "We're better off in the environment that we're in today," he said.

— He is confident Eastern can hold its own in the face of intense new competition on its lucrative flights to Florida.

---

tomers in an effective and economical manner. This requires close control over the channels of distribution and the transportation system.

Distribution channels are the pathways by which goods and services are moved from their place of manufacture to the ultimate consumer. Most goods can be classified as either consumer or industrial. Consumer goods are aimed at the end user, while industrial goods are usually resold or used in manufacturing. Consumer goods and industrial goods flow through different channels.

The manager is faced with many decisions regarding distribution channels. Some goods may be sold directly by the manufacturer to the ultimate consumer. With retail goods there are often intermediaries involved, such as wholesalers and retailers, who are in the distribution chain.

Industrial goods are usually distributed through agents, brokers, jobbers, or industrial distributors. Some of the factors which affect the selection of distribution channel are the kind of goods produced, their size, weight, bulk, and cost. Considerations such as perishability, installation, and maintenance also influence the choice of the distribution channel.

Once the distribution channel has been established, the manager must see that the finished goods move to their destination. This necessitates the use of various shipping methods, including rail, air, boat, pipeline, and truck. The management of distribution is often turned over to a specialized department called the traffic department.

While economic considerations play an important part in this distribution process, other factors are important too. The speed, condition of goods upon arrival, and volume of goods tied up in transit must be considered.

## PERSONNEL CONTROL

There are many noneconomic personnel considerations which influence an organization. Obviously questions of wages, bonuses, and pay differentials must be dealt with. However, the manager must also be concerned with such problems as low morale, personnel attitudes, and promotion practices. Here are some major noneconomic issues dealing with personnel control which must be addressed by managers.

1. *Long-term versus temporary labor.* A manager must decide whether it is best to employ long-term help or temporary labor. Economic considerations aside, this decision affects the attitudes, output, quality, and quantity of work produced by employees. Employees who know they are only temporary may not work as hard as those who feel they have long-term commitments to an organization.

2. *Human labor versus machine.* There are occasions when human labor can be replaced by a machine. Employees who feel their jobs are threatened by automation become resentful and may fail to give their maximum cooperation. Human labor is subject to many problems which are not common to machines. Machines do not go on strike, get sick, or take vacations. However, machines lack creativity and innovative ability. The manager must evaluate the total picture, including the questions of morale, attitudes, and quality of work when selecting one method of production over another.

## SUMMARY

Nonfinancial control deals with the qualitative and quantitative aspects of marketing, production, inventory, distribution, and personnel. New product development seeks to identify new products for manufacture to replace those which lose marketability.

Marketing control deals with the design of sales territories, product mix, and type of customers. Production control is concerned with the flow of goods and services through the production and manufacturing cycle. Routing, scheduling, dispatching, and expediting are important considerations in production control.

Quality control seeks to maintain a specified quality of finished goods. Several techniques are used in quality control, including statistics and sampling.

CHAPTER TWENTY   THE NONFINANCIAL CONTROL PROCESS

Inventory control must balance ordering costs with holding costs. It seeks to define the optimum size of order and the optimum time to order. The economic order quantity (EOQ) is a convenient formula for figuring the most appropriate quantity to order.

Distribution control is concerned with bringing goods and services from the producer to the ultimate consumer. Personnel control deals with problems of morale, personnel attitudes, and promotional practices.

## REVIEW QUESTIONS

1. What is the basic object of new product development?
2. What is the function of market control?
3. List four major elements in production control.
4. What is the function of quality control?
5. Why do ordering costs decrease as larger orders are placed, while holding costs increase?
6. What are the weaknesses in the trial and error method of ordering?
7. Describe the fixed order method of ordering.
8. Why must lead time be considered when placing an order?
9. What is the purpose of safety stock?
10. What problems does temporary labor present in comparison with long-term labor?
11. What role do R & D efforts play in an organization?
12. What problems are presented when human labor is replaced by machines?

## KEY TERMS

Operations management   456
Production control   456
Inventory control   456
Quality control   456
Market control   458
Routing   462
Scheduling   462

Dispatching   462
Expediting   462
Ordering cost   465
Holding cost   465
Lead time   468
Safety stock   469

# Case Incident

United Computer installs and maintains 24-hour bank teller terminals. These devices are leased to various banks in the metropolitan area on a contract arrangement. Since they are sensitive electronic devices, recently a question has arisen as to the best way to control the maintenance and servicing of these terminals. Within the service department, two distinctly different policies have been proposed.

Louis D'Leon, an experienced manager in the department, supports a policy of scheduled preventative maintenance. According to D'Leon, a service representative should be dispatched to each bank to routinely test each terminal every two weeks. Prior experience has shown that service problems and breakdowns rarely occur with a frequency any greater than about once a month. The cost of this additional service and maintenance would be included in the lease contract with the banks.

Another manager in the department, Rita Gibson, believes that an individual per-call maintenance system should be instituted. Gibson thinks United should dispatch maintenance representatives to service the equipment only when they receive word of a specific breakdown from one of their subscribing banks. She feels that this is the best solution to their problem because service problems have been infrequent and limited to relatively minor problems. She does not think that the performance of the bank teller terminals warrants the cost of a complete two-week maintenance schedule.

United is weighing both positions very carefully in order to determine what controls should be instituted in its terminal maintenance department. The two most important factors in their decision will be keeping the overall cost of the maintenance program as low as possible, and yet providing a service program that will satisfy the needs of their customers. If they decide on the wrong maintenance program, it will cost them additional money and eat into their corporate profits. If they do not provide adequate service for their customers, they may lose business to competitors.

## PROBLEMS

1. What are the advantages and limitations of the approach suggested by D'Leon?
2. What are the advantages and limitations of Gibson's approach?
3. What kind of quality control technique should be instituted by United to assure that terminals will be maintained properly?

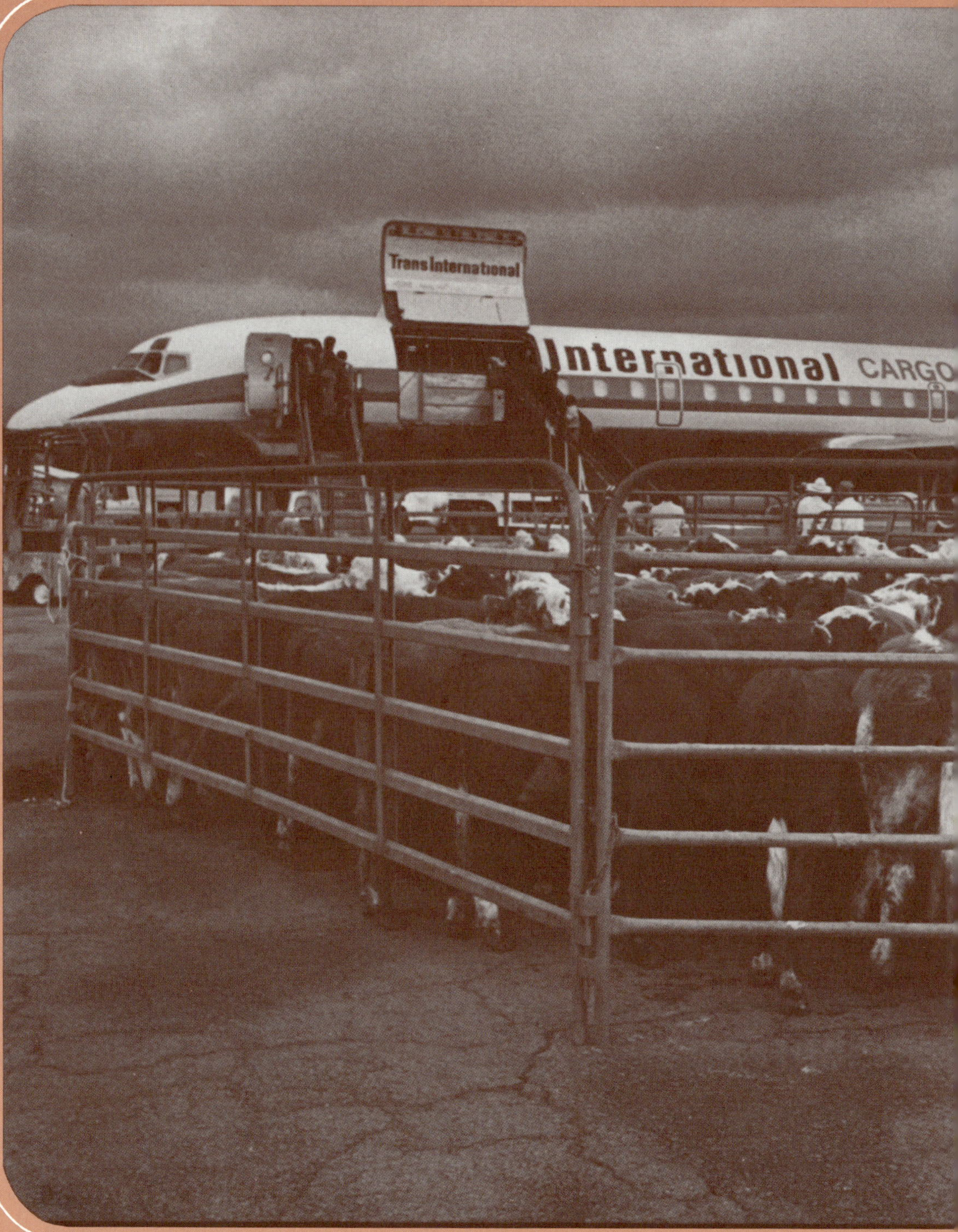
Trans International
International CARGO

# 21

# Controlling the Multinational Corporation

**LEARNING OBJECTIVES**

After studying this chapter, you should be able to:

1. Define key terms related to the multinational corporation.
2. Summarize the growth and interdependency of world trade.
3. List reasons favoring world trade.
4. List some economic associations.
5. List the advantages of multinational corporations.
6. List some limitations of multinational corporations.
7. Describe some problems and risks faced by multinational corporations.
8. Describe the organization and structure of multinational corporations.
9. Describe major management considerations dealing with multinational corporations.
10. Discuss the problem of staffing multinational corporations.

The growth of the multinational corporation (MNC) has had a major impact on management. This chapter explores management's role in the multinational corporation. During the past several decades, the world has seen an increase in the number of corporations which have global marketing, production, distribution, and management philosophies.

This chapter defines basic terms and the factors which have led to the growth of multinational corporations. The chapter describes the interdependency of worldwide businesses, common markets, and joint ventures. The problems and risks of multinational corporations are presented, together with a review of multinational corporation structure, planning, control, and staffing.

## KEY TERMS

New terminology has evolved in the wake of a growing number of organizations engaged in worldwide operations. International joint ventures, common markets, and consortiums are relatively new terms in the manager's vocabulary. Let us define some key terms.

—*Multinational corporation (MNC).* A multinational corporation is a business enterprise with a global orientation. The multinational corporation is usually characterized by sales of fifteen to twenty percent in six or more countries. Some authorities define multinational corporations as having over twenty percent of their ownership in foreign hands. The term *multinational corporation* is used here synonymously with *multinational enterprise* (MNE).

—*International corporation.* An international corporation is one in which the parent company, located in one country, conducts a substantial portion of its business in other countries. It differs from the multinational corporation in that its ownership and management are concentrated in one country.

—*Local corporation.* A local corporation is one in which the major management, ownership, and marketing efforts are directed toward a single country. A local corporation may conduct a limited amount of sales and distribution efforts in one or more other countries.

—*Joint venture.* A joint venture is a union of business organizations or government agencies from several different countries engaged in a common business enterprise. Joint ventures, sometimes called consortiums, are used to undertake major construction or building projects such as oil drilling and exploration operations where large amounts of capital, human resources, or research and development efforts are required. Generally this is beyond the ability of a single business organization or country.

—*Common market.* A common market is an economic business and trading community. Common markets are formed from countries which are located in a common region and where trade barriers and restrictions have been reduced

CHAPTER TWENTY-ONE   CONTROLLING THE MULTINATIONAL CORPORATION    479

or eliminated. Countries participating in a common market allow the free flow of labor, capital, goods, or raw materials between countries. Countries outside the common market face different tariff and trade regulations than those within the market.

## GROWTH AND INTERDEPENDENCY OF WORLD TRADE

During the last several decades there has been a steady and continuing increase in world trade. Figure 21-1 illustrates the growth of world imports and exports from 1960 to 1977. Worldwide exports increased from $128 billion in 1960 to $1125 billion in 1977. Imports of goods increased from $136 billion in 1960 to $1155 billion in 1977. This is the result of a growing interdependence among nations in their worldwide demand for goods and marketing.

Figure 21-2 illustrates the annual percentage change in real Gross National Product (GNP) of various nations. The growing volume of imports and exports is a major impetus behind the expansion of the GNP of the world's leading industrial nations.

## FACTORS FAVORING WORLD TRADE

There are many reasons a nation or business organization engages in world trade. These have many implications for managers, who must plan and direct the sales and marketing activities of large multinational organizations.

Fundamentally, a nation or business offers its goods and services for sale to

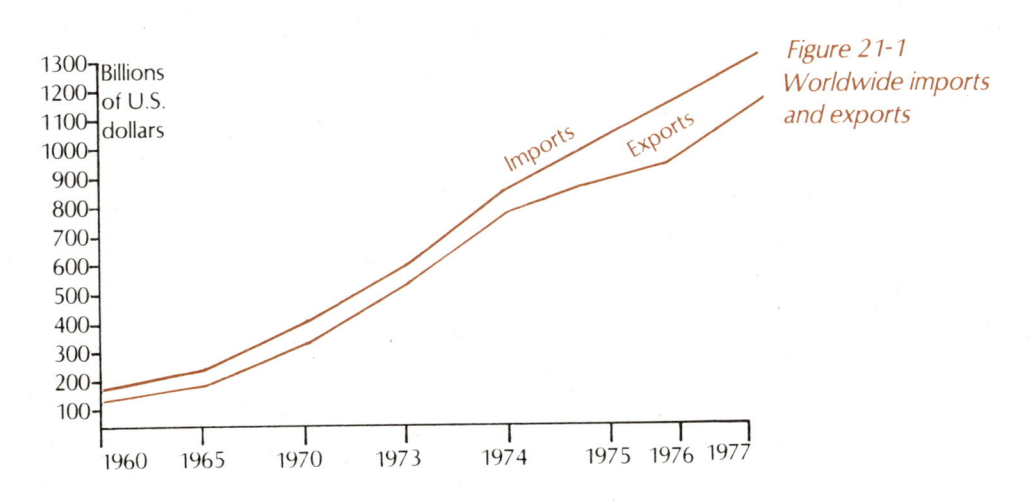

*Figure 21-1 Worldwide imports and exports*

Adapted from *U.S. Statistical Abstract*, 1979 (Washington, D.C.: Government Printing Office, 1979), p. 883.

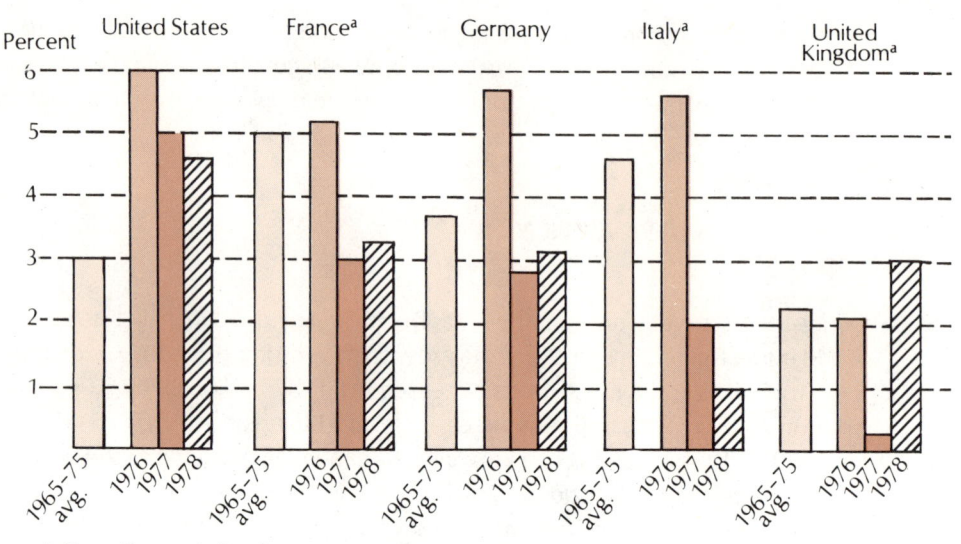

[Figure: Bar chart showing Trends in real GNP (annual percent change) for United States, France(a), Germany, Italy(a), and United Kingdom(a), with bars for 1965-75 avg., 1976, 1977, and 1978.]

a. Gross Domestic Product

Reprinted from the Conference Board, *Road Maps of Industry*, no. 1825, February 1978.

Figure 21-2 Trends in real GNP (annual percent change)

another because it possesses certain advantages. The industry in one country may maintain an absolute advantage in the production of certain goods. Its particular climate, geographic location, or availability of raw materials may make it the only country capable of producing a given good. Thus it is successful at exporting because there is no competition.

A nation may also engage successfully in world commerce because it possesses a relative advantage over other countries. That is, its labor cost, technical skills, climate, or geography place it in a relatively advantageous position over others. Thus the lower labor cost or higher technology available in a country enables it to sell successfully to others.

Low-cost labor in an underdeveloped country means that a business firm can produce labor intensive goods more cheaply than in a country with high labor costs. Terrain, climate, factories, education of the labor force, and raw materials are some of the important factors which favor one nation over another.

## ECONOMIC ASSOCIATIONS

Prior to World War II, there were relatively few economic associations. Economic, trade, and tariff barriers existed between countries of the world. This inhibited the free exchange of labor, goods, and capital between countries. After World War II, many countries, particularly in Europe, became convinced that the elimination of trade barriers and joining into trade alliances were in their best interests. This evolved into the formation of common markets whose goals were economic prosperity and cooperation among members. Following are some of the major economic associations which have led to cooperation between nations, higher living standards, and greater prosperity.

## European Economic Community (EEC)

In 1957, a group of six countries met and drafted the Treaty of Rome, which founded the European Economic Community, or *Common Market.* Initially Belgium, France, Germany, Italy, Luxembourg, and the Netherlands were in the association. Beginning in 1973, Denmark, Ireland, and Great Britain became partners. The EEC is a union of trading nations which has worked toward the gradual elimination of trade barriers, the establishment of a common external tariff, and the coordination of monetary, fiscal, and agricultural policies. The nations in the common market allow a free movement of services, labor, capital, and business enterprises within the community.

## European Free Trade Association (EFTA)

Another trade association, European Free Trade Association, was formed in Europe in 1959. This consisted of Austria, Finland, Iceland, Norway, Portugal,

---

### REAL WORLD
# A Made-in America Japanese Car

Everyone is aware of the success that Japanese management has had in producing automobiles in the Orient and shipping them to the United States and other countries.

But for Kiyoshi Kawashima, president of Honda of Japan, there is a new twist. Because of pressure from the American government and threats of import duties, Kawashima has decided to turn the tables and open an assembly plant to produce Hondas in the United States. His firm will spend over $200 million to build a factory near Columbus, Ohio, which will employ over two thousand workers. The plant will turn out more than ten thousand automobiles using American labor but Japanese design. Kawashima believes in a give and take philosophy. Until recently, United States buyers paid for Japanese expertise and products. Now Honda reciprocates by buying American labor.

Adapted from *Time*, 28 January 1980, p. 64.

Sweden, Switzerland, and, prior to 1973, Denmark and the United Kingdom. This group also worked toward promotion of free trade and economic cooperation through the elimination of tariffs and quotas among themselves. However, they did not establish a common external tariff.

## Other Economic Associations

There are two other common market associations which have an impact on worldwide management of organizations. The Central American Common Market (CACM) includes Costa Rica, El Salvador, Guatemala, Honduras, and Nicaragua. In the Latin American Free Trade Association (LAFTA) are Argentina, Bolivia, Brazil, Chile, Colombia, Ecuador, Mexico, Paraguay, Peru, Uruguay, and Venezuela.

## GROWTH OF MULTINATIONAL CORPORATIONS AND JOINT VENTURES

Just as nations have moved into large associations to stimulate trade, so have business organizations. The multinational corporation resulted from attempts by business organizations to build a worldwide sales, production, and management base. Early business firms engaged in purely local trade. These firms were owned by shareholders in one country and generally sold goods in the same country. Their management philosophy and orientation was only nationwide.

However, as worldwide trade expanded, and as trade associations which allowed free access to markets in other countries were formed, many business firms expanded their operations. This heralded the growth of the large international business firms. International business firms are based in a home country, and focus major sales efforts there. However, sales and production efforts are also aimed at other nations. While ownership may still remain in the home country, these international firms seek to do worldwide business from their home base. These firms are often characterized by a management philosophy which is colored largely by the home country.

As world trade expanded, many companies changed their operations to reflect a truly international character. These firms, often emerging from large international organizations, took on a global base of operations. The modern multinational corporation is characterized by a worldwide management philosophy. A substantial share of its stock is held by nationals of many countries, and its marketing and distribution efforts are based upon worldwide strategies. (See figure 21-3.)

The list of multinational corporations includes General Electric, Unilever, Royal Dutch/Shell Group, and other large corporations. Table 21-1 lists some of the world's largest industrial companies. These firms are characterized by man-

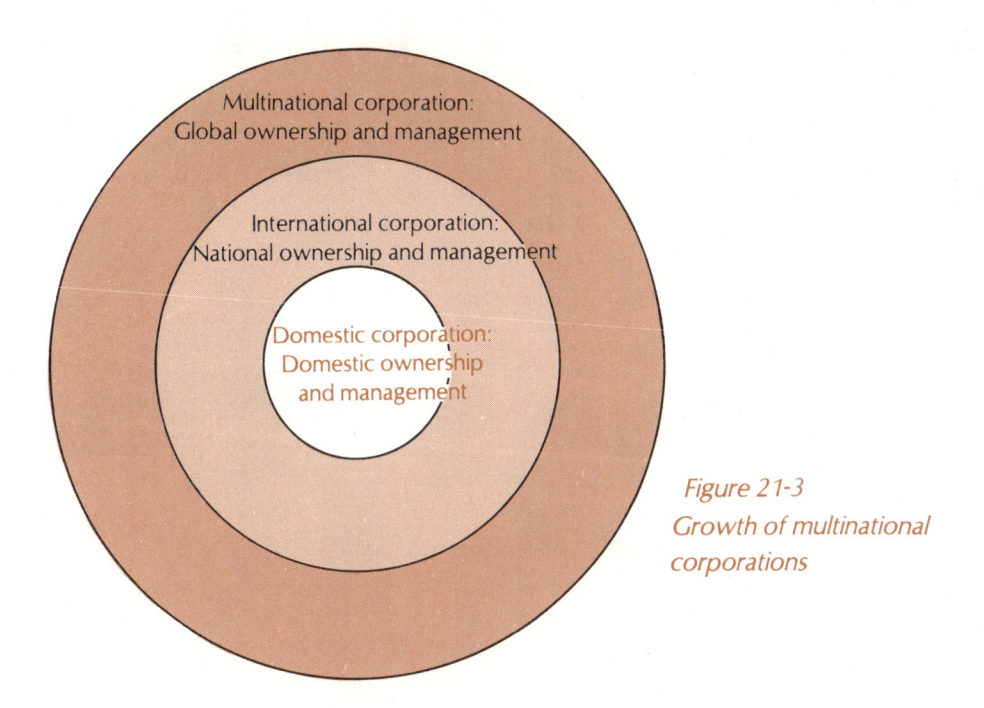

CHAPTER TWENTY-ONE    CONTROLLING THE MULTINATIONAL CORPORATION    483

Multinational corporation:
Global ownership and management

International corporation:
National ownership and management

Domestic corporation:
Domestic ownership
and management

*Figure 21-3
Growth of multinational corporations*

agement philosophies which are influenced by many nations. While their home country may serve as international headquarters, ownership of stock may be worldwide, as is their management orientation.

## Advantages of Multinational Corporations

Many benefits accrue to an organization to operate on a global base.

1. *Profit.* Profit is a major reason for an organization becoming global in operation. Much money is made where organizations take advantage of the benefits offered by various countries.

2. *Expanded market.* Greater sales result where a firm focuses on a global marketing base. Worldwide orientation means that goods can be sold successfully to many markets.

3. *Raw materials.* Multinational corporations have available a larger supply of raw materials. Since these organizations often base production operations in many nations of the world, they can take advantage of availability of raw materials in many countries.

4. *Financial resources.* Greater capital is available to multinational corporations, since they can draw upon the financial resources of many nations. Stockholders from many countries can participate in ownership, thus giving greater economic power to the multinational corporation.

Table 21-1 The twenty-five largest industrial companies in the world (ranked by sales)

| Rank 1978 | Company | Headquarters | Sales ($000) | Net Income ($000) |
|---|---|---|---|---|
| 1 | General Motors | Detroit | 63,221,100 | 3,508,000 |
| 2 | Exxon | New York | 60,334,527 | 2,763,000 |
| 3 | Royal Dutch/Shell Group | London/The Hague | 44,044,534 | 2,084,653 |
| 4 | Ford Motor | Dearborn, Mich. | 42,784,100 | 1,588,900 |
| 5 | Mobil | New York | 34,763,045 | 1,125,638 |
| 6 | Texaco | Harrison, N.Y. | 28,607,521 | 852,461 |
| 7 | British Petroleum | London | 27,407,620 | 853,057 |
| 8 | Standard Oil of California | San Francisco | 23,232,413 | 1,105,881 |
| 9 | National Iranian Oil | Tehran | 22,789,650 | 15,178,157 |
| 10 | International Business Machines | Armonk, N.Y. | 21,076,089 | 3,110,5 68 |
| 11 | General Electric | Fairfield, Conn. | 19,653,800 | 1,229,700 |
| 12 | Unilever | London/Rotterdam | 18,893,176 | 531,337 |
| 13 | Gulf Oil | Pittsburgh | 18,069,000 | 791,000 |
| 14 | Chrysler | Highland Park, Mich. | 16,340,700 | (204,600) |
| 15 | International Tel. & Tel. | New York | 15,261,178 | 661,807 |
| 16 | Phillips' Gloeilampen-fabrieken | Eindhoven (Netherlands) | 15,121,166 | 327,117 |
| 17 | Standard Oil (Ind.) | Chicago | 14,961,489 | 1,076,412 |
| 18 | Siemens | Munich | 13,864,726 | 322,021 |
| 19 | Volkswagenwerk | Wolfsburg (Germany) | 13,332,059 | 275,671 |
| 20 | Toyota Motor | Toyota City (Japan) | 12,768,821 | 529,933 |
| 21 | Renault | Paris | 12,715,866 | 2,222 |
| 22 | ENI | Rome | 12,565,727 | (367,892) |
| 23 | Francaise des Petroles | Paris | 12,509,942 | 60,305 |
| 24 | Atlantic Richfield | Los Angeles | 12,298,403 | 804,325 |
| 25 | Daimler-Benz | Stuttgart | 12,090,806 | 295,054 |

Reprinted from the August 13 issue of *Fortune* Magazine, p. 208; © 1979 Time Inc.

CHAPTER TWENTY-ONE    CONTROLLING THE MULTINATIONAL CORPORATION        485

5. *Lower labor cost.* Hourly labor costs are not the same worldwide. Multinational corporations can concentrate labor intensive manufacturing operations in those countries with the lowest labor cost.

6. *Higher productivity.* Output per man hour varies in different parts of the world. Some labor forces are more skilled and trained than others, hence they can produce more per hour. Multinational corporations can take advantage of this fact and place manufacturing operations in countries which have labor forces with high productivity. Figure 21-4 shows the annual average rate of change in productivity in manufacturing for various nations.

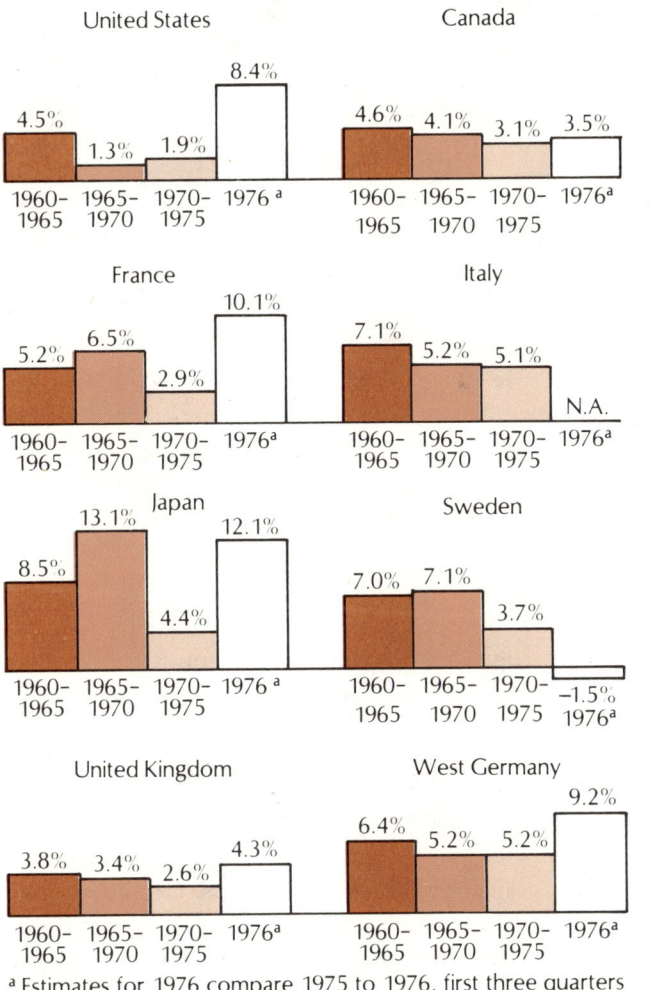

*Figure 21-4*
*Trends in productivity in manufacturing (average annual rate of change)*

United States
- 1960–1965: 4.5%
- 1965–1970: 1.3%
- 1970–1975: 1.9%
- 1976[a]: 8.4%

Canada
- 1960–1965: 4.6%
- 1965–1970: 4.1%
- 1970–1975: 3.1%
- 1976[a]: 3.5%

France
- 1960–1965: 5.2%
- 1965–1970: 6.5%
- 1970–1975: 2.9%
- 1976[a]: 10.1%

Italy
- 1960–1965: 7.1%
- 1965–1970: 5.2%
- 1970–1975: 5.1%
- 1976[a]: N.A.

Japan
- 1960–1965: 8.5%
- 1965–1970: 13.1%
- 1970–1975: 4.4%
- 1976[a]: 12.1%

Sweden
- 1960–1965: 7.0%
- 1965–1970: 7.1%
- 1970–1975: 3.7%
- 1976[a]: −1.5%

United Kingdom
- 1960–1965: 3.8%
- 1965–1970: 3.4%
- 1970–1975: 2.6%
- 1976[a]: 4.3%

West Germany
- 1960–1965: 6.4%
- 1965–1970: 5.2%
- 1970–1975: 5.2%
- 1976[a]: 9.2%

[a] Estimates for 1976 compare 1975 to 1976, first three quarters for the United States and first halfs for other countries.

Reprinted from the *International Economic Report of the President*, January 1977, p. 103.

*"O.K. Whose turn is it to set the moral tone?"*

Reprinted from the *New Yorker,* 25 July 1977.

7. *Larger operating units.* Multinational corporations enable organizations to structure larger operating units. Thus a firm is able to assemble greater amounts of personnel, capital, and manufacturing operations into single units. Multinational corporations can take on research and development projects, and use talented people in many countries, which cannot be done with a smaller operation.

8. *Advantages to host countries.* Many nations foster multinational corporations because of a variety of advantages. Multinational corporations provide a greater tax base and more revenue. Some bring in defense industries or reduce the local unemployment rate.

## Limitations of Multinational Corporations

Multinational corporation operations are not without problems to their owners or their host countries. Following are some of their limitations.

1. *Taxation.* Multinational corporations may face additional taxation because they may pay taxes for operations in both the home country and abroad. Profit from multinational corporation operations may be heavily taxed when brought home.

2. *Governmental restrictions.* Multinational corporations may face governmental restrictions which limit the movement of capital to operations outside the home country. The flow of cash, capital, and foreign investment is very limited in some countries.

3. *Disadvantage to host countries.* The operation of a multinational corporation within a host country may present problems. Some multinational corporations

may transfer manufacturing operations from one country to another, thus creating local unemployment. A multinational corporation may attempt to influence government policy in the host country. Others may disturb internal policies or government programs by the influx of money or ability to avoid local rules and regulations.

## Problems and Risks Faced by Multinational Corporations

While there is an undeniable growth of multinational corporations, there are many problems and risks faced by worldwide operations. Managers must be aware of the following problems if they are to manage multinational corporations successfully.

1. *Legal complications.* Businesses conducted in foreign countries face many local problems. These range from discriminatory rules and regulations to red tape and excessive restrictions on obtaining permits, licenses, and franchises.

2. *Unfair competition.* Some multinational corporations find that they are unable to compete with local firms because of different rules and regulations which apply to them. Special permits or licenses may be granted to local firms, but not to multinational corporations. In other instances, substantial government subsidies to local firms may make it hard for a multinational corporation to compete. Figure 21-5 lists some major industries and the amount of government control in various countries.

3. *Political problems.* Multinational corporations often face political problems in the host country. These range from conflicts with political leaders to oppressive rules and regulations. The continuing threat of political instability, changing political leaders, and internal warfare create difficulties and dangers.

4. *Expropriation of assets.* One of the major threats faced by multinational corporations is the possible takeover of its assets by a host country. In the past, political upheavals and changes in governmental policies have resulted in the nationalization of private property, factories, and other assets. In some cases these have been expropriated with the payment of cash for reinvestment. In other instances, multinational corporations have lost their assets without any repayment. The events in Cuba and recent actions in South Africa illustrate the problem.

5. *Monetary and economic problems.* Differences in currency, exchange rates, and financing make it difficult for multinational corporations to operate in some countries. High interest rates, out-of-control inflation, and restrictions on removal of hard currency limit management alternatives in many countries.

6. *Language difficulties.* Language barriers often create problems in the operation of some multinational corporations in foreign countries. Some nations have

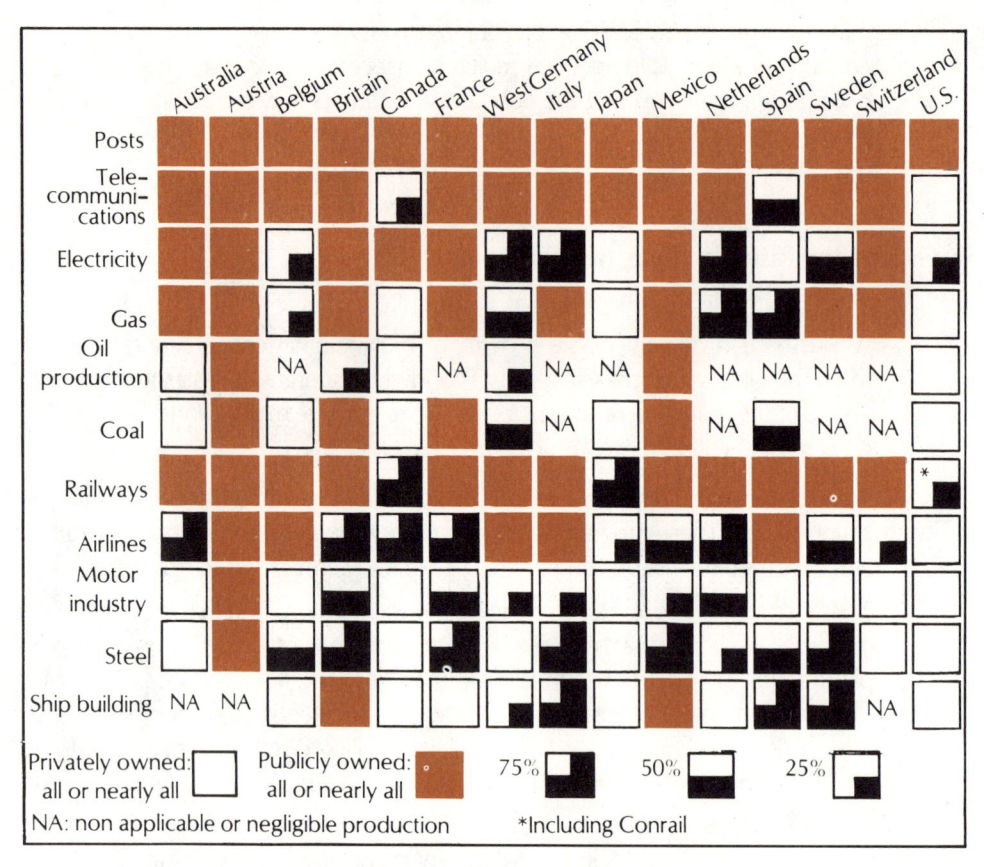

Reprinted from the *Los Angeles Times*, 1 November 1979. Original source: *The (London) Economist*, 30 December 1978.

*Figure 21-5   Government control of industry*

several official languages, and many unofficial ones. Communication between the multinational corporation and the public or local personnel is difficult.

7. *Cultural differences.* Cultural values and ethics vary widely between countries. For example, bribery or payment of money under the table is an accepted way of doing business in some countries, but may violate the laws of the home country. If the multinational corporation fails to buy off local officials, licenses and permits become very hard to obtain.

8. *Time.* In many countries time is valued highly and appointments are kept promptly. In others, appointments may be missed, long delays may be experienced in receipt of goods, or meetings may run on interminably. Religious observances, holidays, dietary laws, or other restrictions often influence the operation of a multinational corporation in a host country.

## ORGANIZING AND STRUCTURING THE MULTINATIONAL CORPORATION

A variety of structures have evolved for the operation of multinational corporations. These range from organizations built around products or foreign geography to functional or other lines. Most organizations which have large multinational corporations have evolved through several phases of growth and development. (See figure 21-6.)

A small local organization may begin by selling on a limited basis to foreign countries. It may not have production facilities or sales offices abroad. As sales volume increases, a foreign sales manager may be appointed to work alongside the domestic sales manager in the home office.

As sales continue to increase, the sales department may be split into two distinct units, one specializing in foreign sales and the other domestic. Each department has its own manager. As these units grow, they are expanded into full operating divisions. In these instances division managers head each unit and have full autonomy over its operations.

If sales and production operations expand in foreign markets, the organization flourishes as a global operation. It uses locally owned subsidiaries or affiliates operated autonomously, with local financing and capital. However, planning and decision making for the subsidiaries are part of a global strategy for the entire organization.

*Language barriers often create problems for multinational corporations.*

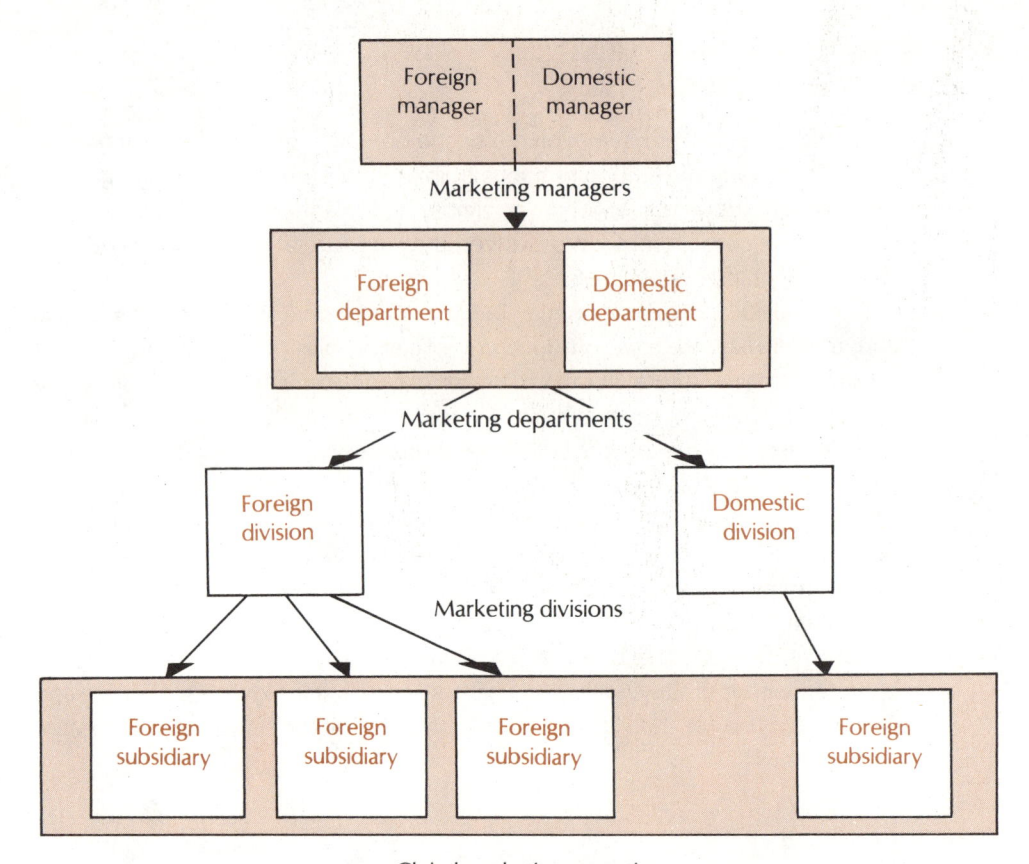

*Figure 21-6 Evolution of foreign marketing operations*

The structure of the operating units may vary depending upon the organization, products sold, sales volume, and kinds of goods manufactured. Two common structures are found in multinational corporations: the geographic and the functional organization.

1. *Geographic organization.* In the geographic organization, responsibility is defined along geographic lines (fig. 21-7). In this situation, a vice president is assigned to handle a given geographic territory. Under the vice president are various managers or division heads, including marketing, personnel, production, and finance. This form of structure stresses geographic lines and makes the organization more responsive to local needs and differences.

2. *Functional organization.* Another form of multinational corporation structure is built around the classical functions (fig. 21-8). In this instance, a vice president is placed in charge of each major function. In turn, the vice president may have

CHAPTER TWENTY-ONE    CONTROLLING THE MULTINATIONAL CORPORATION                491

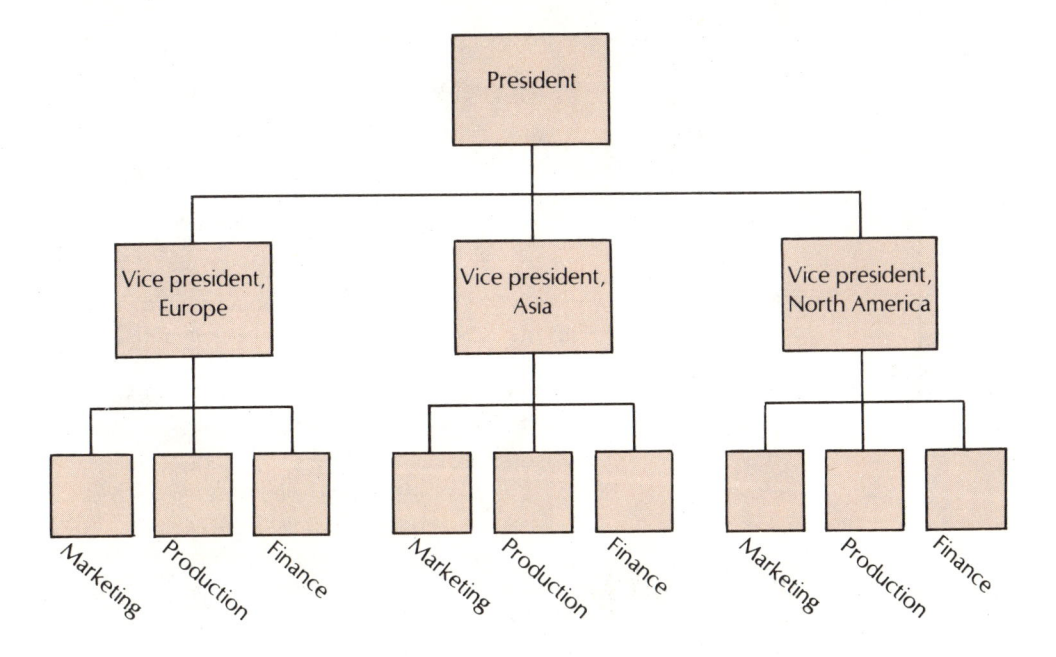

*Figure 21-7 Geographic organization*

managers who are responsible for various geographic territories. The advantage of this form of organization is its stress on functional lines, which ties together the multinational corporation's common efforts in marketing, production, distribution, and finance.

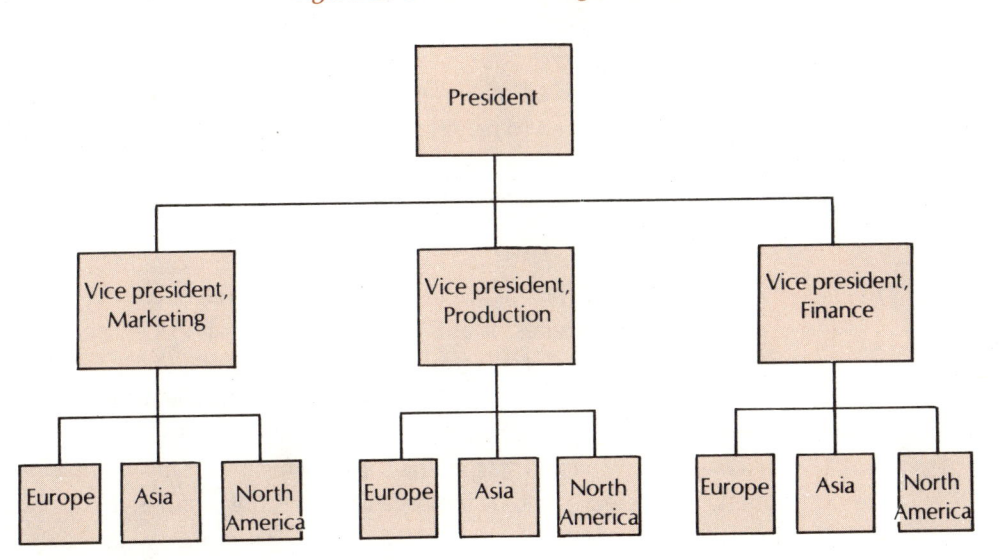

*Figure 21-8 Functional organization*

> **REAL WORLD**
>
> # Wickes Corporation's Retailing Triumph in Europe
>
> Two Wickes Corporation executives, Chairman Daniel FitzGerald and President E. L. McNeely, are not ordinary managers. They had heard the stories about the inability of American retailers to sell successfully to the European market. But they weren't convinced. Under their guidance, Wickes Corporation opened a series of forty-five home improvement centers all over Europe. Others in the industry were sure they would fail, because Europeans are not do-it-yourself remodelers. In the early 1970s, using the supermarket approach, the firm opened stores in England, Holland, and West Germany. For a while it looked like their critics were right. Wickes lost a lot of money in the early years. But then the idea caught hold. Soon Europeans began streaming into these one-stop hardware-lumber stores. In 1978 the European division of Wickes Corporation generated a little under $2 billion of profit, while it accounted for only one-twentieth of the firm's sales.
>
> Adapted from *Fortune,* 13 August 1979, p. 178.

## MANAGING AND CONTROLLING THE MULTINATIONAL CORPORATION

The widespread operation and crossing of national boundaries makes the control and management of multinational corporations a complex and difficult task. Special consideration must be given to national differences, languages, local staffing problems, and communications. Here are some of the major management considerations which must be dealt with in controlling the multinational corporation.

1. *Degree of control.* Management must decide on the degree of control to exercise over each of its subsidiaries or affiliates. A true multinational corporation has a global orientation and is not affected by the influences of a single country. Decisions tend to be decentralized and reflect the local needs of the organization. However, too much decentralization and diffusion of control can lead to a lack of overall direction. Too much control from the top may mean that local problems are not properly addressed, and thus the organization is not responsive to local markets, personnel, and needs.

2. *Communication.* Another major consideration is the communications network necessary for the successful operation of the multinational corporation. Some multinational corporations employ hundreds of thousands of people around the world, with thousands of managers, division heads, and supervisors. Communication can be a major problem. Physical distances and differences in language, time zones, and communication facilities must be overcome. Without sound communication, the multinational corporation cannot function. With a good communications network, the multinational corporation has a strong marketing and distribution advantage over other organizations.

3. *Planning.* Multinational corporation planning must be from a global orientation. Local problems and differences of many diverse operating units must be considered. This is difficult to do where many different interests and people are involved. Planning must take into consideration the long- and short-range plans of many subsidiaries, and tie them together into a unified structure. Deadlines for budgets, submission of plans, and other administrative functions must be coordinated worldwide.

## STAFFING MULTINATIONAL CORPORATIONS

The human resources of the multinational corporation deserve special consideration. Staffing a worldwide organization involves analysis of differences in pay rates, living costs, attitudes, and promotion and hiring policies. Following are some of the major problems which must be addressed when dealing with personnel.

1. *Attitudes of manager.* Managers of multinational corporations must exhibit a global view and consider the total organization rather than local or home country problems alone. This is difficult for some managers. Some may take on a local orientation with little regard for the global character of their decisions. Other managers may be regionally oriented and consider only problems which are related to their regions.

2. *Hiring local personnel.* A decision must be made regarding the number of locals to be hired. There are many factors which affect this decision. Local pay rates are often lower, thus managers can be hired in the host country at low cost. But local managers may also be limited in their managerial training and skills.

There may be government restrictions on the hiring of nationals from other countries. The education, skills, and training of local workers in some countries may be very low. Thus it may require extensive training to prepare them for employment in the multinational corporation. If too many nationals are hired with respect to the number of locals, problems of jealousy and conflict may arise. Locals may resent being placed in low paid positions, while the higher paid jobs go to foreign nationals.

**POSTSCRIPT**

# Government in Industry— No Small Deal

## By Murray Seeger

BRUSSELS, Belgium — Reeling under the blows of spiraling inflation, halting growth, and rising unemployment, governments throughout the industrial world are moving more directly into daily business life.

Auto workers in Britain, gasoline station attendants in Italy, bank tellers in Germany, and potash miners in France — all work, in one way or another, for the government.

In some places state-owned or state-controlled concerns are generally well-run and making money. The Renault auto works in France is an example.

Others, like the British Steel Corp., are old, inefficient, and losing money.

Some businesses, among them Swedish shipbuilding and Norwegian oil, have been nationalized fairly recently. Others, like the tobacco and match monopoly in France, date back to another century. And some were spawned by World War II or the Great Depression of the 1930s, including Volkswagen of Germany and the giant Italian holding company, IRI.

Even the United States, the bastion of capitalism, has dipped a toe in what can only be called socialism, taking over part of the railroad industry, subsidizing broadcasters, and offering loans or loan guarantees to certain industries.

Only Britain and Canada, under recently elected conservative governments, are taking steps to reduce government ownership of business.

Although policies and techniques vary from one country to another, there are some general reasons for government intervention in the economy. Among them:

*Jobs.* Faced with the choice of seeing a major employer fail or propping it up with loans or acquisition, governments will often try to save jobs. They argue that it is better and cheaper to subsidize an uneconomic job than to pay a dole.

*Resources.* Many countries have found that controlling supplies of oil and other natural resources by means of state-owned or state-directed companies is the best means of monitoring the big multinational firms.

*Investment.* In smaller countries, where private investors are cautious, the government is often the only agency willing to invest in new industry or expanding old industry.

*Security.* Certain industries are consid-

Reprinted from the *Los Angeles Times*, 1 November 1979.

ered so vital to a country's national security—ship and aircraft construction are examples—that some governments will prop them up indefinitely.

*Policy.* Many governments are dominated by socialists who believe it to be essential that the state operate certain services and businesses, including banking, in order to control the private sector.

The crucial question is: Do state-owned corporations receive special benefits from their governments that give them an unfair advantage over privately owned corporations?

More specifically, since national companies do not have to make profits, can they cut prices unfairly? Can they get cheap financing through their governments or state-owned banks that other firms cannot get? Do the national companies get exclusive use of domestic markets as a base for overseas expansion? Do governments intervene to help their firms in foreign markets? Can these firms hold down wages with government help? Do the companies make other uneconomic decisions they would not dare make if they had to answer to private stockholders?

Some of these questions have already been asked by competitors of British Steel, which was accused in 1977 of underselling more efficient Japanese steelmakers in Western markets.

The questions might also be asked by American auto makers now that Renault has purchased a substantial portion of the American Motors Corp. and will make some of its cars in Racine, Wis.

And they could be asked of Volkswagen, whose major stockholders are the taxpayers of West Germany. Volkswagen was the first foreign carmaker to open an assembly plant in the United States.

In the most international business of all, banking, three of the five largest banks outside the United States—National Credit Agricole, Paris National Bank and Credit Lyonnais, all of France—are state-owned.

British Petroleum, Veba, Volkswagen and Renault are among the ten largest European corporations and are all moneymakers. The three French banks, plus the Westdeutsche Landsbank of Duesseldorf, also publicly owned, are among the ten largest European banks and are successful.

On the other hand, among the ten biggest money-losing corporations in Europe in 1978 were six state-owned firms—British Steel, Italsider (the Italian steel maker), ENI (Italian oil), Montedison (Italian chemicals), Ensidesa (Spanish steel) and Alfa Romeo (Italian cars). And, of course, it is the taxpayer who makes up the deficits.

Another of the big losers, Cockerill Steel, has sought to resolve a financial crisis by selling a sizable portion of its stock to the Belgian government.

The managers of some state firms feel that they could do better if they were free of the political restraints that have been imposed on them. And few want to see state ownership extended to cover more of their national economies. The poor example of central-planning and state-monopoly operations in Communist Eastern Europe is a powerful influence.

In fact, even though practical politics still call for the state to step in to prevent immediate damage from economic dislocations, many in Europe look for a reversal of the trend in the near future.

3. *Maintenance of families and spouses.* A consideration in placing foreign nationals in various positions in multinational corporations abroad is the problem of providing for spouses and families. Many executives will not relocate unless the multinational corporation provides housing, transportation, and education for their families while they are serving abroad. This may represent a substantial cost in countries where living expenses are high. Educational programs and tutors must sometimes be provided for children.

4. *Promotions.* Employees who are serving assignments in multinational corporation affiliates or subsidiaries must be given equal consideration for promotions and raises. Sometimes employees who are on assignment abroad feel out of touch with the rest of the organization. They develop frustrations, or feel that they are being passed over or kept in an undesirable location. These employees can become alienated and fail to perform their best.

5. *Pay rate differentials.* The establishment of a fair and equitable pay scale for multinational corporation employees is an important consideration. Living standards and cost of living vary widely between countries. Salaries must be high enough to provide a reasonable level of housing, transportation, and comforts for employees assigned to remote multinational corporation locations. Employees who are paid the same salary, even when they are assigned to a high-cost-of-living country, may refuse to accept the assignment.

6. *Conflicts with locals.* Problems sometimes arise between multinational personnel and local citizens. Foreign nationals who are placed in a territory may have a higher living standard than locals, thus causing friction. The organization is often looked to as the mediator for disputes arising between locals and its employees.

## SUMMARY

During the past several decades there has been a steady growth and increase in world trade. Several economic associations have evolved including the European Economic Community, European Free Trade Association, and other associations.

Many firms have evolved from local organizations to multinational corporations with worldwide economic management and marketing bases. The advantages of multinational corporation operations include greater profit, expanded markets, availability of raw materials, financial resources, lower labor costs, and higher productivity.

The limitations of the multinational corporation include taxation, governmental restrictions and disadvantages to foreign countries. The multinational corporation may face legal complications, unfair competition, language difficulties, political problems, and the threat of expropriation of assets in host countries.

The multinational corporation may be organized along several lines including geographical or functional. Many issues arise in dealing with multinational corporations, including degree of control, communication, and planning.

Staffing is a major consideration of the multinational corporation. Attitudes of managers, employment of local personnel, maintenance of families, promotions, and pay rate differentials must be considered.

## REVIEW QUESTIONS

1. How does the multinational corporation differ from the international corporation?
2. Define the term *common market*.
3. Why do business organizations engage in world trade?
4. Discuss why the European Economic Community was formed.
5. How does the European Free Trade Association differ from the EEC?
6. List several advantages of the multinational corporation.
7. What are the disadvantages to the host country of the multinational corporation?
8. What political problems does the multinational corporation face?
9. What cultural problems does the multinational corporation face?
10. Describe the geographic form of multinational corporation organization.
11. Describe the functional form of multinational corporation organization.
12. What communication problems does the multinational corporation face?

## KEY TERMS

Multinational corporation (MNC)   478
International corporation   478
Local corporation   478
Joint venture   478
Common market   478
Economic association   480

## Case Incident

Plastics Products Corp. manufactures and markets a full line of plastic household goods, including such products as kitchen utensils, food storage containers, and household fixtures. These products have enjoyed substantial sales throughout the United States market. A recent marketing research study has shown that they could increase sales to several developing countries by providing a local source of supply, rather than shipping from one central United States warehouse.

Plastic Products has had a long-term relationship with a successful and well-respected South American firm which now distributes but does not manufacture its products in the South American market. It has been so successful that both sales and share of market have increased steadily since their arrangement began. This is greatly due to the fact that their South American distributor understands the particular needs of both retailers and consumers in this part of the world. At the same time, Plastic Products has operated a manufacturing plant in Europe which has been quite successful since it first opened, mainly because it allows a greater degree of production flexibility to meet the current demand of the European market. Also, it has enabled them to bypass many import taxes on goods.

Wendell Douglas, national sales manager for Plastic Products, would like to increase their sales to certain other countries through a licensing and distributorship program such as that now in effect in the South American market. He has been extremely pleased with the relationship with the distributor there. Sales and profits are going up steadily. It eliminates the need for a large capital expenditure in a manufacturing plant. Since this distributorship relationship has worked so well in South America, he feels it can apply to these other countries.

Steve Skiles, plant manager of their major U.S. manufacturing facility, believes that additional plant facilities should be constructed. He reasons that such a facility could carefully coordinate its production to the needs and demands of the new developing market by purchasing locally produced raw materials to keep costs at a much lower level. Finally, he feels that they could learn much from their experience with their manufacturing plant in Europe, which has been so successful. To ensure effective startup of the plant, it would be staffed by key American personnel on a rotating basis.

The executive management at Plastic Products will need to make a decision soon on whether to operate and market their products through a distributorship arrangement or build their own manufacturing facilities in the developing markets. Needless to say, the future growth and profitability of the company may depend on this decision. It will be an important one that will affect the company for many years to come.

## PROBLEMS

1. What are the merits and problems of Douglas' approach?
2. What are the merits and problems of Skiles' approach?
3. What solution to the problem do you favor? Explain.

# Index

Accountability, 196, 204
Accounting
　basic statements of, 435-8
　basic system of, 434-5
Action studies, 333
Activity ratio, 114-15, 438
Affirmative action programs, 67-70
Age
　as a factor in labor force, 60-1
American Motors Corporation, 495
American Woman's Economic Development Corporation (AWED), 323
Arbitration, 285-6
Arithmetic and logic unit (ALU), 180
Arkwright, Richard, 32
ASK Computer Services, Inc., 323
Assembler, 183
Asset, 432
Assistant to positions, 308-10
Associations, economic, 480-2
Atkinson, John W., 352-3
Audits, 416-17
Authority, 195, 203-4, 236
Automatic Sequence Control Calculator, 178
"Avoid verbal orders," 395

Babbage, Charles, 32, 178
Bache Group, Inc., 372
Balance sheet, 435-6
BankAmerica, 144
Barnard, Chester I., 40-1
BASIC, 183
Basic plans, 91
Batch process, 461

Bavelas, Alex, 253-5
Behavioral/reinforcement theory, 345-7
Behavioral science theory, 29t, 41-3
Behavioral theory
　of leadership, 366-73
Behavior modification, 333-4
Bell-shaped curve, 157
Berezin, Evelyn, 323
Berne, Eric, 349-50, 400
"Best estimate"
　in critical-path method, 154
Blake, R.R., 328
Blue collar workers, 59-60
Blue Diamond Coal Co., 64
Board of directors
　function of, 5-6
Boone, Allen, Hamilton, 154
Borman, Frank, 470-1
Born managers
　theory of, 19
Boulding, Kenneth, 44
Brainstorming, 258-9
Break-even-point analysis, 160-3
Brennan, Edward, 305
Bribery, foreign, 65
Budgetary control, 432, 441-8
Budget committee, 443
Budget director, 443
Budgets, 432
　applied considerations of, 448-50
　as a control tool, 418
　as a planning tool, 111
　purpose of, 441-2
　staffing of, 442-3

types of, 443-8
Buggie, F.D., 258-9
Buntrock, Dean L., 159
Burden, 161
Burns, Thomas J., 48
Burroughs Corporation, 65t
Business strategy experiences, 164-5

Cafeteria plan, 350
California
    and air pollution control laws, 74
Capital, 433
    investment of, 6, 58
Carrot and stick
    theory of motivation, 341
Cathode ray terminals (CRTs), 176-7
Central American Common Market (CACM), 482
Centralization, 228-30, 236-7
Central processing unit (CPU), 180-1
Chain channel, 254
Chain of command, 196
Change
    attitudes toward, 320-1
    forces of, 317-18
    impact of, 316-17
    implementation of, 305
    in Lewin's theory, 326-7
    rate of, 319-20
    resistance to, 321
Channel, 385
Chrysler Corporation, 142, 164-5
Circle channel, 254
Circular organizational charts, 232
Civil Aeronautics Board (CAB), 54
Civil Rights Act of 1964, 67
Clausen, A.W., 144
Clayton Act, 54
Clique, 248
COBOL, 183
Cohesiveness, 248
Coleman, Sheldon, 466
Collective bargaining, 55, 284
Collins, Shirley, 323
Committee organization, 223-4
Common Market, 478-9
Communication
    barriers to, 397-8
    definition of, 384
    importance of, 384
    as a management activity, 14
    methods of, 395-7
    in multinational corporations, 493
    process of, 385-8

    ways to improve, 399-400
Communication networks, 253-5, 384, 388-9
    formal and informal, 390-2
Communication theory
    manager's understanding of, 17
Compensation, 271-3, 350
    *see also* Salaries
Competition
    and multinational corporations, 487
Computer languages, 183
Computers
    advantages of, 174
    definition of, 171, 179
    early, 43, 178-9
    elements of, 180-2
    in forecasting, 117
    and human resources inventories, 274
    influence on organizational structure, 228
    in quantitative decision making, 152, 155, 164-5
    trends in use of, 172
    as used by management, 173-4
Computer systems, 182-8
    access to, 185
    problems of, 184-8
    security of, 185, 186-7
Conditions
    for achievement of a plan, 89
    Conferencing, 334
Conflict
    introduction of, 323-4
    kinds of, 324-5
    in organizations, 322-3
Consultants, 306-7, 323, 332-3
Consumer credit, 61
Consumerism, 66
Consumer needs
    as a basis for departmentalization, 213-16
Contact chart, 251-2
Contingency leadership, 373-4
Contingency organizational structure, 227-9
Contingency theory, 21-3, 29t, 47-9
Continuous process, 461
Control
    applied aspects of, 421-2
    areas of, 419-20
    definition of, 410
    major issues in, 422-3
    as a management function, 13
    of multinational corporations, 492
    need for, 411-12
    nonfinancial, 456-72
    process of, 413-15
    tools of, 416-19
Control unit (of computer), 181

# INDEX

Coordination
    as a management activity, 15
Corporation
    structure of, 5-6
Corrective action, 410
Cost-analysis charts, 161
Costs
    types of, 161-2
Credit economy, 61
Criteria of acceptable performance
    of a plan, 89, 93
Critical-path method (CPM), 153-4
Crocker National Bank, 387
Current ratio, 114, 438
Customers' satisfaction
    as a goal, 7
Cybernetics, 410

Data, 112
    in the control process, 416
    definition of, 170
Data banks, 175-7
Davis, Keith, 390
Debt ratio, 114, 438
Decision making, 130-44
    approaches to, 130-5
    definition of, 130
    factors in, 142-3
    as a management activity, 13
Decisions
    group vs. individual, 143-4
    programmed and nonprogrammed, 137-9
Decision tables, 140-2
Decision theory school, 20-1
Decision trees, 139-40
Decoding, 387
Delegation (of authority), 203-5, 235
Department, 196
Departmentalize, 196, 198, 209-16
Deterministic occurrences, 157
Deterministic system, 150
Dewey, John, 132
Directing
    as a management function, 12-13
Dispatching, 462
Distribution channel
    as a basis for departmentalization, 212-13
Distribution control, 470
Distributive management information
    processing, 228
Division of labor, 5-6, 201-3
Dobby, James K., 134
Documenting (organizational structure), 199, 230-2, 235
Dress codes, 268

Drucker, Peter, 119

Eastern Airlines, 470-1
Economic environment, 56-7
Economic order quantity (EOQ), 467-8
Economic theory
    manager's understanding of, 16
Economic trends, 57-8
Electrical accounting machines (EAM), 178
Electronic Discrete Variable Automatic
    Computer (EDVAC), 178
Electronic funds transfer system (EFTS), 61
Ellig, Bruce, 350
Ely, Carole, 323
Emerson Electric, 45
Encoding, 386
Encounter groups, 306
End results
    of a plan, 89
Energy crisis, 70-3
Environmental pollution, 73-4
Environments, business, 54-7
Equity theory, 353-4
Ethics, 64-5
European Economic Community (EEC), 481
European Free Trade Association (EFTA), 481-2
Evaluation
    of employees, 281-2
Executive development, 295, 307-10
    see also Management development
Executive obsolescence, 296
Executives
    see Top-level management
Expectancy theory, 354-6
Expediting, 462-3
Expropriation (of assets of multinational
    corporations), 487
Exxon Corporation, 65t, 448-9

Fact finding, 286
Family businesses, 214-15, 466
Famolare, Joseph P., Jr., 163
Fast, Julius, 396
Fayol, Henri, 37-8
Federal Aviation Administration (FAA), 62
Federal Express, 423
Federal spending, 440
Federal Trade Commission (FTC), 54, 62
Feedback loop, 45-6, 415
Fiedler, Fred E., 48, 373-4
Field interviews, 333
Financial control, 419
Financial plans, 106

Financial theory
   manager's understanding of, 16
FitzGerald, Daniel, 492
Fitzpatrick, Beatrice, 323
Fixed budget, 444
Fixed cost, 161, 433
Fixed order, 466
"Flat" organization, 205, 206-7
Flex-time, 257
Follett, Mary Parker, 38
Food and Drug Administration (FDA), 54
Force field analysis, 327-8
Ford, Henry, 202
Ford Motor Co., 21
Forecasting, 116-18, 424-5
Foreperson
   see Operational-level management
Formal organization, 195
FORTRAN, 183
Fraser, Douglas A., 142
Friends Amis, Inc., 433
Froung, William, 204
Function(s), 11, 210-11
   central, 220
   supporting, 220-1
Functionalize
   see Departmentalize
Functional organization
   of multinational corporations, 490-1
*Future Shock,* 319

Game theory, 159-60
Gantt, Henry L., 35
General Electric, 63
General Motors, 142, 176
General Telephone Company, 402
Geographic organization
   of multinational organizations, 490
Gilbreth, Frank and Lillian, 35-6
Goals
   definition of, 9-10, 81
   of groups, 255-6
   of nonprofit organizations, 86
   of a plan, 92-3
   of profit-making organizations, 84-6
Gordon, Ronald, 433
Gottfried, Ira, 187
Government
   and industry, 486, 494-5
Governmental environment, 54-5
Government influence
   growth of, 62
Grace, J. Peter, 107
Graham, Bette Nesmith, 31
Grapevine, 252-3, 390-2

Green Giant Company, 318
Greiner, Larry, 328
Grievance hearings, 287
Gross National Product (GNP), 57, 479
Group dynamics, 244
Group process
   manager's understanding of, 16
Groups, 244
   interrelationship of, 250-1
   methods of studying, 251-2
   norms and goals of, 255-6
   sanctions of, 256-7
   types of, 249-50
Growth
   as a goal, 7
Gulf Oil Corporation, 65t

Haas Tailoring Company, 418
Hall, E.T., 396
Hammurabi, Code of, 30
Hardware (computer), 171
Harp, Lore, 323
Harrington, Eileen, 64
Harris, Thomas, 402
Hawthorne effect, 40, 423
Hawthorne Study, 39-40
Herzberg, Frederick, 43, 351-2
Hierarchy of human needs, 41-2, 347-9
Holding costs, 465
Hollerith, Herman, 178
Horizontal organizational charts, 231-2
Hub channel, 254-5
Human behavior school, 20
   *see also* Behavioral science theory
Human relations theory, 20, 29t, 38-41, 341-2
Human resources
   acquisition of, 274-81
   control of, 472
   inventory of, 274, 417
   management of, 266-7, 420
   planning of, 267-73
Hunt, Bunker, 372
Hyster Company, 226

IBM Corporation, 63
Incentive, 341
Income statement, 436
Indicators
   lead and lag, 118
Industrial revolution, 31
Inflation rate, 57
Informal organizations, 195
   communication in, 253-5
   leadership of, 257-8
   need for, 248-9

# INDEX

norms and goals of, 255-6
    sanctions of, 256-7
    types of, 249-50
Injunction, 288
Input system, 180
Integrated circuits (ICs), 179
Interest rates, 58
International corporation, 478
Internship programs, 310
Interstate Commerce Commission (ICC), 54, 62
Intuition, 131
Inventory control, 456, 464-70

Japan
    investment in the United States, 481
    lifetime employment in, 286-7
    productivity in, 295
    shareholders' meetings in, 247
    working conditions in, 46-7
Job design, 269-71, 344
Job enrichment, 270-1
Job orientation, 280-1
Job rotation, 307
Job simplification, 270
Job titles
    and sexism, 72-3
Johns-Manville Corporation, 275
Johnson, George E., 396
Joint ventures, 478
    growth of, 482-3
Justice Department, 54, 67

Kapner, Leonard J., 308-9
Kast, Fremont E., 45
Kilkenny, William H., 226
Kimball, G.E., 43
Kinesics, 385
Knight, Charles, 45
Kroc, Ray, 462
Kurtzig, Sandra L., 323

Labor contracts, 285
Labor force
    composition of, 59-61
    outlook for job categories of, 61
Labor force trends, 58-61
Lansing, Sherry, 364
Latin American Free Trade Association (LAFTA), 482
Leader, 362
Leadership, 362
    environment of, 362-3
    as a management activity, 14
    theories of, 365-78

Lead time, 468-9
Learning
    methods of, 301-3
Leavitt, Harold J., 331
LeGrange, Ulyesse, 448-9
Lewin, Kurt, 326-8, 367-8
Liability, 432
Likert, Rensis, 43, 368-9
Linear programming (LP), 155-6
Line channel, 254
Line function, 208
Line management, 442-3
Line organization, 221-2
Line and staff organization, 222-3
Liquidity ratio, 114, 438
Liquid Paper, 31
Local corporation, 478
Lockheed Aircraft Corporation, 65t
Locomotion, 248
Long-range plans, 102-3
Ludwig, Daniel Keith, 115

McClelland, David C., 352-3
McCloskey, Joseph, 43
McDonald's, 462
McDonnell Douglas Corporation, 65t
McGregor, Douglas, 20, 42-3, 350-1
McNeely, E.L., 492
Magnetic ink character recognition (MICR), 180
Management
    definition of, 8
    function of, 5, 11-13
    levels of, 10-11, 206
    philosophies of, 19-23
    purpose of, 4
    social responsibility of, 63-74
    statistics on, 18-19
Management development, 295
    benefits of, 297-8
    desirable abilities in, 298-9
    need for, 296
    *see also* Executive development
Management Grid, 328-30
Management information systems (MIS), 175-88
    advantages of, 177
    elements of, 175-7
Management by objectives, 119-24
    advantages of, 121-2
    limitations of, 123-4
Management theories
    early, 28-31
    modern, 38-49
    post-industrial revolution, 31-8

Manager
  activities of, 13-15
  areas of knowledge of, 15-17
  definition of, 8-9
  in multinational corporations, 493
  need for, 4-6
Manley, Joan, 376-7
Manufacturers Bank, 134
Manufacturing process
  as a basis for departmentalization, 213
Mark I, 178
Marketing
  as a goal, 85-6
Marketing control, 419, 458-9
Marketing plans, 104-5
Maslow, Abraham, 20, 41-2, 347-9
Matrix organization, 226-7
Mayo, Elton, 39-40, 423
Measurement
  in the control process, 414-15
  criteria of, 88-90
  of goal achievement, 86-90
Mechanistic management, 48
Mediation, 285
Memory (computer), 181
Merck & Co., Inc., 65t
Message, 385
Metropolitan Life Insurance Company, 257
Microelectronic circuitry, 179
Mid-level management, 11
  as planners, 109
Minorities
  and affirmative action programs, 67-70
Mobil Oil, 63
Modeling, 152
Mooney, James D., 38
Morale, 344-5
Morse, P.M., 43
Motivation
  contemporary views of, 345-56
  definition of, 340-1
  historical views of, 341-5
Motive, 340
Mouton, J.S., 328
Multinational firms, 478
  advantages of, 483-6
  growth of, 62-3, 482-3
  limitations of, 486-7
  management and control of, 492-3
  organization and structure of, 489-91
  problems and risks faced by, 487-8
  staffing of, 493-6
Munsterberg, Hugo, 38
Murphy, Thomas A., 142, 176

Nader, Ralph, 66
National Bulk Carriers, 115
National Computer Crime Data Center, 186
National Training Systems, Inc. (NTS), 308-9
Need, 341
Need theories, 347-53
Net worth, 432
Neuman, Irving, 418
New Jersey Bell Telephone, 40
New product development, 457-8
Nonbudgetary control, 432
Nonfinancial control, 456-72
Nonprofit organizations
  goals of, 7-8, 86
Nonverbal communication, 396-7
Norms, 247
  of group, 255-6
Northrop Corporation, 65t

Objectives
  definition of, 9-10, 81-2
Occupational Safety and Health Act (OSHA), 66
Ohio State studies, 369-70
"One best way," 33-4
One-time plans, 104
On-the-job training, 106, 303
On-line access (to computers), 176-7
Operational-level management, 11
  as planners, 109-10
Operational plans, 91
Operations management, 456
Operations research, 151
Optical character recognition (OCR), 180
Ordering costs, 465
Orders
  optimum time for, 468-70
  size of, 466-8
Organic management, 48-9
Organizational charts, 231
Organizational development (OD), 295-6, 325-6
  characteristics of, 326-32
  tools of, 332-4
Organizational hierarchy
  definition of, 9
Organizational manuals, 231
Organizational shape, 205
Organizational structure
  centralized vs. decentralized, 228-30
  documenting of, 230-2
  manager's understanding of, 16-17
  problems in, 232-7
  types of, 221-8

# INDEX

Organizations
  goals of, 6-7
Organizing
  definition of, 194
  as a management function, 12, 194
  principles of, 197-216
  steps in, 197-9
Output system, 181-2
Overhead, 161
Owners
  see Shareholders, Sole proprietorship

Palmer, Russell E., 173
Paperwork, 134, 171, 236-7
Parsons, James, 355
Pavlov, I.P., 345-6
Personnel departments, 267
Personnel functions, 267-83
Personnel plans, 106
Personnel review
  as a management activity, 13
Pfizer, Inc., 350
Phillips, Stewart W., 403
Pillsbury Company, 318
Plan(s)
  definition of, 82
  hierarchy of, 107-8
  interrelationship of, 107
  measurement of results, 86-90, 94
  modification of, 94-5
  steps in developing, 91-5
  time element in, 102-4
  types of, 90-1, 104-6
  use of, 90-5
Plan design
  characteristics of, 108-9
Planners, 109-11
Planning, 80-95, 102-24
  advantages of, 80
  as a management function, 12, 14
  in multinational corporations, 493
  need for, 80
  tools of, 111-18
  at various management levels, 95
Planning departments, 109
Plessner, Rene, 214-15
Policy
  definition of, 83
  as a source of conflict, 323-4
Policy making
  as a management activity, 13
Posner, Ronald S., 308-9
Power, 362
  sources of, 363-5
Power center chart, 252

Probability theory, 157
Procedure, 83
Production control, 419, 456, 460-3
Production plans, 105-6
Productivity
  as a goal, 7, 470-1
  as a labor force trend, 59
  of multinational corporations, 485
Product line
  as a basis for departmentalization, 211
Profit, 84, 434
  excessive, 448-9
  as a goal, 6-7, 84-6
  of multinational corporations, 483
Profit ratio, 114, 438
Program (computer), 171, 182-3
Program Evaluation and Review Technique
  (PERT), 154-5
Project manager, 110, 226-7
Project organization, 225-7
Promotions
  in multinational corporations, 496
Psychology
  manager's understanding of, 15, 20
Pyramid structure, 9

Qualitative decision making, 131-2
Qualitative measurement, 87-8
Quality control, 456, 462, 463-4
Quantitative decision making, 132-7, 150-63
Quantitative measurement, 87-8
Quantitative methods
  in decision making, 151-63
  in forecasting, 117-18
  manager's understanding of, 16
Quantitative theory, 43-4
Question team (Q.T.), 403
Queuing Theory, 157-8

Ratio analysis, 418, 438-40
Ratios, 112-15, 438-40
Real-time system, 170-1, 410, 424-6
Recruitment, 274-6
Redactron Corporation, 323
Reddin, William J., 378
Refreezing, 327
Reichhold Chemicals, 355
Reiley, Alan C., 38
Reorganization
  as a source of conflict, 324
Report Program Generator (RPG), 183
Research and development (R&D), 457-8
Responsibility, 196, 204, 236
Responsibility centers, 418-19
Retained earnings statement, 436-7

Revenue, 162, 434
Rewards
   money, 342-3
   job, 343-4
Role, 244
Role playing, 306
Rosenzweig, James E., 45
Routing, 462
Rule
   in decision table, 140
   definition of, 84
Russia
   economic planning system of, 96-7

Safety
   of employees, 66
Safety stock, 469-70
Salaries
   determination of, 271-3
   of managers, 18-19
   in multinational corporations, 496
   of women, 69
   see also Compensation
Sales
   as a goal, 85-6
Sayles, Leonard R., 249-50
Scheduling, 462
Schmidt, Warren, 370
Scientific approach
   to decision making, 132-7
Scientific management, 19-20, 29t, 33-5, 39
Searle, G.D. & Company, 65t
Sears, Roebuck, 305
Sedlik, Jay M., 308-9
Semantics, 384
   principles of, 392-5
Sensitivity training, 306
Sexual harassment, 275
Shakey's Pizza, 372
Shareholders, 5
Sherman Antitrust Act, 54
Shoeffler, Dr. Sidney, 164-5
Short-range plans, 103
Silicon chips, 179
Simon, Herbert, 43, 137
Simulations, 152, 306
Sisters of Loretto
   and Blue Diamond Coal Co., 64
Situational management
   see Contingency theory
Skinner, B.F., 345
Smith, Frederick, W., 423
Social audits, 64
Social environment, 56

Social good
   as an organizational goal, 7-8
Social responsibility
   of management, 63-74
Sociogram, 252
Software (computer), 171
Sole proprietorship, 4-5
Span of control, 196, 205, 206
Specialization of effort, 6
Spoor, William H., 318
Staff development, 299-307
Staff function, 208
Staffing
   as a management function, 12, 266-7
   in multinational corporations, 493-6
   see also Human resources
Stalker, G.M., 48
Standard
   in the control process, 414-15, 416
   definition of, 84
Standard cost, 411
Standing plans, 103-4
Statistics
   on management, 18-19
   as a planning tool, 111-12
Status, 245-6
Status symbols, 246-7
Stimulus-response (S-R) bonds, 346-7
Stochastic system, 150-1
Stockholder democracy, 144
Strategic Innovations, Inc., 258-9
Strategic Planning Institute (SPI), 164-5
Strategic plans, 91
Strategy, 82-3
Strokes, 349
Stubs, 140-1
Subclique, 248
Subordinate
   definition of, 9
   and organizational structure, 222, 224
Supervisors
   see Operational-level management
Supporting plans, 91
Sur la Table, 323
Symbol, 385
   selection of, 392
System, 170
Systems analysis, 151
Systems theory, 21, 29t, 44-6

"Tall" organization, 205, 206-7
Talman Federal Savings and Loan, 268
Tannenbaum, Robert, 370
Task force, 110
Task force organization, 225-6

Taxation
    of multinational corporations, 486
Taylor, Frederick W., 19, 33-5, 341
Team building, 334
Technical obsolescence, 296
Telling, Edward, 305
Termination
    of employees, 282-4
Territory
    as a basis for departmentalization, 211-12
T groups, 306, 334
Therbligs, 36
Thorndike, Edward, 345
Three-dimensional model (of leadership), 378
Throughput, 410-11
Time-Life Books, 376-7
Time series analysis, 117
Timesharing, 171
Time standard, 411
Toffler, Alvin, 319
Top-level management, 10
    compensation of, 273
    as planners, 109
Total cost, 433
Touche Ross and Company, 173
Trade, worldwide, 479-80
Training, 106, 281, 295
    cost effectiveness of, 308-9
    of management, 296-9
    of staff, 303-7
Trait theory, 365-6
Transactional analysis, 400-4
Trends
    affecting management, 57-61
Trial and error, 131-2, 466
Trial promotion, 310
Turnaround time, 411
Turnover
    of inventory, 470
Twentieth Century-Fox Studios, 364
Two factor theory, 351-2

Unfreezing, 327
Union-labor
    as a business environment, 55
    and collective bargaining, 284-5
    disputes, 285-8
    and personnel plans, 106
United Auto Workers Union, 142
United Brands Company, 65t
Unity of command, 207
Urwick, Lyndall F., 38

Vacuum tubes, 178
Variable budget, 444-5

Variable costs, 161, 433
Vector Graphic, Inc., 323
Vertical organizational charts, 231
Vestibule training, 304
Voinovich, George V., 195
Volkswagen, 495
von Bertalanffy, Ludwig, 44
von Neumann, John, 178
Vroom, Victor, 43, 375-6
Vroom-Yetton model, 375-8

Wanderman, Herb, 122-3
Waste Management, Inc., 159
Weber, Max, 33
Weil, Leonard, 134
Well pay, 354-5
Wells Fargo Bank, 134
Western Electric, 39, 423
Wheel channel, 254-5
White collar workers, 59-60
Whitney, Amasa, 332-3
Wickes Corporation, 492
Wilcox, Thomas R., 387
Women
    and affirmative action, 67-70
    as entrepreneurs, 323
    as executives, 364, 376-7
    and job titles, 72-3
    as percentage of work force, 60, 69
    salaries of, 18-19, 69
    and sexual harassment, 275
Woodward, Joan, 48
Workers, 5-6
Worker's compensation laws, 66

X theory, 42-3, 350-1

Y channel, 254
Yetton, Philip, 375-6
Y theory, 42-3, 351

Zero-base budgeting, 445-8
Zone of indifference, 40-1